# PLANNING ARCHITECTURE

# PLANNING ARCHITECTURE

## DIMENSIONS AND TYPOLOGIES

BERT BIELEFELD, ED.

Birkhäuser
Basel

# Contents

1  Introduction _____ 6

2  Human Measure _____ 9

   2.1  Anthropometry and Barrier-Free Accessibility  11

   2.2  Comfort and Physical Spatial Qualities  21

   2.3  Spatial Perception  31

3  Spaces _____ 35

   3.1  External Circulation  39

   3.2  Internal Circulation  61

   3.3  Workrooms and Production Spaces  83

   3.4  Communication Spaces and Dining Rooms  87

   3.5  Sanitary Facilities  101

   3.6  Kitchens  111

   3.7  Storage Spaces  119

   3.8  Ancillary and Staff Rooms  131

   3.9  Technical Equipment Rooms  139

4  Typologies _____ 155

   4.1  Housing  157

   4.2  Office and Administration  197

   4.3  Logistics and Commerce  227

   4.4  Industry and Production  269

   4.5  Education and Research  291

   4.6  Culture and Performing Arts  327

   4.7  Lodging and Food Service  355

   4.8  Healthcare Facilities  383

   4.9  Sports and Recreation  425

   4.10  Public Safety  475

   4.11  Transportation and Infrastructure  495

5  Reference Guide _____ 535

   5.1  Standards and Regulations  537

   5.2  References  553

   5.3  Index  559

   5.4  Picture Credits  565

   5.5  The Authors  567

# 1 Introduction

When transforming a design concept into a feasible project, architects continually oscillate between two levels of consideration: the specific overall design task in the context of a certain planning typology – such as a residential building, office building, school, or hospital – and the individual spatial elements, such as living rooms, office workplaces, sanitary facilities, etc.

*Planning Architecture* has been conceived as a realignment of conventional typology-based design models, which combines the requirements for buildings with the design paths taken by practicing architects.

## 1.1 Structure of the Book

*Planning Architecture* presents planners and designers with a well-conceived planning instrument that is divided into two main parts: "Spaces" and "Typologies," between which the reader can freely switch back and forth, depending on the scale being considered. All the information relevant to planning and design is presented here clearly, in detail and in context.

The *Spaces* section details the fundamentals and planning basics for various room types that are valid for a diverse assortment of typologies. These are treated systematically, with attention given to their requirements, functional relationships, and detailed dimensional specifications.

In the *Typologies* section, the specific requirements and processes pertaining to various building types are explained. This includes not only functional approaches for application in the design process but also explanations of how the various building types are used and of the specific rooms and space requirements.

These two main sections are flanked by the introductory sections *Human Measure,* which describes the demands made on buildings by the "average person" or a person with impairments or disabilities, and the *References* section at the end of the book, which comprises information concerning presentation and dimensions as well as clearly assembled lists of standards and bibliographic references pertinent to the preceding chapters, intended to assist the reader in exploring this book's subject matter in further detail. For the purposes of promoting universal design, issues pertaining to barrier-free accessibility are integrated throughout the entire book.

## 1.2 Use of the Book

This book is structured in such a way that the duplication of content matter is avoided or reduced to a minimum. The ↗ Spaces section is conceived as a reference guide and provides detailed information on spatial design requirements. Since basic information is presented in the ↗ Spaces section, only supplementary information – such as the quantity or required areas of particular rooms – is considered in the ↗ Typologies chapters.

Thus the book may be used as a reference guide for space requirements and because the individual ↗ Typologies chapters introduce the functional particularities of the respective typologies and contain all the essential parameters needed for the design process, it also serves as an aid for design.

For cross-linking the ↗ Spaces and ↗ Typologies sections, various navigation aids are provided. In addition to the orientation furnished by the index at the end of the book and the navigation bar on every page, chapter references at the top of the pages in the typology-related chapters establish a direct link to relevant information in the ↗ Spaces section.

## 1.3 Integration in the Design Process

It goes without saying that a functional approach does not replace the creative and highly individual design processes of architects. It should, however, offer the possibility to directly combine design ideas with functional requirements. Individual design approaches and the contents of drawings must always be adapted to relevant national or regional standards. Due to this great diversity of requirements, no guarantee can be made for the applicability of the dimensions and conditions specified here. The dimensions and clearances presented in this book are therefore to be understood as a design aid and not as binding in a legal or normative sense. Moreover, dimensions that are identified as minimum requirements should be freely adjusted if needed to achieve comfortable conditions.

Figure 1.2.1
Illustration of the navigation aids
used in the book

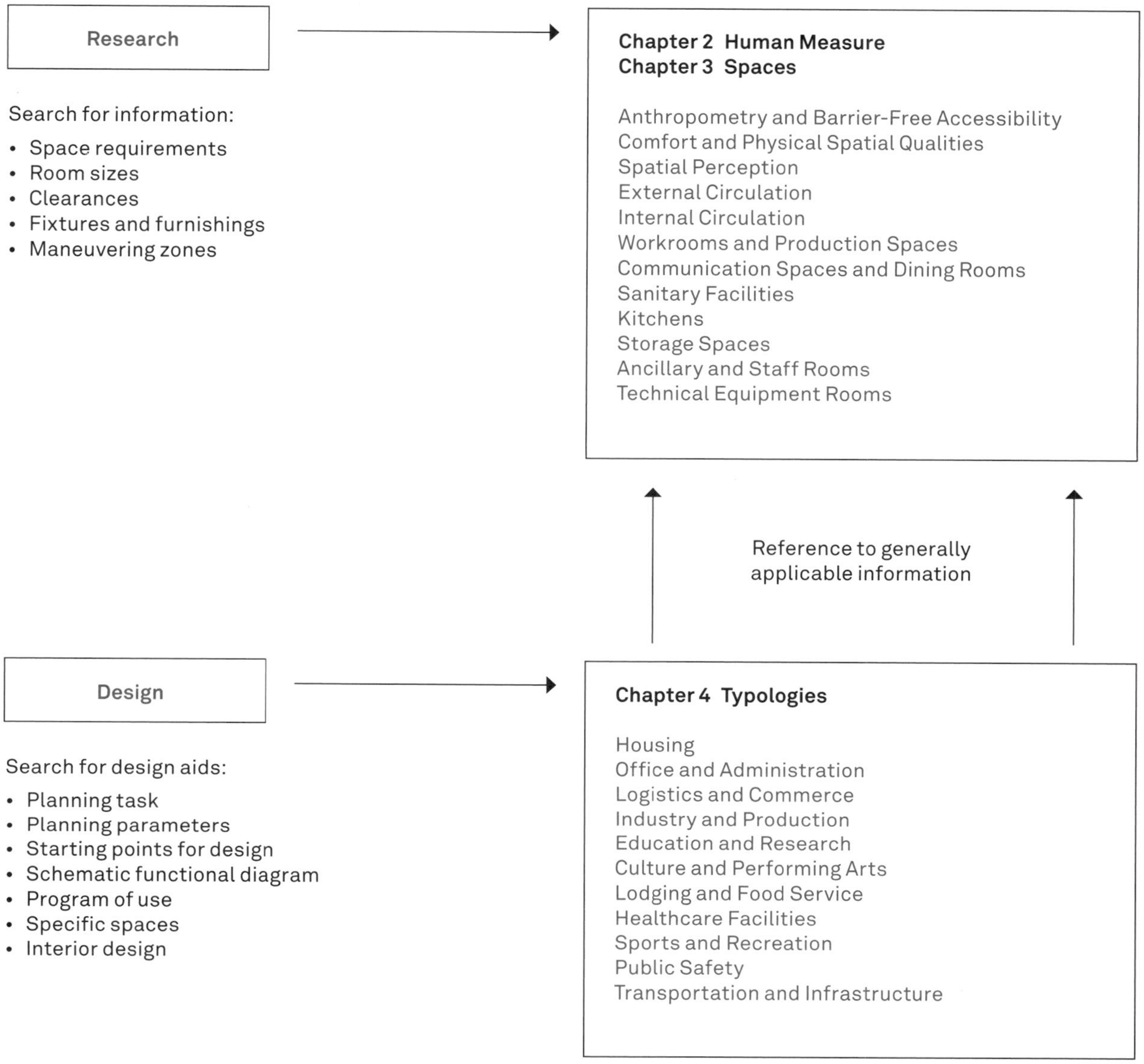

Research

Search for information:
- Space requirements
- Room sizes
- Clearances
- Fixtures and furnishings
- Maneuvering zones

**Chapter 2  Human Measure**
**Chapter 3  Spaces**

Anthropometry and Barrier-Free Accessibility
Comfort and Physical Spatial Qualities
Spatial Perception
External Circulation
Internal Circulation
Workrooms and Production Spaces
Communication Spaces and Dining Rooms
Sanitary Facilities
Kitchens
Storage Spaces
Ancillary and Staff Rooms
Technical Equipment Rooms

Reference to generally
applicable information

Design

Search for design aids:
- Planning task
- Planning parameters
- Starting points for design
- Schematic functional diagram
- Program of use
- Specific spaces
- Interior design

**Chapter 4  Typologies**

Housing
Office and Administration
Logistics and Commerce
Industry and Production
Education and Research
Culture and Performing Arts
Lodging and Food Service
Healthcare Facilities
Sports and Recreation
Public Safety
Transportation and Infrastructure

# 2 Human Measure

## 2.1 Anthropometry and Barrier-Free Accessibility ↗11

2.1.1 **Motor Functions** ↗16

2.1.2 **Sensory Perception** ↗17

2.1.3 **Cognition** ↗19

2.1.4 **Impairments and Disabilities** ↗19

## 2.2 Comfort and Physical Spatial Qualities ↗21

2.2.1 **Room Temperature** ↗21

2.2.2 **Indoor Air** ↗22

2.2.3 **Lighting Conditions** ↗24

2.2.4 **Acoustics** ↗29

## 2.3 Spatial Perception ↗31

2.3.1 **Typology-based Requirements** ↗31

2.3.2 **Spatial Geometry and Proportion** ↗32

# 2.1 Anthropometry and Barrier-Free Accessibility

Because people are the users of buildings, human measure is the main benchmark to use for designing and planning architecture. Whether dealing with an office building, a college, or a restaurant, many fundamentals – both those that are measurable and others that are not – can unfailingly be linked directly to the people using the building.

Our built environment is designed according to the requirements of the people using it. Consequently, room sizes, heights, and transitions as well as the operating elements such as switches, handles, furniture, etc. must be coordinated with human proportions and dimensions – anthropometry – and human ergonomics.

Drastic changes in body heights in the industrialized nations (statistics reveal an increase of about 7 cm in 25 years) constitute a major challenge that needs to be met architecturally, particularly when renovating existing buildings.

When dimensioning areas where many people will congregate, an important factor for the design and planning is how that area will be used. For example, communication areas like the lobby in front of a concert hall require significantly more area per person than do access control points where groups of people wait to pass through.

Figure 2.1.1
Height distribution in Germany
Data source: SOEP

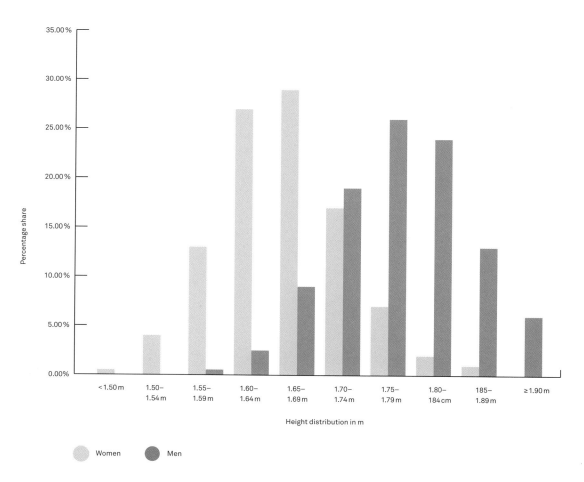

**Figure 2.1.2**
Dimensions (in cm) of people
performing various activities

Table 2.1.1
Planning-relevant body measurements of children, youth, and adults (in cm) as a function of age

Per DIN 33 402 Part 2

| Age | 3 | 5 | 7 | 9 | 11 | 13 | 15 | 16–17 | 18–19 |
|---|---|---|---|---|---|---|---|---|---|
| Height | 93–111 | 106–126 | 118–138 | 127–148 | 134–160 | 149–173 | 155–183 | 155–188 | 156–189 |
| Forward reach | 39–48 | 41–53 | 46–58 | 52–64 | 55–69 | 61–75 | 62–77 | 62–79 | 62–79 |
| Upward reach | 105–127 | 122–144 | 134–159 | 151–179 | 159–192 | 173–210 | 178–219 | 181–219 | 187–226 |
| Eye level | 85–99 | 96–112 | 106–127 | 117–137 | 125–149 | 138–164 | 145–172 | 145–174 | 145–175 |
| Upper body height when seated | 53–62 | 57–70 | 64–75 | 67–78 | 70–82 | 74–92 | 81–94 | 83–97 | 83–98 |
| Eye level when seated | 42–52 | 47–57 | 51–63 | 57–70 | 59–75 | 63–79 | 69–84 | 70–86 | 71–86 |
| Seat height | 19–28 | 25–32 | 28–35 | 30–38 | 34–41 | 36–45 | 39–49 | 39–50 | 39–50 |
| Seat depth | 23–29 | 26–36 | 30–40 | 35–43 | 40–47 | 40–49 | 43–54 | 44–54 | 44–55 |
| Seat width | 25–35 | 27–37 | 29–39 | 31–41 | 32–43 | 33–43 | 33–44 | 34–45 | 37–48 |

| | Men | | | | Women | | | |
|---|---|---|---|---|---|---|---|---|
| Age | 18–25 | 26–40 | 41–60 | 61–65 | 18–25 | 26–40 | 41–60 | 61–65 |
| Height | 168.5–179.0 | 166.5–176.5 | 163.0–183.5 | 160.5–180.5 | 156.0–176.0 | 154.5–172.5 | 161.5–170.5 | 151.0–168.5 |
| Forward reach | 70.0–82.5 | 68.5–82.0 | 68.0–81.0 | 67.5–80.0 | 63.5–76.0 | 63.0–75.0 | 62.0–74.5 | 61.5–74.0 |
| Upward reach | 200.0–224.5 | 199.0–222.0 | 196.0–219.5 | 193.0–215.0 | 185.5–208.5 | 184.5–203.5 | 183.5–200.5 | 182.0–195.5 |
| Eye level | 156.5–178.5 | 154.5–175.0 | 151.0–172.0 | 149.0–169.0 | 145.0–164.5 | 144.0–161.5 | 142.0–159.0 | 139.5–157.0 |
| Upper body height when seated | 87.5–98.5 | 86.5–97.5 | 84.5–96.0 | 83.0–94.5 | 83.0–93.0 | 82.0–91.5 | 80.5–90.5 | 79.0–90.0 |
| Eye level when seated | 76.0–87.0 | 74.5–86.0 | 73.0–85.0 | 71.0–83.0 | 72.0–82.0 | 71.0–81.0 | 70.0–80.0 | 68.5–79.5 |

Figure 2.1.3
Planning-relevant body measurements of children and youth

A = Height
B = Eye level
C = Upward reach
D = Forward reach
E = Upper body height when seated
F = Seat height
G = Eye level when seated
H = Seat depth
I = Seat width

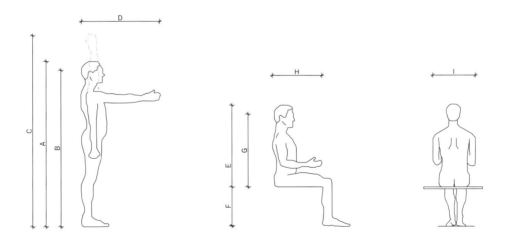

Figure 2.1.4
Area requirements (in m)
for groups of people

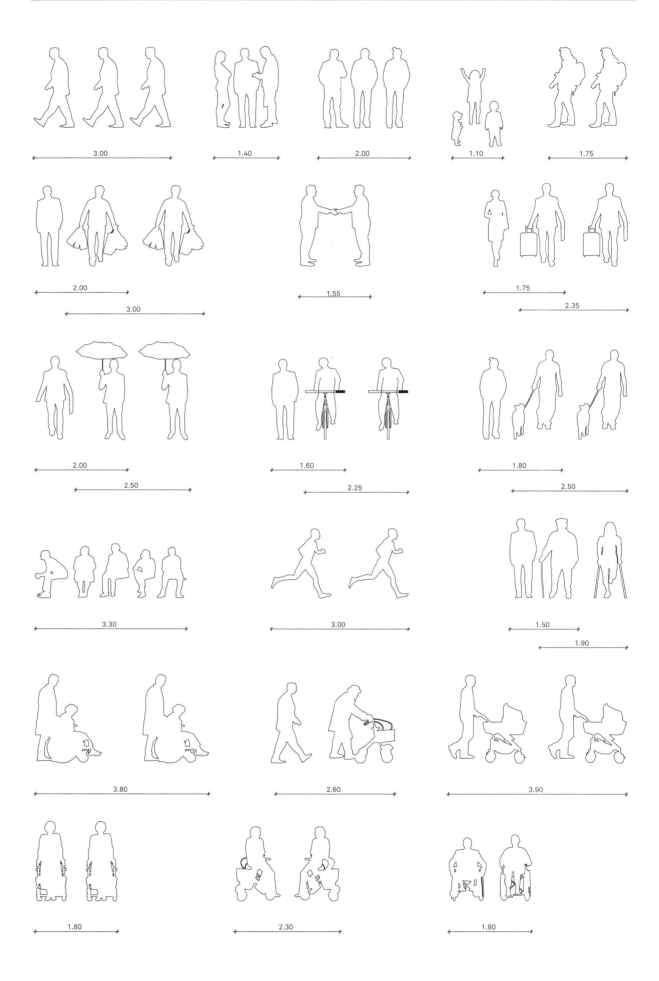

Figure 2.1.5
Area requirements for
waiting lines

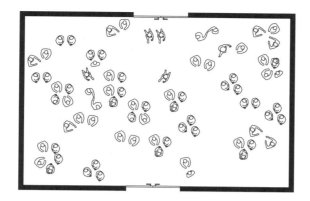

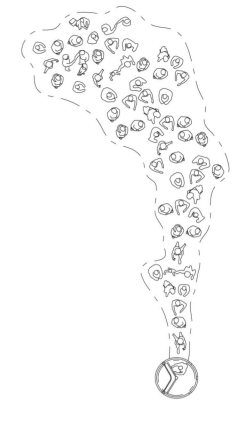

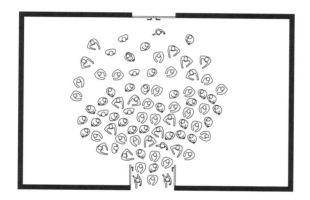

Area of room: approx. 100 m²
Number of persons: 81

Waiting line at an airport
Area occupied: 36.50 m²
Number of persons: 60

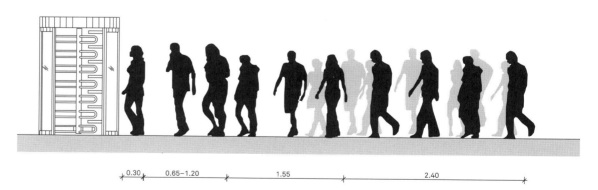

0.30    0.65–1.20    1.55    2.40

Example of a waiting line (in m)

## 2.1.1 Motor Functions

All kinds of dimensional relationships can be derived from people's motor skills. The resultant minimum space requirements for various routine movement sequences and everyday situations at work and at leisure are thus universal. Since the dimensions relate to people's movement capabilities, special user groups – such as small children, the elderly, and wheelchair users – must be considered when planning. Use-specific dimensional requirements are to be found in the relevant chapters for each of the building types.

**Figure 2.1.6**
**Reach ranges (in mm) of wheelchair users**

The reach ranges actually attained from a wheelchair depend on the wheelchair user's personal abilities and the type of wheelchair used.

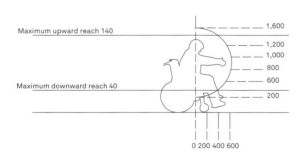

## 2.1.2 Sensory Perception

Virtually all our human senses are involved in the perception of architecture and space: visual perception (seeing), auditory perception (hearing), tactile perception (touching), and olfactory perception (smelling). The dominant means of sensory perception is nevertheless visual detection, which is why the spatial design, operation, and orientation of our environment is mainly shaped visually. For people with sensory impairments, it is therefore essential for them to receive information for perception, orientation, and operation through two different senses. → **Table 2.1.2**

**Figure 2.1.7**
Orientation at the public access to trains

The same scene with normal and impaired vision (cataracts and macular degeneration)

Table 2.1.2
Two-sense principle

| Two-sense principle | Visual | Auditory | Tactile | Olfactory |
| --- | --- | --- | --- | --- |
| **Traffic controls, danger zones** | Display | Acoustic signals | | |
| **Stopping points (train, elevator)** | Display | Announcement | | |
| **Lettering of all types** | Normal characters | | Braille writing | |
| **Orientation outdoors** | Information signs | | Tactile floor markings | Plant scents |
| **Warning systems, e.g., in case of fire** | Warning light | Acoustic warnings | | |

**Figure 2.1.8**
**Braille code**

In comparison to ordinary writing, Braille requires considerably more space. Books in Braille are many times thicker, and even for lettering on such items as information boards and directional signs, sufficient space must be provided.

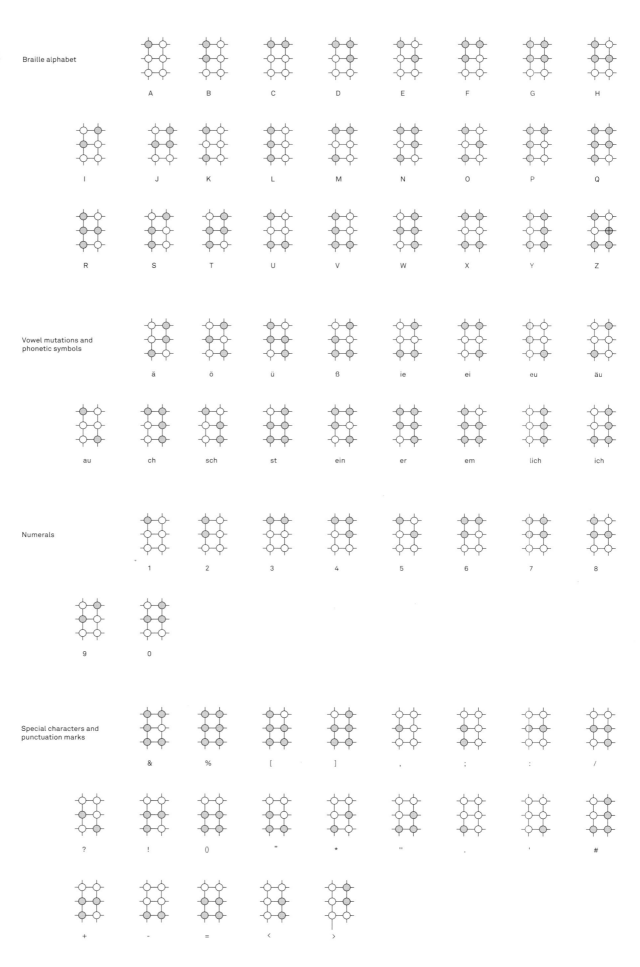

## 2.1.3  Cognition

The superimposition or combination of individual sensory perceptions is what first makes it possible for an overall image to be assembled and evaluated through cognitive perception in the human brain. Thus, the visual stimuli from visual connections, incident light, and the colors in a space are combined with the tactile stimuli and smells of the materials and the acoustics of a room to form an overall impression. Impairments to cognitive perception include many afflictions and traits, such as neural developmental disorders, psychological disabilities or syndromes, dementia, learning disabilities, autism, etc.

## 2.1.4  Impairments and Disabilities

Motor, sensory, and cognitive skills can, under certain circumstances, be impaired or fail to conform to normal levels for a wide variety of reasons. Most notably, the following subgroups can be identified:

- Small children
- Temporarily or chronically ill people
- People with physical disabilities
- People with intellectual disabilities
- Elderly people

It is important to bear in mind that there are gradual transitions in the severity of such impairments. The adherence to normative standards is not to be equated with providing barrier-free accessibility. Rather, it is a matter of sensibly designing the built environment for as many people as possible, which also means accommodating as many different skill sets as possible.

Doing so requires more than just aiding some people with motor impairments by enabling wheelchair use, yet even a wheelchair user's mobility and range of motion can vary greatly due to the type of wheelchair and the user's own abilities.

**Figure 2.1.9**
Spectrum of disabilities and impairments

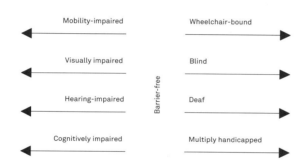

**Figure 2.1.10**
Movement areas (in mm) of people with walking aids or wheelchairs

Since electrically powered wheelchairs mostly tend to be used outdoors, areas of sufficient size must be provided there to ensure their barrier-free use. However, this also applies to interior entrance areas because changes between wheelchairs ordinarily take place inside the building.

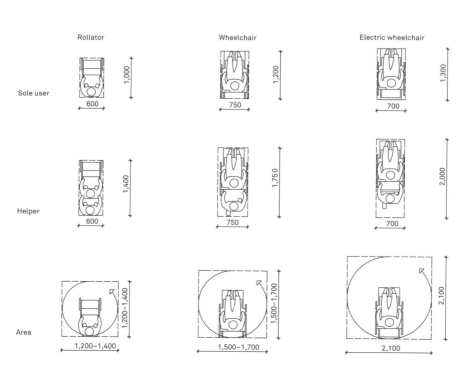

# 2.2  Comfort and Physical Spatial Qualities

In addition to the previously described human skills, people's needs play an important role in the design and planning of buildings with regard to the physical qualities of spaces. These needs differ depending on the building's type and its spatial use as well as the relative activity of the users. Generally speaking, all human needs can be described by a desire for comfort. Comfort cannot, however, be defined one-dimensionally. It is related to a host of factors, including lighting conditions, cleanliness, indoor climate, room acoustics, psychological perception of the space, and not least of all, the basic needs for security, protection, refuge, companionship, communication, clarity, attention, etc. The weight given to each of the various comfort ranges in the context of an overall evaluation of a space depends greatly on the individual.

### 2.2.1  Room Temperature

To start with, there is the physically measurable thermal comfort, which comprises a number of factors: indoor air temperature, average surface temperature of all surrounding surfaces, heat gain (or loss) from floors, air circulation, and relative indoor air humidity, all of which must be maintained within certain limits for occupants to experience a feeling of comfort. If there are no great differences between the air and surface temperatures in a room, people generally judge the climate there to be comfortable. How we perceive an open fire that is burning in a fireplace within an otherwise cold room, however, serves to point out that the factors of thermal comfort are clearly influenced by purely psychological perceptions within the context of cognition.

Figure 2.2.1 (left)
Comfort ranges in relation to room temperature

Depictions according to:

1. Frank, W.: *Raumklima und Thermische Behaglichkeit* (1975)

2. Roedler, F.: *Wärmephysiologische und hygienische Grundlagen* (1960)

3. Leusden, F.; Freymark, H.: *Darstellungen der Raumbehaglichkeit für den einfachen praktischen Gebrauch* (1951)

Table 2.2.1 (right)
Exemplary reference values for the standard interior temperature of various room typologies

Per DIN EN 12831

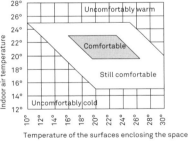

1. Influence of indoor air temperature and temperature of the surrounding surfaces on the perception of comfort

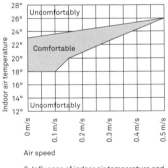

2. Influence of indoor air temperature and air speed on the perception of comfort

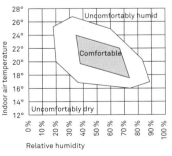

3. Influence of indoor air temperature and indoor relative humidity on the perception of comfort

| Building/room type | Average operating temperature (in °C) of all quality classes of indoor air temperature, in winter |
| --- | --- |
| Individual office | 22 |
| Open-plan office | 22 |
| Conference room | 22 |
| Auditorium | 22 |
| Cafeteria/restaurant | 22 |
| Classroom | 22 |
| Preschool | 22 |
| Department store | 19 |
| Apartment | 22 |
| Bathroom | 25 |
| Church | 18 |
| Museum/gallery | 19 |

## 2.2.2 Indoor Air

Along with favorable temperature, a sufficient supply of fresh air is essential for a positive perception of interior spaces. The fresh air can be supplied mechanically using ventilation or air-conditioning systems, or it can come from natural ventilation. Where natural ventilation is relied upon, it is necessary to check whether a sufficient supply of air can enter through the available openings and whether this means of air exchange is sufficiently energy-efficient and verifiable according to applicable standards.

Figure 2.2.2
Various types of room ventilation

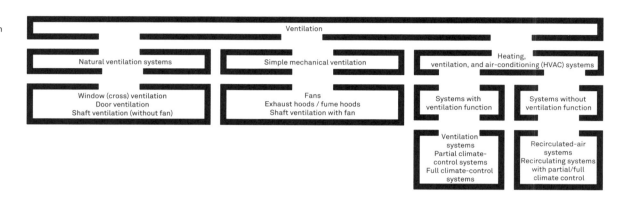

Figure 2.2.3
Basic principles of natural room ventilation

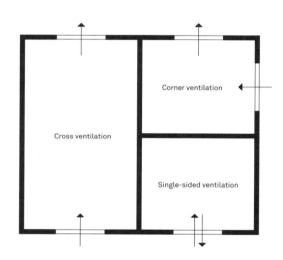

Maximum room depth with window ventilation

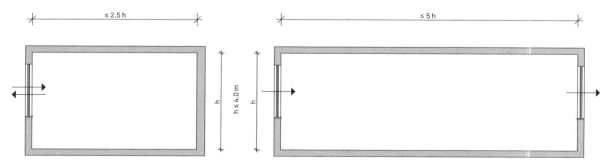

Table 2.2.2 (left)
Exemplary reference values for
the air exchange rate of various
room typologies

Per Pistohl, W; Rechenauer, C.;
Scheuerer, B., *Handbuch der
Gebäudetechnik,* vol. 2, *Heizung,
Lüftung, Beleuchtung, Energie-
sparen*

Table 2.2.3 (top right)
Standard values for the air
exchange rates of various opening
types

Per Pistohl, W; Rechenauer, C.;
Scheuerer, B., *Handbuch der
Gebäudetechnik,* vol. 2, *Heizung,
Lüftung, Beleuchtung, Energie-
sparen*

Table 2.2.4 (bottom right)
Requirements for air quality

Per ASR A3.6 (2012)

| Room type | Hourly air change rate in h$^{-1}$ |
|---|---|
| Assembly spaces | 5.0–10.0 |
| Auditoriums, lecture halls | 6.0–8.0 |
| Big-box stores, department stores | 4.0–6.0 |
| Cafeterias | 6.0–8.0 |
| Cinemas, theaters, etc. | 4.0–6.0 |
| Classrooms | 4.0–5.0 |
| Commercial kitchens | 15.0–30.0 |
| Exhibition halls | 2.0–3.0 |
| Gymnasiums | 2.0–3.0 |
| Kitchenettes | 15.0–25.0 |
| Laboratories | 8.0–15.0 |
| Laundries | 10.0–15.0 |
| Libraries, archives, museums | 4.0–6.0 |
| Living spaces as per EnEV | 0.6–0.7 |
| Locker rooms in gymnasiums | 8.0–10.0 |
| Locker rooms in natatoriums | 8.0–10.0 |
| Meeting rooms | 6.0–12.0 |
| Natatoriums | 3.0–6.0 |
| Offices | 2.0–6.0 |
| Operating rooms | 5.0–20.0 |
| Paint shops | 10.0–20.0 |
| Paint spray rooms | 20.0–50.0 |
| Public toilets | 10.0–15.0 |
| Restaurants, dining areas | 4.0–8.0 |
| Retail stores, salesrooms | 4.0–8.0 |
| Toilets in apartments | 2.0–4.0 |
| Toilets in factories | 8.0–10.0 |
| Toilets in office buildings | 3.0–6.0 |
| Shower rooms in natatoriums | 10.0–15.0 |
| Sickrooms, hospital rooms | 3.0–5.0 |
| Workshops with no exceptional deterioration in air quality | 3.0–6.0 |

**Air exchange rates with window ventilation**

| Type of window ventilation | Hourly air change rate in h$^{-1}$ |
|---|---|
| Windows and doors closed (air exchange through cracks) | 0–0.5 |
| Single-sided ventilation, window tilted, no rolling shutters | 0.8–4.0 |
| Single-sided ventilation, window half open | 5.0–10.0 |
| Single-sided ventilation, window fully open (brief and intense air exchange) | 9.0–10.0 |
| Cross ventilation (brief and intense air exchange via opposing windows and doors) | Up to 45 |

| $CO_2$-concentration [ml/m³]/[ppm] | Measures |
|---|---|
| < 1,000 | No measures (provided that no increase above 1,000 ppm is anticipated) |
| 1,000–2,000 | Check ventilation behavior and improve |
|  | Establish ventilation plan |
|  | Define ventilation measures |
| > 2,000 | Additional measures |
|  | Intensified ventilation |
|  | Reduce the number of people in the room |

### 2.2.3 Lighting Conditions

Depending on the room typology, the lighting conditions are also an important factor for the planning. They include the type of natural or artificial lighting, the necessary brightness – which is measured in terms of illuminance – and the nature of the light itself. The latter includes design elements such as directional and nondirectional light sources, the accentuation of individual areas, the reduction of glare and contrast, and protection from excessive incident solar radiation.

**Figure 2.2.4**
Types of room lighting

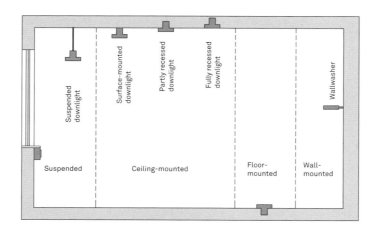

**Figure 2.2.5**
Directed and undirected light sources in a room

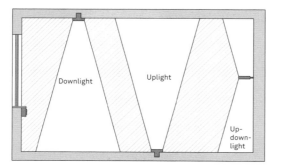
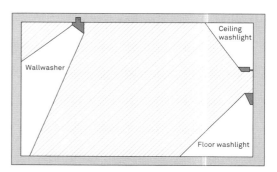

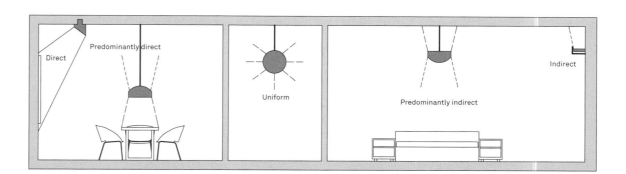

## 2.2.3 Lighting Conditions

### Examples for various natural illuminance values

| Natural illuminance values | E in lx approx. |
|---|---|
| Sunny day outdoors (12 noon) | 100,000 |
| Overcast sky in summer (12 noon) | 18,000 |
| Overcast sky in winter (12 noon) | 5,000 |
| In the middle of a room (winter, overcast, 12 noon) | 300 |
| Nighttime with full moon | 0.25 |

### Mean illuminance values for a selection of various room types as per DIN 12464-1

| Room type | $E_m$ in lx |
|---|---|
| Circulation spaces and corridors | 100 |
| Stairs, escalators | 150 |
| Cafeterias, kitchenettes | 200 |
| Lunchrooms | 100 |
| Dressing rooms, washrooms, bathrooms, toilets | 200 |
| Sanitary facilities | 500 |
| Supply rooms and storage spaces | 100 |
| Rooms for technical drawing | 750 |
| Conference and meeting rooms | 500 |
| Archives | 200 |
| Office spaces (writing, reading, data processing) | 500 |
| Classrooms in primary and secondary schools | 300 |
| Lecture halls, classrooms for night school | 500 |
| Examination rooms (general lighting) | 500 |

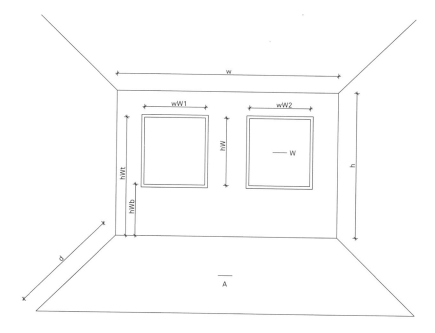

Windows in habitable rooms:
ΣwW = min. 0.55 w
hWt = min. 2.2 m above TOFF (top of finished floor)
hWb = max. 0.95 m above TOFF

Windows in workrooms:
For d ≤ 5 m → W ≥ 1.25 m²
For d > 5 m → W ≥ 1.5 m²
For A ≤ 600 m² → ΣW ≥ 0.1 × A
For 600 m² < A ≤ 2,000 m² → ΣW ≥ 60 m² + 0.01× A
For h ≤ 3.5 m → ΣW ≥ 0.3 × w × h

Applies additionally:
wW = min. 1 m
hW (for predominantly sedentary activities) = min. 1.25 m
hW (for predominantly standing activities) = min. 1 m
hWt = min. 2.2 m above TOFF (top of finished floor)
hWb (for predominantly sedentary activities) = max. 0.95 m above TOFF
hWb (for predominantly standing activities) = max. 1.2 m above TOFF

For workrooms that do not significantly exceed the following values:
h = ca. 3.5 m
d = ca. 6 m
A = ca. 50 m²
the following applies additionally:
ΣwW = min. 0.55 w

**Figure 2.2.7**
Parameters for incoming daylight

Per DIN 5034-1

Determination of the minimum window width (in m)

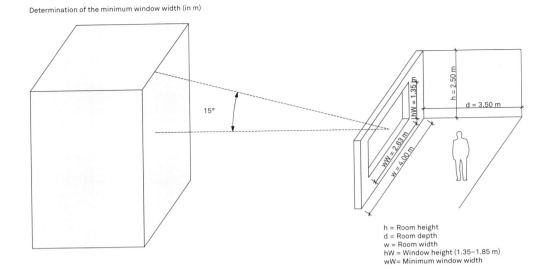

h = Room height
d = Room depth
w = Room width
hW = Window height (1.35–1.85 m)
wW= Minimum window width

Sufficient perceived brightness

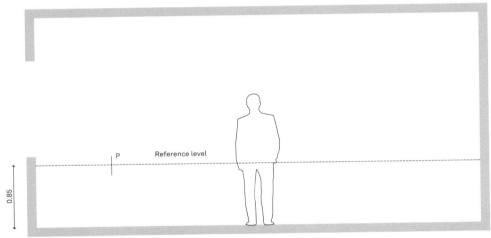

Daylight factor measured at point P (at reference level at half the depth of the space, 1 m distance from the side wall) must be a minimum of 0.9% on average and may not be less than 0.75% at any point.

Angle of obstruction a

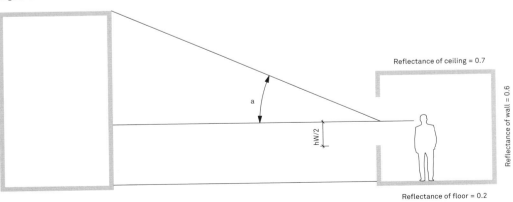

Reflectance of ceiling = 0.7
Reflectance of wall = 0.6
Reflectance of floor = 0.2

Figure 2.2.8
Barrier-free window sizes (in cm)

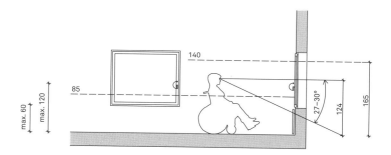

Figure 2.2.9
Alternatives for sun shading/glare protection

a) Vertical folding shutters
b) Vertical louvers
c) Sliding shutters
d) Stationary sun shading element
e) Horizontal folding shutter
f) Horizontal louvers
g) Exterior rolling shutter/blind

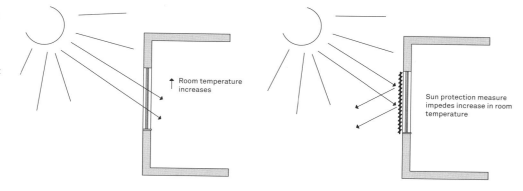

Measures – horizontal section through room

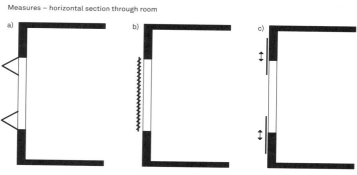

Measures – vertical section through room

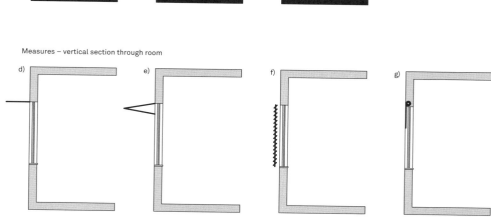

Table 2.2.7
Requirements for various
room types

Based on DIN 5034-1

| Requirement | Habitable room | Workroom (only defined for room height h ≤ 3.5 m, room depth d ≤ 6 m and room area A ≤ 50 m²) | Hospital room |
|---|---|---|---|
| Visual connection to outside | (Total) width of the transparent parts of the window shall be at least 55% of the window wall, the bottom edge of the transparent glazing of the window h (Wb) for predominantly sedentary activities shall be no more than 0.95 m above the floor and no more than 1.20 m above the floor for predominantly standing activities. Top edge of the transparent glazing of the window h (Wt) at least 2.2 m above the floor | | |
| | | • Also for room heights of more than 3.5 m: Height of the rough window opening shall be greater than 1.3 m Width of the transparent part of each window shall be ≥ 1 m<br>• Minimum area of the transparent part of the window for room depths of less than 5 m: 1.25 m² for larger room depths: 1.5 m²<br>• Transparent (total) window surface shall be at least 30% of the room width times the room height, but no less than 10% of the room area. | Notwithstanding the hospital guidelines of some German states, additionally: Bottom edge of the transparent part of the window 0.7 m above the floor; and temporary visual screening to prevent views from outside. |
| Sufficient brightness | Daylight factor D at half the room depth, 0.85 m above the floor, and 1 m away from each side wall: A min. of 0.9% in the middle of the two points and a min. of 0.75% at one of the two points. For rooms with windows in two adjacent walls: 1%. Maximize the reflectance of the enclosing room surfaces. | | |
| Required illuminance | No requirements formulated | Minimum of 60% of the values for artificial lighting specified in DIN EN 12464-1 | No requirements formulated |
| Protection from glare and heat radiation | | Sun protection devices, e.g., rolling shutters, venetian blinds, curtains | |
| Possible period of exposure to sunlight | In at least one habitable room of a dwelling, until the equinox at least 4 hrs. For winter months: on January 17 minimum 1 hr. | No requirements formulated | At least until the equinox: 4 hrs. For winter months: on January 17 minimum 1 hr. |

## 2.2.4 Acoustics

Room acoustics can be an essential design principle, for example in concert halls or religious buildings. In general, the primary concerns are to achieve good speech intelligibility and to limit reverberation times. For this purpose and subject to the use and the number of users, specific requirements are defined for the spatially enclosing elements.

**Table 2.2.8**
Noise abatement parameters for various situations

Per TA Lärm

Individual, brief spikes in noise levels are allowed to exceed the daytime and nighttime immission guide values. Pertinent levels are stipulated in the applicable standards.

### Immission guide values for affected areas outside of buildings

| Immission area | Standard value for the assessment level |
|---|---|
| a) Industrial parks | 70 dB(A) |
| b) Commercial areas | daytime: 65 dB(A), nighttime: 50 dB(A) |
| c) Core areas, village areas, mixed-use area | daytime: 60 dB(A), nighttime: 45 dB(A) |
| d) General residential areas, small housing estates | daytime: 55 dB(A), nighttime: 40 dB(A) |
| e) Residential-only areas | daytime: 50 dB(A), nighttime: 35 dB(A) |
| f) Spa areas, hospitals, nursing homes | daytime: 45 dB(A), nighttime: 35 dB(A) |

### Immission guide values for affected areas within buildings

| | |
|---|---|
| Nonoperational rooms in need of protection | daytime: 35 dB(A), nighttime: 25 dB(A) |

### Immission guide values for rare events

| | |
|---|---|
| Rare events as per section 7.2, for affected areas outside of buildings | daytime: 70 dB(A), nighttime: 55 dB(A) |

**Figure 2.2.10**
Use-specific reverberation times as a function of spatial volume

Per DIN 18041

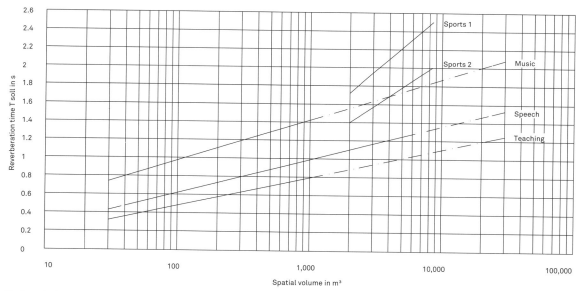

**Use Examples for Diagram**

**Music**
Music classroom with active music-making and singing, council chamber and banquet hall for music performances

**Speech**
Court and council chamber, community hall, assembly room, music rehearsal space in music schools or similar, sports hall and natatorium with spectator seating

**Teaching**
Classroom (except for music), music classroom with audio-visual presentations, group rooms in preschools and day care centers, senior day care centers, seminar room, room for social interaction

**Lecture hall**
Room for tele-teaching, meeting room, conference room, performance space exclusively for electroacoustic use

**Sports 1**
Sports hall and natatorium without spectators, for normal use and/or instructional use by a single class or group (one class or sports group with uniform communication content)

**Sports 2**
Sports hall and natatorium without spectators, for instructional use by multiple simultaneous classes or groups (multiple classes or sports groups at the same time, with varying communication contents)

# 2.3 Spatial Perception

The large majority of rooms are conceived as occupied spaces where people can be expected to spend a lengthy amount of time (that is, not only for transient use – for example, maintenance work in machine rooms). Users develop specific needs or expectations for a particular typology of use based on factors they associate with it. Although all matters should be given precise and purposeful consideration, it is equally important to avoid situations that might be perceived as uncomfortable – and especially spaces that cause anxiety. Even though such perceptions can vary significantly from one person to another, being influenced as they are by their own personal experiences, generally applicable requirement profiles do exist for specific occupied spaces.

### 2.3.1 Typology-based Requirements

Typological references like living, working, learning, entertaining, leisure activities, etc., engender specific spatial requirements that range from objectively characterized and functionally designed environments all the way to entry into an illusory world with the character of adventure or entertainment. These expectations are fundamentally influenced by sociocultural factors, so spatial solutions should be tailored to the society or user group of greatest importance. Especially if personal experience with a particular use is lacking, it is important for the architect to engage with the specific particularities and expectations in relation to the subsequent use – and to understand these.

Figure 2.3.1
Requirement profiles for occupied spaces

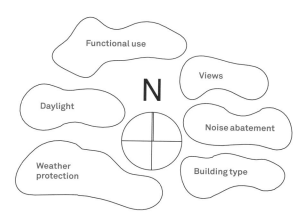

Figure 2.3.2
Example of typology-based expectations for sitting (movie theater vs. lecture hall)

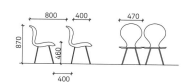

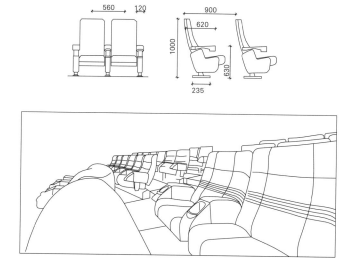

## 2.3.2  Spatial Geometry and Proportion

A room's proportions bring about specific impacts on users: for instance, tunnel-like rooms (with restricted height and width over a long length), tend to have a connecting, corridor-like character, whereas contorted geometries and layouts are difficult to comprehend and are thus often unpleasant or confusing for unfamiliar users. Very high spaces are found especially in religious and public buildings. Thus, on the basis of basic historical elements, spatial proportions that are perceived as pleasant and "well-proportioned" have developed in various cultures.

The relationship between a room's height and its floor area is particularly important in this regard. Thus when room sizes are increased, an increase in the room height is always also recommended. Especially with typical room heights of 2.50 m (as commonly encountered in private residences), deviations of just a few centimeters are very clearly and consciously perceived.

**Figure 2.3.3**
Spatial proportions and effects

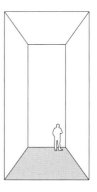
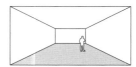
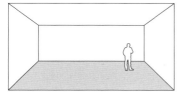
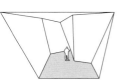

**Table 2.3.1**
Appropriate minimum heights
of occupied spaces

| Orientation for the minimum heights of occupied spaces | |
| --- | --- |
| Floor area (m²) | Minimum clear height (m) |
| ≤ 50 | ≥ 2.50 |
| > 50 ≤ 100 | ≥ 2.70 |
| > 100 ≤ 2,000 | ≥ 3.00 |
| > 2,000 | ≥ 3.30 |

**Figure 2.3.4**
Japanese tatami as an example
of sociocultural principles of room
sizes and organization

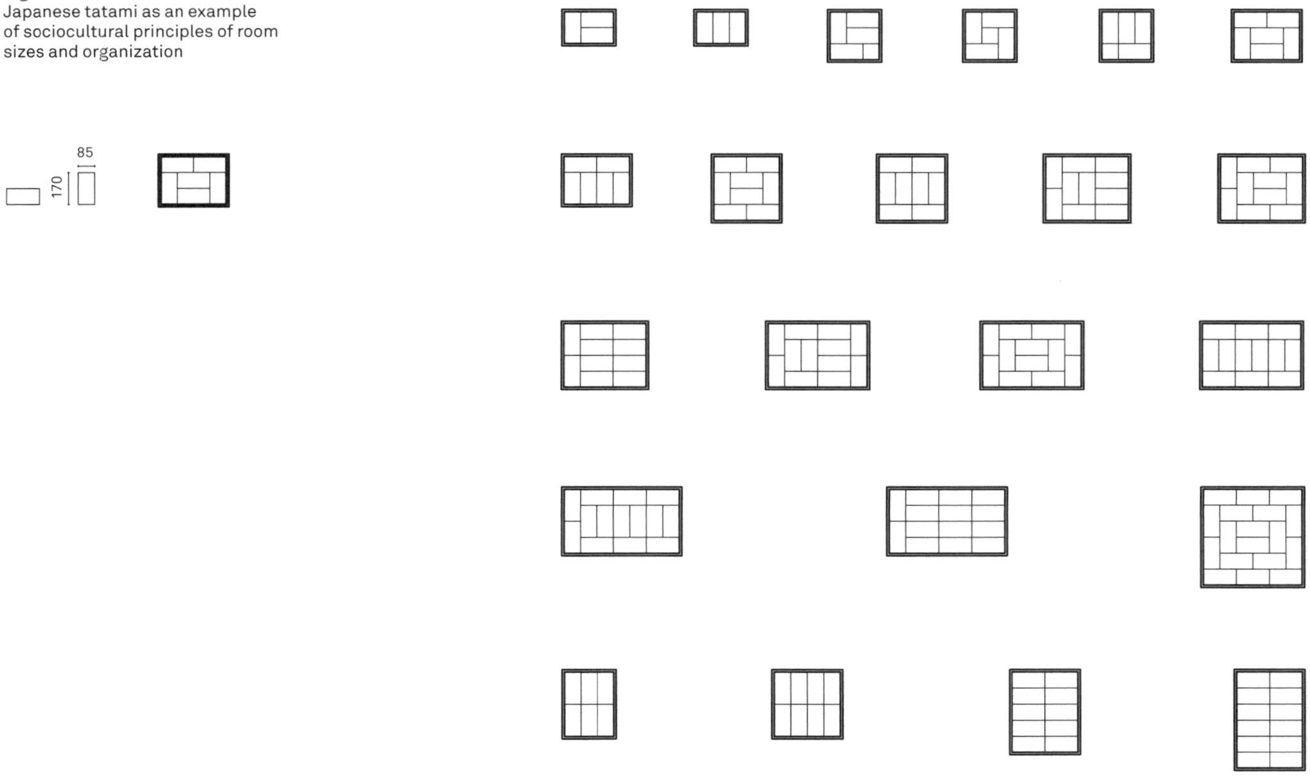

# 3 Spaces

## 3.1 External Circulation [39]

3.1.1 Public Access [39]

3.1.2 Parked Vehicles [45]

3.1.3 Private Exterior Circulation [54]

3.1.4 Mailbox Units [56]

3.1.5 Waste Receptacles [57]

## 3.2 Internal Circulation [61]

3.2.1 Entrance Areas [61]

3.2.2 Corridors [63]

3.2.3 Doors [66]

3.2.4 Stairs [69]

3.2.5 Ramps [74]

3.2.6 Escalators and Moving Walkways [75]

3.2.7 Elevators and Conveying Systems [77]

## 3.3 Workrooms and Production Spaces [83]

3.3.1 Workplaces [83]

3.3.2 Production Spaces [84]

## 3.4 Communication Spaces and Dining Rooms [87]

3.4.1 Lecture, Seminar, and Conference Rooms [87]

3.4.2 Waiting and Seating Areas [94]

3.4.3 Dining Areas [97]

## 3.5 Sanitary Facilities ↗101

3.5.1 Plumbing Fixtures ↗101

3.5.2 Bathrooms and Private Sanitary Facilities ↗104

3.5.3 Public and Commercial Sanitary Facilities ↗105

3.5.4 Piping Routes ↗109


## 3.6 Kitchens ↗111

3.6.1 Kitchen Fixtures and Appliances ↗111

3.6.2 Private Kitchens ↗115


## 3.7 Storage Spaces ↗119

3.7.1 Pallets and Containers ↗119

3.7.2 Types of Storage ↗123

3.7.3 Handling and Transport ↗127


## 3.8 Ancillary and Staff Rooms ↗131

3.8.1 Lunchrooms ↗131

3.8.2 Locker and Changing Rooms ↗132

3.8.3 Medical and First Aid Rooms ↗136

3.8.4 Storerooms and Janitor's Closets ↗137


## 3.9 Technical Equipment Rooms ↗139

3.9.1 Connections to Public Utilities ↗139

3.9.2 Mains Connection Rooms and Meter Rooms ↗140

3.9.3 Distribution Rooms and Shafts ↗142

3.9.4 Heating ↗143

3.9.5 Ventilation ↗146

3.9.6 Water Supply and Wastewater Disposal ↗148

3.9.7 Electric Supply and Data Systems Technology ↗150

3.9.8 Server Rooms and Data Centers ↗151

# 3.1 External Circulation

Infrastructure development for buildings encompasses diverse measures in the public realm and in ensuring access and supply logistics on the property. In addition to roads, bicycle paths, and walkways, this includes access restrictions such as perimeter enclosures, gates, etc., and built elements located on the property (waste container areas, lighting, doorbells, mailboxes, etc.). The connections to public utility services (such as electricity, water supply, sewer, etc.) are also to be planned in this context. ↗Chapter 3.9 Spaces/Technical Equipment Rooms Depending on the building's typology and its function/public impact, in terms of design and organization there may be a clear separation or a smooth transition between the public and private realms. In terms of responsibilities, there is a clear division between the public development of infrastructure carried out by the city/municipality and private development done within the property lines.

### 3.1.1 Public Access

The demands placed on public space vary considerably due to the diversity of uses and users. In addition to logistical considerations (fast and reliable mobility, accommodation of parked vehicles), aspects of residential quality and the social integrity of public spaces are important in planning these spaces. Public spaces and infrastructures are to be designed with attention to aspects of accessibility and are fundamental to the participation of as many people as possible in public life and activities relating to mobility. Thus it is of little help to design a building according to current requirements for accessibility if disabled persons cannot reach it independently via public access routes.

**Figure 3.1.1**
Demarcation of public and private outdoor space

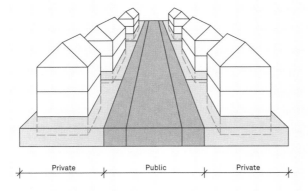

| Private | Public | Private |

**Figure 3.1.2**
Requirements for street spaces

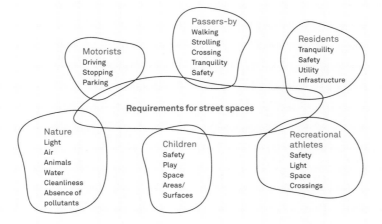

Motorists
Driving
Stopping
Parking

Passers-by
Walking
Strolling
Crossing
Tranquility
Safety

Residents
Tranquility
Safety
Utility
infrastructure

**Requirements for street spaces**

Nature
Light
Air
Animals
Water
Cleanliness
Absence of
pollutants

Children
Safety
Play
Space
Areas/
Surfaces

Recreational
athletes
Safety
Light
Space
Crossings

Figure 3.1.3
Sensible allocation of street
spaces

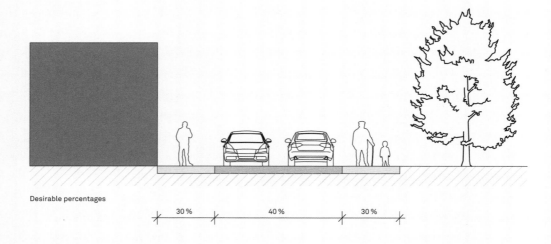

Desirable percentages

|  | 30 % | 40 % | 30 % |

Table 3.1.1
Typical widths of street spaces

Widths of street spaces vary
depending on traffic volume
(vehicles/hr.)

Author's summary, based on
RASt 06

**Street space widths**

| Use | Residential lane | Residential street | Collector road | Neighborhood street | Rural main road | Local thoroughfare |
|---|---|---|---|---|---|---|
| Without public transit | 4.50–10.00 m | 9.00–17.00 m | 11.50–15.50 m | 12.00–17.50 m | 8.50–14.00 m | |
| With public transit bus service | | 11.00–16.50 m | 16.50–26.70 m | 16.50–21.50 m | 11.50–19.50 m | 12.50–21.20 m |
| Use | Local shopping street | Main shopping street | Commercial street | Industrial road | Connecting road | Non-built-up road |
| With public transit bus service | 20.50–30.20 m | 20.50–33.00 m | 16.50–38.00 m | 23.50–30.00 m | 19.70–31.45 m | 15.50–28.60 m |
| With tram | 24.20–34.20 m | 16.50–37.00 m | 16.50–38.00 m | | 19.70–39.70 m | 28.50–34.10 m |

Table 3.1.2 (left)
Typical widths of elements along
roadways

Table 3.1.3 (top right)
Safety clearances for cycling
facilities

Table 3.1.4 (bottom right)
Space required for barrier-free
access

| Element | Space required |
|---|---|
| Advisory bike lane for cyclists on the roadway | 0.50–1.50 m |
| Areas for children to play by the roadside | 2.00 m |
| Areas in front of benches | 1.00 m |
| Areas in front of shop displays | 1.50 m |
| Bikeway | 1.60–2.50 m |
| Bus lane | 3.25 m |
| Curb strip (road verge) with trees | 2.00–2.50 m |
| Curb strip (road verge) without trees | 1.00 m |
| Median | 1.00–2.50 m |
| Parallel parking | 2.30–2.50 m |
| Parking, delivery, loading | 2.50–3.00 m |
| Pedestrian and cycle path | 3.00–5.00 m |
| Perpendicular parking | 5.00–5.50 m |
| Roadside area with frontage road | 7.00–7.50 m |
| Spaces for lingering in front of store windows | 1.00 m |
| Sidewalk | 2.25–7.00 m |
| Waiting areas at bus stops | 2.50 m |

| Distance | Safety clearance |
|---|---|
| From buildings, boundary enclosures, tree pits, traffic facilities, and other built-in elements | 0.25 m |
| From edge of roadway | 0.50 m |
| From parked vehicles (parallel parking) | 0.75 m |
| From parked vehicles (perpendicular or angled parking) | 0.25 m |
| From pedestrian traffic areas | 0.25 m |

| Type of restriction or assistive equipment | Width | Length |
|---|---|---|
| Blind person with white cane | 0.80–1.20 m | – |
| Blind person with guide dog | 1.20 m | – |
| Blind person with escort | 1.10–1.30 m | – |
| Person with baby carriage | 0.80–1.00 m | 2.00 m |
| Person with cane | 0.85 m | – |
| Person with crutches | 1.00 m | – |
| Person in wheelchair | 0.90–1.10 m | – |
| Wheelchair user with escort | 0.90–1.00 m | 2.50 m |

Table 3.1.5
Dimensions of passenger cars

| Vehicle category | Example | Length | Width | Diameter of turning circle | Turning radius |
|---|---|---|---|---|---|
| Subcompact car | | 3.50 m | 1.65 m | 9.60 m | 4.80 m |
| Compact car | | 4.00 m | 1.70 m | 10.60 m | 5.30 m |
| Mid-sized car | | 4.40 m | 1.80 m | 11.00 m | 5.50 m |
| Mid-luxury car | | 4.80 m | 1.85 m | 11.50 m | 5.75 m |
| Luxury car | | 5.00 m | 1.95 m | 11.90 m | 5.95 m |

Table 3.1.6
Dimensions of miscellaneous vehicles

| Type | Example | Length | Width | Height |
|---|---|---|---|---|
| Bicycle | | 1.70–2.00 m | 0.60–0.75 m | 1.00–1.25 m |
| Motorcycle | | 2.00–2.50 m | 0.70–1.00 m | 1.00–1.50 m |
| Quad bike | | 1.75–2.10 m | 1.05–1.25 m | 1.00–1.25 m |

Table 3.1.7
Dimensions of trucks

| Permissible total weight | Length | Width | Height |
|---|---|---|---|
| max. 3.5 t | 5.25–7.45 m | 2.40–2.45 m | 2.45–3.10 m |
| max. 7.5 t | 6.00–8.50 m | 2.45–2.55 m | 3.80 m |
| max. 12 t | 6.50–12.00 m | 2.45–2.55 m | 3.80–4.00 m |
| 40 t | 13.50–18.75 m | 2.55 m | 3.80–4.00 m |
| Truck, 2 axles | max. 13.50 m | max. 2.55 m | max. 4.00 m |
| Truck, min. 3 axles | max. 15.00 m | max. 2.55 m | max. 4.00 m |
| Tractor-trailer | max. 16.50 m | max. 2.55 m | max. 4.00 m |
| Truck-trailer combination | max. 18.75 m | max. 2.55 m | max. 4.00 m |

**Table 3.1.8**
Dimensions of buses

\* Average dimensions based on manufacturers' data

| Type | Number of persons*<br>Seated/standing | Dimensions*<br>Length | Width | Height | Turning circle*<br>Diameter | Turning curve*<br>Radius |
|---|---|---|---|---|---|---|
| **Public transit bus** | | | | | | |
| Low-floor bus, city bus | 30–55 / 75–110 | 12.00–18.00 m | 2.50–2.55 m | 3.00–3.30 m | 21.00–23.00 m | 10.50–11.50 m |
| Regional bus | 40–60 / 20–70 | 12.00–18.00 m | 2.50–2.55 m | 3.15–3.40 m | 21.00–23.00 m | 10.50–11.50 m |
| Minibus | 10–20 / 12–30 | 5.90–9.00 m | 1.95–2.15 m | 2.60–2.90 m | 13.50–17.50 m | 6.75–8.75 m |
| Minivan | < 9 | 4.75–5.30 m | 1.90–2.00 m | 1.90–2.50 m | 11.50–13.80 m | 5.75–6.90 m |
| Double-decker bus | 50–90 / 10–45 | 13.00–14.00 m | 2.50–2.55 m | 3.90–4.00 m | 22.00–24.00 m | 11.00–12.00 m |
| Articulated bus | 35–60 / 80–150 | 17.50–19.50 m | 2.50–2.55 m | 3.00–3.30 m | 22.50–24.50 m | 11.25–12.25 m |
| Bi-articulated bus | 45–60 / < 150 | 23.50–25.00 m | 2.50–2.55 m | 3.00–3.30 m | 22.50–25.00 m | 11.25–12.50 m |
| **Intercity bus (coach)** | | | | | | |
| Intercity bus with toilet | 40–60 | 12.00–14.50 m | 2.50–2.55 m | 3.30–3.75 m | 20.50–24.00 m | 10.25–12.00 m |
| Sleeper bus ("Nightliner") | 6–12 | 12.00–14.00 m | 2.50–2.55 m | 3.70–4.00 m | 20.50–24.00 m | 10.50–12.00 m |

**Table 3.1.9**
Dimensions of construction vehicles

| Type | Length | Width | Height | Turning radius |
|---|---|---|---|---|
| Backhoe loader | 3.40–6.75 m | 1.40–2.35 m | 2.25–3.10 m | 4.00–6.50 m |
| Concrete mixer | 8.00–15.00 m | 2.50–2.55 m | 3.80–4.00 m | |
| Concrete pump | 8.00–15.00 m | 2.50–2.55 m | 3.80–4.00 m | |
| Crawler excavator | 9.10–14.00 m | 2.50–4.85 m | 3.00–4.10 m | |
| Mobile crane | 10.00–22.00 m | 2.55–3.00 m | 3.55–4.00 m<br>(25.00–145.00 m) | |
| Mini-excavator | 3.25–5.50 m | 0.95–2.30 m | 2.25–2.95 m | |
| Self-propelled excavator | 6.25–10.25 m | 2.50–2.75 m | 3.10–3.25 m | 4.50–6.65 m |
| Wheeled front loader | 5.30–10.00 m | 2.30–2.75 m | 2.75–3.65 m | 3.50–7.00 m |
| Bulldozer | 4.00–7.65 m | 2.35–3.00 m | 3.10–4.00 m | |

**Figure 3.1.4**
Design of ramps and ramp transitions for motor vehicles

Ramp inside building: max. 15% grade

Ramp outside: max. 10% grade

Parking ramp: max. 6% grade

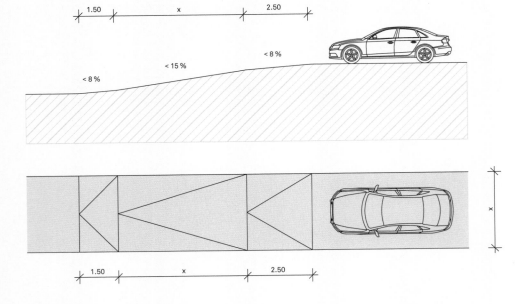

**Figure 3.1.5**
Hammerhead turnarounds for cars

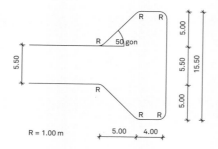

R = 1.00 m

Hammerhead turnaround for vehicles up to 9.00 m long

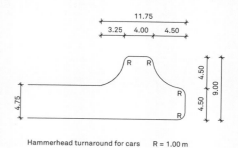

Hammerhead turnaround for cars        R = 1.00 m

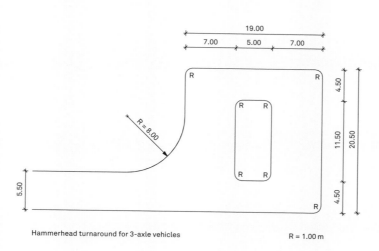

Hammerhead turnaround for 3-axle vehicles                R = 1.00 m

**Figure 3.1.6**
Angled parking for straight-body trucks, trucks with trailers, tractor-trailers, buses, articulated buses

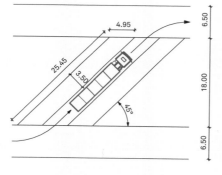

Angled parking for straight-body trucks, trucks with trailers, tractor-trailers, buses, articulated buses

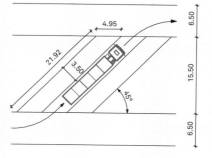

Angled parking for straight-body trucks, tractor-trailers, buses, articulated buses

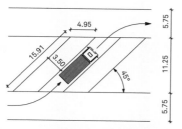

Angled parking for straight-body trucks, 12 m buses

**Figure 3.1.7**
Turning curves for cars

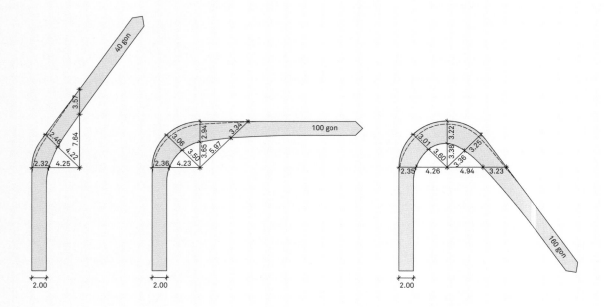

**Figure 3.1.8**
Turning curves for trucks

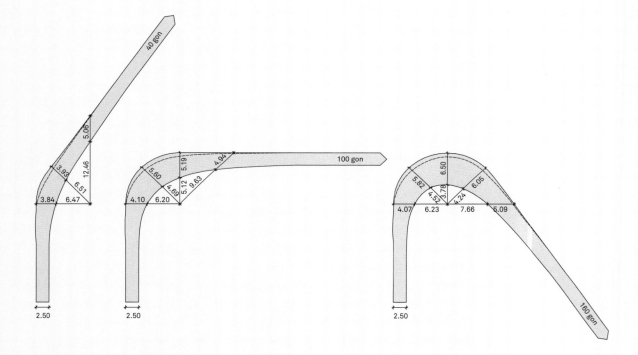

## 3.1.2 Parked Vehicles

One function that occupies large amounts of exterior space is the parking of vehicles – cars, bicycles, buses, and/or trucks – which must be taken into account both in public spaces and on private property. The number of necessary parking spaces is generally determined by statutory minimum standards or user requirements. For all parking spaces, consideration must be given to ensure good vehicular accessibility and ease of entering, exiting, and loading the vehicle. Particularly in high-use areas, the architect must carefully plan the logistics of the parking and waiting areas and should also consider the provision of parking guidance systems.

**Figure 3.1.9**
Dimensions of parking spaces for passenger cars

Minimum dimensions:
2.50 m when confined on both sides
2.40 m when confined on one side
2.30 m when open on both sides

For comfortable use, parking spaces should always have a width of at least 2.50 m so that car doors can be opened approximately 45°.

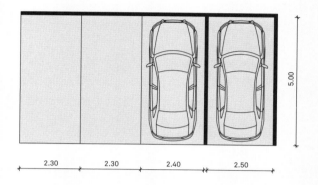

**Figure 3.1.10**
Dimensions of wheelchair-accessible parking spaces

It is important to ensure that a wheelchair-accessible transition is established between the maneuvering zone and the walkway.

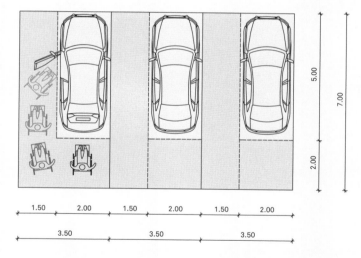

**Figure 3.1.11**
Parking variants and dimensions

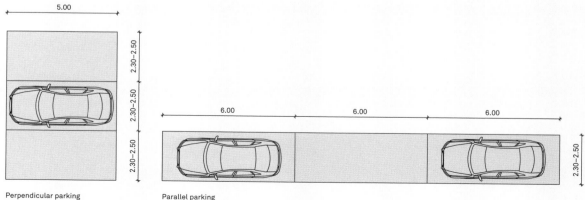

Perpendicular parking          Parallel parking

Table 3.1.10 (left)
Parking aisle depth as a function of parking angle

Table 3.1.11 (right)
Typical carport and garage sizes

| Parking angle [gon] | Parking angle [°] | Parking aisle depth, against wall [m] | Parking aisle depth, bumper-to-bumper interlock [m] |
|---|---|---|---|
| 50 | 45 | 4.85 | 8.25 |
| 60 | 54 | 5.15 | 9.00 |
| 70 | 63 | 5.30 | 9.60 |
| 80 | 72 | 5.35 | 9.90 |
| 90 | 81 | 5.25 | 10.00 |

| Type | Length | Width | Height |
|---|---|---|---|
| Single carport | 5.00–8.00 m | 2.90–3.80 m | 2.10–3.10 m |
| Double carport | 5.00–8.00 m | 5.00–6.00 m | 2.10–3.10 m |
| Single-car garage | 5.10–9.00 m | 2.55–4.00 m | 2.20–3.50 m |
| Double-car garage | 5.10–9.00 m | 5.00–8.00 m | 2.20–3.50 m |

Figure 3.1.12
Parking variants and dimensions

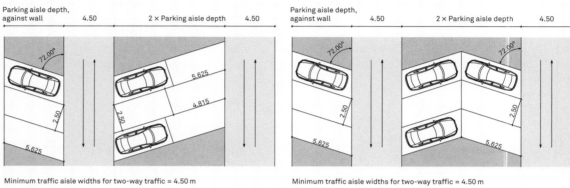

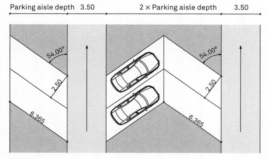

Figure 3.1.13
Minimum space between garage and road

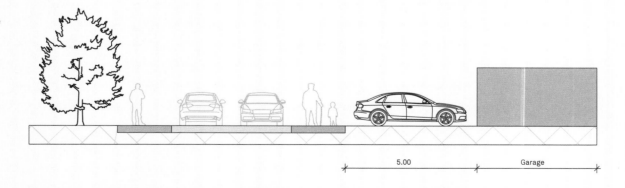

**Figure 3.1.14**
Garage door types in section and plan

a) Rolling door
b) Double-leaf rolling door
c) Telescopic rolling door
d) Folding door
e) Swing-out door, single-leaf
f) Swing-out door, double-leaf (barn doors)
g) Tilt-up door (single-panel) door
h) Overhead sectional door
i) Overhead coiling door

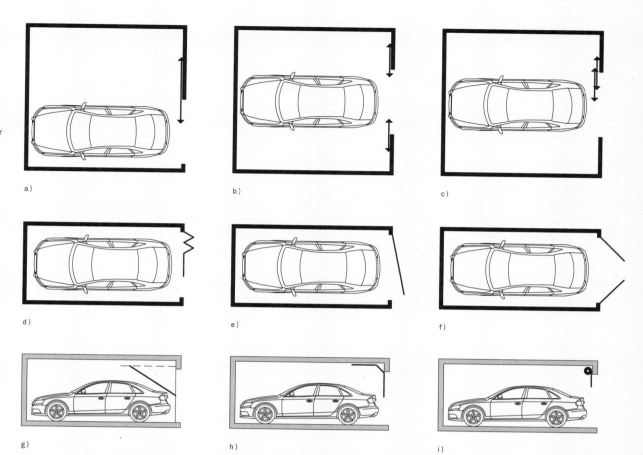

a)    b)    c)

d)    e)    f)

g)    h)    i)

**Table 3.1.12**
Quantity of required parking spaces

Depending on the simultaneity and frequency of use, the minimum amounts shall be increased accordingly.

Per BauO NRW

| Ref. no. | Type | Quantity of parking spaces | Parking spaces, minimum | Percentage of visitors |
|---|---|---|---|---|
| 1 | **Residential buildings and dormitories** | | | |
| 1.1 | Buildings with dwellings | 1 space per dwelling | – | – |
| 1.2 | Children's residences and youth homes | 1 space per 20 residents | – | 75% |
| 1.3 | Senior citizen homes, retirement homes, care homes for people with disabilities | 1 space per 10–17 residents | 3 | 75% |
| 1.4 | Other dormitories | 1 space per 2–5 residents | 2 | 10% |
| 2 | **Buildings with offices, administrative facilities, and medical practices** | | | |
| 2.1 | General office and administrative spaces | 1 space per 30–40 m² usable area | – | 20% |
| 2.2 | Spaces with substantial visitor traffic (customer service desks, dispatch rooms, consultancies, doctors' offices, etc.) | 1 space per 20–30 m² usable area | 3 | 75% |
| 3 | **Sales outlets** | | | |
| 3.1 | Stores with up to 700 m² sales area | 1 space per 30–50 m² usable sales area | 2 | 75% |
| 3.2 | Stores with more than 700 m² sales area | 1 space per 10–30 m² usable sales area | – | 75% |
| 4 | **Places of assembly (except sports facilities), churches** | | | |
| 4.1 | Places of assembly | 1 space per 5–10 seats | – | 90% |
| 4.2 | Churches | 1 space per 10–30 seats | – | 90% |

Table 3.1.12 (continuation)
Quantity of required parking
spaces

Depending on the simultaneity
and frequency of use, the minimum amounts shall be increased
accordingly.

Per BauO NRW

| Ref. no. | Type | Quantity of parking spaces | Parking spaces, minimum | Percentage of visitors |
|---|---|---|---|---|
| **5** | **Sports facilities** | | | |
| 5.1 | Sports fields | 1 space per 250 m² sports area, plus 1 space per 10–15 spectator seats | – | – |
| 5.2 | Multipurpose gyms | 1 space per 50 m² gym floor area, plus 1 space per 10–15 spectator seats | – | – |
| 5.3 | Outdoor and open-air swimming pools | 1 space per 200–300 m² site area | – | – |
| 5.4 | Riding stables | 1 space per 4 horse stalls | – | – |
| 5.5 | Indoor swimming pools | 1 space per 5–10 lockers/clothes hooks, plus 1 space per 10–15 spectator seats | – | – |
| 5.6 | Fitness centers | 1 space per 15 m² sports area | – | – |
| 5.7 | Tennis facilities | 4 spaces per court, plus 1 space per 10–15 spectator seats | – | – |
| 5.8 | Miniature golf courses | 6 spaces per miniature golf course | – | – |
| 5.9 | Bowling alleys | 4 spaces per lane | – | – |
| 5.10 | Boathouses and boat berths | 1 space per 2–5 boats | – | – |
| **6** | **Restaurants and lodging establishments** | | | |
| 6.1 | Restaurants and lodging establishments | 1 space per 6–12 m² guest area | – | 75 % |
| 6.2 | Hotels, pensions, sanatoriums, and other lodging establishments | 1 space per 2–6 beds (for associated restaurant operations: additional spaces per 6.1) | – | 75 % |
| 6.3 | Gaming centers and amusement arcades | 1 space per 20–25 m² arcade/gaming area | 3 | – |
| 6.4 | Dance halls, discotheques | 1 space per 4–8 m² guest area | – | – |
| 6.5 | Youth hostels | 1 space per 10 beds | – | 75 % |
| **7** | **Medical institutions** | | | |
| 7.1 | University hospitals and similar teaching hospitals | 1 space per 2–3 beds (additional spaces per 2.2) | – | 50 % |
| 7.2 | Hospitals, clinics, and sanitarium facilities | 1 space per 10–15 beds | – | 60 % |
| 7.3 | Nursing homes | 1 space per 10–15 beds | 3 | 75 % |
| **8** | **Schools, youth training centers** | | | |
| 8.1 | Elementary schools | 1 space per 30 students | – | – |
| 8.2 | Other general education schools, vocational schools, vocational colleges | 1 space per 25 students, plus 1 space per 5–10 students over 18 years old | – | – |
| 8.3 | Special needs schools for people with disabilities | 1 space per 15 students | – | – |
| 8.4 | Colleges and universities | 1 space per 2–4 students | – | – |
| 8.5 | Nursery schools, day care centers | 1 space per 20–30 children | 2 | - |
| 8.6 | Youth clubs | 1 space per 15 clients | – | – |
| **9** | **Commercial facilities** | | | |
| 9.1 | Craftsmen's shops and industrial businesses | 1 space per 50–70 m² usable area (or per 3 employees) | – | 10–30 % |
| 9.2 | Storage rooms, storage yards, exhibition spaces, and sales areas | 1 space per 80–100 m² usable area (or per 3 employees) | – | – |
| 9.3 | Auto repair shops | 6 spaces per repair bay | – | – |
| 9.4 | Gas station with store | 3 spaces (additional spaces per 3.1) | – | – |

**Figure 3.1.15**
Bicycle dimensions

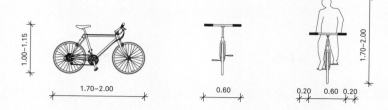

**Figure 3.1.16**
Bicycle parking

Inverted U bike rack      Frame/wheel holder      Hanging bike rack

**Figure 3.1.17**
Parking spaces for bicycles

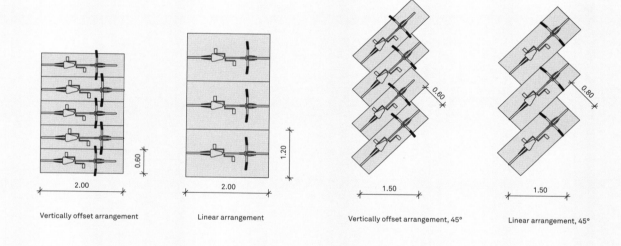

Vertically offset arrangement    Linear arrangement    Vertically offset arrangement, 45°    Linear arrangement, 45°

**Table 3.1.13**
Dimensions of bicycle parking
spaces

| Arrangement | Width in m | Length in m |
|---|---|---|
| Parking space, linear | 1.20 | 2.00 |
| Parking space, vertically offset | 0.60 | 2.00 |
| Parking space (45°), linear | 0.80 | 1.50 |
| Parking space (45°), vertically offset | 0.60 | 1.50 |
| Parking space, rack (narrow spacing) | 0.80 | 2.00 |
| Parking space, rack (comfortable spacing) | 1.20 | 2.00 |
| Parking space, rack, vertically offset (narrow) | 1.00 | 2.00 |
| Parking space, rack, vertically offset (comfortable) | 1.20 | 2.00 |
| Bike box | 1.00 | 2.10 |

**Figure 3.1.18**
Bicycle parking layout with racks

Linear arrangement

Vertically offset arrangement

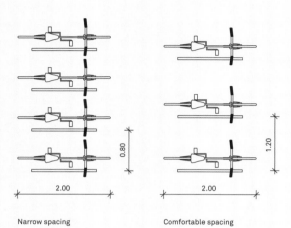

Narrow spacing

Comfortable spacing

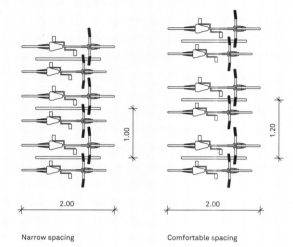

Narrow spacing

Comfortable spacing

**Figure 3.1.19**
Bicycle hanger types

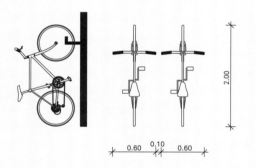

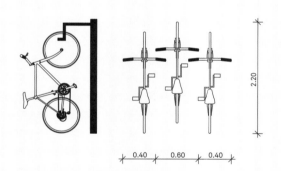

**Figure 3.1.20**
Arrangement of bike boxes

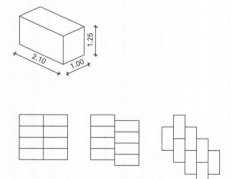

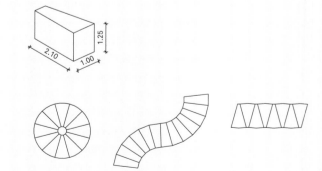

**Figure 3.1.21**
Various types of dock levelers/
plates

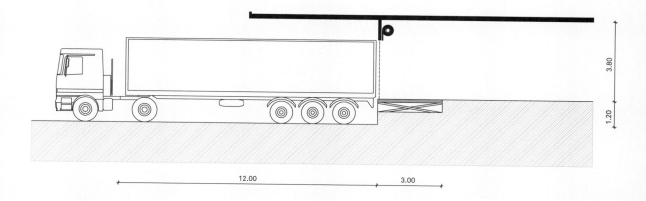

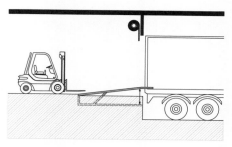

Dock leveler

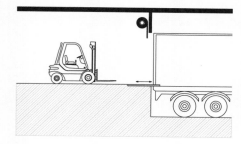

Dock plate

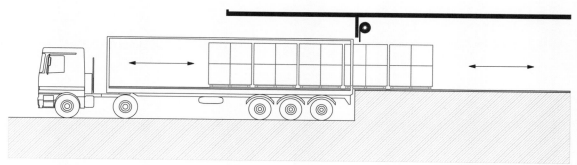

Moving floor shuttle trailer

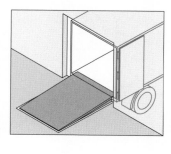

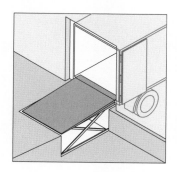

Figure 3.1.22
Loading of containers

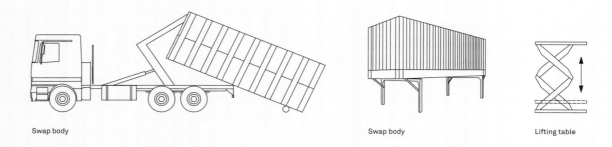

Swap body        Swap body        Lifting table

Figure 3.1.23
Maneuvering area in front
of loading docks

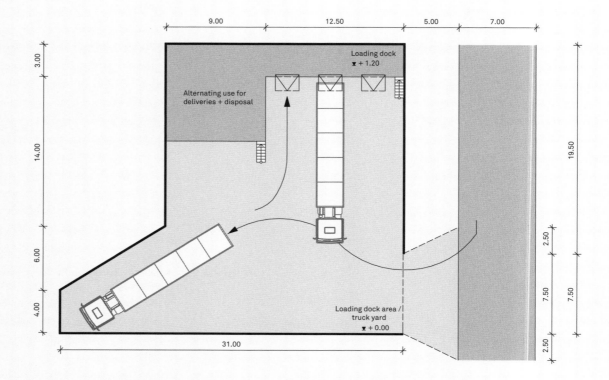

Table 3.1.14
Area requirements for loading
and delivery

| Minimum space required by delivery vehicles | Width | Length |
|---|---|---|
| Delivery vans and small trucks | 2.30 m | 10.00–12.00 m |
| Large trucks | 2.50 m | 12.00–14.00 m |
| Tractor-trailers | 2.50 m | 16.50 m |
| Temporary storage areas for goods | 3–5 m | |

**Figure 3.1.24**
Bus stop platform with waiting area/waiting island

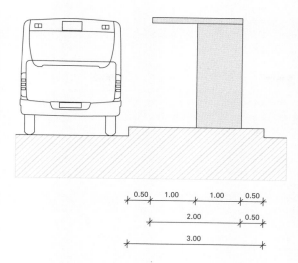

**Figure 3.1.25**
Bus parking lot with passenger islands

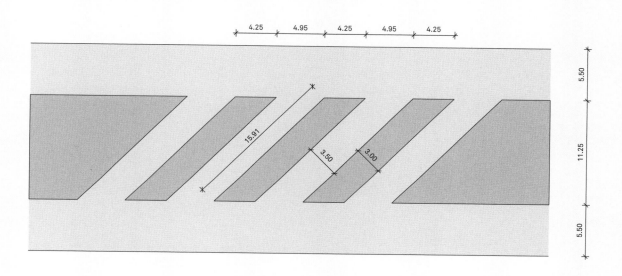

**Figure 3.1.26**
Various types of bus stops

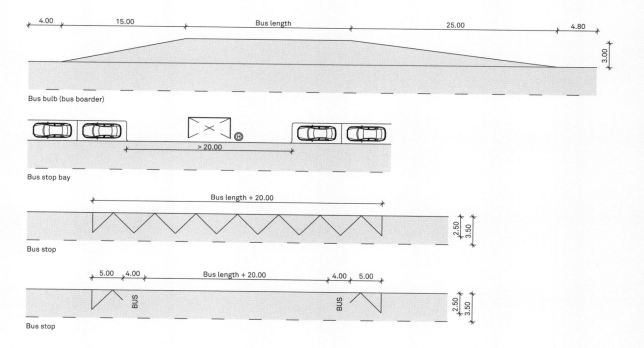

Bus bulb (bus boarder)

Bus stop bay

Bus stop

Bus stop

### 3.1.3 Private Exterior Circulation

Building entrances are ordinarily approached from the public realm via a pedestrian path. But depending on the building typology and logistical needs, a means of access must also be considered for cars, trucks, buses, bicycles, walking aids, wheelchairs, baby carriages, etc. Especially for typologies that are heavily frequented at peak periods (theaters, sports facilities, nursery schools, etc.), suitably effective concepts are needed to accommodate the very high frequencies encountered there briefly. This also includes temporary or long-term parking of vehicles and equipment in private outdoor spaces or buildings.

Buildings should generally be approachable via accessible ramps and paths. Thus any difference in height between street level and the top of the finished floor at the entrance level, which may not be excessive, should receive attention. In exterior areas, various built elements are also used for diverse purposes, which include controlling access to the property, facilitating circulation and logistics on the property, and making a transition to the building. For their design and configuration, the degree of public or private exposure and the security requirements appropriate to the building typology are usually crucial.

**Typical exterior built elements:**
- Entrances such as gates, barriers, doors, etc.
- Physical access control using electronic systems or gates with security guards
- Fences, walls
- Lighting
- Mailboxes
- Waste receptacles and enclosures
- Playgrounds, benches
- etc.

**Figure 3.1.27**
Ramps and passing areas for wheelchair users

The specified requirements also pertain to ramps within buildings.

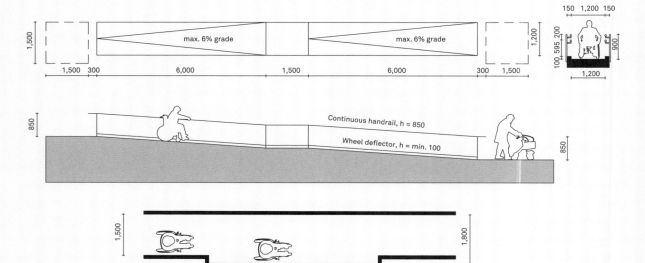

**Figure 3.1.28**
Access control with barrier gates

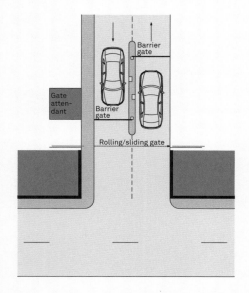
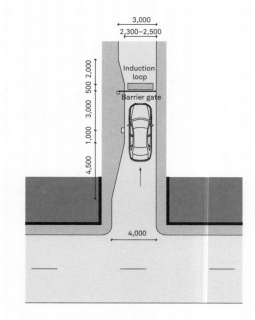

**Figure 3.1.29**
Various access control systems

Exact dimensions vary by manufacturer, so the specified dimensions can only serve as guidelines.

CH = Clear passage height
FH = Fascia height
OH = Overall height

Entry control with voucher system

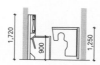
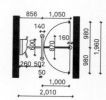

Half-height tripod turnstile

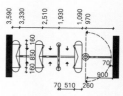

Half-height rotary turnstile

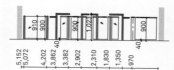

Sensor-controlled speed gates

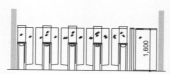
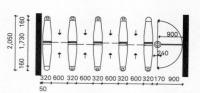

Security revolving door

$CH = 2,100$
$OH = CH + FH$

Full-height security turnstile

Full-height turnstile

### 3.1.4 Mailbox Units

Doorbell and mailbox units represent an interface between public and private space, since they should be publicly accessible and the mailboxes should, where possible, be capable of being emptied directly from the private realm.

Mailbox units can be located outside the building as freestanding elements, on or in the exterior wall, or in the entry area.

**Table 3.1.15**
Dimensions of mail slots

Per DIN EN 13724

**Dimensions for mail slots of mailboxes**

| Size | Height of mail slot | Length of mail slot | Compatible letter formats (max.) |
|---|---|---|---|
| 1 | 30–35 mm (Type 4 up to 40 mm, as long as the space between the bottom of the mail slot and the bottom of the box at the removal side is at least 680 mm) | 325–400 mm | Max. B4 inserted lengthwise, E4 and C3 inserted sideways |
| 2 | 30–35 mm (Type 4 up to 40 mm, as long as the space between the bottom of the mail slot and the bottom of the box at the removal side is at least 680 mm) | 230–280 mm | Max. B4 inserted lengthwise, C4 inserted sideways |
| 3 (only types 1–3) | 35–45 mm | 325–400 mm | Max. B4 inserted lengthwise, E4 and C3 inserted sideways |

**Figure 3.1.30 (left)**
Integration of doorbell/mailbox units within wall cladding

**Figure 3.1.31 (right)**
Practical dimensions for doorbell/mailbox units

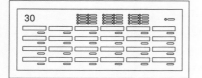

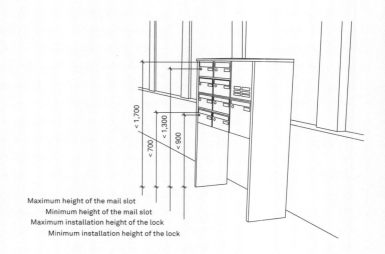

Maximum height of the mail slot
Minimum height of the mail slot
Maximum installation height of the lock
Minimum installation height of the lock

**Figure 3.1.32**
Placement and types of doorbell/mailbox units

a) Freestanding exterior mailbox, directly in front of the building
b) Freestanding exterior mailbox, accessible from the sidewalk
c) Mailbox with mail slot(s) outside, contents removable from inside
d) Mailbox inside the building (problematic access)
e) Mail slot in door

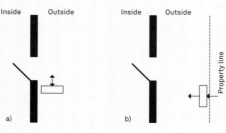

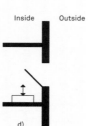

## 3.1.5 Waste Receptacles

For aesthetic reasons and to reduce offending odors, areas for the disposal of waste are located apart from the building and preferably shielded from view. When planning these areas, however, it is important to bear in mind that the containers must be easily and directly accessible for the building's occupants and collection vehicles alike.

In general, the sizes of waste receptacles used in any one locality are standardized, so enclosures can be planned accordingly. For the sake of accessibility, different height levels are desirable so as to ensure that the openings for disposal are also within reach of wheelchair users.

Table 3.1.16
Dimensions of waste containers
As per BS EN 840-1

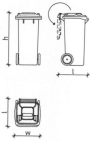

**Part 1 – Containers with 2 wheels with a capacity up to 400 L for comb lifting devices**

| Volume in L | Height (h) in mm | | Width (w) in mm | Length (l) in mm |
|---|---|---|---|---|
| 60 | Type A | max. 1,005 | 448 + 5 | max. 530 |
| | Type B | | 480 + 5 | max. 555 |
| 120 | max. 1,005 | | max. 505 | max. 555 |
| 140 | max. 1,100 | | max. 505 | max. 555 |
| 180 | max. 1,100 | | max. 505 | max. 755 |
| 210 | Type A | max. 1,100 | 546 + 5 | max. 730 |
| | Type B | | | |
| 240 | max. 1,100 | | 580 + 5 | max. 740 |
| 340 | max. 1,115 | | max. 665 | max. 880 |
| 390 | max. 1,100 | | 755 + 5/– 15 | max. 810 |

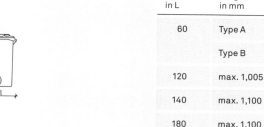

**Part 2 – Containers with 4 wheels with a capacity up to 1,300 L with flat lid(s), for trunnion and/or comb lifting devices**

| Volume in L | Height (h) in mm | Width (w) in mm | Length (l) in mm |
|---|---|---|---|
| 550 | max. 1,370 | 1,370 + 10 | max. 740 |
| 660 | max. 1,370 | 1,370 + 10 | max. 850 |
| 770 | max. 1,370 | 1,370 + 10 | max. 870 |
| 1,000 | max. 1,470 | 1,370 + 10 | max. 1,190 |
| 1,100 | max. 1,470 | 1,370 + 10 | max. 1,190 |
| 1,200 | max. 1,470 | 1,370 + 10 | max. 1,190 |

**Part 3 – Containers with 4 wheels with a capacity up to 1,300 L with dome lid(s), for trunnion and/or comb lifting devices**

| Volume in L | Height (h) in mm | Width (w) in mm | Length (l) in mm |
|---|---|---|---|
| 770 | max. 1,425 | 1,370 + 10 | max. 1,100 |
| 1,100 | max. 1,470 | 1,370 + 10 | max. 1,245 |
| 1,300 | max. 1,480 | 1,370 + 10 | max. 1,245 |

**Figure 3.1.33**
Dimensions of waste collection rooms and enclosures

In building classes 3 to 5, the walls, ceilings, and interior doors of waste collection rooms must have a suitable fire rating. They require constant ventilation and should be capable of being emptied directly from outside the building.

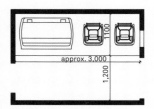

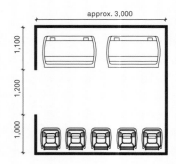

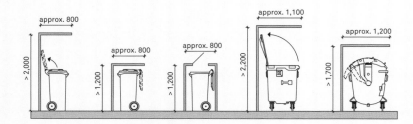

**Figure 3.1.34**
Examples of prefabricated enclosures for exterior areas

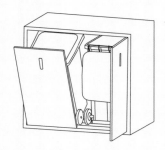

**Figure 3.1.35**
Accessibility of waste receptacles for wheelchair users

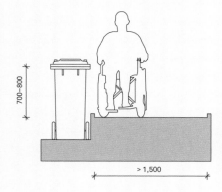

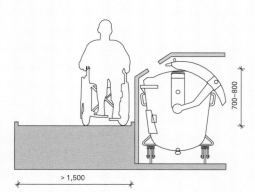

Figure 3.1.36
Dimensions of containers
of various capacities

Symmetrical containers with a capacity
of 2–4 m³ and a maximum width of 1,520 mm
for skip loader vehicles

Asymmetrical containers with a capacity
of 3–5 m³ and a maximum width of 1,520 mm
for skip loader vehicles

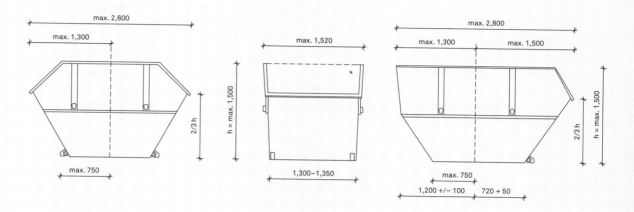

Figure 3.1.37
Loading of containers

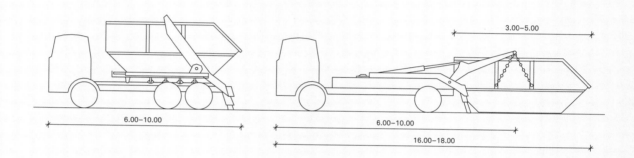

Figure 3.1.38
Exemplary dimensions of trash
compactors

Trash compactors are available in
many shapes and sizes that are
dependent on the waste products
to be processed and the desired
result. Thus consideration must be
given to the specific requirements
and the manufacturer's product
data.

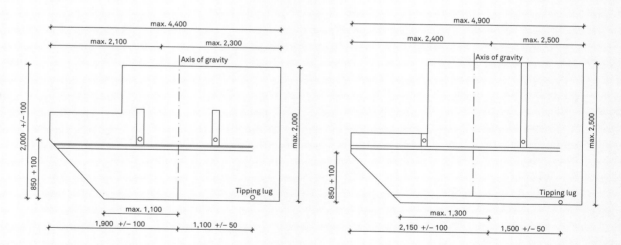

# 3.2 Internal Circulation

The internal circulation of a building ordinarily consists of elements such as entrance areas, corridors, doors, stairs, elevators, etc. Depending on whether a building is public or private, the entrance areas can be designed with open plans and integrated vertical circulation or organized instead in a more functional, spatially efficient, and expedient manner. Of equal importance is whether the internal circulation serves different functional units or solely acts as a distributor within a single functional unit.

### 3.2.1 Entrance Areas

Entrance areas fulfill a variety of tasks pertaining to functions that include communication, access, security, and supervision. The entrance area gives people a first impression, making it the "calling card" of the building. Because they convey initial intuitive information about the building's users (companies or individuals), entrance areas have a very strong psychological impact. Moreover, entrance areas are thermal and acoustic buffer zones. In the case of fire, they serve as an escape route, and for people with disabilities they represent a crucial link between the public realm and functions inside the building.

Figure 3.2.1
Organization of entrance areas
and internal circulation

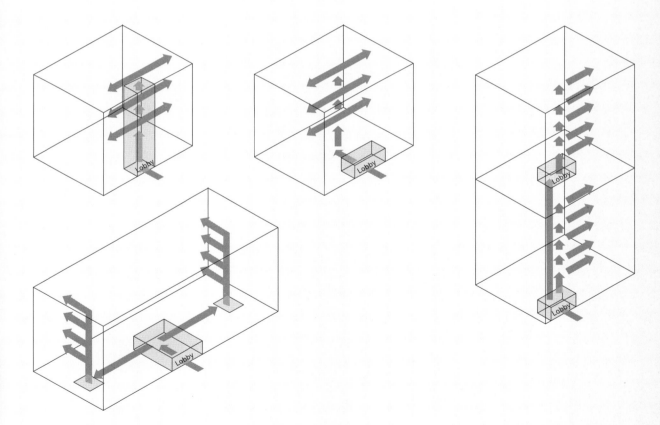

**Figure 3.2.2**
Arrangement of building entrances in relation to the exterior wall

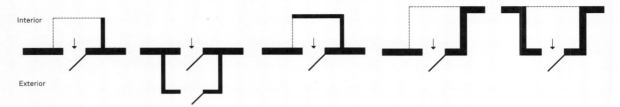

**Figure 3.2.3**
Dimensions of wheelchair-accessible vestibules

Automatic door opener controls must be positioned for operation within reach of wheelchair users, and they should be located at least 1.50 m away from doors (2.00 m from doors swinging toward user).

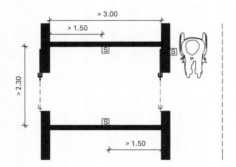

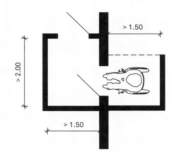

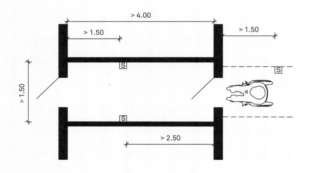

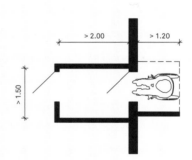

**Figure 3.2.4**
Space requirements for private entrance areas

It is important to create sufficient storage space for baby carriages and strollers, wheelchairs, bicycles, etc., in the entrance area to ensure uninterrupted free movement between inside and outside, depending on the typology.

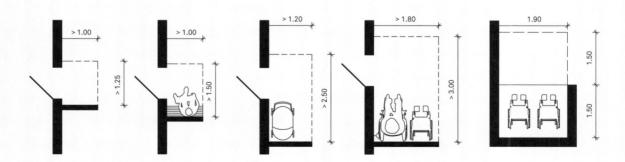

## 3.2.2 Corridors

Maneuvering zones must fulfill a wide variety of requirements. In addition to providing access, corridors can serve as communication areas as well as zones for waiting, resting, or encounters. Depending on the type of use, measures for improving qualities that create a pleasant atmosphere in those spaces, such as natural lighting and views to the exterior, should therefore also be considered.

A distinction must be made between, on the one hand, necessary corridors and maneuvering zones that are classified as escape and rescue routes and which the planner must equip in compliance with the applicable minimum standards and, on the other hand, corridors and maneuvering zones that are not required by the building code and which are used solely for internal circulation. Especially for escape and rescue routes, specific requirements are placed on the clear widths of corridors, the elimination of smoke and fire loads, the surrounding building components, and the paths and doors leading to the exterior. To this end, fire compartmentation in buildings is also essential.

For designing accessible corridors, further measures are also needed in addition to providing sufficient widths for wheelchair users. The elderly and people with impaired mobility require handrails and opportunities to sit at short intervals. Using high-contrast colors on doors, frames, floors, etc. helps by providing guidance to the visually impaired.

**Figure 3.2.5**
Definition of the various opening widths

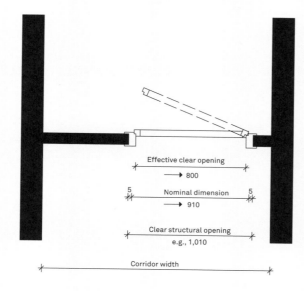

Effective clear opening
→ 800

Nominal dimension
→ 910

Clear structural opening
e.g., 1,010

Corridor width

**Figure 3.2.6**
Minimum widths of corridors as a function of door swing direction

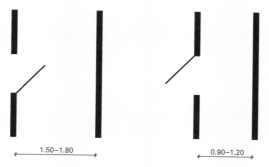 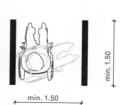 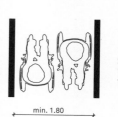

1.50–1.80          0.90–1.20          min. 1.50          min. 1.50          min. 1.80          min. 1.80

**Figure 3.2.7**
Width of corridors for
different uses

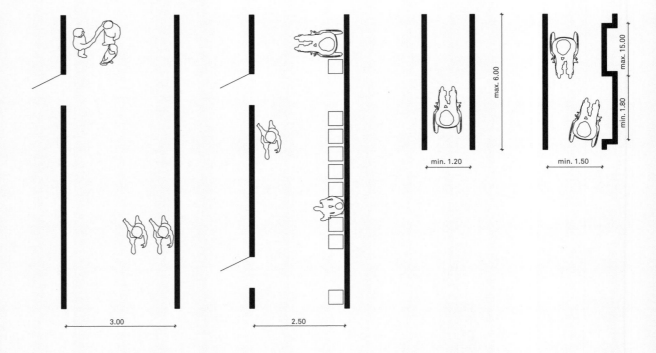

**Figure 3.2.8**
Fire compartmentation within
buildings

The measurements given here
are to be regarded as guidelines
only, since fire compartments
must always be designed for the
specific project site in compliance
with the applicable building codes.
The determination of construction
phases is nevertheless essential
for the design of rescue and
escape routes as well as for the
disposition of stairways.

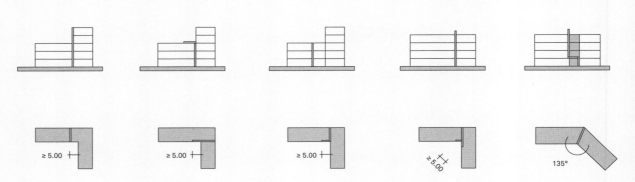

## 3.2.2 Corridors

**Table 3.2.1**
Minimum widths of paths for pedestrian traffic

As per ASR A1.8

| Circulation path | Clear width |
|---|---|
| Minimum width of circulation paths according to number of persons served | |
| max. 5 people | 0.875 m |
| max. 20 people | 1 m |
| max. 200 people | 1.2 m |
| max. 300 people | 1.8 m |
| max. 400 people | 2.4 m |
| At doors, a reduction to the minimum width of corridors can be disregarded if the constriction is not more than 0.15 m. Regardless, the clear width may not be less than 0.80 m at any point. | |
| Aisles to personally assigned workstations, auxiliary stairs | 0.60 m |
| Maintenance aisles, aisles to infrequently used operating equipment | 0.50 m |
| Pedestrian routes between storage facilities and equipment | 1.25 m |
| Pedestrian routes in secondary corridors of storage facilities, used exclusively for loading and unloading by hand | 0.75 m |
| Circulation paths between rail vehicles with speeds of ≤ 30 km/h and without permanent fixtures in the circulation paths | 1.00 m |
| Maneuvering paths | 1.30 m |

**Table 3.2.2**
Maximum escape route length in workplaces

As per ASR A2.3

| Room | Maximum length |
|---|---|
| In ordinary workspaces | 35.00 m |
| Areas with high fire risk, equipped with automatic fire extinguishing devices | 35.00 m |
| Areas with high fire risk, not equipped with automatic fire extinguishing devices | 25.00 m |
| Areas endangered by toxic substances and/or explosion | 20.00 m |
| Areas endangered by explosive materials | 10.00 m |

**Table 3.2.3**
Escape route length as a function of the clear ceiling height in places of assembly

An escape route length of 30 m may not be exceeded unless it is compensated by corresponding room height.

As per MVStättV

| Escape route length | Clear ceiling height |
|---|---|
| ≤ 30.00 m | ≤ 5.00 m |
| ≤ 35.00 m | > 5 ≤ 7.50 m |
| ≤ 40.00 m | > 7.50 ≤ 10.00 m |
| ≤ 45.00 m | > 10.00 m ≤ 12.50 m |
| ≤ 50.00 m | > 12.50 ≤ 15.00 m |
| ≤ 55.00 m | > 15.00 ≤ 17.50 m |
| ≤ 60.00 m | > 17.50 m |

### 3.2.3  Doors

As connecting elements between rooms or maneuvering zones, doors are an important design element. Not every type of door, however, is suitable or approved for every location. Doors are subject to specific requirements, especially along escape and rescue routes and at wheelchair-accessible entrances. As potential bottlenecks, doors play a central role in maintaining the necessary clear width of an escape route and hence they can also determine the necessary corridor width.

For many doors, the direction of swing is often dictated by the function. For instance, all escape and rescue path doors must, as a basic rule, open in the direction of the escape route. In technical rooms, too (such as electrical distribution rooms), outward-opening doors are often necessary. Individual room doors that adjoin an escape and rescue path can ordinarily be oriented inward as desired.

**Table 3.2.4**
Range of applications for various door types

| Door type | Barrier-free | Escape and rescue path | Fire protection |
|-----------|--------------|------------------------|-----------------|
| Hinged door | x | x | x |
| Sliding door | x | | |
| Folding door | x | | |
| Swing door | x | | |
| Revolving door | | | |
| Automatic door | x | (x) | (x) |

**Figure 3.2.9**
Minimum widths for use of wheelchairs or walking aids

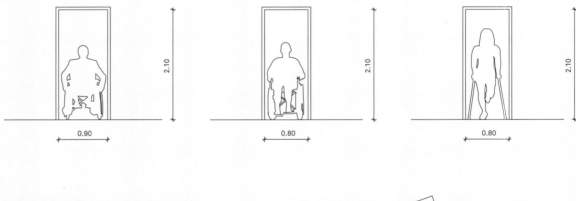

**Figure 3.2.10**
Door types

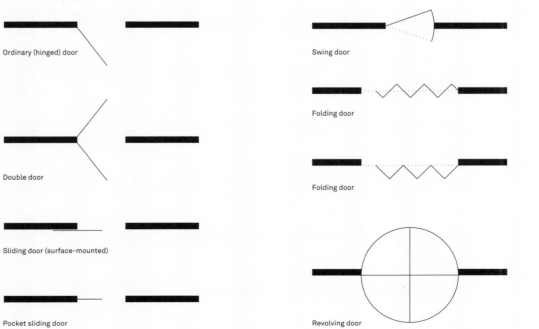

Ordinary (hinged) door

Double door

Sliding door (surface-mounted)

Pocket sliding door

Swing door

Folding door

Folding door

Revolving door

**Figure 3.2.11**
Minimum dimensions for wheel-chair maneuvering areas at doors

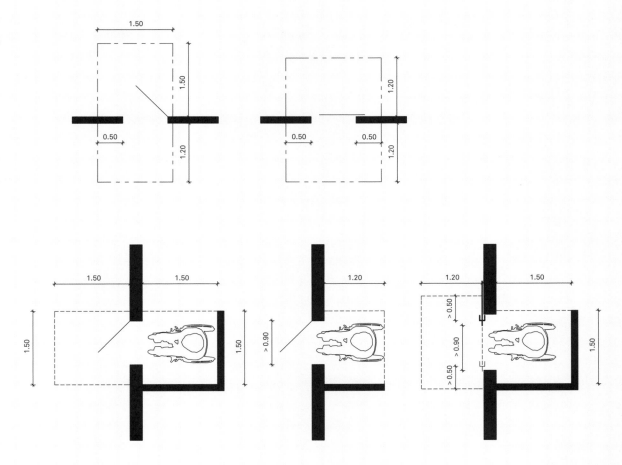

**Figure 3.2.12**
Requirements for the placement of automatic door openers

a) Distance between activation button and hinged door with frontal approach
b) Distance between activation button and hinged or sliding door with side approach
c) Distance between activation button and sliding door with frontal approach

Per DIN 18040

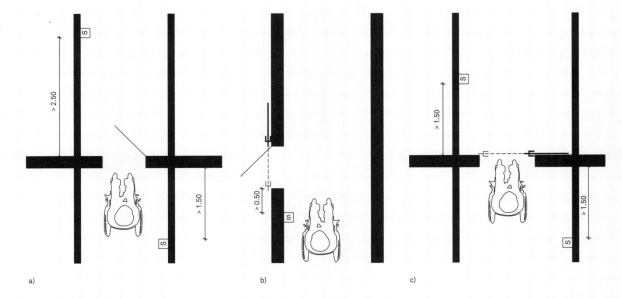

a)

b)

c)

**Figure 3.2.13**
Various revolving door types

Above:
a) Basic position
b) Night closure
c) Middle position "Night/bank function," Closure with controlled entry through additional sliding door
d) Middle position with open sliding door (Emergency egress position)

Below:
a) Basic position
b) Escape opening
c) Free passage

2-leaf revolving door

a)

2.00–4.00

b)

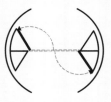

c)

d)

Example:
Outside diameter: 2.30 m
Inside diameter: 2.20 m
Entrance width: 1.34 m

3- or 4-leaf revolving door

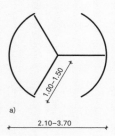

a)

1.00–1.50

2.10–3.70

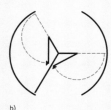

b)

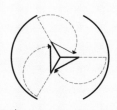

c)

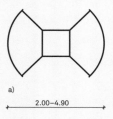

a)

2.00–4.90

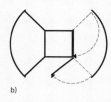

b)

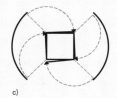

c)

Example:
Outside diameter: 2.30 m
Inside diameter: 2.20 m
Entrance width: 1.474 m

## 3.2.4 Stairs

Stairs and stair enclosures must comply with a myriad of requirements. They serve as escape and rescue routes and as functional or communicative links between different stories or levels.

The geometry and minimum dimensions of a stair are dependent on the type of use, the number of people who might need to flee in an emergency, and the desired ease of use. It is generally very important to identify the number of risers and the geometry of the stairway early on in the design process.

For designing and dimensioning stairs, the following rules apply (r = riser, t = tread):

- Stride length rule: t + 2r = 630 mm (+/− 30 mm)
- Safety rule: t + r = 460 mm (+/− 10 mm)
- Comfort rule: t − r = approx. 120 mm

An intermediate landing must be provided after no more than 18 steps. For determining stair widths, the free escape route width as well as handrails or guardrails and any stairwell openings must be taken into account. Stair railings must be designed so there is neither a risk of injury to children (max. 120 mm gaps) nor a possibility of climbing over the railing.

To enable barrier-free use of the stairs by the visually impaired, highly visible markings and Braille numbering on the handrail are desirable. Similarly, a high-contrast design of the landings and the top and bottom steps is helpful.

Figure 3.2.14
Terminology for stairs

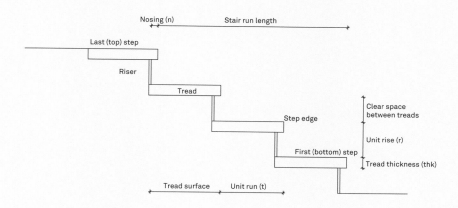

Figure 3.2.15
Typical stair geometries

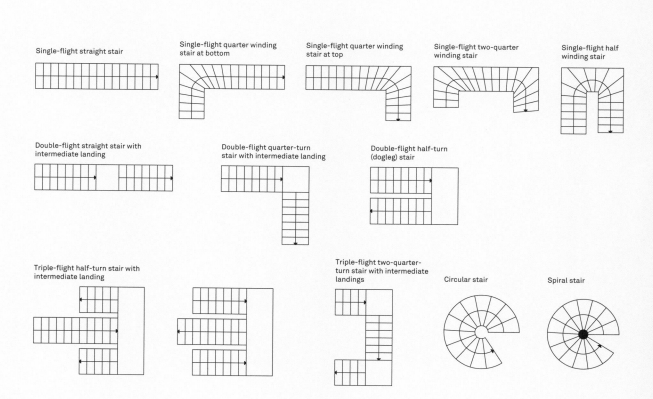

Single-flight straight stair

Single-flight quarter winding stair at bottom

Single-flight quarter winding stair at top

Single-flight two-quarter winding stair

Single-flight half winding stair

Double-flight straight stair with intermediate landing

Double-flight quarter-turn stair with intermediate landing

Double-flight half-turn (dogleg) stair

Triple-flight half-turn stair with intermediate landing

Triple-flight two-quarter-turn stair with intermediate landings

Circular stair

Spiral stair

Figure 3.2.16 (left)
Stair types according to
rise-to-run ratio

Table 3.2.5 (right)
Requirements for stair risers
and treads

As per ASR A1.8

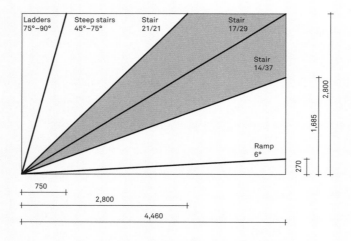

| Construction type | Unit run (t) | Unit rise (r) |
|---|---|---|
| Exterior stairs, child day care facilities | 320–300 mm | 140–160 mm |
| Places of assembly, administrative buildings for public bodies, schools, after school centers | 310–290 mm | 150–170 mm |
| Commercial buildings, miscellaneous buildings | 300–260 mm | 160–190 mm |
| Auxiliary stairs | 300–210 mm | 140–210 mm |

Figure 3.2.17
Stair construction types

a) Double stringer stair
b) Cut-string stair
c) Center stringer stair
d) Solid stair
e) Cantilevered stair
f) Spiral stair
g) Load-bearing-bolt stair
h) Suspended stair

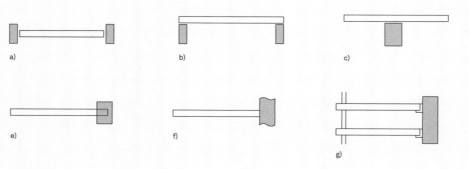
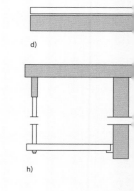

Figure 3.2.18
Break line for stair designs

The break line defines a geometric line where the flights, stair soffit, and railings/handrails change direction.

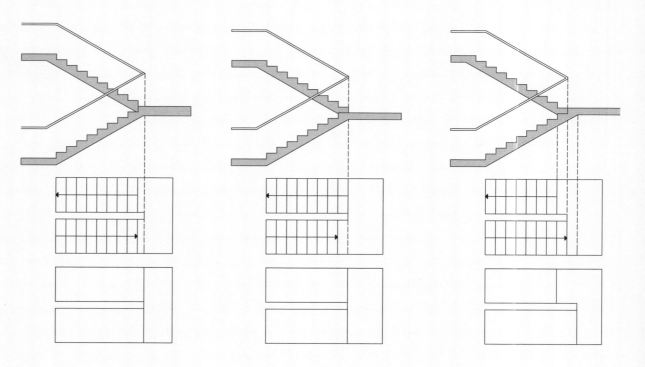

**Figure 3.2.19**
Determining the clear dimensions of stairs

For simultaneous use by multiple people, the clear stair width should be at least 1.25 m.

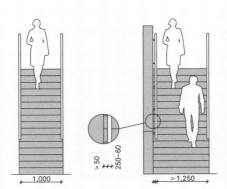
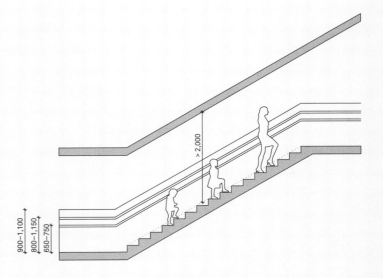

**Figure 3.2.20**
Minimum size of landings

A landing is needed after max. 18 risers
a) Typical buildings
b) Residential buildings with max. 2 apartments

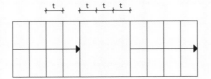
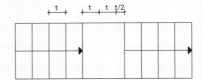

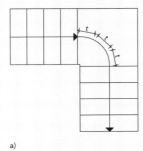

a)

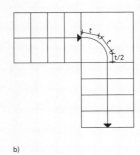

b)

**Figure 3.2.21**
Clearance between doors and stairs

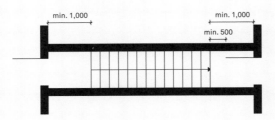
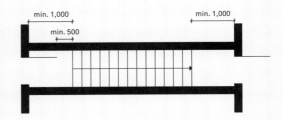

Figure 3.2.22
Guards at stairs and landings,
designed to prevent climbing

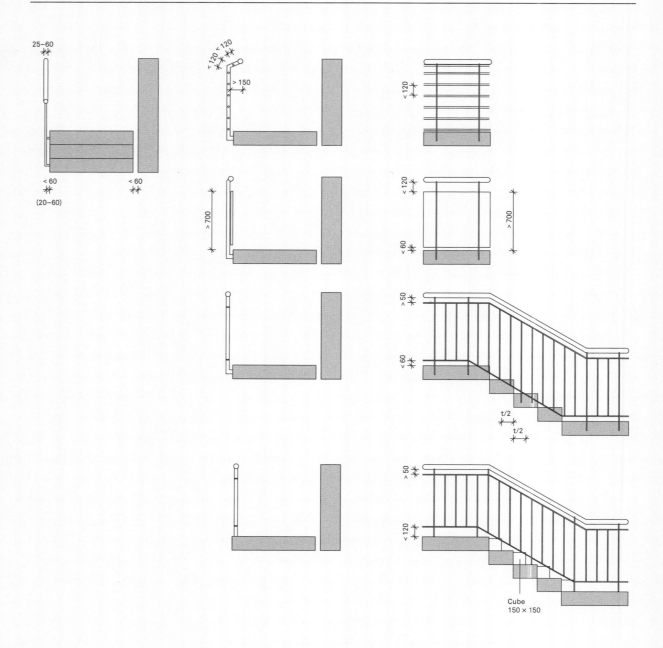

Table 3.2.6
Rough guidelines for total runs
(lengths) of stairs (in m)

Riser/tread ratios calculated
according to stride length rule
2r + t = 630 mm (+/– 30 mm)

| Floor-to-floor height in m | Riser/tread ratio (r/t) in mm | | | | | |
|---|---|---|---|---|---|---|
| | 165/300 | 170/290 | 175/280 | 180/270 | 185/260 | Optimum riser/tread ratio |
| 2.80 | 17 × r/t = **5.10** (2.80) | 16 × r/t = **4.64** (2.72) | 16 × r/t = **4.48** (2.80) | 15 × r/t = **4.20** ( 2.70) | 15 × r/t = **3.90** (2.77) | 17 × 165 / 300 = **5.10** |
| 3.00 | 18 × r/t = **5.40** (2.97) | 18 × r/t = **5.22** (3.06) | 17 × r/t = **4.76** (2.97) | 17 × r/t = **4.59** (3.06) | 16 × r/t = **4.16** (2.96) | 17 × 176 / 277 = **4.70** |
| 3.20 | 19 × r/t = **5.70** (3.13) | 19 × r/t = **5.51** (3.23) | 18 × r/t = **5.04** (3.15) | 18 × r/t = **4.86** (3.24) | 17 × r/t = **4.42** (3.14) | 18 × 177 / 276 = **4.96** |
| 3.40 | 20 × r/t = **6.00** (3.30) | 20 × r/t = **5.80** (3.40) | 19 × r/t = **5.32** (3.32) | 19 × r/t = **5.13** (3.42) | 18 × r/t = **4.68** (3.33) | 19 × 179 / 272 = **5.16** |
| 3.60 | 22 × r/t = **6.60** (3.63) | 21 × r/t = **6.09** (3.57) | 20 × r/t = **5.60** (3.50) | 20 × r/t = **5.40** (3.60) | 19 × r/t = **4.94** (3.51) | 20 × 180 / 270 = **5.40** |
| 3.80 | 23 × r/t = **6.90** (3.79) | 22 × r/t = **6.38** (3.74) | 22 × r/t = **6.16** (3.85) | 21 × r/t = **5.67** (3.78) | 20 × r/t = **5.20** (3.70) | 22 × 173 / 284 = **6.24** |
| 4.00 | 24 × r/t = **7.20** (3.96) | 23 × r/t = **6.67** (3.91) | 23 × r/t = **6.44** (4.02) | 22 × r/t = **5.94** (3.96) | 22 × r/t = **5.72** (4.07) | 23 × 174 / 282 = **6.48** |

**Figure 3.2.23**
Clear escape route widths
in stairways

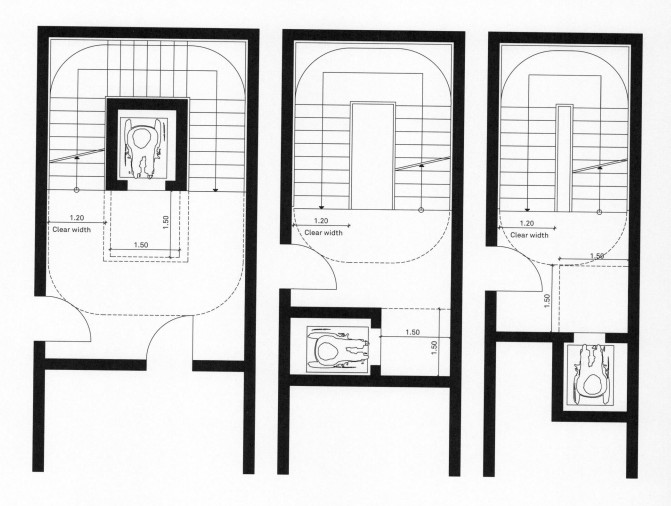

**Table 3.2.7**
Rough guidelines for stairway
widths

Varies as a function of one-/
two-sided handrail and open well
at double-flight stairs

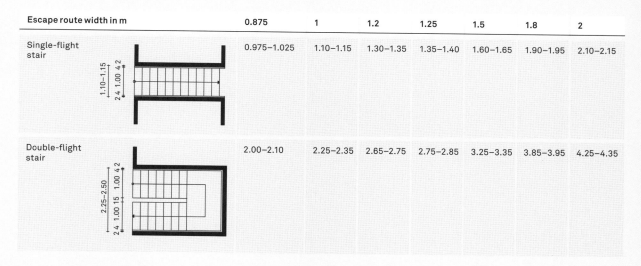

| Escape route width in m | | 0.875 | 1 | 1.2 | 1.25 | 1.5 | 1.8 | 2 |
|---|---|---|---|---|---|---|---|---|
| Single-flight stair | | 0.975–1.025 | 1.10–1.15 | 1.30–1.35 | 1.35–1.40 | 1.60–1.65 | 1.90–1.95 | 2.10–2.15 |
| Double-flight stair | | 2.00–2.10 | 2.25–2.35 | 2.65–2.75 | 2.75–2.85 | 3.25–3.35 | 3.85–3.95 | 4.25–4.35 |

## 3.2.5  Ramps

Ramps represent a good option for bridging small height differences, such as in entrance zones. Ramps that should also be accessible for wheelchair use are subject to specific requirements. They are permitted to have a maximum grade of 6 percent and must be provided with rest plat-

forms after no more than 4 m. In addition to the technical requirements pertaining to widths, lengths, wheel rails, etc., the areas at the ends of the ramp should be sensibly designed to minimize safety hazards.

**Figure 3.2.24**
Technical requirements for accessible ramps

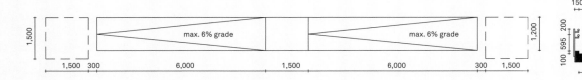

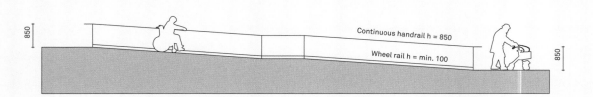

**Figure 3.2.25**
Bike channels/rails on stairs and ramps

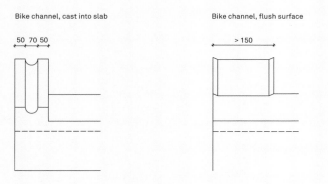

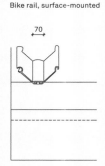

## 3.2.6 Escalators and Moving Walkways

Escalators ensure speedy transport of larger numbers of people between different floor levels. They must be designed for a maximum inclination of 30–35° and their points of connection to the structure must be dimensioned according to the manufacturer's specifications. Depending on whether they are used simultaneously by standing and walking persons, the step width is between 600 and 1,000 mm. Moving walkways can also be used as inclined planes (moving ramps) that accommodate shopping carts or the like. Moving walkways with little or no inclination are used as passenger conveyors for bridging longer distances, such as in airports or shopping malls.

Figure 3.2.26 (left)
Components of escalators

Table 3.2.8 (right)
Overall lengths of escalators for installation (in mm)

The length and width of the openings vary by manufacturer. These are standard dimensions given here only for general orientation.

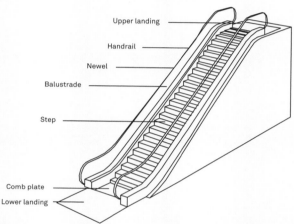

| Floor-to-floor height (H) | Overall length of escalator (30° incline) L = H × 1.732 + 4,731 | Overall length of escalator (35° incline) L = H × 1.428 + 4,825 |
|---|---|---|
| 3,000 | 9,927 | 9,109 |
| 3,500 | 10,793 | 9,823 |
| 4,000 | 11,659 | 10,537 |
| 4,500 | 12,525 | 11,251 |
| 5,000 | 13,391 | 11,965 |
| 5,500 | 14,257 | 12,679 |
| 6,000 | 15,123 | 13,393 |

Overall length of the escalator

Figure 3.2.27
Vertical circulation with escalators/moving ramps

Circulation with escalators must be dimensioned according to the anticipated number of visitors. For relevant circulation paths, such as in train stations, the width should be dimensioned so that both standing and walking persons can use the escalator at the same time.

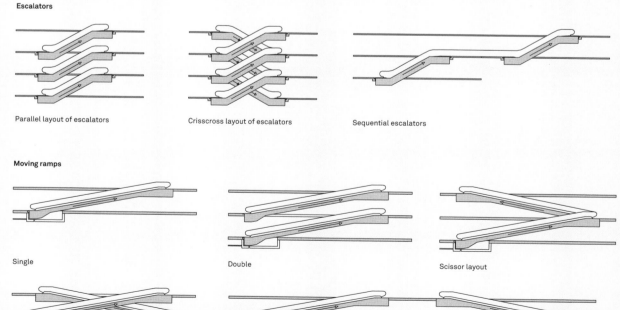

Escalators

Parallel layout of escalators

Crisscross layout of escalators

Sequential escalators

Moving ramps

Single

Double

Scissor layout

Crisscross layout

Opposing directions

**Table 3.2.9**
Floor opening sizes for the installation of escalators

The length and width of the openings vary by manufacturer. These are standard dimensions given here only for general orientation.

| Inclination of escalator | Max. travel height in mm | Width of step in mm | Length of the opening in level I in mm | Length of the opening at level II and above in mm | Width of the opening in mm |
|---|---|---|---|---|---|
| 30° | 6,000 | 600/800/1,000 | 4,450 | Min. 6,476 | 1,200/1,400/1,600 |
| 30° | 8,000 | 600/800/1,000 | 4,850 | Min. 6,876 | 1,200/1,400/1,600 |
| 30° | 6,500/13,000 | 800/1,000 | 4,850 | Min. 7,003 | 1,400/1,600 |
| 35° | 6,000 | 600/800/1,000 | 4,250 | Min. 5,837 | 1,200/1,400/1,600 |

**Figure 3.2.28**
Dimensions of escalators

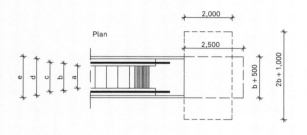

Plan

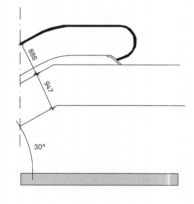

| | in mm | in mm | in mm |
|---|---|---|---|
| a: Step width | 600 | 800 | 1,000 |
| b: Width between handrails | 758 | 958 | 1,158 |
| c: Handrail center spacing | 838 | 1,038 | 1,238 |
| d: Escalator width | 1,140 | 1,340 | 1,540 |
| e: Width of pit | 1,200 | 1,400 | 1,600 |

Connection points
Elevation

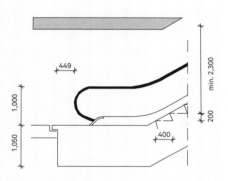

**Figure 3.2.29**
Dimensions of moving walkways

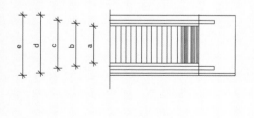

| | in mm | in mm |
|---|---|---|
| a: Pallet width | 800 | 1,000 |
| b: Width between handrails | 958 | 1,158 |
| c: Handrail center spacing | 1,038 | 1,238 |
| d: Moving walkway width | 1,340 | 1,540 |
| e: Width of pit | 1,400 | 1,600 |

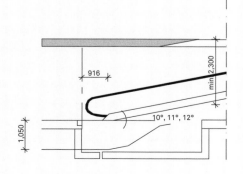

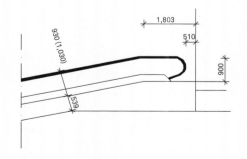

# 3.2.7 Elevators and Conveying Systems

Elevators transport people and freight between stories or different levels of a building. A distinction is made between passenger elevators, service elevators (carries passengers and goods), and freight elevators (no passengers). Passenger elevators are essential for barrier-free circulation in multistory public buildings, but they are also requisite in residential buildings without barrier-free requirements if there are five or more stories. Especially when adapting existing buildings, smaller lifting platforms are often used to overcome small changes in height in order to make the building accessible to wheelchair users. In high-rise buildings, large numbers of users usually necessitate complex control systems that can enable the use of multiple cars in a single shaft, automatically manage available cars with destination selection control, or serve distribution levels with dedicated express elevators. Depending on the type of construction, the planner must, at an early stage, take into account system-dependent shaft pits and headroom clearances as well as separate machine rooms.

**Figure 3.3.30**
Elevator door openings

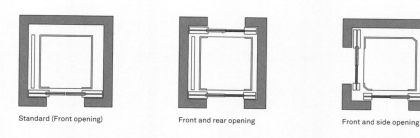

**Figure 3.2.31**
Passenger elevators for residential buildings

Per DIN 15306

**Figure 3.2.32**
Passenger elevators for other buildings

Per DIN 15309

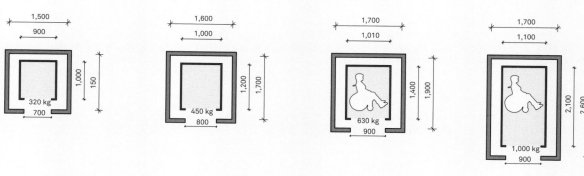

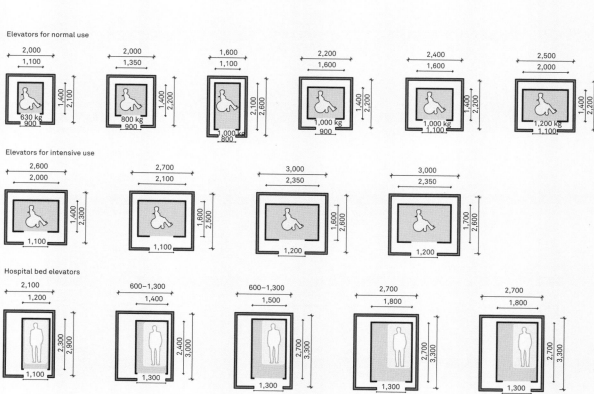

Table 3.2.10
Dimensions of elevators

| Elevator type | Number of persons | Nominal loading (kg) | Car width (CW) | Car depth (CD) | Door width (DW) | Hoistway width (HW) | Hoistway depth (HD) | | Door rough opening (DRO) |
|---|---|---|---|---|---|---|---|---|---|
| | | | | | | | Door one-sided | Doors on opposite sides | |
| | | | | | Standard sizes – all dimensions in mm | | | | |
| Passenger elevators | 3 | 240 | 700 | 900 | 600 | 1,170 | 1,280 | – | 900 |
| | 4 | 320 | 900 | 1,000 | 700 | 1,370 | 1,450 | – | 1,000 |
| | | | 750 | 1,100 | 700 | 1,300 | 1,500 | – | 1,000 |
| | 5 | 400 | 800 | 1,200 | 700 | 1,300 | 1,600 | 1,810 | 1,000 |
| | | 400 | 950 | 1,100 | 700 | 1,420 | 1,500 | 1,710 | 1,000 |
| | | | | | 800 | 1,450 | 1,500 | 1,710 | 1,100 |
| | 6 | 450 | 1,000 | 1,200 | 800 | 1,470 | 1,600 | 1,810 | 1,100 |
| | | | | | 900 | 1,600 | 1,600 | 1,810 | 1,200 |
| | | 480 | 950 | 1,300 | 700 | 1,420 | 1,700 | 1,910 | 1,000 |
| | | | | | 800 | 1,450 | 1,700 | 1,910 | 1,100 |
| | | | | | 900 | 1,600 | 1,700 | 1,910 | 1,200 |
| | | | 1,000 | 1,250 | 800 | 1,470 | 1,650 | 1,860 | 1,100 |
| | | | | | 900 | 1,600 | 1,650 | 1,860 | 1,200 |
| "Barrier-free construction" in accordance with the applicable provisions as per EN 81-70, "Construction of Accessible Buildings" | 8 | 630 | 1,100 | 1,400 | 800* | 1,800 | 1,700 | 1,810 | 950 |
| | | | | | 900 | 2,000 | 1,700 | 1,810 | 1,050 |
| | 10 | 800 | 1,350 | 1,400 | 800* | 1,900 | 1,800 | – | 950 |
| | | | | | 900 | 2,000 | 1,800 | – | 1,050 |
| | 12 | 900 | 1,400 | 1,500 | 800* | 1,950 | 1,850 | 1,910 | 950 |
| | | | | | 900 | 2,000 | 1,850 | 1,910 | 1,050 |
| | 13 | 1,000 | 1,100 | 2,100 | 800* | 1,800 | 2,400 | 2,510 | 950 |
| | | | | | 900 | 2,000 | 2,400 | 2,510 | 1,050 |
| | | | | | 1,000 | 2,200 | 2,400 | 2,510 | 1,150 |
| | | | 1,600 | 1,400 | 900 | 2,150 | 1,850 | – | 1,050 |
| | | | | | 1,000 | 2,200 | 1,850 | – | 1,150 |
| | | | | | 1,100 | 2,400 | 1,850 | – | 1,250 |
| | 15 | 1,150 | 1,200 | 2,100 | 800* | 1,800 | 2,400 | 2,510 | 950 |
| | | | | | 900 | 2,000 | 2,400 | 2,510 | 1,050 |
| | | | | | 1,000 | 2,200 | 2,400 | 2,510 | 1,150 |
| | | | 1,600 | 1,550 | 900 | 2,150 | 1,850 | – | 1,050 |
| | | | | | 1,000 | 2,200 | 1,850 | – | 1,150 |
| | | | | | 1,100 | 2,400 | 1,850 | – | 1,250 |

* 900 mm door width required under German law

Table 3.2.10 (continuation)
Dimensions of elevators

| Elevator type | Number of persons | Nom-inal loading (kg) | Car width (CW) | Car depth (CD) | Door width (DW) | Hoistway width (HW) | Hoistway depth (HD) | | Door rough opening (DRO) |
|---|---|---|---|---|---|---|---|---|---|
| | | | | | | | Door one-sided | Doors on opposite sides | |
| | | | | | | Standard sizes – all dimensions in mm | | | |
| Hospital bed elevators as per DIN 15309 for nominal loading of 1,275 kg or greater | 17 | 1,275 | 2,000 | 1,400 | 1,100 | 2,700 | 2,000 | – | 1,250 |
| | 21 | 1,600 | 2,100 | 1,600 | 1,100 | 2,800 | 2,100 | – | 1,250 |
| | | | 1,400 | 2,400 | 1,300 | 2,300 | 2,850 | – | 1,450 |
| | | | | 2,300 | 1,300 | 2,300 | 2,750 | 2,990 | 1,450 |
| | 24 | 1,800 | 2,350 | 1,600 | 1,200 | 3,050 | 2,100 | – | 1,350 |
| | 26 | 2,000 | 2,350 | 1,700 | 1,200 | 3,050 | 2,150 | – | 1,350 |
| | | | 1,500 | 2,600 | 1,300 | 2,350 | 3,050 | 3,290 | 1,450 |
| | | | | 2,700 | 1,300 | 2,350 | 3,150 | – | 1,450 |

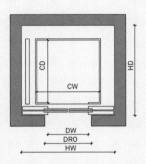

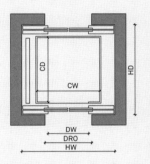

**Figure 3.2.33**
Vertical circulation with elevators

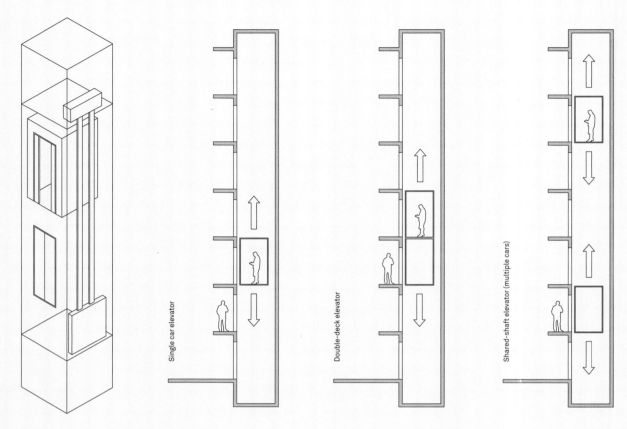

Single car elevator

Double-deck elevator

Shared-shaft elevator (multiple cars)

**Figure 3.2.34**
Elevator door types

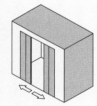 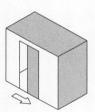 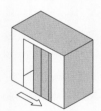 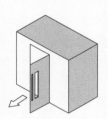 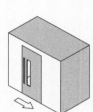

**Figure 3.2.35**
Location of elevator machinery
(rooms)

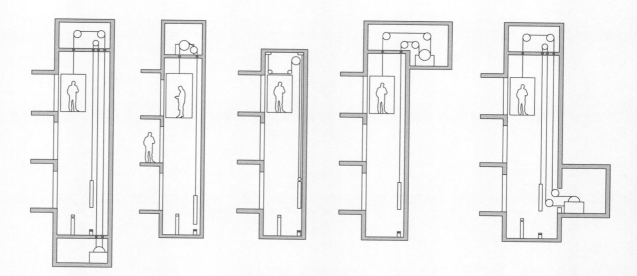

**Figure 3.2.36**
Use of elevators with a wheelchair

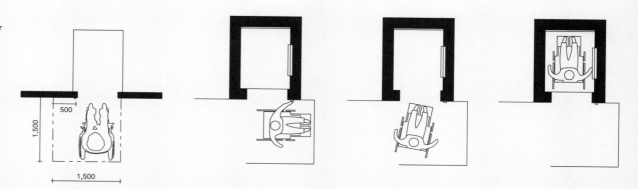

**Figure 3.2.37**
Accessible elevator operating
controls

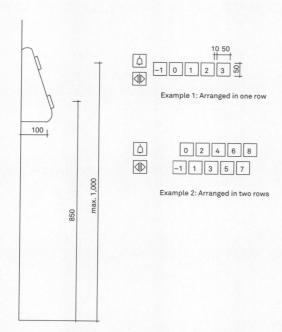

Example 1: Arranged in one row

Example 2: Arranged in two rows

# 3.3  Workrooms and Production Spaces

Workrooms and production spaces are decisively governed by regulations for occupational safety, which are increasingly being standardized internationally and cover all facets of workplace activities. With respect to architectural matters, occupational health and safety regulations impose many requirements on spaces, materials, safety devices, and the physical conditions of the workplace.

## 3.3.1  Workplaces

In addition to providing protection against occupational accidents and safeguarding health, the work environment plays an important role in ensuring the well-being and productivity of workers. The stresses encountered while working are very diverse: the work might be accomplished while sitting, standing, or in motion, and it might require an unvaried posture or be physically strenuous. It can be char- acterized by manual work with one's hands, subservient to production rhythms, or performed as a service that predominantly requires work on a computer. For each specific mode of working, the most optimal environment possible must be ensured in terms of anthropometric requirements, room temperature, natural lighting, etc. In this regard, the requirements for computer workstations are very specific.

**Figure 3.3.1 (left)**
Ergonomic requirements for computer workstations

**Table 3.3.1 (right)**
Minimum ceiling heights for workrooms

Per ASR A1.2

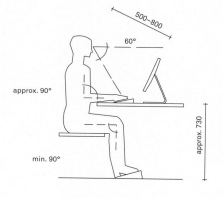

**Minimum ceiling height for workrooms**

| Floor area | Clear ceiling height |
|---|---|
| < 50 m² | 2.50 m |
| 50–100 m² | 2.75 m |
| > 100 m² | 3.00 m |
| > 2,000 m² | 3.25 m |

**Table 3.3.2 (left)**
Typical slip resistance requirements for workplaces

Per DGUV Regel 108-003 and GUV-I 8527

**Table 3.3.3 (top right)**
Working heights and table heights

Per DGUV

**Table 3.3.4 (bottom right)**
Indoor air requirements for workplaces

Per ASR A3.5

The air temperature in workrooms should not be above 26°C under normal circumstances. Lunchrooms, resting rooms, sanitary facilities, and first aid rooms should be continuously kept at 21°C, and shower rooms should be kept at 24°C during use.

| | |
|---|---|
| Outdoor areas | R10–R12 |
| Outdoor parking areas | R10–R11 |
| Outdoor ramps | R12 |
| Interior entrance areas, stairs, corridors | R9–R10 |
| Group activity rooms | R9–R10 |
| Shared kitchens | R11–R12 |
| Commercial kitchens | R12–R14 |
| Sanitary facilities | R10–R11 |
| Dry barefoot areas (such as locker rooms) | A |
| Shower areas, swimming pool decks | B |
| Stairs and ramps leading into water | C |

**Working heights and table heights for various types of standing work**

| Type of work | Working height | Table height |
|---|---|---|
| Fine work | 1,200–1,500 mm | 1,200–1,500 mm |
| Light work | 950–1,200 mm | 900–1,150 mm |
| Heavy work | 900–1,150 mm | 750–1,050 mm |

| Primary posture | Difficulty of work | | |
|---|---|---|---|
| | Light | Moderate | Heavy |
| Sitting | + 20°C | + 19°C | – |
| Standing, walking | + 19°C | + 17°C | + 12°C |

### 3.3.2 Production Spaces

Production processes are generally subject to very stringent and optimized procedures. For this reason, the workplace and the entire work environment (workshops, equipment operating areas, order picking/packing stations, etc.) are optimized with regard to gripping ranges and movement sequences. When the production processes are characterized primarily by the use of automated machines, these are decisive for the organization of surrounding areas and buildings, since short processing paths, optimal machine deployment, and logistical aspects can possibly yield significant competitive advantages. Floor space for machines as well as conveying systems, along with the ancillary technical supply infrastructure and foundations, must be taken into account in combination with maneuvering zones and operator control areas as well as escape routes and fire safety concerns. Required load movements and storage areas might also require consideration together with the legal requirements for occupational health and safety with respect to aspects such as noise abatement and heat. ↗ **Chapter 3.7 Spaces/Storage Spaces** When planning production facilities, flexibility that allows for adaptation or reorientation of processes must also be given consideration.

Figure 3.3.2
Material sequences in the
production process

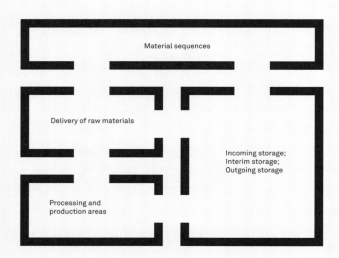

Figure 3.3.3
Planning of production sequences

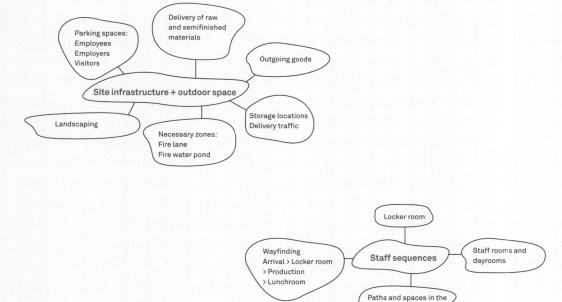

**Figure 3.3.4**
Requirements for rescue routes in production spaces

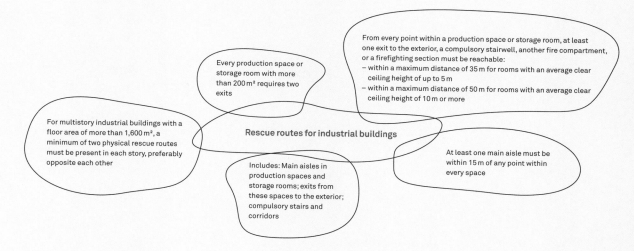

For multistory industrial buildings with a floor area of more than 1,600 m², a minimum of two physical rescue routes must be present in each story, preferably opposite each other

Every production space or storage room with more than 200 m² requires two exits

From every point within a production space or storage room, at least one exit to the exterior, a compulsory stairwell, another fire compartment, or a firefighting section must be reachable:
– within a maximum distance of 35 m for rooms with an average clear ceiling height of up to 5 m
– within a maximum distance of 50 m for rooms with an average clear ceiling height of 10 m or more

**Rescue routes for industrial buildings**

Includes: Main aisles in production spaces and storage rooms; exits from these spaces to the exterior; compulsory stairs and corridors

At least one main aisle must be within 15 m of any point within every space

**Figure 3.3.5**
Options for heating production halls

Radiant heaters

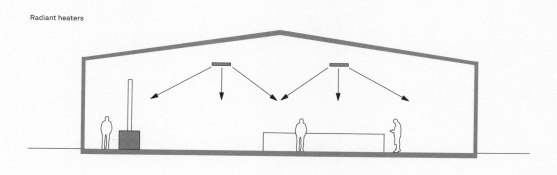

Ambient air heaters

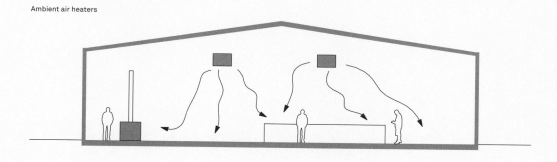

Underfloor radiant heat

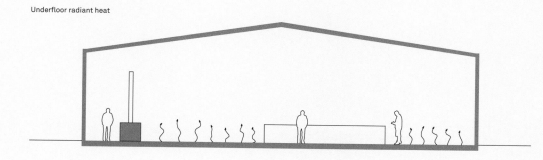

# 3.4 Communication Spaces and Dining Rooms

Communication spaces and dining rooms encompass a multitude of diverse activities and typological features in the private, professional, and leisure sectors. For communication areas it is essential to creatively bring about the implemented or desired cultures of encounter and interaction in order to also convey these intuitively to nonlocal users. For example, the seating arrangement in a seminar or conference room plays an essential role in determining how easily a free and uninhibited discussion can develop. Similarly, the design of waiting areas has considerable influence on the length of waiting time that is perceived as acceptable.

## 3.4.1 Lecture, Seminar, and Conference Rooms

The area requirements for lecture rooms, classrooms, seminar rooms, and conference rooms are directly dependent on the method of communication. Depending on the typology or business segment, highly varied concepts of teaching and communication methods are used, such as presentation style (that is, lecture-style instruction), group projects, panel discussions, guided discussions, free exchange of opinions, etc. For planning and design purposes, it is important to know if the communication processes will be guided or free and democratic, and which furniture layouts are desired for the purpose. If teacher-centered presentations are planned (such as lecture-style instruction), a directional furniture layout ensures a highly efficient use of space. For freer discussions, all the participants should, as far as possible, have eye contact with one another so they can interact as equals. Thus the furniture arrangement must enable this for the given number of participants and, as the circumstances may require, a large portion of the floor area might, for example, be given over to open space within a circular or oval table arrangement.

Table 3.4.1
Rough size of a lecture hall as a function of the number of people accommodated

| Number of persons | Area in m² |
|---|---|
| 50 | 60–70 |
| 100 | 90–110 |
| 120 | 120–130 |
| 150 | 150–200 |
| 200 | ≥200 |
| 300 | ≥350 |
| 400 | ≥400 |
| 500 | ≥500 |
| 700 | ≥700 |
| 1,200 | ≥800 |

**Figure 3.4.1**
Media equipment for meeting, conference, and lecture rooms

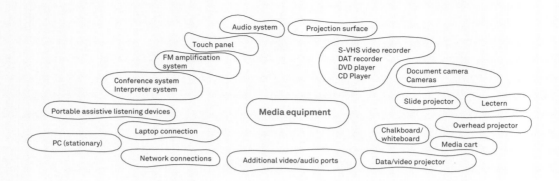

**Figure 3.4.2**
Furniture arrangement as a function of patterns of interaction

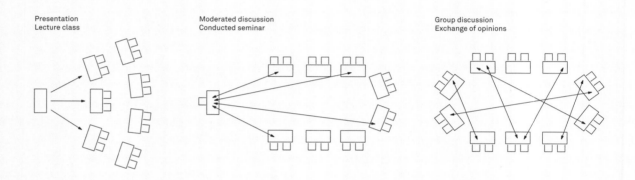

**Figure 3.4.3**
Layout of seating rows in lecture halls and lecture rooms

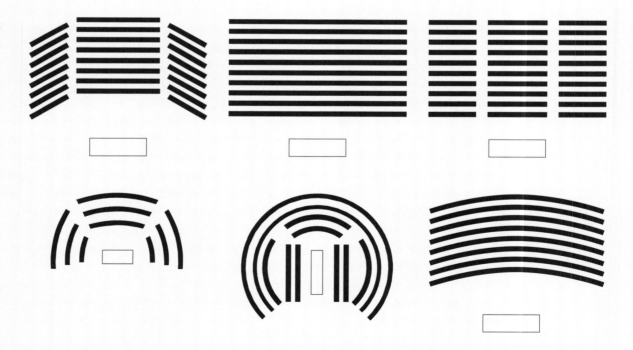

**Figure 3.4.4**
Access to rows of seats

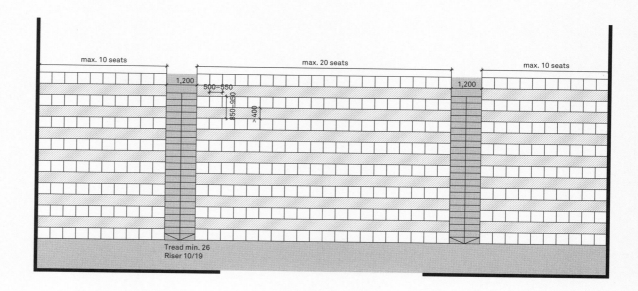

**Figure 3.4.5**
Parameters for raised
seating rows

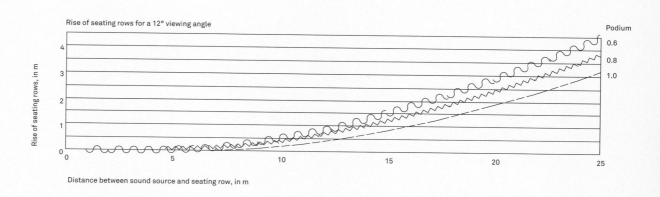

**Figure 3.4.6**
Tiered seating in lecture halls
and lecture rooms

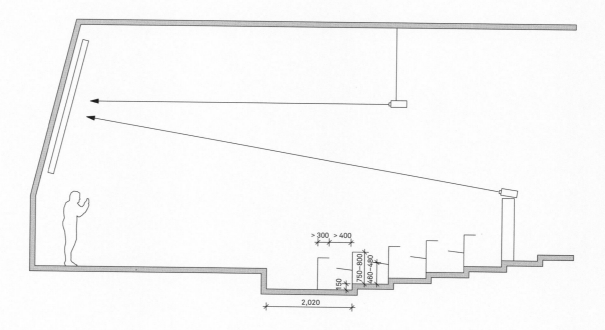

**Figure 3.4.7**
Seminar and conference seating

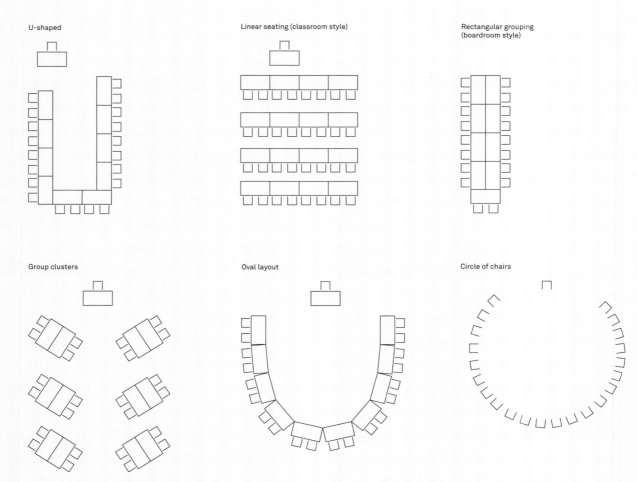

U-shaped

Linear seating (classroom style)

Rectangular grouping
(boardroom style)

Group clusters

Oval layout

Circle of chairs

**Figure 3.4.8**
Table arrangements for
conference rooms

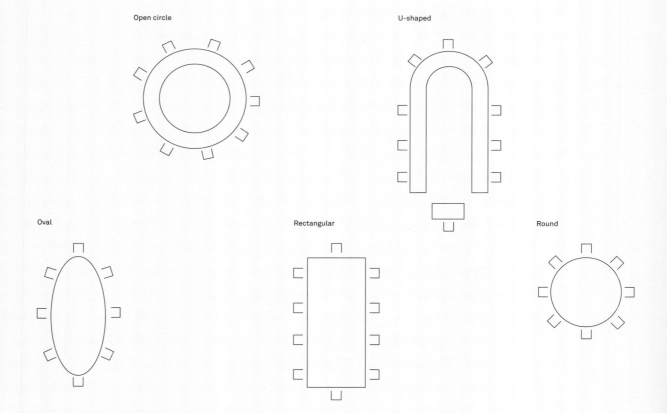

Open circle

U-shaped

Oval

Rectangular

Round

**Figure 3.4.9**
Maneuvering areas at conference and seminar tables

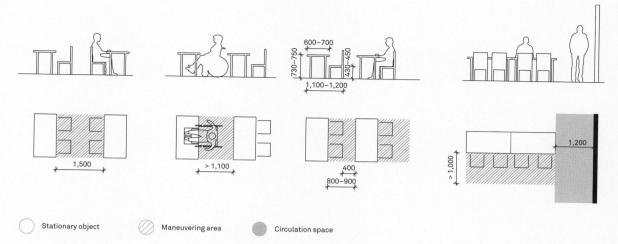

◯ Stationary object    ▨ Maneuvering area    ⬤ Circulation space

**Figure 3.4.10**
Seating furniture in lecture halls and lecture rooms

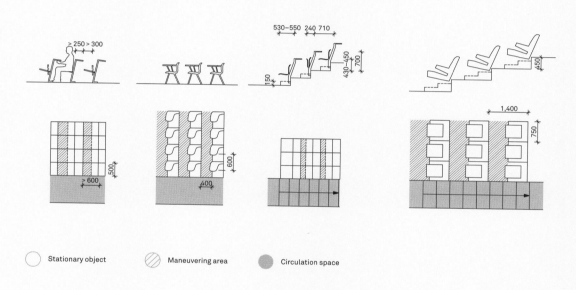

◯ Stationary object    ▨ Maneuvering area    ⬤ Circulation space

**Figure 3.4.11**
Acoustics in lecture halls/rooms

Per DIN 18041

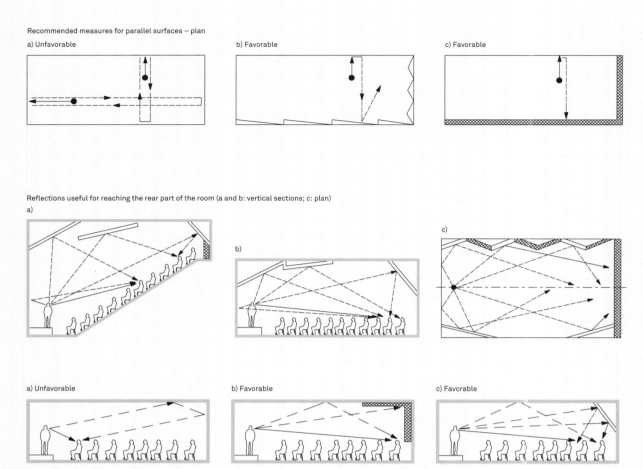

Recommended measures for parallel surfaces – plan

a) Unfavorable    b) Favorable    c) Favorable

Reflections useful for reaching the rear part of the room (a and b: vertical sections; c: plan)

a)

b)

c)

a) Unfavorable    b) Favorable    c) Favorable

**Figure 3.4.12**
Layout of sound-absorbing surfaces

Per DIN 18041

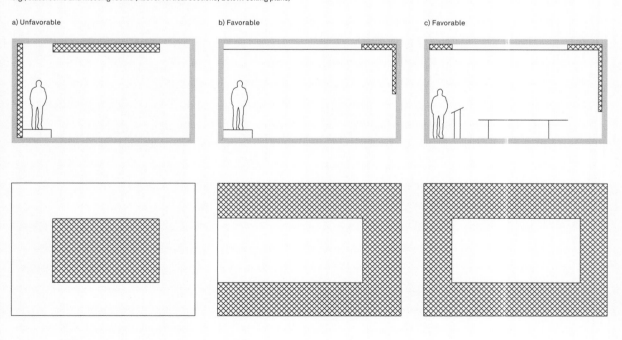

Distribution of sound-absorbing surfaces for small- to moderate-sized rooms,
e.g., classrooms and meeting rooms (Above: vertical sections, Below: ceiling plans)

a) Unfavorable    b) Favorable    c) Favorable

Sound-absorbing material

**Figure 3.4.13**
Lecterns and laboratory benches
in lecture halls and lecture rooms

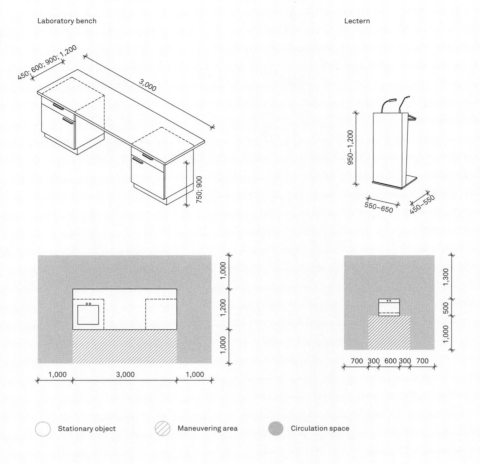

Laboratory bench

Lectern

Stationary object

Maneuvering area

Circulation space

**Figure 3.4.14**
Projection surfaces for video
projectors

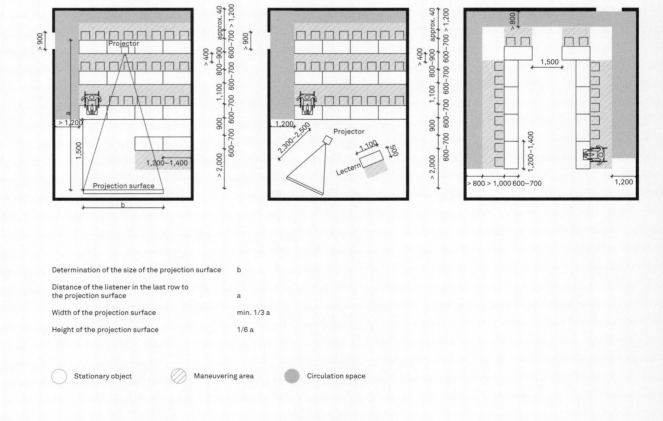

| Determination of the size of the projection surface | b |
| Distance of the listener in the last row to the projection surface | a |
| Width of the projection surface | min. 1/3 a |
| Height of the projection surface | 1/6 a |

Stationary object

Maneuvering area

Circulation space

### 3.4.2 Waiting and Seating Areas

Gathering places and seating areas should be commensurate in terms of density and size with the anticipated number of people and the expectations with regard to the typology. Thus seating areas in private apartments differ greatly from waiting areas at public agencies, infrastructure buildings such as train stations or airports, and medical facilities, or break areas in cultural and recreational facilities. If waiting areas are created, they should be designed to be functional and to have qualities that create a pleasant atmosphere: clear zoning, seating opportunities, play areas for children, and the like provide the comfort appropriate for the typical waiting time. At peak times (before or after theater performances, for example) or for large numbers of people over brief periods of time (at airport gates, for example), areas for sitting and waiting in line should be sufficiently differentiated. For cultural and recreational buildings, combining gathering places and seating areas with food service offerings is also desirable.

**Figure 3.4.15**
Space requirements for waiting areas

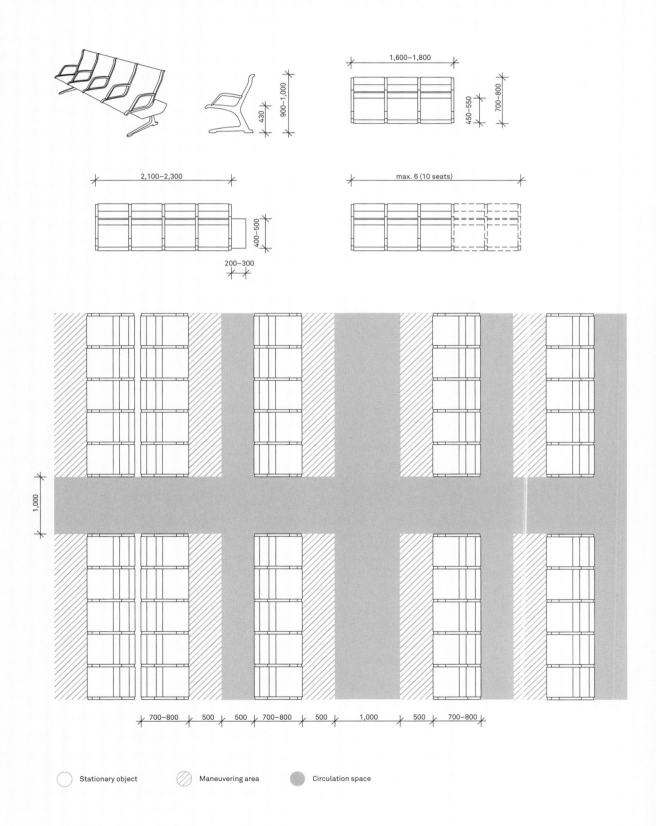

Stationary object    Maneuvering area    Circulation space

**Figure 3.4.16**
Dimensions of typical armchairs
and sofas

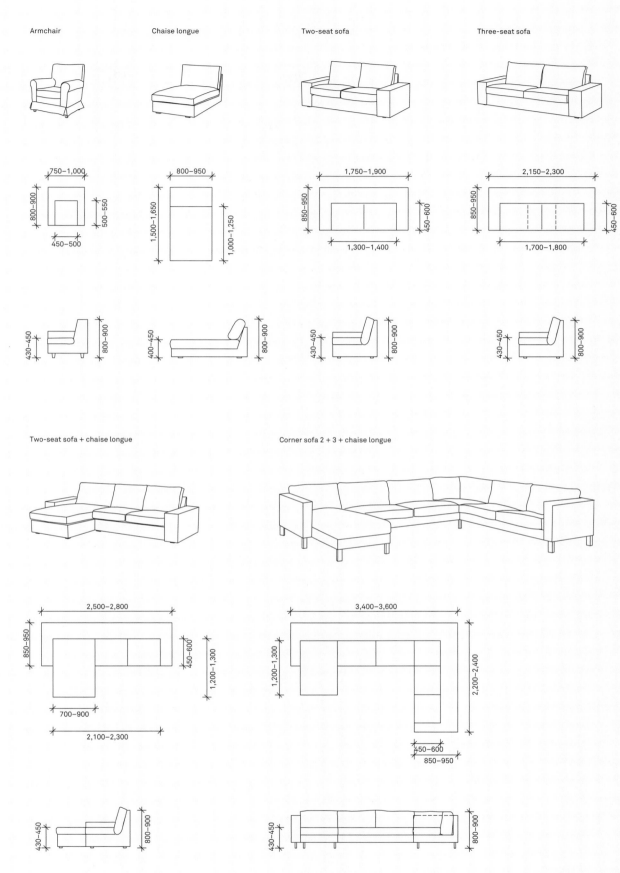

Armchair

Chaise longue

Two-seat sofa

Three-seat sofa

Two-seat sofa + chaise longue

Corner sofa 2 + 3 + chaise longue

**Figure 3.4.17**
Informal seating groups and
lounge areas

**Figure 3.4.18**
Dimensions of typical couch
and side tables

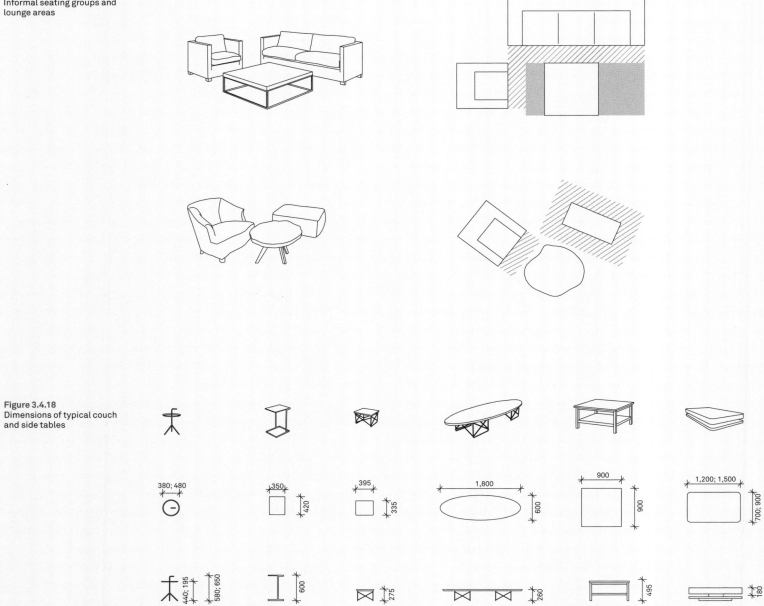

## 3.4.3 Dining Areas

When planning dining areas, it is important to make sure that tables and chairs are arranged with sufficient space for movement so that the users do not interfere with one another while eating: attention must be given to ensure sufficient spacing between the individual chairs, sufficient dimensions for the areas surrounding the tables, and that people have the possibility to pass behind seated guests.

Especially for dining rooms with many tables, paths giving access to the tables should be laid out to avoid impediments by varying the table spacing. To enable wheelchair use, adequate clearance beneath the table and a maneuvering area of 1.50 m × 1.50 m between the table and other furniture or confining parts of the building must be provided.

Table 3.4.2
Clearances behind chairs

| Dimensions for dining areas | Minimum | Comfortable |
|---|---|---|
| Center-to-center spacing of seats | min. 0.60–0.65 m | approx. 0.80 m |
| Depth of table space per person | min. 0.40 m | approx. 0.50–0.60 m |
| Distance between chair and wall | min. 0.30 m | approx. 0.50 m |
| Distance between chair and wall, walking past is possible | min. 0.60 m | approx. 0.90 m |
| Distance between chair and other furniture | min. 0.70 m | approx. 1.0 m |

Table 3.4.3
Minimum floor space for dining areas

| Number of people and arrangement | Width of floor space, in m | Depth of floor space, in m | Floor space, in m² |
|---|---|---|---|
| 2 people, seated opposite | 1.80 | 0.80 | 1.44 |
| 2 people, seated at corner | 1.30 | 1.30 | 1.69 |
| 4 people, 1 person per side | 1.80 | 1.80 | 3.24 |
| 4 people, 2 people per side | 1.80 | 1.20 | 2.16 |
| 4 people, round table | 2.10 | 2.10 | 4.41 |
| 5 people, 1 person at head of table | 1.80 | 1.80 | 3.24 |
| 5 people, 2 chairs + corner bench | 1.80 | 1.90 | 3.42 |
| 6 people, 3 people per side | 1.80 | 1.80 | 3.24 |
| 6 people, 1 person at each end | 1.80 | 2.30 | 4.14 |
| 8 people, 4 people per side | 1.80 | 2.40 | 4.32 |
| 8 people, 1 person at each end | 1.80 | 2.80 | 5.04 |

**Figure 3.4.19**
Minimum spacing in dining areas

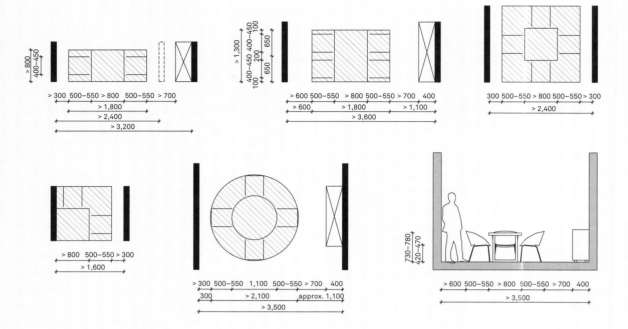

**Figure 3.4.20**
Typical table combinations

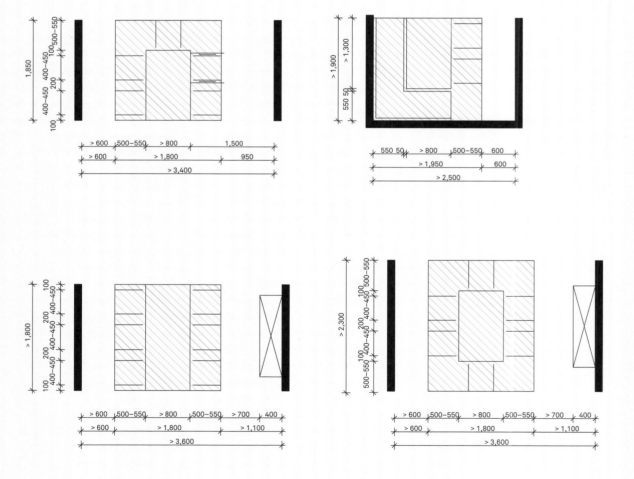

**Figure 3.4.21**
Seating elements and stand-up tables

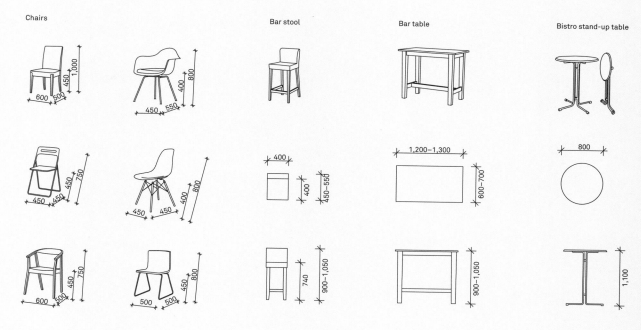

Chairs

Bar stool

Bar table

Bistro stand-up table

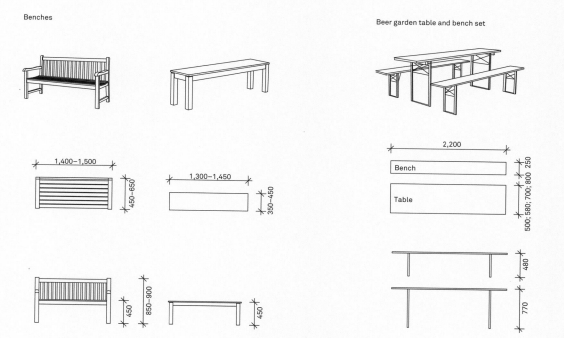

Benches

Beer garden table and bench set

# 3.5 Sanitary Facilities

When planning sanitary facilities, there are significant differences to be taken into account between private bathrooms and public or commercial/operational sanitary facilities. Although minimum dimensions for clearance distances and maneuvering zones apply, private bathrooms are nevertheless usually designed to also create agreeable surroundings.

As a rule, the planner should take into account the needs of wheelchair users by incorporating suitable accessibility of the plumbing fixtures into the sanitary planning. For publicly accessible facilities, requirements for safety and operation from a wheelchair must be observed.

These include: Wheelchair clearance beneath lavatories; mirror at low height or tilted appropriately; shower areas without raised thresholds; seats and grab bars; space for wheelchair next to toilets and showers; toilets at wheelchair height and fitted with hinged grab bars; accessibility of all operating elements (shower controls, toilet paper holder, soap dispenser, etc.); alarm devices on all plumbing fixtures; slip resistance of the flooring; and doors that do not open inward.

Wheelchair-accessible water closets in public facilities must be approachable from both sides, whereas access from one side is generally sufficient for private bathrooms, where custom solutions can be developed to address the individual user's degree of impairment.

### 3.5.1 Plumbing Fixtures

For plumbing fixtures, typical widths, depths, mounting heights, and maneuvering areas must be taken into consideration. These are to be considered as minimums, however, and can be increased commensurate to the building typology and the amount of expected use of the plumbing fixture. Especially in public buildings such as trade fairs, theaters, sports venues, etc., where high numbers of users can be expected simultaneously, considerably larger maneuvering zones should be planned.

Figure 3.5.1
Heights of plumbing fixtures

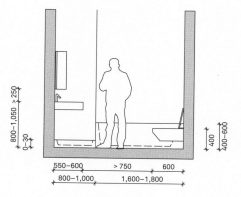

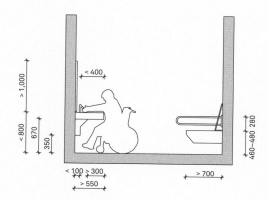

**Table 3.5.1**
Minimum dimensions of plumbing fixtures and maneuvering zones

| Plumbing fixture | Floor space w × d (for standard sizes) | Maneuvering area in front of the fixture w × d (when opposite each other) | Side clearance | Height above finished floor |
|---|---|---|---|---|
| Single basin lavatory | 600 × 550 | 900 × 550 (900 × 750) | 200 | 800–950 |
| Double basin lavatory | 1,200 × 550 | 1,500 × 550 (1,500 × 750) | 200 | 800–950 |
| Lavatory | 450 × 350 | 700 × 450 (700 × 750) | 200 (250 with walls at both sides) | 800–950 |
| WC (flush tank in wall) | 400 × 600 | 800 × 550 (800 × 750) | 200 (250 with walls at both sides) | 400 |
| WC (flush tank in front of wall) | 400 × 750 | 800 × 550 (800 × 750) | 200 (250 with walls at both sides) | 400 |
| Urinal | 400 × 400 | 600 × 600 (600 × 750) | 200 (250 with walls at both sides) | 650–700 |
| Shower basin | 800 × 800 | 800 × 750 | 200 (space between lavatory and shower basin can be reduced to 0) | 0–30 (depending on model and type) |
| Bathtub | 750 × 1,700 | 900 × 750 | 200 (space between lavatory and bathtub can be reduced to 0) | 400–600 (ideal 590) |

**Figure 3.5.2**
Plumbing fixtures and minimum dimensions of maneuvering zones

When laying out plumbing fixtures along a wall, larger clearances should be provided in order to ensure freedom of movement. Where plumbing fixtures are placed opposite each other, the extended maneuvering areas apply (values in parentheses).

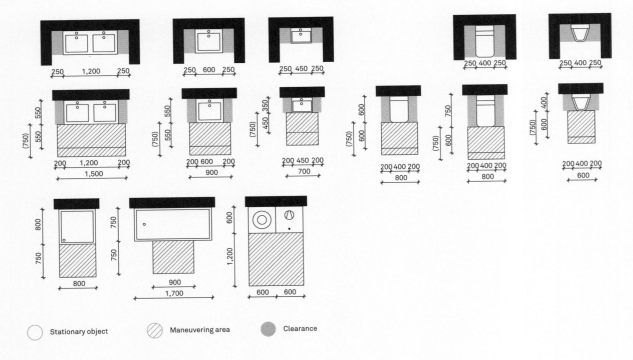

○ Stationary object   ▨ Maneuvering area   ● Clearance

**Figure 3.5.3**
Common shapes and sizes
of showers and bathtubs

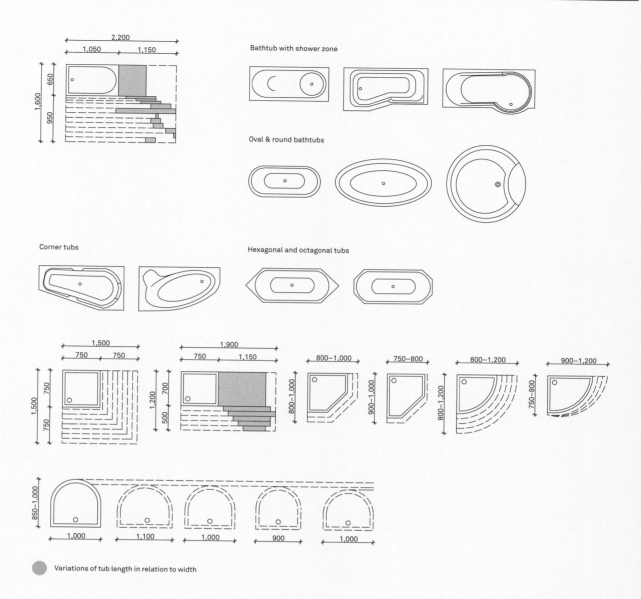

Bathtub with shower zone

Oval & round bathtubs

Corner tubs

Hexagonal and octagonal tubs

⬤ Variations of tub length in relation to width

**Figure 3.5.4**
Wheelchair-accessible plumbing
fixtures and minimum dimensions
of maneuvering zones

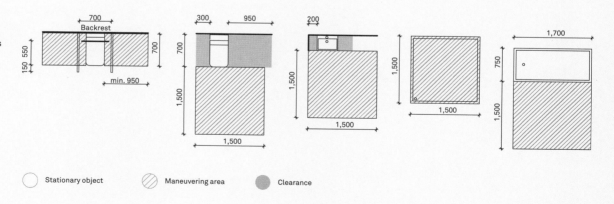

○ Stationary object        ▨ Maneuvering area        ⬤ Clearance

### 3.5.2 Bathrooms and Private Sanitary Facilities

Private bathrooms and toilets are usually designed according to individual user requirements. Minimum requirements for clearances and maneuvering zones can play a decisive role in planning rental apartments, and beyond that, all bathrooms should have qualities that create a pleasant atmosphere. A spatial separation between the toilet and other plumbing fixtures is often made, or indi-vidual plumbing fixtures such as the bathtub are showcased as space-defining elements. In addition to accommodating the plumbing fixtures, sufficient space should also be planned for cabinets and shelf space. Furthermore, washing machines and dryers may need to be integrated if no other places are available for their installation.

**Figure 3.5.5**
Examples of minimum requirements for private toilets and bathrooms

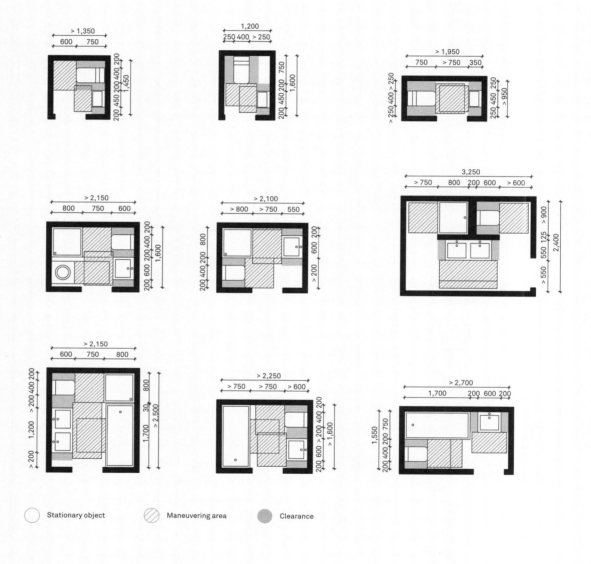

**Figure 3.5.6**
Layout of wheelchair-accessible toilets and shower rooms

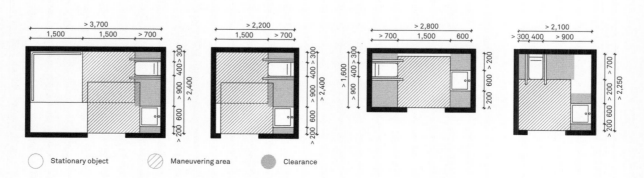

## 3.5.3 Public and Commercial Sanitary Facilities

Public and commercial or industrial sanitary facilities must be laid out in sufficient numbers and within reasonable distances. With a view toward barrier-free accessibility, toilet cores should be designed to be unobstructed and bright and to have separate wheelchair-accessible toilets. These can be accommodated in a separate room or integrated into a larger facility with due regard to the specific requirements. The quantity of necessary plumbing fixtures is specified by the requirements of public law (for example, occupational safety and health standards). Women's and men's toilets, a (unisex) wheelchair-accessible toilet and/or baby changing rooms as well as janitor's closets, if required, are combined in sanitary cores. The planner must take into account that sometimes there may be several people occupying the same area, such as the space in front of the sinks. All the same, privacy must be maintained, by not permitting direct views from the corridor into the toilet areas when the doors open, for instance, and by providing a separate anteroom for the sinks. The provision of screen walls and toilet partitions as well as privacy screens at the urinals ensures sufficient privacy within the toilet room.

In public toilet cores, baby changing areas for infants should always be provided in separate rooms. If the physical conditions do not permit this, a baby changing station should be integrated into the restrooms for both genders as well as the wheelchair-accessible toilet.

Washrooms and shower areas (for example, in production plants, sports facilities, or technical buildings) can be designed with individual stalls or as a group area, depending on the requirements, and combined with a communal changing room with or without partitions. In any case, sufficient shelf space and clothing hooks must be provided and transition zones must be planned between wet and dry areas.

Figure 3.5.7
Minimum dimensions for toilet facilities

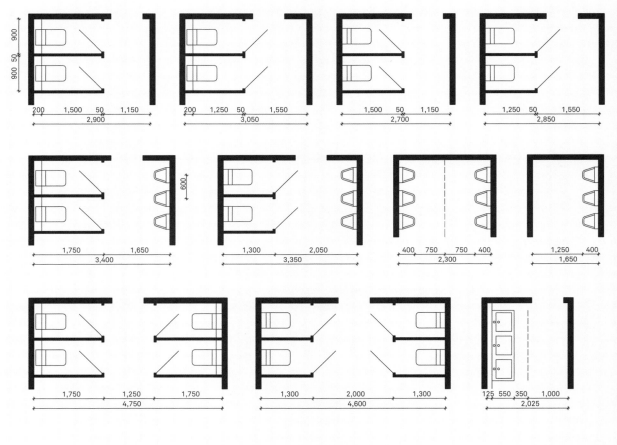

Figure 3.5.8
Wheelchair-accessible toilets and shower rooms (publicly accessible)

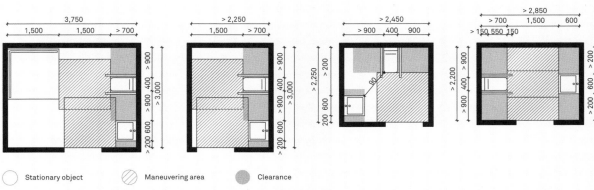

○ Stationary object      ▨ Maneuvering area      ● Clearance

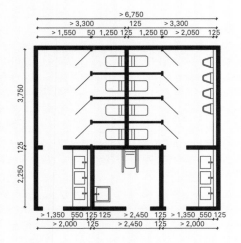
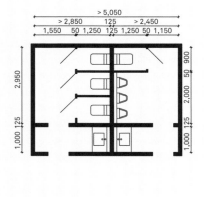
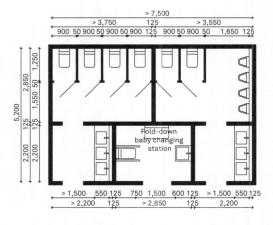

**Figure 3.5.9**
Examples of the layout of
toilet cores

**Figure 3.5.10**
Requirements and layout of
washing and shower areas

Per ASR A4.1

a) open rows of showers and
    shower stalls
b) shower stalls with visual
    screening/splash protection
c) shower stalls with double
    T-shaped visual screening/
    splash protection
d) row of individual shower stalls
    with private drying areas
e) row of shower stalls with
    shared drying area
f) wash positions

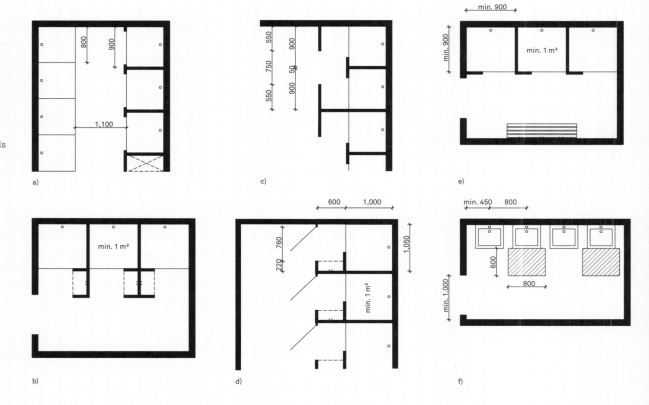

**Figure 3.5.11**
Baby changing areas in toilet
facilities

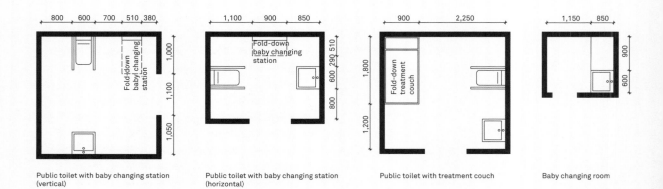

Public toilet with baby changing station (vertical)

Public toilet with baby changing station (horizontal)

Public toilet with treatment couch

Baby changing room

Table 3.5.2
Various minimum requirements for plumbing fixtures in workplaces

| Workplaces | Reference unit (RU) | Number of plumbing fixtures | | | | |
|---|---|---|---|---|---|---|

**Requirements as per VDI 6000 Part 2**

| Workplaces | Number of all employees | WCs (women) | Lavatories | WCs (men) | Urinals | Lavatories |
|---|---|---|---|---|---|---|
| **Total number of employees is known** | 6–10 | 1 | 1 | 1 | 1 | 1 |
| | 11–20 | 1 | 1 | 1 | 1 | 1 |
| | 21–50 | 2 | 2 | 1 | 2 | 2 |
| | 51–75 | 2 | 2 | 2 | 3 | 2 |
| | 76–100 | 4 | 2 | 2 | 4 | 2 |
| | 101–150 | 5 | 3 | 2 | 5 | 3 |
| | 151–200 | 7 | 3 | 3 | 7 | 4 |
| | 201–250 | 8 | 4 | 4 | 8 | 5 |

| Workplaces | Number of employees (female and male) | WCs (women) | Lavatories | WCs (men) | Urinals | Lavatories |
|---|---|---|---|---|---|---|
| **Respective numbers of male and female employees is known** | 6–10 | 1 | 1 | 1 | 1 | 1 |
| | 11–20 | 2 | 1 | 1 | 2 | 1 |
| | 21–50 | 2 | 1 | 2 | 2 | 2 |
| | 51–75 | 4 | 2 | 2 | 4 | 2 |
| | 76–100 | 5 | 3 | 2 | 5 | 3 |
| | 101–150 | 7 | 3 | 3 | 7 | 4 |
| | 151–200 | 8 | 4 | 4 | 8 | 5 |
| | 201–250 | 10 | 5 | 5 | 10 | 5 |

**Requirements as per ASR A4.1**

| Female or male employees | Minimum number for low concurrence (values apply for men and women) | | Minimum number for high concurrence (values apply for men and women) | |
|---|---|---|---|---|
| | WCs/urinals | Lavatories | WCs/urinals | Lavatories |
| max. 5 | 1 (for male employees: 1 addtl. urinal) | 1 | 2 | 1 |
| 6–10 | 1 (for male employees: 1 addtl. urinal) | 1 | 3 | 1 |
| 11–25 | 2 | 1 | 4 | 2 |
| 26–50 | 3 | 1 | 6 | 2 |
| 51–75 | 5 | 2 | 7 | 3 |
| 76–100 | 6 | 2 | 9 | 3 |
| 101–130 | 7 | 3 | 11 | 4 |
| 131–160 | 8 | 3 | 13 | 4 |
| 161–190 | 9 | 3 | 15 | 5 |
| 191–220 | 10 | 4 | 17 | 6 |
| 221–250 | 11 | 4 | 19 | 7 |
| | + 1 for each addtl. 30 employees | + 1 for each addtl. 90 employees | + 2 for each addtl. 30 employees | + 2 for each addtl. 90 employees |

Table 3.5.3
Minimum number of plumbing
fixtures in places of assembly

As per VDI 6000

Statutory requirements such as
regulations governing places of
assembly can impose considerably higher requirements. Here,
0.8–1.2 WCs per 100 visitors are
required, and the quantities may
be reduced depending on the total
number. The legal requirements
applicable for the project site
must therefore be verified in each
instance!

| Visitors | WCs (women) | Lavatories | WCs (men) | Urinals | Lavatories |
|---|---|---|---|---|---|
| **Low concurrence** | | | | | |
| 25 | 1 | 1 | 1 | 1 | 1 |
| 50/100 | 2 | 2 | 1 | 2 | 1/2 |
| 300/500 | 4 | 2/3 | 2 | 4 | 2/3 |
| 700 | 5 | 4 | 3 | 5 | 4 |
| 1,000 | 6 | 4 | 4 | 6 | 5 |
| 1,500 | 8 | 6 | 5 | 8 | 6 |
| 2,000 | 9 | 7 | 6 | 9 | 8 |

- Overall, 1 toilet room each for women and men
- Max. 1,000 visitors: 1 barrier-free stall each for women and men
- Over 1,000 visitors: 2 barrier-free stalls each for women and men

| Visitors | WCs (women) | Lavatories | WCs (men) | Urinals | Lavatories |
|---|---|---|---|---|---|
| **Average concurrence** | | | | | |
| 25 | 1 | 1 | 1 | 1 | 1 |
| 50 | 2 | 2 | 1 | 2 | 1 |
| 100 | 3 | 3 | 1 | 3 | 2 |
| 300 | 5 | 3 | 2 | 5 | 3 |
| 500 | 6 | 4 | 3 | 6 | 4 |
| 700 | 7 | 5 | 4 | 7 | 5 |
| 1,000 | 9 | 6 | 5 | 9 | 7 |
| 1,500 | 11 | 8 | 7 | 11 | 9 |
| 2,000 | 13 | 10 | 9 | 13 | 11 |

- Max. 1,000 visitors: 1 toilet room each for women and men and 1 barrier-free stall each for women and men
- Over 1,000 visitors: 2 toilet rooms each for women and men and 2 barrier-free stalls each for women and men

| Visitors | WCs (women) | Lavatories | WCs (men) | Urinals | Lavatories |
|---|---|---|---|---|---|
| **High concurrence** | | | | | |
| 25 | 2 | 2 | 2 | 2 | 2 |
| 50 | 3 | 3 | 2 | 3 | 2 |
| 100 | 5 | 5 | 2 | 5 | 3 |
| 300 | 8 | 5 | 3 | 8 | 5 |
| 500 | 9 | 6 | 5 | 9 | 6 |
| 700 | 11 | 8 | 6 | 11 | 8 |
| 1,000 | 14 | 9 | 8 | 14 | 11 |
| 1,500 | 17 | 12 | 11 | 17 | 14 |
| 2,000 | 20 | 15 | 14 | 20 | 17 |

- Max. 500 visitors: 1 toilet room each for women and men
- Over 500 visitors: 2 toilet rooms each for women and men
- Max. 1,000 visitors: 1 barrier-free stall each for women and men
- Over 1,000 visitors: 2 barrier-free stalls each for women and men

## 3.5.4 Piping Routes

When designing sanitary facilities and determining the layouts, the piping routes must be planned at an early stage. If the enclosing walls are built of lightweight construction, the plumbing lines can be integrated within them, provided there are no problems with noise abatement. Otherwise, furred or double wall construction of sufficient dimensions must be used. To determine the overall dimensions, the measurements of the largest pipes, including insulation and any anchors or supports, along with any pipe crossings, the constructive assembly of the chase wall (for example, drywall framing), and the outer cladding must be added together.

**Figure 3.5.12**
Minimum dimensions for double wall construction

**Figure 3.5.13**
Typical arrangements of supply and drain lines for plumbing fixtures

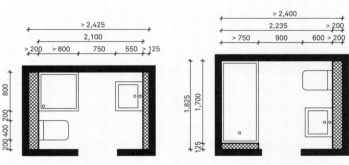 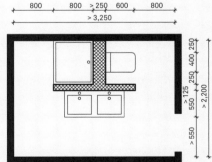

# 3.6 Kitchens

The preparation of food and beverages embraces a broad spectrum, from kitchenettes in private apartments, hotel rooms, or offices to professional commercial kitchens. Even though kitchen areas are often designed on a very individual basis, there are established geometric and hygienic requirements that must be adhered to as minimum standards. As soon as a kitchen is used commercially, local requirements of the authorities for trade supervision and sanitary inspection must be observed in addition. ↗ Chapter 4.7 Typologies/Lodging and Food Service

## 3.6.1 Kitchen Fixtures and Appliances

For residential use, most kitchen fixtures and appliances (such as cabinets, stoves, ovens, refrigerator/freezers) are available with a depth of approximately 60–65 cm and a standard nominal width of 60 cm, which are complemented by additional unit spacings of 30 cm, 45 cm, 90 cm, 120 cm, etc. for cabinetry and other furnishings. In the food and beverage industry, additional sizes are also encountered, which are partly based on modular Gastro-Norm food containers and partly on the size of technical equipment. Due

to the necessary installation density and the hygiene requirements concerning aspects such as joints and clearance distances, detailed kitchen planning that incorporates all desired or requisite kitchen appliances is useful at an early stage. The planner must take into account not only ergonomic requirements such as gripping and work surface heights and adequate spaces for maneuvering within the kitchen, but also clearances and arrangements of appliances that promote effective use.

**Figure 3.6.1**
Drawing symbols for various kitchen elements

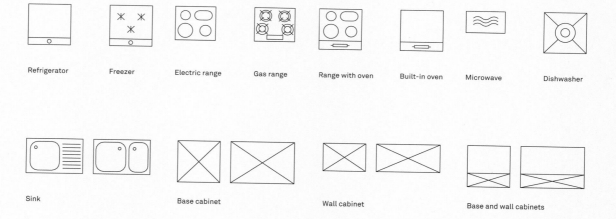

Refrigerator    Freezer    Electric range    Gas range    Range with oven    Built-in oven    Microwave    Dishwasher

Sink    Base cabinet    Wall cabinet    Base and wall cabinets

**Figure 3.6.2**
Typical dimensions for sinks
and cooktops

Minimum widths for sinks per DIN 66354
a) Individual sink unit
b) Sink unit with 1½ bowls
c) Double bowl sink unit without drainboard
d) Double bowl sink unit with drainboard

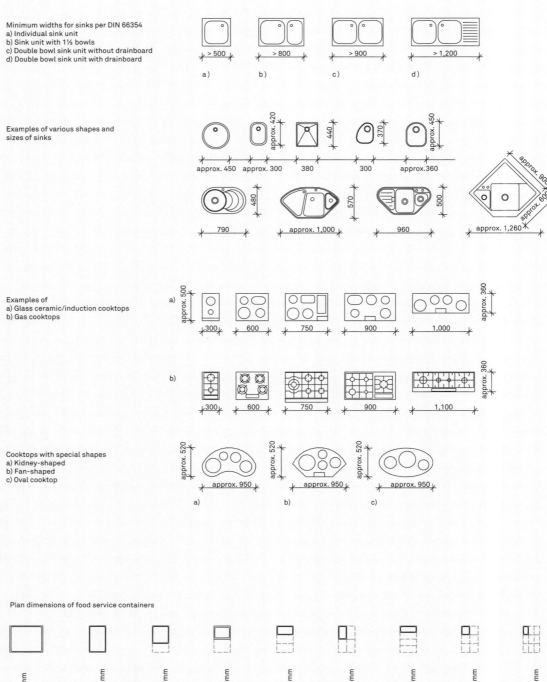

Examples of various shapes and
sizes of sinks

Examples of
a) Glass ceramic/induction cooktops
b) Gas cooktops

Cooktops with special shapes
a) Kidney-shaped
b) Fan-shaped
c) Oval cooktop

**Figure 3.6.3**
Typical dimensions for food
service industry equipment

Plan dimensions of food service containers

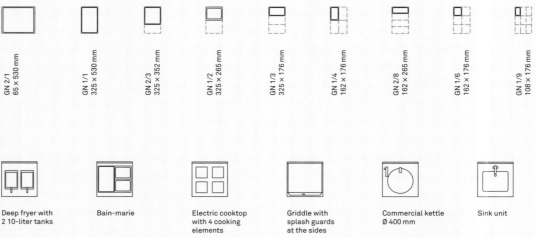

GN 2/1
65 × 530 mm

GN 1/1
325 × 530 mm

GN 2/3
325 × 352 mm

GN 1/2
325 × 265 mm

GN 1/3
325 × 176 mm

GN 1/4
162 × 176 mm

GN 2/8
162 × 265 mm

GN 1/6
162 × 176 mm

GN 1/9
108 × 176 mm

Deep fryer with
2 10-liter tanks

Bain-marie

Electric cooktop
with 4 cooking
elements

Griddle with
splash guards
at the sides

Commercial kettle
Ø 400 mm

Sink unit

Examples of commercial kitchen appliances with dimensions of 700 × 700 × 850 mm (w × d × h).
Other widths (400, 500, 600, 800, 900 mm) and depths (600, 650, 900, 1,100 mm) are also available.

**Table 3.6.1**
Minimum clearances in
kitchen areas

| Required minimum clearances in kitchens in mm | |
| --- | --- |
| Distance between two opposite kitchen counter units (storage surfaces) | 1,200 |
| Distance between kitchen counter unit and opposite wall | 1,200 |
| Distance between two opposite kitchen counter units, wheelchair-accessible | 1,500 |
| Distance between kitchen counter unit and opposite wall, wheelchair-accessible | 1,500 |
| Gaps between kitchen counter unit and adjacent walls | 30 |
| Distance between kitchen counter unit and door/window frames | 100 |

**Table 3.6.2**
Work surfaces and gripping
heights

Per AMK – Arbeitsgemeinschaft
Die Moderne Küche (The Modern
Kitchen Working Group)

| Body height in cm | Optimal and recommended work surface heights | | | Installation height for refrigerator/ freezers, in cm | Installation height for ovens/ microwave ovens, in cm | Shelf heights reachable from a standing position, measured from floor in cm | | |
| --- | --- | --- | --- | --- | --- | --- | --- | --- |
| | Countertop, in cm | Cooktop, in cm | Sink, in cm | | | Base cabinet drawer | Wall cabinet | Tall cabinet |
| 135 | 70 | | 80 | 65–130 | 60–135 | 34 | 140 | 150 |
| 140 | 80 | 70 | 85 | 65–140 | 65–135 | 35 | 145 | 155 |
| 145 | 80 | 70 | 90 | 60–150 | 70–140 | 36 | 150 | 160 |
| 150 | 85 | 80 | 90 | 60–155 | 75–145 | 37 | 155 | 165 |
| 155 | 90 | 85 | 95 | 55–160 | 80–150 | 39 | 160 | 170 |
| 160 | 90 | 85 | 95 | 55–165 | 85–155 | 40 | 165 | 175 |
| 165 | 95 | 90 | 100 | 55–170 | 90–155 | 41 | 170 | 180 |
| 170 | 100 | 95 | 100 | 55–175 | 95–165 | 42 | 175 | 185 |
| 175 | 100 | 95 | 105 | 55–180 | 95–165 | 43 | 180 | 190 |
| 180 | 105 | 100 | | 55–185 | 100–170 | 44 | 185 | 195 |
| 185 | 105 | 100 | | 55–190 | 105–175 | 46 | 190 | 200 |

**Figure 3.6.4**
Wheelchair-accessible kitchen design

Per DIN EN 1116 and DIN 18040-2

Comfort rule: The distance between work surface and elbow height should be 100–150 mm.

Dimension in parentheses: The clear distance above the cooktop must be a minimum of 650 mm. This is also recommended above the sink.

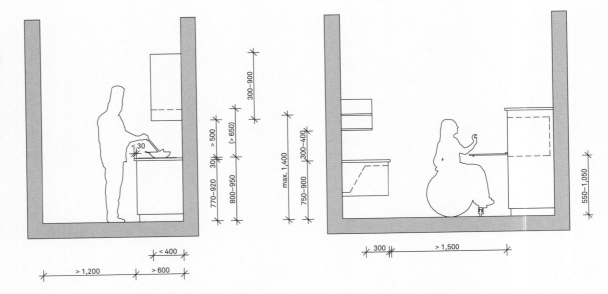

**Figure 3.6.5**
Wheelchair-accessible work areas and heights in kitchens

Per DIN 18040

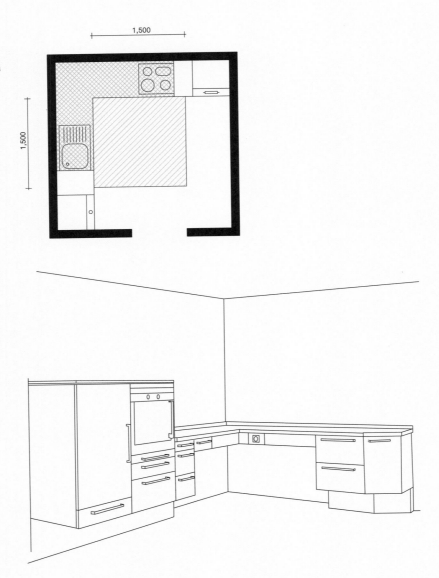

## 3.6.2 Private Kitchens

Kitchens in private residences have evolved from functional spaces designed for optimal efficiency to become a center of life at home. Communication between living, dining, and kitchen areas and the sense of amenity that goes along with it are important to many people, although individuals can have very different opinions of the advantages and disadvantages of open and closed kitchen concepts. To create rental apartments with the highest possible level of acceptance, for example, the design of the kitchen space is an important hallmark of quality. Also when planning individual residential kitchens, minimum standards for clearances and areas should be observed. When planning for wheelchair accessibility, considerably larger kitchen areas are needed because adequate wheelchair clearance must be provided beneath counters and essential kitchen appliances such as the sink and stove, and because wall-hung cabinets are generally not accessible, thus requiring the provision of additional storage space at a height within reach.

Table 3.6.3
Minimum areas for private kitchens

| Kitchen type | Recommended room size |
| --- | --- |
| Kitchenette within a room | approx. 5–6 m² |
| Kitchen for cooking only | approx. 8–10 m² |
| Eat-in kitchen | approx. 8–10 m², of which 5 m² is eating area for 4 people |
| Combined kitchen/living room | min. 15 m² |

Figure 3.6.6
Kitchen layout forms

a) U-shaped
b) G-shaped
c) L-shaped
d) L-shaped with island
e) Single row
f) Double row

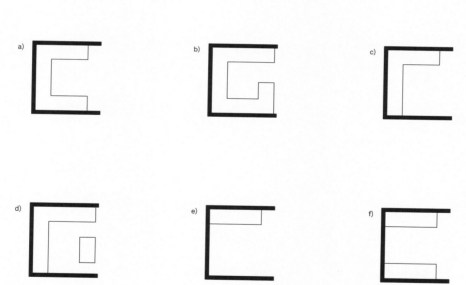

**Figure 3.6.7**
**Zoning of kitchens**

1 Food storage
2 Equipment storage
3 Sink
4 Food preparation
5 Cooking/Baking

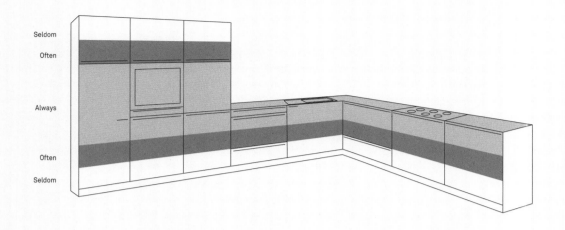

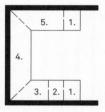
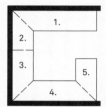
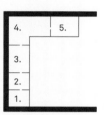

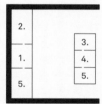
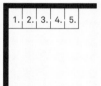
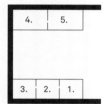

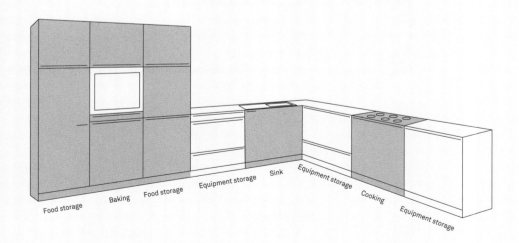

Figure 3.6.8
Examples for the layout of
private kitchens

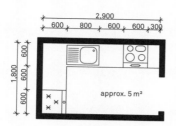

approx. 5 m²

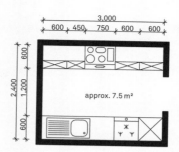

approx. 7.5 m²

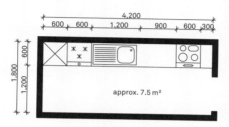

approx. 7.5 m²

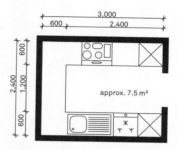

approx. 7.5 m²

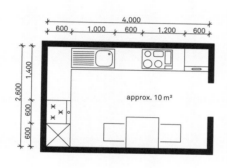

approx. 10 m²

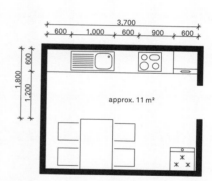

approx. 11 m²

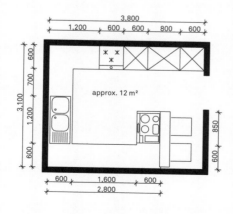

approx. 12 m²

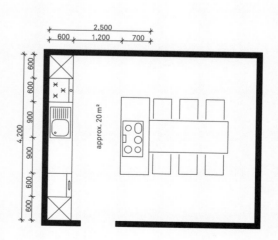

approx. 20 m²

# 3.7 Storage Spaces

Storage rooms must be incorporated when planning almost all types of buildings, although their type, size, and complexity can sometimes differ considerably. Very different terminology is used for the various types of storage, which are generally a consequence of the specific typology or the logistics concept. In addition to storing items in a spatially efficient way, the operation of storage areas is an important aspect when planning storage rooms, especially when, as in logistics buildings, storage of goods is an integral part of the business model. A wide diversity of requirements that depend on the type of stored materials (for example, hazardous substances or food) may need to be taken into account, including security issues and hygienic or climatic conditions.

### 3.7.1 Pallets and Containers

Dependent on the various sizes of items being stored, different standardized systems for transporting and storing these goods with ease and efficiency have become established. The storage room or storage building must be dimensioned accordingly. In addition to disposable packaging/pallets, reusable elements such as Euro pallets, big bags (also known as bulk bags or flexible intermediate bulk containers [FIBC]), intermediate bulk containers (IPC, also known as IBC totes or pallet tanks) and ISO freight containers are used. Many warehouses are therefore specifically coordinated with the standardized 800 × 1,200 mm pallet systems as well as the 20- and 40-foot ISO containers.

Figure 3.7.1
Basic principles of warehouse logistics

**Figure 3.7.2**
Transport pallets for warehouses

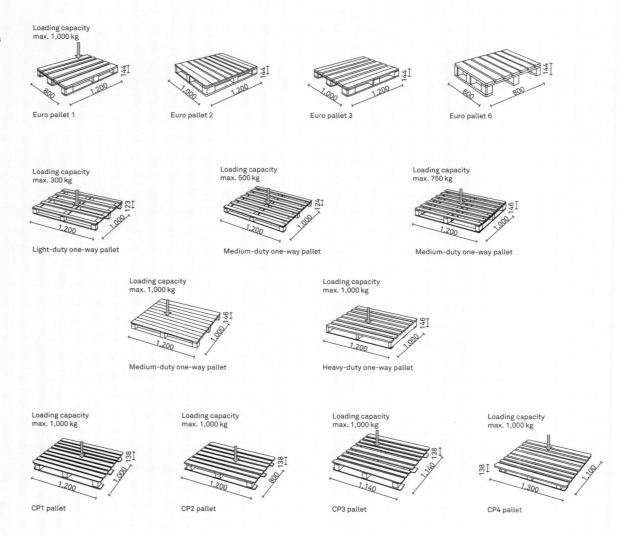

Loading capacity
max. 1,000 kg

Euro pallet 1

Euro pallet 2

Euro pallet 3

Euro pallet 6

Loading capacity
max. 300 kg

Light-duty one-way pallet

Loading capacity
max. 500 kg

Medium-duty one-way pallet

Loading capacity
max. 750 kg

Medium-duty one-way pallet

Loading capacity
max. 1,000 kg

Medium-duty one-way pallet

Loading capacity
max. 1,000 kg

Heavy-duty one-way pallet

Loading capacity
max. 1,000 kg

CP1 pallet

Loading capacity
max. 1,000 kg

CP2 pallet

Loading capacity
max. 1,000 kg

CP3 pallet

Loading capacity
max. 1,000 kg

CP4 pallet

**Figure 3.7.3**
Various types of transport devices

Metal collars for
flat pallets

Pallet-mounted frame
with safety retainers

Metal stacking frame

Middle clamping bracket
for Euro pallet

Wood collars for
Euro/flat pallets

Flat pallet with collar
per DIN 15148/49

Clamping brackets
with mesh dividers

Pallets for full and
half warp beams or
back beams

Box pallet with lid and
removable side panel
per DIN 15142

Attachable pipe
frames

Flat pallet with
stacking frame

Partitionable mesh
box pallet per DIN 15155

Large-capacity or
insulation pallet

2-piece collapsible
pallet converter

**Figure 3.7.4**
**ISO containers**

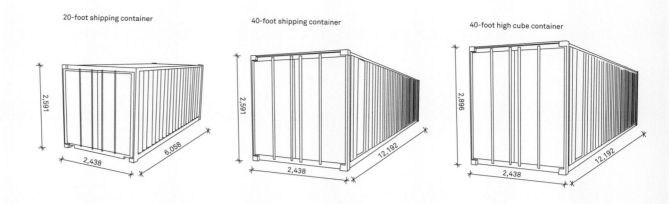

20-foot shipping container

40-foot shipping container

40-foot high cube container

**Table 3.7.1**
**Dimensions of ISO containers (selection)**

| Type | Outer dimensions (L × W × H) | Inner dimensions (L × W × H) | Volume | Empty weight (tare) | Max. capacity | Max. total weight |
|---|---|---|---|---|---|---|
| 20-foot | 6.058 × 2.438 × 2.591 m<br>19' 10½" × 8' × 8' 6" | 5.710 × 2.352 × 2.385 m<br>18' 8 ¹³⁄₁₆" × 7' 8 ¹⁹⁄₃₂" × 7' 9 ⁵⁷⁄₆₄" | 33.0 m³ | 2,250 kg | 21,750 kg | 24,000 kg |
| 40-foot | 12.192 × 2.438 × 2.591 m<br>40' × 8' × 8' 6" | 12.040 × 2.345 × 2.385 m<br>39' 5 ⁴⁵⁄₆₄" × 7' 8 ¹⁹⁄₃₂" × 7' 9 ⁵⁷⁄₆₄" | 67.0 m³ | 3,780 kg | 26,700 kg | 30,480 kg |
| 40-foot high cube | 12.192 × 2.438 × 2.896 m<br>40' × 8' × 9' 6" | 12.040 × 2.345 × 2.690 m<br>39' 4" × 7' 7" × 8' 9" | 76.0 m³ | 3,900 kg | 26,580 kg | 30,480 kg |
| 45-foot high cube | 13.716 × 2.438 × 2.896 m<br>45' × 8' × 9' 6" | 13.556 × 2.345 × 2.695 m<br>44' 4" × 7' 8 ¹⁹⁄₃₂" × 8' 9 ¹⁵⁄₁₆" | 86.0 m³ | 5,050 kg | 27,450 kg | 32,500 kg |
| 53-foot high cube | 16.154 × 2.591 × 2.896 m<br>53' × 8' 6" × 9' 6" | 16.002 × 2.515 × 2.710 m<br>52' 6" × 8' 3" × 8' 10 ¹¹⁄₁₆" | 109.1 m³ | | | |

**Figure 3.7.5**
**Various miscellaneous storage containers**

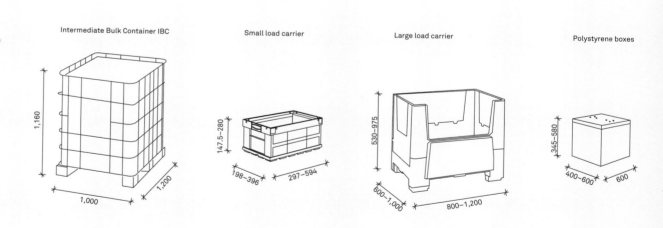

Intermediate Bulk Container IBC

Small load carrier

Large load carrier

Polystyrene boxes

Figure 3.7.6
Typical big bags (FIBC)

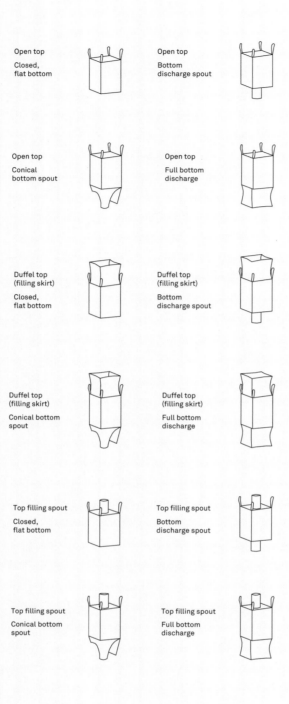

Open top
Closed,
flat bottom

Open top
Bottom
discharge spout

Open top
Conical
bottom spout

Open top
Full bottom
discharge

Duffel top
(filling skirt)
Closed,
flat bottom

Duffel top
(filling skirt)
Bottom
discharge spout

Duffel top
(filling skirt)
Conical bottom
spout

Duffel top
(filling skirt)
Full bottom
discharge

Top filling spout
Closed,
flat bottom

Top filling spout
Bottom
discharge spout

Top filling spout
Conical bottom
spout

Top filling spout
Full bottom
discharge

**Big Bag**

**Type: Standard 4-loop container**

| Measurements | Various footprint sizes | | |
|---|---|---|---|
| Inner dimensions | 760 × 760 mm | 870 × 870 mm | 950 × 950 mm |
| Outer dimensions | 800 × 800 mm | 910 × 910 mm | 990 × 990 mm |
| Diameter of big bag, filled | 1,010 mm | 1,150 mm | 1,250 mm |

| Volume (m³) | Height (mm) | | |
|---|---|---|---|
| 0.3 | 550 | – | – |
| 0.4 | 650 | – | – |
| 0.5 | 800 | 650 | – |
| 0.6 | 900 | 750 | – |
| 0.7 | 1,050 | 850 | – |
| 0.8 | 1,150 | 950 | – |
| 0.9 | 1,250 | 1,050 | 850 |
| 1 | 1,400 | 1,150 | 950 |
| 1.1 | 1,550 | 1,250 | 1,050 |
| 1.2 | 1,650 | 1,350 | 1,150 |
| 1.3 | 1,800 | 1,450 | 1,200 |
| 1.4 | 1,900 | 1,550 | 1,300 |
| 1.5 | – | 1,650 | 1,350 |
| 1.6 | – | 1,750 | 1,450 |
| 1.7 | – | 1,850 | 1,550 |
| 1.8 | – | 1,950 | 1,600 |
| 1.9 | – | 2,050 | 1,700 |
| 2 | – | 2,150 | 1,750 |
| 2.1 | – | – | 1,850 |
| 2.2 | – | – | 1,950 |

## 3.7.2 Types of Storage

The type of storage needed depends on the requirements of the items being stored, the availability, the stored diversity of goods, etc. A basic distinction is made between static vs. dynamic or chaotic storage systems, which are subject to automated processes. Both systems can be organized as compact storage or line storage, and whereas compact storage offers more efficient use of space, line storage enables access to all the stored goods. Further distinctions are made based on the storage height and the loading capacity (for example, high-rise rack, heavy-duty rack) or specific properties, such as storage systems utilizing mobile carousels, paternosters, rolling racks, or mobile shelving.

**Figure 3.7.7**
Criteria for selection of storage type

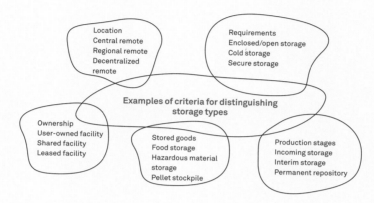

**Figure 3.7.8**
Classification of possible storage systems

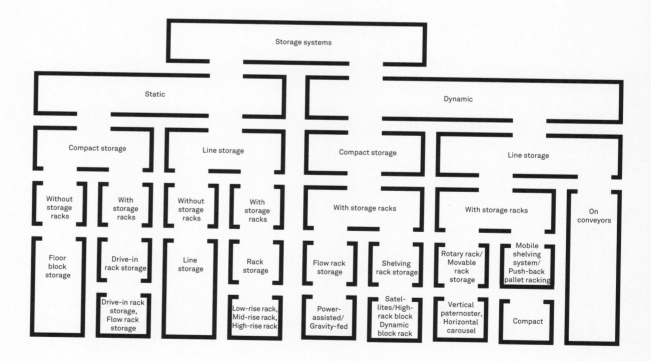

**Figure 3.7.9**
Block, line, and rack storage

Block storage

Line storage

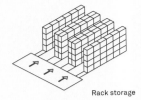

Rack storage

**Figure 3.7.10**
Loading capacities of various shelving systems

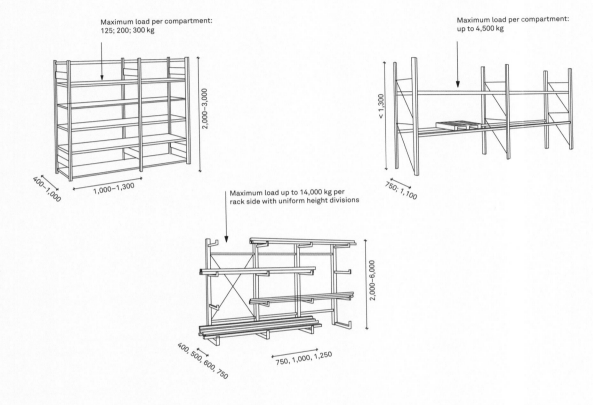

Maximum load per compartment: 125; 200; 300 kg

Maximum load per compartment: up to 4,500 kg

Maximum load up to 14,000 kg per rack side with uniform height divisions

**Figure 3.7.11**
Vertical carousel storage, horizontal carousel storage, mobile pallet storage and flow rack storage

Vertical carousel storage

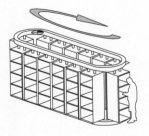

Horizontal carousel storage

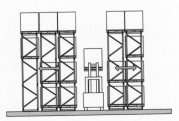

Mobile pallet storage

Flow rack storage

Figure 3.7.12
High-rack storage systems

Automatic small-parts storage

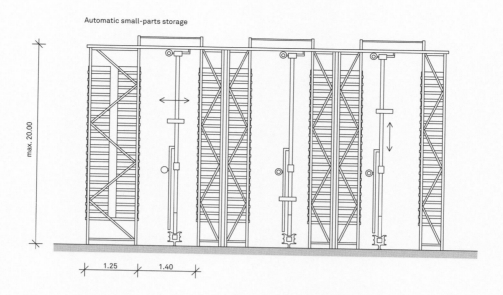

max. 20.00

1.25    1.40

Shuttle systems

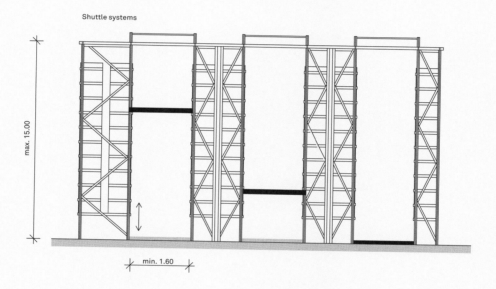

max. 15.00

min. 1.60

High-rack storage (from 6 m)

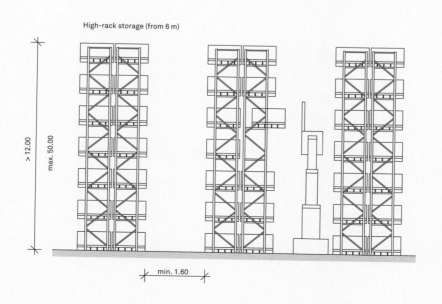

> 12.00    max. 50.00

min. 1.60

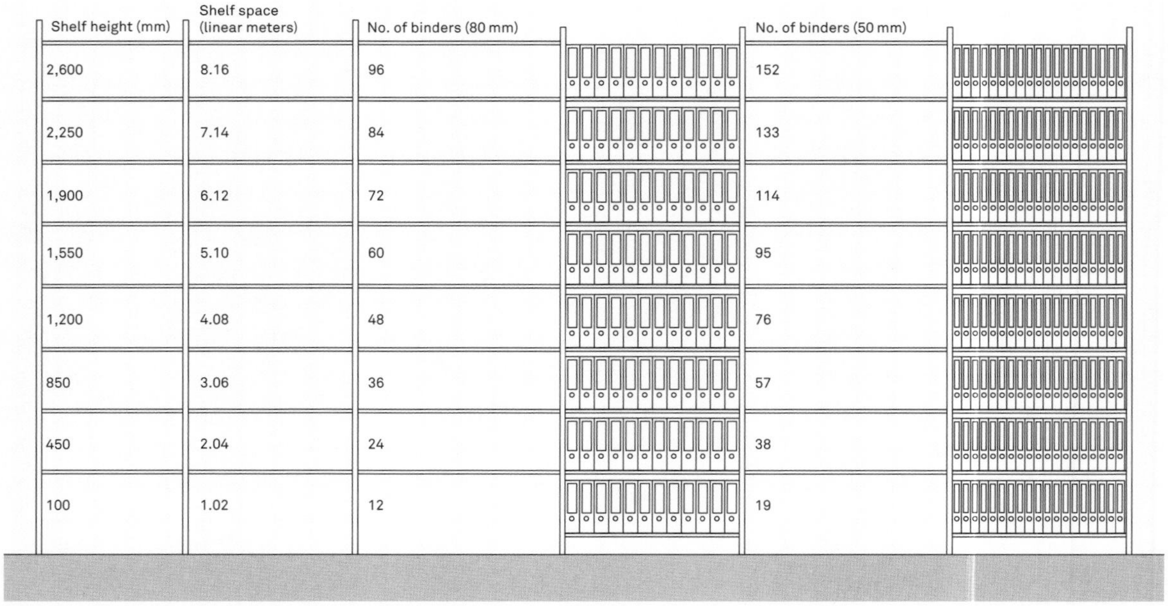

**Figure 3.7.13**
Binder storage in filing shelves

| Shelf height (mm) | Shelf space (linear meters) | No. of binders (80 mm) | | No. of binders (50 mm) | |
|---|---|---|---|---|---|
| 2,600 | 8.16 | 96 | | 152 | |
| 2,250 | 7.14 | 84 | | 133 | |
| 1,900 | 6.12 | 72 | | 114 | |
| 1,550 | 5.10 | 60 | | 95 | |
| 1,200 | 4.08 | 48 | | 76 | |
| 850 | 3.06 | 36 | | 57 | |
| 450 | 2.04 | 24 | | 38 | |
| 100 | 1.02 | 12 | | 19 | |

**Figure 3.7.14 (left)**
Example of mobile shelving

**Figure 3.7.15 (right)**
Mobile shelving elements

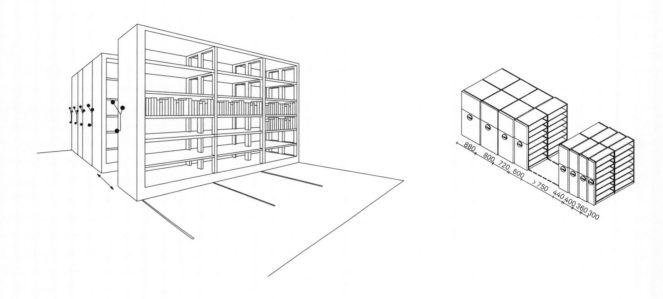

**Table 3.7.2**
Area requirements for mobile shelving

**Area requirements for mobile shelving**

Assumptions:
Height: approx. 2.35 m
Shelf width: 1.40 m

| Mobile shelving | Outer dimension in mm | Shelf space (linear meters) | Number of binders (80 mm ea.) | Binder capacity (50 mm ea.) |
|---|---|---|---|---|
| 3 shelving units | 2,690 | approx. 42.12 | 540 | 828 |
| 4 shelving units | 3,320 | approx. 56.16 | 720 | 1,104 |
| 5 shelving units | 3,950 | approx. 70.20 | 900 | 1,380 |
| 6 shelving units | 4,580 | approx. 84.24 | 1,080 | 1,656 |
| 7 shelving units | 5,210 | approx. 98.28 | 1,260 | 1,932 |

### 3.7.3 Handling and Transport

When planning storage areas, adequate circulation routes and maneuvering areas are to be incorporated for loading and unloading. A decisive factor in this respect is whether operations shall be automated or carried out manually, since automated rack-serving equipment generally requires less space than human-operated ground conveyors like pallet trucks or forklifts. In addition to accommodating the actual warehouse operations, consideration must also be given to the transfer areas, including turning areas, crossing vehicle paths, gates, etc. For automated warehouses, warehouse management systems must be used to provide appropriate areas for stocking and picking as well as packing and shipping stations. ↗ Chapter 4.3 Typologies/Logistics and Commerce

**Figure 3.7.16**
Height limits of various industrial trucks in m

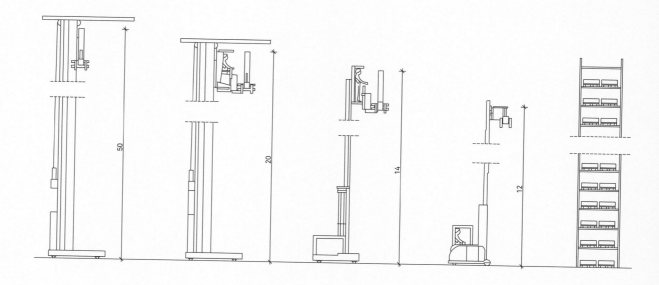

**Table 3.7.3**
Space requirements of conveyor vehicles in mm

Per ASR A1.8

| Vehicle | | | | Remarks | Clear height above traffic routes | |
|---|---|---|---|---|---|---|
| Type | Width | Length | Outside turning radius of wheels | | Trucks with no or low lift height (max. 1,200 mm lift) | High-lift trucks |
| Pedestrian-controlled industrial trucks (walkies) | 800–1,300 | 1,200–2,000 | 1,000–1,600 | | 2,000 | 3,500 |
| Stand-up rider trucks | 900–1,500 | 1,500–2,500 | 1,500–2,000 | | 2,500 | 3,500 |
| Sit-down rider trucks | 900–1,500 | 2,500–3,800 | 1,500–2,500 | Dimensions apply only to forklifts with a carrying capacity of max. 3t | 2,500 | 3,500 |
| Mobile cranes | 1,500–2,500 | 3,500–5,500 | 2,500–7,200 | For mobile cranes with max. 9t carrying capacity | 4,000 | 4,000 |
| Light trucks with max. 1.5t loading capacity | 1,500–2,400 | 4,000–5,000 | 4,000–6,000 | For trucks with 6000 mm vehicle length | 4,000 | 4,000 |

Figure 3.7.17
Space requirements of hand
pallet trucks

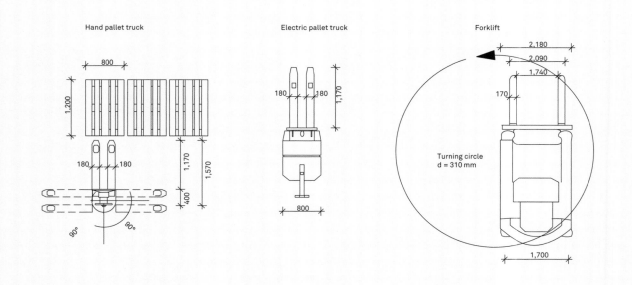

Table 3.7.4
Quantity of pallets as a function
of lifting device type

| Type of lifting device | AST (minimum aisle width) | Number of storage | Number of pallets per m² |
|---|---|---|---|
| Forklift | 2,300 mm | 4 levels | 1.8 |
| Counterbalance truck | 4,000 mm | 4 levels | 1.6 |
|  |  | 6 levels | 2.2 |
| Pallet stacker | 2,300 mm | 4 levels | 1.8 |
|  |  | 6 levels | 2.7 |
| Pallet stacker with telescopic fork | 2,400 mm | 4 levels | 1.7 |
|  |  | 6 levels | 2.6 |
| Reach mast truck | 1,000 mm | 4 levels | 1.7 |
|  |  | 6 levels | 2.5 |
|  |  | 8 levels | 3.2 |
| High rack stacker with swivel traverse fork | 1,000 mm | 4 levels | 2.0 |
|  |  | 6 levels | 2.9 |
|  |  | 8 levels | 4.1 |
|  |  | 10 levels | 5.2 |
| High-rack storage with telescopic platform | 1,500 mm | 4 levels | 2.2 |
|  |  | 6 levels | 3.2 |
|  |  | 8 levels | 4.3 |
|  |  | 10 levels | 5.4 |

**Figure 3.7.18**
Types of conveyors in mm

Belt conveyor

Wheel conveyor

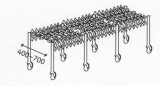

Gravity roller conveyor

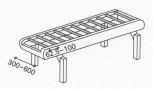

Drag chain conveyor

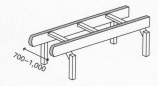

Slat-band chain conveyor

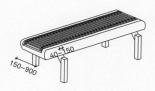

Mesh belt conveyor

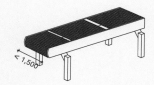

Scraper conveyor

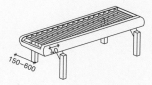

Pallet belt conveyor

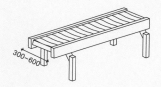

# 3.8 Ancillary and Staff Rooms

For reasons of occupational health and safety, the architect must plan for ancillary and staff rooms in almost all types of buildings. These include lunchrooms, sanitary facilities, first aid rooms, and relaxation areas as well as changing rooms where applicable. ↗Chapter 3.5 Spaces/Sanitary Facilities To facilitate cleaning of the building, the architect must include storage and cleaning rooms in sufficient number and in locations as needed.

## 3.8.1 Lunchrooms

Lunchrooms and break areas give employees a place to stay during work breaks. A minimum of 1 m² per employee is to be provided in addition to the circulation spaces and fixed furniture, with a minimum room size of 6 m². Each lunchroom must have a visual connection to the outside and receive sufficient natural light. If there is no staff canteen or similar facility, employees should be given the opportunity to prepare their own meals or to heat them up in the lunchroom.

**Figure 3.8.1**
Features of lunchrooms

Per ASR A4.2

Floor area: min. 6 m²
1 m²/user (incl. table and chair)
+ Entry/exit
+ Circulation space
+ Other facilities

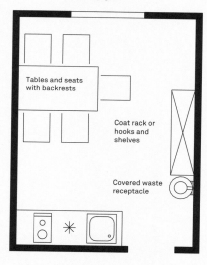

Visual connection to outside and sufficient daylight

Tables and seats with backrests

Coat rack or hooks and shelves

Covered waste receptacle

– Access to drinking water
– Ability to refrigerate and warm up food if there is no canteen

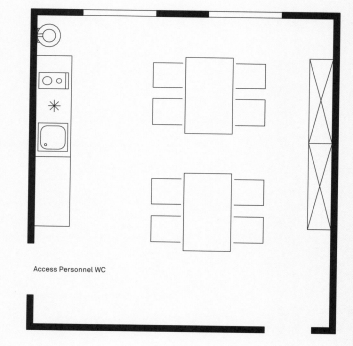

Access Personnel WC

### 3.8.2 Locker and Changing Rooms

Depending on the building typology, locker and changing areas fulfill various purposes and must consequently be planned accordingly. They can, for instance, be combined with a toilet and shower area for users of sports facilities or serve as a warm-up area for actors in a theater. Changing areas are often needed in work environments for hygienic reasons or when it is mandatory to wear uniforms. The spectrum ranges from simple lockers in staff rooms to hermetic separation between clean and dirty areas. Such changing areas serve as vestibules between work areas and the outside. Cloakroom areas are found in many types of buildings and are usually located close to the entrance.

**Figure 3.8.2**
Changing areas serving as access control

Layout of swimming pool locker room

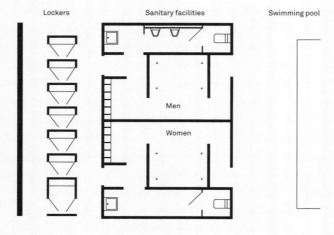

Layout of gymnasium locker room

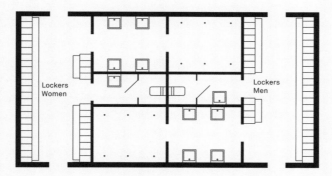

**Figure 3.8.3**
Staff changing areas

Layout of a clean/dirty locker room

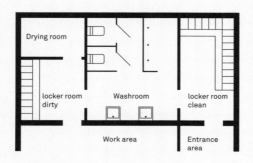

**Figure 3.8.4**
**Various locker systems**

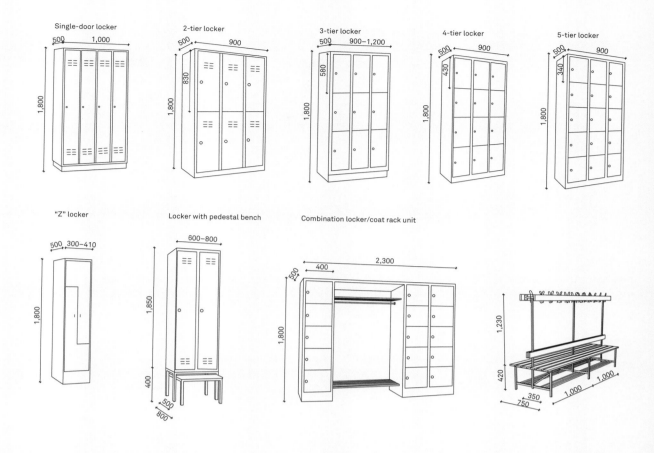

**Figure 3.8.5**
**Principle of changing compart-**
**ments (e.g., in swimming pools)**

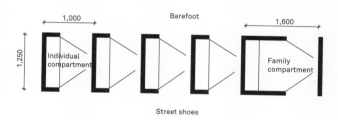

**Figure 3.8.6**
**Maneuvering zones in changing**
**rooms**

For changing areas, a bench
surface of min. 400 mm wide and
300 mm deep shall be provided.
For wheelchair users, additional
transfer areas shall be provided.
The circulation space between
benches must be at least 1,500 mm
wide. If the path serves as the
only passage, 1,800 mm shall be
provided.

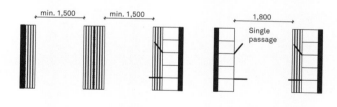

**Figure 3.8.7**
**Changing areas for wheelchair**
**users**

For people with disabilities, accessible individual stalls measuring
a minimum of 1,500 × 2,000 mm
shall be provided commensurate
with the need. Including WC,
shower, folding seat, and sink, a
minimum of 2,200 × 2,850 mm
(without examination table) or
2,900 × 3,600 mm (with examination table) shall be provided.

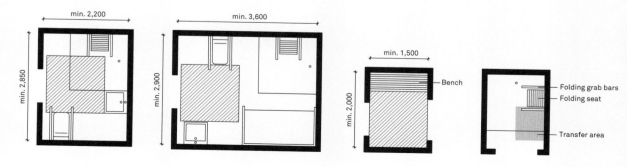

**Figure 3.8.8**
Layouts of changing rooms, locker rooms, and cloakroom areas

Per Ordinance on Workplaces, §34

**Changing room facilities with lockers**

Lockers without bench

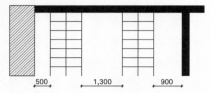

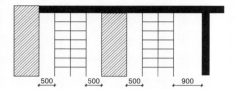

Lockers with bench

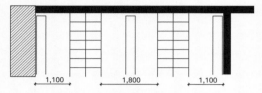

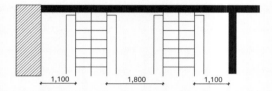

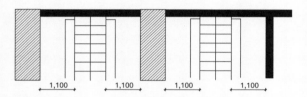

Lockers with kick plate

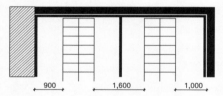

Lockers with movable stools

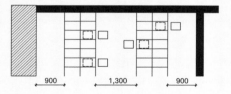

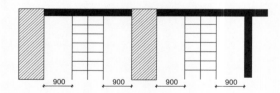

**Changing room facilities with base frames**

Simple hook racks

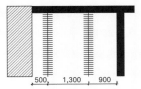
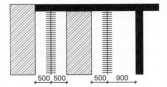

Coat hanger racks

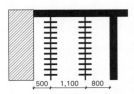
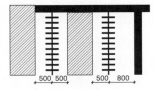

Coat hanger racks with kick plate

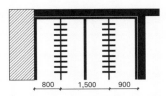

**Changing room facilities with attended cloakroom (theater cloakroom)**

Attended cloakroom, single-sided, with hook rack

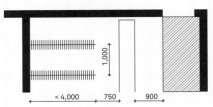

Attended cloakroom, double-sided, with coat hanger rack

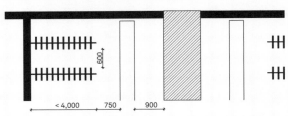

Benches in attended cloakrooms

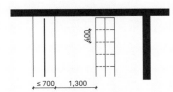

### 3.8.3 Medical and First Aid Rooms

A first aid room is a room where, in the event of an accident, emergency medical care can be provided until the ambulance service arrives, if required. It should be centrally located on the ground floor in order to ensure quick access, even with stretchers. First aid rooms must have an area of at least 20 m². and a clear height of 2.50 m. They contain the following minimum furnishings and equipment: exam-

ination table, dressing trolley, sink with hot and cold water, mirror, soap and disinfectant dispensers, emergency light, telephone, desk, and stretcher as well as sundry first aid materials. There must be a shower and a toilet with direct access from the first aid room, or at least in close proximity to it.

**Figure 3.8.9**
First aid room

Per ASR A4.3

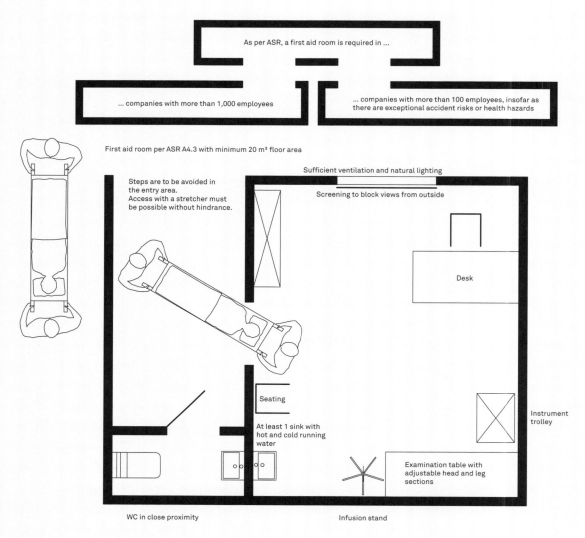

As per ASR, a first aid room is required in ...

... companies with more than 1,000 employees

... companies with more than 100 employees, insofar as there are exceptional accident risks or health hazards

First aid room per ASR A4.3 with minimum 20 m² floor area

Steps are to be avoided in the entry area.
Access with a stretcher must be possible without hindrance.

Sufficient ventilation and natural lighting

Screening to block views from outside

Desk

Instrument trolley

Seating

At least 1 sink with hot and cold running water

Examination table with adjustable head and leg sections

WC in close proximity

Infusion stand

First aid container (modified shipping container as a temporary facility) per ASR A4.3 for temporary workplaces, minimum 12.5 m² floor area

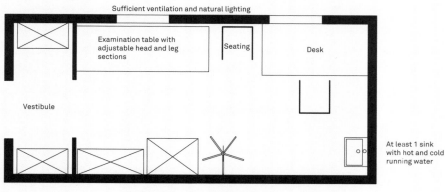

Sufficient ventilation and natural lighting

Examination table with adjustable head and leg sections

Seating

Desk

Vestibule

At least 1 sink with hot and cold running water

Instrument trolley    Infusion stand

### 3.8.4 Storerooms and Janitor's Closets

Storerooms and janitor's closets are needed in every building in sufficient number to enable care and technical maintenance of the building by cleaning personnel and custodial staff. Storerooms for maintaining supplies of small items such as replacement lamps, garden tools, etc., are expediently located in basement areas or near other technical plant areas. Cleaning supply rooms and janitor's closets may need to be established in multiple places within the building (usually close to plumbing cores) in order to avoid long distances. At a minimum, a janitor's closet should contain a janitor's sink with running water, floor space for cleaning equipment, and a shelf for cleaning materials.

Figure 3.8.10 (left)
Janitor's closet

Figure 3.8.11 (right)
Cleaning cart

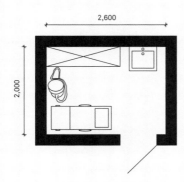

# 3.9 Technical Equipment Rooms

Building services installations are an integral part of a functioning and effective overall concept. Due to increasing requirements for energy efficiency and growing capabilities for networking and controllability of building services, the interdependencies of building parts and system components are becoming ever more complex. Thus the connections to public utility networks, the installation area for building services components such as boilers and ventilation systems, data networks, server equipment, etc., as well as the distribution of the utilities within the building is best planned from the outset.

### 3.9.1 Connections to Public Utilities

The supply mains for water, electricity, gas, communication media, etc., and the sewer mains are typically all within the confines of the public right-of-way. Depending on the type of service needed, applications must be submitted to cities/municipalities, public utilities, or private communications companies in order to obtain the appropriate service connections. The handover point is located either at the property line, in a manhole, or in the service connection room within the building. Branch lines are generally labeled with markings and underground warning tapes in order to ensure they can be identified in the future. When laying out utility connections, different minimum installation depths must be observed in some cases. For sewer lines in particular, the pipe connection heights at the street and the height of the backflow level must be taken into account.

Figure 3.9.1 (left)
Positions of utility lines beneath public right-of-way

Table 3.9.1 (right)
Installation depths of utility lines
As per DIN 18012

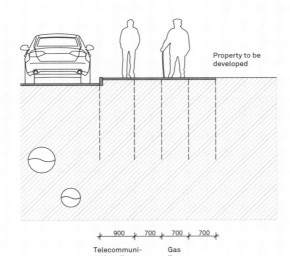

| Type of utility line | Depth under t.o. grade |
|---|---|
| Telecommunications line | 350–600 mm |
| Water line | 1,200–1,500 mm |
| Gas line | 500–1,000 mm |
| Electric power line | 600–800 mm |
| District heating | 600–1,000 mm |

Figure 3.9.2
Principle of building drainage

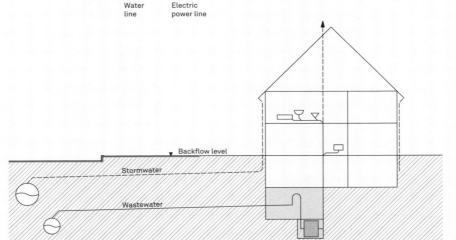

### 3.9.2 Mains Connection Rooms and Meter Rooms

The service connection room, or meter room, is where the interface is made between the supply to the building and the building's internal networks. Whenever possible, meter rooms should be located on the ground floor or in the basement, directly along the exterior wall and facing toward a public street. Depending on the building size and type, meter rooms must be ventilated and enclosed by fire-rated walls. It may be necessary to provide separate rooms for different utilities, so the planner must make al-lowances for such areas early in the design. For the water supply, in addition to providing meters and shut-off valves, additional fittings such as pressure reducers must be provided in some cases. For the electrical supply, the planner must include space for meters and circuit breaker boxes as well as telecommunications and data supply. For the gas supply, in addition to providing shut-off valves, meters, and distribution installations, regulations for avoidance of undetected gas leakage are to be observed.

Table 3.9.2
Service connection room for residential buildings

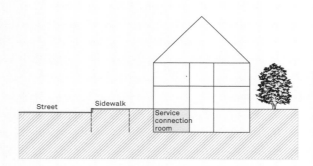

| Without district heating connection | Max. 30 dwelling units | Max. 60 dwelling units |
|---|---|---|
| **With district heating connection** | **Max. 10 dwelling units** | **Max. 30 dwelling units** |
| Depth | > 2.00 m | > 2.00 m |
| Width | > 1.80 m | > 3.50 m |
| Height | > 2.00 m | > 2.00 m |

Figure 3.9.3
Location of the service connection room within the building

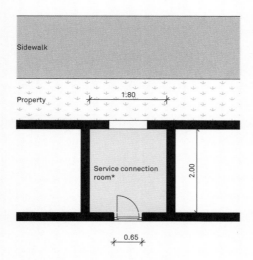

Figure 3.9.4
Service connection room for residential buildings

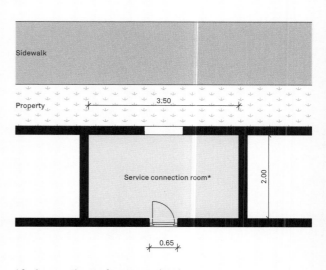

* Service connection room for up to approximately 30 dwelling units (up to approximately 10 dwelling units with district heating)

* Service connection room for up to approximately 60 dwelling units (up to approximately 30 dwelling units with district heating)

**Figure 3.9.5**
Elements within the service
connection room

As per DIN 18012

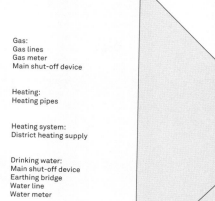

Gas:
Gas lines
Gas meter
Main shut-off device

Heating:
Heating pipes

Heating system:
District heating supply

Drinking water:
Main shut-off device
Earthing bridge
Water line
Water meter

Electricity:
Electric power lines
Transfer box
Electric meter

Communications:
Broadband cable
Telecommunications service

Miscellaneous:
Potential equalization bus bar
with connection lug for grounding
electrode

Gas
Heating
Drinking water

Electricity
Telecommunications

**Figure 3.9.6**
Vertical section through the
utility connections

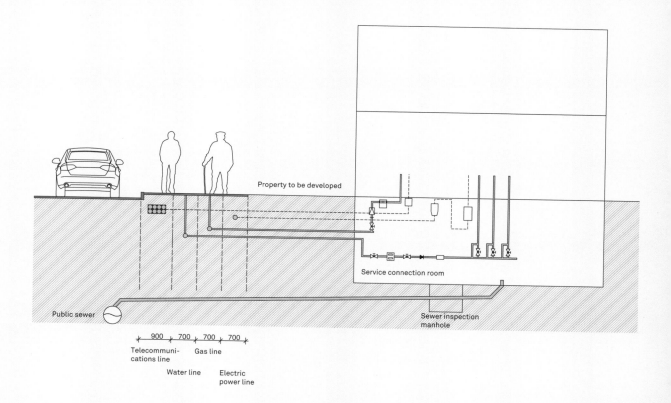

Property to be developed

Service connection room

Public sewer

Sewer inspection
manhole

900  700  700  700

Telecommuni-
cations line

Gas line

Water line

Electric
power line

**Figure 3.9.7**
Utility service feed

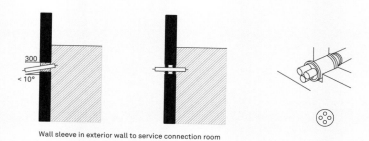

300

< 10°

Wall sleeve in exterior wall to service connection room

### 3.9.3 Distribution Rooms and Shafts

In general, utilities such as heating are either distributed in the basement and fed along multiple vertical risers to the points of use or routed along a central shaft supplying all the stories, with distribution and shut-off/metering possibilities at each floor. Depending on the system chosen, space for shafts and/or distribution rooms must be included in the plans at an early stage. In some cases accessible shafts are also used for locating shut-off valves and distribution points, and in other cases separate distribution cabinets/rooms are located near the shafts. For reasons of fire safety, either the shaft itself is compartmentalized with firestops at each floor level or firestops are used at each point of exit into the individual stories. In both cases, the planner must include adequate installation space for firestopping and fire dampers (in the dimensioning of suspended ceiling plenums, for example). For single shaft ventilation, fireplaces, or if heating is supplied by vented unit heaters, for instance, areas for incorporating shafts or flues must also be provided.

Figure 3.9.8
Vertical and floor-by-floor
(horizontal) distribution of utilities
inside the building

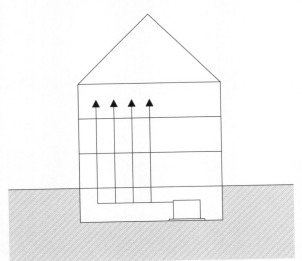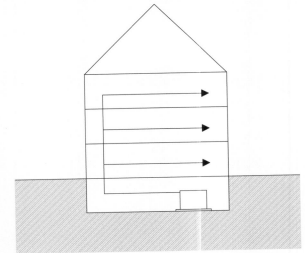

Figure 3.9.9 (left)
Firestopping of utility shafts

Figure 3.9.10 (right)
Example of accessible
utility shafts

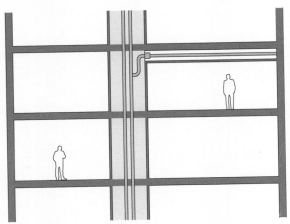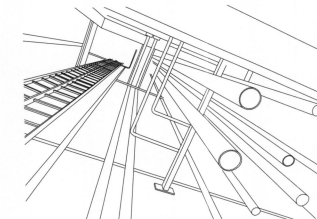

## 3.9.4 Heating

Depending on the heating system used, the requirements concerning separate boiler rooms, distribution systems, and the amount of area to be provided will differ. A building can be heated centrally, using cogeneration units or district heating, for example, or in a decentralized manner by using multiple local heat sources, such as gas unit heaters or electric radiators. Nothing more than heat transfer stations or electric/gas connections may be necessary or, conversely, an elaborate and costly heating plant with high fire protection requirements might have to be planned. Flues must be incorporated in close proximity to heating sources, and in the case of closed systems, supply air shafts are also needed. If fuel is stored locally (for oil or pellet heating systems, for example), suitable delivery routes and fire-resistant containment barriers are to be provided. Especially when utilizing alternative energy sources, the production surfaces and equipment (heat pumps, solar thermal devices, geothermal equipment, etc.) often become a key design factor – affecting the orientation of roof surfaces, for example. Accordingly, architects should coordinate the heating system with the necessary technical consultants beginning at an early stage.

Figure 3.9.11
Elements of an exhaust system for fireplaces and heating systems

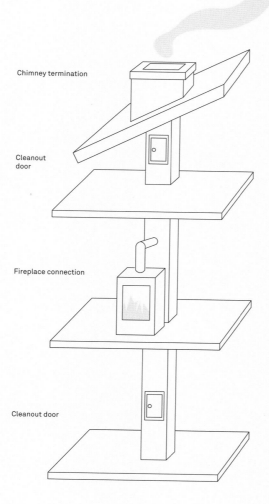

Chimney termination

Cleanout door

Fireplace connection

Cleanout door

**Figure 3.9.12**
Classification of heating systems
Per Klein and Schlenger

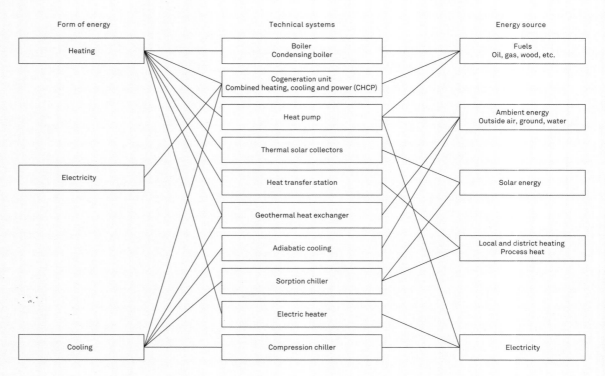

**Figure 3.9.13**
Placement of radiators

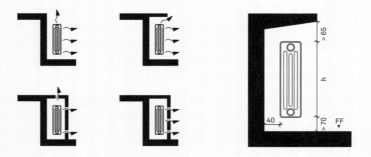

**Figure 3.9.14**
Placement of chimneys with respect to prevailing wind direction

**Table 3.9.3**
Typical sizes of radiators

| Cast-iron radiators | | Steel radiators | | Flat radiators | |
|---|---|---|---|---|---|
| Height [mm] | Depth [mm] | Height [mm] | Depth [mm] | Height [mm] | Depth [mm] |
| 280 | 250 | 300 | 160 | 350 | 65 |
| | 70 | | 250 | | 100 |
| 430 | 110 | | 70 | | 155 |
| | 160 | 450 | 110 | 500 | 65 |
| | 220 | | 160 | | 100 |
| | 70 | | 220 | | 155 |
| 580 | 110 | | 70 | 600 | 65 |
| | 160 | 600 | 110 | | 100 |
| | 220 | | 160 | | 155 |
| 680 | 160 | | 220 | 900 | 65 |
| | 70 | | 70 | | 100 |
| 980 | 160 | 1,000 | 110 | | 155 |
| | 220 | | 160 | | |
| | | | 220 | | |
| Length = 60 mm per section × quantity | | Length = 50 mm per section × quantity | | Length = 400–3,000 mm | |

**Table 3.9.4**
Reference values for sizing open fireplaces

Per Pistohl

| Area of room [m²] | Dimensions of the combustion chamber opening [mm] | | | Flue diameter [mm] | |
|---|---|---|---|---|---|
| | w | h | d | 1-sided | 2- or 3-sided |
| 15–20 | 600–650 | 450–500 | 350–400 | 200 | 225–250 |
| 20–30 | 700–750 | 500–550 | 400–450 | 225 | 250–300 |
| 25–35 | 750–800 | 550–600 | 450–500 | 250 | 300–350 |
| 35–50 | 850–1,000 | 650–700 | 500–600 | 300 | 350 |

**Figure 3.9.15**
Height of chimneys in relation to roof area

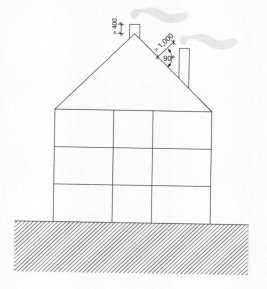
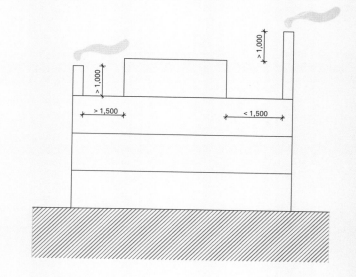

### 3.9.5 Ventilation

Due to high standards for energy efficiency, ventilation systems for reduction of ventilation heat losses and provision of conditioned and fresh air are standard in almost all types of buildings. Heated rooms without windows for a direct connection to the outside must obligatorily be mechanically ventilated. Depending on the air volume needed, ventilation systems can be accommodated as wall-mounted or ceiling-hung units in ancillary spaces, or dedicated rooms or roof areas may have to be provided for the installation of more complex ventilation and air-conditioning equipment. For the purposes of maintenance and replac-

ing components, appropriately dimensioned access openings are essential for long-term operation. Due to their dimensions and possible visual impact, supply and exhaust air openings must also be well planned. If cooling with heat exchangers is intended, locations for these must also be identified early. The interior routing can be accomplished with central ducts and subdistribution branches. In addition to these considerations, sound attenuators, fire dampers, and points of crossing are essential aspects that must be taken into account early on by architects, as they affect matters such as floor-to-floor heights.

Figure 3.9.16
Types of air supply and patterns of air currents

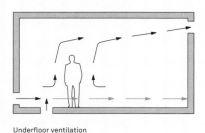

Underfloor ventilation

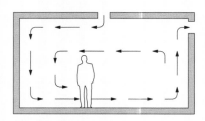

Overhead (fully mixed) ventilation

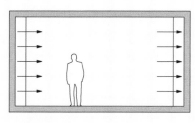

Displacement ventilation

Table 3.9.5
Maximum room depths and opening areas for natural ventilation

Per ASR A3.6

| System | Maximum allowable room depth in relation to clear ceiling height (h) [m] | Opening area needed to ensure minimum air change | |
|---|---|---|---|
| | | For continuous ventilation [m²/person present] | For brief and intense ventilation [m²/10 m² floor area] |
| I Single-sided ventilation | Room depth = 2.5 × h (for h > 4 m: max. room depth = 10 m) (assumed air velocity in cross section = 0.08 m/s) | 0.35 | 1.05 |
| II Cross ventilation | Room depth = 5.0 × h (for h > 4 m: max. room depth = 20 m) (assumed air velocity in cross section = 0.14 m/s) | 0.20 | 0.60 |

Table 3.9.6
Characteristic values for ventilation ducts

| Use | Discharge in m³/h | Daily HVAC hours of operation | Target room temperature for cooling | Net energy demand for hot water |
|---|---|---|---|---|
| | Days of use [d] | [h] | [°C] | [Wh/(m² × d)] |
| Office | 250 | 13 | 24 | 30 |
| Retail/department store | 300 | 14 | 24 | 10 |
| Hotel, standard | 365 | 24 | 24 | 190 |
| Hotel, luxury | 365 | 24 | 24 | 580 |
| Restaurant | 300 | 16 | 24 | 1,250 |

**Figure 3.9.17**
Basic principle of a ventilation
system

WA = Waste air
SA = Supply air
OA = Outside air
EA = Exhaust air

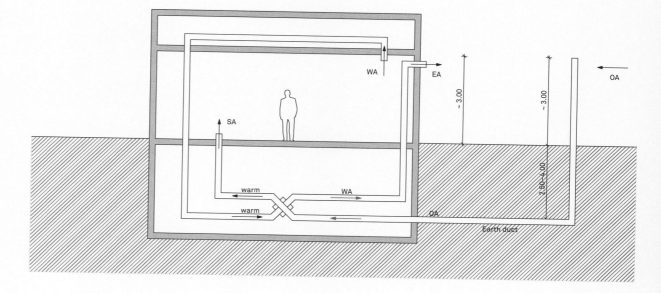

**Figure 3.9.18**
Types of shaft ventilation

In many places, shaft ventilation
is restricted or no longer permitted. In times of concern for
energy efficiency, uncontrolled air
movement must be prevented.
In addition, shaft ventilation does
not work in all weather conditions.

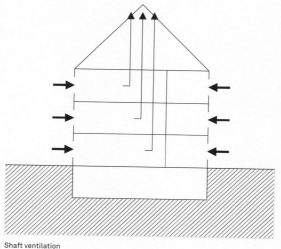

Shaft ventilation

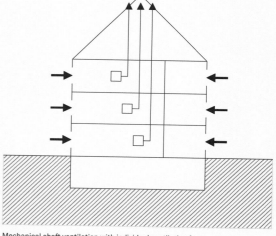

Mechanical shaft ventilation with individual ventilating fans

**Figure 3.9.19**
Space requirements for
ventilation ducts of equal
cross-sectional area

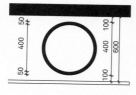

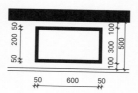

### 3.9.6 Water Supply and Wastewater Disposal

The supply of fresh water must be planned and dimensioned to meet the anticipated demand. In industrialized countries, the presumed water demand is roughly 100–150 liters per person per day, whereas hot water demand is roughly 20–50 liters. Hot water can be produced either by utilizing the heating system or with electric water heaters.

To prevent the formation of legionella and to increase the comfort value by ensuring that hot water is available without waiting, circulation pipes are installed, which increase installation costs and must be well insulated to prevent unwanted energy losses.

For drainage and sewer systems, piping below the backflow level (top of manhole cover in the street) requires pump stations and backflow preventers. In addition, sufficient means for inspection should be incorporated and, depending on the type of building, additional devices such as grease traps may need to be provided.

**Figure 3.9.20**
Basic principle of water supply
with circulation pipes

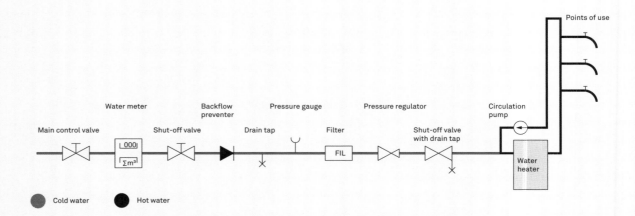

**Figure 3.9.21**
Basic principle of wastewater
disposal

IM = Inspection manhole
BSV = Backflow shut-off valve

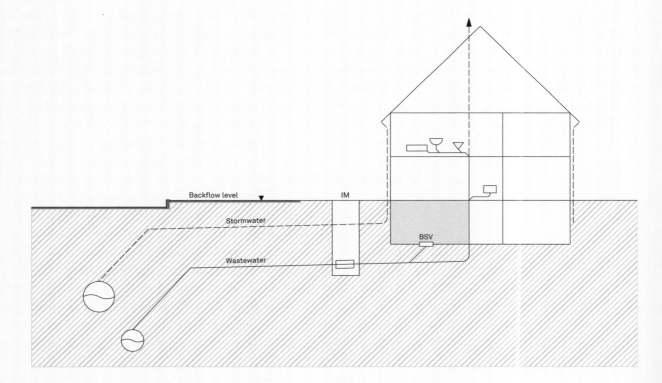

Table 3.9.7
Average water consumption
in liters per person/day

Per BDEW e.V.

| Activity | Water consumption |
|---|---|
| Drinking and cooking | 3 |
| Washing dishes | 7 |
| Cleaning | 7 |
| Personal hygiene | 5–15 |
| Showering | 30–50 |
| Washing laundry | 30 |
| Flushing toilet | 40 |

Table 3.9.8
Electric water heaters

Per RWE

| Electric water heater | Nominal capacity in liters | Rated input in kW | Dimensions in mm Height × Width × Depth | Use |
|---|---|---|---|---|
| Open-outlet water heater | 5 | 2 | 400 × 300 × 200 | Individual supply |
| Storage water heater (open) | 5 | 2 | 400 × 250 × 200 | Lavatory, kitchen sink |
| | 10 | 2 | 500 × 350 × 300 | Lavatory, kitchen sink |
| | 15 | 2, 4 | 600 × 350 × 300 | Kitchen sink |
| | 30 | 4 | 850 × 400 × 350 | Shower |
| | 50 | 6 | 850 × 500 × 500 | Shower |
| | 80 | 6 | 1,050 × 500 × 500 | Bathtub |
| | 100 | 6 | 1,200 × 500 × 500 | Bathtub |
| Hot water tank (closed) | 10 | 2 | 500 × 350 × 300 | Double basin lavatory, sink |
| | 15 | 2, 4 | 600 × 350 × 300 | Kitchen sink |
| | 30 | 4 | 850 × 400 × 350 | Sink and shower |
| | 50 | 6 | 850 × 500 × 500 | Sink and shower |
| | 80 | 6 | 1,050 × 500 × 500 | |
| | 100 | 6 | 1,200 × 500 × 500 | Bathroom supply |
| | 120 | 6 | 1,250 × 550 × 500 | Dwelling supply |
| | 150 | 6 | 1,400 × 550 × 550 | |
| Instantaneous water heater (hydraulic) | – | 18, 21, 24, 27 | 500 × 300 × 200 | Bathroom supply |
| Instantaneous water heater (electric) | – | 18, 21, 24, 27 | 500 × 300 × 200 | Bathroom supply, kitchen supply |
| Floor-standing electric water heater | 200 | 2, 4, 6 | 1,600 × 600 × 700 | Dwelling supply, single-family house |
| | 300 | 3, 6 | 1,800 × 700 × 800 | |
| | 400 | 4, 6 | 1,900 × 800 × 900 | |
| | 600 | 6, 9 | 2,000 × 800 × 1,000 | Central supply, household, commercial, agriculture |
| | 1,000 | 9, 18 | 2,500 × 1,000 × 1,000 | |
| Hot water heat pump with storage | 200–400 | 0.3–0.6 | – | Dwelling supply, single-family house |

### 3.9.7 Electric Supply and Data Systems Technology

The electrical wiring and data systems technology together constitute one of the essential components in most typologies and link a great many building elements and devices. The scope includes the electric power supply, lighting, data and telecommunications connections, the control of building services components, security systems, fire alarm systems, sound equipment and PA systems, measurement and warning devices, etc. Since wiring must be routed through almost all parts of the building, the planning of distribution areas is an important design task. The space requirement for enclosures, circuit breaker boxes, subdistributors, etc., depends, among other things, on how many individual electric circuits are to be installed, which components are needed, and what voltages are used. For larger functional units, separate electrical rooms are usually provided. Especially for emergency power supply, transformer stations, or substations, spaces with particular relevance to fire protection are generally to be situated with a connection to the outside.

The telecommunications and data supply should be fed into the building at a central location, and the means for further distribution within the building depends on the number and location of the connections (for example, via a central telephone system or additional remote server/distribution rooms).

**Figure 3.9.22**
Principles for laying out electrical lines in rooms

Per DIN 18015-3

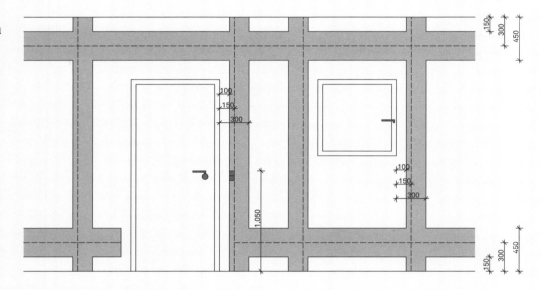

**Figure 3.9.23**
Types of electrical and switchgear cabinets

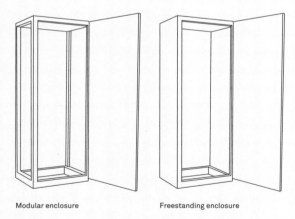

Modular enclosure

Freestanding enclosure

Wall cabinet

19" rack enclosure

Terminal box

**Table 3.9.9**
Typical dimensions of freestanding electrical enclosures, in mm

| w | h | d |
|---|---|---|
| 600 | 1,800 | 4,000 |
| 800 | 2,000 | 5,000 |
| 1,000 | 2,200 | 6,000 |
| 1,200 | | 8,000 |

## 3.9.8 Server Rooms and Data Centers

Due to the high degree of networking common today, many building typologies require server rooms that serve as the hub of communication for telephone service and data traffic or are responsible for storing large amounts of data. These data often constitute the core of businesses, so they must be protected to an exceptional degree against loss due to fire, lightning, water, or power outage, industrial espionage, burglary, or vandalism. For this purpose, levels of security as well as access control and warning systems are established. Despite hermetic separation in some cases, the sup-

ply of building services such as conditioned fresh air must function properly to dissipate the sometimes high heat loads. Likewise, fire-retardant installations shall be provided at least in data centers. Individual server cabinets typically have widths of 600 or 800 mm and a height of 2,000-2,200 mm. The depths vary from 600 to 1,200 mm and are dependent on the built-in components and the need for two-sided use. To facilitate installation and maintenance, server cabinets, aisle widths of 1,000 mm should be provided both in front and behind.

**Figure 3.9.24 (left)**
Example of a server room

**Figure 3.9.25 (right)**
Types of server cabinets

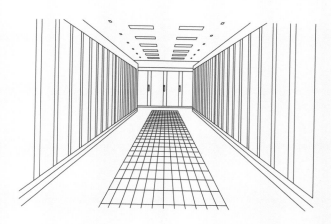

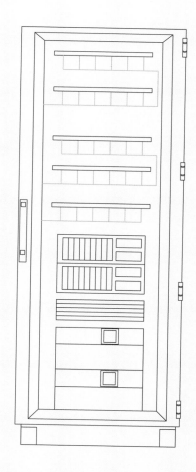

**Figure 3.9.26**
Floor space requirements
of server cabinets

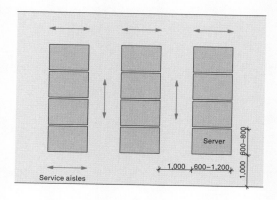

151

Figure 3.9.27
Cooling of server rooms

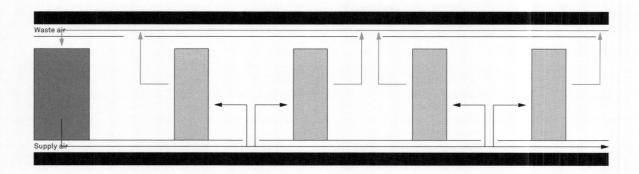

Figure 3.9.28
Zoning of data centers with high security requirements

Zone 1: Semipublic area, including adjoining office areas

Zone 2: Operating areas, ancillary spaces for IT

Zone 3: Technical facilities for operating IT

Zone 4: IT and network infrastructure

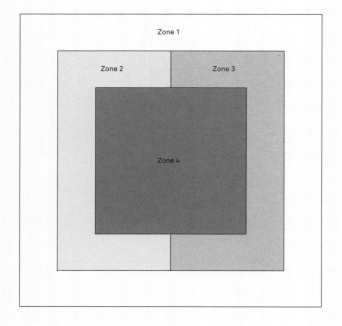

Table 3.9.10
Security requirements to server rooms and data centers
Per TÜV Rheinland

| Requirements | CAT I | CAT II | CAT III | CAT IV |
|---|---|---|---|---|
| **Construction** | | | | |
| Enclosing walls | F 30–WK 1 | F 90–WK 1 | F 90–WK 2 | F 90–WK 2 |
| Shafts | F 30 | min. F 30 | F 90 | F 90 |
| Floors and ceilings | F 90 | F 90 | F 90 | F 90 |
| Clear ceiling height | approx. 2.50 m | approx. 2.50 m | approx. 3.00 to 3.50 m | approx. 3.00 to 3.50 m |
| Clear raised floor height | approx. 0.30 m | approx. 0.30 m | approx. 0.60 m | approx. 0.60 m |
| **Doors and entrances** | | | | |
| Circulation and transport paths (w × h) | min. 1.00 m × 2.50 m | min. 1.00 m × 2.50 m | min. 1.20 m × 2.50 m | min. 1.20 m × 2.50 m |
| Dimensions of doors (w × h) | min. 1.00 m × 2.13 m | min. 1.20 m × 2.25 m (recommended 2.50 m) | min. 1.20 m × 2.25 m (recommended 2.50 m) | min. 1.20 m × 2.25 m (recommended 2.50 m) |
| Fire resistance class | min. T30–RS. | min. T30–RS. | min. T90–RS. | min. T90–RS. |
| Burglar-resistant doors | WK 1 | WK 1 | WK 2 | WK 2 |
| Physical separation from other areas of the data center | No requirements | Yes | Yes | Yes |
| Multiple building entrances with security screening | No requirements | No requirements | Yes | Yes |
| Turnstiles, vestibules, or other facilities for access control | No requirements | No requirements | Yes | Yes |
| No exterior windows near the server room | Additional measures required if present, such as security film or applied frames with grating | Not permissible | Not permissible | Not permissible |
| **Security center** | | | | |
| Dedicated security center for security equipment and surveillance (including protection against breakage and ballistic penetration) | No requirements | If present, recommended | Recommended | Recommended |
| **Electrotechnology** | | | | |
| Transformers | 1 | 1 | 1 (2 recommended) | 2 |
| Emergency diesel generator | Recommended | 1 | 1 (2 recommended) | 2 |
| Fuel supply tank | If present, 8 hrs. | 24 hrs. | 48 hrs. (2 tanks, incl. crossover connections) | 72 hrs. (2 tanks, incl. crossover connections) |
| Connection for rental generator | Yes | Yes, if not present | Yes, for during maintenance | Yes, for during maintenance |

# 4    Typologies

**4.1    Housing** ↗157

**4.2    Office and Administration** ↗197

**4.3    Logistics and Commerce** ↗227

**4.4    Industry and Production** ↗269

**4.5    Education and Research** ↗291

**4.6    Culture and Performing Arts** ↗327

**4.7    Lodging and Food Service** ↗355

**4.8    Healthcare Facilities** ↗383

**4.9    Sports and Recreation** ↗425

**4.10   Public Safety** ↗475

**4.11   Transportation and Infrastructure** ↗495

**Robie House**, Chicago, Illinois, USA, Frank Lloyd Wright, 1910

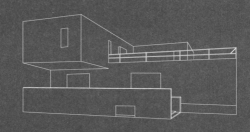

**Gropius House (Masters' Houses)**, Dessau, Germany, Walter Gropius, 1926

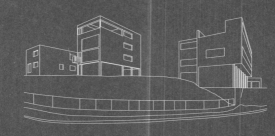

**Weissenhofsiedlung (Weissenhof estate)**, Stuttgart, Germany, various architects, 1927

**Villa Tugendhat**, Brno, Czech Republic, Ludwig Mies van der Rohe, 1930

**Villa Savoye**, Poissy, France, Le Corbusier, 1931

**Schminke House**, Löbau, Germany, Hans Scharoun, 1933

**Fallingwater**, Allegheny Mountains, Pennsylvania, USA, Frank Lloyd Wright, 1937

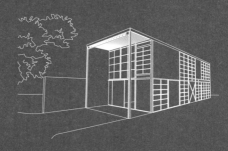

**Eames House**, Los Angeles, California, USA, Charles and Ray Eames, 1949

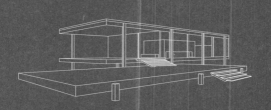

**Farnsworth House**, Plano, Illinois, USA, Ludwig Mies van der Rohe, 1951

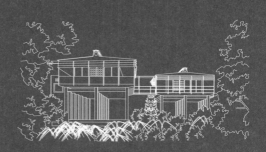

**Maison Tropicale**, prototype for West Africa, Jean Prouvé, 1951

**Unité d'Habitation**, Marseilles, France, Le Corbusier, 1947–52

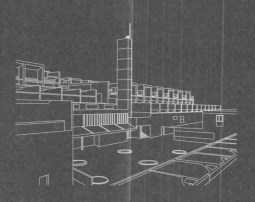

**Halen development**, Herrenschwanden near Bern, Switzerland, Atelier 5, 1955–61

Roland Schneider
Alexander Görg

# 4 Typologies
## 4.1 Housing

### 4.1.1 Building Concept ↗158

4.1.1.1 Planning Parameters ↗158
4.1.1.2 Building Forms ↗162
4.1.1.3 Circulation Systems ↗164
4.1.1.4 Construction and Technology ↗168

### 4.1.2 Program of Use ↗169

4.1.2.1 Internal Organization of Apartments ↗169
4.1.2.2 Single- and Multifamily Dwellings ↗172
4.1.2.3 High-Rise Apartment Buildings ↗177
4.1.2.4 Student Housing ↗179
4.1.2.5 Multigenerational Homes ↗179
4.1.2.6 Residential Group Housing and Retirement Homes ↗180

### 4.1.3 Areas and Rooms ↗182

4.1.3.1 Entrance Areas ↗183
4.1.3.2 Living Rooms ↗184
4.1.3.3 Kitchens and Dining Rooms ↗185
4.1.3.4 Bedrooms ↗188
4.1.3.5 Rooms for Children and Teenagers ↗188
4.1.3.6 Bathrooms ↗190
4.1.3.7 Utility Rooms ↗193
4.1.3.8 Laundry and Drying Rooms ↗193
4.1.3.9 Storage Spaces ↗194
4.1.3.10 Open Area Seating and Winter Gardens ↗194
4.1.3.11 Ancillary Rooms ↗195

# 4.1 Housing

## 4.1.1 Building Concept

### 4.1.1.1 Planning Parameters

The very first buildings known to history served the purpose of human shelter, and thus housing, as a building type, occupies a special place. Residential architecture is closely linked to social aspects. Constant social change continually gives rise to novel forms of housing that seek to accommodate new requirements. Common to all, however, remains the objective of creating a healthy living atmosphere that suits its inhabitants.

At the beginning stage of design and planning, a needs analysis should be carried out with the client or users in order to specify the housing form, the spatial program, and the area requirements. If the design involves an existing building, a detailed analysis of the existing conditions must also be carried out. Many vacant buildings are well-suited to conversion as housing, which may foster urban cohesion and upgrade the surroundings. For all new buildings, as well as the renovation or conversion of existing buildings, aspects of barrier-free accessibility should be taken into account in order to guarantee a living environment that is also adequate over the long term for aging users who may experience increasing disabilities.

Typical Design Parameters:
- Place, context, and infrastructure
- Geometry of the site
- Existing buildings, where applicable
- Building code restrictions
- Spatial program/requirements
- Individual client specifications
- Needs of user groups
- Layout type, building form
- Orientation
- Public/private relationship
- Barrier-free accessibility
- Budget and deadlines

**Client and Users**
The objectives of clients who are also users of a residential property are significantly different from those of investors, developers, or housing associations who, for marketing reasons, generally want to create residential accommodation for a typical, average user group. The spectrum that extends from an individual commissioning the design of a home for their personal needs to a commercial client seeking to optimize profit constitutes a significant planning parameter that determines the direction taken in the design process. → Figure 4.1.1

**Dwelling Unit Sizes/Space Requirements**
When approaching a residential development project from a commercial perspective, the selected quality standard (ranging from minimal to luxury) is the basis for determining the size of the dwelling units to be created. The minimum requirements for individual room sizes can be determined based on the intended use and required furnishings, including maneuvering areas → Table 4.1.1, but psychological aspects of spatial perception should be given as much consideration as functionality. The perception of space is influenced by the height and proportion of a room, by the materials used, and by the window or door openings that lead to the outside or to other rooms. The space requirements increase as functions are further separated, and with a greater number of inhabitants. One- to two-person households usually manage with a layout comprising two rooms plus a kitchen and bathroom. If children are part of the household or more rooms are desired, more space is required. For individually designed luxury apartments or lavish single-family homes, diverse additional uses mean there is no upper limit to the space requirements.

Figure 4.1.1
The client as owner-occupant or investor

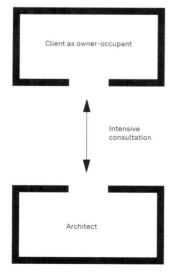

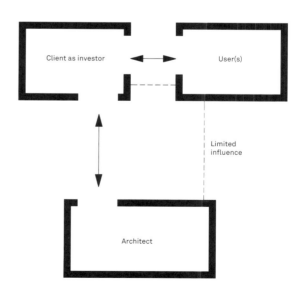

## Subsidized or Social Housing

By making available subsidized housing, the state assumes a duty to care for the welfare of its citizens, and it supports the provision of affordable living space. The details of such programs are determined by numerous regulatory instruments specific to the locality. As a rule, precise specifications are set for aspects such as room and apartment sizes, and minimum requirements for features and amenities are also defined. →Table 4.1.2

Only properties that are built cost-effectively are funded, meaning that increased construction costs lead to a minimization of living space. This close relationship between production costs and dwelling unit size presents a challenge to the designer. For this reason in particular, funding programs that allow the future residents to personally contribute to the work are of interest; in these schemes, owners each take possession of a condominium – which is built to a lower standard – and can then improve the standard themselves.

Table 4.1.1
Recommendations for the sizes of rooms and dwelling units

| Sizes in m² | Single person | | 2 persons | | 3 persons | | 4 persons | | 5 persons | | 6 persons | |
|---|---|---|---|---|---|---|---|---|---|---|---|---|
| | Mini-mum | Com-fort | Mini-mum | Com-fort | Mini-mum | Com-fort | Mini-mum | Com-fort | Mini-mum | Com-fort | Mini-mum | Com-fort |
| Living room | | | 18.0 | 20.0 | 18.0 | 22.0 | 20.0 | 30.0 | 20.0 | 32.0 | 22.0 | 35.0 |
| Living room/bedroom | 25.0 | 30.0 | | | | | | | | | | |
| Living room with dining area | 20.0 | 25.0 | 20.0 | 25.0 | 22.0 | 27.0 | 25.0 | 35.0 | 25.0 | 37.0 | | |
| Dining room | | | 5.0 | 8.0 | 6.0 | 10.0 | 6.0 | 12.0 | 6.0 | 14.0 | 10.0 | 16.0 |
| Office workspace | 2.0 | 5.0 | 2.0 | 5.0 | 2.0 | 5.0 | 2.0 | 5.0 | 2.0 | 5.0 | 2.0 | 5.0 |
| Bedroom | 11.0 | 14.0 | 15.0 | 17.0 | 15.0 | 17.0 | 15.0 | 17.0 | 15.0 | 17.0 | 15.0 | 17.0 |
| Child's room (1 bed) | | | | | 11.0 | 17.0 | 11.0 | 17.0 | 11.0 | 17.0 | 11.0 | 17.0 |
| Child's room (2 beds) | | | | | | | 14.0 | 20.0 | 14.0 | 20.0 | 14.0 | 20.0 |
| Kitchen | 7.0 | 9.0 | 8.0 | 12.0 | 8.0 | 12.0 | 8.0 | 12.0 | 8.0 | 12.0 | 8.0 | 12.0 |
| Kitchenette | 5.5 | 7.0 | | | | | 8.0 | 12.0 | | | | |
| Utility room | | | | | | | | | 6.0 | 9.0 | 6.0 | 9.0 |
| Bathroom | 4.0 | 6.0 | 4.0 | 7.0 | 5.0 | 8.0 | 5.0 | 8.0 | 5.0 | 9.0 | 5.0 | 10.0 |
| Second bathroom/ guest toilet | | | | | | | 4.0 | 6.0 | 4.0 | 6.0 | 4.0 | 7.0 |
| Hallway with closet/ storage room | 2.0 | 6.0 | 6.0 | 7.0 | 6.0 | 7.0 | 7.0 | 10.0 | 7.0 | 10.0 | 7.0 | 12.0 |
| Dwelling unit size (without balcony) | from 38.5 | to 65.0 | from 55.0 | to 76.0 | from 69.0 | to 98.0 | from 76.0 | to 129.0 | from 93.0 | to 151.0 | from 104.0 | to 188.0 |

Table 4.1.2 (left)
Appropriate habitable areas (exemplary standards)

Source: Guidelines for Subsidized Social Housing in Lower Saxony, Regulations on Housing Subsidies (Wohnraumförderungsbestimmung, WFB)

Table 4.1.3 (right)
Minimum requirements for room sizes

Excerpt from DIN 18011, which was rescinded in 1990, but is still used as a base reference

| For rental apartments, the following habitable areas are deemed appropriate: | |
|---|---|
| Single person | up to 50 m² |
| Two-person household | up to 60 m² |
| Three-person household | up to 75 m² |
| Each additional household member | additional 10 m² |
| Per severely disabled person | additional 10 m² |
| Per single parent | additional 10 m² |

| Room | 1–4 persons | Each additional person |
|---|---|---|
| Living room with dining area | 18–20 m² | + 2 m² |
| Living room without dining area | 18 m² | + 2 m² |
| Bedroom, 1 bed | 8 m² | |
| Bedroom, 2 beds | 12 m² | |
| Storage space | 2% of habitable area (minimum 1 m²) | |

## Analysis of Residential Environment

Another important aspect is the context in which the building will be constructed. Users' decisions for or against an apartment or house often depend on the direct residential environment. Short distances help to make daily life easier. A detailed analysis of the local environment helps in finding the right location.

This includes the urban surroundings and its density, emissions and views, and building code restrictions, as well as the building's access to public transit and the surrounding infrastructure. → **Figure 4.1.2** The desire to benefit from a fully developed infrastructure can normally only be met in an urban context.

**Figure 4.1.2**
Schematic analysis of residential environment

Based on: *Wir bauen ein Haus*, Vienna: Österreichisches Institut für Bauforschung, 1987

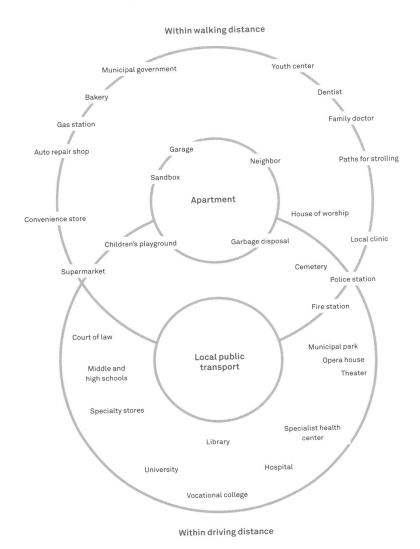

**Figure 4.1.3**
External factors with impact on a residential property

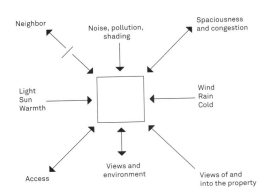

## Orientation

Whereas the orientation of apartments is usually dictated by urban constraints, at least when the disposition of individual spaces is unrestricted, any habitable rooms should not be located facing north. Within an urban context, in addition to ensuring adequate daylight, it is particularly important to carefully plan the relationship of the dwelling unit to the outside and to protect it against noise and other sources of pollution.

Where exposure to daylight is only available from two opposite sides, this has a significant effect on the depth of the building; the depth of solar penetration depends on the cardinal direction (north–south: approximately 7–10 m/ east–west: up to approximately 14 m). In the case of buildings and apartments with exposure on only one side, the layout is typically arranged along the facade with the windows. Where there is no opportunity for cross ventilation it may be necessary to install mechanical ventilation.

**Figure 4.1.4**
Orientation of dwelling units

a) Single orientation: providing adequate daylight for the inner areas is difficult; depth of rooms is limited.
b) Front-to-back orientation: secondary areas are located centrally; greater room depths are possible with an east–west orientation.
c) Three-sided orientation: very good daylighting options; usually at the end of a building or row of houses.
d) Oriented outward to all sides: allows full freedom in designing the layout; typical for detached single-family houses.
e) Oriented to an inner courtyard: difficult to provide good daylight while maintaining privacy.
f) Two-sided orientation at a corner: secondary areas occupy the inner corner; good daylight possible for other areas.

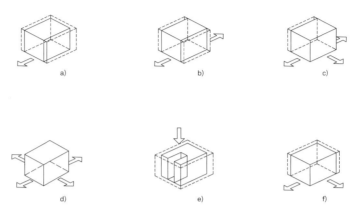

**Figure 4.1.5**
Orientation of rooms by cardinal direction

The orientation should also take into account user habits: for example, since users who have daytime jobs are generally not at home during the day, it makes the most sense for the living room with patio or balcony to be located toward the west.

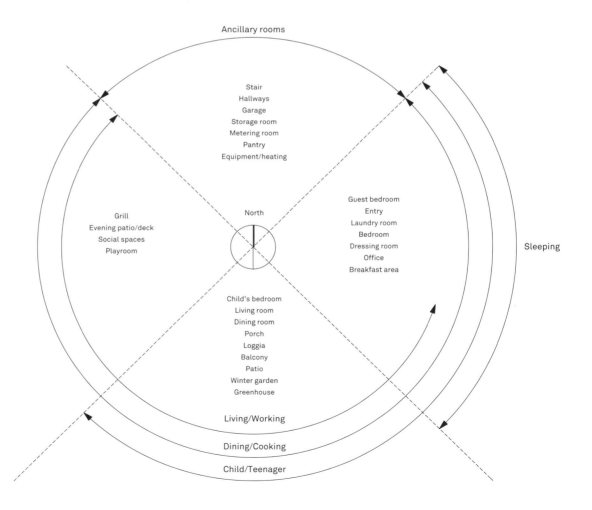

## 4.1.1.2 Building Forms

No other building type offers so many different building forms that are dependent on the individual project parameters as does housing. The forms taken by housing units range from detached single-family homes to mass housing in large configurations. ↗ **4.1.2 Program of Use** Individual structures such as single- and multifamily homes can normally be found on the edges of cities or in rural areas. → **Figure 4.1.6** Large structures are typical for denser urban development and for mass housing. → **Figure 4.1.7**

The selection of the building form depends on the project parameters and, usually, on the urban design context, the available public access, and any development restrictions that may apply. → **Figure 4.1.9** Parking spaces for private cars must also be taken into account, which can be located in an open area, integrated into the building at ground level, or placed in underground parking garages. Where the car parking facilities are situated has a major effect on the geometry of the building and its position on the site. → **Figure 4.1.8**

**Figure 4.1.6**
Examples of different forms of individual building structures

The degree to which street frontage appears open or closed depends on the building forms used, such as freestanding homes, duplex houses, and row houses. In new housing developments covering larger areas, intentional variation enables creation of protected private yards as well as open configurations with detached single-family homes.

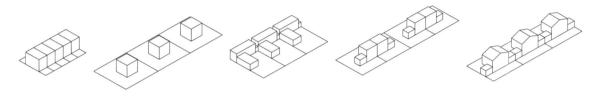

**Figure 4.1.7**
Examples of different forms of large building structures

These examples of building forms for apartment buildings yield very different exterior spaces. Tall buildings in various forms require appropriate spacing between them and therefore create large outdoor areas with a public character, while perimeter block developments create a clear separation between private and public open spaces.

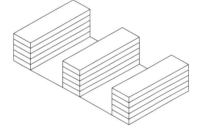
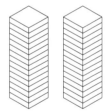
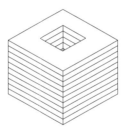

**Figure 4.1.8**
Parking arrangements

Parking options:

(Left) Parking in the open area away from the building; vegetation provides screening.

(Center) Parking at ground level inside/beneath the building; reduced distance between building and road.

(Right) Underground parking garage; ramp determines the distance from the road.

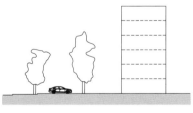
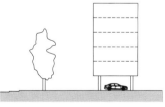
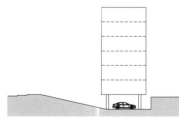

**Figure 4.1.9**
Examples of multistory residential
buildings in an urban context,
including the different circulation
systems

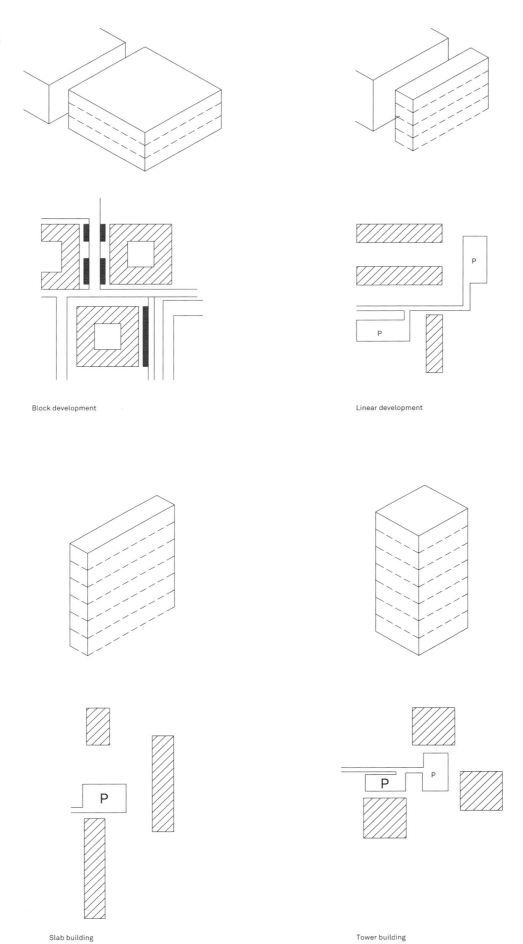

Block development

Linear development

Slab building

Tower building

### 4.1.1.3 Circulation Systems

Circulation systems can provide a clear order to building layouts or they can be intentionally complex and differentiated. Furthermore, since circulation systems are subject to building code regulations because they must also serve as escape routes in the case of emergencies, their design also depends on the number of units and users that are being served. From an economic point of view, it is desirable to keep the proportion of circulation area as low as possible. Greater building depths can be achieved by using double-loaded corridors. → **Figure 4.1.10**

**Shared Vertical Access Types**
In multistory residential buildings, the apartments are linked vertically via shared stairs and elevators. This type of building, in which the apartments are directly accessed via the vertical circulation, is mostly found in inner-city locations where the available sites are restricted in size. Depending on the number of apartments accessed on a single level, a differentiation is made among buildings with one, two, three, or multiple dwelling units per stair. → **Figure 4.1.11** The stair is commonly located on the inside or the north side of the building. In buildings with two apartments per floor, the two dwelling units are frequently mirror images of each other, whereas in buildings with three apartments there is an additional central apartment that is frequently smaller and faces south. In buildings with multiple apartments per floor, such as in larger apartment complexes, various options are possible for circulation. It is generally useful to position ancillary rooms directly adjacent to the stair where they act as a buffer zone for rooms such as bedrooms that should be shielded from noise. → **Figure 4.1.12**

**Figure 4.1.10**
Building depths for multistory housing with single- and double-loaded corridors

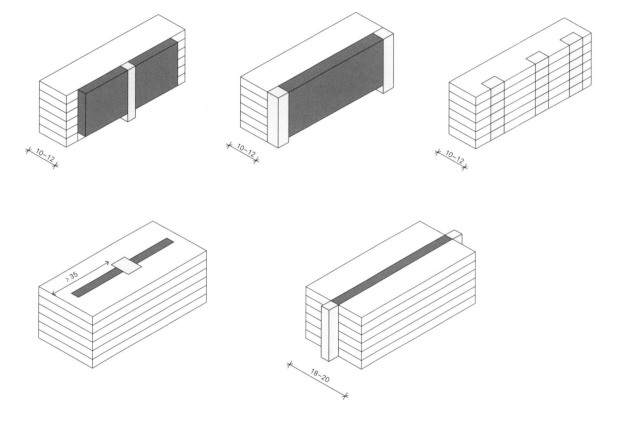

**Figure 4.1.11**
Layouts with vertical circulation that provides access to one, two, and three apartments per floor (from left to right)

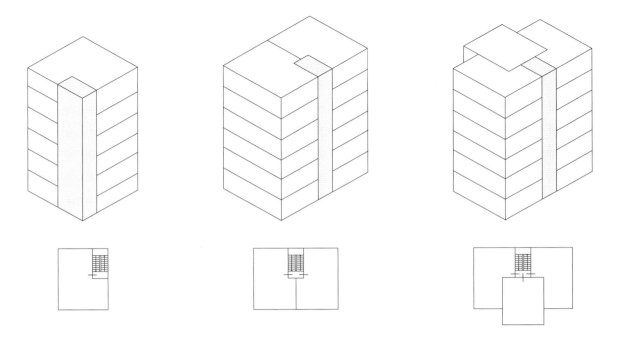

**Figure 4.1.12**
Orientation of functional areas

Traditional orientation of functional areas in buildings with several apartments per floor; ancillary rooms are situated adjacent to the stair, living rooms are arranged in mirror fashion, and bedrooms are farthest away from the neighboring apartment.

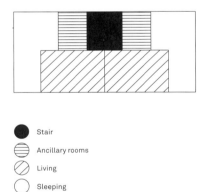

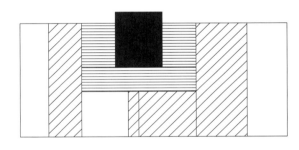

● Stair

⊜ Ancillary rooms

⊘ Living

◯ Sleeping

### Corridor Access Types

With corridor access, there is no limit to the number of apartments that are given access. → **Figure 4.1.13** Owing to the maximum length of escape routes, however, the number of compulsory stairs is subject to regulations governing emergency egress. Buildings with this type of circulation are frequently elongated in form and appearance. In buildings where the access corridor runs down the middle, serving units on two sides, the system is referred to as a double-loaded corridor. → **Figure 4.1.14** This type of circulation system is commonly used in buildings with an east–west orientation. Artificially lit internal corridors with long, straight runs are often perceived as anonymous and negative. By creating wider areas, zones are established that can be meaningfully incorporated into the use concept in various ways, depending on the user group: as shared social areas, a bay where families can park baby carriages and strollers, a seating area for senior citizens, etc. Placing windows at regular intervals enables views to the outside that make it possible to experience the time of day inside the building.

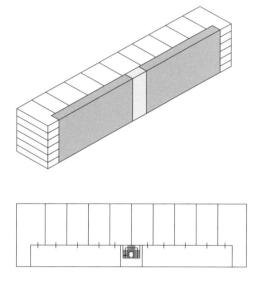

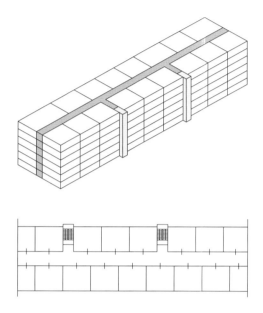

Figure 4.1.13 (left)
Single loaded (one-sided) circulation system in a linear building (corridor or access gallery)

Figure 4.1.14 (right)
Double-loaded corridor running along the middle of a linear building

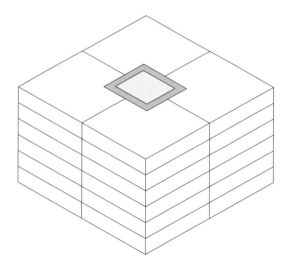

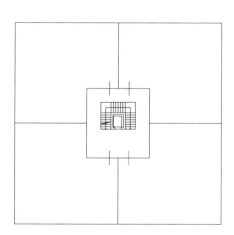

Figure 4.1.15
Point-type circulation system with a corridor surrounding the central core

### Duplex Apartments

An alternative to the single-loaded circulation system is a building with duplex apartments, which are also known as maisonettes. → **Figure 4.1.16** In this type of building, a central corridor exists only in every second or third floor and provides access to duplex apartments on the lower floor and the upper floor (both with double-sided orientation). Duplex apartments create interiors similar to those of multistory houses, but allow developments with greater density. Here, an open stair links a living space of at least two stories, in which only the smaller floor area is connected to the corridor/stair.

### Circulation System via Access Gallery

Apartments with access via an outdoor gallery benefit from a specific orientation. → **Figure 4.1.17** These apartments are accessed from one side via an outdoor corridor, meaning that the apartments can have smaller, north-facing windows along the gallery (such as bands of transom windows) and can be opened up with a primary orientation toward the south. However, access galleries are also a source of noise, so bedrooms should not be located along them. These buildings are less deep than buildings with double-loaded central corridors and are usually placed on an east–west axis so that the apartments have northern and southern aspects.

Offsetting the access gallery below the main floor level can be a means of creating privacy and preventing views to the inside; they can also be used for accessing duplex apartments. Furthermore, it is possible to increase the quality of circulation spaces and to create shared areas by providing narrower and wider spaces, and offsets. → **Figure 4.1.18**

**Figure 4.1.16**
Cross section through different types of duplex apartment circulation systems

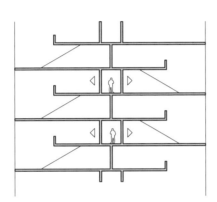
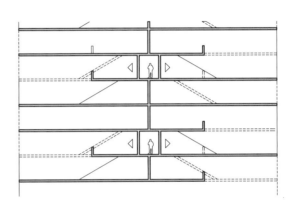

**Figure 4.1.17**
Example of an open gallery access circulation system with stair at one side

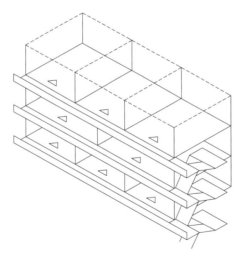

**Figure 4.1.18**
Different types of circulation systems via access balconies

Circulation systems via access balconies can be arranged at all floor levels (left), on every other floor for the purpose of providing access to duplex apartments (center) or as an independent element detached from the building (right).

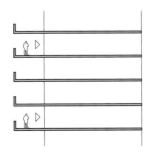
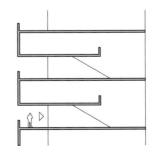
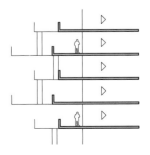

**Necessary Corridors and Stairs**

The design of the necessary corridors and stairs has to take the respective regionally applicable laws and guidelines into account, as well as any fire safety concept for the building. In Germany, the maximum length of mandatory corridors with access at one end only is 15 m. Doors to a required stair, to the lobby of a emergency egress stair, or into the open must not be at a distance of more than 35 m from any habitable room and any basement floor. It is always necessary to provide two rescue routes that are separate from one another and that lead directly into the open. The two rescue routes can be accessed via a joint necessary corridor. The doors to the rescue routes must comply with the respective requirements. ↗ **Chapter 3.2.2 Spaces/ Internal Circulation/Corridors**

It may be necessary to provide an emergency egress stair, which is a fire- and smoke-resistant stairway consisting of noncombustible materials. → **Figure 4.1.19** Where such emergency egress stairs have an external facade, smoke can escape directly to the outside (opening casements on stair landings). These stairways must not accommodate any other functions, and must not contain any flammable materials. They also should be accessed via self-closing fire doors. Any necessary stairs located on the inside require a pressurized ventilation system, which can generate positive air pressure in order to keep the space free from smoke. ↗ **Chapter 3.2.4 Spaces/Internal Circulation/Stairs**

## 4.1.1.4 Construction and Technology

Solid construction is the predominant construction method in both multistory apartment buildings and single-family residences. Timber construction is increasingly used in single-family and also in multiple family housing. Grid axes in buildings that are organized in a regular construction grid as in office buildings are not often used in residential developments. Exceptions may be multistory housing, apartment blocks, or residential developments with parking garages.

More demanding requirements regarding the energy efficiency of buildings result in more complex services installations in housing as in other developments. To accommodate the services installations it is important to consider the routing of services (e.g., of ventilation ducts). → **Figure 4.1.21** The basic consideration is whether the routing for installations is to be fully enclosed or whether there should be access for revisions or even the option of completely changing the structure. → **Figure 4.1.20** ↗ **Chapter 3.9.3 Spaces/ Technical Equipment Rooms/Distribution Rooms and Shafts**

**Figure 4.1.19**
Schematic plan of an emergency egress stair

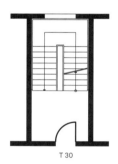
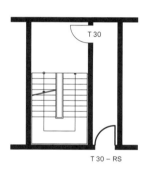

T 30                    T 30 – RS

**Figure 4.1.20 (left)**
Possible installation levels

1  Basic provision with window ventilation + radiator

2  Upmarket provision with ventilation system + surface heating; ventilation pipes within the primary construction

3  Upmarket provision with ventilation system + surface heating; separate installation level in the floor construction

4  Upmarket provision with ventilation system + surface heating; additional installation level in the suspended ceiling

**Figure 4.1.21 (right)**
Installation of services in vertical ducts

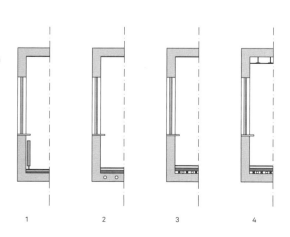

1          2          3          4

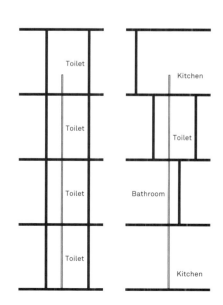

## 4.1.2  Program of Use

There is an increasing differentiation of use functions and forms of living together required by users. In addition to the need for apartments for classic user groups such as single persons, young couples, and families, there is increasing demand for users such as senior citizens, patchwork families, single parents, and couples without children (DINKs: Double Income No Kids). A good mix of living and working should be provided when designing new residential quarters, and flexible models of childcare should be taken into consideration. In order to accommodate changing requirements and the resulting faster conversion cycles, housing projects should make adequate allowance for social and demographic changes by providing the highest possible degree of flexibility in use. Residential accommodation with flexible layouts that can easily be modified will be usable in the long term and improve the lasting value of the property.

### 4.1.2.1  Internal Organization of Apartments

The layout of apartments and houses has to accommodate various user needs, including areas for retreat. Communication areas can be living rooms, dining rooms, and to an extent also kitchens. Bathrooms, utility and storage rooms, and possibly also kitchens have a more functional, serving character. Depending on the system/room concept, the different areas can either be strictly separated (cellular layout) or deliberately connected or integrated into a single room (open layout). →Figure 4.1.23 The most common solution is to combine living and entertainment functions including kitchen and dining area but keeping all other, rather more private rooms, organized in a cellular layout.

The internal circulation system of an apartment defines the pathways and differentiates private areas and areas that are more open to the outside, which can also include work areas. Parallel circulation systems provide an option for a deliberate multiplication of movement processes and spatial links. In larger units with several inhabitants and a greater number of individual rooms it is important to ensure that private areas are arranged such that they are somewhat sheltered from shared areas where communication takes place.

A distinction is made between:
- apartments with a central circulation area that is also used for living,
- apartments with a central circulation area for the purpose of distribution only,
- apartments with corridors for best possible individualization,
- studio apartments in which most functions take place in a single room and the circulation is determined by the user.
→Figure 4.1.24

Vertical circulation elements inside apartments can either be integrated into the layout configuration or designed as independent elements. In the case of split-level arrangements, the stair is often integrated into the living space. →Figure 4.1.26 The most common form of vertical circulation is via stairs with one, two, or three flights, with or without landings. ↗Chapter 3.2.4 Spaces/Internal Circulation/ Stairs

Apartments arranged on several levels provide the opportunity for separating living rooms and shared rooms from individual rooms and bathrooms on separate floors. →Figure 4.1.28 Furthermore it is possible to differentiate the areas for living and working within the building in this way. →Figure 4.1.29 The integration of the stair into the living room minimizes the area used for circulation and subdivides large spaces without strict separation. With air spaces and galleries it is possible to create transitional zones across several floors that lend themselves to communication.

Figure 4.1.22
Basic needs associated
with housing

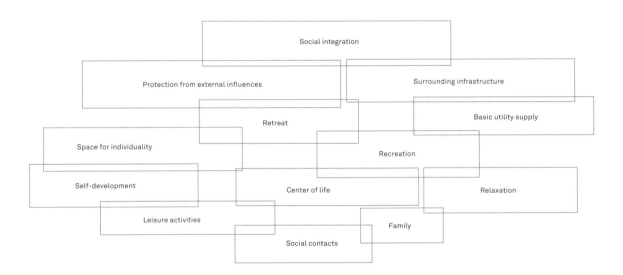

169

**Figure 4.1.23**
Open layout of housing unit (left) with flowing transitions between rooms; detailed cellular layout (right) with central corridor circulation system

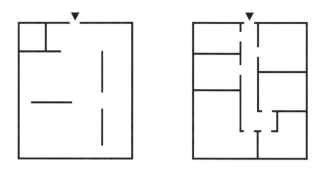

**Figure 4.1.24**
Schematic room layout: central circulation area with living function (left), central circulation area for distribution only (center) corridor circulation system (right)

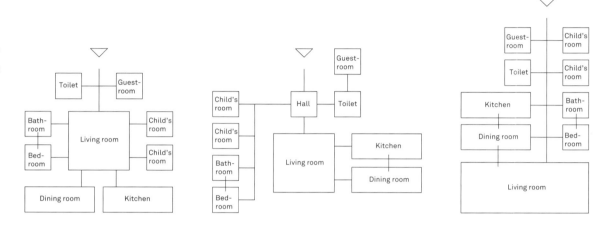

**Figure 4.1.25**
Vertical and horizontal circulation systems: circulation via stairs, corridors, and open space

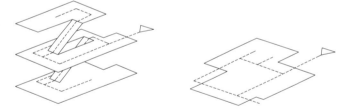

**Figure 4.1.26**
Residential building with split-level circulation system

Residential buildings with split-level arrangements are convenient solutions for sloping terrains and also provide an additional separation between public, semipublic, and private room functions.

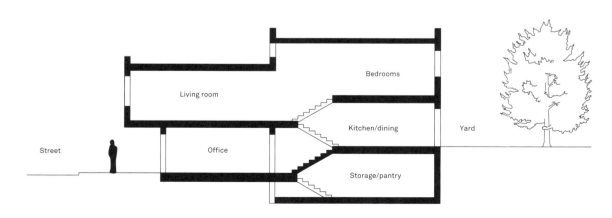

**Figure 4.1.27**
Layout example of studio apartments accessed by a central
corridor

In studio apartments all functional areas are accommodated
in a single room with the exception
of the bathroom, which is in a
separate room, and kitchens
usually arranged in a recess.

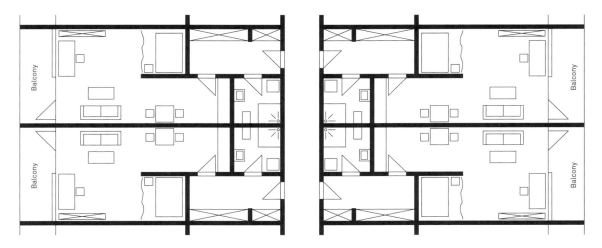

**Figure 4.1.28**
Zoning options, by way of example
on sloping terrain

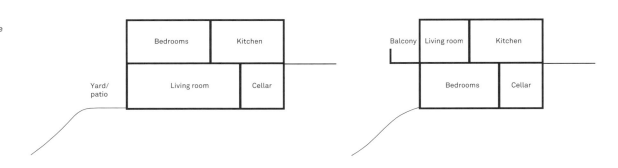

**Figure 4.1.29**
Access options for living and
working areas

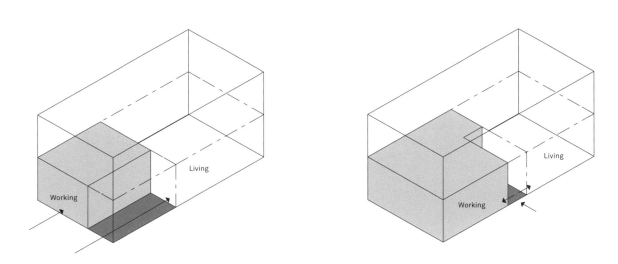

## 4.1.2.2 Single- and Multifamily Dwellings

When designing multiple-family dwellings, self-containment of the units needs to be considered as well as the internal organization of the units themselves, be they apartments or single-family dwellings ↗ **Chapter 4.1.2.1 Internal Organization of Apartments**. Where there are several residential units in a building, some of the use functions can be shared and arranged in a central location. → **Figure 4.1.30** Furthermore, multistory residential buildings often contain different sizes of apartments, ranging from studio apartments through to duplex apartments, which in turn requires an appropriate circulation system and, if applicable, ancillary areas.

Where a number of private parties join together, this can be called an owner's association, a housing society, or self-help building group. Building groups can be formed for the purpose of building multiple-family dwellings, buildings with mixed uses, or a number of individual buildings or townhouses. Developments of this kind can include shared rooms and facilities. It may be possible for such a group to finance facilities such as fitness, leisure, and party rooms, or even swimming pools. Shared rooms may also include guest apartments to be used by visiting relatives or friends of all the parties involved. It is also possible to include additional apartments outside the units occupied by the building group to be used for letting purposes, with the profit being shared by the group.

Figure 4.1.30
Functional scheme of an apartment in a multifamily dwelling

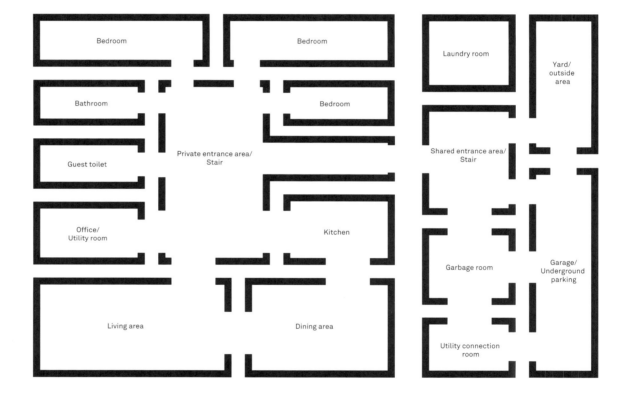

### Freestanding Single- and Multifamily Dwellings

As a rule, freestanding single-family dwellings have a net floor area of at least 110 to 150 m² and are designed for families with children. The rooms normally include children's rooms, parents' bedroom, kitchen, living room, utility room, bathroom, and guest WC spread over two floors. Depending on the size of the site and the topography of the terrain, larger units with a floor area of over 300 m² are common. In addition to the full stories, it is possible to create additional space in the loft or recessed attic of dwellings with sloping roofs. → **Figure 4.1.31** Ancillary rooms are often provided in basements in order to keep the first-floor areas free for more important functions.

The large-scale layout of a development comprising single-family dwellings is largely determined by the distances between the units. These distances are necessary to ensure adequate daylight/solar irradiation to the houses, depending on their height and roof shape. Yards and green areas can be screened from the public realm by placing garages at the boundary.

A more economical way of building single-family units is in the form of freestanding two- and three-family dwellings. It is important to remember that buildings with more than two residential units are subject to more exacting fire safety and sound insulation regulations.

### Duplex Houses

Duplex houses are buildings that share a common separating wall, although each unit stands on its own plot of land; they are often designed as the exact mirror image of one another. → **Figure 4.1.32** Since no space is needed between the houses, they make more efficient use of the site. Duplex houses must be separated from each other in terms of structure, sound insulation, and fire safety.

### Row Houses

Row houses, also commonly known as townhouses, make use of the same principle as in a duplex house, except that multiple single-family dwellings are built adjacent to each other in a row, thus minimizing the required plot size. → **Figure 4.1.33** We speak of row houses when three or more buildings occur in a row. The units at the end of a row are simply called end-of-row houses (UK: end-of-terrace). Row houses may be arranged to occupy an entire housing block, or may be broken up into various groups. Rows of houses can also be arranged at an angle and linked via a corner building.

Row houses have a lower transmission heat loss owing to their smaller facade area and can be built on a smaller site, resulting in a more economical provision of services and access. The typical townhouse layout (layout of a mid-row house) is usually perpendicular to the road with the external walls forming the shorter sides of the unit and the party walls the longer sides. → **Figure 4.1.34** Owing to this orientation and the options for letting daylight into the building, the maximum depth is restricted to approx. 14 m. Ancillary rooms and stairs are often located at the core of the building, which does not necessarily require daylight. → **Figure 4.1.35**

**Figure 4.1.31 (left)**
Additional living space in the loft

The loft area of single-story single-family dwellings can be used in different ways, depending on the shape of the roof; possible roof shapes are double-pitched roof (left), monopitch roof with gallery (center) and flat roof with a recessed attic floor (right).

**Figure 4.1.32 (right)**
Freestanding single-family homes and duplex houses on individual sites

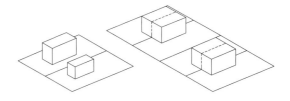

**Figure 4.1.33**
Ways of adding together row houses

Group of townhouses with a corner house (top); row of townhouses with middle and end houses (bottom left). By staggering the townhouses (bottom right) it is possible to achieve better privacy in front of and behind the units.

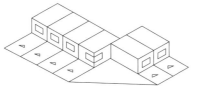

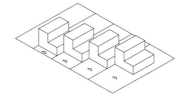

**Figure 4.1.34**
Floor plan orientation for
row houses

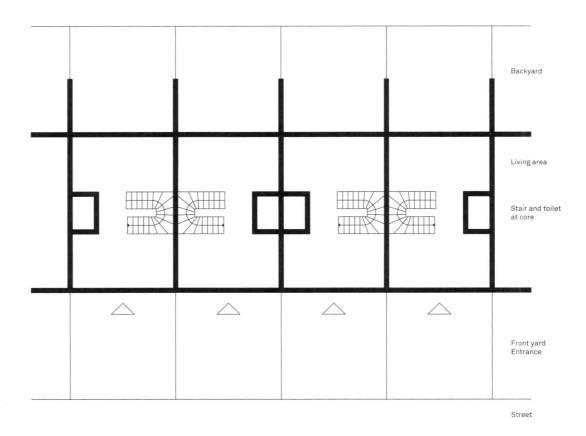

Backyard

Living area

Stair and toilet
at core

Front yard
Entrance

Street

**Figure 4.1.35**
Alternative stair positions in
row houses

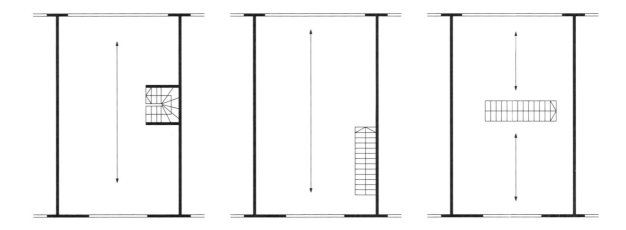

## Linked Townhouses

By linking row houses and varying specific aspects of the individual units, such as mirroring floor plans or adding vertical or horizontal projections and/or recesses, numerous variations can be created. With little additional cost, it is thereby possible to create a differentiated appearance and to provide more individually designed spaces. →Figure 4.1.36

## Courtyard Houses

In a courtyard house, an enclosed courtyard is formed by parts of the building and/or garden walls. The building may enclose the yard in L-shaped or U-shaped form, allowing natural light to enter the yard from the other sides. →Figure 4.1.37 In a two-story development, private yards can be created in this way in spite of the close proximity of the neighboring buildings.

## Atrium Houses

An atrium house features an extreme form of private outdoor space, the atrium, which is surrounded by rooms on all sides, thereby providing them with natural light. This is particularly beneficial in providing better daylighting to deep buildings. →Figure 4.1.38

## Stepped Buildings

These houses offer a unique relationship to outdoor space but are not very spatially efficient. The usually generous exterior space is made possible by a stepped arrangement of the residential units. Such stepped housing developments may either follow the natural slope of the terrain, adapting to the existing topography, or can be designed as an artificial landscape on flat ground, with ancillary and storage rooms or parking in the areas without any natural light. →Figure 4.1.39

## Linear Apartment Buildings

While freestanding single and multiple-family houses are usually found in rural and suburban areas, linear apartment buildings are typical of block developments in higher-density urban areas. In this case, the orientation and daylight are predetermined by the road layout and neighboring buildings, and the structure and access to the apartments have to be individually designed. The height of the development – particularly the elevation facing the street – is usually restricted by local development plans. Buildings in this type of linear block development have elevations facing the street and the courtyard at the back. This can create a conflict with the preferred cardinal orientation in the interior of the apartments. It is common to divide such buildings into three parts (first floor, upper floors, penthouse floor) to accommodate different uses, such as retail shops, offices, residential units, and possibly exclusive penthouse apartments.

**Figure 4.1.36**
Quinta Monroy in Iquique, Chile (2004), by Alejandro Aravena (Elemental)

A modified row of houses was chosen here in order to give owners the opportunity to expand their units over the single-story areas. The basic house type measures 30 m² and costs USD 7,500; it can be expanded by its owners to reach sizes up to 90 m². The illustration to the left shows the complex upon initial completion, with empty spaces for expansion between the houses; to the right, residents have already filled some of the spaces to create additional living space.

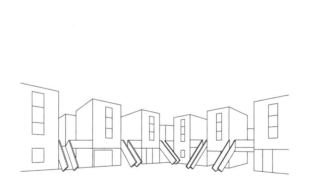

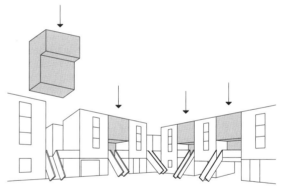

**Figure 4.1.37 (left)**
Courtyard houses as a group of attached buildings

**Figure 4.1.38 (right)**
Row of introverted atrium houses with internal courtyards

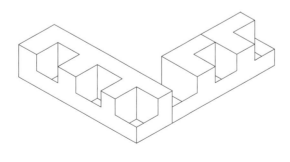

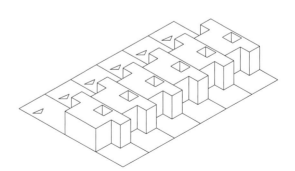

**Figure 4.1.39**
Stepped housing development

Houses stepped in this way normally receive daylight only from one side. By using an L-shaped layout embracing the terrace, the quantity of spaces receiving direct daylight is increased.

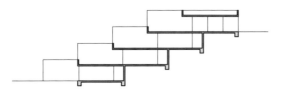

### Corner Buildings

Corner buildings constitute a special building type in urban contexts. These buildings have two streetside facades as well as minor elevations to the rear. Whereas linear block buildings ordinarily have a backyard, which may accommodate communal areas and/or private yards for ground-floor apartments, the position of a corner building often hinders use of the quiet rear of the building, thus fully exposing the inhabitants to noise from the street. The prominent position of such buildings at the intersection of two streets gives them special importance. → Figure 4.1.41

### Solitary Buildings

Solitary buildings are multistory residential buildings that could be seen as the transition between single-family dwellings in rural areas and inner-city blocks in central locations. Examples range from extremely luxurious single-family city homes to cluster developments on a site with several point-shaped buildings. Outside urban areas, this type of solitary character is more often found in the form of a slab building. The main considerations leading to this type of design are the creation of a green area as a buffer zone and access to daylight on four sides. However, such developments have a high land requirement and are therefore rather uneconomical. On the first floor it is possible to accommodate shared-use functions as well as apartments.

**Figure 4.1.40**
Oderberger Strasse, Berlin, BARarchitekten, 2010

Even though the internal subdivision is very complex, with various offsets and intermediate levels creating a wide range of spatial units, the facade nevertheless follows a classic division into three. Studios and galleries are on the first floor, with commercial and office uses, and finally apartments, above.

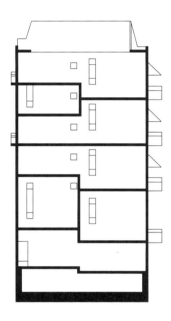

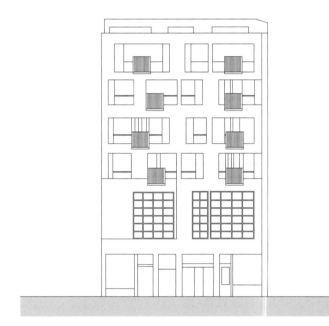

**Figure 4.1.41**
Typical historical example of a corner building in a perimeter block

### 4.1.2.3  High-Rise Apartment Buildings

There is no uniform international definition of what constitutes a high-rise building, and the requirements for such buildings can vary considerably. A construction grid for the primary construction and the alignment of access cores that have a bracing function are important design features, particularly if parking garages are included beneath the building. The construction grid and fit-out grid for internal walls and facade connections should be aligned so that an economical facade construction is possible using grid and element facades.

Smaller residential high-rise buildings differ a little in scale from other multistory apartment buildings, and are therefore widely accepted in the housing market. However, the perception and acceptance of high-rise developments in metropolitan regions needs careful consideration. The functionality and user acceptance of residential megablocks in the sense of a "vertical city" – with several tens of thousands of users/inhabitants – as they are being developed as prestigious projects in Asia, have yet to be established in the long term.

Potential conflicts with significant historic buildings and other negative impacts on the neighborhood (such as shading) should be examined as part of a compatibility study that takes into account the urban context and adjacent buildings. In view of the fact that the lower stories are usually less attractive for housing owing to noise emissions and poor exposure to sunlight, a mixed use is recommended. High-rise buildings with mixed use normally have a plinth building (actually designed as a separate part of the building) or a plinth area that is used for retail, offices, medical practices, and other facilities. High-rise buildings with apartments only could make use of the first floor for shared and ancillary rooms.

High-rise apartment buildings are becoming increasingly popular, particularly in Asian and Arab countries. This type of building is not a new phenomenon, but many projects in the past experienced problems with user acceptance. In many instances, high-rise buildings dating from the 1970s and 1980s are equated with social housing and/or low-quality apartments which, over the years, has led to a change in tenant and owner structures. High operating costs, the absence of any sustainable building services concepts, and constructions involving harmful substances make the modernization of many high-rises from that time uneconomical, so that the only remaining option is demolition. Current projects try to counteract this negative image by using ecological energy concepts, futuristic facade designs, luxurious interiors, and penthouse-type layout concepts. Another element in the marketing of such inner-city buildings is the provision of loggias and balconies, which provide a view over the urban panorama. Furthermore, additional service and leisure facilities within the building increase the attractiveness in the sense of an all-inclusive housing concept.

Key design issues are spatial perception, the attractiveness of internal circulation areas, and the development of social relationships in the sense of neighborhood networking.

**Figure 4.1.42**
Potential positive and negative aspects of high-rise apartment buildings

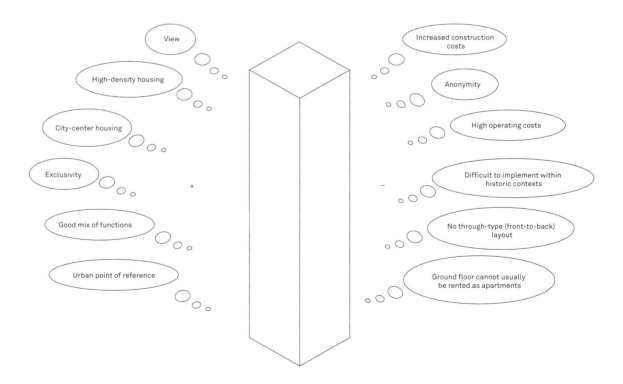

### Layout and Orientation

As in other forms of residential buildings, the internal layout organization can be arranged relatively freely. Owing to the dimensions of these buildings, apartments can only be oriented toward two cardinal directions. A "front-to-back" layout is difficult to achieve owing to the depth of the building and the vertical circulation structures, which are usually placed centrally. Nevertheless, it is possible to create attractive rooms with high-quality comfort in high-rise buildings using duplex units.

Depending on the position of the building, the directly adjacent outside spaces are either public spaces or can form a small public park, but they cannot be used as private outside areas. For this reason, features such as loggias, balconies, and terraces that provide outside space close to the home are of greater importance in high-rise apartment buildings. With the help of vertical gardens and glazed atria it is possible to create high-quality green areas for the purpose of retreat, even in inner-city locations. Penthouse apartments lend themselves to the provision of roof terraces with panoramic views.

### Associated Uses, Service and Leisure Facilities

Depending on the size and immediate environment of the high-rise apartment building, it may be opportune to provide service and leisure facilities directly in the building, creating a mixed use.

Possible facilities may include: porter's lodges with reception service, security personnel, laundries, health facilities, food shops, retail shops, banks, hairdressers, fitness studios, swimming pools, cinemas, restaurants, rooms of worship and prayer, and public toilets.

### Circulation System and Escape Routes

Generally speaking, circulation in high-rises relies on the use of elevator systems. Each story must be serviced by at least two elevators. In very high buildings, elevator groups are provided for different story sections, and express elevators may also be used. The requirements for fire brigade elevators require special attention. Necessary stairways are usually only used as escape routes, owing to the long distances. Necessary corridors can be designed either as central corridors or as corridors surrounding vertical access cores. The minimum width of escape routes must be a clear 1.20 m; this width must be provided between any projecting balusters or handrails. → **Figure 4.1.43–45,** ↗ Chapter 3.2 Spaces/Internal Circulation

**Figure 4.1.43 (left)**
Layout scheme of a high-rise apartment building with central circulation core (emergency egress stair) and corridor surrounding the core (10 apartments per floor)

In accordance with the German guideline on high-rise buildings, a fire-rated emergency egress stair in addition to a necessary stairway is accepted in lieu of a second necessary stairway in buildings with a height of up to 60 m. In buildings higher than 60 m, both necessary stairways must be designed as emergency egress stairs.

**Figure 4.1.44 (right)**
Layout scheme of a high-rise apartment building with a circulation core along one facade (emergency egress stair), elevator lobby, and two dead-end corridors (7 apartments per floor)

**Figure 4.1.45**
Layout scheme of a high-rise apartment building with central corridor and two stairs at the facade (5 apartments per floor)

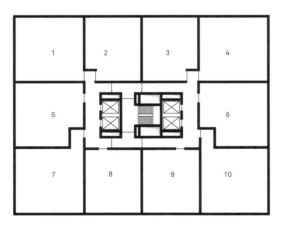

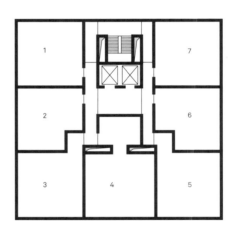

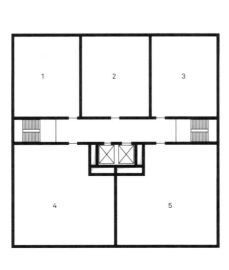

### 4.1.2.4  Student Housing

Student housing offers economical accommodation to students in small apartments or in the form of small shared units. Characteristic of shared apartments are uniform private retreat options in the form of a personal sleeping and working place, at least two shared bathrooms, one large central kitchen, and communal areas for flexible use. → **Figure 4.1.46** Minimum and maximum sizes of space per student are laid down in regulations similar to those for social housing.

In addition to the studios and shared accommodation, there are larger shared kitchens and rooms for small study groups and shared activities that allow increased networking. Nevertheless, there should be an option for more privacy and also autonomy, a mixture of social life and private sphere with clearly defined private areas.

### 4.1.2.5  Multigenerational Homes

Multigenerational homes, as well as self-build cooperatives, are buildings based on a concept in which different user groups and diverse user requirements call for mixed-use and shared communication areas. Owing to this diversity, these residential buildings differ significantly from the standard housing that is commonly found in the rental market. These projects may include shared rooms and facilities that would be unattainable for an individual, but are affordable to the community. → **Figure 4.1.47** The multigeneration concept fosters communities of younger and older persons who can support each other. These homes can range from a project that merely provides shared outdoor areas to one with the atmosphere of an extended family spanning generations.

**Figure 4.1.46**
Layout of student accommodations in a dormitory

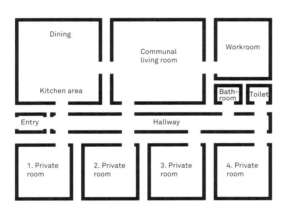

**Figure 4.1.47**
Possible functional areas in a multigenerational home

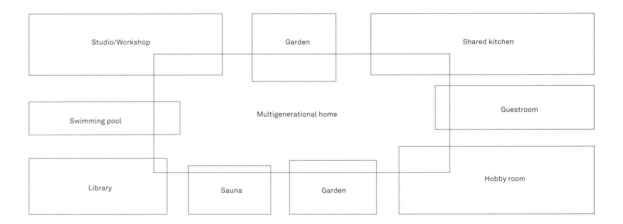

## 4.1.2.6 Residential Group Housing and Retirement Homes

A residential (or community) group home is a term that embraces (supervised) homes for the elderly and group homes for young people or disabled persons who rely on sustained support, as well as residential groups for persons sharing similar life circumstances, such as young single mothers.

The heterogeneous social and age structure of community groups can result in positive synergy effects. Old people will be less lonely since they have contact with young persons and children, and young persons benefit from the exchange with experienced senior persons. Likewise, disabled persons are better integrated. ↗ **Chapter 2.1 Human Measure/Anthropometry and Barrier-Free Accessibility**

The core of community group dwellings is the shared living area, which can often be joined with the dining and cooking area. →**Figure 4.1.48** Adequate sizing of the individual private rooms is important for persons to be able to retreat into their private sphere as well as share space with the community. Depending on the use structure, it may be necessary to provide additional rooms for care personnel or therapy/treatment.

A number of very different housing concepts exist for housing senior citizens. Apartments and housing developments designed for the use of senior citizens can make it possible for residents to continue coping with their everyday lives. However, these housing developments, which usually include a care element, are rather more like individual rental apartments that provide emergency call facilities in addition to barrier-free accessibility. All these apartments are designed to be barrier-free and suitable for wheelchair users; they also offer additional services such as care and support by trained personnel. The accommodation for the service personnel is provided in a separate unit close by.

In cases where more intensive care is required, other types of apartment have to be provided, which are described in ↗ **Chapter 4.8 Typologies/Healthcare Facilities.** In order to make it possible for senior citizens and/or persons requiring care to remain in their homes as long as possible, the use of living areas and bedrooms of individual housing units must be flexible, including a small cooking area and a care room. ↗ **Chapter 2.1 Human Measure/Anthropometry and Barrier-Free Accessibility**

For special user groups, such as persons with dementia, additional protected outside areas and walkways should be provided that make it possible to spend time out in the open without risk. →**Figure 4.1.51**

**Typical Functions in a Retirement Home**
- Reception
- Administration
- Central cafeteria
- Building code restrictions
- Apartments, rooms
- Nurses' room
- Needs of user groups
- Specially equipped bathrooms
- Physical activity rooms
- Kitchen
- Laundry, including decentralized rooms
- Storage areas
- Additional services such as newspaper kiosk, hairdresser, physiotherapy, chapel

**Figure 4.1.48 (left)**
Schematic layout of residential group housing

**Figure 4.1.49 (right)**
Senior citizen apartment with bedroom, combined living, dining and cooking area, balcony, and accessible bathroom

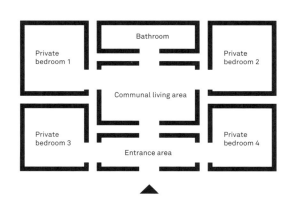

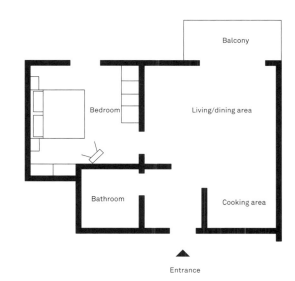

**Figure 4.1.50**
Sample layout of senior citizen group housing with associated communal and ancillary rooms

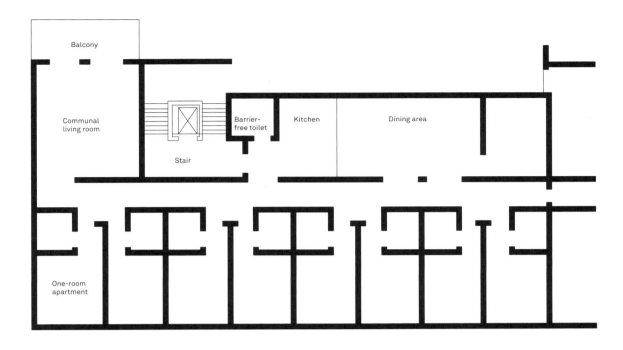

**Figure 4.1.51**
Internal courtyard with walkway in a home for dementia patients

Outside areas in homes for senior citizens, and in particular for persons with dementia, can be provided in inner courtyards so that residents are protected from noise and road traffic. Landscaped circular pathways create a pleasant atmosphere and make orientation easier for patients.

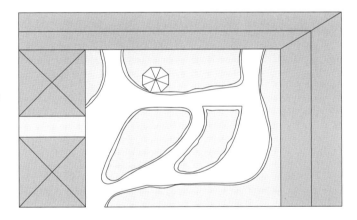

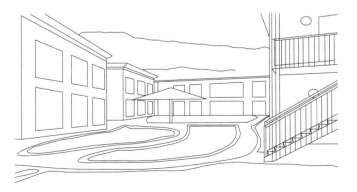

### 4.1.3  Areas and Rooms

**External circulation**  ↗Chapter 3.1

**Entrance areas**  ↗183  ↗Chapter 3.2.1

**Stairs, elevators**  ↗Chapter 3.2.4, ↗Chapter 3.2.7

**Corridors, internal circulation**  ↗Chapter 3.2.2

**Living rooms**  ↗184  ↗Chapter 3.4.2

**Workplaces**  ↗Chapter 3.3.1

**Kitchens**  ↗185  ↗Chapter 3.6

**Dining areas**  ↗185  ↗Chapter 3.4.3

**Bedrooms**  ↗188

**Rooms for children and adolescents**  ↗188

**Bathrooms and toilets**  ↗190  ↗Chapter 3.5

**Utility rooms**  ↗193

**Laundry and drying rooms**  ↗193

**Storage spaces**  ↗194  ↗Chapter 3.7

**Outdoor seating areas**  ↗194

**Utility connection and technical equipment rooms**  ↗195  ↗Chapter 3.9

**Waste container areas**  ↗195  ↗Chapter 3.1.5

**Parking spaces and garages**  ↗195  ↗Chapter 3.1.2

## 4.1.3.1 Entrance Areas

Entrance areas can be designed in many different ways depending on the type of building and number of residential units. In high-rise apartment buildings, a distinction is made between the main building entrance area and the apartment entrance areas (hallways). The entrance areas for multistory residential buildings include the actual entrance door with lobby, access to the stairs and elevators, and usually a bell and letterbox system, as well as storage areas for prams and wheelchairs, access to ancillary and storage rooms, and/or parking garages. If required, there may also be a porter/concierge facility. → **Figure 4.1.52**

The entrance area of the apartments should have enough space for wardrobes, movement, and a mirror. In order to provide barrier-free access, a room depth of 1.60 m has to be included in the design. → **Figure 4.1.54**, ↗ **Chapter 3.1.4 Spaces/External Circulation/Mailbox Units**, ↗ **Chapter 3.2.1 Spaces/Internal Circulation/Entrance Areas**

**Figure 4.1.52**
Entrance area: seating with integrated storage; built-in closet with clothing rods, shelves, and drawers

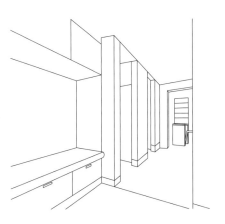
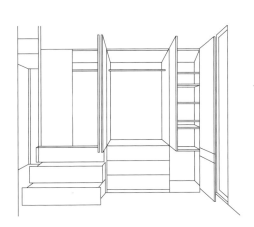

**Figure 4.1.53**
Requirements for the entrance to a dwelling unit

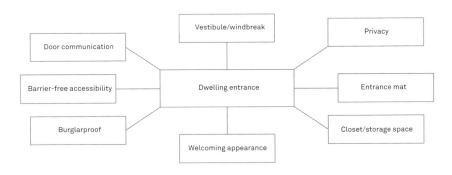

**Figure 4.1.54**
Minimum requirements for a barrier-free apartment entrance

Apartment entry

Apartment entry with wheelchair storage space

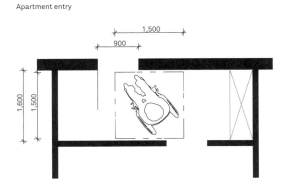
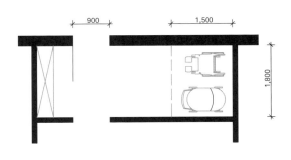

### 4.1.3.2 Living Rooms

As a rule, the living room forms the core of the apartment; the relationship between the living room and the other areas is an important factor in determining the apartment's use quality. Direct access to the garden or balcony via large balcony doors opens the living space to the outside; an orientation toward the south or west is preferable. Two-story areas, vertical connections, and cross views within living rooms create a more generous, open, and communicative ambiance. In large spaces with various use zones, the room height should be proportional to the size. → **Table 4.1.4**

In order to provide some zoning in what is usually the largest room in an apartment, it is possible to reduce the height of some partial areas. The kitchen and dining area can be combined particularly well with the living room in an L-shaped layout, as the different areas can be used separately from one another, depending on the furnishing. ↗ **4.1.3.3 Areas and Rooms/Kitchens and Dining Rooms** Smaller desks or an escritoire can also be placed directly in a living room or separately in a workroom.

Cellular layouts are conducive to privacy and retreat from the common area but do not encourage communication. Various uses of individual, separated rooms may include: television room, home cinema, family room with a fireplace, and a library/reading room.

When designing classic living areas or living rooms, it is important to ensure that adequate space is provided for seating and other furniture in individual configurations. → **Figure 4.1.56,** ↗ **Chapter 3.4.2 Spaces/Communication Spaces and Dining Rooms/Waiting and Seating Areas**

**Figure 4.1.55 (left)**
Accommodation of various functions within a living area

**Figure 4.1.56 (right)**
Living room as a separately enclosed space

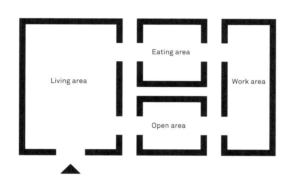

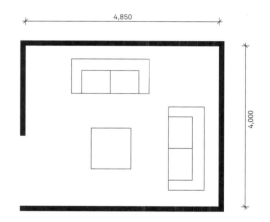

Table 4.1.4
Minimum heights and comfortable heights for habitable rooms

| Floor area | Minimum height | Comfortable height |
|---|---|---|
| Up to 10 m² | 2.30 m | 2.50 m |
| Up to 20 m² | 2.40 m | 2.60 m |
| Up to 50 m² | 2.50 m | 2.75 m |
| 50 m² – 100 m² | 2.75 m | 2.90 m |
| Over 100 m² | 3.00 m | 3.20 m |

### 4.1.3.3 Kitchens and Dining Rooms

Numerous different concepts exist with respect to the integration of kitchens, ranging from a small kitchenette in a one-room apartment via a small, purpose-designed kitchen in a separate room to a large living kitchen with integrated seating corner through to an open-plan kitchen in the living room. The relationships to the other functional areas are determined by criteria such as frequency and intensity of use, use as an essential family and communication center, and the avoidance of odors in the living areas. → **Figure 4.1.57,** ↗ Chapter 3.6 Spaces/Kitchens, ↗ Chapter 3.4.3 Spaces/Communication Spaces and Dining Rooms/Dining Areas

The kitchen should have easy access from the outside. A storeroom directly adjacent to the kitchen is helpful. The connection between a kitchen and a separate dining room can be via a door or a pass-through. Sliding doors make it possible to separate or connect the kitchen and dining room as required.

**Figure 4.1.57**
Possible intercommunication between kitchen and other rooms

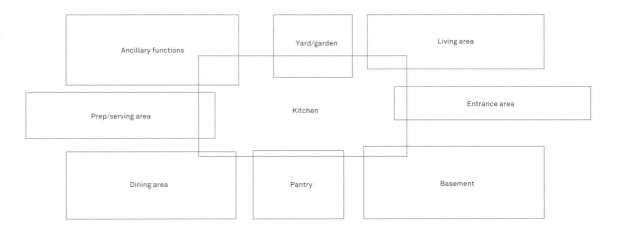

**Figure 4.1.58**
Minimalist cupboard-fitted kitchen

**Figure 4.1.59**
Cellular layout: kitchen and dining room with separate entries

Individual rooms create a small-scale spatial feeling in the dining room and kitchen, but they provide more wall area for furnishing with cabinets and shelves.

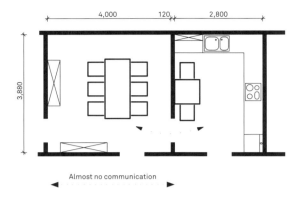
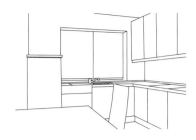

Almost no communication

**Figure 4.1.60**
Connection between kitchen and dining room via a pass-through

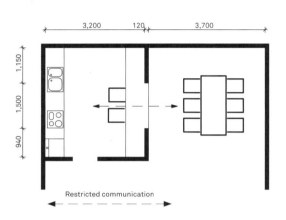
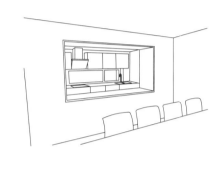

Restricted communication

**Figure 4.1.61**
Combined cooking and dining area: an L-shaped layout with a link to the living area

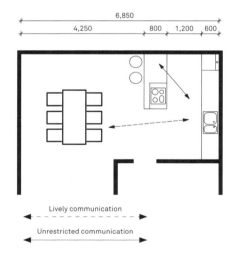

Lively communication

Unrestricted communication

**Figure 4.1.62**
Combination of a row of fitted kitchen furniture and a freestanding cooking island with dining area

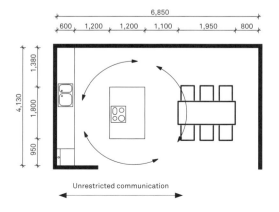
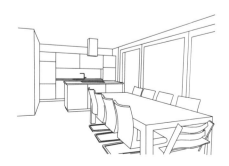

Unrestricted communication

Figure 4.1.63
Examples of open-plan kitchens

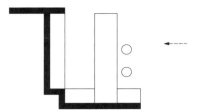

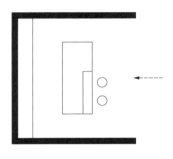

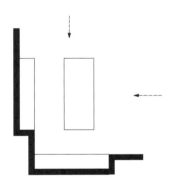

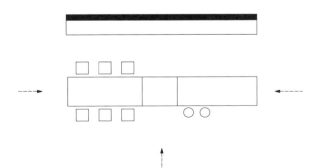

### 4.1.3.4 Bedrooms

The position of bedrooms within an apartment should be remote from potential sources of noise, and away from the street. Within a residential unit, it is common to arrange several bedrooms in the direct proximity of a shared bathroom. Individual en suite bathrooms are another option, and common in some countries.

In bedrooms for adults it may be necessary to provide larger areas to accommodate a baby cot, changing table, or other equipment. →Figures 4.1.64 and 4.1.66

### 4.1.3.5 Rooms for Children and Teenagers

Depending on the age of the child or teenager, the use of the respective room is subject to constant change. The size of a room that can accommodate various changes over time should be 15 m² to 18 m² (min. 12 m²). Raised platform beds or cupboard beds can help with the furnishing of small rooms. →Figures 4.1.67 and 4.1.68

**Figure 4.1.64**
Standard dimensions of beds

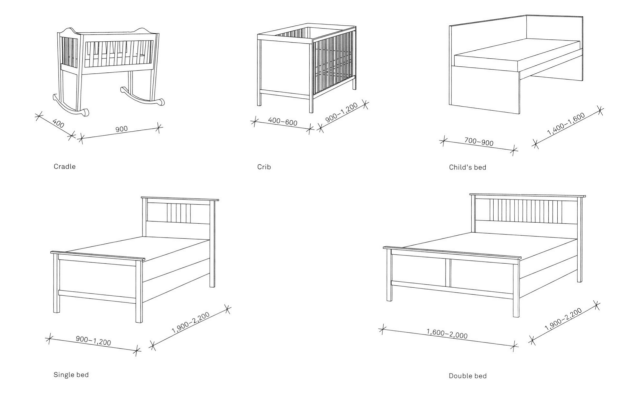

Cradle

Crib

Child's bed

Single bed

Double bed

**Figure 4.1.65**
Barrier-free bed arrangement

In a barrier-free bed arrangement, the two long sides of the bed should be kept clear and there should be adequate distance to furniture and adjoining walls. This guarantees that the bed is accessible to wheelchair users and care personnel in sheltered accommodation.

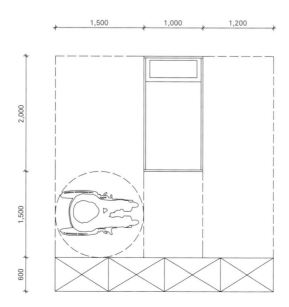

**Figure 4.1.66**
Furniture and movement space
in the bedroom

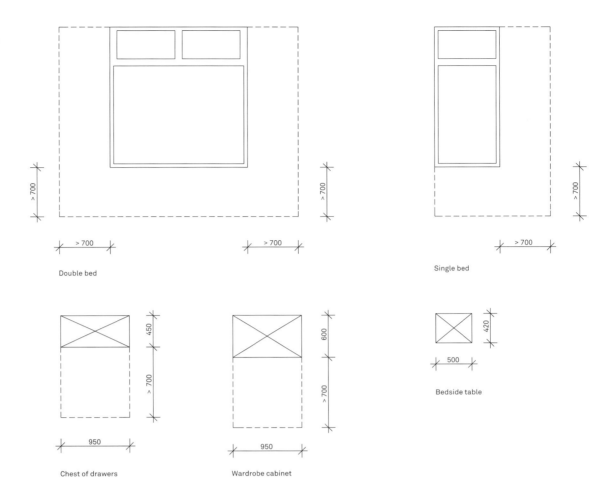

Double bed

Single bed

Chest of drawers

Wardrobe cabinet

Bedside table

**Figure 4.1.67**
Child's room as single-bed room
and as two-bed room with storage
units as room dividers

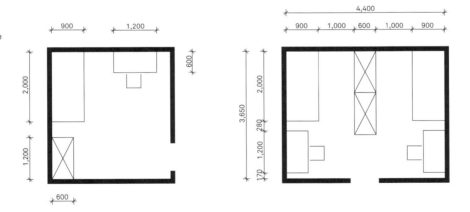

**Figure 4.1.68**
Examples showing the space
gained with a raised platform bed

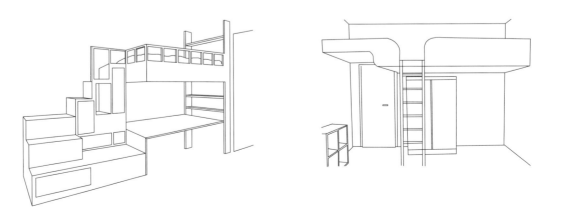

### 4.1.3.6 Bathrooms

A basic distinction can be made between full bathrooms with a bathtub (with or without a separate shower), bathrooms with a shower but no bathtub (¾ bath), and separate rooms with just a sink and a toilet (½ bath). Full and three-quarter bathrooms should be located close to bedrooms and other private rooms. In small apartments and single-family homes, the bathroom can also be used as a laundry room by accommodating a washing machine. Natural light and ventilation should ideally be provided, but where this is not possible, mechanical ventilation must be provided.

Increasingly, bathrooms are no longer used solely for personal hygiene, but are equipped with saunas, special bathtubs, or whirlpools and thereby have an upgraded function.

Depending on the number of users and the overall size of the residential unit, storage facilities for towels and hygiene articles should be provided in the bathroom. Depending on the layout, it may be possible to include a dirty laundry chute to a room below. Family bathrooms should have two washbasins. The provision of a second toilet in a separate room provides greater flexibility during the busiest use periods. Additional WCs and/or guest WCs should be located in the more public part of the apartment.
↗ **Chapter 3.5 Spaces/Sanitary Facilities**

**Figure 4.1.69**
Variations for directly linking bathroom and bedroom

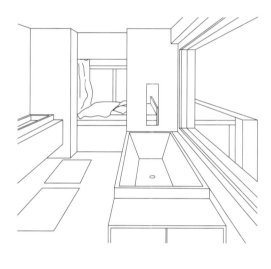

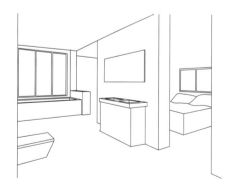

**Figure 4.1.70**
Bathroom with two points of entry

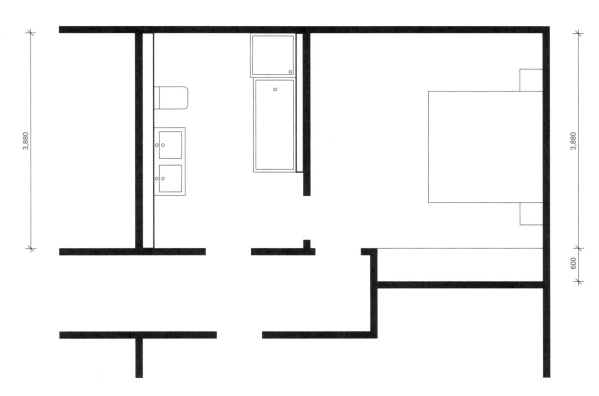

**Figure 4.1.71**
Family bathroom adjacent to bedrooms, with sole access from the hallway

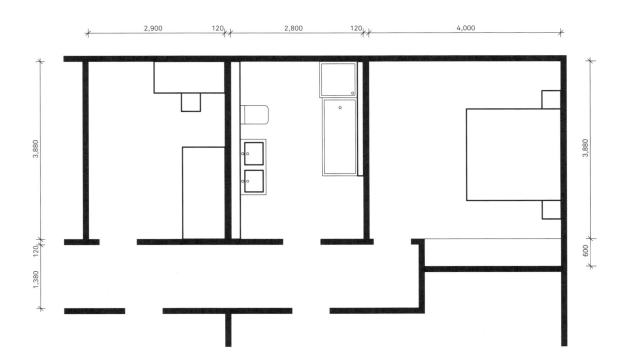

**Figure 4.1.72**
Barrier-free design of
a shower room

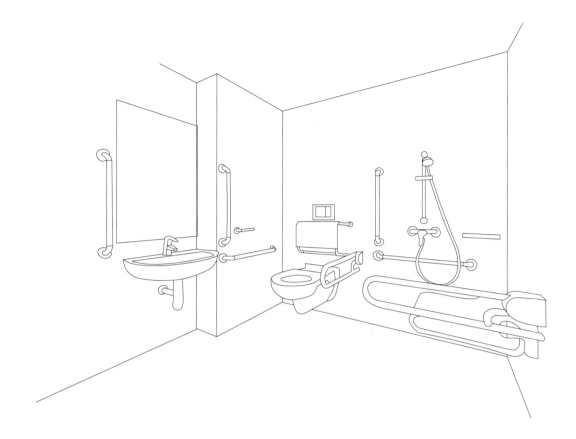

**Figure 4.1.73**
Examples of various bathroom
furnishing options

### 4.1.3.7 Utility Rooms

Utility rooms should measure at least 8 m² and should have a window for natural light and ventilation. These rooms should have space for a washing machine, tumble dryer, ironing board, drying stand, and storage facilities for provisions, household hardware, cleansing agents, and household equipment. In addition, consideration should be given to a work surface, a slop sink, and a drainage outlet in the floor. → **Figure 4.1.74** Since washing machines and tumble dryers cause considerable noise, it is advisable to place the utility room away from the bedrooms and living areas.

### 4.1.3.8 Laundry and Drying Rooms

In multifamily dwellings and in multistory residential buildings, it is advisable to provide laundry and drying rooms for shared use. These rooms should have space and electrical connection points for washing machines and possibly a tumble dryer, as well as a slop sink. Owing to the high relative humidity, laundry and drying rooms should have good ventilation. For a three-family dwelling, the size of the room should be 10 m²; an additional 3 to 4 m² should be allowed for each additional residential unit. → **Figure 4.1.75**

**Figure 4.1.74**
Example fit-out of a utility room within an apartment

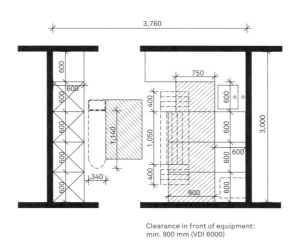
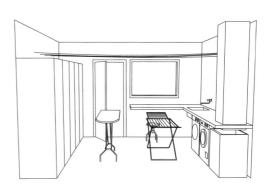

Clearance in front of equipment:
min. 900 mm (VDI 6000)

**Figure 4.1.75**
Layout of a laundry and drying room in a multifamily dwelling

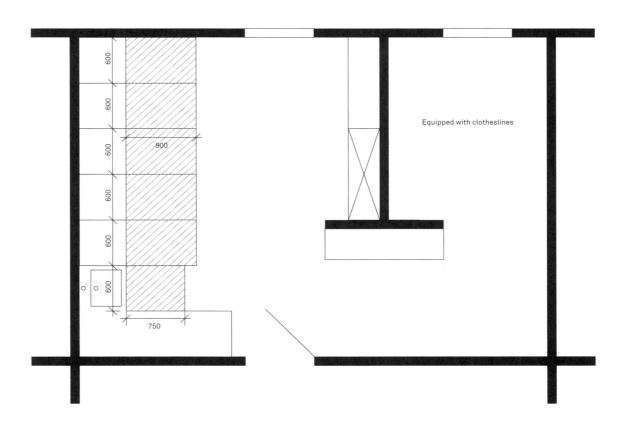

Equipped with clotheslines

### 4.1.3.9 Storage Spaces

Each apartment should be allocated a storage area of 2 percent of the habitable floor space, but at least 6 m². There should be a storage area of at least 1 m² inside the apartment. A good solution is to supply both an individual storage area within the apartment, as well as a larger, central area near the building entrance or in the basement. ↗ Chapter 3.7 Spaces/Storage Spaces

### 4.1.3.10 Open Area Seating and Winter Gardens

If possible, each apartment should have its own outdoor seating area or access to a shared garden or roof terrace. → Figure 4.1.76 Possible options include:

- Balcony (projecting platform)
- Patio (ground-level paved open space)
- Porch (covered deck)
- Loggia (covered area recessed into the building)
- Atrium (open-roofed central courtyard)
- Winter garden (lean-to structure, glazed on all sides).

Winter gardens and balconies, loggias, etc., with additional folding glass panels can also have the function of buffering the room behind against the climate, as well as making the external space usable during the change of seasons. In multistory developments it is important to remember that balconies and loggias cast a shadow over any window openings in the floor below.

Open area seating should have a floor area of at least 4 m² so that, with a depth of approx. 1.40 m to 1.50 m, it is possible to place a dining table with chairs and still have adequate circulation space. When designing an open area seating space, the orientation toward the south and any shadowing should be taken into consideration. For example, in Central Europe an orientation toward the southwest or west is advantageous if the space is to be used in the afternoon or evening. By contrast, breakfast terraces and balconies should face southeast. In order to improve the quality of the space, adequate shading and visual screening should be provided. → Figure 4.1.77

Figure 4.1.76
Balcony, roof terrace, loggia, atrium/inner courtyard

  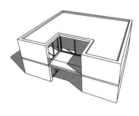 

Figure 4.1.77
Visual screening in the form of vegetation, structures or a difference in level

Vegetation

Screening element

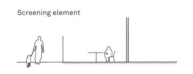

Visual screening for privacy from neighbors above

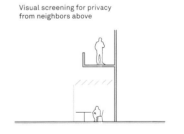

Raised level, bank

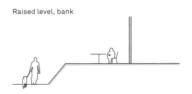

Wall

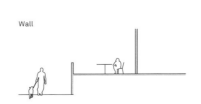

Visual screening for privacy from neighbors above

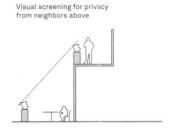

### 4.1.3.11 Ancillary Rooms

**Public Services Connection Rooms and Plant Rooms**
In smaller dwellings there is normally no need for a separate room for the public services connections. A common solution is to have one room for plant and services connections, which could be in the basement or on the first floor. Alternatively, it is possible to install ventilation and heating plant in the loft space. In larger residential developments, separate rooms for large services installations, such as ventilation and heating systems, are required. ↗ Chapter 3.9 Spaces/Technical Equipment Rooms

**Garbage Disposal**
Garbage collection points serving residential buildings are usually outside the building. In larger, multistory residential buildings or in high-density inner-city areas, a good solution may be the provision of garbage chutes. → **Figure 4.1.78** These chutes should have good ventilation and be located separate from any habitable rooms. Furthermore, garbage chutes must be fire-resistant in order to prevent any spread of fire from floor to floor. ↗ Chapter 3.1.5 Spaces/External Circulation/Waste Receptacles

**Parking Lots and Garages**
Parking lots on the open ground or in garages usually have to be included in the planning application for the project and are subject to local parking and garage regulations. As a rule, at least one car parking lot should be provided for each residential unit. Parking spaces can be provided on open ground, in separate or attached garages, at ground level within buildings, or underground as parking garages. → **Figure 4.1.79** For larger housing developments or perimeter block developments, it is possible to provide parking garages beneath internal planted courtyards. Private garages may include parking space for a car and also other functions, such as storage areas, workbenches, space for waste receptacles and gardening equipment, etc. ↗ Chapter 3.1.2 Spaces/External Circulation/Parked Vehicles, ↗ Chapter 4.11 Typologies/Transportation and Infrastructure

**Figure 4.1.78**
Garbage chute door

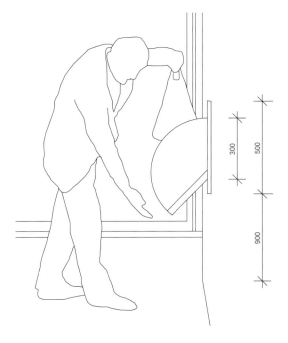

**Figure 4.1.79**
Options for positioning parking lots and garages for a single-family dwelling

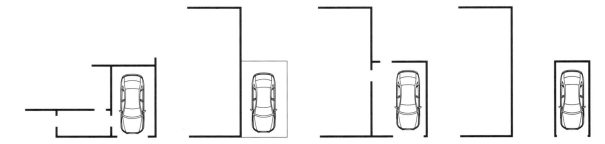

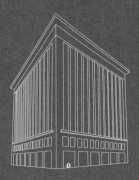

**Wainwright Building**, St. Louis, Missouri, USA,
Louis H. Sullivan, 1891

**Chilehaus**, Hamburg, Germany, Fritz Höger, 1924

**IG Farben Administration Building**, Frankfurt am Main,
Germany, Hans Poelzig, 1931

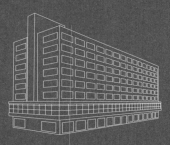

**Berolinahaus**, Alexanderplatz, Berlin, Germany,
Peter Behrens, 1932

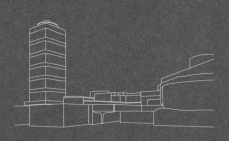

**Johnson Wax Headquarters**, Racine, Wisconsin, USA,
Frank Lloyd Wright, 1939

**UN Headquarters**, New York, USA, Le Corbusier,
1951

**Seagram Building**, New York, USA, Ludwig Mies
van der Rohe, 1958

**Olivetti Building**, Frankfurt am Main, Germany,
Egon Eiermann, 1972

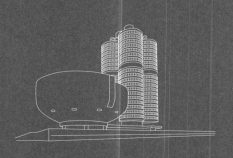

**BMW Tower**, Munich, Germany, Karl Schwanzer, 1973

**AT&T Building**, New York, USA,
Philip Johnson, 1984

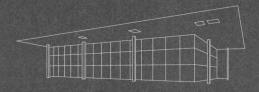

**Plenary Hall**, Bonn, Germany, Günter Behnisch, 1992

**Swiss Re Tower**, London, Great Britain,
Norman Foster, 2004

Bert Bielefeld
Roland Schneider

# 4 Typologies
# 4.2 Office and Administration

### 4.2.1 Building Concept ↗198

4.2.1.1 Planning Parameters ↗198
4.2.1.2 Building Forms ↗199
4.2.1.3 Circulation Systems ↗200
4.2.1.4 Construction and Technology ↗203

### 4.2.2 Program of Use ↗204

4.2.2.1 General Office and Administration Buildings ↗204
4.2.2.2 Public Administration ↗205
4.2.2.3 Banks ↗207

### 4.2.3 Areas and Rooms ↗208

4.2.3.1 Entrance Areas ↗209
4.2.3.2 Office Spaces and Workplaces ↗212
4.2.3.3 Meeting and Conference Rooms ↗222
4.2.3.4 Ancillary Rooms ↗224

# 4.2  Office and Administration

## 4.2.1  Building Concept

### 4.2.1.1  Planning Parameters

Pure office and administration buildings are primarily used by companies providing services and by public authorities. Generally speaking, however, every company and every private, public, or charitable organizational unit needs an administrative area of some sort. Furthermore, offices are integrated into many different building types and thus do not necessarily occur as an independent type.

An important planning parameter is the number of workplaces required, since this information is usually the most suitable for determining the floor area and space needs. In the next step, the type of workplaces (cellular offices, open-plan offices, etc.) needs to be determined as well as what other functional and ancillary areas are needed. Owing to the different space requirements, the overall usable area that needs to be provided in the building usually averages between 20 and 40 m² per workplace. It is possible to use sample office layouts to determine the required floor area per workplace; as a rule this floor area adds up to 40 to 70 percent of the total usable area, depending on the number of ancillary functions (cafeteria, conference areas, etc.) called for. The circulation areas alone take up between 10 and 30 percent of the total floor area.

It is essential, right at the beginning of the design process, to clarify the relationship between various departments within the administrative structure (for example, using functional diagrams) and, together with the client, to determine the respective requirements for the office workplaces to be created as well as any special interests relating to them. → Figure 4.2.1

**Typical Design Parameters:**
- Place, context, and infrastructure
- Geometry of the site
- Building code restrictions
- Spatial program/requirements
- Number of workplaces
- Office type(s), working methods
- Necessary ancillary functions
- User group needs
- Layout type, building form
- Representational purposes
- Relationship of public and internal areas
- Accessibility
- Budget and deadlines

Figure 4.2.1
Diagram for identifying the relationships between departments

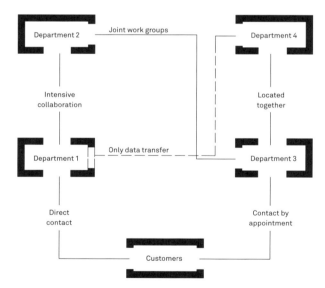

### 4.2.1.2 Building Forms

The basic shape of the building and its layout are often determined by restrictions imposed by the site and by conditions set in building codes, as well as by the location of circulation cores and fire compartments. On this basis, adequate building forms have to be found to suit the particular project.

#### Linear Buildings
Linear or slab buildings are among the classic office building forms. Buildings with very different depths can be achieved by varying the circulation system, using single- or double-loaded corridors or double corridors. Additional circulation cores can be used to link several linear buildings. Another option is to connect linear buildings with point-block towers. → **Figure 4.2.2**

#### Point-Block Buildings
Especially on restricted sites in expensive inner-city locations, a point-block building is often the only form in which an office building can be accommodated. Once a building reaches a certain height, however, the economy achieved by minimizing the horizontal circulation areas is offset by expensive vertical circulation and fire safety measures. → **Figure 4.2.3**

#### Spine-and-Fingers Buildings
The spine-and-fingers type of layout – with multiple wings, or fingers, perpendicular to a continuous spine along one side – makes it possible to site buildings in such a way that the courtyards between the fingers, which open out to one side only, face away from roads or other sources of noise. When the fingers are located adjacent to an existing building, the new building intermeshes with the existing outdoor areas. Especially when expanding existing office complexes, such a layout offers many design options for linking old and new. → **Figure 4.2.4**

#### Courtyard Buildings
In courtyard buildings, the protected inner courtyard can be used as a private outdoor area that is largely shielded from environmental noise emissions. Offices located along the facades of inner courtyards benefit from natural ventilation without being exposed to noise. However, the complete seclusion of the inner courtyard creates an isolated situation with few opportunities for interconnecting with existing buildings. Passages at the ground floor level can provide public access to the inner courtyard and likewise serve as covered outdoor areas. → **Figure 4.2.5**

**Figure 4.2.2 (left)**
Examples of linear buildings

**Figure 4.2.3 (right)**
Examples of point-block buildings

**Figure 4.2.4 (left)**
Examples of spine-and-fingers buildings

**Figure 4.2.5 (right)**
Examples of courtyard buildings

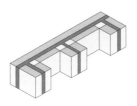 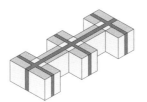 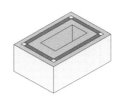 

### 4.2.1.3 Circulation Systems

Conventional office layouts, such as those with cellular and group offices, can be served by single-loaded or double-loaded corridors, whereas combi-offices – which feature a combination of cellular and group offices – can be served by double corridors. → **Figure 4.2.6** With open-plan offices and in high-rise buildings there is also the option of providing access without corridors; in this system the open-plan office is reached directly from the circulation core. By combining different layout types and circulation systems it is possible to achieve different building depths; nevertheless, the dimensions of individual rooms and the thicknesses of walls can vary significantly, depending on the project.

#### Single-Loaded Corridor

Single-loaded corridors do not make very efficient use of the available floor area. They can, however, make sense where the building depth is limited due to a narrow site, in the case of transparent and prestigiously designed buildings, where a building is organized around an atrium, or where the corridor is used to create a barrier along major roads. Furthermore, single-loaded corridors are useful in cases where an existing building is expanded on one side or an administrative tract is added in front of an industrial or production building. Vertical circulation cores, including sanitary facilities and ancillary spaces, can be accommodated along the corridor on the same side as the offices. → **Figure 4.2.7**

#### Double-Loaded Corridor

In this circulation system, which makes significantly more efficient use of the available floor area, cellular and group offices are located on both sides of a central corridor. Such buildings should – if possible from an urban design standpoint – be oriented with regard to the sun, such that none of the offices solely face due south. In buildings with only cellular offices, the spatial quality can be improved by utilizing translucent or transparent office partitions and/or by positioning intermediate zones along the facade. → **Figure 4.2.8**

#### Double Corridors

Workrooms and lunchrooms need natural daylight as well as a view to the outside, and for this reason they must be positioned along the exterior walls of the building. The central space between the two corridors can, however, be used for conference rooms, ancillary spaces (storerooms and archives), staff kitchens, and copier rooms (↗ **Combi-offices, p. 217**), and the space next to central vertical circulation cores can accommodate sanitary facilities, janitor's closets, and technical equipment rooms, in order to keep the facades free for workrooms requiring daylight. Thus the middle zone cannot receive daylight and must be equipped with mechanical ventilation. → **Figure 4.2.9**

**Figure 4.2.6 (left)**
Circulation systems with single- and double-loaded corridor, and with a double corridor

**Figure 4.2.7 (right)**
Single-loaded corridor system

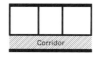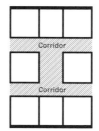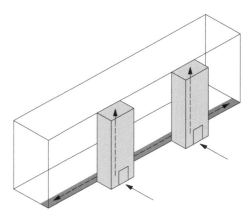

**Figure 4.2.8 (left)**
Double-loaded corridor system

**Figure 4.2.9 (right)**
Double corridor system

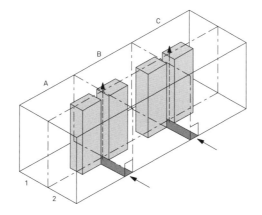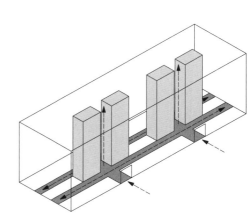

### Circulation without Corridors

By completely omitting corridors it is possible to make efficient use of the available floor space; nevertheless, escape and rescue routes must be kept unobstructed between the areas used for workplaces or otherwise occupied by furniture. This is typical for open-plan offices, but may also apply to high-rise buildings with small floor plates due to their vertical circulation. As a rule, the vertical circulation cores in high-rise buildings take up much of the floor area because the transport of all occupants and services is accommodated centrally.

In buildings without corridors it is nevertheless mandatory to comply with the local regulations pertaining to fire compartments; depending on the applicable building code, it may also be necessary to provide protected corridors. For larger units, compensatory measures using sprinkler and fire alarm systems must be clarified with consulting engineers and receive approval from the fire safety authority. → **Figure 4.2.10**

### Determining Building Depth

When the design primarily comprises cellular and group offices, with their need for natural daylight, the resulting building layout usually takes on a long and narrow rectangular form. The ideal depth of rooms receiving daylight is approximately 1.5 times the height of the windows. If additional internal connecting doors are provided for cellular and group offices, it is possible to achieve greater depths for the rooms and hence the building. → **Figure 4.2.11**, → **Table 4.2.1**

### Escape Routes and Fire Compartments

The applicable building codes specify the maximum permitted distances to the nearest compulsory escape stairwells and the maximum permitted length/size of fire compartments. In Germany, the maximum permitted distance to a compulsory escape stairwell is 35 m. The maximum size of fire compartments is 40 × 40 m, and mandatory corridors must be separated into sections with a maximum length of 30 m by self-closing smoke control doors. These requirements result in a number of possible combinations for the layout of cellular and group offices. In addition to the classic linear form of building, it is possible to design variations that range from courtyard blocks to spine-and-fingers type layouts. Buildings with open-plan offices usually have a more compact layout.

**Figure 4.2.10**
Circulation system without corridors

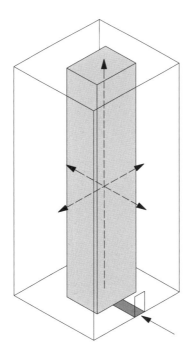

Figure 4.2.11
Determining the building
depth on the basis of different
circulation systems

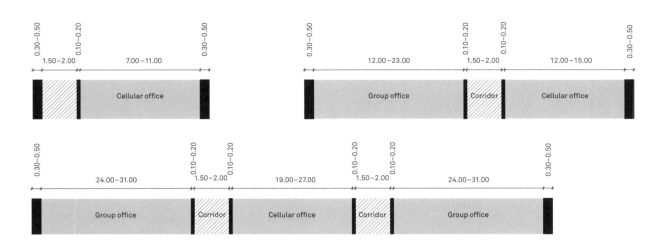

Table 4.2.1
Typical building depths for
different circulation systems

|  | Single-loaded corridor | Double-loaded corridor | Double corridors |
| --- | --- | --- | --- |
| **Cellular offices** | 7–11 m | 12–18 m | 19–26 m |
| **Group offices** | 7–14 m | 12–24 m | 22–32 m |
| **Cellular and group offices** |  | 12–21 m | 22–28 m |

Table 4.2.2
Minimum widths of circulation
routes and doors

Per ArbStättV and ASR A1.8

| Number of persons (occupant capacity) | Width (modular dimension in m) |
| --- | --- |
| ≤5 | 0.875 m |
| ≤20 | 1.00 m |
| ≤100 | 1.25 m |
| ≤250 | 1.75 m |
| ≤400 | 2.25 m |
| Minimum width of circulation route to a permanent workplace | 0.60 m |
| Minimum width of service routes | 0.50 m |

Table 4.2.3
Maximum distances to exits and/
or stairwells

Per ArbStättV

| | |
| --- | --- |
| In rooms, generally | 35 m |
| In rooms with fire risk, without sprinkler system | 25 m |
| In rooms with fire risk, with sprinkler system | 35 m |
| In rooms with exposure to toxic substances | 20 m |
| In rooms subject to explosion hazards | 20 m |
| In rooms exposed to potentially explosive materials | 10 m |

### 4.2.1.4 Construction and Technology

It makes sense to determine the building depth and spacing of the planning grid at an early stage because these have a major impact on how efficiently the available space is used. The building grid affects the facade, for instance, as well as the spacing of partitions, the interior design and furniture layout, and floor, ceiling, and fit-out elements. → Figure 4.2.12 Where parking garages are situated beneath buildings, the construction grid must be coordinated with the grid of the parking spaces.

As a rule, office workplaces require a number of technical installations. Each workstation needs a connection to the data network, which can be installed in the cavities beneath hollow or raised floors, in installation ducts, or in the ceiling plenum. Ventilation and air-conditioning installations must be carefully laid out to ensure good comfort levels in the workplace. Owing to the excellent thermal insulation provided by modern building envelopes and the high thermal loads generated in group and open-plan offices in particular, cooling can be a more critical task in these buildings than heating.

Supply lines can be installed in the cavity beneath raised floors, in the ceiling plenum, or within installation ducts mounted along the exterior walls at sill level. For this reason, the floor-to-floor height is an important design parameter in the early stages of design. → Figure 4.2.13

Table 4.2.4
Typical grid dimensions for office and administration buildings

| 0.5 × grid | 1 × grid | 1.5 × grid | 2 × grid | 3 × grid | 4 × grid | 5 × grid | 6 × grid | 7 × grid | ... |
|---|---|---|---|---|---|---|---|---|---|
| 0.60 m | 1.20 m | 1.80 m | 2.40 m | 3.60 m | 4.80 m | 6.00 m | 7.20 m | 8.40 m | ... |
| 0.625 m | 1.25 m | 1.875 m | 2.50 m | 3.75 m | 5.00 m | 6.25 m | 7.50 m | 8.75 m | ... |
| 0.675 m | 1.35 m | 2.025 m | 2.70 m | 4.05 m | 5.40 m | 6.75 m | 8.10 m | 9.45 m | ... |
| 0.75 m | 1.50 m | 2.25 m | 3.00 m | 4.50 m | 6.00 m | 7.50 m | 9.00 m | 10.50 m | ... |

Figure 4.2.12
Correlation between load-bearing structure and fit-out grid

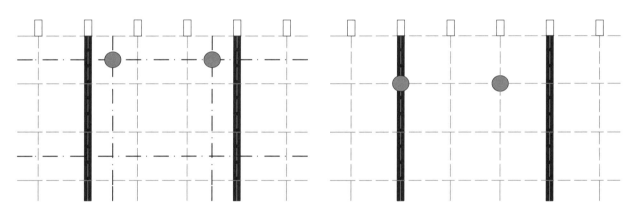

Figure 4.2.13
Dimensions of floor-to-floor heights for offices with different installation systems

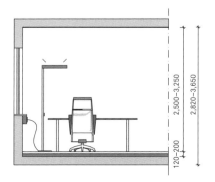
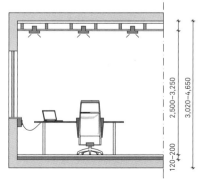
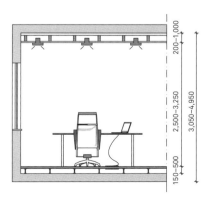

## 4.2.2  Program of Use

A single office and administration building may accommodate a wide range of different user groups and functions. Buildings might require public access and may also need to fulfill representational functions; they may provide office space for purely internal use, in a monofunctional way, or house diverse companies that offer additional functions, such as retail stores, restaurants, representational areas, and communication spaces.

In addition to the office workers themselves, it may be necessary to accommodate visitor groups with varying access rights, and who might possibly need to be spatially separated from one another. Especially in buildings for banks and insurance companies, therefore, the demarcation between areas with public access (and a customer-friendly atmosphere) and security-relevant parts of the building must be given careful attention.

### 4.2.2.1  General Office and Administration Buildings

For office and administration buildings, any additional functional areas have to be provided as a modular extension to the workplaces required by the program. ↗4.2.3.2 **Areas and Rooms/Office Spaces and Workplaces** Where buildings fulfill a representational function or regularly receive flows of visitors, public areas such as lobbies, customer service areas, conference rooms, and waiting areas should be located near the entrance area and be separated from workrooms used only by the employees. If the building is located in an area with inadequate infrastructure, it may be necessary to provide more generous areas for breaks and relaxation, as well as a cafeteria or other food service facility.

In many cases it is important to provide smaller, informal communication areas within the departments in addition to conventional conference spaces. ↗4.2.3.3 **Areas and Rooms/Meeting and Conference Rooms** Such areas can be integrated with a staff kitchen, designed as informal meeting places within a central zone, or accommodated by dedicated meeting rooms. By contrast, central seminar and conference rooms should have an anteroom serving as their own lobby and when possible, should be located in close proximity to the main lobby.

Cafeterias and cafés in office and administration buildings ↗**Chapter 4.7 Typologies/Lodging and Food Service** are often located on the ground floor since this offers the option of extending the seating area to the outside and there is easier access for external guests, who then do not have to cross any secured areas. Alternatively, outdoor seating areas for cafeterias or cafés can be located on roof terraces.

**Typical spaces needed in office and administration buildings:**
- Reception areas/customer service areas
- Office areas
- Centralized and/or decentralized meeting rooms
- Break rooms and communication areas
- Ancillary spaces
- Food service and recreational facilities (where applicable)
- Representational facilities (where applicable)

**Figure 4.2.14**
Schematic functional layout of office and administration buildings

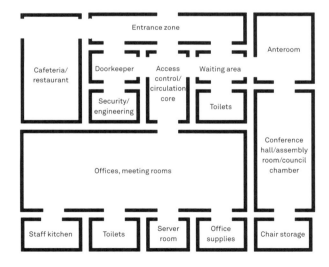

## 4.2.2.2 Public Administration

In public and semipublic administration buildings, such as town halls, tax offices, administrative district offices, governmental administration buildings, etc., security aspects play an important role in the design and often conflict with the objective of creating a transparent building that is welcoming to all citizens. This usually means that different zones must be provided, in which the degree of security increases commensurate to the size of the unit being administered (small municipalities, cities, states, federal governments, etc.).

Places of assembly, such as parliament halls, council chambers, and plenary rooms, require large amounts of space, which must be accommodated in addition to the general office and administration areas. The seating layout for representatives and government officials can be arranged in linear, elliptical, or circular fashion. It is possible to provide seating for visitors and the press by extending the geometric pattern of the main seating and providing separate guest access, or by providing independent seating boxes or additional tiers of seats. Visitor seating should also be separated from the parliament seating in terms of security provisions. ↗ Chapter 3.4.1 Spaces/Communication Spaces and Dining Rooms/Lecture, Seminar, and Conference Rooms

**Typical public administration buildings:**
- Parliaments/government administration buildings
- Ministries/central authorities
- Town halls/municipal offices
- Embassies/consulates
- Central/national banks
- Public safety buildings (↗ Chapter 4.10 Typologies/Public Safety)

**Rooms with specific functions required in town halls and parliament buildings:**
- Citizens' services
- Separate application points (where required)
- Offices and reception areas of politicians/delegates
- Meeting rooms
- Conference rooms/faction chambers/committee chambers
- Council chambers/plenary rooms/halls of parliament
- Waiting areas
- Exhibition areas
- Representational spaces

Figure 4.2.15
Typical schematic layout
of a town hall

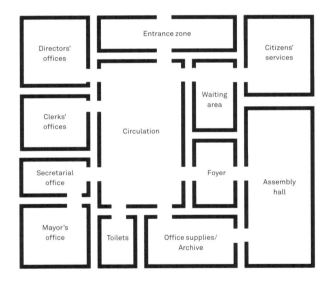

**Figure 4.2.16**
Examples of different seating
layouts in parliament buildings

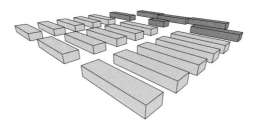

Straight rows of seats, e.g.,
State Parliament of Mecklenburg-
Vorpommern, Schwerin

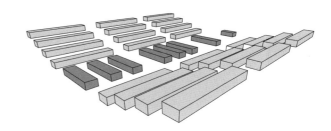

Opposite seated rows with central
zone, e.g., House of Lords, London

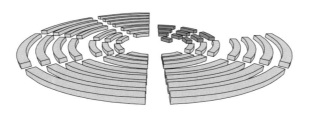

Circular plenary hall, e.g.,
German Reichstag, Berlin

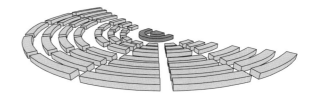

Horseshoe shape, e.g., US House of
Representatives, Washington, DC

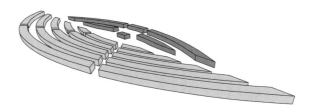

Arced shape, e.g., Bavarian State
Parliament, Munich

Representatives

Government, Stenographers, Lectern

### 4.2.2.3 Banks

The design of banks and savings and loan associations needs to combine representational and service functions with security requirements that can be very exacting. Whereas the facilities used by Internet banks are rather similar to classic office and administration buildings, the design of bank buildings and branches with customer traffic is largely influenced by their individual service concepts. Automated teller machines (ATMs) and self-service areas usually have direct access from the outside and may also be arranged as a zone preceding the banking hall. The banking hall, which usually has an open-plan layout and generally includes teller stations, is intended for personal customer service and may also offer access to separate meeting and consultation rooms. The teller stations can be designed in the form of individual counters with service points, as classic counters with a small back office area, or as a mixed form combining elements of both systems. In large banking halls it is important to provide clear signage to help customers find their required service. For more extensive consultations, a reception point, waiting areas, and small meeting rooms should be easily accessible from the main public area. In addition to the main area for day-to-day customer business, larger branches often have to provide separate facilities geared to the varied needs of different customer groups, distinguishing among private individuals and small, medium, and large business customers. While consultation rooms for private customers can be accessed directly from the banking hall, it may be more practical to arrange separate access for the areas for business customers.

Services such as safe storage in vault rooms and safe deposit boxes may also be provided; they must be shielded from view and are subject to special security arrangements. Safe deposit boxes are usually provided both in the publicly accessible area and in the secure vault area. For security reasons, staff access and cash deliveries should be arranged via a separate secondary entrance. Automated teller machines (ATMs) must be accessible from the back in order to facilitate filling and servicing.

**Rooms with specific functions in banks and savings and loan associations:**
- 24-hour self-service area/ATMs
- Banking hall
- Teller stations
- Consultation/meeting rooms
- Waiting areas
- Separate areas for private, business, and key account customers (where required)
- Offices/internal administration
- Vault rooms, safe deposit boxes
- Ancillary rooms
- Deliveries/secondary entrance

**Figure 4.2.17**
Schematic layout of functions in a bank

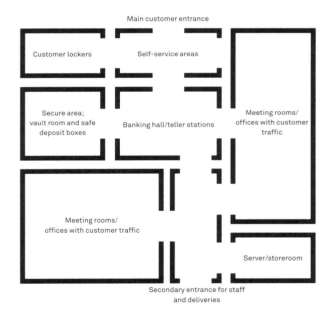

**Figure 4.2.18**
Schematic layout of self-service facility

ATM = Automated teller machine
BSP = Bank statement printer
SSB = Self-service banking machine

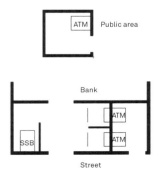
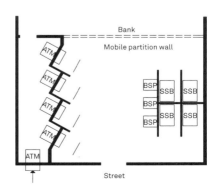

### 4.2.3  Areas and Rooms

**External circulation**  ↗ Chapter 3.1

**Entrance hall**  ↗ 209  ↗ Chapter 3.2.1

**Custodian's office**  ↗ 209

**Staircases, elevators**  ↗ 211  ↗ Chapter 3.2.4, Chapter 3.2.7

**Corridors, internal circulation**  ↗ 211  ↗ Chapter 3.2.2

**Workplaces**  ↗ 212  ↗ Chapter 3.3.1

**Customer contact areas**  ↗ 211

**Cellular offices**  ↗ 215

**Group offices**  ↗ 216

**Combi-offices**  ↗ 217

**Open-plan offices**  ↗ 219

**Nonterritorial workspaces**  ↗ 220

**Meeting rooms**  ↗ 222  ↗ Chapter 3.4.1

**Conference rooms**  ↗ 222  ↗ Chapter 3.4.1

**Staff kitchens**  ↗ 224  ↗ Chapter 3.6

**Cafeteria**  ↗ Chapter 4.7, Chapter 3.4.3

**Lunchrooms**  ↗ 224  ↗ Chapter 3.8.1

**Toilets**  ↗ 225  ↗ Chapter 3.5

**Storage/archive rooms**  ↗ 224  ↗ Chapter 3.7.2

**Server rooms**  ↗ 224  ↗ Chapter 3.9.8

**First aid rooms**  ↗ Chapter 3.8.3

**Janitor's closets**  ↗ 225  ↗ Chapter 3.8.4

**Mechanical equipment rooms**  ↗ Chapter 3.9

### 4.2.3.1 Entrance Areas

Entrance areas may be purely functional access points to a building or they may be designed with prestigious styling to fulfill a representational function, such as multistory entrance halls with central reception desks and generous circulation arrangements.

**Rooms with specific functions that may be required in the entrance area:**
- Entrance hall
- Lobby
- Reception
- Custodian's office
- Security installations
- Waiting area
- Customer contact area
- Sanitary facilities
- Internal mail room
- Storage rooms
- Mechanical equipment rooms

#### Building Access/Circulation

The access to nonpublic office buildings can be controlled using a security system or by security staff from a custodian's office. In public office buildings with customer traffic, the lobby/reception area with registration desk and information point forms the boundary for visitors between external and internal zones; this area should also provide a direct view of the parking lot and/or the outside area around the building. Depending on the security concept, the custodian or reception staff will control visitor traffic and show visitors how to reach their intended destination. → **Figure 4.2.19** It is also possible to combine the custodian's office with a mail room and/or parcel storage area.

#### Reception and Waiting Areas

The reception area may include a waiting area with sanitary facilities, and lead to the internal circulation system. Depending on the number and type of functional units, reception and waiting areas can be located centrally in the main lobby or decentralized, usually close to the circulation core. → **Figure 4.2.20**

In office buildings with retail premises on the ground floor ↗ **Chapter 4.3 Typologies/Logistics and Commerce** units on the upper floors have their own reception and waiting areas that are separate from the retail customer circulation areas. ↗ **Chapter 3.4.2 Spaces/Communication Spaces and Dining Rooms/Waiting and Seating Areas**

Reception areas on the ground floor should also provide barrier-free access to toilet facilities. In order to streamline the installation, the sanitary facilities should be located in the same position on all floors, preferably next to the stairwells. Waiting areas that include visitor toilets can also be positioned within view of the reception area. ↗ **Chapter 3.1.3 Spaces/External Circulation/Private Exterior Circulation**

**Figure 4.2.19**
Alternative concepts of open access

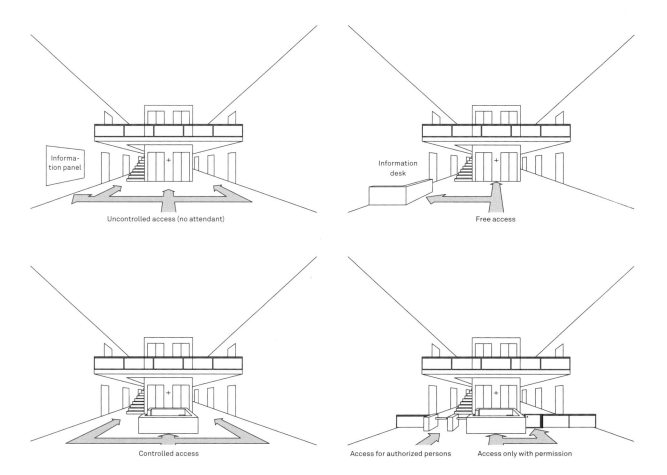

Uncontrolled access (no attendant)

Free access

Controlled access

Access for authorized persons    Access only with permission

**Figure 4.2.20**
Elements of a circulation core

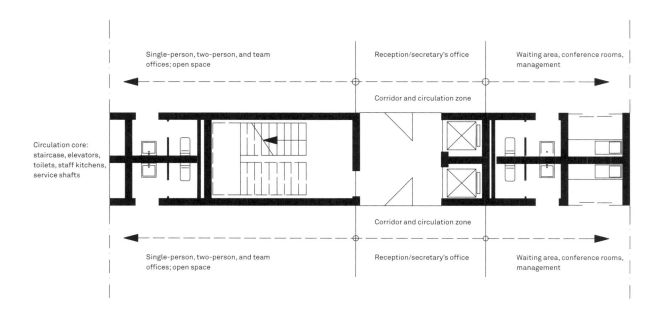

Single-person, two-person, and team offices; open space

Reception/secretary's office

Waiting area, conference rooms, management

Corridor and circulation zone

Circulation core: staircase, elevators, toilets, staff kitchens, service shafts

Corridor and circulation zone

Single-person, two-person, and team offices; open space

Reception/secretary's office

Waiting area, conference rooms, management

**Figure 4.2.21**
Example of a decentralized reception with waiting area

**Figure 4.2.22**
Example of a centralized reception in an entrance hall

**Customer Service/Citizens' Services**

Where customer service points with reception and counter are provided in the public entrance area, these points should be equipped like fully functional workplaces. Sufficient space for customer queues waiting to register, waiting areas with seating, and any technical equipment, such as waiting ticket dispensers and digital waiting indicators are just as necessary as access to sanitary facilities.

**Internal Circulation**

Access to the vertical circulation system should be easy to find and direct from the entrance zone with lobby and reception/custodian's office. The number of required elevators is determined by the applicable building code but it may be necessary to provide additional elevators where significant numbers of visitors are expected or to reduce waiting times. ↗ Chapter 3.2.7 Spaces/Internal Circulation/ Elevators and Conveying Systems A comprehensive guide system with appropriate signs should be provided to indicate where companies/departments can be found in the building. Depending on the location of the building it may be necessary to provide car parking in a parking garage beneath the building; if that is the case, appropriate access to the entrance area or internal circulation needs to be included in the design.

Figure 4.2.23
Examples of customer
service points

### 4.2.3.2   Office Spaces and Workplaces

The following basic forms of office layouts can be distinguished: cellular offices, group offices, open-plan offices, and combi-offices. In addition, it is possible to combine the above types of layouts in order to create more varied office landscapes. The design of workrooms for highly qualified employees in particular tries to ensure that these staff members are comfortable at their workplaces and can choose between different options to suit their preferences or type of activity.

When designing offices for a large number of employees careful consideration must be given to the balance between efficient utilization of the space available and individual employee requirements. → **Table 4.2.5** In addition to the space for the workplace itself, areas for furniture and circulation have to be provided in the offices.

**Figure 4.2.24**
Factors influencing the design of office workplaces

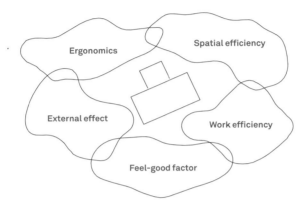

**Table 4.2.5 (left)**
Qualities of different types of office layout

**Table 4.2.6 (right)**
Approximate minimum space requirements

| Advantages and disadvantages of the different basic office layouts | | | |
|---|---|---|---|
|  | Flexibility | Communication | Quietness |
| Cellular office | – | – | ++ |
| Group office | + | ++ | + |
| Open-plan office | ++ | o | – |
| Combi-office | ++ | ++ | o |

| | |
|---|---|
| Workroom for one person | ≥8 m² |
| Workroom for two persons | ≥13 m² |
| Workroom for three persons | ≥18 m² |
| Each additional workplace | +≥5 m² |

**Table 4.2.7 (left)**
Clear minimum height of offices with different sizes

**Table 4.2.8 (right)**
User areas around desks

Per ArbStättV

| | |
|---|---|
| Floor area up to 50 m² | ≥2.50 m |
| Floor area up to 100 m² | ≥2.75 m |
| Floor area up to 2,000 m² | ≥3.00 m |
| Floor area over 2,000 m² | ≥3.25 m |
| Clear room height at workplaces and circulation areas under sloping ceilings | ≥2.50 m |

| | |
|---|---|
| Unobstructed movement area | 1.50 m² |
| Minimum depth of personally assigned workplace | 1.00 m |
| Minimum depth of other workplaces | 0.80 m |
| Minimum depth of visitor/meeting places | 0.80 m |

Table 4.2.9
Depth and height of rooms of
different basic office layout types

| Office layout type | | Persons | Room depth | Room height |
|---|---|---|---|---|
| Cellular office | | 1 to 4 | 5 to 7 m | ≥ 2.50 m |
| Group office | | 5 to 25 | 5 to 10 m | ≥ 2.50 to ≥ 3.00 m |
| | Small groups | 5 to 8 | 5 to 7.5 m | ≥ 2.50 to ≥ 2.75 m |
| | Large groups | 8 to 25 | 7.5 to 10 m | ≥ 2.75 to ≥ 3.00 m |
| Combi-office (cellular and group offices) | | 1 to 25 | 5 to 10 m | ≥ 2.75 to ≥ 3.00 m |
| Open-plan office | | 25 to > 100 | 15 to 30 m | ≥ 3.00 to ≥ 3.25 m |

Table 4.2.10
Comparison of the properties
of different office types

| Properties | Cellular offices | Group offices | Combi-offices | Open-plan offices |
|---|---|---|---|---|
| Number of workplaces | 1–4 persons | Usually 8–12, small groups 5–8, max. 20–25 persons | Flexible design, see cellular/group offices | From 25 persons, often more than 100 persons |
| Room depths | Approx. 5.00 to 6.00 m | Approx. 5.00 to 10.00 m | See cellular/group offices + approx. 5.00 to 7.00 m for the combi-zone | Varies, usually approx. 15.00 to 30.00 m |
| Room widths | Approx. 2.60 to 5.00 m | Approx. 7.00 to 30.00 m | Flexible design, see cellular/group offices | Varies, usually up to approx. 40.00 m |
| Used for | Administration and office workers, service areas with external customers, leading management staff, managing director | Team-oriented and net-worked working in small groups | Suitable for a range of different staff structures owing to the varied spaces | Administration and office workers, call centers, IT services |
| Working atmosphere | Quiet, individual, uncom-municative | Team-oriented, communi-cative, can be noisy | Team work and meetings in the combi-zone; concentrated work in cellular offices is also possible due to the com-bination cellular, group, and open-plan offices | Good communication, but usually acoustic and visual disruptions, imper-sonal work environment |
| Personal choice of workplace design | Individual design is possible | Restricted to the respec-tive desk space | See cellular/group offices | Restricted to the respec-tive desk space |
| Services installation | Possible via partitions or wall-mounted ducts | Via floor ducts, raised floors and floor boxes, or suspended ceilings | Via floor ducts, raised floors and floor boxes, or suspended ceilings | Congested installation in suspended ceilings and raised floors |
| Lighting | Natural/artificial, can be individually controlled | Natural/artificial, can be controlled by the group | Natural near the facade/artificial at greater dis-tance from the facade | Only artificial possible |
| Ventilation | Natural/artificial, can be individually controlled | Natural (small groups), otherwise artificial, can be controlled by the group | Natural possible near the facade/artificial at greater distance from the facade | Only artificial possible |

**Figure 4.2.25**
Minimum space requirement
for workplaces

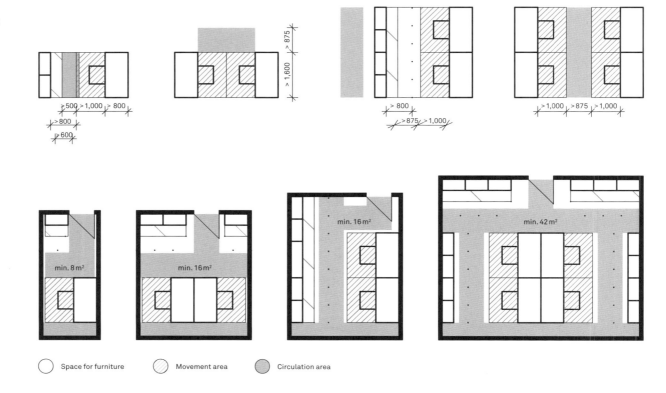

◯ Space for furniture       ▨ Movement area       ⬤ Circulation area

**Figure 4.2.26 (left)**
Space-saving desk layout
concepts

**Figure 4.2.27 (right)**
Examples of distances and
heights at workplaces

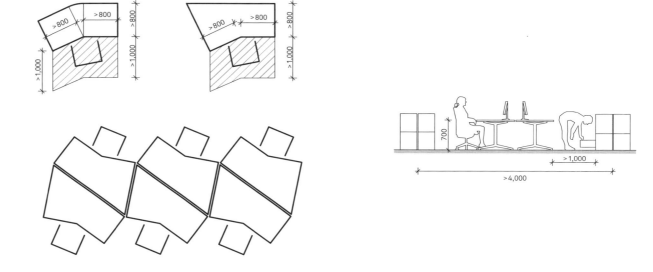

**Figure 4.2.28**
Differences in the use-related
accommodation of employees

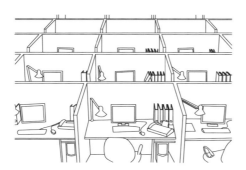

## Cellular Offices

Cellular offices are individual, separate office rooms arranged along circulation corridors. Depending on the spacing of the fit-out grid and the number of workplaces, cellular offices measure between 2.60 and 5.00 m in width and between 5.00 and 6.00 m in depth.

Most cellular offices are used by one, two, or a maximum of four persons. Office rooms for one or two persons require a relatively large amount of space per person. In terms of efficient use of space, four-person offices are comparable to small group offices. In practice, cellular offices are often found in combination with other types of office layout. The workplaces in cellular offices are usually allocated to permanent members of staff on a long-term basis. Exceptions are cellular offices that are made available to external consultants or auditors.

Since cellular offices are separated from one another, it may be an advantage – in the case of highly complex, strongly networked processes – to link individual offices by interconnecting doors. However, this arrangement also requires additional circulation areas within the cellular offices. In office buildings where there are cellular office rooms only, meeting rooms and communication areas, such as a staff kitchen, become rather more important for the purpose of maintaining good communication.

Figure 4.2.29
Schematic design of cellular offices

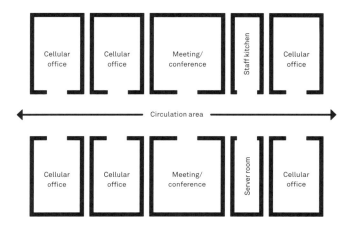

Figure 4.2.30
Example of cellular offices

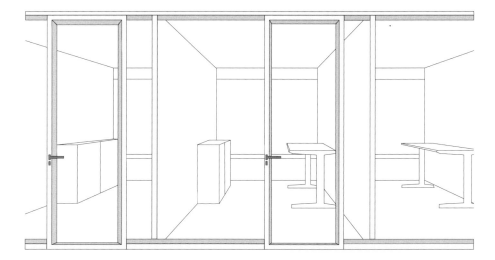

### Group offices

Group offices are separate rooms that are usually arranged along circulation corridors. Depending on the spacing of the fit-out grid and the number of workplaces, group offices measure between 7 and 30 m in width and between 5 and 10 m in depth. As with cellular offices, the individual rooms are usually accessed via a central corridor.

The provision of group offices is a reaction to the bad experiences made with open-plan offices; the idea is to combine the advantages of cellular offices with those of open-plan offices. By using a compact furniture layout it is possible to achieve good spatial efficiency. In larger group offices it may be necessary to create different zones by placing furniture or inserting half-high partition walls or planters. This not only creates visually distinct working areas but also introduces sound-absorbing surfaces that help to reduce noise levels. The problem of acoustic disruptions should also be addressed by choosing appropriate materials for the floor finish and suspended ceilings (such as fitted carpet and perforated acoustic ceiling panels). A frequent problem are telephone conversations, especially when several take place at the same time. This problem, which may impact on the concentration of colleagues, can be avoided by providing communication facilities in additional rooms, such as meeting and conference rooms or small cellular offices, where staff can make longer phone calls. Another option for dealing with the problem of acoustic interference is to install specially designed work cubicles with sound-absorbing separating walls. Group offices enhance communication and make it possible to allocate tasks in an uncomplicated manner. There is no need to leave the room for smaller meetings or for making arrangements with colleagues.

Where services are installed in floor boxes, the desk layout should be designed at an early stage because floor boxes should not be located in the area of the office chair casters or of the legroom beneath the desk.

Figure 4.2.31
Schematic design of group offices

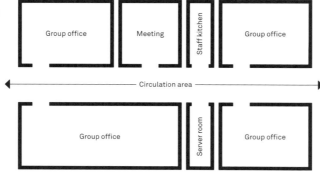

Figure 4.2.32
Example of "work bay" furnishing in group offices

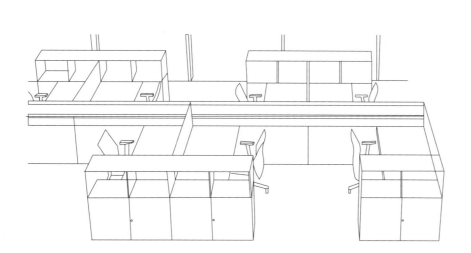

**Combi-offices**

Combi-offices are a combination of offices along the external walls of the building with a central, multifunctional corridor zone. The office rooms along the outside walls can be cellular, group, or also open-plan offices. The combi-zone tends to be between 5 and 7 m deep and also functions as the circulation area. It can be used in a number of ways to suit the respective requirements and, owing to its open structure, it retains its changeable character. Where work processes require individual spaces as well as flexibility, the combi-office concept may be the most suitable.

The idea is that the combination of cellular, group and open-plan offices with the combi-zone allows for team work and meetings as well as concentrated work in quiet spaces. The partition walls between the office rooms and the corridors should have large translucent or transparent sections in order to allow light to come in.

Where combi-zones are primarily used for additional communication areas or as staff facilities, the spatial efficiency is reduced compared to a combination of group and cellular offices with circulation corridors only; on the other hand it is possible to locate those offices that need to be close to an outside wall along the "expensive" external wall, which means that the shape of the building can be more compact. In general it can be said that a combi-zone significantly improves the value of the spatial situation and creates new vistas across the entire building.

**Rooms/functions that may be located in a combi-zone:**
- Meeting rooms
- Open communication areas
- Staff kitchen with lunch areas
- Communication center (fax, printer, etc.)
- Coatrooms
- Archive
- Library
- Temporary workplaces, telephone areas, "thinking retreat" cubicles, etc.
- Ancillary facilities such as server and storage rooms, and toilet units
- Circulation areas such as staircases, elevators, ducts

Figure 4.2.33
Schematic design of
combi-offices

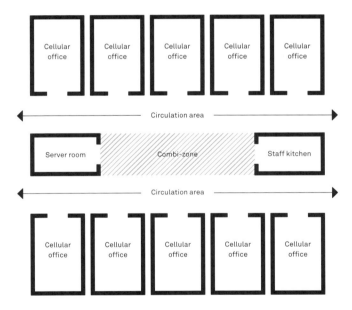

217

**Figure 4.2.34**
Example of a furniture layout
in a combi-zone

**Figure 4.2.35**
Examples of different types
of seating furniture for use in
combi-zones

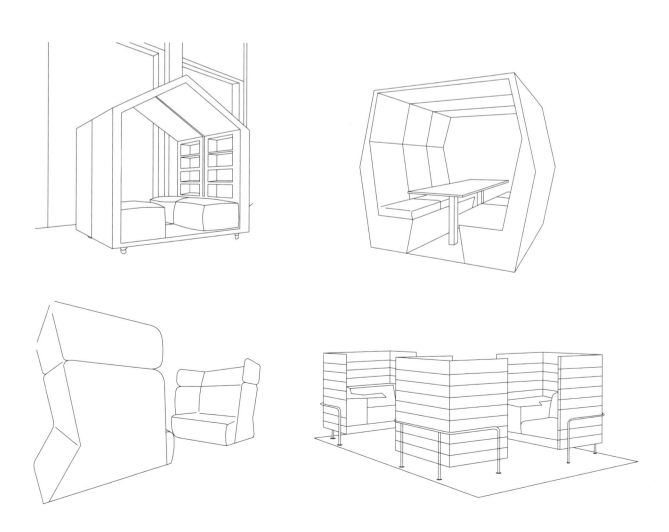

### Open-Plan Offices

As a rule, open-plan offices are offices without corridors, which can be significantly larger than 1,000 m² in floor area. Open-plan offices make very efficient use of the available floor area; however, the gross building volume is substantially larger compared to other types of office layout because of the raised floors and suspended ceilings, and the required room height. In order to provide at least a token relationship to the outside, no workplace should be located more than 20 m distant from a window. In view of the fact that mobile partition walls and furniture are used to create separate spaces, this type of office layout guarantees maximum reversibility and flexibility. It is relatively easy to re-group teams in different spaces, and there is no need to allocate workplaces to employees on a permanent basis.

Generally speaking, open-plan offices support good communication; however, the great number of employees also leads to acoustic and visual interference. The main challenge when designing this type of office is therefore to create comfortable working conditions, taking into account the likely noise levels as well as furniture layout options and services installations. Specially equipped retreat areas (thinking retreat cells) provide space for concentrated work or telephone conversations; the quality of the interior can be improved by creating varied zones and using variations of furniture.

Figure 4.2.36
Schematic design of
open-plan offices

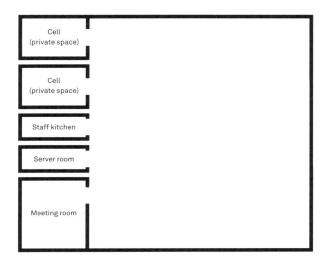

Figure 4.2.37
Example of furniture layout
in an open-plan office

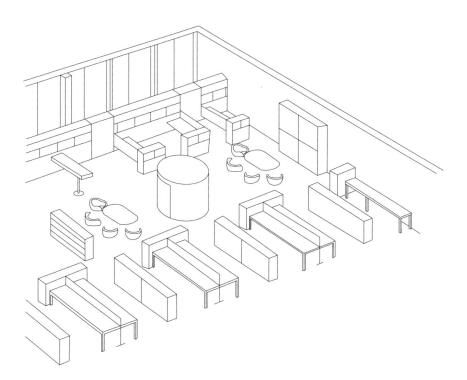

### Nonterritorial Work Environments

A new form of structuring offices is offered by nonterritorial work environments such as "net and nest," "flex office space," "business club," and "desk sharing," which do not provide permanent desks or fixed workplaces for office workers but instead offer a choice of different workplace situations for different tasks. There are many different concepts for nonterritorial work environments, but most of them are similar in their organizational structure. Generally speaking, all office layout types can be used for nonterritorial concepts but open-plan offices are best suited.

Nonterritorial office arrangements address the fact that in many companies some of the workplaces are not occupied because all of the employees are typically not working in the office at the same time as they may be away on business travel, customer visits, etc. The permanent provision of workplaces that are only used part of the time is very expensive in the long run, which is why "desk sharing" has meanwhile become established in some large companies.

Ideally, open office concepts are tailored to the individual requirements of each company employee. Participatory procedures enable employees or labor representatives to directly take part in the development process. The starting point is usually consideration of the various tasks to be performed by the employees; these may involve concentrated work phases with minimal disturbance or phases of open communication and teamwork, during which concepts are developed, results are discussed, and/or advanced training takes place. Other important aspects may entail customer involvement or representation of the work and development process to the public in order to present innovative corporate structures or attract qualified personnel.

**Figure 4.2.38**
Grouping of functions in nonterritorial work environments

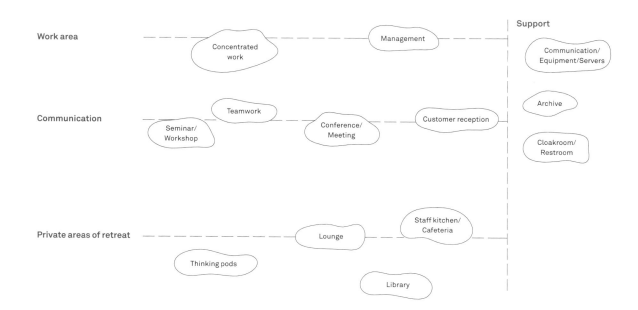

**Figure 4.2.39**
Schematic layout example of a nonterritorial work environment

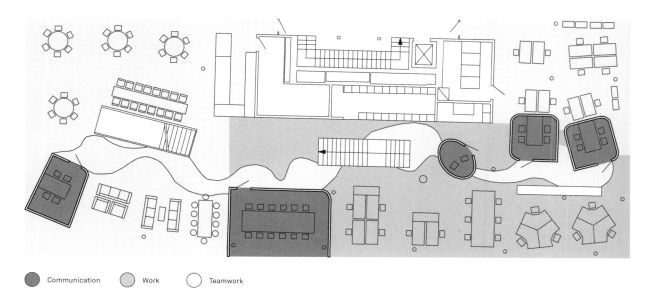

Figure 4.2.40
Examples of staff lounges in
nonterritorial work environments

### 4.2.3.3  Meeting and Conference Rooms

**Meeting Rooms**

Depending on the size of the office units, meeting rooms may be provided internally for shared use or they can be allocated to certain departments or even individual persons. Meeting rooms should be within easy reach, which is why there should be one on each floor of the building. The exact position and design of the room has to be determined in accordance with the intended function of the room. For example, meeting rooms used by management or the human resources department should always provide the necessary privacy.

Meeting rooms used by external visitors should be located so that they are easily accessible. Direct access from the reception area or secretariat ensures that external visitors do not have to walk through other departments on the way to the meeting room. Where there is a need to split team meetings into groups, an additional small meeting room should be available nearby or it should be possible – in larger meeting rooms – to use mobile partitions to create separate areas.

Meeting rooms for up to three persons do not require special technical equipment. In meeting rooms for up to twelve persons it may be necessary to provide not only tables and chairs but also a screen or monitor, and computer connections for networking. All rooms with screens and monitors should have a black-out facility. Rooms that can be divided need separate doors to the corridor. Furthermore, both parts of the room should be adequately provided with furniture and media equipment. ↗Chapter 3.4.1 Spaces/Communication Spaces and Dining Rooms/ Lecture, Seminar, and Conference Rooms

**Conference Rooms**

Conference rooms are similar to meeting rooms but are designed for much larger gatherings. Conference rooms are used for larger meetings, conferences, congresses, conventions, training sessions, symposia, or plenary meetings. The furniture layout can vary to suit the respective event. In view of the large number of people congregating, the location of such rooms in the building should be easily accessible. ↗Chapter 3.4.1 Spaces/Communication Spaces and Dining Rooms/Lecture, Seminar, and Conference Rooms

**Figure 4.2.41 (left)**
Example of furniture layout in a small meeting room

**Figure 4.2.42 (right)**
Example of (U-shaped) furniture layout in a large conference room

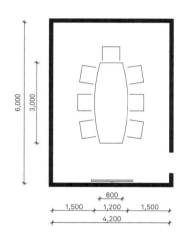

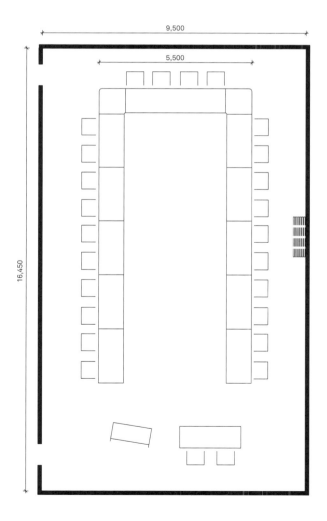

Figure 4.2.43
Examples of furniture layout in
partitionable meeting/conference
rooms

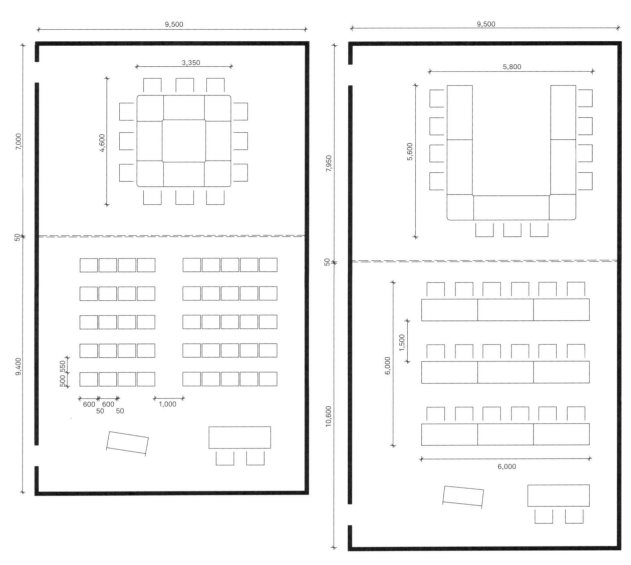

Figure 4.2.44
Meeting room with display
panel or screen

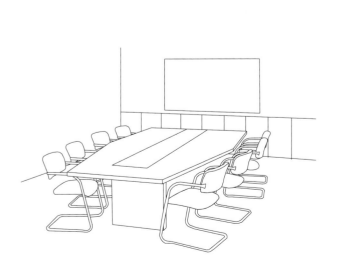

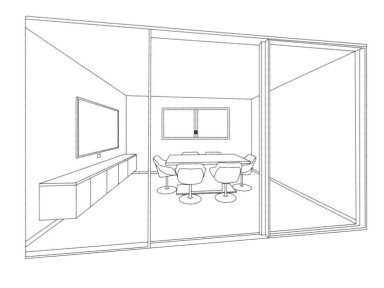

### 4.2.3.4  Ancillary Rooms

**Staff Kitchens**

Staff kitchens should be easily accessible to all members of staff. However, in order to simplify the services installations, these kitchens are usually located near circulation cores or toilet facilities. Smaller staff kitchens should, as a minimum requirement, include a sink, a refrigerator and worktops for kettles and coffee machines, as well as storage space for sufficient crockery and cutlery. Where there are no separate lunchrooms or staff facilities, staff kitchens should also include a seating area. ↗ **Chapter 3.6 Spaces/ Kitchens**

**Lunchrooms**

From a workforce of 10 people it is mandatory to provide staff/lunch areas. These areas don't necessarily have to be provided in the form of separate rooms. Usually there is sufficient space in the office workplaces to take a meal and spend break times. There are exceptions, however, such as densely furnished open-plan offices or semipublic office workplaces with customer traffic at government agencies and banks. In any case, attractively designed lunchrooms or areas certainly improve the working atmosphere in the office. ↗ **Chapter 3.8.1 Spaces/Ancillary and Staff Rooms/Lunchrooms**

**Storage, Server, and Archive Spaces**

There are different types of storage rooms: those used for the storage of consumables; and those for items that are rarely used. The size of storage rooms depends largely on the required function. Permanent storage spaces should be accommodated in basement floors. On the upper floors of buildings, rooms with poor daylighting (for example, next to circulation cores) can also be used for storage, especially for consumables. Chair and furniture storage facilities are required near conference and meeting areas. ↗ **Chapter 3.7 Spaces/Storage Spaces,** ↗ **Chapter 3.9.8 Spaces/Technical Equipment Rooms/Server Rooms and Data Centers**

**Figure 4.2.45**
Example of a staff kitchen in the combi-zone

**Toilets**

The number of toilets provided must be sufficient for the number of employees. Sanitary facilities can be positioned next to circulation cores where they are centrally located and can be reached directly from the respective entrance area, which means that they can also be used by external visitors. In large offices with many staff it is appropriate to provide separate toilet areas for staff. The provision of barrier-free sanitary facilities must be considered in all cases. ↗ Chapter 3.5 Spaces/Sanitary Facilities

**Janitor's Closets**

There should be a central janitor's closet on every floor. Where floors are subdivided into several functional units, each self-contained unit should have a janitor's closet or at least a water draw-off point with a slop sink. Janitor's closets can be positioned directly next to staff kitchens or circulation cores. ↗ Chapter 3.8.4 Spaces/Ancillary and Staff Rooms/Storerooms and Janitor's Closets

Table 4.2.11
Number of toilets to be provided in offices

Per ArbStättV

| Number of staff | Men | | Women |
| | Number of toilets | Number of urinals | Number of toilets |
| --- | --- | --- | --- |
| Up to 5 | 1 | 0 | 1 |
| Up to 10 | 1 | 1 | 1 |
| Up to 25 | 2 | 2 | 2 |
| Up to 50 | 3 | 3 | 3 |
| Up to 75 | 4 | 4 | 4 |
| Up to 100 | 5 | 5 | 5 |
| Up to 130 | 6 | 6 | 6 |
| Up to 160 | 7 | 7 | 7 |
| Up to 190 | 8 | 8 | 8 |
| Up to 220 | 9 | 9 | 9 |
| Up to 250 | 10 | 10 | 10 |

**Le Bon Marché department store**, Paris, France, Louis-Auguste Boileau/Gustave Eiffel, 1876

**Galeries Lafayette**, Paris, France, Ferdinand Chanut/Jacques Grüber, 1912

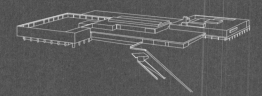

**Southdale Center**, Edina, Minnesota, USA, Victor Gruen, 1956

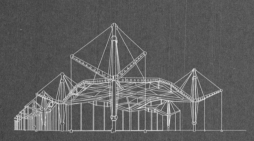

**The Spectrum Building**, Swindon, Great Britain, Norman Foster, 1982

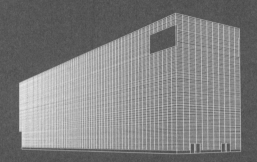

**High-bay warehouse**, Sedus Stoll AG, Waldshut, Germany, Sauerbruch Hutton, 2003

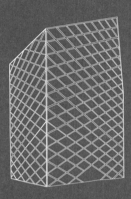

**Prada Aoyama**, Tokyo, Japan, Herzog & de Meuron, 2003

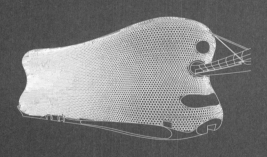

**Selfridges department store**, Birmingham, Great Britain, Future Systems, 2003

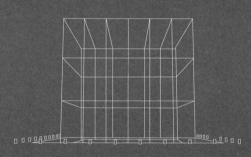

**Apple Store**, New York, Bohlin Cywinski Jackson, 2006

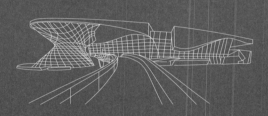

**BMW Welt**, Munich, Germany, Coop Himmelb(l)au, 2007

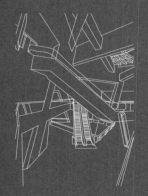

**Westside Shopping and Leisure Center**, Bern, Switzerland, Studio Daniel Libeskind, 2008

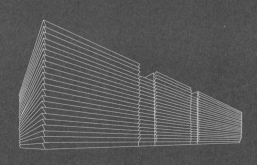

**Logistics Center**, Ernsting's family, Coesfeld-Lette, Germany, Nabo Gaß/Wortmann Architects, 2011

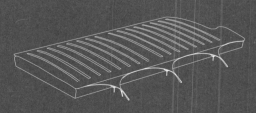

**G. Park Blue Planet**, Chatterley Valley, Great Britain, Chetwoods Architects, 2013

# 4 Typologies
## 4.3 Logistics and Commerce

Bettina Sigmund

**4.3.1 Building Concept** ↗228

4.3.1.1 Planning Parameters ↗228
4.3.1.2 Building Forms ↗230
4.3.1.3 Circulation Systems ↗233
4.3.1.4 Construction and Technology ↗238

**4.3.2 Program of Use** ↗239

4.3.2.1 Logistics Buildings ↗239
4.3.2.2 Sales Premises ↗244
4.3.2.3 Trade Fairs ↗250

**4.3.3 Areas and Rooms** ↗251

4.3.3.1 Entrance Areas ↗252
4.3.3.2 Logistics Spaces ↗255
4.3.3.3 Sales Rooms ↗259
4.3.3.4 Ancillary Spaces ↗266

# 4.3 Logistics and Commerce

## 4.3.1 Building Concept

### 4.3.1.1 Planning Parameters

Logistics buildings are used for allocating goods to supply production facilities, as an intermediate stop in the transport of merchandise to and from production, commerce, and end customers, and also for the return of goods. Buildings for trade and commerce cover a wide spectrum of typologies and dimensions, ranging from individual store concepts to huge shopping malls.

In order to design logistics and commerce buildings, it is necessary to consider the buildings throughout the process chain, from production ↗ **Chapter 4.4 Typologies/ Industry and Production** to the sale of goods. Logistics buildings in particular are characterized by complex, need-adapted transport processes and dependencies. They may be integrated in industrial and commercial complexes or constitute standalone buildings. Key considerations for design are the optimization of material flows and the efficient use of space. Buildings for commerce must allow flexible use and be laid out clearly, and they may also convey a public image.

**Typical planning parameters:**
- Place, context, and site geometry
- Existing infrastructure
- Options for delivery access
- Building law restrictions, such as emissions control
- Spatial program and needs
- Requirements of the logistics chain and material flow
- Workplace requirements
- Type of goods
- Necessary secondary functions
- Needs and expectations of customers
- Layout type and building form
- Budget and deadlines

**Design of Logistics Buildings**
Logistics facilities are characterized by optimum use of the available floor space and building volume. A modular concept without space-consuming structures integrates all module sizes from the product to the building grid; this is most often based on standardized unit sizes such as those of Euro pallets. An important value is the storage volume, which can be optimized with an appropriate column grid and shelving layout. Characteristics that are important for investors are flexible use, extendability, layout for third-

party use, the possibility of subdividing the space for multiple users, and standardized equipment and fixtures. Properties such as high-bay warehouses, refrigerated storage warehouses, and depots for hazardous goods are usually designed specifically for the respective function. Given that such buildings are typically used for about twenty to thirty years, it is important that the design allows for easy changes to the interior fit-out and building services.

All functions within logistics buildings are arranged with the aim of optimizing the flow of goods. This has priority over the circulation of persons. For the planning of goods flows, it is important to avoid returns or crossovers; likewise, all routes for goods and persons should be as short as possible. → **Figure. 4.3.1**

**Standard requirements for logistics buildings:**
- Single-story building
- Building height 10–12 m (beneath beams)
- Sprinkler system/ESFR sprinklers
- Heating
- Office space 5–10% of total area
- Building size min. 10,000 m² (divisible where necessary)
- Floor load-bearing capacity > 5,000 kg/m²
- Spread foundations preferable
- Concrete slab with no or few joints
- Floor levelness tolerances per DIN 18202
- Reinforced concrete columns, column spacing > 12 × 24 m
- Roof structure according to economic demands
- Slightly inclined roof
- Facade consisting of sandwich elements
- Maneuvering area > 35 m
- One gate per 1,000 m² floor area
- One ground-level vehicle door per section
- Two-sided access for cross-docking warehouses
- Site coverage 45–60%
- Controlled access to the site; site fully fenced
- Adequate parking for cars, trucks, and trailers
- Space for expansion
- Capable of being subdivided (multiple users)
- Usable by third parties

(Source: Jones Lang LaSalle, *Logistics Buildings Report 2013*)

Figure 4.3.1
Common layout options for the flow of goods in logistics buildings

One-sided access:
U-shaped flow of goods

Two-sided access:
Straight flow of goods

Two-sided access:
L-shaped flow of goods

### Design of Sales Premises

The design of sales premises must take into account the type of customers and their consumption behavior. The sales system distinguishes between open and closed sales. With open sales, the customer can choose one or more entrances and exits, and cash registers are distributed freely throughout the space. In closed sales systems, the customer is forced to pass the cash register at the exit. →**Figure 4.3.2** Specialty stores use a sales approach of serving the customer with specialized advice. In the open system, the customer decides whether specialist advice is needed. The preselection system offers product information on labels or on the goods to help the customer make a selection. In a self-service system, customers make their own selection, pick up the goods, and take them independently to the checkout counter.

The layout of the circulation integrates all function zones in the sales room and ancillary rooms. It is the basis for the design of customer routes, escape routes, goods transport routes, and furnishing, lighting, and floor plans. The customer route planning conforms to the walking habits of the consumer, and should help customers with orientation. The logic of the route layout should not require explanation. →**Figure 4.3.3** In order to ensure that customers pass through many merchandise zones, a circular route should be adopted. The furniture and shelving should be flexible and easy to change in a modular pattern in order to facilitate the presentation of goods.

**Figure 4.3.2**
Open and closed sales systems

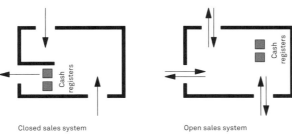

Closed sales system          Open sales system

**Figure 4.3.3**
Examples of route layout systems

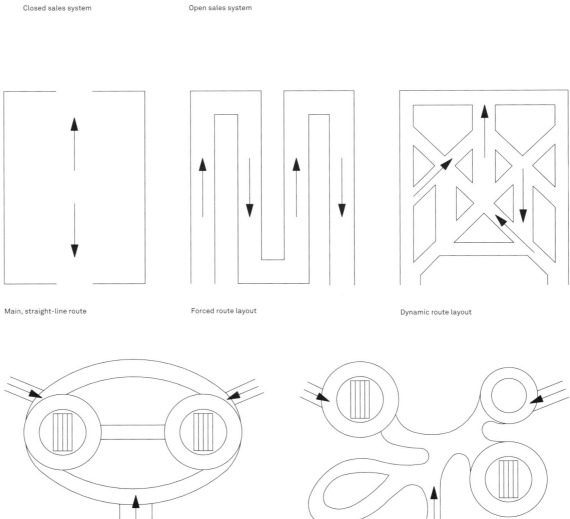

Main, straight-line route          Forced route layout          Dynamic route layout

Circular route layout          Open route layout

## 4.3.1.2 Building Forms

### Individual Premises

Stores: The terms *retail shop* and *store* are commonly used to refer to smaller retail establishments with floor areas of up to 500 m². Units with a sales area of 800 m² or more are classed as large-scale. Usually, these units are located on the first floor of multistory buildings or consist of units in shopping centers and malls. All units have a sales area, staff rooms, and storage areas. →**Figure. 4.3.4**

Single-story commercial buildings: Supermarkets are mostly built as single-story shed buildings. Standardized construction systems are typically used to benefit from lower building costs and short construction times. Large spans enable flexible use of the floor space. Simple timber or steel roof structures are often set atop these low-rise single-story buildings. →**Figure. 4.3.5**

Single-story buildings for logistics: Buildings used for logistics tend to be high, of a single-story construction and with large spans. Multistory buildings are rather rare owing to the complex processes, the structural load-bearing requirements, and fire protection regulations. Clear heights are at least 8 m, but are usually between 10 and 15 m. In addition, 2.50 m has to be added to allow for the roof construction and building services installations. The size of logistics buildings usually starts at 5,000 m²; larger units of 10,000 m² or more should allow for flexible subdivision. →**Figure. 4.3.6**

High-bay warehouses: These buildings are usually fully automated and are often more than 12 m high; they are classed as special industrial buildings. Structurally and logistically, it is possible to construct and use buildings with a height of up to 50 m. These buildings feature steel rack shelving which typically also serves as the structure that supports the facade and roof. This is referred to as silo-type construction. →**Figure. 4.3.7**

**Figure 4.3.4 (left)**
Volumetric forms of individual retail units

**Figure 4.3.5 (right)**
Volumetric forms of retail supermarkets

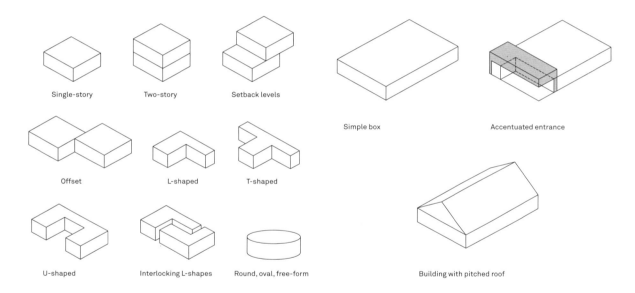

Single-story · Two-story · Setback levels

Offset · L-shaped · T-shaped

U-shaped · Interlocking L-shapes · Round, oval, free-form

Simple box · Accentuated entrance

Building with pitched roof

**Figure 4.3.6 (left)**
Common volumetric forms of logistics buildings

**Figure 4.3.7 (right)**
Volumetric form of a high-bay warehouse (silo-type construction)

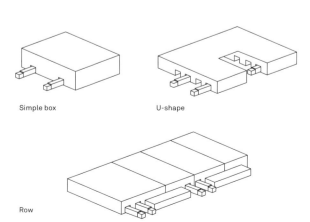

Simple box · U-shape

Row

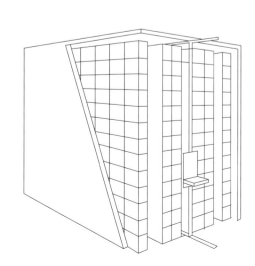

**Larger Sales Premises**

Multistory buildings: Multistory department stores are usually found in inner-city locations, often as freestanding buildings. With the help of generous glass roofs, it is possible to create impressive atria and stairwells. In these establishments, the merchandise is presented in open selling areas organized by departments and sections. It is also possible that part of the floor area is sublet to brand chains, which will design their space to their own brand requirements.

Arcades: Shopping arcades and indoor shopping streets are roofed-over street-like spaces lined with retail premises, with sales areas often located on two or more floors. Traditional arcades are public access links between urban block zones, and usually have several access points. Shopping streets should not be less than 5 m wide. Deliveries can be arranged from the rear or via an underground delivery system. → **Figure 4.3.8**

Shopping malls: Retail facilities and services are accommodated together in an air-conditioned complex. Such buildings or complexes are characteristically large volumes with a total floor area of at least 10,000 m². Entrances and the display windows of the shops are grouped around an atrium, the mall, which also serves as circulation area. Shopping malls can often be huge, sometimes with more than 100,000 m² of floor space, in which case they are referred to as mega-malls or supermalls. → **Figure 4.3.9**

Clusters: A cluster of sales premises forms a central supply facility. The diverse buildings integrate different functions similar to an historical urban structure and can be adapted to the scale of the neighborhood using small-scale formats.

Pedestrian zones: Owing to the large number of vehicles, city centers often separate traffic from pedestrian and shopping areas. For pedestrian zones to work well, they should provide a combination of functions in addition to retail premises, such as restaurants, service providers, cultural and leisure facilities, as well as housing and work-related property. Relevant characteristics for these zones are the quality of the urban street design, safety and cleanliness, and the development of a pedestrian infrastructure. → **Figure 4.3.10**

Logistics centers: A large building or complex of buildings used for logistics is referred to as a logistics center when it has a floor area of more than 10,000 m². These centers will combine turnover, storage, and administration functions for different companies, as well as bundled services such as assembly, labeling, and packaging.

Freight centers: Freight centers are interfaces for at least two transport modes. Goods are transferred from rail, water, or air transport to road-based transport. Likewise, these centers are used for the transfer of goods from long-distance to local means of transport, and for the bundling of deliveries. The centers consist of clusters of buildings of different logistics service providers.

Logistics zones: Logistics parks (privately operated, approximate size 100 ha) and pure logistics estates have become increasingly popular. The proximity of various industrial and commercial enterprises creates synergy effects. This arrangement can often be found near conurbations with very good transport links.

Figure 4.3.8
Volumetric forms of a shopping arcade and a multistory department store

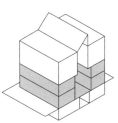

Arcade

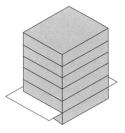

Multistory building: department store

**Figure 4.3.9**
Volumetric forms of
shopping centers

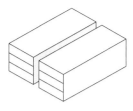

Linear buildings with shopping street

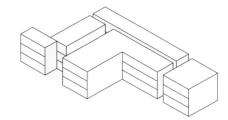

L-shaped layout with some areas wider than others

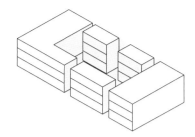

Circular arrangement around a center,
also in U-shape

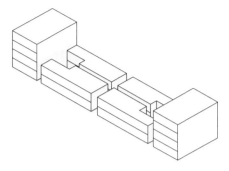

Anchors: popular stores act as "magnets" to
activate the flow of shoppers

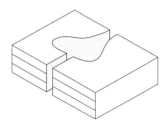

Both the atrium and the entire building are
free-form

**Figure 4.3.10**
Volumetric forms of cluster
developments and a pedestrian
zone

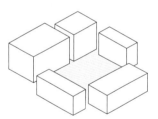

Arrangement of freestanding buildings

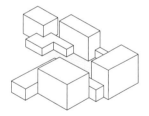

Arrangement of buildings with link elements

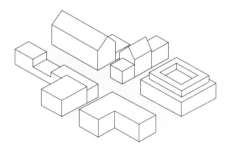

Urban development with pedestrian zone

## 4.3.1.3  Circulation Systems

### Access to Logistics Buildings

The means and form of access to logistics buildings depends on the type of freight transport network: road as well as water, rail, and air. Goods transport generates increased traffic volumes with the corresponding noise and pollution emissions, particularly in the case of 24-hour operation. The plots should be rectangular and offer the option to extend. Road surfaces should be constructed with sufficient load-bearing capacity for heavy loads. Access and exit points to and from the site should be separate; the direction of travel should be counterclockwise. A depth of at least 35 m is required for maneuvering trucks. At dead-end roads it is necessary to provide a turning area or loops for turning; however, a better solution is to provide a continuous route around the building. Depending on the goods stored, security devices should be provided, including items such as fences, access control, entrance and exit barriers, a porter's lodge, and external lighting. Parking lots for staff and visitors are frequently located outside the fenced-off area. → **Figure 4.3.11**

The difference in level between road surface and the floor of the building depends on the transport vehicle, and is usually around 1.20 m in order for the truck load delivery area to be level with the floor. ↗ **Chapter 3.1.1 Spaces/External Circulation/Public Access**

In the case of single-sided delivery, the maximum depth and width of the building is determined by the size of the fire compartments. A number of fire compartments can be combined to form larger complexes, and it is also possible to construct an identical building with reverse layout along the closed rear wall. About 70 percent of the building floor area can be used as storage area. In cross-docking buildings, the goods "flow" through the building and are re-picked/packaged/labeled as orders come in. The incoming and outgoing processes for goods are combined to allow for the docking of as many trucks as possible. Owing to the increased number of trucks, there is a greater need for external parking places and swap trailers. There is a special form of building for courier, express, and parcel services (CEP), in which automated conveyor technology yields a reduction in the building depth. → **Figure 4.3.12**

Within logistics buildings, all routes must be at least 1.25 m wide and secondary corridors for manual operation only must be at least 0.75 m wide. All other corridor widths have to be laid out to suit the dimensions of the vehicles used. → **Figure 4.3.13** The length of the racks depends on the maximum length of the escape routes. Rescue paths have to be provided at both ends of the rows of shelving.

Figure 4.3.11
Circulation areas for logistics buildings

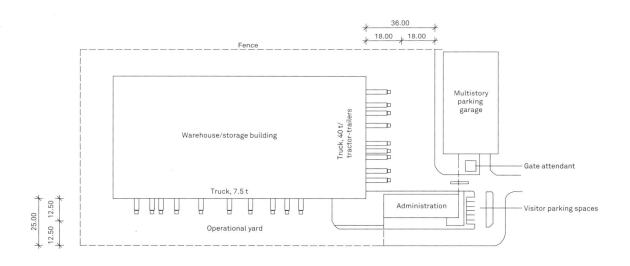

Figure 4.3.12
Different access options

Source: Juhr 2010

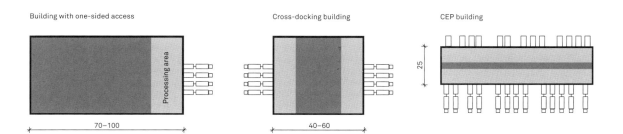

233

**Figure 4.3.13**
Circulation routes and safety distances for transport within buildings

Source: Illustration based on Groenmeyer, Logma Logistics, and Jungheinrich AG

Pedestrian traffic

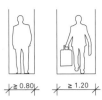

Shared pedestrian and vehicular traffic

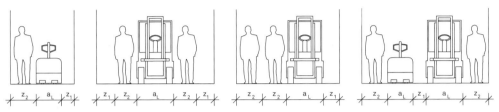

Additional width for pedestrian traffic in the case of high speeds and large transport loads

Avoid central drive lane if possible; it is better to separate pedestrian and vehicular traffic

Vehicular traffic

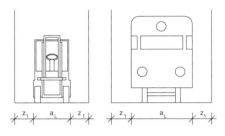

Special form: narrow aisle

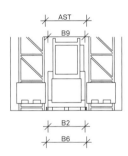

B2    Load axle width, vehicle width

B6    Clear dimension between the guide rails

B9    Width of cabin/swiveling reach frame

AST   Clear dimension of working corridor width; permitted deviation of working corridor from the center line is +/− 5 mm over 20 m

Calculation

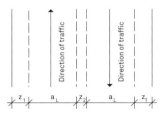

Aisle width $B = 2\,a_L + 2\,z_1 + z_2$

$a_L$ = Width of transport vehicle

$z_1$ = Additional width
        0.5 m for vehicular traffic ($\leq$ 20 km)
        0.4 m for vehicular traffic ($>$ 20 km)

$z_2$ = Additional width
        0.75 m for pedestrian and vehicular traffic

**Access to Sales Premises**

Customers' access to sales premises needs to have a certain style and should be located at the front; usually there is also an access point for staff and deliveries at the rear – in the case of larger premises, this can be via a delivery yard. For the delivery of goods it is necessary to provide adequate vehicular access and loading space, together with unrestricted handling space. Where this is not possible within the site boundaries of the property, loading bays may be provided on the public road with appropriate time limitations. As a general rule, parking lots for deliveries, staff, and customers have to be provided; the number depends not only on the relevant regulations, but also on the maximum number of customers expected. → **Table 4.3.3** For large premises it is possible to arrange customer access via a parking garage or atria integrated into the building.

The width of corridors is determined by the size of the sales area and the number of customers expected. → **Figure 4.3.16** Main paths are the primary circulation routes for customers and lead to the exits and emergency exits. Secondary paths are connecting routes, for example, between rows of shelving. Rule of thumb: the height of the goods display units determines the width of the corridor. Therefore, if a shelf is 1.60 m high, the corridor should be at least 1.60 m wide.

In multistoried sales premises, special regulations with regard to fire compartments and escape routes must be complied with. Escalators are not permitted for use as mandatory stairs. It makes sense to provide one escalator for each 1,000 m² of sales area. In order to slow down the walking speed when going down, normal staircases may be used. Moving walkways are employed in self-service supermarkets where shopping carts are used. Elevators are an important component of barrier-free circulation; they should be visible from the main route and the stairwell, and should be located in the axis of the staircase.

Figure 4.3.14
Atria as internal circulation
and rest area

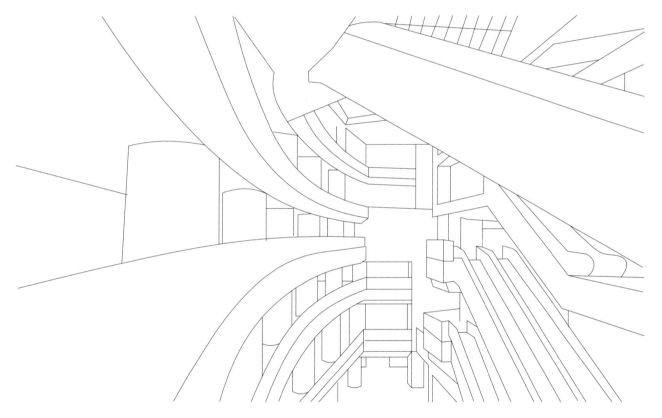

**Table 4.3.1**
Circulation parameters in sales premises

Source: Ordinance governing sales premises (VkVO)

| Internal circulation | Sales area ≤ 500 m² | Sales area > 500 m² |
|---|---|---|
| Mandatory exits | Sales area ≤ 100 m² = 1 exit<br>Sales area > 100 m² = 2 exits | 2 exits |
| Door widths | 1.00 m | ≥ 2.00 m<br>Calculation: 0.3 m per 100 m² |
| **Length of rescue path** | **Sales room** | |
| Main routes within the sales area | ≤ 10 m | |
| Sales room | ≤ 25 m | |
| Miscellaneous rooms | ≤ 35 m | |
| Corridor, shopping mall with smoke and heat exhaust | Extra ≤ 35 m | |
| **Size of fire compartments (per floor)** | **Without sprinkler** | **With sprinkler** |
| Ground floor | ≤ 3,000 m² | ≤ 10,000 m² |
| Other floors, multistory | ≤ 1,500 m² (max. 3 floors and total ≤ 3,000 m²) | ≤ 5,000 m² |

**Table 4.3.2**
Circulation parameters for logistics buildings

Sources: Industrial Buildings Directive (IndBauRL), Workplace Directive (ASR)

| Internal circulation | |
|---|---|
| Mandatory exits | ≥ 200 m² area = min. 2 exits |
| Width of corridors | Main routes ≥ 2.00 m<br>The layout of circulation routes to be calculated to DIN 18225 and Industrial Buildings Directive (IndBauRL) |
| **Length of rescue path** | |
| Main routes within the building | ≤ 15 m |
| Buildings up to 5 m high | ≤ 35 m/with sprinkler: ≤ 50 m |
| Buildings up to 10 m high | ≤ 50 m/with sprinkler: ≤ 70 m |
| Escape passage through shelf unit | Width of escape route through a shelf unit depends on the number of persons:<br>up to 20 persons: ≥ 1.0 m wide, height ≥ 2.0 m<br><br>• Length of rescue route depends on the height, fire protection measures, and the fire hazard of the stored goods<br>• Distance measured in a straight line, actual walking distance max. 1.5 times the straight-line distance |
| **Size of fire compartments** | **Fire compartment with automatic fire extinguishing system**<br><br>≤ 10,000 m² per Industrial Buildings Directive (IndBauRL) | **Firefighting compartment with automatic fire extinguishing system**<br><br>≥ 10,000 m² possible in the case of an individual fire protection concept per DIN 18230-1 |

**Table 4.3.3**
Guidelines for car and truck parking spaces

Source: Lehder 1998

| Sales premises | Number of car parking spaces | Proportion for shoppers |
|---|---|---|
| Stores, business premises | 1 space for every 40 m² of usable sales area, at least 2 spaces per store | 75% |
| Stores and business premises with low customer traffic | 1 space for every 50 m² of usable sales area | 75% |
| Supermarkets | 1 space for every 10–20 m² of usable sales area | 90% |
| Shopping centers and large-scale retail stores with a usable sales area of > 1,000 m² outside central urban areas | 1 space for every 15 m² of usable sales area | 90% |
| **Logistics properties** | **Number of car parking spaces** | **Number of truck parking spaces** |
| Logistics buildings | 1 space for every 300 m² of usable area | 1 space for every 400 m² of usable area |

**Figure 4.3.15**
Schematic illustration of access options to shops, department stores, and shopping centers

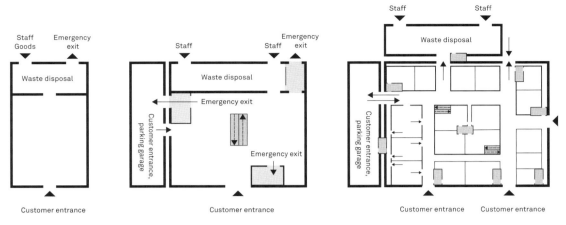

**External access for simple retail areas**

**Access for multistory sales premises/ department stores:**
An additional point of access for customers is possible via a parking garage. Emergency exits and egress stairways from the upper sales floors must be reachable from every location within a maximum distance of 25 m.

**Access for shopping centers/malls:**
Supply and disposal often are handled via a separate delivery yard.There is a variety of customer entrances. Additional rear access to the retail areas for deliveries and personnel is common. Sales rooms generally require two emergency exits. Escape routes within the retail area must not exceed a maximum of 25 m, plus 35 m escape route in mall areas with SHEVS or sales premises with a sprinkler system.

**Figure 4.3.16**
Circulation widths for primary and secondary paths in sales premises

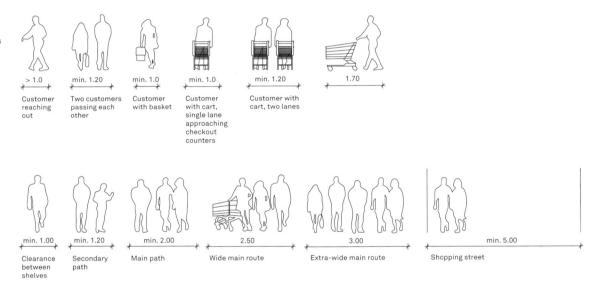

**Figure 4.3.17**
Width of staircases depending on the size of retail premises and number of customers

↗ Chapter 3.2.4 Spaces/Internal Circulation/Stairs
↗ Chapter 3.2.6 Spaces/Internal Circulation/Escalators and Moving Walkways
↗ Chapter 3.2.7 Spaces/Internal Circulation/Elevators and Conveying Systems

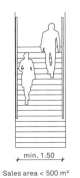

min. 1.50

Sales area < 500 m²

2.00

Sales area > 500 m²

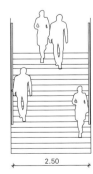

2.50

## 4.3.1.4 Construction and Technology

Logistics buildings consist of building envelopes without internal partition walls, except for those needed for staff and administration rooms. The structure consists of steel and reinforced concrete construction, depending on the operating equipment used in the building and the static and dynamic loads, such as those generated by integrated crane systems. A column grid of 24 × 24 m or 24 × 12 m, or one extended to 24 × 36 m, has proven to be expedient in allowing for the flexible use of standard logistics facilities. → **Figure 4.3.18,** ↗ Chapter 4.4.1 Typologies/Industry and Production/Building Concept

Small retail shops – particularly in existing buildings – may have unusually shaped layouts, while larger premises prefer rectangular and open areas. The design of circulation routes and goods displays should take the column grid pattern into account. A common building grid is based on a 10 × 10 m grid, which is further subdivided by a smaller-scale fit-out grid. → **Figure 4.3.19**

**Figure 4.3.18**
Standardized grid versions

Source: Groenmeyer 2012

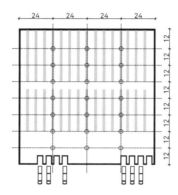 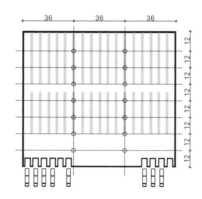 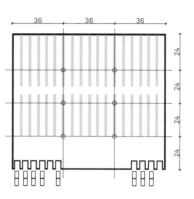

**Figure 4.3.19**
Building and furnishing grids

Rough allocation of circulation and functional areas for initial schematic design purposes. The specific dimensions are an outcome of the accessible area and the anticipated number of people to be accommodated.

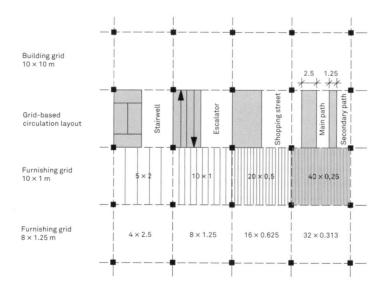

## 4.3.2 Program of Use

In logistics buildings as well as retail premises it is important to lay out the flow of material and people to maximum benefit. In logistics buildings it is usual for the flow of goods to have top priority, while members of staff have to adjust to the resulting layout. In sales premises, customers determine the layout, while storage requirements and staff movement are considered supportive functions.

### 4.3.2.1 Logistics Buildings

Logistics buildings are operated as owned or leased premises by industrial or trading companies, or by logistics service providers. Users may include industrial and production companies and retail, wholesale, and mail-order companies, as well as logistics service providers such as post, parcel, express delivery, and freight-forwarding (haulage) companies.

New forms of distribution require efficient provision of infrastructure linked with the logistics buildings to be designed. Given the increase in online and multichannel trade, a close-knit network of new types of logistics buildings is on the increase, including e-fulfillment centers along with CEP, sorting, and delivery centers. E-fulfillment centers also include provisions for e-commerce services such as online shopping, call center management, and the handling of returns. As part of what is known as omnichannel retail, online orders are dispatched directly from the regional retail branch stores.

In CEP transshipment hubs, shipments by the parcel and post service providers are handled at high speed. Such buildings are designed around a fully automated conveyor and sorting system, the so-called sorter. A room height of 8 m is sufficient. CEP centers require many gate access points for loading the many trucks and vans making inbound and outbound deliveries. A minimum area of 15 percent should be allowed for office and staff facilities.

**Figure 4.3.20**
Diagram of functions in a logistics building

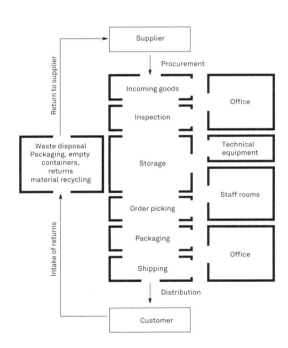

**Table 4.3.4**
Number of staff and external operatives depending on logistics model and type of building

\* The numbers represent average values which may deviate widely upward or downward, depending on the individual case.

\*\* External operatives include: truck drivers, security personnel, IT service providers, cleaning staff, facility maintenance staff, telecommunications staff, and canteen workers

Source: Ansiedlungshandbuch Logistik.NRW, 2012

| Building type | Number of staff per hectare* | Size of lot, average* | Internal staff, average* | External staff, average** |
|---|---|---|---|---|
| Fast-turnover buildings (cross-dock operations) | 40–70 | 1.5 hectares | 30–50 | 30–55, incl. 17–33 drivers |
| Storage buildings | 51–85 | 1 hectare | 30–50 | 21–35, incl. 10–17 drivers |
| Distribution buildings: regional distribution centers | 85–121 | 1 hectare | 50–70 | 35–51, incl. 23–33 drivers |
| Distribution buildings: European distribution centers | 70–105 | 6 hectares | 400–600 | 22–35, incl. 3–5 drivers |
| High-bay warehouses | 56–104 | 2 hectares | 80–150 | 33–57, incl. 17–33 drivers |
| Special storage | 52–137 | 1 hectare | 30–100 | 22–37, incl. 7–13 drivers |

Table 4.3.5
Requirements of different types
of logistics buildings

Based on Münchow 2012, source:
Logivest

| Building requirements by user type | | Required | | | | | |
|---|---|---|---|---|---|---|---|
| | | Standard new building | Auto-motive | Food-stuffs | Haulers | CEP | Mail order |
| Essential for location/site | Customer | | | x | | x | x |
| | Supplier | | x | x | | | |
| | Logistics network | | x | x | x | x | x |
| Clear height in warehouse | 8.0 m | | | | x | x | x |
| | 1.0–1.4 m | x | x | x | x | | |
| Gate access | Via ramp for 7.5 t truck | x | | x | x | x | x |
| | Via ramp for 40 t truck | x | x | x | x | x | x |
| | Ground level (lateral loading and unloading) | 1/5,000 m² | x | | | | |
| | Van ramp (utility and cargo vans) | | | | | x | |
| | 1 gate/1,000 m² | x | x | x | | | |
| | 2 to 10 gates/1,000 m² | | | | x | x | |
| Maneuvering area | For 7.5 t truck (approx. 20/25 m shunting distance) | | x | x | x | x | x |
| | For 40 t truck (approx. 35 m shunting distance) | x | x | x | x | x | x |
| | For vans and delivery vehicles | | | | | x | |
| Parking on paved surfaces | Trucks | x | x | x | x | x | x |
| | Swap trailers | x | x | x | x | x | x |
| | Cars | x | x | x | x | | x |
| Use | Storage | x | x | x | x | | x |
| | Order picking | x | x | x | | | x |
| | Production, assembly, service activities | x | x | x | | | x |
| | Fast turnover | | | | x | x | |
| Special requirements | Refrigerated building | | | x | for specialists | for specialists | in special cases |
| | Deep-freeze building | | | x | for specialists | for specialists | in special cases |
| | Hazardous goods storage | | | | for specialists | for specialists | |
| Level for order picking or storage | On same level | x | x | | x | x | x |
| | Possible on different levels | | | VAS only | | | x |
| Office and staff facilities | > 5% of storage floor area | | x | | | | |
| | 5% of storage floor area | | | | | | |
| | 5%–10% of storage floor area | x | | x | | | x |
| | 10%–15% of storage floor area | | | | x | x | |
| Special criteria | Railway siding | | useful | | useful | | in special cases |
| | Inland waterway transport | | useful | | useful | | |
| | Air freight | | useful | | useful | useful | |
| | Hazardous goods storage | | | | useful | useful | |

### Logistics Processes

Goods/articles within logistics buildings are conveyed through different zones: when the goods arrive they are identified and recorded, a quality check is carried out, and they are assigned to a storage location. The storage zone refers to the actual storage area. The operator zone is the area required for reaching the shelves manually or with a transport system. Except in special cases, order picking cannot be carried out using an automated process since articles may vary in shape, weight, and size. It is important for the order-picking operative that the workplace is clearly organized, that it is ergonomically designed, and that articles are easy to reach quickly. At the goods dispatch point, the goods are placed ready for dispatch and packaged, and the dispatch is recorded. → **Figure 4.3.21**

**Figure 4.3.21**
Schematic layout of zones and functional areas

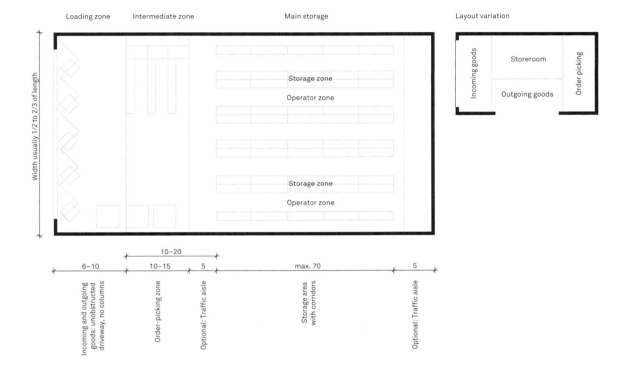

### Storage and Order Picking

When designing logistics facilities, various zones need to be taken into account. → **Figure 4.3.22** Their size and structure, however, are determined mainly by the type of goods. Piece goods are bundled together into larger units, which are the basis for selecting the storage and shelving systems, means of transport, and the control system. A basic distinction is made between block, linear, and shelf storage. A storage management system, which is usually automated, assigns the storage location for the item upon arrival. Order picking involves sorting and putting together the goods that make up a customer order. In the "goods to man" system, the product is conveyed to the order-picking operative via automated conveyor; in the "man to goods" system, the operative retrieves the goods from the storage facility and transports them to the packing station. ↗ **Chapter 3.7.2 Spaces/Storage Spaces/Types of Storage**

Figure 4.3.22
Layout of the different zones

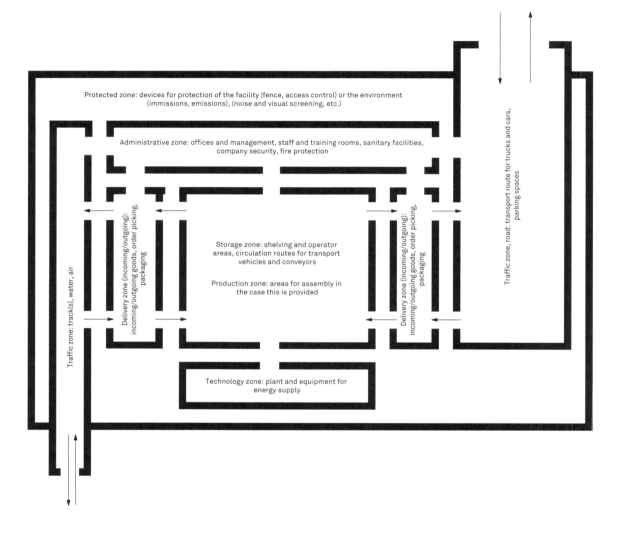

Protected zone: devices for protection of the facility (fence, access control) or the environment (immissions, emissions), (noise and visual screening, etc.)

Administrative zone: offices and management, staff and training rooms, sanitary facilities, company security, fire protection

Storage zone: shelving and operator areas, circulation routes for transport vehicles and conveyors

Production zone: areas for assembly in the case this is provided

Technology zone: plant and equipment for energy supply

Traffic zone: track(s), water, air

Delivery zone (incoming/outgoing): incoming/outgoing goods, order picking, packaging

Delivery zone (incoming/outgoing): incoming/outgoing goods, order picking, packaging

Traffic zone, road: transport route for trucks and cars, parking spaces

Figure 4.3.23
Design of storage and shelving
systems according to material/
goods

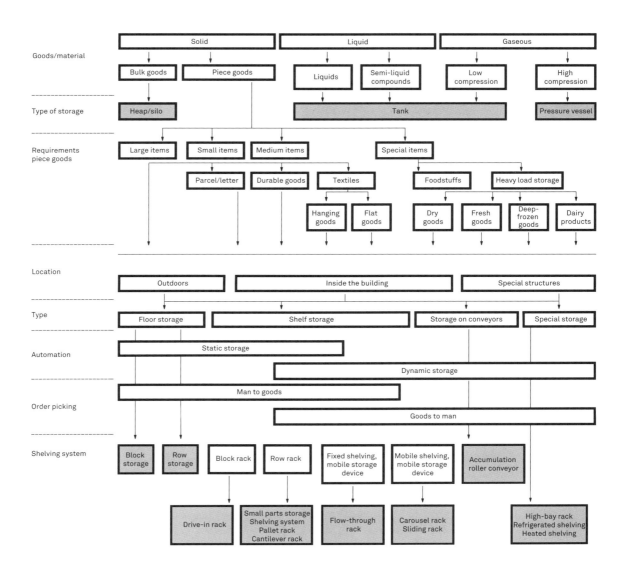

## 4.3.2.2 Sales Premises

It is not until they come together in the sales room that the customer, goods, and staff form a unit. The arrangement and presentation of goods creates a positive environment for the customer. There are three main approaches to designing the interior of sales rooms with a view to creating a certain atmosphere:

- strong design orientation that focuses on individual products;
- design that emphasizes customer comfort, creating a feel-good atmosphere;
- design with an eye on price, emphasizing the value-for-money aspect.

Supporting functions, such as the storeroom and administration, are not noticed by the customer.

### Sales Areas
A lobby zone at the entrance serves as distribution point and gives customers an opportunity to find their bearings. The main route leads to the display area. The speed of walking is controlled by the width of the route. Long, straight routes – but also chaotic routes – fatigue the customer.

The objective of shop design is to extend the stay of the customer in the shop. The vertical design of displays and shelving units is based on zones of impact and reach.

Arena principle: In this system, the goods are displayed in terraced form. From the entrance, the customer can view the entire range on offer. The view is confined by the walls of the sales room. Products on the more distant shelves are highlighted with lighting and visual merchandising.

Aisle principle: The arrangement of tall rows of shelving directs the view along the aisles. The aisles can only be accessed from the side via cross-links. Orientation is supported by a guide system. The aisle principle is the principle most often used in supermarkets.

Shop-in-shop principle: In large premises, the sales areas may be subdivided into concession areas that are leased to third-party operators. These may require their own checkout area and furniture. It is important that the different units are integrated into the overall area while still being clearly distinct from adjoining spaces. → **Figure 4.3.25**

**Figure 4.3.24**
Triangular relationship between customer, staff, and goods

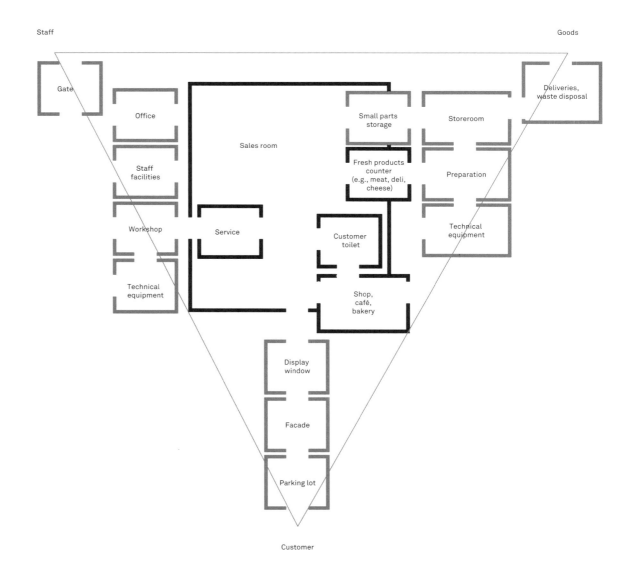

**Figure 4.3.25**
Common layout concepts for
sales areas

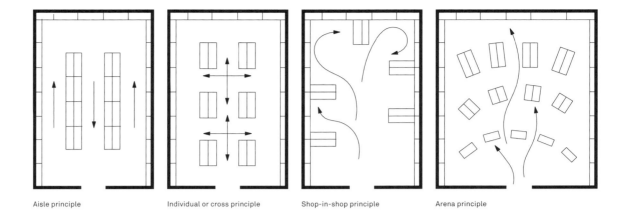

Aisle principle          Individual or cross principle          Shop-in-shop principle          Arena principle

**Figure 4.3.26**
Height zones of impact and reach,
in mm

↗ Chapter 2.2 Human Measure/
Comfort and Physical Spatial
Qualities
↗ Chapter 3.3 Spaces/Workrooms
and Production Spaces

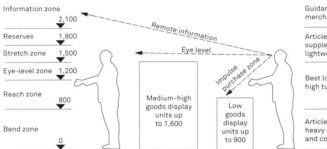

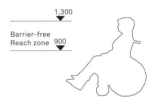

Information zone 2,100

Reserves 1,800

Stretch zone 1,500

Eye-level zone 1,200

Reach zone 800

Bend zone 0

Remote information

Eye level

Impulse purchase zone

Medium-high goods display units up to 1,600

Low goods display units up to 900

Guidance system, signage,
merchandise information

Articles with poor stock turnover,
supplementary articles,
lightweight articles

Best location for items with
high turnover rate, basic items

Articles with rather poor turnover,
heavy items, supplementary items,
and conspicuous items

Barrier-free
Reach zone 900      1,300

**Table 4.3.6**
Typical forms of sales premises
for consumer goods

| Type of sales premises | Merchandise | Building form |
|---|---|---|
| Boutique | Textiles, jewelry, accessories, etc. | Usually in the form of a retail shop within buildings |
| Department store | Many product segments, may include food | Usually multistory buildings in inner cities with more than 6,000 m² sales area |
| Shopping center | Diverse product segments, sometimes in the form of boutiques; may include leisure facilities | Usually two- to three-story centers of more than 10,000 m² with optimized connections for individual transport |
| Flagship store | Stores for certain brands aimed at specific target groups | Unique architecture as lifestyle or concept store in top city locations |

## Sales Depots

Wholesale market: the goods offered by wholesalers are usually stored in boarded shelving on several floors and are sold to retailers. Wholesalers may specialize in certain goods or may offer a wide range of goods. Cash-and-carry wholesalers are self-service outlets with a wide range of goods that require cash payment and customer transport.

Factory outlet: manufacturers may offer their products for sale directly at the factory or they may join with others in a factory outlet center (FOC). An FOC will typically have more than twenty merchants and a sales area in excess of 5,000 m². Factory outlet centers are usually located on the outskirts of cities and often try to imitate an urban setting.

Self-service depots: furniture retailers, construction material suppliers, and garden centers generally operate a cash-and-carry system where customers obtain the merchandise directly from a self-service warehouse. The store may be laid out such that customers are guided along a circular route, along which the goods are displayed, before passing through a market hall–like arrangement that finally leads to a self-service, depot-type warehouse area. Most flat-pack products are stored in transport packaging on shelving and pallet racks; the routes are designed for use by shoppers and forklift trucks alike.

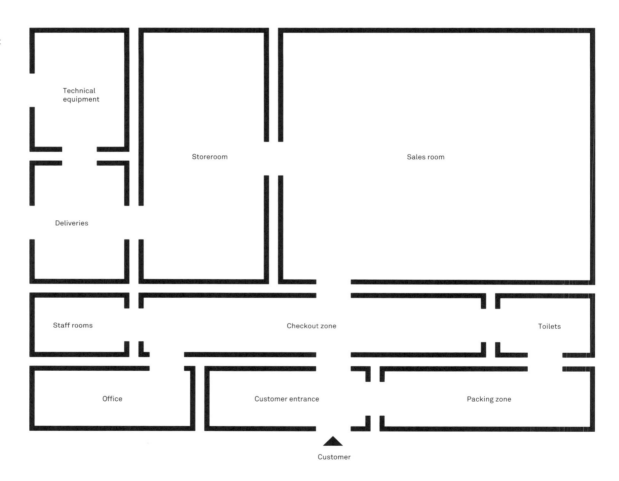

**Figure 4.3.27**
Schematic layout of sales depot

**Groceries**

Supermarket: By stacking the goods on shelves, self-service supermarkets create the impression of a warehouse. A circular route guides customers along all goods sections, ending at the checkout next to the packing station. Where fresh foods are sold it is necessary to provide special storage and cold rooms for meat, dairy products, deep-frozen products, and fruit and vegetables, as well as appropriate preparation rooms. In order to keep distances short, fresh goods are arranged in the sales room near the storage area at the rear. → **Figures 4.3.28 and 4.3.29**

Specialty food store: Specialty food stores usually provide service at one or more fresh products counters. The goods are presented on display shelves, in display cases, behind counters for fresh and refrigerated goods, and in self-serve areas. Depending on the goods offered, it is necessary to provide special rooms for preparation and cooking, as well as refrigerated and frozen storage rooms and spaces for required equipment such as airlocks or slide rails, etc. All vertical and horizontal surfaces must be washable. → **Figures 4.3.30–4.3.32**

Food logistics: Cold and frozen storage warehouses are special facilities that constitute part of the cold chain for food products. Commercial cold storage warehouses are the interface between industry and trade, and serve as buffers for excess production and seasonal fluctuations. By providing subdivisions with different sections it is possible for some rooms to be used for dry storage at normal temperature. Cold storage warehouses are governed by foodstuffs hygiene regulations (e.g. VO [EG] Nr. 852/2004). → **Figure 4.3.33**

Figure 4.3.28
Schematic diagram of supermarket with full range of goods

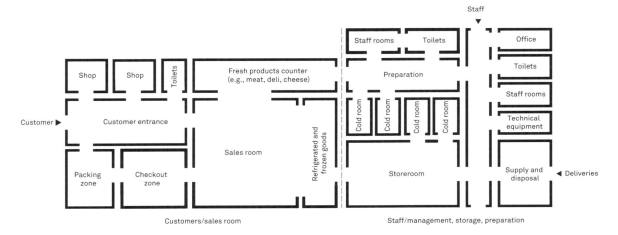

Figure 4.3.29
Schematic layout of discount
supermarket

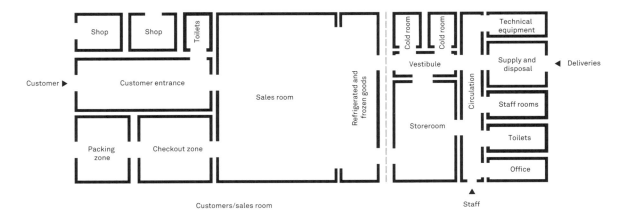

**Figure 4.3.30**
Schematic layout of a bakery

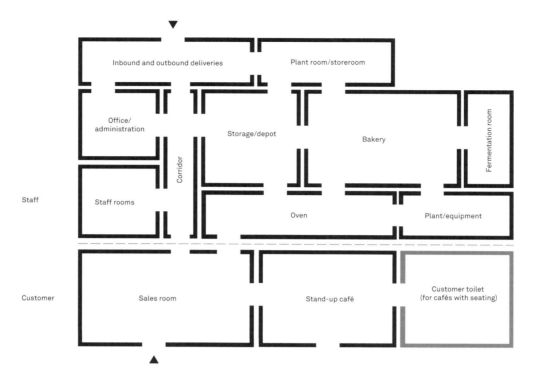

**Figure 4.3.31**
Schematic diagram of
a butcher shop

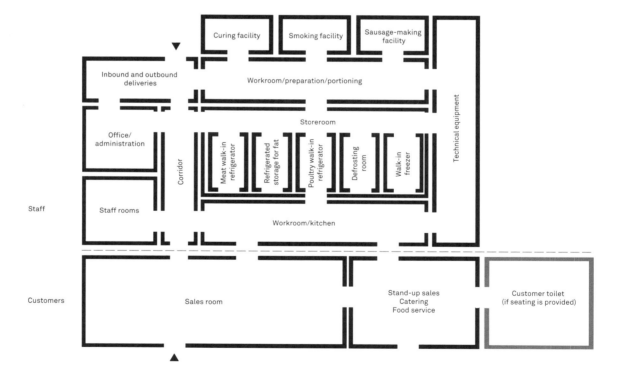

**Figure 4.3.32**
Schematic diagram of
greengrocer shop

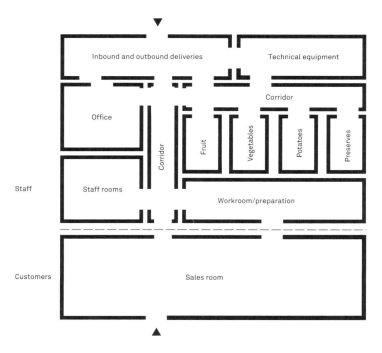

**Figure 4.3.33**
Schematic layout of cold storage

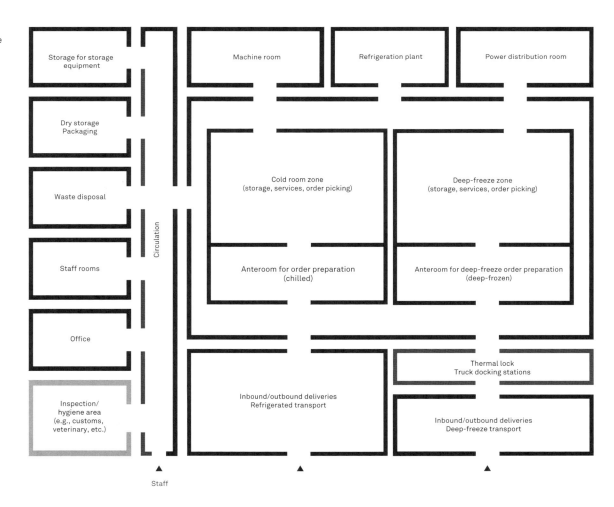

### 4.3.2.3 Trade Fairs

International trade fair buildings should have exhibition floor space of at least 100,000 m² and about the same amount of area for service, ancillary, and circulation zones. Trade fair grounds are usually laid out in a modular fashion. With the appropriate layout of service, storage, sanitary, and restaurant modules, it is possible to combine or separate the halls as required. Access points for exhibition visitors should be separate from those for exhibitors and deliveries. In the case of multistory halls, deliveries are made via external ramps for trucks, or via goods lifts, otherwise at ground level via delivery yards. → **Figures 4.3.34 and 4.3.35**

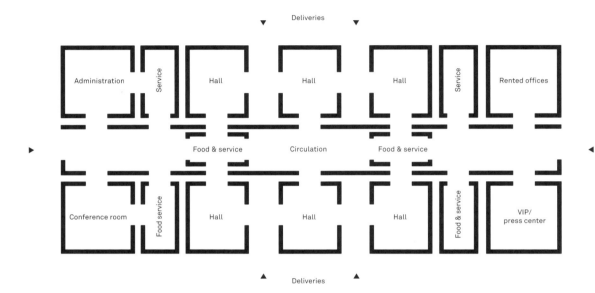

**Figure 4.3.34**
Schematic layout of trade exhibition venue

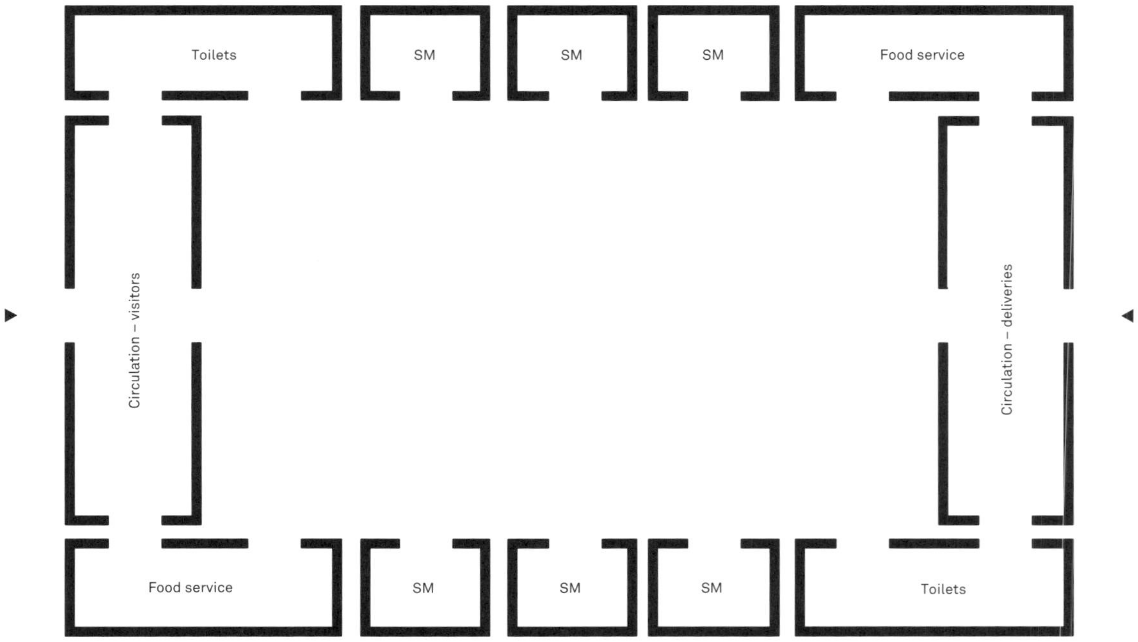

**Figure 4.3.35**
Schematic layout of trade exhibition hall

SM = support module (storage, office, technical equipment, etc.)

## 4.3.3 Areas and Rooms

**External circulation** ↗Chapter 3.1

**Parking spaces** ↗Chapter 3.1.2

**Gates, loading platforms, ramps** ↗252 ↗Chapter 3.1.2, ↗Chapter 3.1.3

**Entrance areas** ↗252 ↗Chapter 3.2.1, ↗Chapter 3.2.3

**Stairs, elevators** ↗Chapter 3.2.4, ↗Chapter 3.2.7

**Escalators and moving walkways** ↗Chapter 3.2.6

**Corridors, internal circulation** ↗Chapter 3.2.2, ↗Chapter 3.2.3

**Workplaces** ↗Chapter 3.3

**Incoming goods** ↗255

**Storeroom** ↗255 ↗Chapter 3.7

**Order picking** ↗255

**Sales rooms** ↗259

**Merchandise area** ↗259

**Customer area** ↗259

**Checkout area** ↗259

**Meeting rooms** ↗Chapter 3.4.1

**Kitchens** ↗Chapter 3.6

**Waste disposal** ↗267 ↗Chapter 3.1.5

**Lunchrooms/break areas** ↗Chapter 3.8.1

**Locker and changing rooms** ↗Chapter 3.8.2

**Sanitary facilities** ↗267 ↗Chapter 3.5

**First aid rooms** ↗Chapter 3.8.3

**Storerooms and janitor's closets** ↗Chapter 3.8.4

**Technical equipment rooms** ↗Chapter 3.9

### 4.3.3.1 Entrance Areas

**Gates, Loading Platforms, Ramps**
The docking facility for trucks at logistics buildings can be designed in different ways. Loading ramps may also be necessary at retail premises when goods are delivered/collected by trucks without lift platforms. Reversing approaches to the ramp should be from the left so that drivers can use the left-hand rear-view mirror during shunting. The docking angle at sawtooth and docking ramps can vary between 15° and 45°. In logistics buildings, at least one gate with side-loading option and a ground-level vehicle door should be provided for each building section.

**Entrance Areas to Sales Premises**
Entrances have to be designed to suit the number of visitors and must be barrier-free. → **Figures 4.3.37 and 4.3.38** For larger sales premises, a vestibule with automatic doors, and possibly with an air curtain system and entrance mat, should be provided. → **Figure 4.3.39**

Figure 4.3.36
Different types of docking arrangements

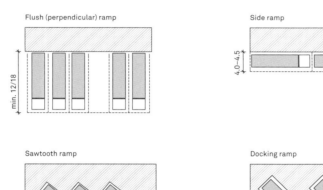

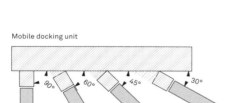

Table 4.3.7
Guide values for the number and types of doors

Source: Juhr 2010

| Type of door | Dimensions (width × height) |
| --- | --- |
| Standard loading door | 2.75–3.00 m × 3.00–3.20 m |
| Side-loading option | 12.00 m × 3.00–3.20 m |
| Ground-level vehicle door | 3.50 m × 4.20 m |
| **Deliveries** | **1 door for each** |
| One-sided docking | 1,000 m² |
| Cross-docking building | 120–150 m² |
| CEP building | 1 door for each 40–60 m² |

**Figure 4.3.37**
Examples of various entrance
and store window layouts for small
retail premises ≤ 500 m²

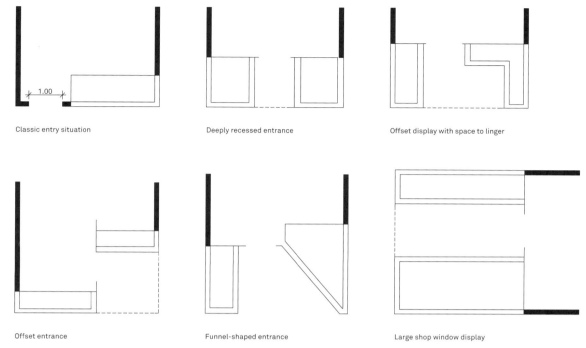

Classic entry situation

Deeply recessed entrance

Offset display with space to linger

Offset entrance

Funnel-shaped entrance

Large shop window display

**Figure 4.3.38**
Examples of entrance and store
window systems for retail
premises of more than 500 m²,
and in shopping centers

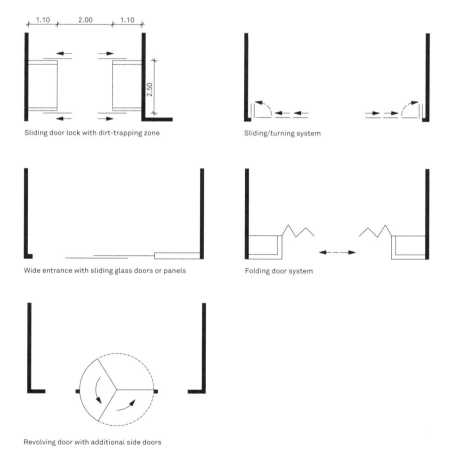

Sliding door lock with dirt-trapping zone

Sliding/turning system

Wide entrance with sliding glass doors or panels

Folding door system

Revolving door with additional side doors

**Figure 4.3.39**
Air curtain systems and
dirt-trapping zone

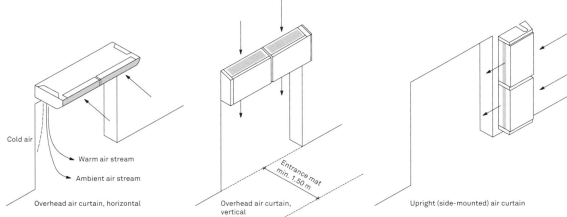

Cold air

Warm air stream

Ambient air stream

Overhead air curtain, horizontal

Entrance mat
min. 1.50 m

Overhead air curtain,
vertical

Upright (side-mounted) air curtain

**Figure 4.3.40**
Types of shop window systems

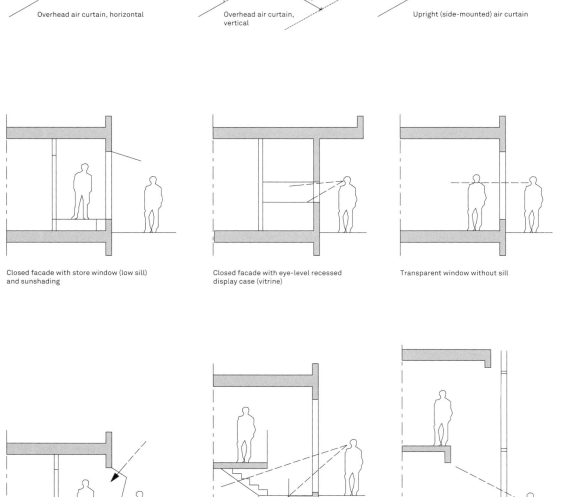

Closed facade with store window (low sill)
and sunshading

Closed facade with eye-level recessed
display case (vitrine)

Transparent window without sill

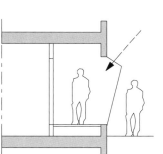

Low-glare, slanted shop window panes

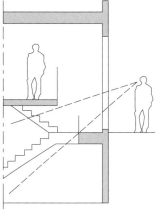

Transparent window with downward view

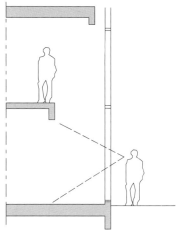

Facade with multistory glazing, with upward view

## 4.3.3.2 Logistics Spaces

### Incoming and Outgoing Goods

Incoming goods are recorded at scanner stations or terminals. Depending on requirements, it is possible to use anything from a hand-held terminal to a full-screen industrial or vehicle terminal.

### Warehouse

The loading and unloading of row racks takes place from the warehouse aisles, either manually or using automated storage and retrieval (S/R) equipment. Space utilization can be optimized by providing storage and order-picking platforms. → **Figure 4.3.41**

Rack systems: Rack systems are distinguished by the degree of automation and the type of access. These days, standard equipment includes mixed forms of highly automated, seamlessly linked systems in which storage and conveyor systems form a unit in logistics buildings. → **Figure 4.3.42**, ↗ Chapter 3.7 Spaces/Storage Spaces

Storage units: Depending on the storage system and the goods, different types of racks are used for storage. The range includes stackable bins, boarded shelving, pallet racks, and container racks. ↗ Chapter 3.7.1 Spaces/Storage Spaces/Pallets and Containers

Transport and conveyor systems: Within the building, conveyor systems and vehicles are used for the transport of goods. The capacities of racks and industrial trucks (forklifts), their operating range, speed, load-bearing capacity, and handover points have to be precisely matched. A distinction is made between overhead, suspended, and floor-based conveyor systems, which may be manually operated or automated. → **Figure 4.3.43**, ↗ Chapter 3.7.3 Spaces/Storage Spaces/Handling and Transport

### Order Picking

Workplaces for order picking in automated systems usually feature a conveyor system and the handling element at which the actual activity takes place. Partial orders run through different order-picking zones before they are brought together to complete the order. These tasks are usually performed by high-performance automated sorting systems. → **Figure 4.3.46**

Figure 4.3.41
Storage and order-picking platforms

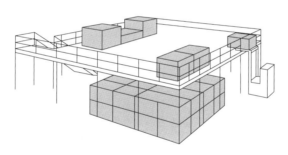
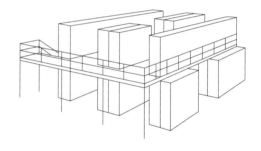

**Figure 4.3.42**
Selection of automated
rack systems

Based on Jungheinrich AG

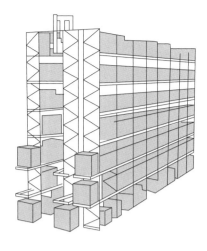

Automated pallet rack

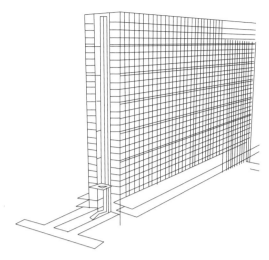

Automated small parts rack

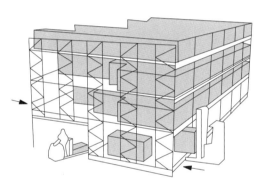

Drive-through rack

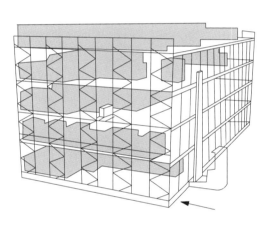

Drive-in rack

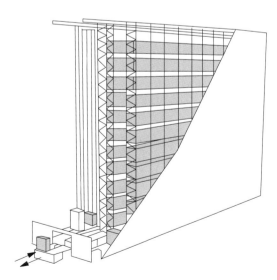

Automated high-bay warehouse

Figure 4.3.43
Overview of different conveyor
systems to overcome differences
in height

Based on Führer 1999

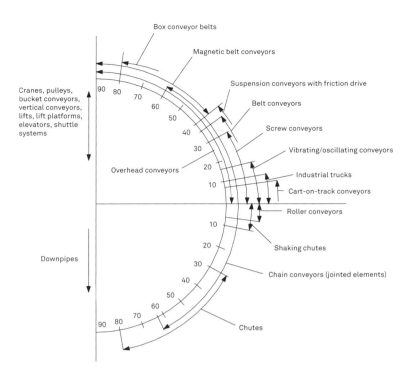

Figure 4.3.44
Selection of order-picking
carriages and vehicles

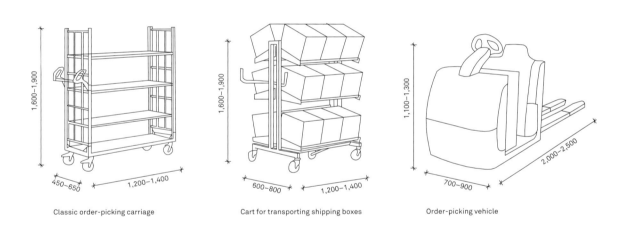

Classic order-picking carriage

Cart for transporting shipping boxes

Order-picking vehicle

Figure 4.3.45
Examples of sorting devices

Source: Fraunhofer Institute for
Material Flow and Logistics (IML),
based on Jünnemann/Schmidt

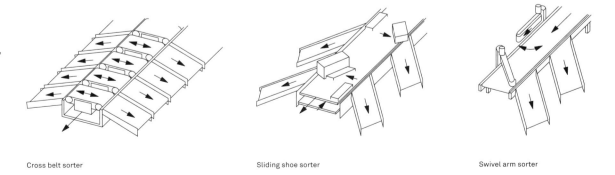

Cross belt sorter

Sliding shoe sorter

Swivel arm sorter

**Figure 4.3.46**
Examples of arrangements
of order-picking processes

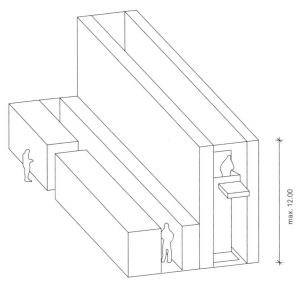

max. 12.00

Manual arrangement

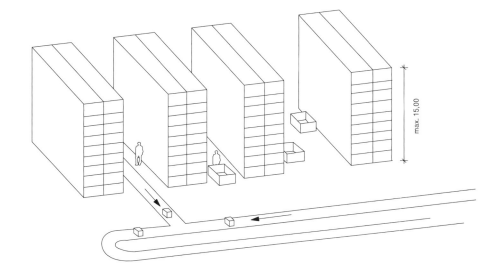

max. 15,00

Partly automated arrangement

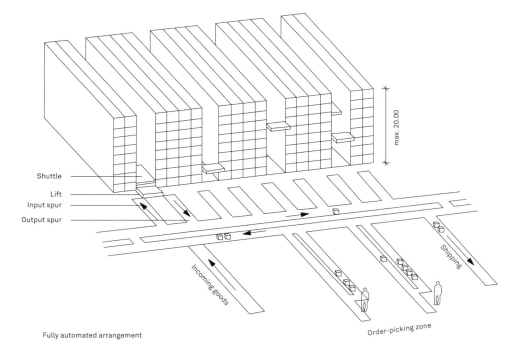

max. 20.00

Shuttle
Lift
Input spur
Output spur

Incoming goods

Shipping

Order-picking zone

Fully automated arrangement

### 4.3.3.3 Sales Rooms

Sales rooms can be subdivided into areas for merchandise, customers, and miscellaneous support functions (cash registers, fitting rooms, etc.). Aisles between the merchandise display furniture are considered part of the sales area, whereas ancillary areas such as display windows, stairs, storerooms, and offices are not included. Permanent work areas in the sales room should have natural light if possible, and provide a view to the outside.

**Merchandise Area**
The display fixtures used in self-service and preselection systems are open and transparent so that the goods are presented in full view and can be easily handled. Goods consisting of small parts are arranged in suspension systems. Special offers are promoted and arranged on tables; shoppers expect shelves to contain goods sorted by segment.

**Customer Area**
The type and size of transport device required by customers depends on the type of goods. Manufacturers offer various shopping cart types with different load capacities. As a general rule, 1 cart is needed for every 5 m² of sales area. → **Figure 4.3.56 and Table 4.3.8**

**Service and Support**
A variety of service and support functions can be offered, from information centers and waiting areas through to restaurants and childcare facilities. → **Table 4.3.9** It is desirable to provide seating at busy path crossings, whereas fitting rooms should be located in less frequented sales areas. → **Figure 4.3.59**

**Checkout Area**
It is common to provide additional functions at or near individual checkout counters or central cashier facilities, such as an information desk, packaging station, complaint desk, and returns/exchange facility. In supermarkets the standard checkout facilities consist of cash registers with conveyor belts and scanners; in addition, self-service checkout stations are becoming increasingly popular. → **Figure 4.3.60** For all these variants, it is important to provide sufficient space for a customer waiting line.

Figure 4.3.47
Selection of freestanding
shelving systems

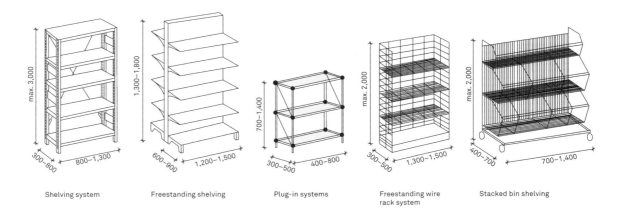

Shelving system     Freestanding shelving     Plug-in systems     Freestanding wire rack system     Stacked bin shelving

Figure 4.3.48
Selection of wall shelving systems

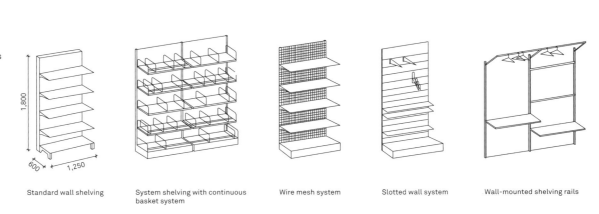

Standard wall shelving     System shelving with continuous basket system     Wire mesh system     Slotted wall system     Wall-mounted shelving rails

**Figure 4.3.49**
Selection of special shelving

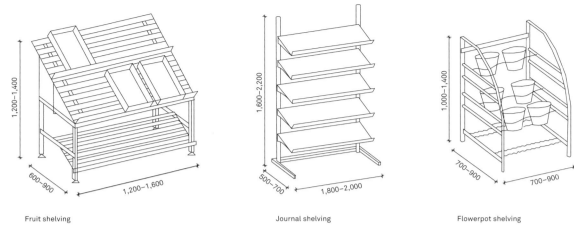

Fruit shelving

Journal shelving

Flowerpot shelving

**Figure 4.3.50**
Selection of island shelving units

Standard island unit with shelves

Island unit with header element

Island unit with mesh wall and continuous shelves

**Figure 4.3.51**
Stand systems

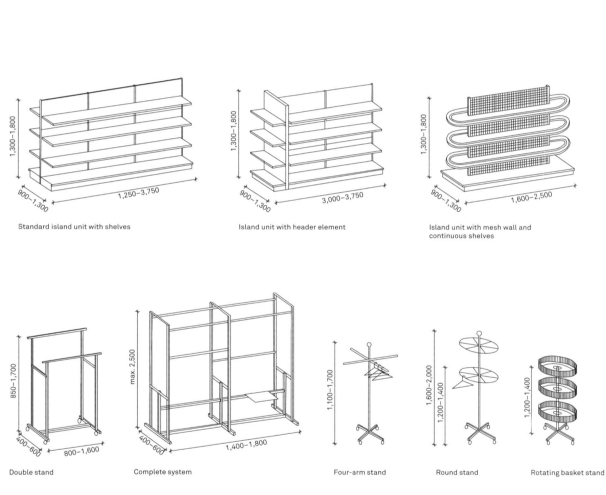

Double stand

Complete system

Four-arm stand

Round stand

Rotating basket stand

**Figure 4.3.52**
Rummage baskets and sales tables

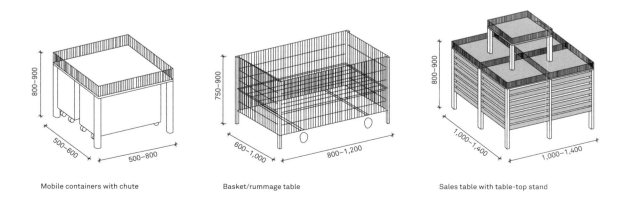

Mobile containers with chute

Basket/rummage table

Sales table with table-top stand

**Figure 4.3.53**
Different types of tables

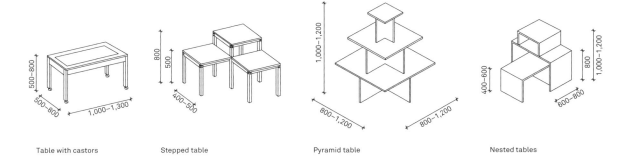

Table with castors          Stepped table          Pyramid table          Nested tables

**Figure 4.3.54**
Display cases

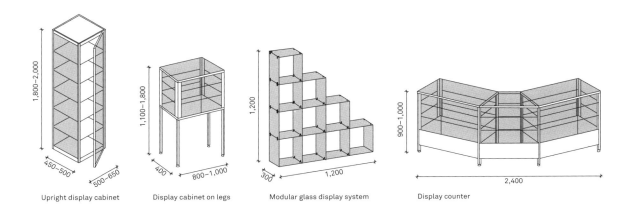

Upright display cabinet          Display cabinet on legs          Modular glass display system          Display counter

**Figure 4.3.55**
Refrigerated units

In order to avoid condensate in refrigerated display units it is necessary to provide fans, an evaporator, a compressor, a condenser to release heat, and the coolant pipes. Where several refrigerated units are installed together, they are usually controlled via a combined refrigeration system.

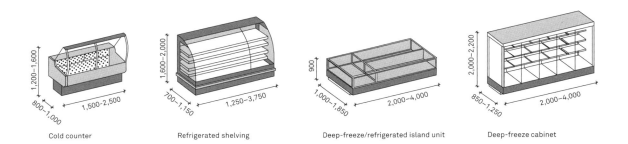

Cold counter          Refrigerated shelving          Deep-freeze/refrigerated island unit          Deep-freeze cabinet

Figure 4.3.56
Examples of shopping carts
and baskets

Source: Wanzl Metallwarenfabrik
GmbH

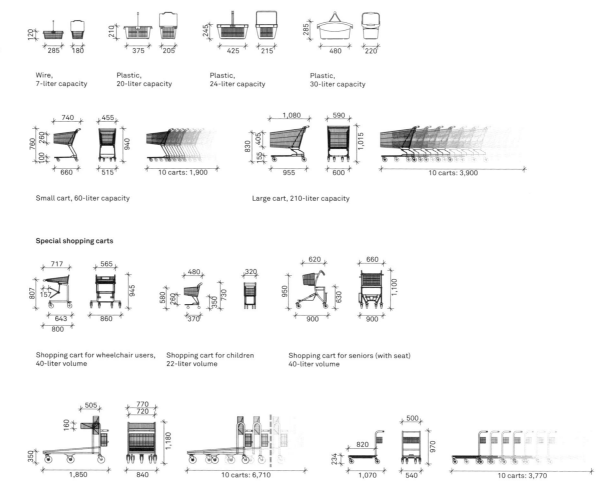

Wire,
7-liter capacity

Plastic,
20-liter capacity

Plastic,
24-liter capacity

Plastic,
30-liter capacity

Small cart, 60-liter capacity

Large cart, 210-liter capacity

**Special shopping carts**

Shopping cart for wheelchair users,
40-liter volume

Shopping cart for children
22-liter volume

Shopping cart for seniors (with seat)
40-liter volume

Self-service cart for large/bulky items (e.g., beverage crates, building materials, furniture, garden supplies)

Table 4.3.8
Shopping carts required
for different types of retail
premises

Based on Wanzl Metallwarenfabrik
GmbH

| Type of retail premises | Range of goods | Sales area (average) in m² | Sales area (min. and max.) in m² | Capacity of carts and baskets in L | Carts per 100–150 m² | Space required in m² per 10 carts |
|---|---|---|---|---|---|---|
| Convenience store | Food | 150 | 100–250 | 60–75 | 22 | 1.8 |
| Self-service grocery store | Food | 300 | 250–400 | 60–99 | 27 | 1.8 |
| Local supermarket | Food | 650 | 400–800 | 75–100 | 20 | 2.1 |
| Department store supermarket | Food | 1,100 | 800–1,500 | 90–130 | 19 | 2.3 |
| Food department | Food | 1,000 | 400–1,500 | 60–90 | 17 | 1.8 |
| Discounter | Food | 450 | 300–600 | 60–130 | 17 | 2.3 |
| Regional superstore | Food/Non-Food | 2,600 | 1,500–5,000 | 100–130 | 16 | 2.3 |
| Hypermarket | Food/Non-Food | 8,900 | 5,000 or more | 130–212 | 13 | 2.7 |
| Drugstore | | 250 | 200–400 | 60–75 | 25 | 1.8 |
| Drugstore | | 450 | 400–600 | 60–90 | 22 | 1.8 |

**Table 4.3.9**
Common service and
support functions

Based on Gretz 2000

| Goods-related services | Needs-related facilities | Repair and assembly | General service functions |
|---|---|---|---|
| • Customer advice<br>• Information terminal<br>• Buy-and-collect service<br>• Fitting rooms<br>• Tasting areas<br>• Demonstration areas<br>• Sample installations<br>• Gift wrapping | • Seating<br>• Customer toilets<br>• Baby changing room<br>• Play area for children<br>• Childcare<br>• Food service | • Repairs<br>• Alterations tailor<br>• Assembly service | • Customer cloakroom<br>• Baggage room<br>• Photo service<br>• Photocopy service<br>• Cash dispenser<br>• Ticket sales<br>• Hairdresser<br>• Beautician<br>• Shoe repairs<br>• Key cutting service |

**Figure 4.3.57**
Examples of service counters,
information desks, and
multimedia information terminals

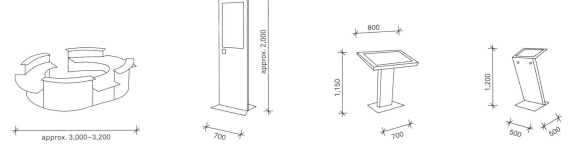

Classic information and advice
desk for three employees

Multimedia information terminal

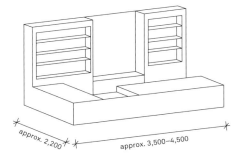

Service counter with cash register and packing station

**Figure 4.3.58**
Packing station and disposal
equipment

Source: Wanzl Metallwarenfabrik
GmbH

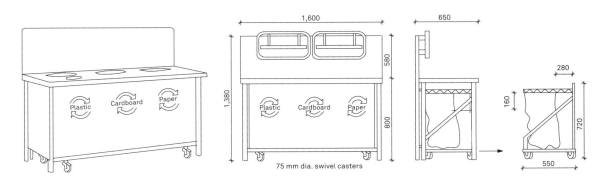

**Figure 4.3.59**
Exemplary layouts of fitting rooms

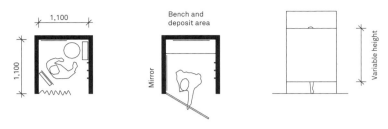

Standard fitting room, height of cabin, and privacy screen can vary; solid partitions, panels or simple frames between booths

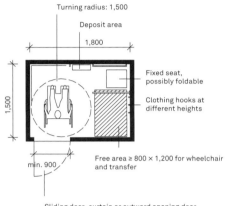

Turning radius: 1,500

Deposit area

Fixed seat, possibly foldable

Clothing hooks at different heights

Free area ≥ 800 × 1,200 for wheelchair and transfer

Sliding door, curtain or outward opening door

Wheelchair-accessible fitting room

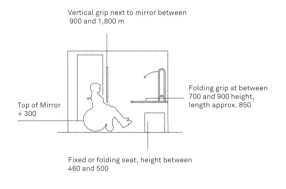

Vertical grip next to mirror between 900 and 1,800 m

Top of Mirror + 300

Folding grip at between 700 and 900 height, length approx. 850

Fixed or folding seat, height between 460 and 500

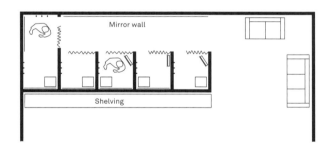

Changing booths behind the sales zone with quiet zone

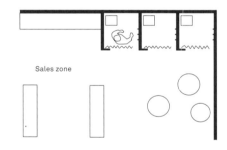

Access to booths visible from the sales room

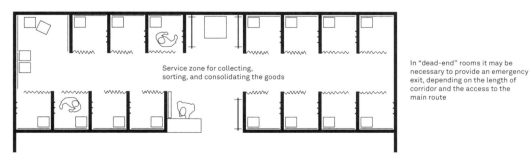

Service zone for collecting, sorting, and consolidating the goods

In "dead-end" rooms it may be necessary to provide an emergency exit, depending on the length of corridor and the access to the main route

Larger changing zone, including service areas and staff supervision

**Figure 4.3.60**
Selection of different types
of checkout systems

Source: STOREbest GmbH &
Co. KG

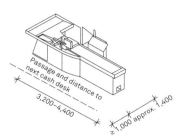

Individual cash desk with front operation

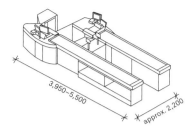

Discount tandem cash desk with long conveyor belt

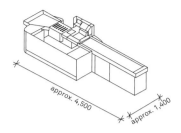

Individual cash desk in home improvement
store, including roller flap downstream of
the frontal workplace to facilitate fast cash
transactions for heavy and large items/data

Mobile checkout counter

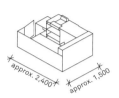

Individual checkout counter for
use in a beverage store

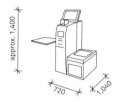

Self-service checkout station

## 4.3.3.4 Ancillary Spaces

Ancillary spaces are needed to serve internal work processes and to ensure the operation of sales premises and logistics buildings. These may include administration, staff rooms, workrooms, storage facilities, as well as delivery and waste disposal areas.

### Support Areas

In sales premises the staff entrance is separate from the customer entrance and combined with a porter or time recording facility. The administration, break, and staff rooms follow on from there. Depending on the complexity and size of the premises it may be necessary to provide offices for an operations manager and for accounts and human resources departments, as well as meeting and training rooms. Classic offices should be provided for administrative functions. Sometimes, retail premises require office workplaces in the sales room; this makes it possible for staff to be available to give advice to customers and carry out office activities at the same time. In trade premises with 10 or more members of staff it is mandatory to provide break and staff rooms with natural lighting. It may be necessary to provide additional workrooms for goods ma-nipulation, workshops, or preparation rooms for foodstuffs close to the goods storage facility.

In logistics buildings the proportion of space required for administrative and staff rooms is relatively low at 5 to 15 percent. Administrative functions should be situated near the main entrance. A foyer serves as a distribution point for visitors, operatives, and office workers. Manager's offices or dispatchers' rooms should be located inside the warehouse near the points for incoming and outgoing goods. This is where external drivers and delivery staff report. Administrative and staff functions are provided in a separate office building, in a multistory structure within the warehouse, or on a mezzanine level at a height of + 5 m above the entryways. Separate break rooms and staff facilities should be provided for management staff and warehouse operatives as well as external drivers. ⌐ Chapter 3.3 Spaces/Workrooms and Production Spaces, ⌐ Chapter 3.4 Spaces/Communication Spaces and Dining Rooms, ⌐ Chapter 3.8 Spaces/Ancillary and Staff Rooms, ⌐ Chapter 4.2 Typologies/Office and Administration, ⌐ Chapter 4.4.3.4 Typologies/Industry and Production/Areas and Rooms/Administration

Table 4.3.10
Ancillary areas in sales premises and logistics properties

| Sales premises | Logistics property |
|---|---|
| In the sales room:<br>• Display windows, display cases, passages<br>• Paths, corridors, stairs, escalators, elevators<br>• Offices in the sales area<br>• Customer toilet | In/adjacent to the depot:<br>• Manager's office<br>• Toilets for visitors/external drivers |
| In the support area:<br>• Administration<br>• Workshops<br>• Dayrooms<br>• Toilets, washrooms, lockers<br>• Meeting rooms<br>• Sick room<br>• Ancillary spaces/café | In the support area/mezzanine level:<br>• Administration<br>• Meeting/training<br>• Break rooms (separate rooms for management staff, depot employees, and external drivers)<br>• Toilets, washrooms, lockers (separate male and female, separate for depot employees and management staff)<br>• Server and IT rooms, archive, etc.<br>• First aid room if needed<br>• Rooms for supervisory authorities (such as customs, veterinary office) if needed |
| Deliveries/storage:<br>• Incoming goods<br>• Shipping<br>• Labeling<br>• Goods handling<br>• Decorations, advertising<br>• Storeroom<br>• Technical equipment room | Supply/disposal:<br>• Loading ramps/doors<br>• Storeroom<br>• Technical equipment room for sprinkler system, transformers, mechanical systems, etc. |
| Outdoor areas:<br>• Courtyard, open areas, landscaping<br>• Loading platform<br>• Parking spaces | Open areas:<br>• Access control, barrier, optionally porter's lodge<br>• Operational yard<br>• Parking spaces, swap trailers<br>• Truck parking spaces<br>• Car parking spaces for staff and visitors |

## Sanitary Facilities

Where sales premises require specific work clothing, separate changing rooms have to be provided for men and women. Where the work involves the preparation of foodstuffs, a preparation room with separately connected staff room and toilet, as well as separate washrooms, and a first aid room are required. In premises with more than 5 members of staff it is mandatory to provide separate staff toilets for men and women, which must not be used by customers. Regulations governing customer toilets apply only for premises with sales areas in excess of 2,000 m². However, many smaller sales premises provide sanitary facilities to the public on a voluntary basis. Where such premises include restaurants with seating it is a mandatory requirement to provide customer toilets.

In logistics buildings, the staff rooms and sanitary facilities should be located between the entrance and the workplaces; in the case of very large complexes, additional decentralized facilities should be provided close to the workplaces – the distance must not be more than 100 m. Separate sanitary facilities should be provided for logistics operatives and office workers. Furthermore, separate wash and changing rooms have to be provided for male and female logistics operatives. ↗Chapter 3.5 Spaces/Sanitary Facilities, ↗Chapter 4.4.3.5 Typologies/Industry and Production/Areas and Rooms/Ancillary Spaces

## Storerooms, Deliveries, and Waste Disposal

Sales premises often maintain a reserve room or stockroom for keeping small stocks of merchandise and replacement parts readily at hand. This storeroom will occupy the largest portion of the ancillary areas. However, with shorter delivery intervals it is possible to reduce the floor space required. This means that the size of the ancillary area, which according to a rule of thumb should be one third of the sales area, is now frequently smaller. In retail operations, the most popular storage system is shelving; the shelving units for foodstuffs need to include cold storage cells. When designing storage areas it is important to take the increased fire load into account. Waste disposal rooms must be large enough to store the waste from at least two days. ↗Chapter 3.7 Spaces/Storage Spaces, ↗Chapter 3.9 Spaces/Technical Equipment Rooms

Table 4.3.11
Numbers and sizes of selected elements in loading yards of department stores and shopping centers

Source: EAR 05

| | Sales area in m² | | | |
|---|---|---|---|---|
| | 5,000–10,000 m² | 10,000–15,000 m² | 15,000–20,000 m² | 20,000–30,000 m² |
| Truck bays at the loading ramp (–) | 2–3 | 3–4 | 4–5 | 5–6 |
| Storage area for deliveries (m²) | 100 m² | 120 m² | 180 m² | 250 m² |
| Number (–) and size of freight elevators (m) | 1: 2.00 × 3.00 m<br>1: 2.00 × 4.20 m | 2: 2.00 × 3.00 m<br>1: 2.00 × 4.20 m | 3: 2.00 × 3.00 m<br>1: 2.00 × 4.20 m | 2: 2.00 × 3.00 m<br>2: 2.00 × 4.20 m |
| Elevator lobbies (m²) | 20 m² | 30 m² | 40 m² | 40 m² |
| Areas for:<br>Waste disposal (m²)<br>Empty containers (m²)<br>Paper bale storage (m²) | 30 m²<br>20 m²<br>15 m² | 30 m²<br>40 m²<br>25 m² | 50 m²<br>60 m²<br>35 m² | 100 m²<br>80 m²<br>35 m² |
| Stationary press with container (m)<br>Channel baler with container (m) | 3.00 × 9.00 in front of the loading ramp<br>2.50 × 9.00 in front of the loading ramp | | | |

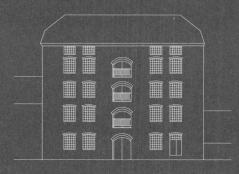

**Cromford Mill textile factory**, Ratingen, Germany, Rutger Flügel, ca. 1789

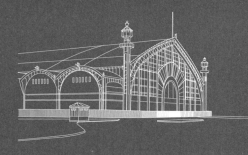

**Galeries des Machines**, Paris, France, Contamin & Duter, 1889

**Hackesche Höfe**, Berlin, Germany, Kurt Berndt & August Endell, 1906

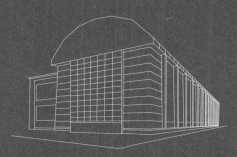

**AEG Turbine Factory**, Berlin, Germany, Peter Behrens, 1909

**Fagus Factory**, Alfeld an der Leine, Germany, Walter Gropius, 1914

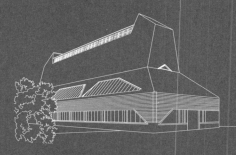

**Friedrich Steinberg Hat Factory**, Luckenwalde, Germany, Erich Mendelsohn, 1923

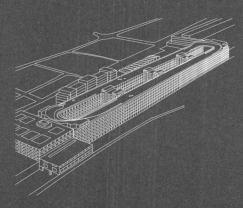

**Fiat Factory**, Lingotto (Turin), Italy, Giacomo Mattè-Trucco, 1923

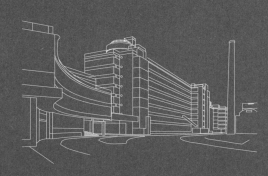

**Van Nelle Factory**, Rotterdam, The Netherlands, Brinkmann and van der Vlugt, 1930

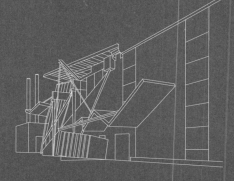

**Funder Werk3**, Sankt Veit an der Glan, Austria, Coop Himmelb(l)au, 1989

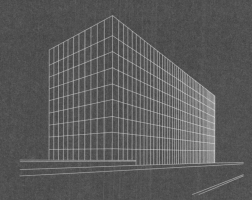

**Hôtel industriel Berlier**, Paris, France, Dominique Perrault, 1990

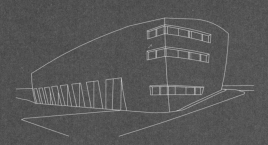

**Altenried carpentry shop**, Hergatz, Germany, Baumschlager/Eberle, 1994

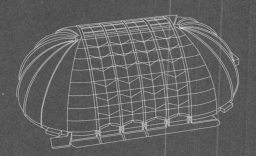

**CargoLifter Hall**, Briesen/Brand, Germany, SIAT, 2000

# 4 Typologies
## 4.4 Industry and Production

Nils Kummer

**4.4.1 Building Concept** ↗270

4.4.1.1 Planning Parameters ↗270

4.4.1.2 Building Forms ↗272

4.4.1.3 Circulation Systems ↗274

4.4.1.4 Construction and Technology ↗276


**4.4.2 Program of Use** ↗280

4.4.2.1 Large-Scale Operations ↗280

4.4.2.2 Small Businesses, Craftsmen's Workshops ↗284

4.4.2.3 Operations with Special Cleanliness or Safety Requirements ↗285


**4.4.3 Areas and Rooms** ↗286

4.4.3.1 Entrance Areas 287

4.4.3.2 Storage Areas ↗288

4.4.3.3 Assembly and Fabrication ↗288

4.4.3.4 Administration ↗288

4.4.3.5 Ancillary Spaces ↗289

# 4.4 Industry and Production

## 4.4.1 Building Concept

### 4.4.1.1 Planning Parameters

Industrial architecture encompasses a diverse range of premises, from small craftsmen's workshops to large production sites. As a rule, the production processes and economic aspects are of utmost concern. For the company, a more efficient building means lower production costs and a higher rate of return for their financial investment. At the same time, the structure must be flexible enough to accommodate future changes in the production process.

The basic aim of industrial architecture is to create a spatial enclosure for the production and further processing of commercial goods, and for their storage and distribution; individual buildings may combine various functions or may be specialized for purely monofunctional use, such as with a warehouse. ↗ **Chapter 4.3 Typologies/Logistics and Commerce** Production and processing, however, represents the central element of industrial architecture.

**Typical Workflow and Conditions**
- Suppliers and sales markets
- Site geometry, context, and infrastructure
- Building code restrictions
- Production processes
- Production conditions
- Production layout
- Number of employees
- Needed/desired ancillary uses
- Building type and form
- Representational purposes (public image)
- Security and access control
- Budget and deadlines

**Production Workflow and Conditions**
The production workflow establishes the basis for the design, which is later refined to incorporate additional functions. Inquiries must be made into numerous internal conditions that will vary depending on the product, and which will have an impact on both the product and the building. Especially for large-scale industry, it is necessary for architects to coordinate their work with various departments and specialists. → **Figure 4.4.1**

**Planning factors related to production conditions:**
- Hygiene
- Lighting
- Energy supply
- Emission of and protection from harmful substances
- Pollution control, ventilation
- PWIS-/dust-free environment
- Explosion protection
- Transport paths, conveyance systems
- Loads/dynamic loads
- Safety
- Machinery and product sizes
- Impact protection

**Figure 4.4.1**
Fundamental production workflow

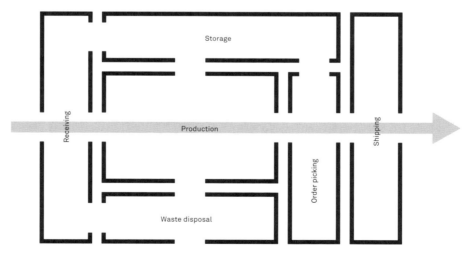

**External Factors of Production**

External factors of production are parameters that not only influence the economic efficiency of a building but can also determine the siting of the building in relation to its surroundings. → Figure 4.4.2 Thus the proximity to customers or suppliers, as well as the availability of personnel capable of carrying out highly specialized processes, for instance, can play a major role in selecting the site. Demand determines the production volume and thus the number of production lines and the amount of the floor space needed. Legal regulations may limit space availability by placing restrictions on the overall building size or the buildable area. The potential for future expansion of the floor space can be crucial to the flexibility and efficiency of the building.

**Production Layout**

The production layout is usually specified by the manufacturer or specialized consulting engineers. These specifications can vary from mere lists of required square footage or numbers of machines, as for most small companies, to precisely determined production layouts with prescribed routing and material flows. With due regard to the minimum legal requirements, the task for the building designer is thus either to design the supporting structures and the floor areas so that the specified requirements are not affected or, on the basis of the given equipment sizes, to lay out movement and circulation areas so as to establish the initial dimensioning. Large, open areas are generally restricted by legal requirements for fire compartmentation. → Table 4.4.1, ↗ Chapter 3.3.1 Spaces/Workrooms and Production Spaces/Workplaces

Figure 4.4.2
Factors influencing production processes

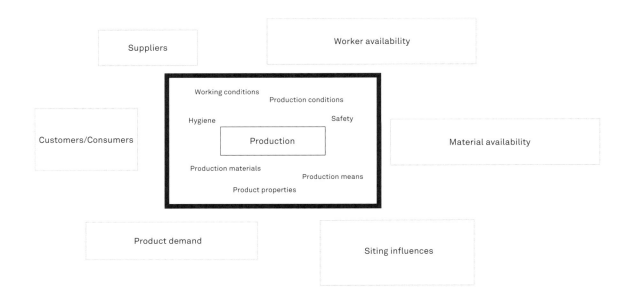

Table 4.4.1 (left)
Fire compartment sizes in m²

Based on the Model Industrial Buildings Directive (M-IndBauRL)

1  Width of the industrial building ≤ 40 m and heat exhaust area as per DIN 18230-1 ≥ 5%

2  Heat exhaust area (as per DIN 18230-1) ≥ 5%

3  For low-rise buildings, the Model Building Code (MBO, Musterbauordnung) permits a maximum size of 1,600 m²

| | Number of stories | | | | | | | | |
|---|---|---|---|---|---|---|---|---|---|
| | 1 | | 2 | | 3 | | 4 | 5 | |
| | Fire resistance rating of the load-bearing and bracing elements | | | | | | | | |
| | F0 | F30 | F30 | F60 | F90 | F60 | F90 | F90 | F90 |
| K1 | 1,800[1] | 3,000 | 800[2,3] | 1,600[2] | 2,400 | 1,200[2,3] | 1,800 | 1,500 | 1,200 |
| K2 | 2,700[1] | 4,500 | 1,200[2,3] | 2,400[2] | 3,600 | 1,800[2] | 2,700 | 2,300 | 1,800 |
| K3.1 | 3,200[1] | 5,400 | 1,400[2,3] | 2,900[2] | 4,300 | 2,100[2] | 3,200 | 2,700 | 2,200 |
| K3.2 | 3,600[1] | 6,000 | 1,600[2] | 3,200[2] | 4,800 | 2,400[2] | 3,600 | 3,000 | 2,400 |
| K3.3 | 4,200[1] | 7,000 | 1,800[2] | 3,600[2] | 5,500 | 2,800[2] | 4,100 | 3,500 | 2,800 |
| K3.4 | 4,500[1] | 7,500 | 2,000[2] | 4,000[2] | 6,000 | 3,000[2] | 4,500 | 3,800 | 3,000 |
| K4 | 10,000 | 10,000 | 8,500 | 8,500 | 8,500 | 6,500 | 6,500 | 5,000 | 4000 |

Table 4.4.2 (right)
Safety classes for fire protection

Based on the Model Industrial Buildings Directive (M-IndBauRL)

| Safety class | Measure(s) within the fire compartment |
|---|---|
| K1 | None |
| K2 | Automatic fire alarm system (FAS) |
| K3.1 | Automatic FAS and full-time plant fire department with squad of min. 6 firefighters |
| K3.2 | Automatic FAS and plant fire department with group of min. 9 firefighters |
| K3.3 | Automatic FAS and plant fire department with 2 squads |
| K3.4 | Automatic FAS and plant fire department with 3 squads |
| K4 | Self-activating fire-extinguishing system |

## 4.4.1.2 Building Forms

### Industrial Sheds

Where the lot is of sufficient size, industrial shed buildings, most commonly as single-story structures with long-span roof structures, offer the advantage of flexible and column-free floor space to accommodate the production workflow. Production layouts can be planned, reorganized, or expanded without any restrictions. The internal transport of goods and materials as well as incoming and outgoing deliveries all take place on a single level. In addition, the production-level floor can withstand heavy loads by transmitting them directly into the ground without major effort. → **Table 4.4.3**

The basic structure of the shed buildings consists of columns and trusses that are arrayed one behind the other in a series or combined to form a spatial system. Additions along the sides can be made to create a multiple-bay structure, or the trusses can be arranged to span in all directions, acting together as a space frame. → **Figure 4.4.3**

The girders of the roof structure can have a wide variety of forms and details: solid sections, perforated/cellular, cable-trussed, pitched or double-tapered (drainage slope), and lattice trussed. → **Figure 4.4.4** In choosing a type, not only structural calculations (dimensions) and architectural considerations (material and appearance) play a role, but also building services (cable/duct/pipe routing) and, of ultimate importance, economic aspects. Available choices of material include reinforced concrete, steel, and wood construction.

Figure 4.4.3
Basic structure of shed buildings

Column/Truss/Girder

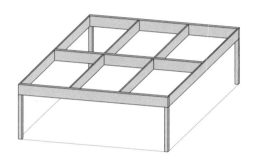

Space frame

Figure 4.4.4
Girder types

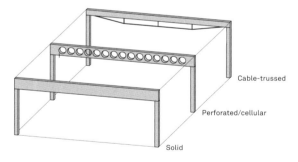

Cable-trussed

Perforated/cellular

Solid

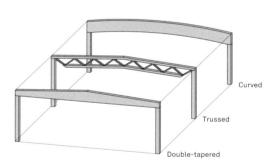

Curved

Trussed

Double-tapered

Table 4.4.3
Advantages and disadvantages of industrial sheds

| Advantages of industrial sheds | Disadvantages of industrial sheds |
|---|---|
| Ground-level access | Occupies large area |
| High load-bearing capacity, low foundation costs | Unfavorable A/V ratio |
| Large span lengths | Usually high infrastructure costs |
| Sometimes has benefits for fire protection | |
| Uniform daylighting possible | |
| Flexible production layouts and changing products possible | |

## Multistory buildings

Urban density, sloping terrain, a small lot size, or advantages in the production workflow can make it sensible to accommodate the facility in a multistory building. →**Table 4.4.4** The prerequisite for such a building is a product that is limited in size and weight and a production process that can benefit from expeditious vertical transport (such as textile manufacturing). Buildings that house various producers or even distinct uses on different floors are equally feasible as multistory buildings or single-story workshop buildings.

The basic system is similar to that of industrial sheds: the vertical, load-bearing elements are walls made of masonry or reinforced concrete, which can also be interspersed with or replaced by columns. The columns can be integrated into the facade plane or freestanding within the space. The horizontal load-carrying members are most commonly prefabricated beams.

## Dimensions and Ceiling Heights

The space requirements, span lengths, and ceiling heights can be defined as consequences of the production layout, the sizes of the products and machinery, and the necessary movement and storage areas. To determine the clear height that is needed, equipment heights, storage rack heights, suspended utility lines (electric, ventilation, exhaust air, industrial gases, compressed air), lighting, cranes and conveying equipment, maneuvering space for production, product heights, and stacker heights are all significant. The latter are also decisive for the design of doors and gates. When, for instance, a portion of the production hall is to be built as a double-story structure for administrative offices, this also impacts the floor-to-floor height. →**Figure 4.4.5**

In multistory buildings, beams can be laid out in one of two directions: perpendicular to the exterior wall they facilitate better daylight exposure because the facade plane is systematized only by columns, and in the longitudinal direction they simplify the routing of utility lines for building services, which must pass through or under the beams less often. →**Figure 4.4.6**

**Figure 4.4.5**
Height relationships

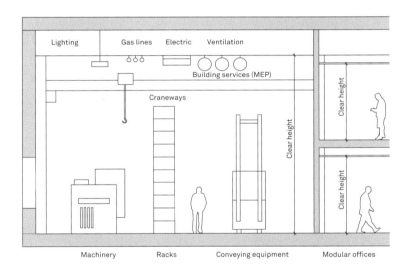

**Figure 4.4.6**
Building services section

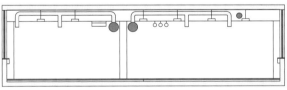

Beams in the transverse direction

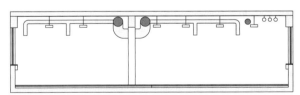

Beams in the longitudinal direction

**Table 4.4.4 (left)**
Advantages and disadvantages of multistory buildings

**Table 4.4.5 (right)**
Ceiling heights

Based on the Technical Rules for Workplaces (ASR A1.2)

| Advantages of multistory buildings | Disadvantages of multistory buildings |
|---|---|
| Small lot size | Low load-bearing capacity |
| Short distances | Higher construction costs |
| Simple ventilation | Limited flexibility |
| Good daylighting | |

| Floor area | Minimum clear ceiling height |
|---|---|
| 0–50 m² | 2.50 m |
| 51–100 m² | 2.75 m |
| 101–2,000 m² | 3.00 m |
| > 2,000 m² | 3.25 m |

## 4.4.1.3 Circulation Systems

Besides the production and storage areas, the movement and circulation areas are to be designed of sufficient size with due regard for the legal requirements. Depending on the pertinent fire protection regulations, a 2-meter-wide main aisle that leads to an outside exit or to another protected area (different fire compartment, stair, etc.) must be accessible within 15 meters from any point in a production or storage space. → **Figure 4.4.7** The maximum distance (straight line) is dependent on the ceiling height. → **Table 4.4.6** For areas larger than 200 m², two exits must be provided. For multistory buildings with over 1,600 m² of floor space, two exits are required on opposite sides of each floor.

**Figure 4.4.7**
Main aisles

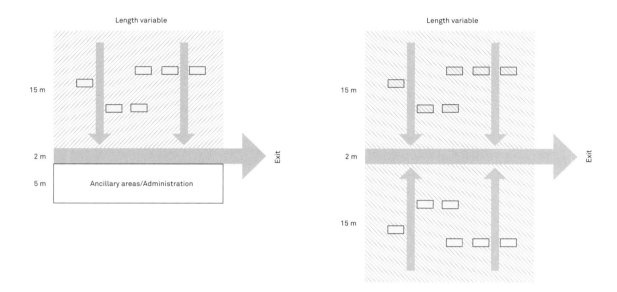

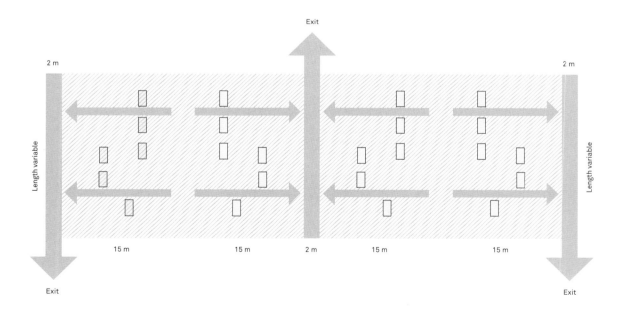

**Table 4.4.6**
Escape route lengths

Based on the Model Industrial
Buildings Directive (M-IndBauRL)

| Average clear ceiling height | Maximum distance to the exit | |
|---|---|---|
| | | With FAS/fire-extinguishing system |
| Up to 5 m | 35 m | 50 m |
| Interpolation, e.g., 8 m | 44 m | 62 m |
| Over 10 m | 50 m | 70 m |

**Table 4.4.7**
Circulation paths

Requirements based on the
Technical Rules for Workplaces
(ASR A1.8) The width of escape
routes is to be coordinated with
local valid regulations.

1  The minimum width of circulation paths derives from the
widths of escape routes as
defined in ASR A2.3. These
are based on the number of
persons served. At doors, a
reduction to the minimum width
of corridors can be disregarded
if the constriction does not
exceed 0.15 m. Regardless, the
clear width may not be less
than 0.80 m at any point.

**Minimum width of the paths for pedestrian traffic**

| Circulation path | Clear width |
|---|---|
| max. 5 people[1] | 0.875 m |
| max. 20 people[1] | 1.00 m |
| max. 200 people[1] | 1.20 m |
| max. 300 people[1] | 1.80 m |
| max. 400 people[1] | 2.40 m |
| Aisles to personally assigned workstations, auxiliary stairs | 0.60 m |
| Maintenance aisles, aisles to infrequently used operating equipment | 0.50 m |
| Pedestrian routes | |
| • Between storage facilities and storage equipment | 1.25 m |
| • In secondary corridors of storage facilities, used exclusively for loading and unloading by hand | 0.75 m |

### 4.4.1.4 Construction and Technology

Since industrial buildings must usually be built very quickly and economically, it is expedient to prefabricate components in a factory to the greatest extent possible, in order to allow the construction work on-site to proceed quickly. In determining the structural grid, girder lengths of between 12 and 24 m turn out to be particularly favorable for the roof structure, especially since traffic regulations cause the transportation costs to rise significantly for unit lengths of 30 m or more. → **Table 4.4.8** In multistory buildings, depths of 12–15 m can usually be spanned without columns. High loads and/or wide column spacing will yield systems that require purlins. As an alternative to fixed-frame structures, bracing can be provided by roof diaphragms and cross bracing.

**Roofs**

Lengthwise, the grid spacing depends on the maximum span of the roof covering (or substructure, where applicable), on the grid sizes of the facade elements, and the interior equipment as well as the requirements of all necessary facade openings.

A maximum girder spacing of 7 m is often chosen in order to use lightweight roofing of metal decking set directly on the structural members. Beyond this distance, secondary beams (purlins) must be supplied along the length of the building. These are also often used to allow placement of the corrugated metal deck such that its valleys lead toward the drainage, thus providing additional protection against standing water. → **Figure 4.4.9**

More massive roof coverings are chosen mostly for reasons of fire safety – for better fire resistance – or for structural reasons when the roof will be actively used (building services, PV system, green roofs, etc.). → **Tables 4.4.9– 4.4.11**

**Figure 4.4.8**
Requisite maneuvering areas

Based on the Technical Rules for Workplaces (ASR A1.8/Circulation areas) and the Model Industrial Buildings Directive (M-IndBauRL)

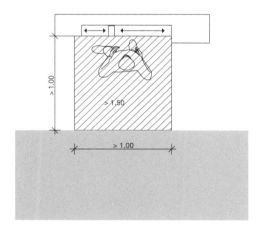

Floor space + Functional area

Maneuvering area

Circulation space

Workplaces side-by-side

**Figure 4.4.9**
Drainage

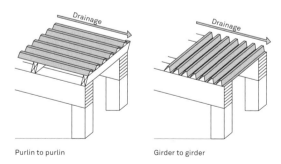

Purlin to purlin

Girder to girder

Table 4.4.8 (left)
Transport dimensions

Per the German Road Traffic Licensing Regulations (StVZO) §32 and §29

Table 4.4.9 (right)
Span lengths of roof elements

| Maximum permissible limit for road transport | Without special permission | With regional long-term authorization |
|---|---|---|
| Length | 15.50–18.75 m | 23.00 m |
| Width | 2.55 m | 3.00 m |
| Height | 4.00 m | 4.00 m |
| Total weight | 40 t (with more than 4 axles) | 41.8 t |

| Roof element | Typical span length |
|---|---|
| Corrugated metal deck | 7.50 m over two bays |
| Precast autoclaved aerated concrete (PAAC) panels | Up to 6.00 m |
| Prestressed concrete hollow core slabs | Up to 15.00 m |
| Double-tee roof panels | Up to 15.00 m |
| Folded structures, shells | Up to 20.00 m |
| Precast purlins with rectangular cross section | Up to 17.50 m |
| Prestressed concrete purlins | Up to 20.00 m |
| Concrete truss/girder | 12.00–24.00 m |
| Prestressed concrete truss/ girder | Up to 50.00 m |

Table 4.4.10 (left)
Standard values for construction thicknesses of roof elements

1 Selected: steel profile l/300; 1 mm thick, double span, 1.25 mm material thickness, system: Hoesch
2 As above, but with a 9 m span and 1.5 mm material thickness

Table 4.4.11 (right)
Typical span lengths for multistory buildings

| Thickness [mm] for span of 6 m/10 m | Roof load 1.5 kN/m² | Roof load 2.5 kN/m² | Roof load 3.5 kN/m² |
|---|---|---|---|
| Precast autoclaved aerated concrete (PAAC) elements | 225/– | 250/– | 275/– |
| Precast double-tee slabs | 260/360 | 260/360 | 260/460 |
| Precast concrete panels | 220/– | 220/– | 220/– |
| Prestressed concrete elements | 120/260 | 160/260 | 180/260 |
| Corrugated metal deck[1] | 102.6/158[2] | 137/– | 153/– |

| Floor elements | Typical span lengths |
|---|---|
| Solid floor slabs | 4.50 m |
| Precast slabs with cast-in-place topping | 3.00 m (max. 5.00 m) |
| Prestressed precast slabs | 8.00–12.00 m |
| Prestressed concrete hollow core slabs | 16.00–18.00 m (1.20 m wide) |
| Double-tee slabs | Up to 17.50 m |
| Prestressed double-tee slabs | Up to 20.00 m |

### Reinforced Concrete Structures

For economic reasons, reinforced concrete structures with repetitive elements are usually constructed of precast reinforced concrete (PRC) elements as simply supported girders on fixed columns. Due to their transport dimensions, the girders are delivered separately, then placed atop the columns and structurally joined on-site. With this system, the girders can also be made of steel or wood. → **Figure 4.4.10**

### Steel Structures

Steel columns are chiefly built as portal frames with pinned (hinged) bases and rigidly connected corners (made on-site) at the eaves. The columns are often tapered toward the bottom to save material. With high dynamic and horizontal loads (such as from a craneway), the base points are also fixed, which significantly increases the complexity and expense of the foundation. → **Figure 4.4.11**

### Wood Structures

The three-hinged frame with a structural member split in the middle, which is joined on-site using a hinged connection, is most commonly found in wooden structures. Here, the rigid corner is easy to manufacture in advance. On the construction site, however, the two halves of the frame, which are split for reasons of transport, can be joined more easily with a hinged connection. → **Figure 4.4.12**

### Arches and Space Frames

Arched structures are a special type of frame structure that enable very long spans and high clear heights. The construction of grids and space frames, which can also be restrained and curved, yields nondirectional structures that enable load transfers in two directions. → **Figure 4.4.13**

Figure 4.4.10 (left)
Column/girder

Figure 4.4.11 (right)
Portal frame

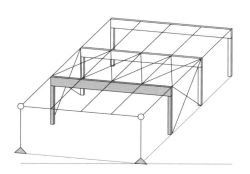

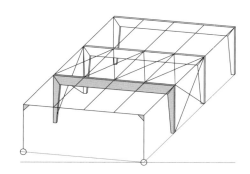

Figure 4.4.12
Three-hinged frame

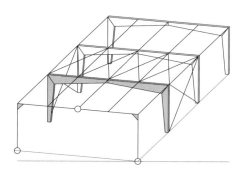

Figure 4.4.13
Constrained articulated arch

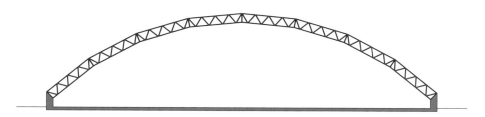

### Natural and Artificial Lighting

Despite large room depths, the natural lighting of industrial sheds can be ensured by installing domed skylights and skylight bands or sawtooth roofs. → **Figure 4.4.14** Artificial lighting is usually provided with linear luminaires suspended from the ceiling and supplemented in places by task luminaires. In multistory buildings, natural light comes from the facades and artificial lighting comes from the ceilings.

### Routing of Utility Lines

The large volumes of space and the high rates of air exchange that are needed usually necessitate mechanical ventilation. Here, displacement diffusers in proximity of the workstations are expedient, but these must be designed so they can be adapted to changing production layouts. Likewise, production-related air supply and exhaust systems, coolant lines, electrical cable trays, technical gas lines, and compressed air lines must all be designed for flexibility. This is usually accomplished using horizontal distribution along the ceiling. Where a craneway extends across the width of the building, floor ducts with outlets at regular intervals or linear covers suitable for heavy loads are advantageous. → **Figure 4.4.15**

The heating of the large space is usually accomplished by heating the room air or via radiant panels on the ceiling. In combination, however, static radiators or underfloor heating can also represent a sensible system, particularly with regard to the quality of the workstation environment.

### Technical Equipment Rooms

Technical equipment rooms and especially ventilation stations are usually located on the roof or in side areas with the shortest possible distances for the utility lines to the outlets. ↗ **Chapter 4.2 Typologies/Office and Administration**, ↗ **Chapter 3.3.1 Spaces/Workrooms and Production Spaces/Workplaces**

Figure 4.4.14
Natural lighting options

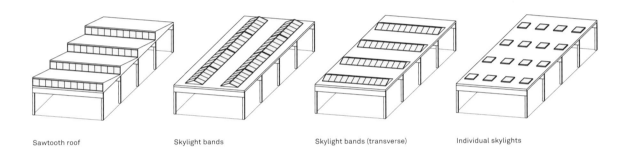

Sawtooth roof          Skylight bands          Skylight bands (transverse)          Individual skylights

Figure 4.4.15
Routing of Utility Lines

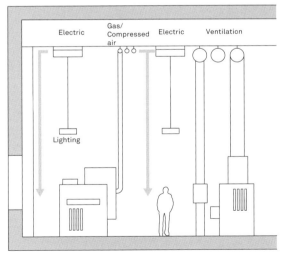

Ceiling system

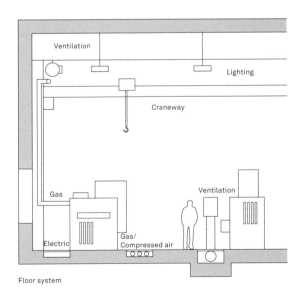

Floor system

## 4.4.2 Program of Use

Industrial production can be divided into various industrial sectors. → **Figure 4.4.16** As with the differentiation between single-story shed buildings and multistory buildings, the programs of use also differ fundamentally, depending on the form and the size of the industrial operation. The main parameters regarding the use are the flows of materials and people.

### 4.4.2.1 Large-Scale Operations

For larger production facilities, the internal flow of materials is decisive for ensuring efficient and profitable production. Incoming and outgoing deliveries (receiving and shipping) should always take place separately from the movement of persons so as to avoid obstructions. Especially in cases where delivery traffic is high, sufficient curve radii as well as parking and interim storage areas should be provided. Incoming and outgoing deliveries can use the same paths, but may not be allowed to interfere with each other. The transport path between the processing stations and the storage areas should be minimized. In large companies, precise requirements are defined with regard to logistics and production planning. Sankey diagrams (→ **Figure 4.4.18**) and workflow planning help to optimize paths and material quantities.

Production staff are usually guided over a short distance to their workstations or to a separate staging area that has changing rooms and sanitary facilities and serves as a transitional zone. → **Figure 4.4.19**

Visitors/customers and administrative staff often use the formal public entrance areas. The administrative block can be accommodated as a separate building or integrated as part of the production hall, although the differing ceiling heights mean that the offices are typically designed to occupy two or more levels. If the offices are added as an annex to the front or side of the building, it is possible to afford views of the production area. → **Figure 4.4.20, ↗ Chapter 4.2 Typologies/Office and Administration**

For large companies, safety and security play an important role: suppliers, visitors, and staff only gain access to the plant grounds after signing in and submitting to a security check. Cost-effectiveness is increased through the consolidation of checkpoints.

**Figure 4.4.16**
Industrial sectors

Categories as per ISIC/NACE

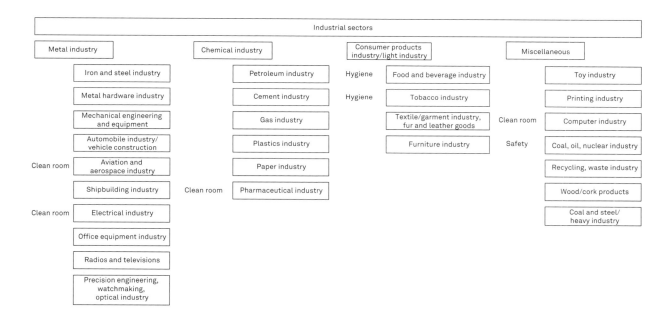

**Figure 4.4.17**
Functional diagram of
a production building

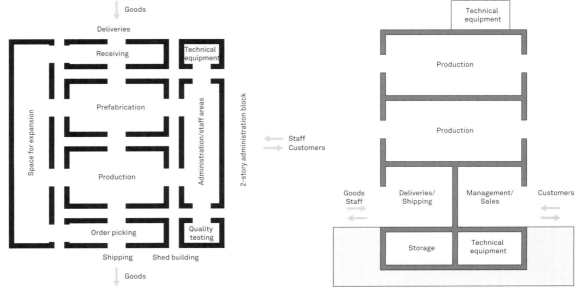

Typical layout of industrial buildings

Typical section of a multistory building

**Figure 4.4.18 (left)**
Material flow test with the
aid of a Sankey diagram

**Figure 4.4.19 (right)**
Connecting path

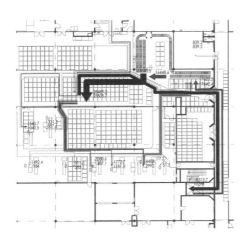

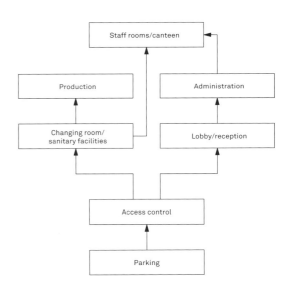

**Figure 4.4.20**
Placement of the adminis-
trative block

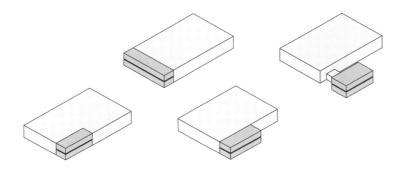

Depending on the product, various types of production can be distinguished:

**Workbench Production**
In small craftsmen's workshops, workbench production corresponds to preindustrial practices: all the steps of work are carried out by one person in one place. Typical examples are goldsmiths, shoemakers, watchmakers, dental technicians, etc.

**Workshop Production**
With workshop production, the various steps and types of work are separated at stations that are within shared spatial surroundings. This requires the work of several people.

**Factory Production**
In factory production, identical steps in executing the work are combined into spatially discrete areas (metalworking shop, paint shop, grinding shop, etc.). The workflow depends on the location of the machinery and the products (such as small batch production, furniture industry).

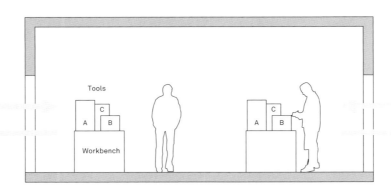

**Figure 4.4.21**
Workbench production

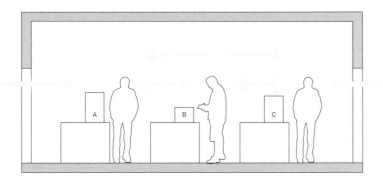

**Figure 4.4.22**
Workshop production

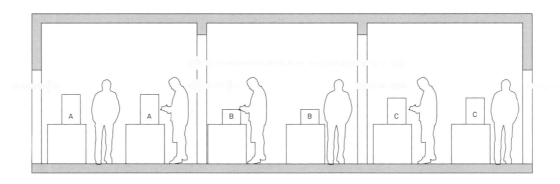

**Figure 4.4.23**
Factory production

### Assembly Line Production

Assembly line production, or continuous flow production, is well suited to making a uniform product at high production rates. In general, the assembly line is the symbol of industrial production. The workpiece is automatically transported along successive steps and the individual operations are executed at a consistently uniform pace.

### Batch Production

Batch production, which is similar to assembly line production in that the steps are also arranged one behind the other, permits different working speeds and rhythms at the stations and dispenses with the rigid connection of the workstations. Typical sectors are the automobile, furniture, and textile industries.

### Group Production (Cell Production)

A hybrid form combining workshop and batch production, in which the operations are performed according to the continuous flow principle by a group within a spatial unit. This group sometimes assumes sole responsibility for the planning and allocation of tasks (as in automobile production).

### Construction Site Fabrication

For stationary products (those bound to a specific place), workers and their means of production are brought to the site of production. Shipyards constitute a special form of construction site fabrication. Although the production or repair takes place in a fixed place, whether a building or a dock, the size of the product makes it necessary to transport people, materials, and equipment to the site of the work. The same is true to some extent for aircraft construction.

Figure 4.4.24
Assembly line production

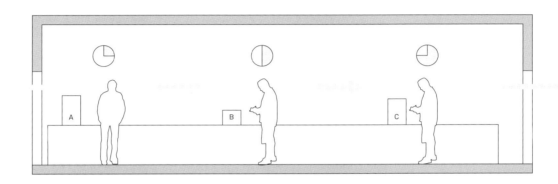

Figure 4.4.25
Batch production

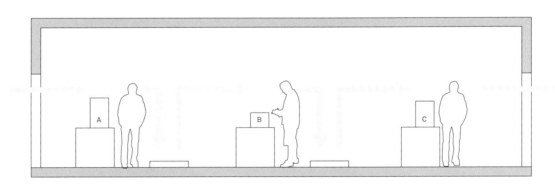

Figure 4.4.26
Group production

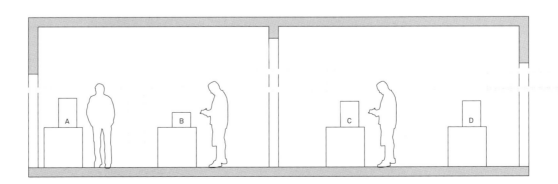

## 4.4.2.2 Small Businesses, Craftsmen's Workshops

The enterprises of those engaged in trades that work with wood, metal, and plastics are mainly found in industrial or business parks, where the production areas are augmented by storage and administrative areas, usually in conjunction with a small showroom area. For businesses involving a broader variety of trades, machinery and work areas are set up for multifunctional use in such a way that they are as freely accessible as possible. The dimensions of the individual workpieces are ordinarily key for determining the clearances between the machinery. Open floor space for final assembly and extensive space for material storage (partly as roofed-over exterior space) may need to be provided, along with space for truck deliveries.

Wood processing, in particular, produces large amounts of shavings and sawdust that must be collected and removed for reasons of health and safety. Suitable ductwork can be installed in the floor or below the roof, although the latter option may reduce the available clear height.

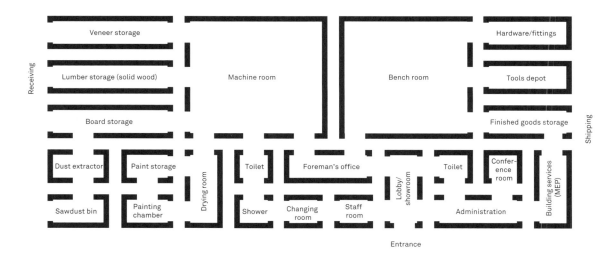

**Figure 4.4.27**
Functional diagram of a carpentry shop or wood processing plant

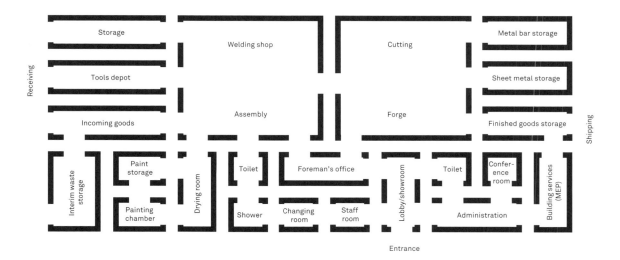

**Figure 4.4.28**
Functional diagram of a metal workshop

### 4.4.2.3 Operations with Special Cleanliness or Safety Requirements

Many industrial sectors place special demands on the indoor air or the adherence to exact temperatures, humidity levels, or air conditions. This may, on the one hand, pertain to the avoidance of specific substances or to dust particles in the air in general or, on the other hand, to compliance with stringent hygienic requirements. Such requirements have implications for the way employees work as well as on the construction of the building.

**Absence of PWIS**

Industrial operations with paint shops or powder-coating facilities must prevent paint-wetting impairment substances (PWIS) from damaging the quality of the end product. Specifically, in these cases it is of importance to forgo the use of materials containing silicone. This places high demands on the selection of the production materials, on the employees (gloves, cosmetics, etc. without silicone substances), and also on the components used to construct the building (waterproofing materials, paints, joint sealants, etc.).

**Hygiene**

All production plants that process food intended for human consumption must abide by elementary rules of hygiene in order to prevent health risks, which include:

- Personal hygiene including training and health
- Hygiene requirements for the premises
- Cleaning and disinfection of surfaces and equipment
- Product hygiene including temperature control
- Requirements for conveyance/transport, including storage
- Traceability and incoming and outgoing goods inspection, including reference samples
- Waste disposal
- Pest prevention and control
- Drinking water analysis

This affects the building primarily in the vicinity of employee entrances, changing rooms, etc., as well as in the selection of the materials used for interior fit-out. Floors, walls, and ceilings must be easy to clean and disinfect, and the floors must be slip-resistant. In addition, special requirements apply to maintaining a closed cold chain, especially at the transitions between transport, storage, and processing.

**Clean Room**

Particularly in the electronics industry, but also in some segments of the pharmaceutical industry, it may be necessary to minimize all foreign particles in the air. This may pertain to cabins, specific areas, or the entire production floor, and it encompasses various classes of purity. In these cases there are special requirements for hygiene and staff clothing. In addition to requiring a change of clothes, the transition to the protected area is made via special airlocks, which remove dust and other particles prior to entry by suction, abrasion, or dust control matting. Accordingly, the building must also be airtight and provide a ventilation system with appropriate filters and flow control technology. → **Table 4.4.12**

**Explosion Protection**

Many production processes require the handling of substances that can be explosive as a result of their diffusion, through contact with other materials or energy sources, or due to vibration. They can be liquids, gases, or even solids and dusts, and conditions pertain to their processing as well as their storage in both indoor and outdoor areas. In addition to the appropriate operational handling of materials, such as compliance with maximum limits, retention measures for liquids, periodic measurements, etc., structural measures are also necessary depending on the risk potential:

- Separation of hazardous areas into discrete fire compartments
- Separation of facilities and storage areas by distance or partitions
- Sealing of pipe penetrations
- Installation of siphons and separator traps at floor drains
- Avoidance of unnecessary areas of potential accumulation by constructing smooth surfaces and avoiding projections
- Provision and maintenance of clear escape routes

Table 4.4.12
Sector-dependent clean room definitions

In Germany, detailed information is provided in the Technical Rules for Operational Safety (TRBS) and the Technical Rules for Hazardous Substances (TRGS).

| Sector | Main contamination | Main standard |
| --- | --- | --- |
| Semiconductor technology | Particles | US Federal Standard 209E, replaced by ISO 14644-1 and ISO 14644-2 |
| Astronautical engineering | Particles | ECSS-Q-ST-70-01 |
| Food technology | Microorganisms | VDI 2083 |
| Pharmaceutics | Bacterial count | EU-GMP Guidelines, Appendix 1: Manufacture of Sterile Medicinal Products |

### 4.4.3  Areas and Rooms

**External circulation**  ↗287 ↗Chapter 3.1

**Entrance areas**  ↗287 ↗Chapter 3.2.1

**Gate**  ↗287

**Stairs, elevators**  ↗Chapter 3.2.4, ↗Chapter3.2.7

**Corridors, internal circulation**  ↗Chapter 3.2.2

**Workplaces**  ↗288 ↗Chapter 3.3.1

**Storage areas**  ↗288 ↗Chapter 3.7.2

**Assembly/fabrication**  ↗288 ↗Chapter 3.3.2

**Administration**  ↗288 ↗Chapter 4.2

**Foreman's office**  ↗288

**Locker rooms**  ↗289 ↗Chapter 3.8.2

**Meeting rooms**  ↗Chapter 4.2

**Kitchens**  ↗289 ↗Chapter 3.6

**Canteen/cafeteria**  ↗289 ↗Chapter 4.7, ↗Chapter 3.4.3

**Break rooms**  ↗289 ↗Chapter 3.8.1

**Toilets**  ↗289 ↗Chapter 3.5

**Server rooms**  ↗Chapter 3.9.8

**First aid rooms**  ↗Chapter 3.8.3

**Janitor's closets**  ↗Chapter 3.8.4

**Mechanical equipment rooms**  ↗Chapter 3.9

### 4.4.3.1 Entrance Areas

Aside from perhaps providing a formal entrance area for visitors, outdoor areas play a subordinate role. In addition to providing the necessary widths and radiuses for areas for vehicular traffic, it is especially important to coordinate the slopes and spot drain locations. The number of parking spaces depends chiefly on the statutory requirements but also on the simultaneity of use (shift duty, sick days, business travel, etc.). →**Table 4.4.13**

#### Gate

For large-scale operations, the gate is usually a detached building sited on the company grounds before reaching the parking lots, but it can also be incorporated into a spatial sequence in the reception area. In addition to controlling the flow of goods and/or people, the gate can be the place where visitors obtain information and passes (visitor registration), thus necessitating additional features such as counters, a waiting area, and possibly exhibition areas. In most cases, turnstiles are also used to control employee access and for time-keeping purposes and/or issuing keys.

As the central point of access, technical control centers (lighting, FAS, intruder alarm, instrumentation and control, camera surveillance, etc.) can be sensibly located here. If there is a need to control car or delivery traffic, barrier equipment with intercoms must be provided. ↗**Chapter 3.1.3 Spaces/External Circulation/Private Exterior Circulation**

#### Receiving

The control and inspection of deliveries can take place at a gate, the reception area, or the receiving department manager's office. Canopy structures guarantee that deliveries made outside remain dry. Impact protection and guide frames help with larger trucks, and the use of ramps, loading bays, and loading platforms can compensate for height differences. Outdoor storage areas, disposal areas, and washing areas are usually located near the receiving department. ↗**Chapter 3.1.2 Spaces/External Circulation/Parked Vehicles**, ↗**Chapter 4.3 Typologies/Logistics and Commerce**

**Figure 4.4.29**
Schematic site plan for an industrial building

↗ Chapter 3.1 Spaces/
External Circulation

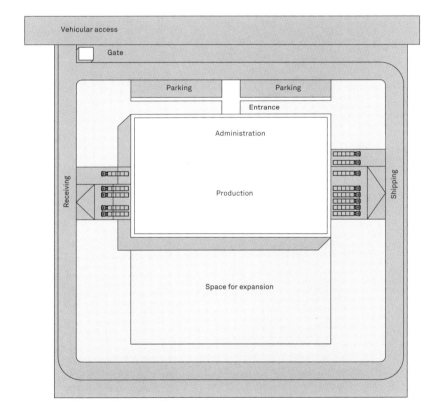

**Figure 4.4.30 (left)**
Detached entry gate for pedestrian and vehicular control

**Table 4.4.13 (right)**
Requirements for parking spaces

As per Bavarian Ordinance Governing Parking Facilities (GaStellV)

| | Required parking spaces | Portion of total allocated for visitors |
|---|---|---|
| Craftsmen's shops and industrial plants | 1 space per 70 m² net area or 1 space per 3 employees | 10% |
| Storage rooms, storage yards | 1 space per 100 m² net area or 1 space per 3 employees | – |

## 4.4.3.2 Storage Areas

Storage areas are an important factor for design. For instance, sufficient areas must be provided for raw materials, additives, hazardous substances, supplier products, intermediate products, end products, recyclable materials, and waste materials. Storage needs range from that of the extended production of seasonal items with long storage periods (such as fireworks) to JIT (just in time) production, which largely dispenses with warehouse stocks and each vendor part is obtained when it is needed in the production process. Thus the dimensioning of storage areas is always dependent on the specifics of production. ↗Chapter 3.7 Spaces/Storage Spaces, ↗Chapter 4.3 Typologies/Logistics and Commerce

## 4.4.3.3 Assembly and Fabrication

By far the largest areas within industrial buildings are those used for assembly and fabrication, and these must therefore be optimized with respect to manufacturing processes and space requirements. The starting point is the equipment layout planning, which comprises operating and service areas, protective zones, maintenance accessibility, and the supply of building services. → **Figure 4.4.31** For smaller equipment layouts, flexible feeding from the ceiling is possible; for larger equipment, it may be necessary

to design foundations or equipment pads at an early phase of the planning. Ideally, machinery will be positioned in rows or clusters so that distinct transport routes and walkways result. When planning workbenches or welding cabins, the sizes of the products to be made must be taken into account so as to avoid any interference with the work done at adjacent workstations. → **Figure 4.4.33**

## 4.4.3.4 Administration

The administrative areas of industrial buildings contain all the typical elements of an office building, and are therefore discussed in **Chapter 4.2 Typologies/Office and Administration.**

### Foreman's Office

The foreman's (or supervisor's) office or cabin is a special, production-oriented type of office space. These rooms may be located off to the side on the ground floor, as standalone cabins within the main production space, on a mezzanine, or combined with meeting rooms and/or storage areas on two levels. They are typically made with modular, insulated partition systems that can be relocated as needed and adapted to fit the production layout. Depending on the manufacturer, a two-story modular office group can reach a height of approximately 8.00 m.

**Figure 4.4.31 (left)**
Example of equipment installation

Based on the Technical Rules for Workplaces (ASR A1.2) and VBG

**Figure 4.4.32 (right)**
Two-story foreman's office

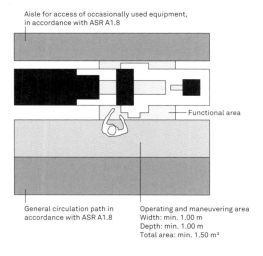

Aisle for access of occasionally used equipment, in accordance with ASR A1.8

Functional area

General circulation path in accordance with ASR A1.8

Operating and maneuvering area
Width: min. 1.00 m
Depth: min. 1.00 m
Total area: min. 1.50 m²

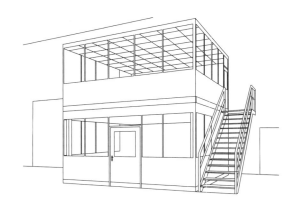

**Figure 4.4.33**
Examples of workbenches and welding cabins

↗ Chapter 3.3 Spaces/Workrooms and Production Spaces

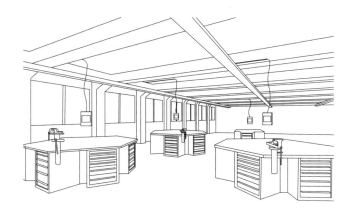

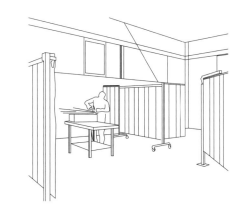

## 4.4.3.5 Ancillary Spaces

### Staff Rooms and Communal Areas

In many companies, depending on the surrounding infrastructure and the number of employees, social spaces are provided to meet the needs of the employees and for a pleasant general working climate. Legally prescribed staff facilities must offer at least 1 m² per simultaneously present employee (room size > 6 m²) and may not be more than 100 m nor more than one story away from all work areas. In addition, canteens, child care facilities, fitness rooms, and lounge areas are also often provided. ↗ Chapter 3.4 Spaces/Communication Spaces and Dining Rooms, ↗ Chapter 3.8.1 Spaces/Ancillary and Staff Rooms/Lunchrooms, ↗ Chapter 4.7 Typologies/Lodging and Food Service

### Sanitary Facilities

Separate sanitary facilities are generally provided for different user groups, such as production staff (with changing rooms and washrooms), administrative staff, visitors (accessible from reception area), as well as for specific social areas such as the canteen or cafeteria and sports facilities. → Table 4.4.14 The sanitary facilities may also not be further from any work areas than a maximum of 100 meters or one story. ↗ Chapter 3.5.3 Spaces/Sanitary Facilities/Public and Commercial Sanitary Facilities

### Changing Rooms

Changing rooms, also known as locker rooms, are generally provided for the production staff and serve as a transitional zone between the entrance and the production area. While in many companies the change from civilian clothing to workwear or protective clothing is intended to protect the employee, in the case of clean room production it mainly serves to protect the product. Changing rooms are usually coupled with sanitary facilities and separated by gender. Depending on hygiene requirements, the changing rooms might additionally be separated into dirty and clean areas. ↗ Chapter 3.8.2 Spaces/Ancillary and Staff Rooms/Locker and Changing Rooms

Table 4.4.14
Washing facilities

Based on the Technical Rules for Workplaces (ASR A4.1)

**Category A** for activities in moderately dirty environments

**Category B** for activities in very dirty environments

**Category C** for activities in extremely dirty environments, if compelling health concerns exist, for activities involving substances with strongly offending odors, when personal protective equipment covering extensive parts of the body is worn, for activities performed under exceptional climatic conditions (heat, cold) or under wet conditions or requiring strenuous physical labor.

| Maximum number of employees ordinarily permitted to use a washroom | Category A | | Category B | | | | Category C | | | |
| --- | --- | --- | --- | --- | --- | --- | --- | --- | --- | --- |
| | Washbasins | | Washbasins | | Showers | | Washbasins | | Showers | |
| | Minimum number for simultaneous use | | | | | | | | | |
| | Low | High | Low | High | Low | High | Low | High | Low | High |
| up to 5 | 1 | 2 | 1 | 2 | 1 | 1 | 1 | 2 | 1 | 2 |
| 6–10 | 2 | 3 | 1 | 2 | 1 | 2 | 2 | 3 | 1 | 3 |
| 11–15 | 3 | 4 | 2 | 3 | 1 | 2 | 3 | 4 | 2 | 4 |
| 16–20 | 3 | 5 | 2 | 4 | 2 | 3 | 3 | 5 | 2 | 5 |
| 21–25 | 4 | 6 | 3 | 5 | 2 | 3 | 4 | 6 | 3 | 6 |
| 26–30 | 4 | 6 | 3 | 5 | 2 | 3 | 4 | 7 | 3 | 7 |
| 31–35 | 5 | 7 | 3 | 6 | 2 | 3 | 5 | 9 | 4 | 9 |
| 36–40 | 5 | 8 | 4 | 7 | 2 | 4 | 5 | 10 | 4 | 10 |
| 41–45 | 6 | 9 | 4 | 8 | 2 | 4 | 5 | 12 | 4 | 12 |
| 46–50 | 6 | 10 | 4 | 9 | 2 | 4 | 6 | 13 | 5 | 13 |
| 51–55 | 7 | 11 | 4 | 9 | 3 | 5 | 6 | 14 | 5 | 14 |
| 56–60 | 8 | 12 | 5 | 11 | 3 | 5 | 6 | 15 | 5 | 15 |
| 61–65 | 8 | 12 | 5 | 11 | 3 | 5 | 7 | 16 | 6 | 16 |
| 66–70 | 8 | 12 | 5 | 11 | 3 | 5 | 7 | 16 | 6 | 16 |
| 71–75 | 9 | 13 | 5 | 12 | 3 | 5 | 8 | 17 | 7 | 17 |
| 76–80 | 10 | 14 | 6 | 12 | 4 | 6 | 8 | 18 | 7 | 18 |
| 81–85 | 10 | 14 | 6 | 12 | 4 | 6 | 9 | 18 | 8 | 18 |
| 86–90 | 10 | 14 | 6 | 13 | 4 | 6 | 10 | 19 | 9 | 19 |
| 91–95 | 10 | 14 | 6 | 13 | 4 | 7 | 11 | 20 | 10 | 20 |
| 96–100 | 11 | 15 | 6 | 14 | 4 | 7 | 11 | 20 | 10 | 20 |
| Per additional 30 | + 2 | + 3 | + 1 | + 3 | + 1 | + 2 | + 2 | + 3 | + 2 | + 3 |

**Bauhaus**, Dessau, Germany, Walter Gropius, 1926

**Goetheanum**, Dornach, Switzerland, Rudolf Steiner, 1928

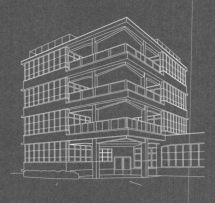

**Openluchtschool (open air school)**, Amsterdam, The Netherlands, Johannes Duiker, 1931

**Max Taut School**, Berlin, Germany, Max Taut, 1932

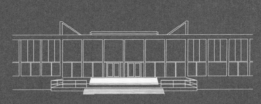

**S. R. Crown Hall**, Chicago, Illinois, USA, Ludwig Mies van der Rohe, 1958

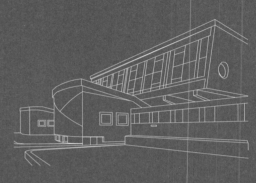

**Geschwister Scholl comprehensive school**, Lünen, Germany, Hans Sharoun, 1962

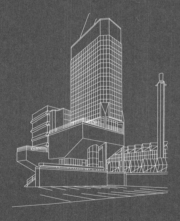

**Leicester University Engineering Building**, Leicester, Great Britain, James Stirling/James Gowan, 1963

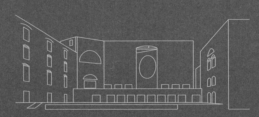

**Indian Institute of Management**, Ahmedabad, India, Louis Kahn, 1974

**Hysolar Research Institute**, University of Stuttgart, Germany, Günter Behnisch, 1989

**Luginsland nursery school ("Schiff im Weinberg")**, Stuttgart, Germany, Günter Behnisch, 1990

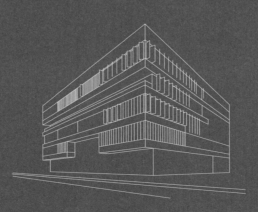

**Ørestad College**, Copenhagen, Denmark, 3XN Architects, 2006

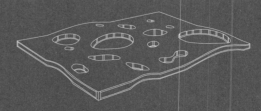

**Rolex Learning Center**, Lausanne, Switzerland, SANAA, 2010

Mareike Borkeloh
Mathias Hölzinger

# 4 Typologies
# 4.5 Education and Research

## 4.5.1 Building Concept ↗292

4.5.1.1 Planning Parameters ↗292
4.5.1.2 Building Forms ↗296
4.5.1.3 Circulation Systems ↗297
4.5.1.4 Construction and Technology ↗300

## 4.5.2 Program of Use ↗303

4.5.2.1 Child Day Care Centers ↗303
4.5.2.2 Schools ↗306
4.5.2.3 Colleges and Universities ↗309
4.5.2.4 Research Facilities ↗310
4.5.2.5 Libraries ↗311

## 4.5.3 Areas and Rooms ↗312

4.5.3.1 Entrance Areas ↗313
4.5.3.2 Group Activity Rooms in Child Day Care Facilities ↗313
4.5.3.3 Classrooms in Schools ↗315
4.5.3.4 Lecture Halls in Colleges and Universities ↗315
4.5.3.5 Specialized Classrooms and Laboratories ↗317
4.5.3.6 Communal Spaces ↗321
4.5.3.7 Cafeterias ↗323
4.5.3.8 Libraries ↗323
4.5.3.9 Administrative Spaces ↗324
4.5.3.10 Ancillary Spaces ↗324

# 4.5 Education and Research

## 4.5.1 Building Concept

### 4.5.1.1 Planning Parameters

Each stage, from childcare to school and onward to academic and scientifically oriented programs of study and research activities, involves distinct use-specific concepts and spaces. The design of educational and research buildings must, on the one hand, take into account a long service life and, on the other, be able to flexibly adapt to the ever-changing requirements and curricula of school systems and institutions of higher education.

Usually, the design of the building is preceded by an extensive analysis of the demand, in which the catchment area and the surrounding infrastructure are assessed. Both the location and size of the establishment are determined on this basis.

Typical planning parameters are:
- Place, context, and infrastructure
- Geometry of the site
- Building code restrictions
- Spatial program and needs
- Necessary secondary functions
- Layout type and building form
- Educational concepts
- Needs of the user groups
- Duration and concepts of use
- Public-private relationships
- Barrier-free accessibility
- Budget and deadlines
- Integration of exterior space
- Integration of existing buildings

**Orientation and Connection to the Outdoors**
The provision of outdoor spaces is an important design parameter for all types of buildings; situations can range from a direct connection between indoor and outdoor spaces in child day care facilities to informal and recreational use of the outdoor spaces surrounding college and university buildings. Where buildings are close to busy roads, the outdoor spaces should be protected from noise emissions through appropriate placement of the building structures. Likewise, the orientation of rooms toward daylight and toward outdoor areas that are protected from noise plays an important role in the development and health of children and young people. →Table 4.5.1

**Pedagogic and Didactic Spatial Concepts**
In order to embody various pedagogic and didactic principles in the building, closed, open, and semiopen concepts can be used for the group activity rooms, classrooms, and workrooms. →Table 4.5.2

The closed concept (also referred to as the separative model) provides user groups, such as specific groups of children, school classes, or seminar participants, with their own room in order to foster a better sense of group identification and promote undisturbed learning within the group. →Figure 4.5.1

In the semiopen concept, the objective is to enable education in separate areas or clusters but still allow for the option of combining areas and mixing or separating user groups in response to different interests. Most often groups of rooms or clusters are arranged around and share general-purpose common areas and specific room functions. →Figure 4.5.3

With an open concept (also referred to as the integration model), space is subdivided either acoustically or optically for various temporary and individual groupings that may be based on random association, shared interests, or personal relationships. An open concept is designed in the form of open spaces with learning landscapes, common rooms, or classrooms and seminar rooms that are linked to one another, and should provide areas for both retreat and communication. →Figure 4.5.2

The design for a specific spatial concept includes not only the classrooms, common spaces, and rooms for research, but also the layout and integration of spaces for ancillary functions and the teaching staff. These can be additive and kept separate from the other functions of the building, gathered in a central location, or they can be decentralized and partly or wholly integrated in the various areas. →Figure 4.5.4

Table 4.5.1
Orientations of different types of rooms for optimum daylight

|  | North | South | West | East |
|---|---|---|---|---|
| Group activity rooms | − | ++ | + | + |
| Teaching rooms | + | + | ++ | ++ |
| Workshops/ateliers/laboratories | ++ | − | + | + |
| Auditoriums | + | + | ++ | ++ |

++ optimum orientation   + possible orientation   − unfavorable orientation

Figure 4.5.1 (left)
Closed spatial concept

Figure 4.5.2 (right)
Open spatial concept

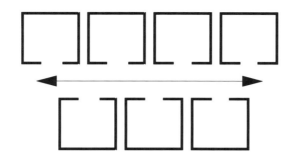
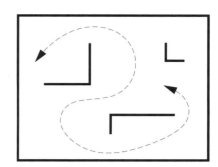

Figure 4.5.3
Semiopen spatial concept

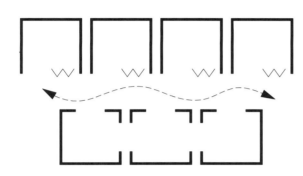
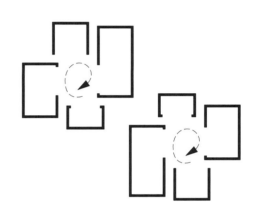

Table 4.5.2
Spatial relationships of educational concepts (examples)

| | Guiding idea | Spatial design | Characteristics |
|---|---|---|---|
| Montessori | • Education fostering self-reliance, without compulsion, direction, or control<br>• Develop enjoyment of learning<br>• Play exclusively with Montessori learning aids | Closed concept: clear and simple spaces | • Open space for exercise and appropriation by the children<br>• Shelves that are freely accessible at all times for storing toys along the walls |
| Waldorf | • Education in accordance with Rudolf Steiner's anthroposophical philosophy<br>• Harmony with the aim of providing protection, order, and comfort<br>• Play and learning as an exercise of free will, as a means of assimilating experiences, and for molding fantasy | Closed concept: organic/natural design | • Clear structuring into thematic areas |
| Freinet | • Free development of personality and critical interaction with the environment<br>• Self-responsibility of the child as well as collaboration and mutual responsibility<br>• Self-determined learning defined by the class council instead of teacher-directed forms of learning | Closed concept: clear, divisible spaces | • Separable areas within the classroom yield subject-oriented work corners or studios<br>• Separation of areas determined by the pupils |
| Reggio | • No set concept > adequate solutions are sought for each facility in relation to its sociocultural context<br>• Stimulation and challenge as well as comfort and refuge<br>• Children follow their own interests and rhythm<br>• Children participate in everyday activities | Open spaces | • No definitive statement about the spatial structure. Instead: adequate solutions are sought for each facility<br>• Transparency and openness based on spatial connections and expansive glazed areas |

Figure 4.5.4
Models for the spatial organization of functional areas

**Additive model**

In nonintegrated layouts the different functional areas of educational
and research buildings are separate.

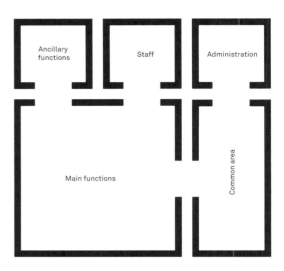

**Partially integrated model**

In partially integrated layouts, secondary functions such as team/staff
rooms or decentralized specialized rooms are placed near the general
education or research areas.

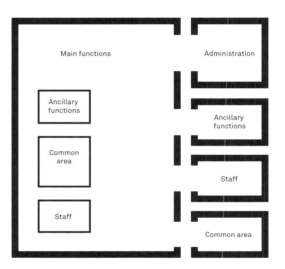

**Integrated model**

In integrated layouts, the different functional areas are located together,
creating a type of interior landscape.

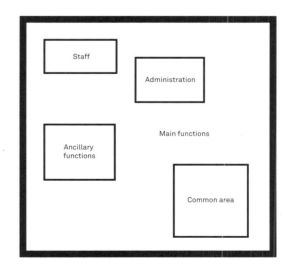

## Campus Organization/Multiple Institutions

In the case of large organizations such as universities with several separate units or school centers with different school types, it is possible to use two different models. Where several units and organizational structures or parts of structures are combined in a building or in a compact campus one talks about an integrated model, since there is a functional relationship between the units and some functions are shared. Where units of an establishment are spread out across the town or city, or where they are allocated in a single building but without any functional relationships to one another, one speaks of an additive model. → Figure 4.5.5

Figure 4.5.5
Models of spatial and functional organization

**Integrated model**

<u>In an urban context</u>
A number of different establishments and service providers are spatially connected.
> Buildings are accessible for external users.

<u>Within the building</u>
Several functional areas are combined.
> Formation of multifunctional clusters or an open spatial landscape

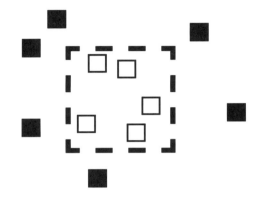

**Additive model**

<u>In an urban context</u>
Several units are networked to form a local educational landscape.
> Shared use of resources and improved communication

<u>Within the building</u>
Separate arrangement of different functional areas
> No spatial connection

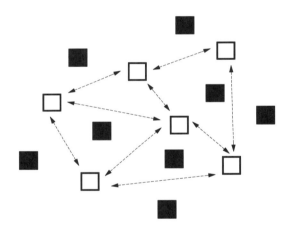

## 4.5.1.2 Building Forms

### Compact/Freestanding Buildings
The more compact building forms include linear buildings as well as nondirectional and cluster-like buildings. In view of the fact that group activity areas and classrooms should be arranged along outer walls to allow for sufficient natural daylight, it may be necessary to provide inner courtyards. With the help of these it is possible to arrange main functional areas on both sides of a corridor. → **Figure 4.5.6**

### Building Complexes/Conglomerates
In order to achieve a functional or atmospheric division of different functional areas, it is possible to differentiate the physical spaces of building complexes and combinations in a number of different ways. → **Figure 4.5.7** Furthermore it is possible to define different relationships between the inside and outside and to create group-specific allocations and/or shared areas with the arrangement of the building volumes and the design of the outside space.

### Multifunctional Buildings or Building Complexes
The combination of educational and research facilities with other facilities or uses, such as working and living, requires the spatial combination of different components within a single complex. This can be achieved by stacking, arranging sections in buildings, or in the form of extensions. Examples are company day nurseries, combined educational facilities consisting of a day nursery and school, or training and research facilities within a company. Depending on the type of combined use, it may be possible to benefit from synergy effects due to the spatial and functional juxtaposition. → **Figure 4.5.8**

**Figure 4.5.6**
Compact/freestanding buildings

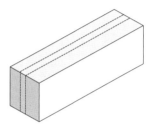
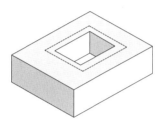
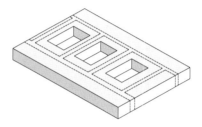

Linear building with courtyards          Nondirectional building with courtyard          Cluster-like building form with courtyards

**Figure 4.5.7**
Building complexes

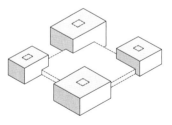
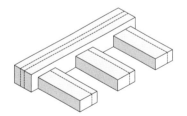
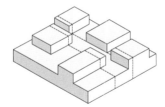

Linked individual buildings          Spine building with finger extensions          Stacked building complex

**Figure 4.5.8**
Multifunctional buildings/building complexes

a) Stacked
b) In building sections
c) As extension

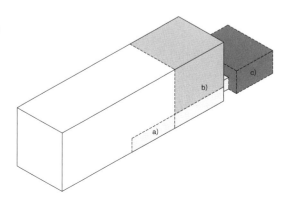

### 4.5.1.3 Circulation Systems

Staircases and corridors in education and research buildings must have a minimum clear width of 1.20 m. Where these spaces are used by larger numbers of people at the same time, the width should be significantly increased. The clear circulation space must not be reduced by doors opening into the space or by fitted components. The maximum length of necessary corridors with only one escape route direction is 10 m. → **Table 4.5.3**

Circulation areas in education and research buildings should always be designed to double up as places for communication and for people to spend time in, taking into account building code requirements. In addition to areas for breaks inside and outside, the distribution and circulation areas are important design elements for the acceptance of user groups. By combining different systems it is possible to create different zones and to enhance the versatility of their use options. → **Figures 4.5.10 – 4.5.12**, ↗ **Chapter 3.2 Spaces/Internal Circulation**

Figure 4.5.9
Planning parameters for
circulation system

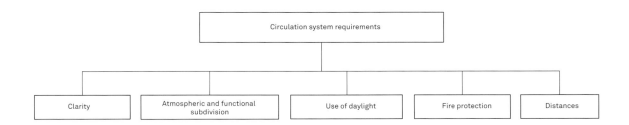

Table 4.5.3
Minimum dimensions for
circulation zones

1   Exits from staff rooms with
less than 200 m² floor area

| | Exits from staff and teaching rooms | Necessary corridors | Necessary staircases |
|---|---|---|---|
| Child day care centers | 0.90 m | 1.50 m | 1.20 m |
| Schools (as per German School Design Directive) | 0.90 m | 1.50 m | 1.20 m |
| Universities (as per VStattVO) | 0.90 m [1]<br>1.20 m | 1.20 m | 1.20 m |

Table 4.5.4
Application of circulation systems

| | Child day care centers | Elementary schools | Secondary schools | Colleges and universities | Research institutions |
|---|---|---|---|---|---|
| Single-loaded circulation | ● | ● | | | ● |
| Double-loaded circulation | ● | ● | ● | | ● |
| Access from hall or courtyard | ● | ● | ● | ● | ● |
| Mixed types | | ● | ● | ● | ● |

● better suited   ● less suited

**Figure 4.5.10 (above)**
Built-in fixtures as play options
in circulation zones

**Figure 4.5.11 (centre)**
Circulation zone used as a
relaxation area, including
integrated lockers

**Figure 4.5.12 (below)**
Opening of a group work area
toward the circulation zone

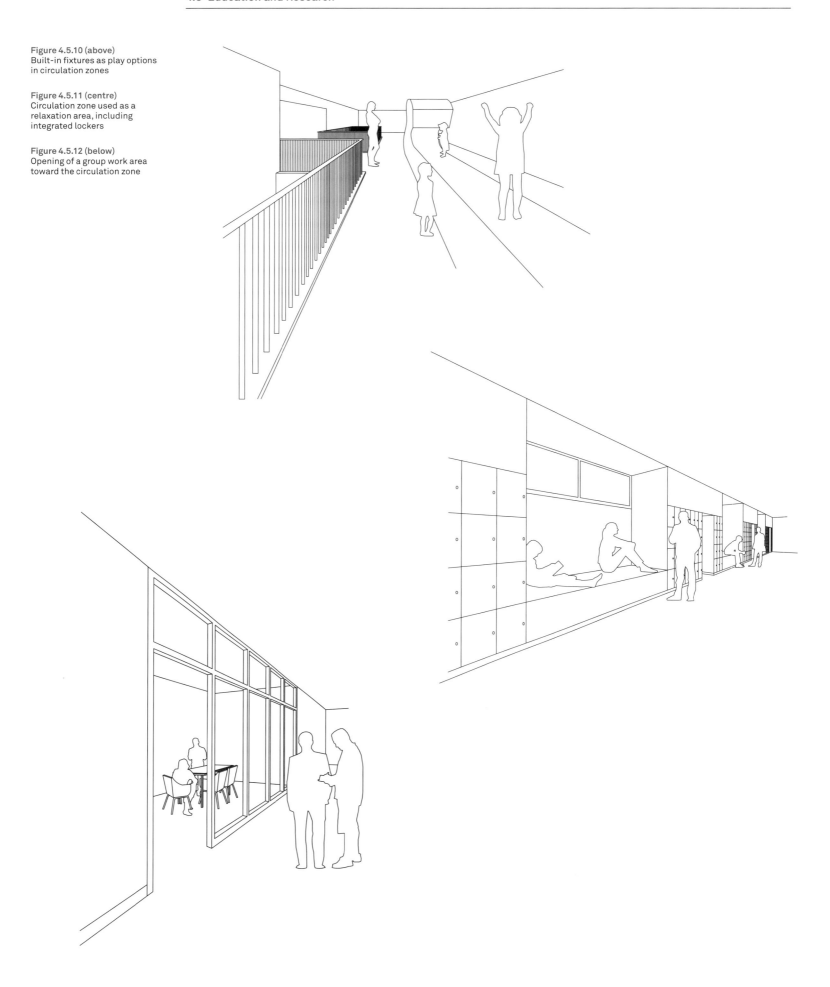

Single-loaded Circulation

In narrow buildings the horizontal circulation can be arranged using a single-loaded system. The shallow depth of the building makes it possible to use even very narrow sites. In urban situations with increased noise emissions, single-loaded circulation can be used as a noise buffer. On the negative side, this type of layout results in long access routes, poor orientation and a relatively high cost per unit of floor area. → **Figure 4.5.13**

Double-loaded Circulation

Double-loaded circulation is used when group and teaching rooms are arranged on both sides of a corridor. An east–west orientation allows for optimum natural light from both sides; however, the circulation routes are on the inside of the building. Double-loaded circulation systems shorten the internal distances between various functional areas. → **Figure 4.5.14**

Access from a Hall or Courtyard

Halls and courtyards can be used to provide horizontal and vertical access and can also have a positive effect on orientation within the building, acting as a central point. This creates flexibly usable space for meeting and communication. → **Figure 4.5.15**

Mixed Types

In large developments it is often necessary to use a combination of the systems shown in order to achieve an economical and clear circulation system for complex layouts. An example is a circulation system with main and secondary corridors, both of which can be single-loaded or double-loaded. In this system, the main circulation works as a multifunctional area with adjoining shared areas, while the secondary corridors form self-contained units. When used in combination with a guide system, this layout allows for good orientation in the building. → **Figure 4.5.16**

Figure 4.5.13 (left)
Single-loaded circulation

Figure 4.5.14 (right)
Double-loaded circulation

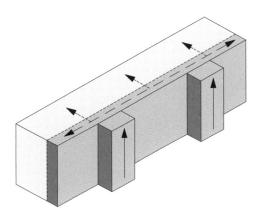

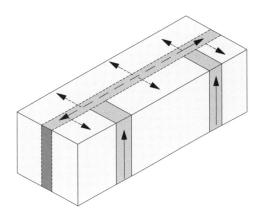

Figure 4.5.15 (left)
Access from a hall or courtyard

Figure 4.5.16 (right)
Circulation via main and secondary corridors

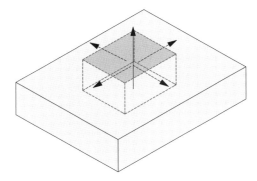

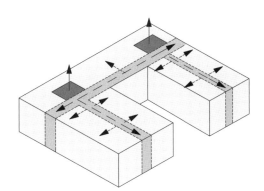

## 4.5.1.4 Construction and Technology

### Load-Bearing Structure

Due to the required sizes of group activity rooms, class-rooms, and auditoriums, large, column-free floor spans are needed, thus making these rooms decisive for determining the overall structural system. Due to fire-protection requirements, education and research buildings are usually built of solid (masonry or concrete) construction unless they are intended solely for temporary use.

### Building Services

Where these buildings are used by large numbers of people, it is common to provide mechanical ventilation or air-conditioning systems, which are intended to improve the room air quality and avoid overheating of the interior. However, a more sensible solution is to prevent overheating by appropriate orientation of the building, providing adequate daylight but preventing solar heat gain with appropriate devices in the facades.

A special situation exists in specialist rooms and laboratories, which usually require high levels of technical equipment; this has an effect on the space to be provided for machinery and the amount of services installations, and hence the story height. For this reason, it is recommended to define the necessary services installations at an early design stage and to carry out a risk analysis in order to determine the installation levels in ducts and in the voids above suspended ceilings. → Table 4.5.5 This analysis should check that the routes of installations and ducts do not collide; ideally the different types of installations are allocated to different levels, thus avoiding any crossovers. An open installation underneath the ceilings of the laboratories is generally recommended. → Figure 4.5.17 This means that the service installations can easily be accessed for the purposes of maintenance and any future modifications; in addition, extra fire-protection measures in corridors are avoided.

Table 4.5.5
Technical services for laboratories

As per Braun and Grömling 2005

| Heat, ventilation, and air-conditioning (HVAC) | Fluids | | | Electrical services |
| --- | --- | --- | --- | --- |
| | Refrigeration and cooling water | Water/wastewater | Gases/other fluids | |
| • In rooms with high heat output, internal rooms, and laboratories<br>• Ventilation systems for filtering, heating, and cooling<br>• Air intake station in the basement, supply air via ventilation ducts and air outlets<br>• Air outlet on the roof, Discharge via exhaust vents and air ducts | • Cooling via HVAC systems for the purpose of process cooling and circulation cooling for experiments<br>• Cooling aggregates in the equipment room in the basement or the attic<br>• When locating cooling aggregates and recooling units it is necessary to consider noise emissions, vibrations, and the potential for mist development | • Potable water, process water, demineralized water, and ultra-pure water<br>• As a rule, wastewater and laboratory water services must be installed separately<br>• Fire-extinguishing water reservoirs may be located outside and used as part of the landscaping | • Types of supply: central storage, group storage, individual bottles<br>• It is advisable to provide routings for media that are selected at a later date<br>• Demand for nitrogen should be clarified at an early stage, since the<br>• nitrogen tank must be located outside the premises in a building-like enclosure with delivery zone | • These are largely determined by the volume of data traffic and the number and rating of consumer units<br>• It is advisable to provide reserves for future upgrades<br>• An emergency power network supplied by a diesel generator should be provided |

Figure 4.5.17
Routing of utilities

* Height depends on the services to be installed

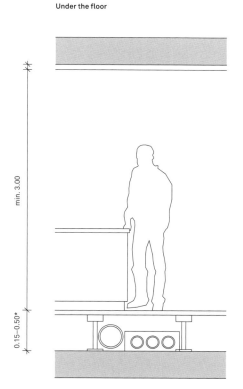

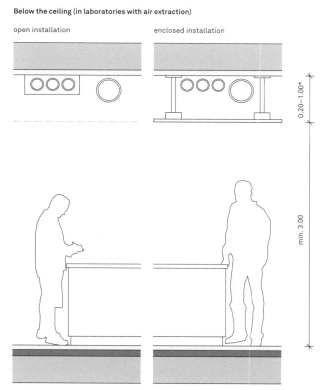

### Daylighting

The supply of daylight to group and teaching rooms can be arranged via windows in the elevation or via skylights, taking into account any solar screening systems. → **Figure 4.5.18** The height of the windows above the work surface determines the depth of the room supplied with daylight. In order to allow unrestricted views to the outside, the sill height of windows should be aligned with the worktops (that is, at table height) and fall guards. In day nurseries and primary schools, windows with low sill heights create a direct spatial connection between the group rooms and play/break areas. Protected exterior space allocated next to the interior makes it possible to open windows/doors irrespective of the weather and protects the interior against excessive light in the height of summer. → **Figure 4.5.19**

A good room acoustics design is just as relevant as the supply of daylight. In group and teaching rooms in particular where many children and young people congregate, suitable sound insulation and reduced reverberation time are essential for the interior quality of a room. ↗**Chapter 2.2 Human Measure/Comfort and Physical Spatial Qualities**

Figure 4.5.18
Natural lighting of group, teaching and research rooms

**Lateral daylight systems**

**Lateral window**  With lateral windows, the light strength reduces toward the center of the room. The actual depth of daylight depends on the height of the window. As a design guideline for daylight reaching the depth of the room, one can assume a window height of 2.5 times the height of the work surface.

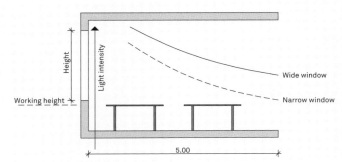

**Light shelves**  The installation of light shelves as part of lateral windows improves the lighting in the depth of the room. These shelves reflect light from the upper area of the window into the rear area of the room. External light shelves can also be used as solar screening for workplaces near the window.

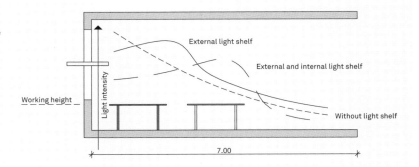

**Clerestory fenestration bands**  Lateral clerestory fenestration bands provide daylight deep into the room. The degree of light coming into the room is determined by the position, size and height. Optimal lighting is achieved when the distance from the (narrow) fenestration band to the opposite wall is equal to the distance from the work surface to the bottom of the band (wide fenestration bands: 1.5 times the distance).

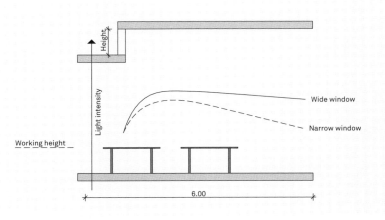

Figure 4.5.18 (continuation)
Natural lighting of group, teaching
and research rooms

### Lateral daylight systems

**Lateral window and clerestory fenestration band**

A combination of lateral window and clerestory fenestration band creates an even distribution of daylight.

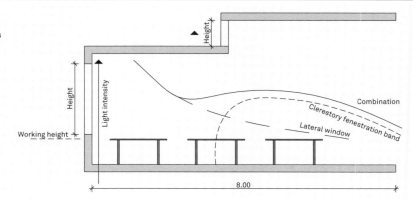

### Overhead daylighting

**Skylights**

In single-story buildings or on upper floors, daylight can be provided via skylights. In this case, the amount of daylight coming into the building depends on the size of the opening and the height of the duct. An even distribution of daylight can be achieved by using several skylights.

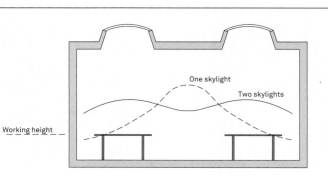

**Shed roof**

Shed roofs are well suited to providing an even distribution of daylight to workplaces in large rooms. The side of the room facing the openings receives more light.

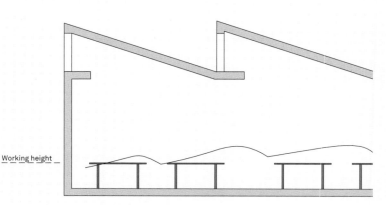

Figure 4.5.19
Relation of the interior of day nurseries and/or primary schools to the outside

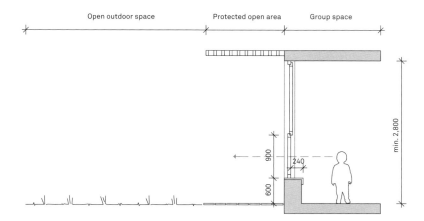

## 4.5.2 Program of Use

Users of education and research facilities usually have very different requirements for the building depending on the age structure, which must be reflected in the design. For small children in particular, it is important to adjust the height of windows, door handles, seats, and sanitary appliances appropriately. Generally, all education and research facilities should be barrier-free in order to allow for the integration and inclusion of users with disabilities. Generally speaking, functional and technical requirements (such as specialist rooms, laboratories) become more prominent as the level of education becomes more specialized. In addition, the views of the teaching and administrative staff must be taken into account for all typologies. Options may include an integrated retreat or administration room (in a day nursery or a research laboratory, for example) through to independent administration tracts. Depending on the type of building, rooms should also be provided for the self-organization of the respective user group (such as a teachers' room, conference area, or committee rooms).

### 4.5.2.1 Child Day Care Centers

Day nurseries are often the first place outside the home where small children can gain experience. For this reason, it is important for the design to strike a balance between communicative meeting areas and protected individual areas.

**Typical rooms in day nursery establishments are:**
- Group activity rooms
- Communal spaces
- Resting/sleeping areas
- Movement/multipurpose rooms
- Storage rooms
- Age-appropriate toilets and washrooms
- Wardrobes with lockers for each child
- Corridors for play and movement
- Meeting room
- Office (facility director)

- Staff room and staff toilet
- Wheelchair-accessible toilet
- Kitchen, cold room
- Lobby, entrance area, vestibule, information boards, etc.
- Storage room/space for baby carriages

The entrance area of a day nursery establishment should include seating areas, a wardrobe for grown-ups, space for information boards, display cabinets or brochure stands, and, just outside or in the transitional area, parking space for baby carriages, strollers, scooters, and bicycles. The day rooms of small children and staff should be separate from the freely accessible entrance area. Depending on the organization's security requirements, access control facilities are provided which, via a control button at a higher level, prevent small children from leaving the building and unauthorized persons from entering from the outside.

By including group, common, and rest areas, different options for play, observation, and sensory experience are provided. Communal areas and secure corridor areas, movement spaces, sanitary facilities, and outside areas all help children to meet beyond the immediate group formation. Retreat and resting areas for small children can be arranged separately or as part of the group activity rooms. If the day care center also looks after older children for the whole day, it is appropriate to provide separate rooms for undisturbed rest or sleep.

In close proximity to the group, a coatroom area for children should be provided in the design, including seating, shelving, clothes pegs, and shoe racks. The area should also provide sufficient space for taking off and putting on coats.

The area for the care staff and administration can be included in the establishment or, in the case of larger organizations, be accommodated in a separate administration tract. In addition to a room for the director of the day care center and a conference area, there should be changing facilities with lockers and a wash facility, a staff toilet and a staff lounge. → **Figure 4.5.21**

**Figure 4.5.20 (left)**
Schematic layout of a child day care center/nursery school

**Figure 4.5.21 (right)**
Schematic layout of the staff area in a child day care center or nursery school

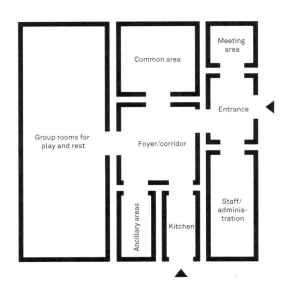

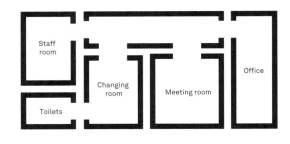

### Crèche (Day Nursery)

Day nurseries offer day care for very small children aged from two months to three years. Children's groups may be subdivided into baby and infant groups. In view of the very different developmental stages of babies and small children, the designer should – above all – ensure that there is a balance between the need for babies' rest and seclusion and small children's need to explore and move about. In view of this requirement, day nurseries are usually smaller establishments. → Figure 4.5.22

### Nursery School/Child Day Care Center

Nursery schools are places for children from the age of three to school age, hence they are also called preschools. If a nursery school has been designed as a full-day facility, the spaces provided should include an area for eating as well as a room for quiet rest. Full-day child care facilities are a combination of the above two types of facilities, usually with a layout similar to that of a nursery school. → Figure 4.5.23 There are also establishments that take children between the ages of three months and school age, for which sometimes the term "children's home" is used. These facilities are open all day and look after children in mixed age groups or age-specific groups. The special challenge in the design of a day care facility lies in the different daily processes and needs of children of different ages.

### After-School Care

Children between school age and the end of their fourteenth year (or until they progress to seventh grade) may spend the afternoon, after the close of school, in an after-school care where they will have lunch, be supervised when doing their homework, and can spend the afternoon in leisure pursuits. In addition to the facilities provided in conventional kindergartens, an after-school care will need an eating area, a fully equipped kitchen, a resting room, rooms for reading/homework, and rooms for small groups and meetings. Conventional group activity rooms don't normally have to be provided because of the diverse functional requirements. Instead, there will be rooms with different functions such as art rooms, workshops, and movement rooms, in order to cater for various leisure activities. → Figure 4.5.24

---

Table 4.5.6
The minimum space requirement for group activity rooms in different care arrangements

The space requirement and size of groups are usually subject to statutory regulations in the various states or determined by the guidelines for grant funding.

| | Dayroom | Ancillary room | Secluded sleeping area |
|---|---|---|---|
| **Separated age groups** | | | |
| Crèche (day nursery) | 40 m² | 20 m² | min. 1.5 m²/child |
| Nursery school | 45–50 m² | 20 m² | – |
| Full-day preschool | 40–50 m² | 20 m² | min. 1.5 m²/child |
| **Mixed age groups** | | | |
| 2 months to 6 years | 60 m² (provided by one or two rooms) | – | min. 1.5 m²/child |
| 3 to 14 years old | 60 m² (spread over three rooms) | – | min. 1.5 m²/child |
| 2 months to 14 years | 60 m² (in a family-type living situation) | – | min. 1.5 m²/child |

---

Table 4.5.7
Group sizes in different facilities

| | Size of group |
|---|---|
| Crèche (day nursery) | 10 children |
| Preschool | 17 to 25 children (depending on age composition) |
| After-school care | 25 children |
| Day care center | 10 to 25 children (depending on age composition and whether age groups are mixed or separated) |

**Figure 4.5.22**
Schematic layout of a crèche

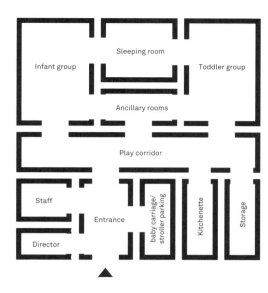

**Figure 4.5.23**
Schematic layout of a nursery
school/child day care facility

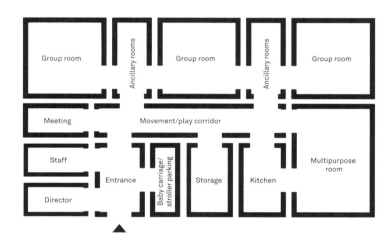

**Figure 4.5.24**
Schematic layout of an
after-school care facility

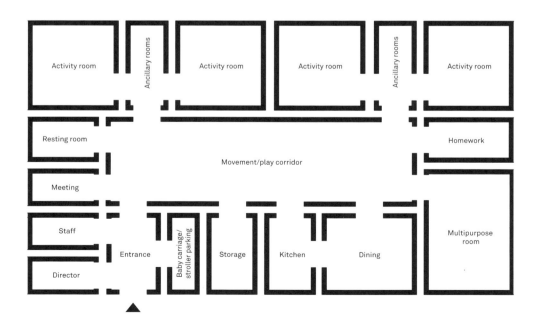

## 4.5.2.2  Schools

Due to different educational forms and ever-changing pedagogical concepts, the program of use for school buildings has to be established individually for each project, in consultation with all the parties involved. In particular, the functional cohesion within the classroom in the case of closed and semiopen concepts or the learning areas in open concepts need to be very carefully planned in order to achieve suitable spaces for the implementation of the respective educational concept and to develop attractive learning and leisure zones for the students. In schools with a full-day program in particular, the provision of different facilities for learning, resting, communication, movement and leisure pursuits is important for a stimulating environment.

Typical rooms in school establishments are:
- Classrooms and special subject rooms
- Assembly hall/multipurpose room
- Library/media center
- Cafeteria, incl. ancillary spaces and kitchen ↗ Chapter 4.7 Typologies/Lodging and Food Service
- Gymnasium, incl. ancillary spaces ↗ Chapter 4.9 Typologies/Sports and Recreation
- Centralized and decentralized toilet facilities
- Coatrooms
- Audio/visual room
- Teachers' room and work spaces
- Conference room
- Principal's office suite, incl. secretary's office and ancillary rooms
- Meeting room
- Rooms for staff and toilets, staff rooms
- Wheelchair-accessible toilet
- Lobby, entrance area, vestibule, information boards, etc.
- Storage rooms
- Facility manager's room

The generous entrance area, which may also be used for events and as a place for students to spend their breaks, should allow good orientation within the building and be easy to monitor. The foyer may include a seating area, a kiosk or café, vending machines, a custodian's office, and a notice board or display cabinet, and should be close to toilet facilities for students, teachers, and guests, the assembly hall, library, and the administration and communal areas. These areas are used as meeting places by students of different ages and from different grades, and provide a setting for the transition between the educational focus and the larger world outside. → Figure 4.5.25

With a starting point at the foyer, the classrooms and other teaching rooms and, in the case of multistory buildings, the staircases, should be arranged so that they can be found easily and quickly. It should be possible to use classrooms and teaching rooms for a variety of functions, which means that it should be possible to link up rooms.

Furthermore, the design of school buildings should take into account the work and non-work-related requirements of teaching and administrative staff. Opportunities for an exchange with colleagues are just as important for teachers as are secluded work spaces and retreat facilities. In addition to a general staff room, the main focus here is on the teachers' room, which can be used as workroom, meeting room, and for rest purposes. In addition to storage areas, there should be a central conference table and individual workplaces for at least 25 percent of the teaching staff. Independent of the size of the school, the teachers' room should have a net usable area of at least 60 m². It should be located close to the administrative area with good access to the school principal's and secretary's offices. In view of the fact that the need for teachers' work places can no longer covered exclusively by central teachers' rooms, it is also possible to provide smaller office areas in the direct proximity to the teacher room or decentralized near the classrooms. These areas need to have space for filing various documents for all teaching staff, as well as desks available for temporary work in a quiet environment. → Figures 4.5.26 and 4.5.27, ↗ Chapter 4.2 Typologies/Office and Administration

Table 4.5.8
Space requirements for general learning and teaching areas by schooling stage

1 Includes: classrooms, group activity rooms, retreat rooms, multipurpose rooms (decentralized full-day areas), leisure areas (including circulation areas that can be used for educational purposes)

| | Space requirement[1] per student | Remarks |
|---|---|---|
| Primary stage | 4.5–5.5 m² | Can be freely distributed depending on the educational concept |
| Secondary stage I | 4,5–5,5 m² | |
| Secondary stage II | 3,5–4,5 m² | |

**Figure 4.5.25**
Schematic layout of a school

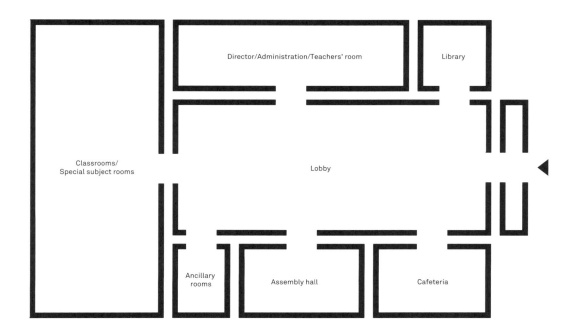

**Figure 4.5.26**
Schematic layout of a school administration area (access via waiting area)

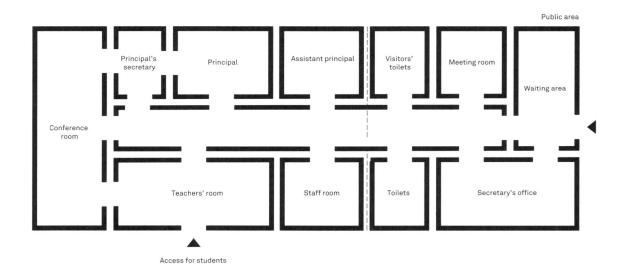

**Figure 4.5.27**
Schematic layout of a teachers' area

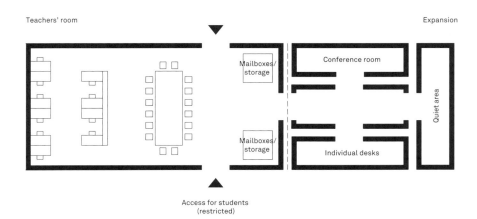

### Primary Schools

When designing primary schools, also known as elementary schools, special attention needs to be paid to the age structure of the students, their physical size and an appropriate, easy-to-monitor building structure. In larger establishments it is common to locate several classrooms of the same grade near each other – for example, in clusters – in order to create functional units that are comfortable for children and easy to monitor. In addition, primary schools have shared areas such as a multifunction room, specialized classrooms, and/or a library. → **Figure 4.5.28**

### Secondary and Comprehensive Schools

Secondary schools, or middle and high schools, usually serve larger catchment areas than the more decentralized primary schools, and are therefore mostly considerably larger. Defining the internal organization of secondary schools is an important design task because specialized classrooms for art and music and for science and technology are commonly grouped together, thus making it necessary for students to swiftly change rooms between lessons. The aim is to create short and easy-to-follow circulation paths and distinct places of identification. Students of different age groups are often grouped within individual parts of the school, and a secondary school may be combined with a primary school to constitute a comprehensive school. → **Figure 4.5.29**

### Vocational and Trade Schools

The emphasis in vocational and trade schools is on providing targeted training for a specific vocation. In addition to conventional classrooms for general education subjects, these schools need significantly more specialist subject classrooms or workshops with a high level of equipment. Vocational schools may cover the following subjects in their curricula:

- Commerce and banking
- Administration
- Manual trades and technical vocations
- Art and design
- Education.

In view of the different levels in demand for certain vocations, it is common to find several vocational schools for specialist subjects grouped together in an educational center. This makes it possible to share general teaching facilities and common functions, as well as certain teaching staff.

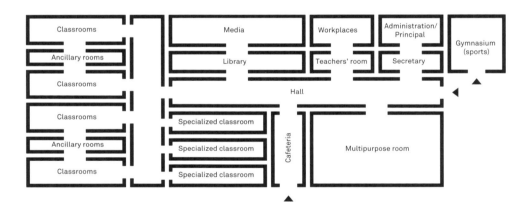

**Figure 4.5.28**
Schematic layout of a primary (elementary) school

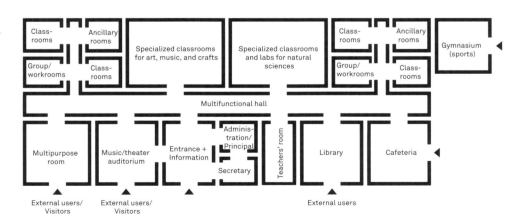

**Figure 4.5.29**
Schematic layout of a high school

## 4.5.2.3 Colleges and Universities

Due to their complex functional organization and space requirements, colleges and universities generally occupy several buildings, which may be located on a central campus or distributed throughout an urban area. A university campus strengthens the relationship between different university sections and allows an efficient layout of central areas such as a central foyer, central library, central cafeteria, main lecture hall, and sports facilities. Additional central functions are administration units such as the dean's office, department offices, the registrar, and ancillary units such as the facility manager's office, sanitary facilities, building service equipment rooms, etc. A central university area should have a generous layout and function as an entrance area to the entire university as well as a place of communication with a distinct identity, from where all areas of the university can be easily accessed. A straightforward, barrier-free guide system is a mandatory requirement for a university.

The central area and the separate entrance areas to the university buildings should have direct access to toilet facilities, waiting zones, service facilities, and a facility to provide information.

The core task of the university as a teaching and research organization takes place in the faculties, departments or institutes which are usually located in specific buildings or parts of buildings and are therefore the direct destination of students in their everyday activities. Depending on their subject orientation, size, number of students, and spatial arrangement, these units will have seminar and lecture rooms, laboratories, workshops, operating theaters, exhibition areas, specialist libraries, and cafeterias or canteens. In addition there will be offices for the administration of the unit and for the teaching staff. At this level, the design should also provide meeting and conference rooms for self-administration, decentralized marking and meeting areas for the tutoring of students, and spaces for exchanges between the teaching staff.

Laboratories and workshops are usually located separately at or near ground level to allow for deliveries. The location of teaching and research staff in relation to laboratories/workshops has to be decided in each specific case. Where there is intensive teaching or research input it is necessary to allocate rooms in close proximity, whereas in situations where rooms are used by different groups, a centralized arrangement of the offices and staff facilities allows easier exchanges between colleagues and often better organization of the building. → **Figure 4.5.30**, ↗ **Chapter 4.2 Typologies/Office and Administration**

**Figure 4.5.30**
Schematic layout of colleges and universities

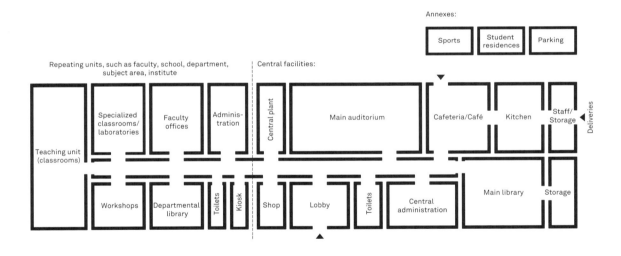

### 4.5.2.4 Research Facilities

Pure research facilities primarily serve the purposes of confirming scientific hypotheses and searching for new findings, as well as documenting and publicizing them, so that the programs of use for research facilities – which may need to accommodate change – must satisfy numerous technical, legal, and economic requirements.

In spite of the significant differences in the orientation of various research facilities, there are some similar functional areas. These are areas for experimental research, for theoretical work, service and infrastructure facilities, and communication and optional teaching areas.

Building sections accommodating experimental research require standard laboratories and fixed workplaces for scientists, and all necessary specialist laboratories (clean-room laboratories, S3 safety laboratories, etc.) as well as central laboratories with large equipment. Areas for theoretical work will need conventional office spaces as well as writing and evaluation spaces within the laboratory areas. These are often designed in the form of individual quiet offices, sometimes called "thinking cells," which are part of the laboratory landscape. The experimental and theoretical work areas are supported by additional service facilities. These may include washrooms, autoclave rooms, or weighing rooms which may be arranged centrally or in close proximity to the laboratory areas. → **Figure 4.5.32**

Other facilities such as libraries, workshops, and separate storage areas may be arranged somewhat further away from the laboratory areas.

In the field of research, communication between scientists often sparks new ideas. This calls not only for meeting rooms, but also – and in particular – for informal spaces in the building such as circulation areas, a cafeteria, break areas, staff and leisure facilities where communication can take place. → **Figure 4.5.31**

**Figure 4.5.31**
Functional areas in research institutes

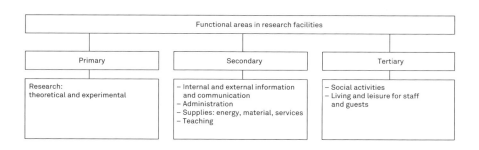

**Figure 4.5.32**
Schematic layout of a research establishment

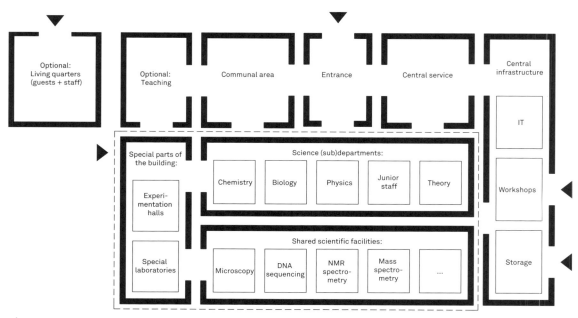

### 4.5.2.5 Libraries

Libraries and media centers support the dissemination and transfer of knowledge, and they can be designed as stand-alone buildings or as facilities within other educational and research facilities. Libraries usually consist of four different functional areas – the entrance with security, the media area, the reading area, and library administration. The entrance area usually requires electronic registration facilities associated with the lending/hand-out counters, and large coatroom and locker areas to compensate for the fact that there is a restriction on taking bags, jackets, or coats into the library. In addition, there are often information facilities (such as boards or counters) and sanitary facilities both inside the library and in the entrance area. The entrance area should be designed so that it can be easily monitored and allow smooth handling of the registration process, while the media area should make efficient use of the available space. Depending on the type of storage, the library may include electronic catalogues, computer workstations and systems for physical forms of information (such as bookshelves, registers, cabinets, and drawers). Media areas can have open access (open stacks), access restricted to persons with prior authorization (limited access), or access restricted to staff only (closed stacks). ↗ Chapter 3.7.2 Spaces/Storage Spaces/Types of Storage In the reading area, a certain privacy and quiet are important. This area should include reading desks with and without electronic devices as well as group work areas, which may have to be provided in separate rooms.

Figure 4.5.33
Schematic layout of libraries

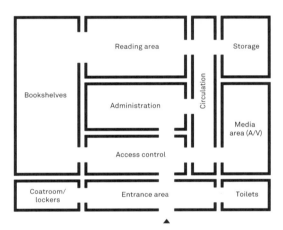

311

### 4.5.3 Areas and Rooms

**External circulation** ↗Chapter 3.1

**Entrance areas** ↗313 ↗Chapter 3.2.1

**Stairs, elevators** ↗Chapter 3.2.4, ↗Chapter 3.2.7

**Corridors, internal circulation** ↗Chapter 3.2.2

**Group activity rooms, day nurseries** ↗313

**Teaching rooms** ↗315

**Auditoriums** ↗315 ↗Chapter 3.4.1

**Specialized classrooms, laboratories** ↗317

**Common areas** ↗321 ↗Chapter 3.4.2

**Cafeterias** ↗323 ↗Chapter 3.4.3, ↗Chapter 4.7

**Libraries** ↗323

**Administration** ↗324 ↗Chapter 3.3.1, ↗Chapter 4.2

**Teachers' rooms, conference rooms** ↗324 ↗Chapter 3.4.1

**Kitchenettes** ↗Chapter 3.6

**Toilets** ↗324 ↗Chapter 3.5

**Storage/Archive rooms** ↗Chapter 3.7.2

**Server rooms** ↗Chapter 3.9.8

**First aid rooms** ↗Chapter 3.8.3

**Janitor's closets** ↗Chapter 3.8.4

**Mechanical equipment rooms** ↗Chapter 3.9

### 4.5.3.1  Entrance Areas

As already described for the various typologies in ↗ Chapter 4.5.2 Program of Use, entrance areas of all educational and research buildings need to accommodate additional functions, and sometimes also serve to represent the organization so that these areas should benefit from a generous design. Most entrance areas will have information boards, orientation systems, and areas for waiting and meeting. Day nurseries require additional parking space for baby carriages, strollers, and bicycles. In schools the entrance areas serve as central distribution points, providing access to numerous functions such as classrooms and teacher areas, the cafeteria, assembly hall, library, etc. Similar to university buildings, these entrance areas may also need to represent the institution and provide space for meeting, lectures, ceremonies, and performances.

The access situation and orientation in the building must always be designed to be barrier-free. In larger facilities there may also be a need for a barrier-free guide system, a contact person such as a custodian/superintendent, and an access control system.

### 4.5.3.2  Group Activity Rooms in Child Day Care Facilities

The design of the group room in a day nursery should allow for periods of rest and of activity, and should provide the setting for various movement, play, exploration and meeting activities. On the one hand, group rooms should have adequate open space for movement and activities and, on the other hand, it is desirable that some areas are dedicated to rest, to play, or as places of retreat. All furniture should be designed to suit the physical size of the children.

**Typical functions in group activity rooms of day nurseries are:**
- Themed play corners or play carpet
- Area for chairs
- Shelves and cupboards
- Lavatories
- Desk for care person
- Lavatories
- Optionally fitted kitchen
- Transitional area to the outside

Fitments such as podiums, intermediate floor levels, sight-protected retreat niches, or a mezzanine level for learning new ways of behavior can provide intelligent extra storage space without infringing on the space available for movement. However, the risk of injury to children must be minimized and appropriate fall guards must be provided.

**Figure 4.5.34**
Space requirement for a seating circle

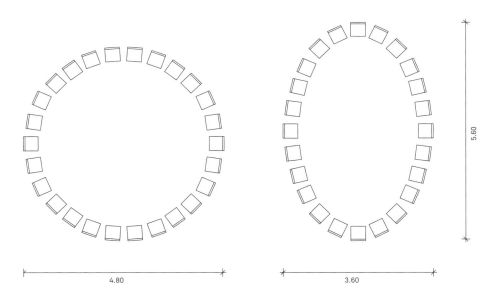

**Figure 4.5.35 (above)**
Group room with shelf elements
for the purpose of space division

**Figure 4.5.36 (center)**
Window seating as transition
between indoor and outdoor
spaces

**Figure 4.5.37 (below)**
Covered open area as an extension
of the group room or classroom

## 4.5.3.3 Classrooms in Schools

Classrooms should have a quiet and concentrated atmosphere for learning but should also allow a flexible use option, in particular in full-day schools or schools with special educational concepts such as that of the "moving classroom." For an average class of 25 students, the classroom should have a minimum size of 65 m². Often smaller rooms for special purposes are connected, sometimes with a visual link, or several classrooms can be linked up via mobile walls. Depending on how long the students stay in the rooms, there may be a need to consider hygiene aspects more carefully – such as lighting, acoustics, and fresh air. Due to frequent changes in educational concepts and the day-to day rhythm of school life, classrooms should be designed to be flexible, without fixed furnishings.

**Typical furniture and fittings required in classrooms:**
- Tables and chairs for students
- Desk/table for teacher
- Black-/whiteboards, possibly with fold-out/ tilt option
- Media technology if required
- Shelves/drawers for the students
- Storage for teaching material
- Shelves for classroom library
- Lockable cupboard for teacher
- Lavatories
- In primary schools, also play areas if required
- In specialized classrooms, special furniture/ equipment

## 4.5.3.4 Lecture Halls in Colleges and Universities

Lecture halls and auditoriums usually provide space for 100 to 800 people and are commonly subject to regulations for places of assembly, meaning that there are stricter requirements for escape and rescue routes, fire safety, and furnishings. The layout of lecture halls is usually rectangular or trapezoidal. → **Figure 4.5.42** Trapezoidal layouts make it possible to accommodate a larger audience with good conditions.

The number of seating rows in lecture halls should not exceed 30. Aisles with a width of at least 1.20 m must lead directly to an exit. A maximum of ten seats are permitted in a row from either side of an aisle, so the maximum number of seats in a block with aisles on both sides is 20 per row. The walking distance from any seat to the nearest exit may not exceed 30 m. ↗ **Chapter 3.4.1 Spaces/Communication Spaces and Dining Rooms/Lecture, Seminar, and Conference Rooms**

In lecture halls it is common to provide raised seating and stepped walkways. The riser of each step must not be more than 19 cm and not less than 10 cm. The tread must be at least 26 cm.

Depending on the university's curriculum, it may be necessary to install extensive technical equipment near the front of the lecture auditorium. The basic equipment includes multilayered whiteboards, retractable projection screens, options for regulating the lighting, microphones and loudspeakers, electric outlets, internet access, and a water connection with janitor's sink. Lecture halls should be capable of being completely darkened and may also be designed without any windows to the outside.

**Figure 4.5.38 (left above)**
Classroom with front-facing furniture and built-in shelving for the storage of teaching material

**Figure 4.5.39 (right below)**
Classroom with a viewing panel to the adjoining smaller room for special activities

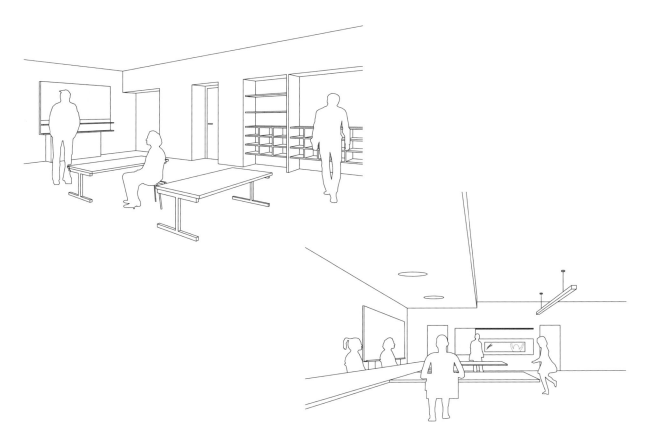

**Figure 4.5.40**
Furnishing examples
for classrooms

Examples of seating arrangements for 24 students in lessons

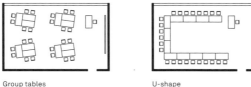
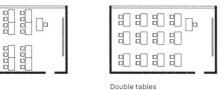

Group tables   U-shape   Rows   Double tables

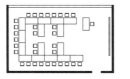
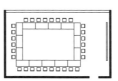
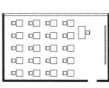

U-shape with infill   Square   Single tables

**Figure 4.5.41**
Minimum dimensions for the
arrangement of tables in teaching
rooms

1   For 6-to-10-year-olds with max.
2 seats next to each other
2   For 10-to-19-year-olds with
max. 2 seats next to each other
or 6-to-10-year-olds with more
than 2 seats next to each other
3   For 10-to-19-year-old students
with more than 2 places next to
each other

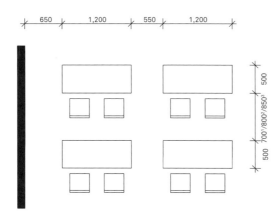

**Figure 4.5.42**
Room shapes and options for
access to lecture halls

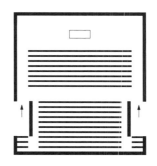

**Table 4.5.9**
Size categories of tables and
chairs in educational institutions
(dimensions in mm)

1   ± 10 mm for chairs with a seat
inclination between – 5° and
+ 5°
2   ± 10 mm for tables for use with
chairs with a seat inclination
between – 5° and + 5°
3   At least
4   Per user
5   Can be reduced to 400 mm
(only if necessary due to
confined space).
6   Can be reduced to 550 mm
(only if necessary due to
confined space).

| Grade | 1 | 1–4 | 2–7 | 5–13 | 7–13 | 9–13 |
|---|---|---|---|---|---|---|
| Seating height[1] | 310 | 350 | 380 | 430 | 460 | 510 |
| Effective seating depth[2] | 270 | 300 | 340 | 360 | 380 | 400 |
| Seating width[3] | 280 | 320 | 340 | 360 | 380 | 400 |
| Height of tabletop[2] | 530 | 590 | 640 | 710 | 760 | 820 |
| Maximum depth of tabletop | 500[5] | 500[5] | 500 | 500 | 500 | 500 |
| Maximum length of tabletop[4] | 600[6] | 600[6] | 600[6] | 600 | 600 | 600 |

## 4.5.3.5 Specialized Classrooms and Laboratories

Specialized classrooms and laboratories require very specific designs, since these rooms usually serve a very specific function for which all necessary materials and equipment has to be provided. In many establishments rooms with specialist functions are grouped together in order to be able to share equipment, installations, and materials. → Figure 4.5.43

**Depending on the type of facility, typical specialized classrooms and laboratories include:**
- Day nurseries: workroom, mud room, creative room, music room, children's kitchen, children's restaurant, music room, reading room, resting room, homework room, theater room
  Special requirements: open shelving to allow free access to the necessary materials, security, spaces that reduce inhibitions and anxiety while promoting curiosity
- Schools: natural science rooms, music rooms, drawing rooms, workshops, computer rooms, theatre rooms, student kitchen
  Special requirements: the level of equipment increases with the grades — multifunctional, scientific multipurpose rooms for the younger students, monofunctional use in traditional specialized classrooms for older students
- Colleges and universities: natural science laboratories, technical laboratories, digital laboratories, workshops, music rooms, computer rooms, collections, language laboratories, medical laboratories
  Special requirements: a high level of technical equipment is required; different equipment is needed for teaching-related practical laboratories and research-related laboratories

Laboratories serve a wide range of different research fields and therefore the equipment needs to be specified to suit the particular purpose. In the fields of chemical, biological, and medical research in particular, many standardized equipment components have been developed for laboratory spaces, the configuration of which depends on the type of activity. → Table 4.5.10

For the design of independent research facilities or those associated with a university, the requirements for hygiene and safety may be more extensive and/or stringent depending on the field of research. → Table 4.5.11 In addition, the building structure may need to be suitable for specialist requirements such as:

- Handling of hazardous materials
- Biological work with/without genetic technology
- Protection against espionage
- Occupational safety

In biosafety laboratories, various types of airlocks make an important contribution to safety, cleanliness, and hygiene. Airlocks separate the contaminated area from the clean area and ensure that staff and materials can be reliably cleaned and disinfected to avoid contamination with contagious germs. → Table 4.5.12 and Figure 4.5.53

Figure 4.5.43 (left)
Functional areas of specialized classrooms and laboratories

Table 4.5.10 (right)
Equipment components for laboratory workplaces

As per Braun, Grömling

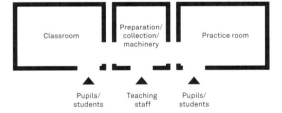

| Component | Requirements/characteristics |
|---|---|
| Electrical raceway | • High-voltage, three-phase, and low-voltage current |
| Laboratory bench | • Surface material to suit the type of use |
| Storage shelves | • Mounted above laboratory benches<br>• Easily accessible storage of materials and equipment that are frequently needed |
| Wall-mounted cabinet | • Frequently required items, documents<br>• Glass doors to avoid 'dead' storage space |
| Laboratory sink | • Size as required<br>• Disinfection device for hands-free operation<br>• With drainboard, eye wash station, purified water if required<br>• Base cabinets with first aid equipment/waste collection |
| Fume hood | • Work with noxious substances (harmful to health)<br>• May require a filter cabinet or air wash facility |
| Writing space | • For recording results<br>• Connection for computer and other equipment<br>• Base cabinets<br>• Can be positioned within the row of laboratory furniture or separately near a window |
| Special components | • Safety cabinet, equipment cabinets, exhaust hood, etc. |

**Figure 4.5.44**
Minimum dimensions for the arrangement of laboratory workplaces

a) Laboratory bench without passage for other persons

b) Laboratory bench with passage for another person

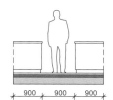

c) Passage between two lab benches

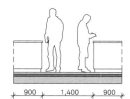

d) Two laboratory benches without passage for other persons

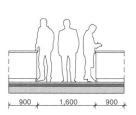

e) Two laboratory benches with passage for other persons

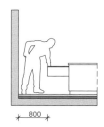

f) Two laboratory benches with drawers, without passage for other persons

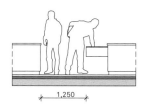

g) Laboratory benches with drawers, with passage for another person

**Figure 4.5.45 (left)**
Student lab bench in specialized science classrooms

**Figure 4.5.46 (right)**
Experiment bench for teaching demonstrations

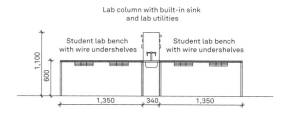

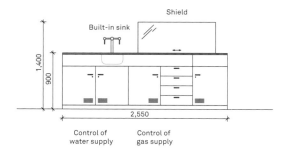

**Figure 4.5.47 (left)**
Laboratory workplace in universities, with wall duct and panel for media

* May include, as required:
Supply lines (gas, water, vacuum)
Electrical services (outlets, fuses/automatic circuit breakers)
An upgrade must be possible at any time.

**Figure 4.5.48 (right)**
Wall-mounted fume hood

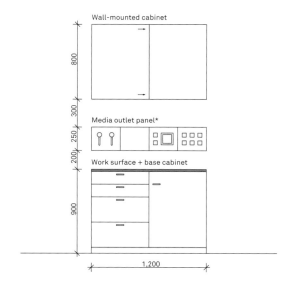

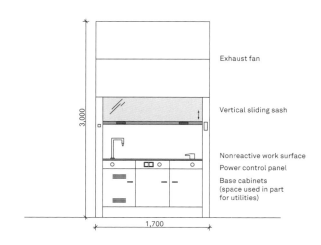

**Figure 4.5.49**
Student laboratory with 24 workplaces

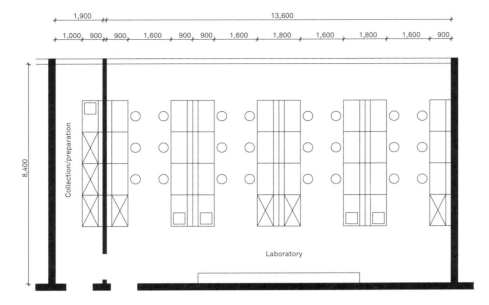

**Figure 4.5.50 (left)**
Work areas and equipment required for molecular biology laboratories

**Figure 4.5.51 (right)**
Work areas and equipment required for chemistry laboratories

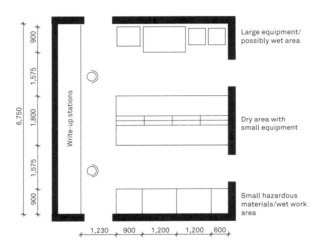

Equipment required: Lab benches, laboratory sinks, tall laboratory cabinets, storage space for equipment

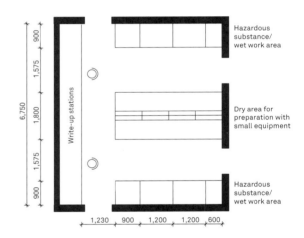

Equipment required: fume hood, point extraction of air, hazardous materials cabinet, chemicals cabinet, lab benches, laboratory sinks, heat/drying cabinet, storage space for equipment

**Figure 4.5.52**
Work areas and equipment required in physics laboratories

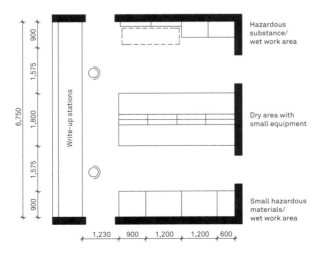

Equipment required: Lab benches, laboratory sinks, tall laboratory cabinets, storage space for equipment

Table 4.5.11
Protection grades for biotechnol-
ogy work with genetic material

As per Genetic Engineering Safety
Ordinance (GenTSV)

| Risk group | Safety measures (selection) |
|---|---|
| 1 – No hazard for people and the environment | • General laboratory standard<br>• Surfaces of walls, ceilings and floors must be resistant to the materials used<br>• At least one lavatory with eye wash station<br>• ... |
| 2 – Low risk for people and the environment | • Measures for the previous risk group<br>• Additionally identified with "biohazard" sign<br>• Windows must be kept closed during work<br>• Lavatory with disinfectant dispenser and disposable towels<br>• Use of Class 2 safety lab benches<br>• All surfaces must be easy to clean and decontaminate, and must be impervious to water<br>• ... |
| 3 – Moderate risk for people and the environment | • Measures for the previous risk groups<br>• Windows must be generally kept closed<br>• Spatial division between the laboratory and the safety area<br>• Access via an airlock containing lavatory with contact-free faucet and counterlocking doors<br>• Air extraction via high-performance aerosol filter<br>• Maintenance of negative pressure<br>• Work with infected material to be carried out at a safety lab bench or in a suitable (isolation) room<br>• Cavities should be avoided by installing fittings/cabinets from floor to ceiling<br>• ... |
| 4 – High risk for people and the environment | • Measures for the previous risk groups<br>• Creation of a distinct separate area, if possible in a separate building<br>• Windows must be closed and locked, break-proof and sealed<br>• Access to each room must be via a three-chamber airlock with shower, disinfection and washbasin<br>• It must be possible to hermetically seal off the workplace<br>• Independent, separate ventilation system<br>• Air extraction via two-stage, high-performance aerosol filters<br>• An observation window should be included<br>• A hatch autoclave system is to be provided in the transition area for sterilization<br>• ... |

Table 4.5.12
Airlocks in laboratory areas

| Airlocks for persons | Material airlocks (also for vehicular access) |
|---|---|
| Wet shower | Immersion airlock |
| Air shower | Gas immersion airlock |

Figure 4.5.53
Clean room laboratory of safety
grade 4 with three-chamber
airlock

* Three-chamber airlock: with
personal showers and auto-
clavable containers for worn
protective clothing, lavatories,
disinfection facilities, cabinets
for street clothing, switch and
control cabinet, differential
pressure display, and airtight
self-closing doors

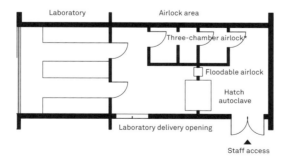

## 4.5.3.6 Communal Spaces

Communal spaces are used by a large number of people from inside and sometimes outside the organization, irrespective of their age group and grade. When these spaces are allocated centrally in the building, they may develop into places for meeting and communication, creating a sense of identity. Alternatively, such spaces may be at the periphery of a building with a direct relationship to the outside. → **Figure 4.5.54**

### Multipurpose Rooms

Multipurpose rooms are often the largest rooms in educational and research facilities, and offer space for many varied activities or are used to provide options for greater flexibility.

**Multipurpose rooms commonly have the following functions (depending on type):**
- Child day care facilities: athletics, free play, resting, therapeutic activities, educational activities in large groups, theater performances, parents' meetings, lectures, parties, celebrations, sports lessons
- Schools: assemblies, events, parties, celebrations, performances, exhibitions, workshops, athletics, concerts
- Colleges and universities: assemblies, informational events, parties, celebrations, performances, exhibitions, trade fairs, lectures
- Research institutes: informational events, lectures, seminars, congresses

Additional functional areas are listed in → **Table 4.5.13**.

It follows that multipurpose rooms in different institutions and with different use frequencies need to be designed to accommodate the different functions, which can involve elements such as acoustics, escape routes, etc.

In order to achieve greater flexibility, it is desirable to provide adjacent rooms that can be used separately (such as storage rooms) or be connected via movable partition walls. → **Figure 4.5.55**

### Open Areas

Open areas are important features in any type of educational facility for relaxation, communication, and play. The open areas of day nurseries and schools are subdivided into three zones: the break/play area, the green space, and the sports area. The break/play area and green space should be located directly adjacent to the educational establishment and should be easy to monitor. In order to make it possible for students to spend time outside also in poor weather conditions, it may be appropriate to provide covered areas. For schools in particular, the break area is also a key place of learning. It is a place where social contact and communication across different grades take place. The size of the break area should provide at least 3 m² per student.

The outdoor premises are highly valued as educational facilities, especially as the venue for sports (↗ **Chapter 4.9 Typologies/Sports and Recreation**). The emphasis in the design for these areas is on team sports such as football, basketball, or handball. In addition it is possible to provide facilities for endurance sport and track and field sports. As a rule, schools should provide open-air sports facilities when they have eight or more grades with sport on the curriculum, unless the school has an arrangement for sharing existing sports facilities elsewhere. These facilities should include a grass playing field, an all-weather field with adjacent long-jump and high-jump facilities, and – with the exception of elementary schools – a shot-put facility.

**Figure 4.5.54**
Position of common rooms within a facility

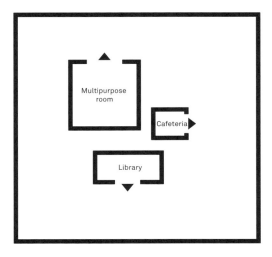

Centralized

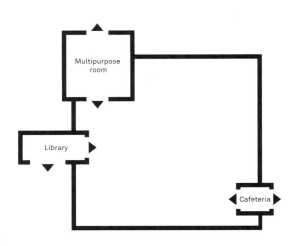

Decentralized

**Figure 4.5.55**
Schematic layout of a multipurpose room in schools/colleges

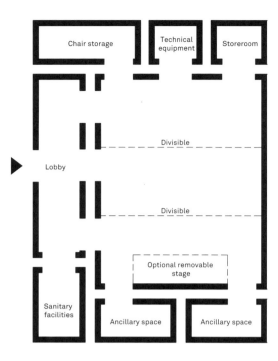

**Table 4.5.13**
Additional functional areas
associated with multipurpose
rooms for various facilities

| | Child day care centers | Elementary schools | Secondary schools | Colleges and universities | Research institutions |
|---|---|---|---|---|---|
| Lobby | – | – | ● | ● | ● |
| Sanitary facilities | – | ● | ● | ● | ● |
| Technical equipment | ● | ● | ● | ● | ● |
| Ancillary spaces | ● | ● | ● | ● | ● |
| Chair storage | ● | ● | ● | ● | ● |
| Storeroom | ● | ● | ● | ● | ● |
| Removable stage | ● | ● | ● | ● | ● |

● Mandatory   ● Optional, depending on use concept   – Not required

**Table 4.6.14**
Space requirement for outside
areas at day nurseries

| Number of children using the area at the same time | 10 | 20 | 30 | 40 |
|---|---|---|---|---|
| Minimum size of outside area | 120 m² | 240 m² | 360 m² | 480 m² |
| Standard size | 150 m² | 300 m² | 450 m² | 600 m² |
| Ideal size | 200 m² | 400 m² | 600 m² | 800 m² |

**Table 4.5.15**
Space requirement for break areas

| Number of students | 500 | 1,000 | 1,000 | 2,000 |
|---|---|---|---|---|
| Minimum size of break area (school) | 1,500 m² | 3,000 m² | 4,500 m² | 6,000 m² |
| Standard size | 1,500 m² | 5,000 m² | 7,500 m² | 10,000 m² |
| Ideal size | 5,000 m² | 10,000 m² | 15,000 m² | 20,000 m² |

## 4.5.3.7 Cafeterias

Cafeterias are not only places for eating, but also for communication and relaxation. For this reason it may be appropriate to provide other functions in addition to the dining area, such as reading rooms, lounges, and resting areas. In large institutions where these facilities are heavily frequented at certain periods, it is essential to optimize sequences so as to avoid long lines at the serving area, cash registers, or tray return, and to ensure that the atmosphere is agreeable, with reduced noise levels. →**Figure 4.5.56**

## 4.5.3.8 Libraries

In the design of libraries, it is important to provide separate areas for the use of media and for reading. In the media area, different types of storage systems are used which are designed to ensure efficient use of the area combined with ease of location and good usability for the respective user group. →**Figure 4.5.57** Reading areas primarily feature typical workplaces and should have adequate lighting, digital connections, or computers. Seating can be arranged individually, in rows, or in groups. →**Figure 4.5.58**, ↗**Chapter 3.7.2 Spaces/Storage Spaces/Types of Storage**

**Figure 4.5.56**
Schematic layout of the serving area in a cafeteria

↗Chapter 3.4 Spaces/Communication Spaces and Dining Rooms
↗Chapter 3.6 Spaces/Kitchens
↗Chapter 4.7 Typologies/Lodging and Food Service

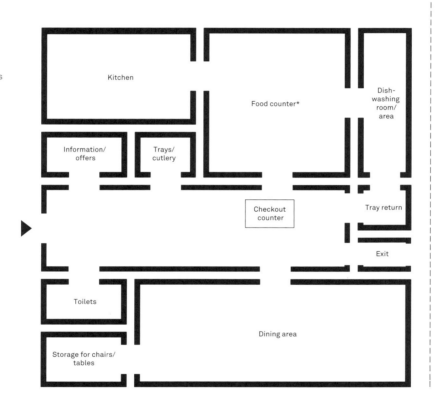

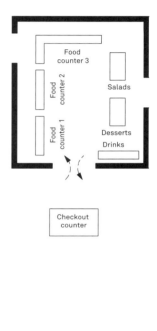

* Layout of serving area

**Figure 4.5.57 (left)**
Age-appropriate shelving systems in libraries

**Figure 4.5.58 (right)**
Minimum space requirements for reading areas in libraries

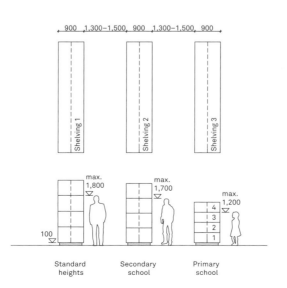

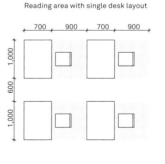

Reading area with single desk layout

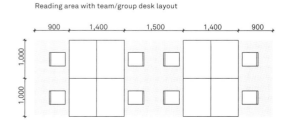

Reading area with team/group desk layout

## 4.5.3.9  Administrative Spaces

Administration rooms and ancillary areas are directly or indirectly allocated to the respective main functions. While smaller facilities such as day nurseries or schools will have a central administration unit close to the building entrance, larger establishments such as universities require a central administration unit as well as specific decentralized units in the departments. →Table 4.5.16

Administration responsibilities include superintendent activities and facility management. If these tasks are carried out by a person who is constantly present, the spaces needed beyond a central point of contact include a workshop, material and equipment storage, and possibly a superintendent's apartment. ↗Chapter 3.3 Spaces/Workrooms and Production Spaces, ↗Chapter 4.2 Typologies/Office and Administration

## 4.5.3.10  Ancillary Spaces

**Sanitary Facilities**
The design of sanitary facilities is directly related to the number of users, their age, and developmental stage. →Table 4.5.17 With the exception of most small day nurseries, toilet facilities need to be separated by gender. All facilities need to provide barrier-free toilet cubicles.

In day nurseries for small children, it is suggested that the design focus on the child's experience with the element of water. Taking into account the age of children, fitments must be set at the appropriate height and enough space must be allocated for care staff to provide help. → Figure 4.5.59 It may also be necessary to provide changing and wash areas.

In the design of schools, toilet facilities need to be provided close to the teaching rooms and near the break areas, as well as – if appropriate – near specialized classrooms. While the toilet facilities associated with a classroom should be in direct proximity of the classroom, general toilet facilities may be up to 40 m away on the same floor. Toilet facilities for use during recess should be accessible from the schoolyard and must be separated by gender.

In colleges and universities, the sanitary facilities should be located centrally at different locations on the premises. Separate facilities need to be provided for cafeterias, libraries, and auditoriums where large numbers of students congregate. For office areas, decentralized toilet facilities should be provided within a short distance on the same floor. ↗Chapter 3.5 Spaces/Sanitary Facilities

Table 4.5.16
Administrative spaces required depending on type of facility

| | Child day care centers | Elementary schools | Secondary schools | Colleges and universities | Research institutions |
|---|---|---|---|---|---|
| Secretary | | ● | ● | ● | ● |
| Director/principal/president | ● | ● | ● | ● | ● |
| Information area | ● | ● | ● | ● | ● |
| Staff room (teachers and other employees) | ● | ● | ● | ● | ● |
| Teachers' room | | ● | ● | | |
| Workplaces for teaching staff | | ● | ● | ● | ● |
| Meeting rooms | ● | ● | ● | ● | ● |
| (Parental) meeting rooms | | ● | ● | | |
| Student council | | ● | ● | ● | |
| Additive administrative areas (human resources, finance, building and technology, etc.) | | | | ● | ● |
| Special administrative areas (examination board, teaching units, dean's offices, institutes, academic departments, etc.) | | | | ● | ● |

**Figure 4.5.59**
Installation height of sanitary fittings according to age

Up to 6 years old

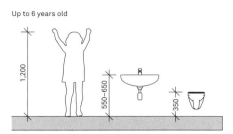

7–11 years old

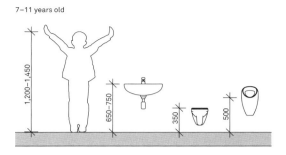

12–15 years old

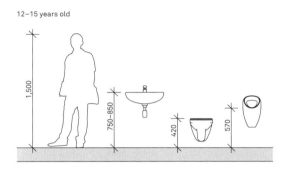

**Tab 4.5.17**
Sanitary fixtures required depending on type of facility

1 Includes: mirror, hook rail for washcloths and towels, shelf for tooth-brushing utensils, soap dispenser
2 Includes: mirror, soap dispensers, disinfectant dispenser, paper towel dispenser, container with lid
3 Includes: mirror, soap dispenser, paper towel dispenser, container with lid
4 Includes: mirror for seated and standing use, soap dispenser, paper towel dispenser, container with lid, hot air hand dryer

| Type of facility | Sanitary facilities | Sanitary fixtures required | | | | |
|---|---|---|---|---|---|---|
| | | Lavatories | | Toilets | | Urinals |
| | | Women | Men | Women | Men | |
| Crèche (day nursery) | Washroom Toilet room Potty room | 1 washbasin per 2–6 children[1] In addition: 1 lavatory and 1 lavatory for staff[2] | | 1 toilet for 8–10 children | | – |
| Preschool After-school care Day care center | Washroom Toilet room | 1 lavatory per 2–6 children[1] | 1 lavatory per 2–6 children[1] | 1 toilet per 6–10 children | 1 toilet per 6–10 children | 1 urinal per 10 children |
| | | In addition: 1 lavatory and 1 lavatory for staff[2] 1 shower per 10 children | | – | | – |
| Preschool Kindergarten | Toilets near classroom | 1 washbasin[3] | | 2 toilets | | – |
| Elementary school Secondary school | General toilets | one lavatory per floor[3] | one lavatory per floor[3] | 2 toilets per floor | 1 toilet per floor | 1 urinal per floor |
| Preschool Kindergarten Elementary school Secondary school Vocational school College/University | Toilets near break area | 1 lavatory per 60 persons[3] | 1 lavatory per 60 persons[3] | 1 toilet per 25 persons | 1 toilet per 50 persons | 1 urinal per 25 persons |
| General | Staff toilets | 1 lavatory per 20 persons[3] | 1 lavatory per 20 persons[3] | 1 toilet per 20 persons | 1 toilet per 20 persons | 1 urinal per 20 persons |
| General | Accessible toilets | 1 lavatory per floor[4] | 1 lavatory per floor[4] | 1 toilet per floor | 1 toilet per floor | – |

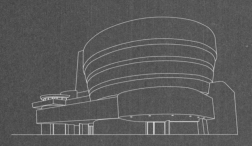

**Solomon R. Guggenheim Museum**, New York, Frank Lloyd Wright, 1959

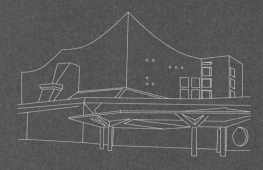

**Philharmonie**, Berlin, Germany, Hans Scharoun, 1963

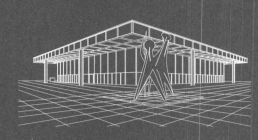

**Neue Nationalgalerie (New National Gallery)**, Berlin, Germany, Ludwig Mies van der Rohe, 1968

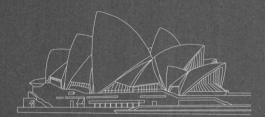

**Sydney Opera House**, Sydney, Australia, Jørn Utzon, 1973

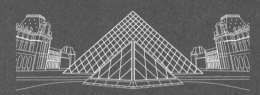

**The Louvre (entrance pavilion)**, Paris, France, I. M. Pei, 1989

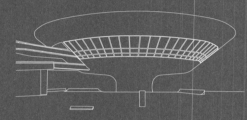

**Museu de Arte Contemporânea**, Niterói, Brazil, Oscar Niemeyer, 1996

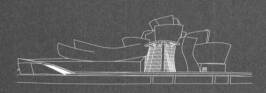

**Guggenheim Museum**, Bilbao, Spain, Frank O. Gehry, 1997

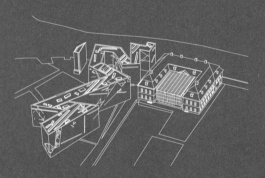

**Jewish Museum**, Berlin, Germany, Daniel Libeskind, 1999

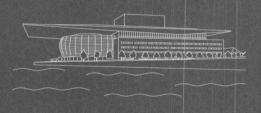

**Royal Opera House**, Copenhagen, Denmark, Henning Larsen, 2004

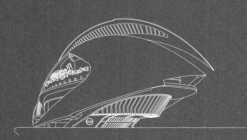

**Palau de les Arts Reina Sofía**, Valencia, Spain, Santiago Calatrava, 2005

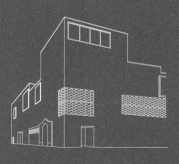

**Kolumba**, Cologne, Germany, Peter Zumthor, 2007

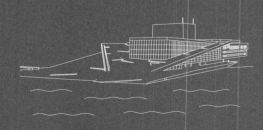

**Opera House**, Oslo, Norway, Snøhetta, 2008

# 4 Typologies
## 4.6 Culture and Performing Arts

Mathias Hölzinger

### 4.6.1 Building Concept ↗328
4.6.1.1 Planning Parameters ↗328
4.6.1.2 Building Forms ↗330
4.6.1.3 Circulation Systems ↗331
4.6.1.4 Construction and Technology ↗332

### 4.6.2 Program of Use ↗334
4.6.2.1 Museums ↗334
4.6.2.2 Stage Theaters, Opera Houses, Concert Halls ↗338
4.6.2.3 Cinemas ↗341
4.6.2.4 Multipurpose Arenas ↗341

### 4.6.3 Areas and Rooms ↗342
4.6.3.1 Entrance Areas ↗343
4.6.3.2 Exhibition Spaces (Galleries) ↗344
4.6.3.3 Performance Spaces ↗345
4.6.3.4 Rehearsal Rooms ↗351
4.6.3.5 Administration and Workshops ↗352
4.6.3.6 Ancillary Rooms ↗352

# 4.6 Culture and Performing Arts

## 4.6.1 Building Concept

Museum and performing arts buildings usually have a strong impact on urban space and are very much in the public focus. Alongside serving intrinsic purposes such as the presentation of cultural artifacts and performances to members of the public, these buildings generally also convey social and political attitudes that document the reality of life or the style of the day like a snapshot in time.

The design of cultural buildings has to bridge the gap between external representation and internal neutrality to create a restrained context for exhibitions and performances. In view of the many options for thematic orientation and the particular requirements of a specific site, each project presents its designers with the challenge of creating an applicable and appropriate architectural and spatial concept at the scale necessary for the intended exhibitions and performances.

### 4.6.1.1 Planning Parameters

Since most museum and performing arts buildings are constructed in downtown environments, the design process starts with an exploration of the urban setting, looking at aspects determined by the urban context as well as building codes and regulations. This yields parameters for the project site, building height, and suitable means of access and site circulation. Frequently, the design for a particular project must be negotiated because such a building may not clearly comply with local development plans or harmonize with the surrounding buildings. In such cases, preliminary discussions with authorities and political stakeholders can help sound out opportunities and limitations.

**Typical Planning Parameters:**

- Place, context, and infrastructure
- Site geometry
- Building code restrictions
- Representational aspects (public image)
- Appropriateness of scale
- Spatial program/space requirements
- Exhibits/type(s) of performance
- Use concepts (such as education/outreach programs)
- Required flexibility/neutrality
- Number and size of exhibition spaces
- Number and size of performance spaces
- Required ancillary functions
- Expectations/needs of user groups
- Layout type, building form
- Public–private spatial relationship
- Barrier-free accessibility
- Budget, deadlines, running costs

In dealing with the internal disposition of the building, the most important task in the planning process is to establish the quantity and dimensions of the key exhibition and performance spaces. If no detailed data is available, the area and space requirements can usually be deduced from the type and quantity of exhibits to be shown and/or from the types of performances or the number of audience members anticipated.

Museum and performing arts buildings are subdivided into one or more areas that are accessible to the public, which include the main exhibition and performance spaces and which usually do not require a direct relationship to the outside, and a non-public area that includes the necessary ancillary spaces and office workplaces that generally do require a connection to the outside.

Table 4.6.1
Subjects covered by museums and commonly exhibited objects

| Museum type | Thematic orientation | Commonly exhibited items |
|---|---|---|
| Art museums | Art (historical and modern), architecture, design, fashion, film, photography | Paintings and other images (prints, photographs, drawings, etc.), plans, sculptures, models, furniture, statues, installations using computer technology |
| Historical and archaeological museums | History, biographies of historically important people, archaeology | Images (prints, photographs, drawings, etc.), models, historical remnants, excavated objects, relics, statues, installations using computer technology |
| Natural history museums | Biology, earth history, geology, zoology, botany, ethnology | Skeletons, taxidermy specimens, models (reproductions of flora and fauna), installations using computer technology |
| Folklore and local history museums | Folklore, local history, design of the cultural landscape | Historical everyday utensils, furniture, models, paintings, images (prints, photographs, drawings, etc.) |
| Historic buildings | Historic properties (palaces, castles, monasteries, and other important buildings) | Furniture, paintings, images, statues |
| Natural science and technology museums | Infrastructure, transportation, technology, industry, mining, chemistry, physics, astronomy, human medicine, pharmaceutics | Excavated objects, skeletons, taxidermy specimens, models, vehicles, machines, measuring devices, musical instruments, installations using computer technology |
| Specialized museums | Cultural history, history of religious faith, ethnic history, history of toys, music history, the art of brewing, literary history, firefighting history, musical instruments, etc. | Everyday utensils, relics, furniture, models, paintings, images (prints, photographs, drawings, etc.), vehicles, machines, measuring devices, musical instruments, installations using computer technology |

## Museums

The purpose of museums is to permanently or temporarily present selected exhibits, or to otherwise make them accessible to the public. Often, permanent exhibits are complemented by changing or special exhibitions. In addition, storage facilities which have only restricted public access, at most, are ordinarily also needed. Reviewing the exhibition content makes it possible to infer the types of possible exhibits and thereby establish an initial basis for the design of the main exhibition spaces. → **Table 4.6.1**

The scale of the objects to be exhibited determines to a great extent the size and proportions of the spaces. In order to attain a generous ambiance, the principal exhibition spaces should in any case have a clear height of at least 4 m, so that the exhibits have sufficient distance to the floor and ceiling and its impact on the viewer is thus not impaired by any limitations of the exhibition space. This minimum requirement must be taken into account at an early stage, as it may result in significant building heights that must be given proper consideration within the urban context.

Another important factor influencing the size and depth of spaces is the viewing distance. This should be based on the optimal human field of vision, which is approximately 18° wide and approximately 25° high. → **Figure 4.6.1**

Even though the primary objective of designing a museum is to create spaces suitable to the presentation of exhibits, with regard to the personnel required for operations and potentially high operating and maintenance costs, it is nevertheless important to give early consideration to area and space efficiency.

## Performing Arts Buildings

Buildings for the performing arts are venues where public performances take place, such as the staging of operas, musicals, and theatrical plays or the presentation of films. The designer's attention is usually focused on the central performance space and its lobby, since its operation requires the support of highly sophisticated stage technology as well as a large area, not accessible to the public, containing rehearsal rooms, dressing rooms, administration facilities, storage spaces, etc. In addition to the central performance space, additional, smaller performance spaces are often also required.

The most important planning parameters are the thematic orientation, or function, of the performing arts building and the associated acoustic and visual requirements, as well as the likely number of patrons. These can be used as the initial basis for design. → **Table 4.6.2** As a rule of thumb, the space needed for each visitor to a performance space is 4–9 m³.

Figure 4.6.1
Field of vision for exhibits

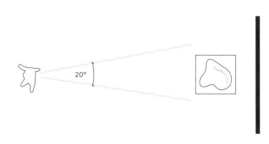
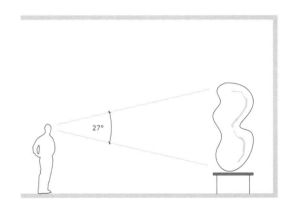

Table 4.6.2
Comparison of different performing arts building types

++ very high importance
+ high importance
o ordinary importance
– subordinate importance

| Type of performing arts building | Opera house | Theater | Music hall |
| --- | --- | --- | --- |
| Typical performances | Operas, operettas, plays, musicals, musical performances | Operas, operettas, plays, musicals, musical performances | Musical performances |
| Complexity of stage technology | ++ | ++ | o |
| Acoustic requirements | + | o | ++ |
| Visual requirements (sight lines) | ++ | ++ | – |
| Number of patrons commonly accommodated | 1,000–3,000 | 1,000–3,000 | 500–2,000 |

## 4.6.1.2 Building Forms

The key exhibition and performance spaces also determine the form of the building to a great extent, since they constitute prominent spatial volumes, both in terms of their floor area and their room height. Whereas the technical requirements for the stage area are relatively minor for straightforward music performances, the presentation of operas and theatrical plays needs sophisticated stage planning owing to the complex technical equipment required; the conspicuous fly loft (fly tower) can be up to 40 m high and thus frequently exceeds the height of other parts of the building.

The form and dimensions of museums are similarly dependent on the size of the exhibits and the overall scope of the collection to be presented. While, for example, historical machines or vehicles require factory-like exhibition spaces with a structure that is suitable for supporting heavy loads, art collections can often be presented in smaller-scale exhibition rooms. → **Figures 4.6.2 and 4.6.3**

Museums and performing arts buildings may take a solitary, additive, or integrative form. → **Figure 4.6.4** Solitary building forms expressively reveal the unique function of the building to the outside and often have an overriding sculptural shape that conceals the exhibition and performance spaces within. Additive building forms express the interior spatial structure on the exterior, and often individual exhibition or performance spaces are designed as distinct building volumes that are accessed via shared lobby areas. Integrative building forms subsume exhibition or performance spaces within a uniform surrounding envelope – which may take the form of a perimeter block development as a typical concept used in response to dense inner-city locations.

The characteristic design of museum and performing arts buildings tends to have closed elevations, since the focus is on the interior without any reference to the outside. Only the entrance area and the lobby are open to the outside and allow a view into the building interior.

**Figure 4.6.2 (left)**
Example of an art museum (Städel Museum, Frankfurt am Main)

**Figure 4.6.3 (right)**
Example of a transport museum

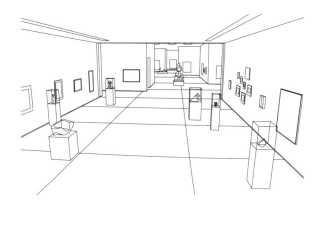
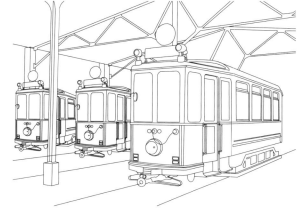

**Figure 4.6.4**
Different building forms: solitary, additive, and integrative

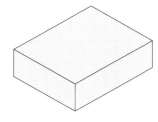
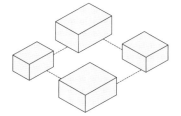
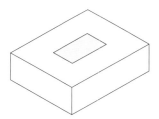

◯ Exhibition or performance space

### 4.6.1.3 Circulation Systems

Access to gallery and performance spaces is usually gained via a generous and impressive lobby. In addition, sufficient escape and rescue routes must be provided for the potentially large number of visitors. Access to public and private areas should be strictly separated.

**Lobby**
The lobby is primarily a connecting circulation space but is also often additionally used for the purposes of communication and assembly, and it must therefore offer an agreeable ambiance for a large number of people, even during times of peak use. Since the coat check rooms, ticket counters/box offices, toilets, any restaurants, gift shops, etc., and the actual gallery and performance spaces are accessed via the lobby, it is the central focus of the overall complex. Where several gallery and performance spaces are served, it is possible to stagger the circulation areas.

The public circulation should be concentrated in a key location within the building. It may be situated as a buffer zone adjacent to the building entrance, as an atrium providing internal and protected communication and circulation space, or as space surrounding a central exhibition or performance space. → **Figure 4.6.5** Clear vistas across the interior of the building aid visitors with orientation.

**Escape Routes**
The escape routes from the principal exhibition and performance spaces must have a minimum width of 1.20 m and must be exclusively reserved for pedestrian circulation. If galleries and other public areas are connected, these areas must not overlap the areas reserved for rescue routes. Any furniture and exhibits placed there may only consist of hardly flammable material. In buildings with higher numbers of patrons (such as theaters or cinemas), the corridors must be significantly wider. → **Table 4.6.3** The minimum increment for increasing the corridor width is 0.60 m.

The maximum walking distance from any point of a gallery space or auditorium to a necessary stair or exit must not be more than 30–35 m (in accordance with the current ordinance governing places of assembly). Where the height of the room is greater than 5 m, it may be permitted to extend that distance in accordance with building regulations. Each necessary stairway must be located in a distinct, continuous enclosure that leads from the upper floors into the open. It is normally not permitted to provide escape routes via window openings in museum and performing arts buildings. This means, as a rule, that it must be possible to reach two escape route stairways from any point in the building. Whether an internal stairway can be considered to be a necessary stair should be discussed in detail with the local fire department or fire protection authority. Similarly, an analysis of specific fire risks should be carried out in cooperation with the local fire department or fire protection authority at the design stage.

Fire protection measures for museums and performing arts buildings consist of measures for fire prevention, firefighting and organizational measures, with the purpose being to rescue persons and also, in the case of museums, to protect any unique cultural objects from destruction in the case of a fire.

**Figure 4.6.5**
Circulation arrangements

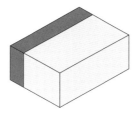 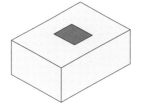 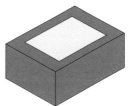 

Exhibition/performance

Circulation

**Figure 4.6.6**
Examples of museum circulation systems oriented to the outside (left) and the inside (right)

Left: German Mining Museum, Bochum

Right: Solomon R. Guggenheim Museum, New York

**Table 4.6.3**
Determining the clear width of escape routes

| Type | Number of patrons | Clear width of escape route |
|---|---|---|
| Outdoor places of assembly | per 600 | 1.20 m |
| Indoor places of assembly | per 200 | 1.20 m |
| Stage area | (not specified) | 0.90 m |

## 4.6.1.4  Construction and Technology

### Load-Bearing Structure

Gallery and performance halls usually require large internal spaces not obstructed by columns. In museums, such large open spaces ensure long-term usability, as temporary light-weight constructions can be inserted to suit different functions; in performing arts buildings, the absence of columns means that audience members' view of the stage is not obstructed. The load-bearing structure is usually not visible, as it is used to integrate the required technical installations. Solid building components are preferred for sound insulation purposes and to provide an adequate buffer between the interior and exterior climate.

### Lighting

When designing the lighting, a distinction must be made between the more introverted gallery and performance spaces and the secondary areas such as cafés, restaurants, event rooms, administration offices, library, staff rooms, and workshops, as these secondary areas usually require direct natural daylight. By contrast, performance spaces must normally be able to be fully darkened; for this reason, they are often internal rooms without windows and have lighting that features continuously variable dimming.

In galleries it is important for the lighting to be even and controllable so that objects on display are not adversely affected and perception of the exhibits remains unchanged throughout the different times of day. Depending on the exhibit, different illuminance strengths apply, ranging from a maximum of 50 lux for very sensitive items to about 200 lux for sensitive objects. Brighter lighting can be provided for nonsensitive exhibits. The illuminance can be achieved with artificial light and, in certain cases, also with daylight. If the lighting includes a daylight component, it must be directed and controlled using daylight control devices. Direct daylight should only be used via facade and roof openings oriented toward the north. → **Figure 4.6.7**

Daylight and artificial light can be combined in lighting ceilings with built-in daylight filters and additional luminaires. Daylight can be filtered using baffle strips or reflectors to divert the light, or translucent material such as matt glass, natural fabric, or plastic. → **Figure 4.6.8**

It is now common to use LED luminaires for the artificial lighting of exhibition spaces. The ranges of light colors and brightness of these systems makes it possible to illuminate the exhibits appropriately and to create different atmospheric effects without any changes in installation.

**Figure 4.6.7**
Options for using daylight
in exhibition spaces

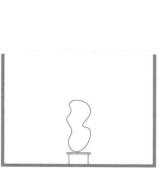  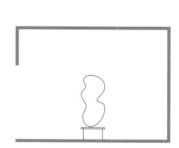

Daylight via translucent ceiling

Daylight via north-facing clerestory window

Daylight via sidelight from the north

**Figure 4.6.8**
Examples for lighting via
light ceilings

Left: Lighting elements in the underground extension to the Städel Museum, Frankfurt am Main

Right: Continuous light ceiling at the Fondation Beyeler, Basel

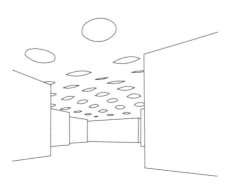 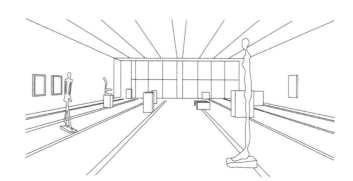

**Services Installations, Heating, and Ventilation**
Museum and performing arts buildings require extensive services installations in order to ensure an adequate interior climate.

In the case of sensitive exhibits in exhibitions, it is important to ensure that temperatures remain constant in the winter and summer months, and that the limit of 16°C is maintained in winter and that of 22°C is not exceeded in summer. Other important aspects for gallery spaces are the variations in daytime and nighttime conditions and the differences in situations with and without crowds of visitors. The conditions have to be kept largely constant, since many materials, such as wood, canvas, oil paint, or metals, may relatively quickly suffer damage when exposed to significant fluctuations in the room climate. When designing museum buildings that accommodate changing exhibits, it is important to ensure that the storage areas where exhibits are stored before and after being exhibited have the same climate conditions as those of the exhibition area itself. Where exhibits or fittings need an electrical supply, it is important to provide sufficient outlets either in the ceiling or in floor boxes, particularly where exhibits are regularly changed and a flexible layout is required.

In performing arts buildings, extensive service and technical installations are required in the stage area. The design of these is normally carried out by engineers specialized in the design of stage technology. In addition, performing arts buildings may need extensive ventilation systems for the performance rooms. A relatively high rate of air exchange of at least 20 m³/h is required; nevertheless, it is important to ensure that spectators are not exposed to draught or noise.

In order to accommodate the ducts, which may have large cross sections, and to save space, it may be possible to place these installations in separate shafts behind installation walls or beneath the corridor ceilings. → **Figure 4.6.9** This can help to maintain a clear room height while nevertheless providing full service to the principal exhibition spaces.

**Acoustics**
In performing arts buildings in particular, the design of the acoustic system determines the quality of the building. For this reason, specialist sound engineers will be involved in the design process in cooperation with the architects in order to achieve optimum acoustics based on the shape and finishes of the performance rooms. ↗ **Chapter 2.2.4 Human Measure/Comfort and Physical Spatial Qualities/ Acoustics**

Figure 4.6.9
Location of installations in the corridor area

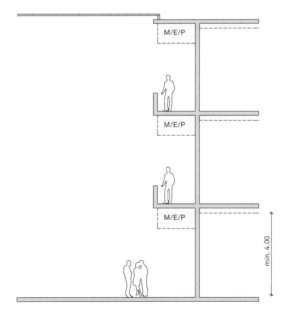

## 4.6.2  Program of Use

Museums, galleries, and other exhibition spaces are used to present collections of a wide range of exhibits. For a visit to be a positive experience, visitors expect there to be enough space and peace to enjoy the exhibits; other important aspects are good lighting, a bookstore or museum shop where an exhibition catalogue can be purchased, and possibly a museum café with restroom facilities. These buildings are primarily used by people moving past the exhibits in a more or less purposeful way.

By contrast, performing arts buildings have a less linear function. Initially and prior to the start of the performance, patrons gather in the entrance area or lobby where there may also be a bar offering refreshments during waiting times or intermissions. In the performance hall itself, audience seats are arranged in front of the stage in a way that ensures optimum visibility. From the perspective of the patrons, therefore, their experience of the building is mainly concentrated on the relatively stationary use of two spaces: the lobby and the performance space. The spatial program is rounded out with ancillary spaces for artists and personnel – such as wardrobes, practice rooms, storage for stage equipment, etc. – which are not accessible to visitors.

### 4.6.2.1  Museums

Although the publicly accessible gallery spaces are of prime importance to museums, as a rule, a large share of the space in these buildings is dedicated to areas that are not accessible to the public. The proportion of public to private (non-public) areas varies considerably owing to the diversity of exhibition spaces, but gallery areas generally take up approximately 30–60 percent of the accessible public space.

The public area of a museum includes not only the exhibition galleries themselves, but also the entrance area with ticket counter, and ancillary spaces that include restroom facilities along with a checkroom or lockers. In addition, space may have to be provided for events, lectures, staff rooms, conferences, a café, restaurant, library, and bookstore or gift shop. As a rule, the circulation area for accessing the public parts of museums takes up 20–40 percent of the usable floor area.

Areas that are not accessible to the public include offices, a library, archive, repository, workshops, and equipment rooms. These spaces usually take up 30–50 percent of the total usable floor area of museum buildings.

**Typical spaces in the public area of museums:**
- Entrance, lobby
- Ticket counter
- Coat check facilities
- Toilets
- Café/restaurant
- Bookstore/gift shop
- Spaces for permanent exhibitions
- Spaces for temporary exhibitions
- Event/conference rooms
- Demonstration room
- Library
- Education center

**Typical spaces in the non-public area of museums:**
- Separate entrance (optional)
- Administration offices
- Meeting rooms
- Staff rooms (toilets, changing rooms, break room, kitchenette, etc.)
- Repository/archive
- Library (for research purposes)
- Conservation workshops and prep rooms
- Specialist workshops (such as carpentry shop)
- Storage
- Deliveries/receiving
- Security checkpoints
- Janitors' facilities
- Technical equipment rooms

Figure 4.6.10
Flow of visitor movement in museum and performing arts buildings

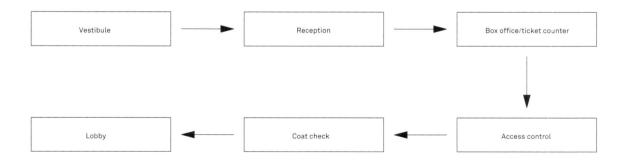

Figure 4.6.11
Schematic layout of a museum

Deliveries

Interim storage

Repository/archive

Library

Corridor

Corridor

Administration entrance

Workshops

Administration/staff

Exhibition spaces (galleries)

Toilets

Ticket counter/ membership desk

Lobby/access control

Coat check

Café/ restaurant/ bar

Entrance/reception

Bookstore/ gift shop

Vestibule

**Organization and Circulation**

A basic question concerning the design of a museum is whether the building will house one single exhibition with permanent exhibits, or whether it is intended to accommodate either a range of changing exhibitions or several exhibitions at the same time. This has an important impact on the design of the entrance area, on the internal building concept, and generally on the overall layout and sequence of spaces. →**Figure 4.6.12**

Exhibition areas can be organized with a variety of different circulation layouts. →**Figure 4.6.13** Some circulation takes place in the exhibition areas, since exhibitions are often arranged in a subject or time sequence where several rooms are connected.

Single-space Concepts

In single-space concepts, the exhibition area is only subdivided by exhibits or exhibition furniture when this is required for a particular exhibition. Visitors can mostly move about freely, but their routes may also be determined by fixed elements.

Linear Spatial Sequences

Linear spatial sequences lead visitors through a range of different galleries. In that case, the end point of the exhibition is usually in a different place to the starting point. The visitor is guided through the different rooms, which restricts free movement to an extent.

Continuous Circuit

Where the entrance and exit of an exhibition are adjacent to each other – albeit in different rooms – the route through an exhibition can be arranged in a circular fashion. In this case, the visitor is guided through the different rooms, and again free movement is somewhat restricted.

Spatial Network/Main and Secondary Rooms

Where several rooms of a similar size connect and visitors can choose their route through these rooms, the circulation is in the form of a room network. This also applies to exhibitions that are arranged in one large main room and several smaller secondary rooms, which can be accessed at will. Usually it is necessary to cross the main room to enter the smaller rooms.

The advantage of this type of organization is that the secondary rooms can be used as extensions of the main room if this is required for the purpose of the exhibition.

House-within-a-house Concept

Where secondary rooms and circulation areas are arranged along all the external walls, the house within a house concept can be used to present the exhibition as a completely independent space within the building.

**Non-Public Areas**

When designing the non-public areas of museums, the organization of the processes must be taken into account. There must be adequate interim storage space available for incoming and outgoing exhibits. It must be possible to transfer the exhibits with ease and to ensure their safety and security to a sufficient degree, such as when transporting highly valuable or easily damaged objects. In an ideal situation, a separate delivery area accessible to vans should be provided from where the exhibits can be transported to the storage and exhibition areas while protected from the weather and, if necessary, via security checkpoints.

In addition, workshops for the restoration or preparation of exhibits may need to be provided in the non-public area but have direct access to the exhibition area. This is of key importance, particularly for larger exhibits and for implementing different exhibition concepts and presentation sequences.

When designing the administration suite for a museum, it is important to ensure that it has a separate access point. If the building includes libraries and repositories, it may be practical to also access these areas from the same point, since it is usually necessary to strictly control and register visitors. →**Figure 4.6.14**

Figure 4.6.12
Schematic building concepts with differing circulation patterns

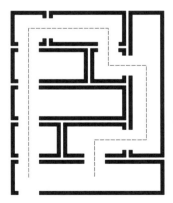
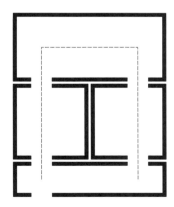
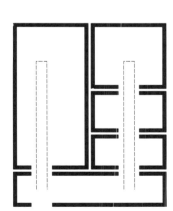

Figure 4.6.13
Different circulation patterns
for an exhibition

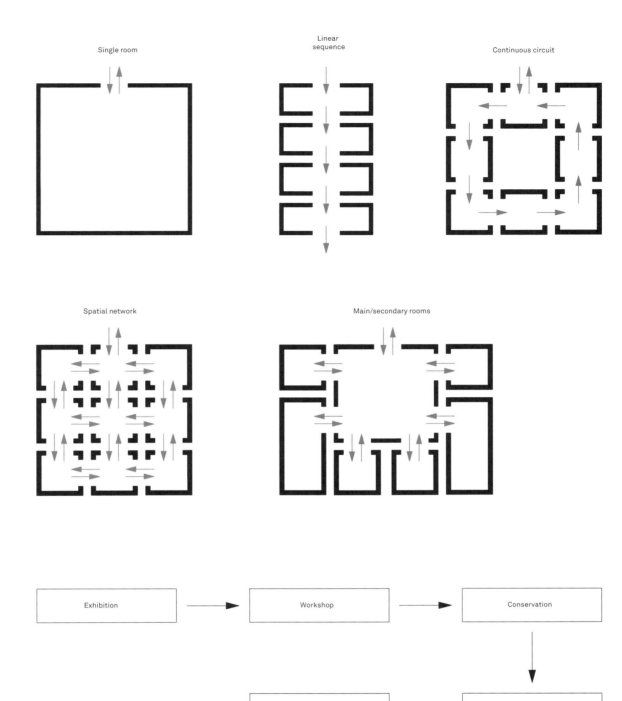

Single room

Linear
sequence

Continuous circuit

Spatial network

Main/secondary rooms

Figure 4.6.14
Flow of exhibits

Exhibition → Workshop → Conservation

Conservation → Interim storage → Delivery

## 4.6.2.2 Stage Theaters, Opera Houses, Concert Halls

In classic stage theaters and opera houses, the space taken up by the performance spaces varies between 20 and 30 percent of the total footprint area because large-scale stage designs require appropriately flexible production, storage, and changing areas. →Figure 4.6.15

In music halls, this proportion is significantly larger, in spite of the usually smaller number of visitors. Here, the key performance rooms usually take up 50–70 percent of the total footprint area. The reason for this is that music halls require much less space for stage technology, and thus the performance room itself takes up a greater proportion.

At the beginning of the design phase it is necessary to establish what public areas are to be integrated, and what prominence they should have. As a rule such areas take up 20–50 percent of the total publicly accessible usable floor area. In addition to the entrance area with box office and checkrooms, lobby, and ancillary areas with restrooms, the design may include areas for events, lectures, cabaret, chamber music, food and beverage service, etc. The circulation areas for accessing the public section of performing arts buildings with a central performance space, including the lobby, may take up 10–20 percent of the overall footprint area.

**Typical rooms in the public area of performing arts buildings:**
- Entrance, lobby
- Ticket counter
- Visitor coatrooms
- Toilets
- Cafés, restaurants
- Shops
- Main performance spaces (concert hall, theater, cinema, etc.)
- Secondary performance spaces (ancillary stages, chamber music, cabaret, etc.)
- Event/lecture rooms

**Typical rooms in the non-public area of performing arts buildings:**
- Separate entrance
- Administration/management offices
- Meeting rooms
- Staff rooms (toilets, changing rooms, break rooms, kitchenettes, etc.)
- Stage, orchestra pit
- Projection room, sound technology
- Rehearsal rooms (orchestra, ballet, rehearsal stage, etc.)
- Artists' dressing rooms, makeup rooms
- Repositories (costume collection, equipment, props, etc.)
- Stage backdrops
- Archive
- Workshops
- Storage
- Delivery area
- Cafeteria, kitchen
- Custodian's office
- Mechanical equipment rooms

**Non-public Areas**

The area in opera houses and theaters that is not accessible to the public primarily serves the operation of the stage with ancillary areas and stage technology. The area of the main stage, its wings and the backstage area alone may take up 30–50 percent of the total floor area. In total, the private area usually takes up 60–80 percent and includes a range of different functions. These may include administration areas, rehearsal rooms for song, music, drama, and dance, as well as workshops and plant rooms in addition to storage areas for costumes, props, and stage backdrops.

A general distinction is required as to which parts of the stage have direct access and which parts have indirect access. Areas directly involved with performances must be closely linked to each other. These typically include the green room, technical areas, prop rooms, toilets, and dressing rooms, all of which may be used by musicians, actors, or singers during performances. In addition there are the wings and the backstage as well as the trap room and fly loft.

The repository, archive, and storage areas should be accessible to a van in order to ensure that backdrops and props can be delivered at any time protected from the weather. Workshops need to be provided for the construction, repair, and restoration of costumes, stage backdrops, and props. Depending on the size of the building, it may be appropriate to include a canteen for artists and staff, which – depending on the operational organization (external suppliers/service providers or complete in-house organization) – may have to be designed for up to 500 people.

**Figure 4.6.15**
Distribution of space as illustrated by the Royal Opera House, Copenhagen

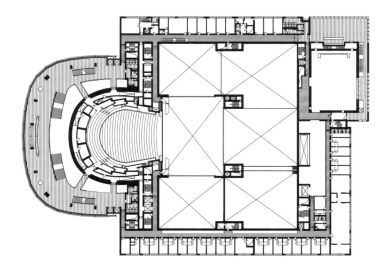

**Figure 4.6.16**
Schematic layout of opera
houses and stage theaters

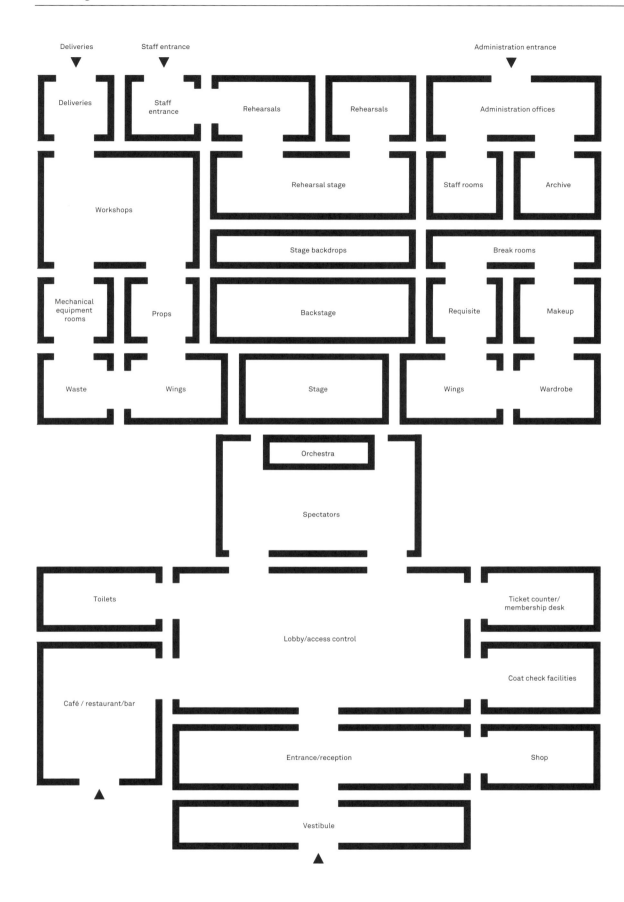

**Figure 4.6.17**
Schematic layout of concert halls

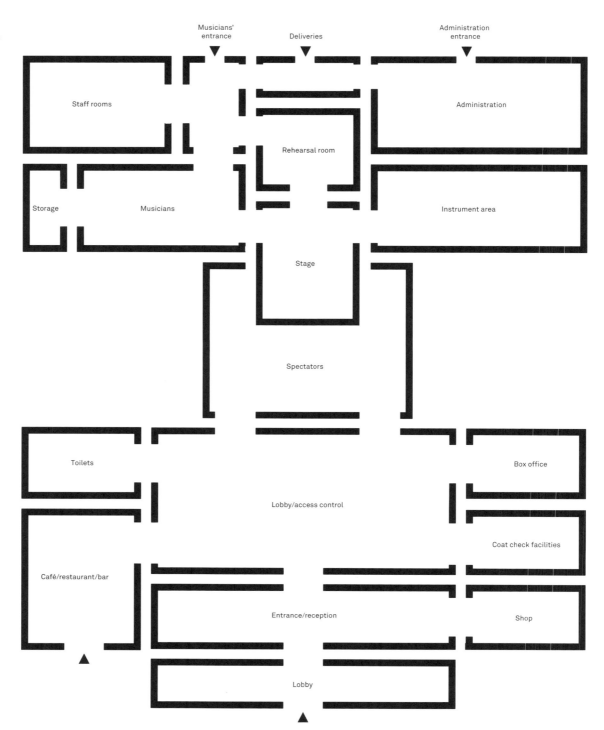

Musicians'
entrance

Deliveries

Administration
entrance

Staff rooms

Administration

Rehearsal room

Storage        Musicians

Instrument area

Stage

Spectators

Toilets

Box office

Lobby/access control

Coat check facilities

Café/restaurant/bar

Entrance/reception

Shop

Lobby

**Figure 4.6.18**
Building structure with functional
areas oriented toward the inside
and outside

1  Administration/rehearsals
2  Stage area
3  Food/beverage service
   (optional)
4  Entrance/lobby/stair
5  Performance hall

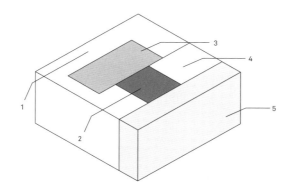

### 4.6.2.3 Cinemas

In designing movie theater buildings, or cinemas, the main focus is put on the internal building organization and on presenting the choice of current and upcoming movies with large posters and/or electronic displays. The technical and acoustic design of cinemas is usually performed by specialist consultants. Like stage theaters and opera houses, cinemas are introverted buildings with mostly closed facades and without any particular reference to the outside. Only the entrance and lobby areas, possibly with a snack counter, bar, and restaurant, are open to the outside. Cinemas often contain bars and restaurants.

**Typical rooms in a cinema:**
- Entrance, lobby
- Box office
- Coat check facilities
- Toilets
- Cafés, restaurants, kiosk
- Break zones
- Shops
- Movie screens
- Projection room, sound technology
- Management
- Staff rooms (toilets, changing rooms, break room, kitchenette, etc.)
- Storage
- Mechanical equipment room

As a rule, cinemas contain 3 to 15 screens in auditoriums of various sizes. The capacity of the various auditoriums may range from 10 to 600 seats. Most newly designed cinemas have between 7 and 14 screens in order to be able to present the range of current movies. The internal organization and lobby and entrance areas usually have to comply with the same requirements as other performing arts buildings.

### 4.6.2.4 Multipurpose Arenas

Multipurpose/multifunctional arenas are used for a range of events and are large enough to be used for sports events, trade shows, and concerts. In order to be able to use these venues for different functions, it must be possible to change the flooring and to set up items like podiums, stages, and grandstands in variable configurations. → **Figure 4.6.20** In addition to the areas for events, space is needed for a reception area with ticketing facilities, an information/service desk, and coat check facilities, as well as for restaurants and ancillary areas with toilets and technical equipment rooms. Often, large sports venues such as track and field or football stadiums are also designed as multipurpose arenas in order to accommodate different types of functions. ↗ **Chapter 4.9 Typologies/Sports and Recreation**

Figure 4.6.19
Schematic layout of a cinema

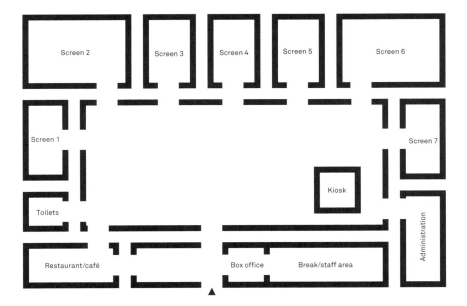

Figure 4.6.20
Variable use/seating layouts in multifunctional arenas

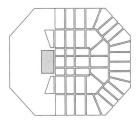

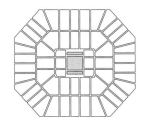

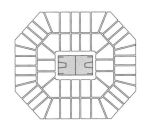

Concert/show (stage at one end)          Show/sport (such as center-stage concert, boxing)          Sport (such as basketball, ice hockey)

### 4.6.3  Areas and Rooms

**External circulation**  ↗Chapter 3.1

**Entrance hall**  ↗343  ↗Chapter 3.2.1

**Ticket counter/box office, information**  ↗343

**Stairs, elevators**  ↗Chapter 3.2.4, ↗Chapter 3.2.7

**Corridors, internal circulation**  ↗Chapter 3.2.2

**Exhibition spaces**  ↗344

**Performance spaces**  ↗345  ↗Chapter 3.4.1

**Movie theaters**  ↗350

**Orchestra rehearsal rooms**  ↗351

**Rehearsal stage rooms**  ↗351

**Dance and ballet rehearsal rooms**  ↗351

**Administration**  ↗352  ↗Chapter 3.3.1, ↗Chapter 4.2

**Workshops**  ↗352  ↗Chapter 3.3, ↗Chapter 4.4

**Makeup, artists' dressing rooms**  ↗352  ↗Chapter 3.8.2

**Storage/archives**  ↗352  ↗Chapter 3.7.2

**Coat check facilities**  ↗352  ↗Chapter 3.8.2

**Kitchenettes**  ↗Chapter 3.6

**Restaurants, cafés, bars**  ↗Chapter 4.7, ↗Chapter 3.4.3

**Break rooms**  ↗Chapter 3.8.1

**Restrooms**  ↗352  ↗Chapter 3.5

**Server rooms**  ↗Chapter 3.9.8

**First aid rooms**  ↗Chapter 3.8.3

**Janitorial rooms**  ↗Chapter 3.8.4

**Mechanical equipment rooms**  ↗Chapter 3.9

### 4.6.3.1 Entrance Areas

In view of the fact that the facades of museum and performing arts buildings are usually closed, the entrance and lobby areas assume an important function as transfer zones, and are the focal points for visitors to the building. These areas include a reception counter, a box office, access control facilities and usually also coat check rooms and possibly cafés, restaurants, bars, museum shops, and toilets, as well as smaller event rooms that can be used flexibly and separately. Any restaurants, cafés, or the like should also be able to serve customers at off-hours, that is, independent of the opening times for the rest of the building, which means they require separate access from the outside.

Generally, entrance areas and access to the coat check facilities and access control points should be designed generously, because they also serve as waiting areas and places where people congregate during events. Where separate entrance zones are provided – for example, with concert halls – waiting areas should also be provided in front of the entrances, commensurate to the number of seats served by each entrance. Barrier-free accessibility and ease of circulation are important factors for public acceptance of the building – particularly in the case of multistory premises – and must be coordinated with internal circulation patterns, access control, and audience movement during intermissions. ↗ Chapter 3.2.1 Spaces/Internal Circulation/Entrance Areas, ↗ Chapter 3.4.2 Spaces/Communication Spaces and Dining Rooms/Waiting and Seating Areas, ↗ Chapter 4.7 Typologies/Lodging and Food Service

**Rooms that may be needed in the building's entrance area:**
- Lobby
- Reception counter
- Box office/ticket counter
- Access control
- Coat check facilities, lockers
- Shop
- Café, restaurant, bar
- Toilets
- Event rooms, possibly with separate lobbies

**Figure 4.6.21**
Examples of lobby designs

Top left: Transparent lobby with staircase in the Harpa Concert Hall, Reykjavik

Top right: Unbroken contact between exhibition and circulation achieved with a continuous ramp, Solomon R. Guggenheim Museum, New York

Bottom left: The structure and the performance hall can be seen from the lobby at the Berlin Philharmonie

Bottom right: Arrangement of different functions in the multi-story lobby of the Royal Opera House, Copenhagen

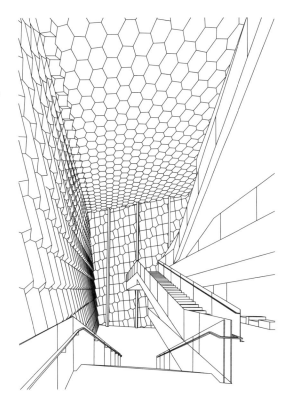

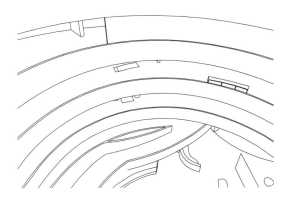

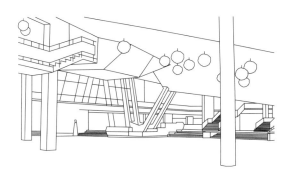

## 4.6.3.2 Exhibition Spaces (Galleries)

Where galleries are used for temporary exhibitions, the means of separating different exhibition areas need to be highly flexible and neutral in terms of backdrop for the exhibition. A wide range of different areas/rooms or room sequences can be created using lightweight partition wall systems, which can be moved as and when required without structural changes. → Figure 4.6.22

Where exhibitions only have a short duration, it is also possible to install mobile walls and room dividers for the structuring of the space and circulation route. Mobile systems are available in the form of straight and curved walls, as consoles, and as different types of display cabinets. → Figure 4.6.23

Between lightweight fitments within exhibition spaces, appropriate movement zones – and possibly also escape routes – must be allowed for. Movement zones must be at least 1.20 m wide; in museums and similar buildings, the corridors and movement zones within galleries are usually more than 2.00 m wide. → Figure 4.6.24

**Figure 4.6.22 (left)**
Creating different circulation routes using movable partition walls in different types of exhibitions

On the left-hand side, the layout shows a separation of exhibition and movement areas, whereas on the right-hand side, the partition walls are used to define the route for visitors, directing them in a given sequence to the various exhibits.

**Figure 4.6.23 (right)**
Examples of mobile presentation devices

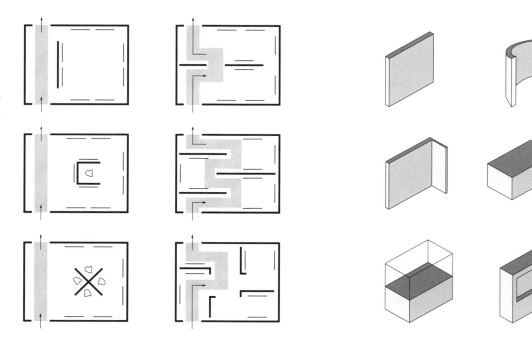

**Figure 4.6.24**
Space requirement for exhibition objects

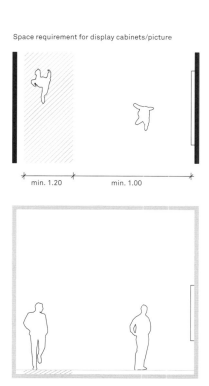

Space requirement: art object displayed freestanding

20°

min. 1.20

27°

min. 1.20

Space requirement for display cabinets/picture

min. 1.20     min. 1.00

min. 1.20     min. 1.00

### 4.6.3.3 Performance Spaces

**Stage Theaters and Concert Halls**
Depending on the type of performance, the stage in a performance space can be positioned in a number of different ways. In rooms dedicated to concerts only, the stage area can be placed centrally in the performance room. The audience will be seated in galleries and balconies. Such concert halls provide a high-quality perception of the performance for a maximum number of visitors, and in many cases they also improve the acoustics, because the galleries and balconies screen the straight wall surfaces and thus reduce reverberation time. → **Figure 4.6.25**

Another option for arranging the stage is to position it in front of the audience (proscenium stage). In this case, any galleries and balconies will also help to improve the acoustics by obscuring any free wall surfaces with offset and angled surfaces, as will the audience itself. For operas and theater performances, it is usual to use a stage placed in front of the audience, because the large spaces required for the organization of a play, including stage technology, large supporting areas, and wings, are not available in the center of a performance room. → **Figure 4.6.26**

The proportion of the central auditorium, which is particularly important in opera houses and theaters, is primarily determined by how well the audience can view the stage. The distance between the portal line and the last row of seats in theaters should not exceed 24 m, since with a greater distance the facial expressions of the actors can no longer be recognized. In opera houses the distance may be greater, up to a maximum of 32 m. The width of the portal can also be determined using these distances. Taking the last row of seats as the starting point and allowing for a horizontal viewing angle of the human eye of 30°, the stage portal should be approximately 13 m wide at a distance of 24 m and approximately 17 m wide at a distance of 32 m. The maximum perception angle of the human eye without head movement is about 110°. This determines the minimum distance required between the first row of seats and the stage. → **Figure 4.6.27**

For determining the width of an auditorium, it helps to start with double the width of the proscenium arch. On the central axis of the proscenium arch and the auditorium, mark a fixed point (P) behind the stage on that central axis at a distance that is twice the width of the proscenium. Connect this point with the end points of the proscenium line and extend these two lines, which will mark the maximum width of the auditorium and rows of seating. The fact that the seats on the side cannot see all of the stage area is accepted with this procedure.

Figure 4.6.25
Example of a central stage
(Berlin Philharmonie)

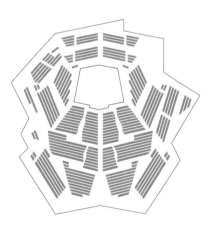

Figure 4.6.26
Example of a proscenium stage
(Opera House, Cologne)

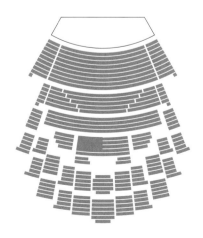

**Figure 4.6.27**
Determining the width of the
auditorium in stage theaters
and opera houses

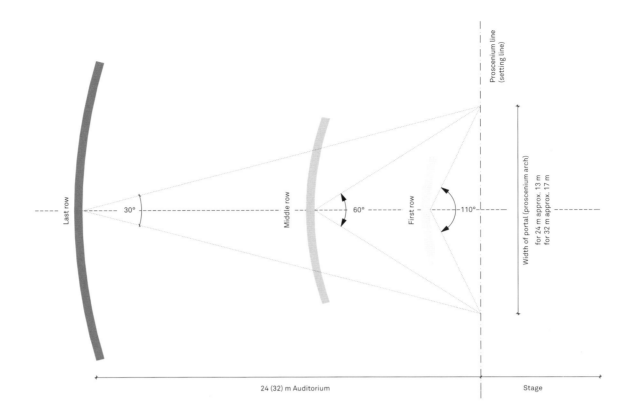

**Figure 4.6.28**
Straight and curved rows
of seating

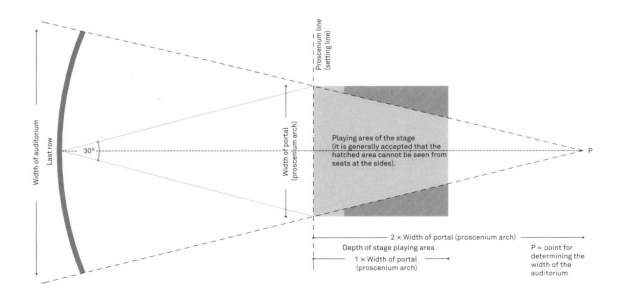

In addition to determining the maximum length and width of the auditorium, it is also important to position the audience seats in order to optimize viewing of the performance. For this reason, the floor in central performance rooms often slopes down toward the stage, and the seats are arranged offset. The maximum incline of aisles without steps is 10 percent. Where a steeper slope is required, for example owing to the incline of the seating, aisles with steps must be provided. ↗ Chapter 3.4.1 Spaces/Communication Spaces and Dining Rooms/Lecture, Seminar, and Conference Rooms The steps in aisles must have a riser of at least 10 cm and no more than 19 cm, and a tread of at least 26 cm. The floor area in front of the rows of seating and the floor of standing area rows must be at the same level as the initial step of the stepped aisle in order to minimize any risk of tripping.

The rows of seating can be arranged parallel in straight lines or in a curved layout facing the stage. When the rows of seating are offset, the audience has a clearer view of the stage. Spectators can see the stage by looking straight ahead and have a clearer comprehension of the entire performance space. → Figure 4.6.29

The rows of seating should always be mounted fixed and provide a minimum walking width of 40 cm. Each individual seat must be at least 50 cm wide. Folding seats reduce the distance required between rows, as the requirement for minimum walking width applies to the seats when folded up. → Figure 4.6.30

The seating in performance spaces should be arranged in blocks of a maximum of 30 rows. Aisles with a minimum width of 1.20 m must be provided between the blocks. These aisles should lead directly to an exit. A maximum of ten seats may be placed next to each other in each row, starting from the aisle, which means that a maximum of 20 seats per row are possible in each block. → Figure 4.6.31

It is possible to provide boxes along the walls of the auditorium. This helps to improve the acoustic properties, and also increases the audience capacity of a performing arts building. In some performing arts buildings, the seating in boxes represents the majority of seats. → Figure 4.6.32

The maximum height at which a box can be provided is determined by the possibility of viewing the stage from the highest seat. The requirement is that from this seat, a space of at least 2 m high at the back of the stage can be seen. → Figure 4.6.33

The orchestra and its conductor can be accommodated in a sunken area between the stage and the house – known as the orchestra pit. This arrangement allows the audience an unobstructed view of the singers, actors and stage backdrops. As a rule, the conductor should be placed where he can be seen by the orchestra as well as the singers on the stage. Even though the orchestra pit impacts the acoustics of the music, it provides many advantages for the performance overall. The area behind and next to the stage remains available to the singers and actors and, during longer intermissions, it is possible for musicians to leave and return to the orchestra pit unnoticed. It should be possible to cover the orchestra pit with appropriate devices should the performance not involve an orchestra, or when the orchestra is placed on the stage itself. A minimum area of 2 m² must be provided for each musician in the orchestra pit. → Table 4.6.4, ↗ Chapter 3.4.1 Spaces/Communication Spaces and Dining Rooms/Lecture, Seminar, and Conference Rooms

Figure 4.6.29
Straight and curved rows of seating

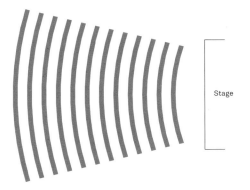

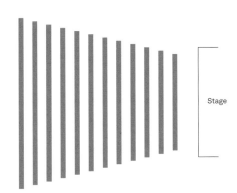

**Figure 4.6.30**
Rows of seating in performing arts buildings

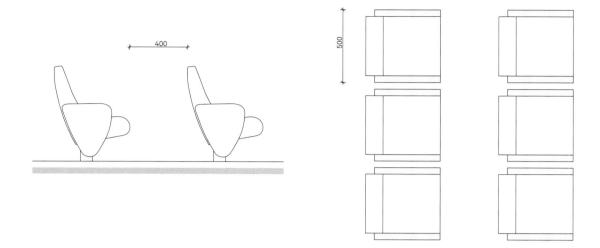

**Figure 4.6.31**
Maximum number of rows of seating in blocks

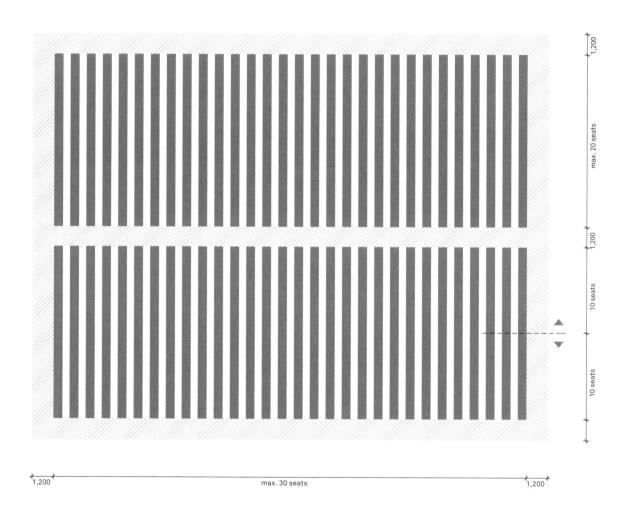

**Figure 4.6.32**
Balconies in a central perfor-
mance hall (Royal Opera House,
Copenhagen)

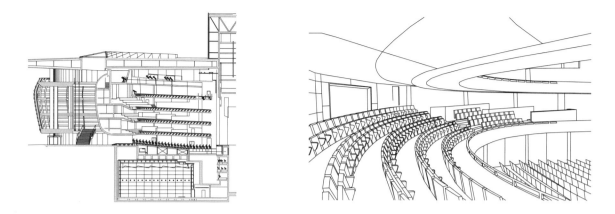

**Figure 4.6.33**
Section through a performance
room and stage area of a classic
theater and opera house

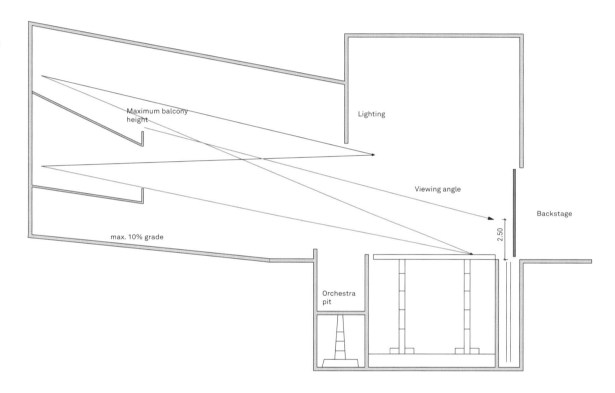

**Table 4.6.4**
Dimensions of orchestra pits

| Type of orchestra | Number of musicians | Minimum floor area of orchestra pit |
|---|---|---|
| Symphony orchestra | 70 to 90 | 140 m² to 180 m² |
| Chamber orchestra | 15 to 25 | 30 m² to 50 m² |

## Movie Theaters

The required size of movie theaters results from the operator's requirement profile and the operator's program concept. Various circulation variations can be applied for the arrangement of the seats, depending on the number of viewers. → **Figure 4.6.34**

As with stage theaters and opera houses, seats must be mounted fixed and there must be a minimum distance between rows of 40 cm. Likewise, each individual seat must be at least 50 cm wide. However, user expectations usually call for significantly larger dimensions. Since it is common for cinemas to use stepped aisles, it is important to ensure that the tread of each of the steps with a row of seats is at least 1.20 m wide. → **Figure 4.6.35**

Movies are projected through the back wall of the movie theater, which means that a projection room must be provided behind each auditorium. The projection outlet for the auditorium must not be lower than 2 m above the floor level of the last row of seats, in order to prevent the image from being fully or partly obscured by persons in the audience. → **Figure 4.6.35** In modern cinemas, movies are usually projected in widescreen formats. The ratio of the sides of the screen is either 2.35:1 or 1.85:1. The size of the image depends on the distance of the projector to the screen. → **Figures 4.6.36 and 4.6.37**

**Figure 4.6.34**
Circulation options in movie theaters

**Figure 4.6.35**
Cross section through a movie theater

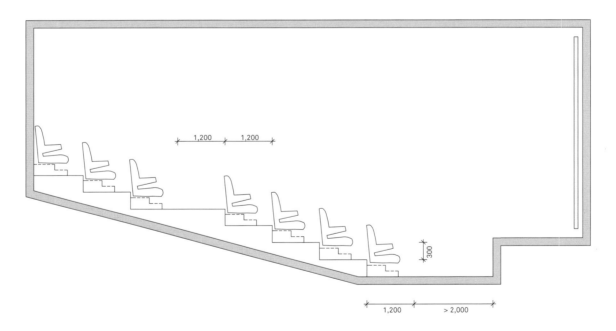

**Figure 4.6.36 (left)**
Layout of a movie theater

**Figure 4.6.37 (right)**
Common projection formats for movie theaters

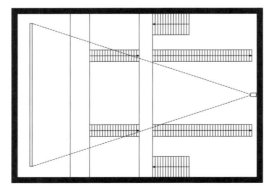

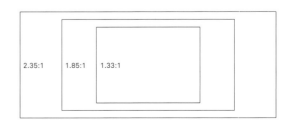

### 4.6.3.4 Rehearsal Rooms

In theaters, opera, and concert halls it is usual to provide several rehearsal rooms in order to free up the main stage; in these rooms, the performance conditions are largely authentically replicated in order to create good conditions for the preparation for performance.

**Orchestra Rehearsal Room**

Orchestra rehearsal rooms do not need any openings to the outside and have exacting requirements with respect to sound-absorbing room surfaces. For this reason, these rooms can be allocated to a place inside the building where there are no windows. The size of an orchestra rehearsal room is determined by the number of musicians. For each musician, at least 3 m² of floor area and 8 m³ of space volume should be provided. The seating arrangement for the orchestra is normally in a semicircular layout so that every musician has a good view of the conductor. → **Figure 4.6.38**
The number of seats for musicians in the orchestra rehearsal room corresponds to the size of the orchestra. In addition to sound-absorbing surfaces and walls, floors and ceilings, it may also be necessary to provide variable wall and ceiling surfaces to create a changeable acoustic environment.

**Rehearsal Stage Room**

Rehearsal stage rooms do not require any openings to the outside and must have a full blackout facility. Similar to rehearsal rooms for orchestras, they are ideally placed on a windowless side of the building or in its interior. In order to create comparable conditions and to be able to maintain the schedule, the rehearsal stage should have exactly the same dimensions as the main stage. Around the perimeter of the rehearsal stage, a corridor with a width of at least 1.00 m should be provided to allow actors to join the action on stage from different sides. In addition to the stage, the rehearsal room may also require an area for the orchestra, which can be accommodated in a pit. In addition, and in support of the rehearsals, a director's area, an area for costume makers, prop makers, and technicians should be provided. In order to accentuate the dimensions of the stage, it is a good idea to raise the rehearsal stage above the main floor and, if possible, to also provide the same room height as that of the main stage in order to create realistic rehearsal conditions. → **Figure 4.6.39**

**Dance and Ballet Rehearsal Room**

Dance and ballet rehearsal rooms should have windows to the outside, but may also require a blackout facility. Their size is largely related to the size of the main stage in order to create comparable rehearsal conditions. Dance and ballet rehearsal rooms are fitted with handrails on all sides, and some of the walls are also fitted with full-sized mirrors. The mirrors allow dancers to check their movements from different sides. In addition, a sprung floor should be provided to cushion the impact following jumps. → **Figure 4.6.40**

**Figure 4.6.38**
Example of an orchestra rehearsal room

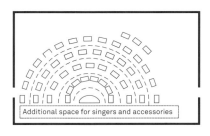

**Figure 4.6.39**
Example of a rehearsal stage room

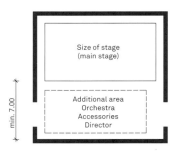

**Figure 4.6.40**
Example of dance and ballet rehearsal room

### 4.6.3.5 Administration and Workshops

The size of office and administration facilities in museum and performing arts buildings depends on the number of staff, and should have windows to the outside and a separate entrance. In addition, all necessary secondary areas must be provided, such as kitchenettes, toilets, and meeting rooms.

Furthermore, a range of workshops may be required, for example for the production of stage sets or exhibition elements, or for the restoration of exhibits. In theaters and opera houses in particular, it is important to ensure that the workshops and connecting corridors are appropriately sized for the items required on stage. ↗ Chapter 3.3 Spaces/ Workrooms and Production Spaces, ↗ Chapter 4.2 Typologies/Office and Administration, ↗ Chapter 4.4 Typologies/ Industry and Production

### 4.6.3.6 Ancillary Rooms

**Ticket Counter/Box Office, Information Desk, and Visitors' Cloakroom**
For museum and performing arts buildings to function properly, servicing the flow of visitors must be well organized. In view of the high number of visitors at peak periods, typically at the box office on the night of the performance, enough ticket counters and sufficient space for queuing should be provided without restricting other functional areas. It is usually a good idea to combine the box office with the information counter. → Figure 4.6.41

The cloakroom area should be near the information counter and box office. The size of the cloakroom should be determined in consultation with the client, as this tends to vary considerably in museum and performing arts buildings. Cloakrooms in theaters and opera houses may need to be relatively large in order to cope with the number of visitors, and therefore need to be taken into consideration at an early stage in the design. For the purpose of returning coats, the length of the return table should be 1 m per 20 visitors. → Figure 4.6.42, ↗ Chapter 3.8.2 Spaces/Ancillary and Staff Rooms/Locker and Changing Rooms

**Dressing and Makeup Rooms**
Dressing and makeup rooms are normally located in the private part of the building. Ideally they should have windows to the outside and the benefit of natural light. It is important that these rooms be in direct proximity to the stage area, and therefore can also be used by the artists during performances. The size of these rooms depends largely on the space requirement for lockers, tables, and seating. In addition, wash facilities and mirror walls have to be provided, and possibly also a daybed for short rests. → Figure 4.6.43, ↗ Chapter 3.8.2 Spaces/Ancillary and Staff Rooms/Locker and Changing Rooms

**Restrooms**
The number of restrooms required depends on the applicable statutory provisions for places of assembly. In performing arts buildings, consideration must be given to the peak usage of these facilities during the intermissions. The requirements in museums are less exacting. → Table 4.6.5, ↗ Chapter 3.5 Spaces/Sanitary Facilities

**Repositories, Storage Rooms, and Archives**
With respect to repositories, storage rooms, and archives in museum and performing arts buildings, a distinction needs to be made between rooms for the long-term storage of valuable items such as art objects and antiques, costumes, and props, and rooms for the storage of simpler objects such as furniture or stage props. The space requirement of these rooms depends largely on the objects to be stored or archived. Permanent storage spaces should be accommodated in the lower floors. In museums it is important to ensure that repositories and storage rooms are appropriately climate-controlled in order to ensure the correct storage conditions for holdings when they are not on exhibit. Where exhibitions change at fairly frequent intervals, it is important to ensure that exhibits can be delivered to the climate-controlled repository and storage areas quickly, easily, and securely without being exposed to the weather. It is possible to save space in repositories, storage rooms, and archives by using specialized storage systems. Examples are rail-based shelving systems in repositories and suspended racks or rolling carts for printed matter. ↗ Chapter 3.7 Spaces/Storage Spaces

**Figure 4.6.41**
Information counter and box office
in theaters and opera houses

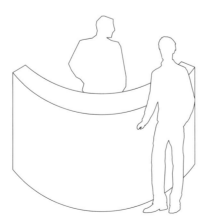

Information counter with box office

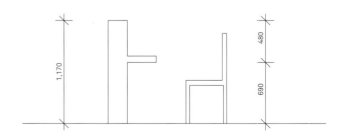

**Figure 4.6.42**
Coat check facility for a theater

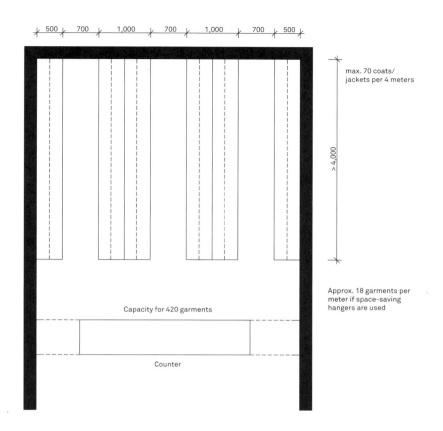

500 | 700 | 1,000 | 700 | 1,000 | 700 | 500

> 4,000

max. 70 coats/
jackets per 4 meters

Approx. 18 garments per
meter if space-saving
hangers are used

Capacity for 420 garments

Counter

**Figure 4.6.43**
Makeup rooms for stage theaters
and opera houses

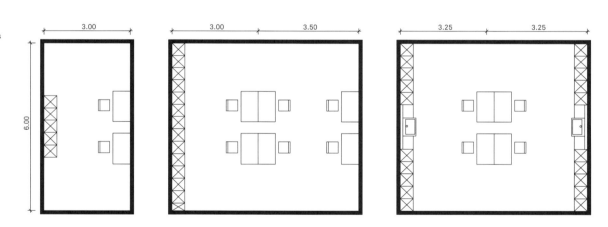

3.00

6.00

3.00 | 3.50

3.25 | 3.25

**Table 4.6.5**
Number of plumbing fixtures
required in museums

| Number of visitors per 120 minutes | Number of plumbing fixtures | | | | |
|---|---|---|---|---|---|
| | Women's toilets | Lavatories | Men's toilets | Urinals | Lavatories |
| Up to 50 | 2 | 1 | 1 | 2 | b |
| 51 to 100 | 3 | 3 | 1 | 3 | 2 |
| 101 to 150 | 4 | 3 | 2 | 4 | 3 |
| Over 151 | 5 | 3 | 3 | 5 | 3 |

**Imperial Hotel,** Tokyo, Japan, Frank Lloyd Wright, 1923

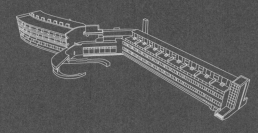

**Ledigenheim on the WuWA housing estate,** Wrocław, Poland, Hans Scharoun, 1929

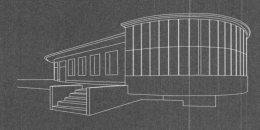

**Kornhaus,** Dessau, Germany, Carl Fieger, 1930

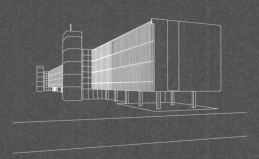

**Brasilia Palace Hotel,** Brasilia, Brazil, Oscar Niemeyer, 1958

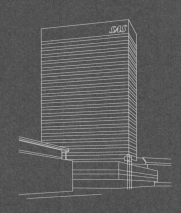

**SAS Hotel,** Copenhagen, Denmark, Arne Jacobsen, 1960

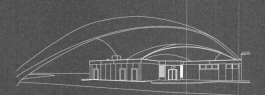

**Deitingen Süd Service Area,** Deitingen, Switzerland, Heinz Isler, 1968

**Nakagin Capsule Tower,** Tokyo, Japan, Kisho Kurokawa, 1972

**Cube House,** Rotterdam, The Netherlands, Piet Blom, 1978

**Hôtel de Thermes,** Dax, France, Jean Nouvel, 1992

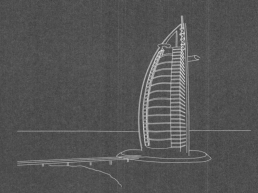

**Burj Al Arab,** Dubai, United Arab Emirates, Atkins, 1999

**Empire Riverside Hotel,** Hamburg, Germany, David Chipperfield, 2007

**Marina Bay Sands,** Singapore, Mosche Safdie, 2010

Ann-Christin Siegemund

# 4 Typologies
## 4.7 Lodging and Food Service

### 4.7.1 Building Concept ↗356

4.7.1.1 Planning Parameters ↗356
4.7.1.2 Building Forms ↗357
4.7.1.3 Circulation Systems ↗358
4.7.1.4 Construction and Technology ↗359

### 4.7.2 Program of Use ↗360

4.7.2.1 General Functional Areas in Accommodation Premises ↗360
4.7.2.2 Specific Lodging Establishments ↗362
4.7.2.3 General Food Service ↗365
4.7.2.4 Specific Food Service Facilities ↗366

### 4.7.3 Areas and Rooms ↗368

4.7.3.1 Entrance Areas ↗369
4.7.3.2 Hotel Rooms ↗369
4.7.3.3 Kitchen and Serving Area ↗375
4.7.3.4 Seating Area ↗381
4.7.3.5 Management ↗381
4.7.3.6 Ancillary Spaces ↗381

# 4.7  Lodging and Food Service

## 4.7.1  Building Concept

### 4.7.1.1  Planning Parameters

Lodging establishments and restaurant operations may be a constituent of another building type, such as a canteen within an office building; integrated into another building without any functional relationship, such as a ground-floor restaurant in an apartment building; or comprise a separate building of its own, such as a hotel or stand-alone restaurant. The range of designs stretches from atmospherically designed, individual rooms of specific users to systematized and reproducible franchises. All lodging establishments and restaurant operations are highly dependent on the satisfaction of their users. This means that – for the purpose of the design – the general target group orientation, the quality level, and the quality requirements of the target group have top priority.

> Typical planning parameters are:
> - Place, context, and infrastructure
> - Geometry of the site
> - Building code restrictions
> - Spatial program and needs
> - Integration in a larger building (optional)
> - The brief (individual through to chain premises)
> - Quality requirement
> - Target group requirements
> - Necessary secondary functions
> - Occupation rates (beds, seats)
> - Barrier-free accessibility
> - Budget and deadlines

**Culinary Classifications**

For the purpose of the design it is possible to determine certain catering classifications since these – depending on the assessment system – not only depend on the service and the quality of the service, but also on certain space characteristics and fit-outs. In terms of the star classification of hotels, this includes a minimum number of parking spaces, minimum room sizes, a minimum number of certain types of rooms, clear space given a specific amount of furnishing, the number of power outlets, and the existence of an individually controllable air-conditioning system.

However, worldwide uniform requirements for the classification system do not exist. Frequently systems are regulated at national level and, for hotels, regulation is voluntary. Within Europe, lodging establishments and restaurants are organized under the umbrella organization HOTREC – Hospitality Europe. In this context, hotel associations from currently 15 countries have come together under the Hotelstars Union, the function of which is to work out and implement a joint catalogue of criteria. A common subdivision is that of five categories, such as from 1 to 5 stars.

**Calculation of Space Requirement**

As a rule, the first space computations are based on the required standards and the associated stipulations for rooms or dining seats. In the hotel industry, the gross floor area (GFA) is determined per hotel room (and hotel class) on the basis of guide values. However, in view of the fact that these guide values are not binding, the sizes can vary significantly depending on the type of hotel and hotel operator. → **Table 4.7.1** In the next step, the space requirement for the other functional areas is added on the basis of the computed overall gross floor area. → **Table 4.7.2** As a general rule, about 75 percent of the floor area is used directly by the guest. The remaining area is needed for the administration and operation of the business, with the administration frequently taking place outside the actual lodging establishment, especially in the case of privately run premises.

In catering premises, the calculation of the space requirement relies primarily on the size, type of business, and furnishing layout. Space is computed separately for each area based on the number of seats. → **Table 4.7.3**

The space layout in catering facilities depends largely on operational requirements. Depending on the business concept, the serving and preparation of food may also take place separately.

Table 4.7.1
GFA per hotel room

| Type of hotel | ★ (Low-Budget) | ★ ★ (Standard) | ★ ★ ★ (Comfort) | ★ ★ ★ ★ (First Class) | ★ ★ ★ ★ ★ (Luxury) |
|---|---|---|---|---|---|
| **GFA in m² per room** | 15–30 | 30–50 | 35–60 | 60–80 | 80–110 |

Table 4.7.2 (left)
Space allocation in hotels

Table 4.7.3 (right)
Space requirement in restaurants (figures in m²/guest)

Source: Schneider Bautabellen für Architekten

| Function | Percentage of area |
|---|---|
| Lodging | 55 % |
| Food service/events (without kitchen) | 15 % |
| Operational/equipment rooms | 15 % |
| Additional facilities | 8 % |
| Courtyard/entrance/reception | 5 % |
| Management | 2 % |

| Function | ≤ 100 guests | ≤ 250 guests | ≥ 250 guests | |
|---|---|---|---|---|
| Food preparation | 0.7 | 0.51 | 0.51 | |
| Storage (incl. deliveries) | 0.55 | 0.65 | 0.58 | |
| Serving | 0.08 | 0.08 | 0.07 | |
| Cleaning | 0.1 | 0.12 | 0.1 | |
| Consumption (guest room) | Good restaurant | Pension | Basic restaurant | Pizzeria |
| | 1.9 | 1.5 | 1.7 | 1.5 |

## 4.7.1.2 Building Forms

### Lodging

A range of different building forms are used for lodging establishments. The design of individual, stand-alone buildings depends on the given site, the building code regulations, and the operator, as well as the respective business concept. Common shapes of individual buildings include linear developments and point-block buildings, as well as free shapes. In larger vacation resorts it is common to develop the accommodation in the form of groups of many individual buildings. Alternatively, lodging establishments such as hotels may be built to occupy a portion of a multistory building along with additional functions, or as a building that constitutes part of a continuous street front. → Figure 4.7.1

### Food Service

Individual buildings that are used exclusively as restaurants are particularly common with large franchise restaurant chains. Independent restaurants, which are those not affiliated with a chain, are by contrast often incorporated into existing buildings and even on different floors of various types of buildings. Where it is intended to carry out a change of use to establish such premises, not only conceptual design considerations have to be taken into account, but also the conditions imposed by the building code.

Food service facilities often form part of large-scale building forms. For example, facilities in shopping malls typically feature a very open design; often the seating area is separate from the sales and support areas and integrated in intermediate zones within the customer circulation areas. Often, large areas known as food courts are specifically allocated to fast-food outlets. The food is prepared in compactly designed areas and sold from behind counters. The food is then consumed in central seating areas that are shared by customers of all the outlets. Food service facilities catering to large groups of people, such as canteens and refectories, are associated with hospitals and universities as well as office and factory buildings.

Figure 4.7.1
Building forms – lodging

1 Freestanding building
2 Part of a larger building
3 Part of a street front
4 Building ensemble

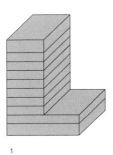 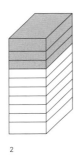 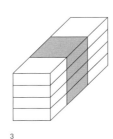 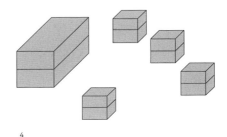

1      2      3      4

Figure 4.7.2
Building forms – food service

1 Part of a large building structure (such as within a shopping center/business)
2 Top of a building (such as a sky bar)
3 Ground floor commercial unit
4 Freestanding building

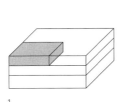 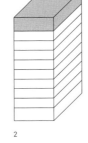 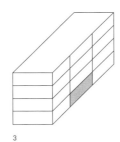 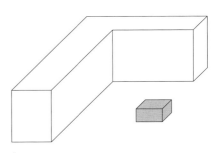

1      2      3      4

### 4.7.1.3 Circulation Systems

**External Circulation**

Access from outside for guests is generally via a formal entrance area with a prestigious character, whereas the entry point for personnel and deliveries is preferably concealed at the back of the house.

The design of parking spaces depends on the operating system of the premises and the intended standard. → **Table 4.7.4** Wherever possible, parking spaces should be offered in the direct vicinity. In the case of inner city hotels, car parking is often provided in underground parking garages. The calculation of parking spaces for gastronomy businesses depends on whether the respective unit is part of a larger complex with walk-in customers, and therefore has to account for fewer external guests. ↗**Chapter 3.1.2 Spaces/External Circulation/Parked Vehicles**

**Internal Circulation**

In internal circulation too, different provisions have to be made for guests and staff.

For guests, access is arranged to the various parts of the business via the entrance area or lobby (in the case of a hotel). The size and number of passenger elevators for guests should be determined on the basis of waiting periods at peak times (arrival, departure, meal times). Where a hotel has an underground parking garage, access should be provided via a separate elevator, or at least a mandatory stop of the main elevator, which can be viewed from the lobby in order to be able to exert a measure of control. Where it is intended that suites or certain areas are accessible directly via an elevator and only by certain persons, an additional control system should be provided in the design. Corridors to hotel rooms are usually double-loaded, that is, they have rooms on both sides. Since stairs in hotels are rarely used by guests, they primarily serve to comply with relevant fire safety regulations. Specially designed staircases with a generous feel may be provided as a link between commonly used levels such as the lobby and an events area.

For restaurants and bars, it is important to provide general circulation and escape routes within the public area and to ensure at an early stage that these will not be hindered by subsequent furniture layouts.

The design of staff routes follows primarily functional considerations in order to organize the operation of the business as efficiently as possible. If needed, the service area should include elevators for passengers, passengers and goods, or goods only. ↗**Chapter 3.2.1 Spaces/Internal Circulation/Entrance Areas,** ↗**Chapter 3.2.2 Spaces/Internal Circulation/Corridors,** ↗**Chapter 3.2.4 Spaces/Internal Circulation/Stairs,** ↗**Chapter 3.2.7 Spaces/Internal Circulation/Elevators and Conveying Systems**

Table 4.7.4
Parking space requirements

Source: Enclosure to No. 51.11
VV BauO NRW (North Rhine-Westphalia Building Code)

| Type of use | Number of parking spaces | Proportion reserved for guests |
|---|---|---|
| Places of assembly | 1 space per 5–10 seats | 90% |
| Restaurants | 1 parking space per 6–12 m² seating area | 75% |
| Hotels, pensions, sanitariums, and other lodging establishments | 1 space per 2–6 beds, where there is an associated restaurant, extra spaces as for restaurants or hotels | 75% |
| Dance halls, discotheques | 1 space per 4–8 m² seating area | |
| Youth hostels | 1 space per 10 beds | 75% |

Figure 4.7.3
Elements of hotel circulation systems for guests

1 Lobby
2 Ancillary areas (via staircases and elevators)
3 Guest rooms (via elevators)
4 Underground parking garage (via separate elevator)
5 Staircases as escape routes
6 Stairs/Elevators

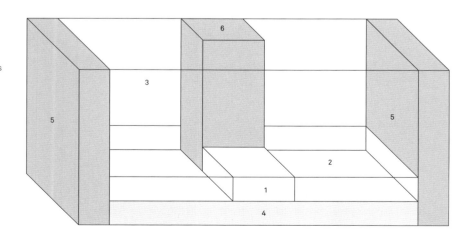

### 4.7.1.4 Construction and Technology

Different requirements apply to the dimensions of the different rooms in the business in accordance with its respective function. The design of the load-bearing structure of multistory hotel businesses is affected by a number of input variables resulting from the guest rooms, lobby, underground parking garage, and ancillary areas.

Appropriate grid dimensions can be determined based on the width of guest rooms and taking into account the furniture layout and the mandatory width of circulation routes. Depending on the furnishing concept, the minimum dimensions vary between 2.90 m and 3.50 m. → **Figure 4.7.5** In order to make the most efficient use of the relatively expensive facade surface, the required room size is often achieved by extending the depth of the room. However, it is important to ensure that the room's proportions are not distorted. For a double room of 22 m² including a 5 m² bathroom, the depth of the room is approximately 6.40 m to 7.70 m.

In contrast to the highly regular grid layout of the guest rooms, the lower stories with lobby, restaurants, and events areas require large spaces, preferably without columns, and the load transfer from above needs to be considered at an early stage in the design. Similarly, any planned underground parking garages require their own grid dimensions. ↗ **Chapter 3.1.2 Spaces/External Circulation/Parked Vehicles**

Figure 4.7.4
System of main spatial elements in a multistory hotel

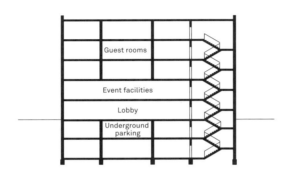

Figure 4.7.5
Minimum widths of guest rooms

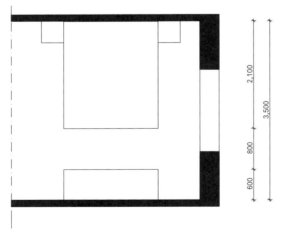
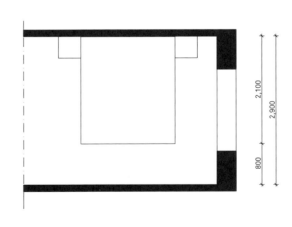

## 4.7.2 Program of Use

The design of lodging establishments and restaurants focuses on certain target groups as temporary users. For example, a catering business may be designed for the regular provision of meals for many people in the form of a canteen or refectory, or it may be aimed at very specific user groups, for example in the case of dining as an experience or a gourmet restaurant. Similarly, the specific orientation towards certain target groups is also important for lodging establishments.

In hotels and restaurants it is usual to refer to the area used only by staff as the "back of house" and the area open to guests as the "front of house." The public area should provide an atmosphere that is appropriate for the intentions of the operating concept. The design of the staff areas is much more functional and is largely determined by guidelines for working conditions, as well as hygiene requirements.

### 4.7.2.1 General Functional Areas in Accommodation Premises

**User Groups**
In the accommodation business, a basic distinction can be made between business travelers and tourists. Business travelers generally stay for only a few days. For them, the most important aspects are proximity to trade exhibitions or their business appointments and easy access to public transportation. For hotels that primarily serve as conference venues, locations outside towns may be appropriate. In order to allow guests to work in their hotel, it is imperative to provide a desk and an Internet connection in each guest room. To accommodate conferences and meetings with fewer people, it is necessary to provide meeting rooms as well as larger event rooms. Since lobbies are also often used as meeting points, appropriate seating and food service should be provided.

Businesses serving the tourist industry vary a great deal. Important parameters for the analysis of target groups are the duration of stay, the composition of the travelers – for example, families, couples without children, or groups – and the purpose of the trip. For example, hotels may specialize in older guests, in students, in families, or in quiet facilities without children. In this case, the individual lifestyle of the guests plays an important part in the design and services on offer. Distinctive features are, for example, particularly eye-catching or, conversely, a rather understated design; specific designs for certain user groups; or a design focusing on the proximity to nature, elegance, or exclusivity. Premises may also cater to special dietary requirements or offer additional, adventure-type leisure activities such as climbing tours. In consideration of the purpose of the guests' trip, hotels can be categorized as city, beach, or adventure hotels.

**Functional Areas**
Lodging establishments comprise five functional areas with a clear separation between guests and staff. → Figure 4.7.6 External and internal circulation routes provide access to the respective back-of-house areas and the transition to the guest areas. Transition areas between guests and staff in hotels are the reception (management → back office → front office/lobby) and housekeeping (laundry storage → hotel corridor → guest room).

In lodging establishments, the lobby is the central point of arrival for guests. The actual lodging area accounts for the largest part of the premises. It includes guest rooms of all types, the hallways connecting them, and any associated service rooms.

**Figure 4.7.6**
Functional areas in lodging establishments

### Wellness

The provision of wellness or other leisure facilities in hotels is not an obligatory requirement in any of the HOTREC star categories. Usually, spa and wellness areas include a range of facilities, though these are not governed by uniform minimum standards or typical classification. → **Figure 4.7.7** However, under HOTREC regulations, an indoor pool of at least 40 m² would attract the same number of points as an individually controllable air-conditioning system or extra-wide beds. In order to qualify as a wellness hotel, additional requirements must be met. According to the German Hotel Association, a wellness hotel should at least fulfill the requirements of the three-star standard and, in addition, should be located close to nature, be run in an environmentally friendly manner, and include special health-oriented cuisine. ↗ **Chapter 4.9 Typologies/Sports and Recreation**

### Events

The events area of a hotel should be as independent of the other hotel functions as possible. This therefore requires dedicated internal circulation, associated sanitary facilities and, depending on the size, its own banquet kitchen or a link to the restaurant kitchen. → **Figure 4.7.8** Where artists or speakers feature in an event, they should be provided with a preparation room.

Where it is intended to offer a range of rooms or different types of events, it is important to consider a wide range of styles and the possibility of creating rooms with different atmospheres. For example, conferences require different lighting concepts compared to cocktail receptions or weddings. The size of the rooms can be modified with the help of mobile partition walls.

The space requirement per person in the actual conference rooms depends primarily on the chosen type of seating. → **Table 4.7.5** Since different furnishing is needed to suit different types of events, it may be appropriate to provide furniture storage close by.

Where a venue provides space for more than 200 people, it is necessary to comply with the requirements for places of congregation. ↗ **Chapter 3.4 Spaces/Communication Spaces and Dining Rooms**

### Food Service as a Component of Lodging Establishments

It is common for lodging establishments to provide various levels of catering to their guests. These may range from simple hotel bars offering drinks and snacks to breakfast rooms through to large dining facilities with several restaurants. In larger hotels and inns in particular, it is common to provide restaurant facilities to external patrons.

Figure 4.7.7
Functional zones in wellness areas

| Changing area | Fitness/sport | Pool area |
| --- | --- | --- |
| | Sauna area | Wellness services |

Figure 4.7.8
Functional zones in events areas

| Preparation | | |
| Storage | Conference rooms | Break area |
| Kitchen | | |
| Toilets | Conference rooms | Lobby |

Table 4.7.5
Space requirement per participant in events venues

See DIN 15906

| Type of seating | |
| --- | --- |
| Row seating | 1.0–1.2 m² |
| Tables in block form | 1.6–2.5 m² |
| Parliament-type seating plan | 1.8–2.5 m² |
| Tables in U-layout (with additional activity area) | 3.0–3.5 m² |
| Open chair arrangement (moderation/interaction) | 2.5–8.0 m² |

## 4.7.2.2 Specific Lodging Establishments

Lodging establishments can be categorized by their specific characteristics, such as the location, type of building and guest rooms, purpose of stay, services offered, and other facilities.

### Examples of different types of accommodation as listed in DIN EN ISO 18513:
- All-suite hotel
- Aparthotel/apartment hotel
- Apartment facility/residence
- Boarding house
- Canal barge
- Camping trailer (travel trailer)
- Campground/RV park/vacation park/vacation camp
- Chalet/bungalow/vacation home
- Farmhouse
- Folding caravan
- Hotel
- Inn
- Motel
- Motor home/camper van
- Mountain chalet
- Pension
- Private lodging/private room
- Spa hotel
- Tent
- Touring caravan/caravan (travel trailer)
- Trailer tent (pop-up camper)
- Vacation retreat/children's recreation home
- Vacation motor home/vacation camping trailer/ mobile home (trailer home)
- Vacation resort/vacation center/holiday village
- Youth hostel

### Hotels/Pensions/Inns

With respect to location, a distinction can be made between city, country, mountain, or beach hotels and motels. Types of buildings include farmsteads, mountain chalets, bungalow facilities, etc. Facilities that are chosen for a particular purpose are, for example, vacation, rehabilitation, wellness, or sports hotels. Other types include family hotels and youth hostels. Common terms such as inn, pension, room-and-breakfast-only hotel, and hotel describe facilities of various sizes and levels of service. While inns generally will mostly provide restaurant services and only have a few guest rooms in addition, pensions are smaller lodging establishments, usually family-managed, that mainly cater to their own guests. Hotels with room and breakfast-only service may have a large number of beds and offer a higher service level, although catering is restricted to breakfast only. Accommodation businesses are not referred to as hotels unless they have at least 20 guest rooms; in addition, there is a higher level of service, such as daily cleaning, additional services, and more catering options in bars and various restaurants, which are open to hotel guests as well as external patrons. → **Figure 4.7.9**

### Serviced Apartments/Boardinghouses

Serviced apartments or also boardinghouses can be classified as somewhere between residential buildings and accommodation premises. The residential units offered are fully equipped, but in contrast to hotels are let for longer periods. In addition, the space offered is somewhat more generous compared to common hotel rooms; for example, apartments may have several rooms and usually also their own cooking facilities. Similar to hotels, residents will enjoy additional facilities such as a reception, laundry service, room service, etc. → **Figure 4.7.10**

Figure 4.7.9
Schematic illustration
of hotel layout

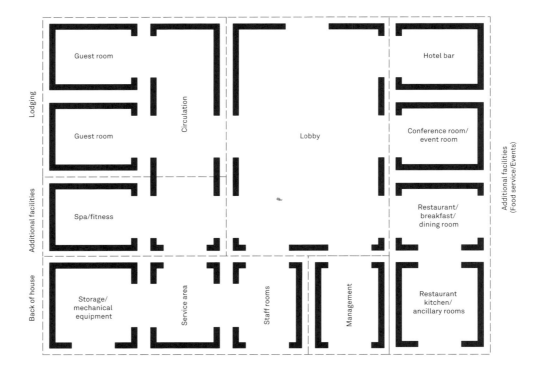

### Group Accommodation (Hostels)

Hostels may be located both in rural areas and in city centers. Depending on the facilities offered, the rooms in youth hostels can vary a great deal. Likewise, the number of beds can vary enormously although the average is approximately 140 beds. Sleeping facilities are offered in various sizes, as dormitories (usually 4 to 8 beds), leader bedrooms, family rooms (possibly with bathroom), single and double bedrooms. Dormitories and bedrooms should include seating and lockers in line with the number of beds. It is also possible to provide a washbasin. Sanitary facilities are usually offered for multiple use and should be close to the sleeping areas. Additional toilets are needed close to the dayrooms. Dayrooms should be provided of various sizes to cater for different functions, most appropriately as multipurpose rooms. Depending on the concept, a kitchen may be provided for guests' use or, alternatively, for use by staff who provide meals. In addition, it is possible to include café or sports facilities in the design similar to other types of accommodation. → **Figure 4.7.11**

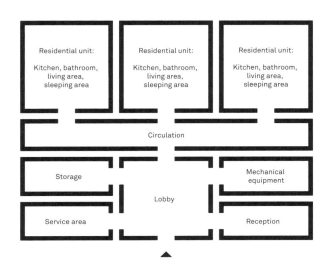

Figure 4.7.10
Schematic layout of accommodation

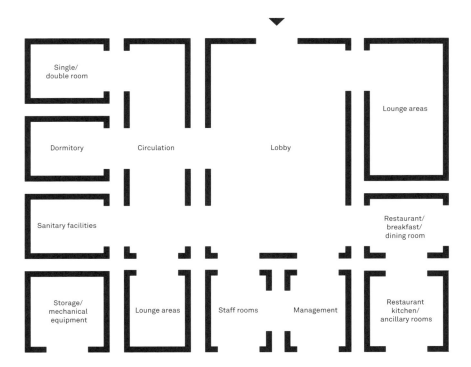

Figure 4.7.11
Schematic layout of group accommodation/hostel

## Motels

Motels offer travelers the opportunity to stay one or a few nights close to a major road. The advantage of these types of accommodation is that they are close to the road network and also usually offer parking directly in front of the room. Often these buildings are only one or two stories high. The rooms are accessible from the parking area, usually via a corridor with single loading, that is, rooms to one side only, with any upstairs corridors being open.

The reception area may include a security device to check incoming vehicles/persons. In addition to the reception, a small office should be provided and, in the case of 24-hour service, a sleeping area. The guest rooms are usually single, double, or twin bedrooms with bathroom, and sometimes with a small kitchenette. As in other accommodation premises, service rooms are needed close to the guest rooms. → Figure 4.7.12

## Vacation Resorts

Vacation resorts are developments with numerous chalets, bungalows, or vacation homes and associated leisure facilities, such as playgrounds, sports facilities, restaurants, and shops. The clientele primarily consists of families and groups (of young people). The interior fit-out of vacation homes can vary a great deal, from basic houses with multibed rooms to interiors that include a private sauna and whirlpool. Where it is intended to attract mostly families, it is important to ensure that the homes and outdoor playgrounds are suitable for children.

## RV Parks/Campgrounds

The largest amount of area at an RV park/campground is taken up by the sites for parking RVs or pitching tents and for means of access, that is, by the layout of outdoor spaces. However, these facilities also need indoor spaces, including a reception/managment office, snack bar or kiosk, and sanitary facilities.

**Figure 4.7.12**
Schematic layout of a motel

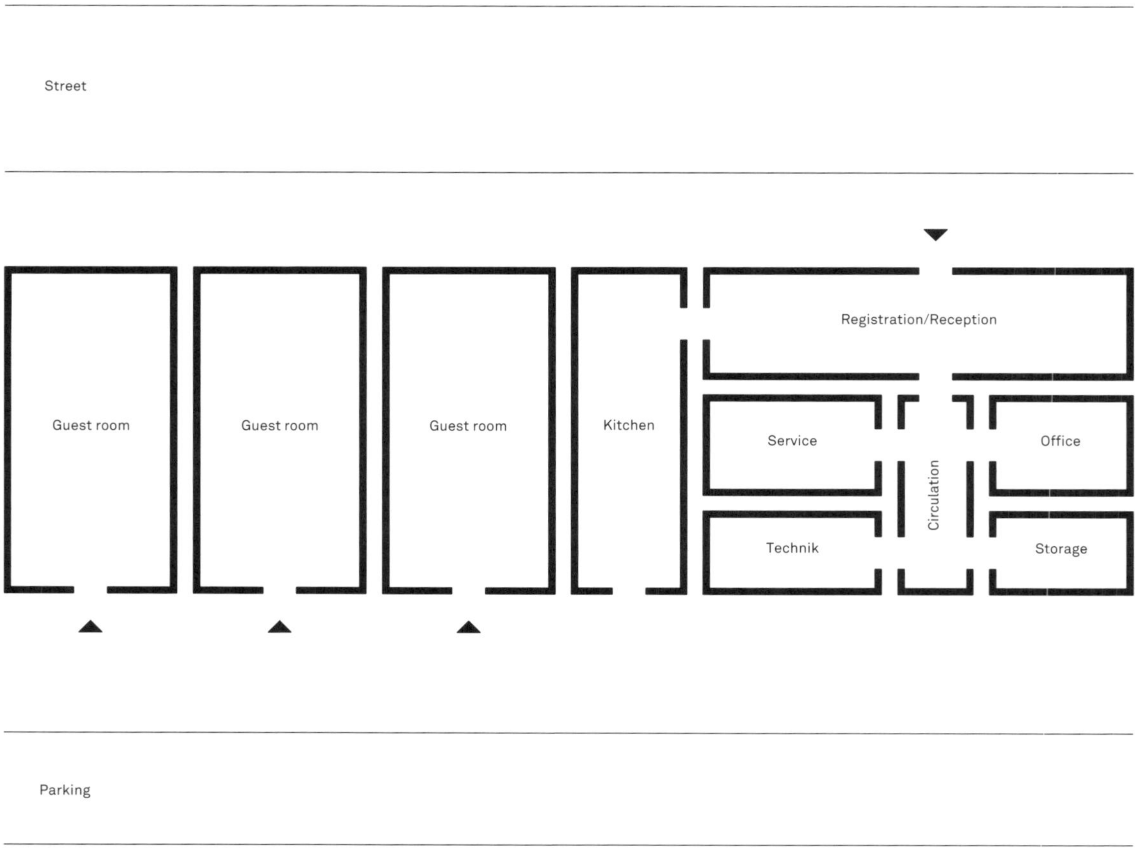

## 4.7.2.3 General Food Service

### User Groups

Food service operations are often categorized by the type of user, the context, the concept, or key services offered. It is important to distinguish whether, for instance, a facility will serve a large number of people with a wide selection of food and beverages, such as a school cafeteria or a canteen, or offer a limited menu to a small group of restaurant guests – or, for that matter, whether the main focus will be on serving drinks or on serving meals.

### Functional Areas

Roughly speaking, restaurant facilities include three functional areas: dining area, kitchen, and management. → **Figure 4.7.13** The dining and kitchen areas are naturally linked through the serving of meals. The design of this transition can take various forms, but a clear demarcation is often lacking, especially in franchise restaurants and in upmarket restaurants that increasingly feature open kitchens for so-called display cooking.

### Public Area

The public area in food service businesses includes the actual dining area as well as ancillary spaces such as coatrooms and restroom facilities. Access can be from the road via a small lobby or, within a building, directly into the public area.

It is usual to provide an additional bar or counter area within the public area for serving drinks. If no table service is offered, it is also possible to locate the buffet and counter service directly within the public area. In addition to interior public areas it is also possible to utilize outside courtyards or terraces for outside seating/dining areas.

### Kitchen

The size, equipment, and layout of commercial kitchens largely depend on the chosen production processes, the type of food offered, and the number of meals to be prepared. ↗ **4.7.3.3 Areas and Rooms/Kitchen and Serving Area** In addition to these requirements specified by the owner/user, other conditions are important for the design, such as those relating to building regulations as well as work and hygiene regulations. Food preparation in the kitchen involves several preparation work steps, for some of which it is necessary to provide separate areas.

The three basic areas in a commercial kitchen are storage, including deliveries, the actual kitchen, and a warewashing area. Adjacent to the kitchen and cleaning area should be the food service. In addition it is necessary to provide changing rooms, sanitary facilities, and staff rooms, and possibly an office for the head chef. → **Figure 4.7.14 and Table 4.7.6**

**Figure 4.7.13 (left)**
Schematic layout of functional areas in food outlets

**Table 4.7.6 (right)**
Allocation of kitchen space

See Alfons Goris, ed., Schneider Bautabellen, 18th ed. (2008), p. 146.

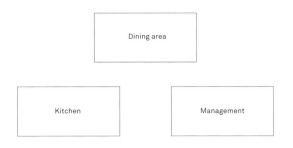

| Functional areas in proportion to the overall kitchen space | |
| --- | --- |
| Functional area | Proportion of space in % |
| Deliveries and waste removal (incoming goods, presorting, waste storage, etc.) | 11 |
| Goods storage | 40 |
| Kitchen | 25 |
| Warewashing area | 12 |
| Staff area (changing and staff rooms) | 12 |

**Figure 4.7.14**
Functional areas and processes in commercial kitchens

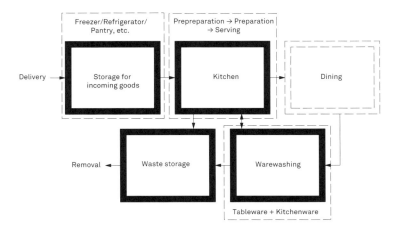

## 4.7.2.4 Specific Food Service Facilities

As mentioned already, food service facilities may be categorized under many different criteria. Cafeterias and canteens as well as caterers and food service facilities in hospitals or residence halls can be grouped into the category of communal food service. A characteristic of communal food service is that only a limited range of meals is offered and only at certain times, but in large quantities.

All other food service operations can be collectively referred to as individual food service businesses. In this category, each portion of food is prepared individually, according to the wishes of the patron. This category also includes chain food outlets, in which processes such as ordering, storage, and preparation are unified and centrally controlled. Additional classification criteria can be the type of food/drink offered or the service provided.

**Examples of food service businesses:**
- Sit-down restaurants
- Takeout restaurants
- Cafeterias
- Caterers
- Snack bars and refreshment stands
- Ice cream parlors
- Cafés
- Taverns and pubs
- Bars and nightclubs
- Discotheques and dance halls

### Restaurants
Restaurant is a generic term that applies to most outlets of individual food-service establishments. In contrast to snack bars, takeaway stands, and the like, there is greater emphasis on service and on serving diners indoors. Furthermore, the range of food on offer is more extensive. Special features relating to the outlet's service, type of food, or premises can be expressed by supplementing the word, as in the case of hotel restaurant, self-service restaurant, or fast-food restaurant.

### Catering
Catering primarily involves the production of food to be consumed at a different location. The service includes delivery of the prepared food as well as final preparation and serving of the food on site, either as a buffet or with table service. Furthermore, beyond the food and beverages, accessories such as dishes, cutlery, tables, and linen are also typically supplied, all of which require additional storage space.

Private persons will use the services of caterers mostly in the context of special events. Nevertheless, catering services also include regular deliveries of individual warm meals, for instance to older people. In addition, caterers provide their services to large establishments such as schools, hospitals, and canteens. In view of the fact that such establishments ordinarily have fully equipped kitchens, they are able to use a number of different processes – such as cook & chill, cook & freeze, and sous-vide – in addition to the traditional cook & hold. ↗ 4.7.3.3 Areas and Rooms/Kitchen and Serving Area

### Cafeterias and Canteens
Refectories and canteens usually serve educational establishments or companies, and are normally only accessible to certain user groups. Food is dispensed from counters or partly from counters and partly in the form of buffets. Important considerations for the design of refectories and canteens are the logistics processes in order to avoid delays at the food-dispensing points, the cash register, and the tray-return point(s) at peak periods.

### Snack Stands
Takeaway stalls generally offer food to take away, although there are also establishments such as snack bars, where a few seats are available to eat indoors. The food on offer is rarely changed and comprises rather more simple meals, often consisting of convenience products. As a rule, meals are prepared and portioned directly in front of the customer. The food is handed over and paid for across a counter.

### Cafés and Ice Cream Parlors
Ice cream parlors mostly offer ice cream and nonalcoholic drinks. Importance is given to the design of the public area in general, along with the presentation of the product. Patrons may be served at tables and/or from a counter; often there is also a display case and counter that allows patrons who are outside to be served directly.

Cafés, on the other hand, offer cakes and pastries, which can preferably be chosen by patrons from display cases rather than from a menu.

### Bars
Bars are places of entertainment and therefore the atmosphere and setting play an important role. This is supported by the choice of furniture and, in particular, appropriate lighting design. In addition to providing a seating area and bar for the sole purpose of consumption, it is common to include additional areas for live music and/or other types of entertainment. In these premises, the preparation of food is of secondary importance.

**Figure 4.7.15**
Schematic layout of food
service outlet

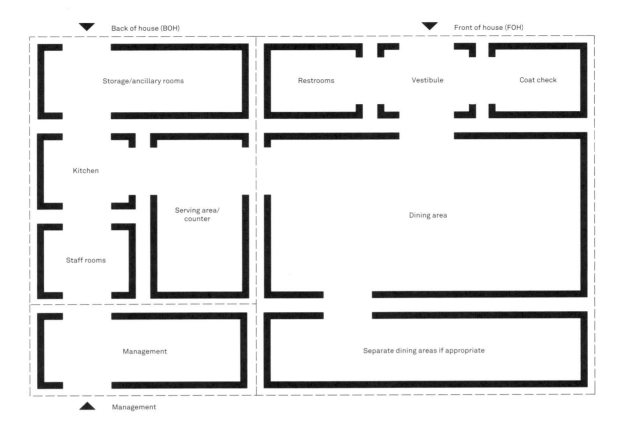

Back of house (BOH)

Front of house (FOH)

Storage/ancillary rooms

Restrooms

Vestibule

Coat check

Kitchen

Serving area/
counter

Dining area

Staff rooms

Management

Separate dining areas if appropriate

Management

### 4.7.3 Areas and Rooms

**External circulation** ↗ Chapter 3.1

**Entrance areas** ↗ 369 ↗ Chapter 3.2.1

**Stairs, elevators** ↗ Chapter 3.2.4, ↗ Chapter 3.2.7

**Corridors** ↗ Chapter 3.2.2

**Reception, lobby** ↗ 369 ↗ Chapter 3.2.1

**Hotel rooms** ↗ 369 ↗ Chapter 4.1

**Guest bathrooms** ↗ 372 ↗ Chapter 3.5

**Hotel-room kitchens** ↗ 374 ↗ Chapter 3.6, ↗ Chapter 4.1

**Service rooms** ↗ 375

**Guest rooms** ↗ 381

**Kitchens (food service)** ↗ 375 ↗ Chapter 3.6

**Common areas** ↗ Chapter 3.4.2

**Cafeterias** ↗ Chapter 3.4.3, ↗ Chapter 4.7.3.3

**Management** ↗ 381 ↗ Chapter 3.3.1, ↗ Chapter 4.2

**Restrooms** ↗ 381 ↗ Chapter 3.5

**Storage spaces** ↗ Chapter 3.7.2

**First aid rooms** ↗ Chapter 3.8.3

**Janitorial/Service rooms** ↗ 381 ↗ Chapter 3.8.4

**Mechanical equipment rooms** ↗ Chapter 3.9

### 4.7.3.1  Entrance Areas

Restaurants and bars are usually entered via a small vestibule in order to avoid drafts from opening doors in the seating area. External walls are often designed of movable glass elements so that the seating area can be opened to the outside during the summer. Where food outlets are located on the inside of a larger building complex, it is possible to omit the entrance area.

In lodging establishments, the central entrance area and distribution point is the lobby, which has to combine various different functions. → **Figure 4.7.16** In addition, the lobby has a strong representational character, because this is where the guest is welcomed and obtains a first impression of the interior. As part of the lobby it is common to provide a lounge in addition to the entrance area and reception. Other options include multipurpose areas with Internet access or a hotel bar and breakfast area.

The reception desk is part of the lobby and the place of the first direct contact between guests and staff, as well as providing a link to the back-of-house area. Staff in the front office is in charge of checking-in and checking-out, and perform other administration and service activities for guests. The reception counter needs work surfaces and counter surfaces at two levels, as well as a passage to the guest area. In addition, there should be enough storage space for materials and equipment, and possibly also a safe for keeping valuables on behalf of guests. A luggage room should be provided close to the reception area.

### 4.7.3.2  Hotel Rooms

The design of hotel rooms is largely determined by the level of comfort provided, which has to comply with the intended star category of the hotel. The range of rooms is considerable and varies significantly in type, fit-out, and size. Types of rooms in accordance with EN ISO 18513:

- Single room
- Double room
- Twin-bed room
- Multiple-bed room
- Family room
- Dormitory
- Junior suite
- Suite
- Apartment
- Studio
- Interconnected rooms
- Duplex/maisonette

However, for any one hotel one should reduce the different types and dimensions to a minimum in order to be able to provide more efficient servicing and maintenance. Hotel rooms normally have an entrance area with a space for luggage and clothes, a bathroom, and the sleeping area. In addition it is common to provide space for items such as a desk or extra seating. → **Figure 4.7.17** Suites, apartments, studios, and family rooms will have additional functions provided within the space or in other connected rooms. With regards to the furniture of the accommodation it is important to use the internationally accepted designation of beds in relation to their sizes. → **Table 4.7.7**

There are no specific regulations regarding the size of rooms. However, from 14 m² the room size is included in the point system of the star classification. Depending on the respective accommodation concept, rooms may also include features usually associated with private residences. ↗ **Chapter 4.1 Typologies/Housing**

Since hotel rooms are normally used in the mornings and evenings it is important to design the lighting accordingly and to provide as many variable control options as possible.

**Figure 4.7.16**
Schematic layout of a lobby

| Restrooms | | |
| Stair/elevator | Lounge | Multipurpose area |
| Luggage room | | |
| Office | Reception | Entrance area |

**Figure 4.7.17**
Functional areas in hotel rooms

| Entrance | Bathroom |
| Additional functions | Sleeping |

Table 4.7.7
Bed sizes and designations

| EU | | USA | | UK | |
|---|---|---|---|---|---|
| Designation | Size in cm | Designation | Size in cm | Designation | Size in cm |
| Small Single | 80 × 200 | – | – | Small Single | 75 × 191 |
| Single | 90 × 200 | Single/Twin | 97 × 191 | Single | 91 × 191 |
| Large Single | 100 × 200 | Extra-long twin | 100 × 203 | Super Single | 107 × 191 |
| – | – | – | – | Small Double | 120 × 198 |
| Double | 140 × 200 | Double/Full | 137 × 191 | Double | 137 × 198 |
| King | 160 × 200 | Queen | 152 × 203 | King | 152 × 198 |
| Super King | 180 × 200 | King | 193 × 203 | Super King | 183 × 198 |
| – | – | California King | 180 × 213 | – | – |

Figure 4.7.18
Sample layouts

Left: King standard USA;
right: Double twin standard EU

Figure 4.7.19
Examples of a double bedroom
and a four-bed room with bunk
beds

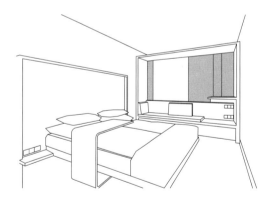
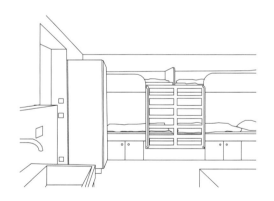

Table 4.7.8
Selection of minimum requirements for allocating stars

Source: HOTREC

| Area | Criterion | ★ | ★★ | ★★★ | ★★★★ | ★★★★★ |
|---|---|---|---|---|---|---|
| Sleeping comfort | Single beds at least 0.90 × 1.90 m; double beds at least 1.80 × 1.90 m | x | x | x | | |
| | Single beds at least 0.90 × 2.00 m; double beds at least 1.80 × 2.00 m | | | | x | x |
| | Modern and well-kept mattresses with a thickness of at least 13 cm | x | x | x | x | x |
| | Washable rug in front of the bed | | | | | x |
| | Darkening device (such as curtains) | x | x | x | x | |
| | Blackout device (such as roller shutters or blackout blinds) | | | | | x |

Table 4.7.8 (continuation) Selection of minimum requirements for allocating stars

Source: HOTREC

| Area | Criterion | ★ | ★ ★ | ★ ★ ★ | ★ ★ ★ ★ | ★ ★ ★ ★ ★ |
|------|-----------|---|-----|-------|---------|-----------|
| Room amenities | Wardrobe or recess of adequate capacity | x | x | x | x | x |
| | Clothes compartments | | x | x | x | x |
| | Appropriate number of uniform clothes hangers | x | x | x | x | x |
| | Coatroom or coat hooks | x | x | x | x | x |
| | Hanging facility for clothes bag (outside the wardrobe) | | | x | x | x |
| | 1 chair | x | x | | | |
| | 1 seat per bed, of which at least 1 chair | | | x | x | x |
| | 1 comfortable seat (upholstered armchair/sofa) with side table/ledge | | | | x | x |
| | 1 additional comfortable seat (upholstered armchair or double-seated sofa) in double rooms and suites | | | | | x |
| | Table, desk, or writing board | x | x | | | |
| | Table, desk, or writing board with a clear work surface of at least 0.5 m² and suitable desk lighting | | | x | x | x |
| | Power outlets in the main room | x | x | x | x | x |
| | Additional power outlet near the desk | | | x | x | x |
| | Appropriate room lighting | x | x | x | x | x |
| | Bedside table/bedside ledge | | | x | x | x |
| | Reading light by the bed | | x | x | x | x |
| | Central switching of room lighting from the bed | | | | | x |
| | Power outlet close to the bed | | | x | x | x |
| | Dressing mirror | | | x | x | x |
| | Suitcase stand | | | x | x | x |
| | Wastebasket | | | x | x | x |
| Safe/safety deposit box | Deposit facility (for example, at reception) | x | x | | | |
| | Central safe (for example, at reception) | | | (x) | x | x |
| | Safe in the room | | | (x) | x | x |
| Entertainment electronics | Radio program (reception also possible via television set or central sound system) | | | x | x | x |
| | Color television with remote control | x | x | | | |
| | Color television of a size appropriate to the room conditions, including remote control and channel list | | | x | | |
| | Color television of a size appropriate to the room conditions, including remote control, channel list, and current TV program guide | | | | x | x |
| Telecommunications | Fax machine at reception | x | x | x | x | x |
| | Telephone accessible to hotel guest | x | x | x | x | x |
| | On request, (mobile) room telephone, including operating instructions in several languages | | | x | | |
| | Room telephone, including operating instructions in several languages | | | | x | x |
| | Internet access in public areas (for example, DSL, WLAN) | | | (x) | x | x |
| | Internet access in the room (for example, DSL, WLAN) | | | (x) | x | x |
| | Internet terminal accessible to the hotel guest | | | | x | |
| | Internet PC in the room on request | | | | | x |

**Selection of additional minimum requirements**

| Area | Criterion | ★ | ★ ★ | ★ ★ ★ | ★ ★ ★ ★ | ★ ★ ★ ★ ★ |
|------|-----------|---|-----|-------|---------|-----------|
| Drinks | Drinks available in the room | | | x | x | x |
| | Minibar | | | | (x) | x |

**Guest Bathroom**

Hotels usually provide a standard bathroom with shower and/or bathtub, a barrier-free version of the same, and a larger bathroom in suites. Special conditions apply in hostels, where shared sanitary facilities are usually outside the bedrooms, and at campgrounds, where they are gathered at one or more central locations. For the room layout design, the position of the bathrooms is essential; a handed layout with two bathrooms using one vertical installation duct should be chosen to maximize efficiency. → **Figure 4.7.20** There is no regulated minimum size for hotel bathrooms; however, the hotel classification according to HOTREC does not allocate points for room sizes below 5 m². The bathroom fit-out also depends on the type of hotel, as well as specific requirements. → **Tables 4.7.9 and 4.7.10,** ↗ **Chapter 3.5 Spaces/Sanitary Facilities**

Table 4.7.9
Minimum requirements for bathroom equipment in the different star categories

Source: HOTREC

| Criterion | ★ | ★★ | ★★★ | ★★★★ | ★★★★★ |
|---|---|---|---|---|---|
| 100% of rooms with shower/toilet or bathtub/toilet | x | x | x | x | x |
| Shower facility with curtain/cubicle | x | x | x | x | x |
| Washbasin | x | x | x | x | x |
| Washable bath mat | | x | x | x | x |
| Appropriate lighting at washbasin | x | x | x | x | x |
| Mirror | x | x | x | x | x |
| Electric outlet close to mirror | x | x | x | x | x |
| Adjustable makeup mirror | | | | x | x |
| Towel holder or hook | x | x | x | x | x |
| Heater in the bathroom (also towel warmer) | | | x | x | x |
| Shelf | x | x | x | | |
| Generous shelf area | | | | x | x |
| Toothbrush tumbler | x | x | x | x | x |
| 1 hand towel per person | x | x | x | x | x |
| 1 bath towel per person | | x | x | x | x |
| Hairdryer | | | x | x | x |
| Bathroom stool | | | | | x |
| Waste receptacles | x | x | x | x | x |

Figure 4.7.20
Position of bathrooms in
hotel rooms

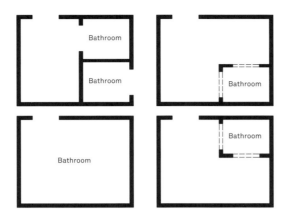

Table 4.7.10
Fixtures for sanitary facilities

Source: VDI 6000, Part 4

| Fixture | Accessories |
|---|---|
| Toilet | Tissue holder, wall-mounted |
| | Spare tissue box, spare tissue holder, wall-mounted |
| | Toilet brush set, wall-mounted |
| Lavatory unit | Shelf, for example in the form of<br>• Glass or porcelain shelf above the lavatory<br>• Horizontal surface on top of the installation wall<br>• Storage shelf with built-in basin<br>• Lavatory with horizontal surface as combined unit |
| | Flat mirror above the lavatory |
| | Shaving mirror, adjustable |
| Bathtub | Integrated grip or grip mounted on the wall |
| | Screen when used as a shower, in the form of<br>• Folding doors<br>• Horizontal or vertical folding or gliding systems<br>• Shower curtain |
| | Holder for soap, shampoo, sponge, etc. |
| Shower | Grip mounted on the wall |
| | Shower enclosure as fixed screen in the form of<br>• Hinged doors<br>• Folding systems<br>• Sliding doors for entrance from the side or the corner |
| | Holder for soap, shampoo, sponge, etc. |
| Bidet | Towel holder |
| | Soap holder |
| Urinal | |

**Kitchens in Hotel Rooms**

Kitchens are not only provided in vacation homes and apartments, but also in some types of accommodation with a self-catering option, such as motel rooms, youth hostels, studios, or apartments, where they may be in a separate room or in the form of kitchen furniture within the main room. The requirements are similar to those in regular housing. → **Table 4.7.11**, ↗ **Chapter 3.6 Spaces/Kitchens**

Table 4.7.11
Kitchen fixtures and equipment in hotel rooms

Source: VDI 6000, Part 4

| Fixture | Accessories |
|---|---|
| Sink with drainboard | Waste receptacle |
| Refrigerator | |
| Cooktop | |
| Exhaust hood | |
| Small appliances | Microwave, coffee machine, electric water boiler, etc. |

### 4.7.3.3 Kitchen and Serving Area

The design of commercial kitchens is largely governed by building code regulations, safety at work, food hygiene, regulatory standards, and the operator's cooking methods. A distinction can be made between different types of commercial kitchens. Central kitchens are used to prepare food that is subsequently served via warm-up/satellite kitchens or distribution kitchens. Warm-up kitchens receive the ready-prepared food in chilled or frozen form for reheating and serving. Distribution kitchens receive the food when it is already prepared and still warm so that it only needs to be kept warm until it is served. Other design considerations are the size of the kitchen, which depends on the number of portions to be prepared (small, medium, large kitchen).

Another distinctive characteristic is the arrangement of the kitchen in relationship to the patrons. In snack stands the food is prepared directly in front of the customer. There is no kitchen and no dining room, and food is handed across a counter that separates the customer area from the work/preparation area. Restaurant kitchens are allocated to separate rooms where they cannot be seen by the patrons, unless display cooking is part of the concept. As the food is distributed by the service personnel, there is no contact between patrons and the kitchen.

Another distinctive characteristic is the method of portioning and distributing the food. Food may be portioned into individual servings, which can also be done via conveyor, large container portions, and by order. Food may be

Table 4.7.12
Guide values for kitchens and ancillary spaces, in m² per seat

Source: Alfons Goris, ed., Schneider Bautabellen, 18th ed. (2008)

| Area | ≤ 100 guests | ≤ 250 guests | > 250 guests |
|---|---|---|---|
| **Deliveries and waste removal** | **0.2** | **0.2** | **0.2** |
| Receiving | 0.07 | 0.06 | 0.05 |
| Storage manager | 0.03 | 0.02 | 0.04 |
| Head chef's office | 0.05 | 0.04 | 0.03 |
| Waste storage | 0.10 | 0.11 | 0.12 |
| **Goods storage** | **0.35** | **0.45** | **0.38** |
| Prechilling room | | 0.03 | 0.03 |
| Refrigerated storage – meat | | 0.05 | 0.04 |
| Refrigerated storage – dairy | | 0.04 | 0.03 |
| Refrigerated storage – vegetables | | 0.04 | 0.04 |
| Walk-in freezer | | 0.04 | 0.04 |
| Cold kitchen | 0.02 | 0.02 | |
| Food waste cold storage | 0.02 | 0.02 | |
| Dry storage | 0.02 | 0.02 | 0.02 |
| Vegetable storage | 0.09 | 0.07 | 0.04 |
| Beverage storage | | 0.03 | 0.02 |
| Wine cellar | | 0.04 | 0.03 |
| Tableware storage | 0.04 | 0.03 | 0.03 |
| **Kitchen** | | | |
| Meat preparation | 0.1 | 0.08 | 0.05 |
| Vegetable preparation | 0.1 | 0.08 | 0.06 |
| Hot kitchen | 0.3 | 0.2 | 0.2 |
| Cold kitchen (garde manger) | 0.2 | 0.15 | 0.2 |
| Assembly/portioning | 0.08 | 0.08 | 0.07 |
| Warewashing | 0.1 | 0.12 | 0.1 |

distributed by personal service to the table, by distributing individually portioned food or food in large containers across the counter, or via self-service from a buffet.

The design of kitchens is based on the system adopted by the food outlet, which can range from catering through to food preparation in fully equipped kitchens. → **Figure 4.7.21**

The main areas required in commercial kitchens are those for storage (including deliveries), the actual kitchen, and warewashing areas; these can be further subdivided into prepreparation, preparation, and distribution, depending on the production method and size of the business. It may be necessary to provide separate rooms for the preparation of fish and poultry.

**Figure 4.7.21**
Processes of different production methods

See DIN 10506

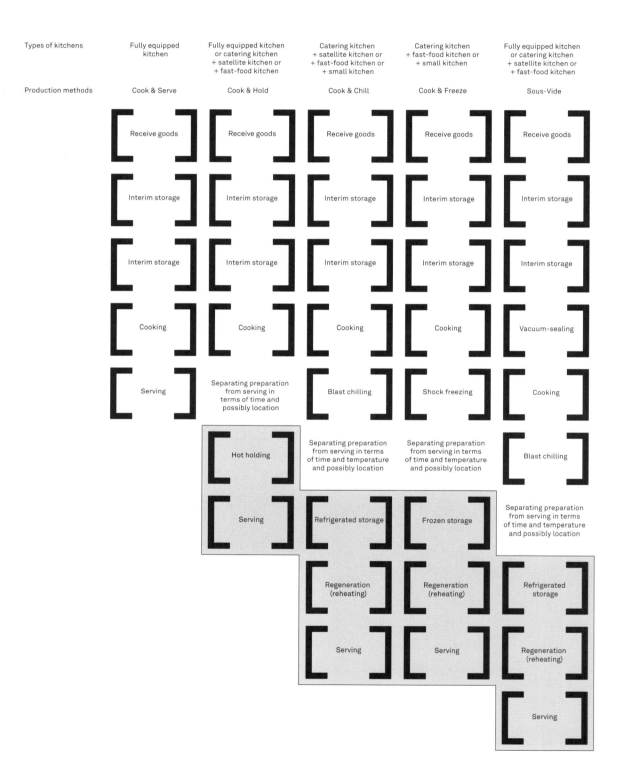

| Types of kitchens | Fully equipped kitchen | Fully equipped kitchen or catering kitchen + satellite kitchen or + fast-food kitchen | Catering kitchen + satellite kitchen or + fast-food kitchen or + small kitchen | Catering kitchen + fast-food kitchen or + small kitchen | Fully equipped kitchen or catering kitchen + satellite kitchen or + fast-food kitchen |
|---|---|---|---|---|---|
| Production methods | Cook & Serve | Cook & Hold | Cook & Chill | Cook & Freeze | Sous-Vide |
| | Receive goods | Receive goods | Receive goods | Receive goods | Receive goods |
| | Interim storage | Interim storage | Interim storage | Interim storage | Interim storage |
| | Interim storage | Interim storage | Interim storage | Interim storage | Interim storage |
| | Cooking | Cooking | Cooking | Cooking | Vacuum-sealing |
| | Serving | Separating preparation from serving in terms of time and possibly location | Blast chilling | Shock freezing | Cooking |
| | Hot holding | Separating preparation from serving in terms of time and temperature and possibly location | Separating preparation from serving in terms of time and temperature and possibly location | | Blast chilling |
| | Serving | Refrigerated storage | Frozen storage | | Separating preparation from serving in terms of time and temperature and possibly location |
| | | Regeneration (reheating) | Regeneration (reheating) | | Refrigerated storage |
| | | Serving | Serving | | Regeneration (reheating) |
| | | | | | Serving |

### Prepreparation and Preparation

Pre-preparation requires primarily horizontal work surfaces and rinsing/washing facilities. However, for reasons of economy, commercial kitchens and communal catering establishments in particular often rely on semiprepared or prepared components, which means that the prepreparation area can be comparatively small. Depending on the requirements and size, the preparation area may contain equipment such as deep fryers, griddles, convection ovens, bain-maries, pasta boilers, bulk boilers, tilt fryers, conventional and/or convection ovens, and gas or electric stoves, as well as other special equipment. → **Figure 4.7.23** In addition, work surfaces are needed for tableware, foodstuffs, etc., as well as for plating and possibly for keeping plated food hot. The different fittings should be arranged to allow for an optimum work process as well as for central supply and disposal. Overall, an area of approx. 0.5–0.7 m² per seat is required for the prepreparation and preparation of cold and hot food.

### Storage Spaces

Storage rooms are required both for the supply side and the disposal side. Depending on the foods to be stored, a distinction is made between dry areas and wet areas and between different items to be stored (such as waste, fresh meat, vegetables) as well as between different temperature zones. Since different storage temperatures are required for foodstuffs and, depending on the production method, more chilled or frozen goods may need to be stored, it is usually necessary to provide several refrigerated storage facilities. Refrigerated storage rooms are available as prefabricated walk-in units with or without a floor and as refrigerator or freezer cabinets. Shelf elements for storage rooms are available with shelf depths of between 30 and 80 cm; the length of the units should not exceed 150 cm. Alternatively, it is possible to use commercial chillers and freezers for small quantities, which are designed for standardized commercial containers. Drinks and bottles of wine are stored in dedicated chillers with individual temperature zones.

Food waste must be stored as cold as possible outside the kitchen and where any odor nuisance can be avoided. Furthermore, waste storage rooms and the removal of waste should be concealed from the public areas.

### Warewashing

The warewashing (dishwashing) area is used for cleaning kitchenware as well as tableware, and should therefore be close to the kitchen as well as the dining room. In commercial kitchens, the cleaning process takes place in several steps. → **Figure 4.7.24** The items to be washed up may have to be cleared of any food remains and manually presorted before they can be placed into warewashing machines – more commonly known as dishwashers. This requires sufficient work surfaces on the "unclean" side as well as a waste bin or chute and a sink with a hand-held sprayer. Different kinds of warewashing machines can be used, the main distinction being machines for washing glassware and those for dishes and cutlery. → **Figure 4.7.25** After the items have been cleaned, they must be returned to their respective storage places. Even in small kitchens it is desirable to separate "clean" and "unclean" sides as much as possible. → **Figure 4.7.26**

Figure 4.7.22
Example layout of an
institutional kitchen

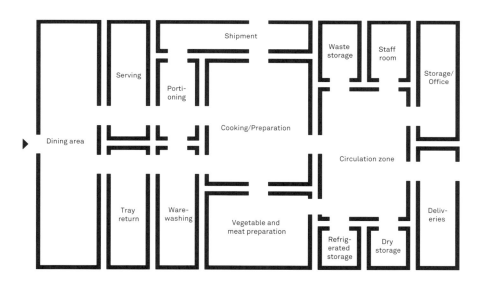

**Serving Food**

The method of serving the food can be distinguished into three basic alternatives that affect the design of the facility:

1. Waitstaff serving food that has been portioned in the kitchen; this requires a pass-through shelf at the handover point (or pass), including a food-warming device. The pass can be in the kitchen, adjacent to the dining area, or take the form of a hatch from the kitchen to the dining area so that the waitstaff does not have to enter the kitchen.

2. Where food is served using the counter system, meals are portioned from a selection of larger containers of ready-prepared food; here the food is handed over directly to the patron by staff across a counter, with the process visible to the patrons. In this zone it is important to observe the hygiene regulations for kitchens, particularly in the area used by staff, which also has a direct connection to the kitchen. In addition, preprepared individual portions may be held available for patrons to serve themselves.

3. In the case of a conveyor or buffet arrangement, patrons serve themselves. However, whereas patrons helping themselves from a buffet portion their meals themselves from larger containers, the meals in a conveyor arrangement are already portioned.

For food service via a counter, conveyor, and buffet arrangement, areas must be provided within the dining area. It is possible to control the route that patrons take by providing an island or linear arrangement of fixed elements. Since payment is made before the food is consumed, separate cashier stations need to be provided, unless payment takes place at the counter. It is also common to find combinations of counter and buffet arrangements. → **Figure 4.7.27**

Since it is necessary to maintain certain temperatures during the plating, transport, and serving of prepared food, different presentation and serving furniture is used in commercial establishments. Options include chilled, neutral, and warming cabinets. In addition, in cafés, snack bars, ice cream parlors, and for serving food from buffets, it is also common to use ice cream counters and panoramic refrigerators to present the food to patrons. → **Figure 4.7.28** When food is prepared in front of the patron, it is also possible to provide a combination of work surface and chilled food storage in the form of saladette counters.

**Figure 4.7.23**
Typical equipment for commercial kitchens

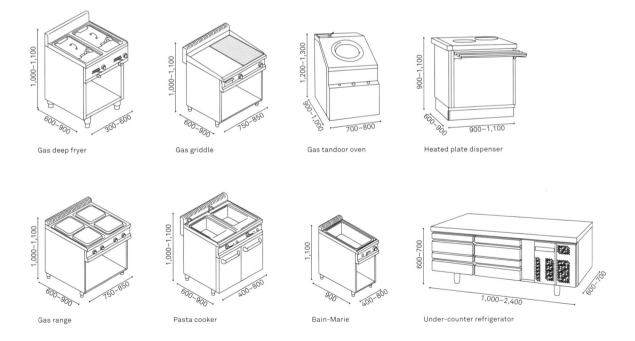

Gas deep fryer    Gas griddle    Gas tandoor oven    Heated plate dispenser

Gas range    Pasta cooker    Bain-Marie    Under-counter refrigerator

**Figure 4.7.24**
Washing-up cycle

Per DIN 10510

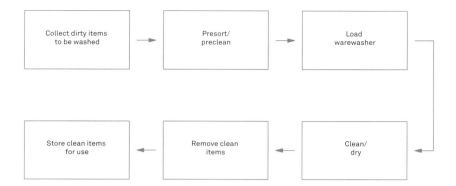

**Figure 4.7.25**
Types of dishwashing machines

Per DIN 10510 and DIN 10512

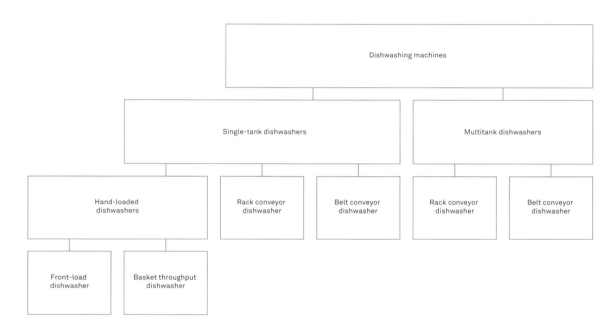

**Figure 4.7.26**
Example of a small washing-up area

1  Intake and precleaning
2  Cleaning
3  Sorting and return

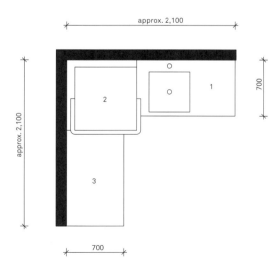

**379**

**Figure 4.7.27**
Buffet arrangements and
counter layouts

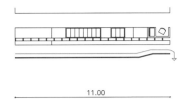

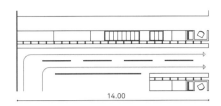

11.00

14.00

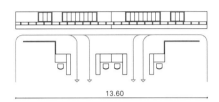

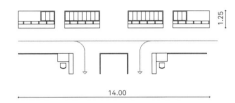

13.60

14.00

1.25

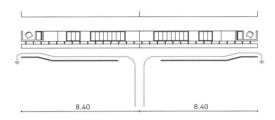

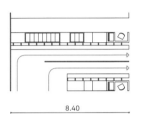

8.40          8.40

8.40

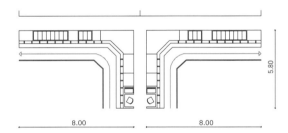

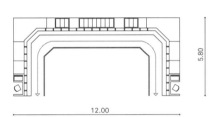

8.00          8.00

12.00

5.80

5.80

**Figure 4.7.28**
Presentation and food-serving
cabinets

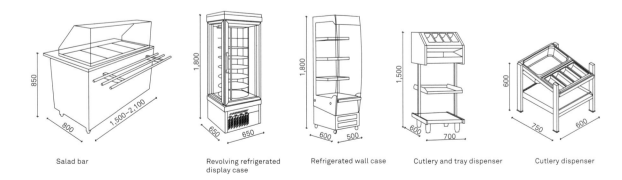

Salad bar

Revolving refrigerated
display case

Refrigerated wall case

Cutlery and tray dispenser

Cutlery dispenser

### 4.7.3.4  Seating Area

The size and design of seating areas depends primarily on the type of business. However, the initial design is usually based on the planned number of seats or standing spaces, and the expected customer turnover. The space requirement for seats depends on the type and arrangement of tables, which is why the final computation of capacity cannot be carried out until a furniture layout has been designed. Generally speaking, the requirement for space increases with higher standards. As a rule, it is possible to base the design on a space requirement of 1.00–1.25 m² per patron. ↗ Chapter 3.4.3 Spaces/Communication Spaces and Dining Rooms/Dining Areas

Next to the seats for patrons, terminals or service stations are required for serving the food, where additional cutlery, the menus, and other items are stored. In higher-class restaurants, these areas are preferably moved to the background. In self-service restaurants, elements such as sideboards and tray return carts are located in the dining area instead of being accommodated in the kitchen, as with other concepts. Circulation routes within seating areas should be designed in accordance with building code regulations, distinguishing between main and secondary routes. ↗ Chapter 3.2.2 Spaces/Internal Circulation/Corridors

### 4.7.3.5  Management

Management tasks address business matters, staff supervision, and customer relations as well as public relations. However, not every food service operation or lodging establishment requires a larger management suite (except for the workplaces at reception) on site. In some cases, management tasks are carried out at external locations.

In lodging establishments, a distinction is made between front-office (see lobby) and back-office areas (purely internal administration activities), which should be very closely connected. In addition to offices, it may be appro-priate to provide a server room, an archive, and a central monitoring station.

Usually the administration premises required for food outlets are smaller than those for accommodation businesses. In smaller establishments it is usually sufficient to provide one office for general administrative activities and the organization of deliveries. Larger businesses will tend to outsource the administrative function, as in the accommodation business. Franchise restaurants and other food outlet chains in particular are characterized by central organization, which reduces to a minimum the management required on site. ↗ Chapter 4.2 Typologies/Office and Administration

### 4.7.3.6  Ancillary Spaces

**Sanitary Facilities**
Restroom facilities are to be located adjacent to dining areas and in the public areas of lodging establishments. These facilities should include at least one barrier-free toilet. → Table 4.7.13, ↗ Chapter 3.5.3 Spaces/Sanitary Facilities/Public and Commercial Sanitary Facilities

**Service Rooms in Hotels**
Service rooms are located on each floor and are used for storing cleaning materials and equipment. Their size depends on the number of personnel involved and the number of rooms to be cleaned in the respective area. These rooms are used to store service trolleys (→ Figure 4.7.29) of various sizes as well as vacuum cleaners and the necessary sheets and towels. For the linen, shelving space of at least 20 × 40 cm per room served should be provided. Service rooms are most appropriately located near service ducts and in places where guest rooms cannot easily be accommodated. Depending on the logistics system, it may also be an option to provide a service elevator. ↗ Chapter 3.8.4 Spaces/Ancillary and Staff Rooms/Storerooms and Janitor's Closets

Table 4.7.13
Sanitary fixtures required in food outlets

See GastStättV

| Dining room area | Women's toilets | Men's toilets | Urinals |
|---|---|---|---|
| Up to 50 m² | 1 | 1 | 1 |
| 50 to 150 m² | 2 | 1 | 1 |
| 150 to 300 m³ | 4 | 2 | 4 |
| Over 300 m² | to be determined individually | | |

Figure 4.7.29
Service trolley

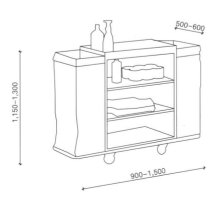

**General Hospital,** Vienna, Austria, Joseph Quarin, 1784

**Rudolf Virchow Hospital,** Berlin, Germany, Ludwig Hoffmann, 1899

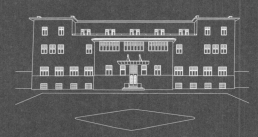

**Sanatorium Purkersdorf,** Austria, Josef Hoffmann, 1905

**Sanatorium Zonnestraal,** Hilversum, The Netherlands, Jan Duiker, 1928

**Terrace Hospital,** Waiblingen, Germany, Richard Döcker, 1928

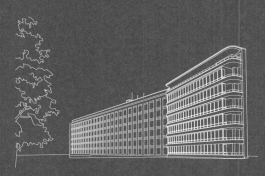

**Tuberculosis sanatorium,** Paimio, Finland, Alvar Aalto, 1933

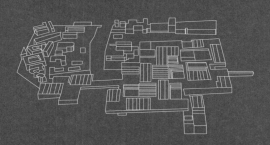

**Hospital (not built),** Venice, Italy, Le Corbusier, 1964

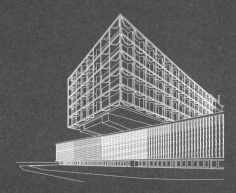

**Steglitz Clinic,** Berlin, Germany, Curtis & Davis Architects with Franz Mocken, 1969

**Klinikum am Urban,** Berlin, Germany, Hans Peter Poelzig, 1970

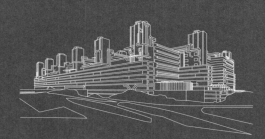

**Aachen University Clinic,** Aachen, Germany, Weber, Brand and Partners, 1985

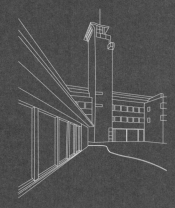

**Oslo State Hospital,** Norway, Medplan AS Architects, 2002

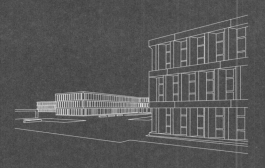

**AZ Groeninge Hospital,** Kortrijk, Belgium, Baumschlager Eberle, 2007

Barbara Weyand

# 4 Typologies
# 4.8 Healthcare Facilities

### 4.8.1 Building Concept ↗384

4.8.1.1 Planning Parameters ↗384
4.8.1.2 Building Forms ↗386
4.8.1.3 Circulation Systems ↗388
4.8.1.4 Construction and Technology ↗391

### 4.8.2 Program of Use ↗392

4.8.2.1 Hospitals and Clinics ↗392
4.8.2.2 Psychiatric Hospitals ↗392
4.8.2.3 Rehabilitation and Health Resort Facilities ↗395
4.8.2.4 Residential Care Homes ↗395
4.8.2.5 Hospices and Palliative Care Wards ↗396
4.8.2.6 Group Practices and Doctor's Offices ↗396

### 4.8.3 Areas and Rooms ↗399

4.8.3.1 Diagnostics and Therapy ↗400
4.8.3.2 Patient Rooms ↗411
4.8.3.3 General Service and Special Areas ↗420
4.8.3.4 Supply and Disposal ↗421

# 4.8 Healthcare Facilities

## 4.8.1 Building Concept

Architects are often faced with designing a wide range of different types of healthcare facilities, such as hospitals, which combine facilities for various medical fields, and more specialized facilities such as psychiatric clinics, along with medical practices and facilities for rehabilitation, long-term treatment, and nursing. Over time, hospitals have been transforming from welfare establishments to commercial health enterprises that act as competitive service providers. At the same time, owing to progress in medical science, hospitals are subject to constant change, which influences the processes within and relationships between the medical disciplines, and which requires modular and flexible building structures.

### 4.8.1.1 Planning Parameters

Typical planning parameters:
- Place, context, and site geometry
- Topography, orientation
- Existing buildings, construction during ongoing operation?
- Options for access to infrastructure
- Building regulation restrictions, such as emission limits
- Operating concept and spatial program
- Current and future requirements
- Workplace requirements
- Necessary ancillary functions
- Length of stay/patient expectations
- Layout type, building form
- Budget and scheduling
- Public funding criteria/guidelines (if applicable)

**Site and Location Criteria**
The site represents one of the most important design criteria. Where completely new healthcare facilities are planned on larger sites, it is possible to opt for low-rise buildings, and the operating concept can be designed without any external constraints. The ideal site will have enough space for interim buildings and future extensions. In the case of health resorts and rehabilitation centers in partic-ular, environmental factors such as air quality and noise pollution play an important role in the selection of the site. It is also important to check the aerodynamics resulting from surrounding buildings in order to avoid excessive air movement in outside facilities, and to ensure that the area has an ample supply of fresh air. Consideration needs to be given to the fact that healthcare facilities themselves are the source of noise – such as from ambulance sirens and helicopters – and air pollution, for example from incinerators and food service facilities.

In many cases, an existing facility needs to be extended or remodeled. Hospitals in particular are often located in inner-city areas. In this case, the existing ensemble and the surrounding buildings provide a specific framework for the integration of the new buildings. The modernization and restructuring of an existing facility usually requires several construction phases. In this case, it is important to ensure that the ongoing hospital activities are not exposed to dust, noise, and other inconveniences. →Figure 4.8.1

**Topography and Orientation**
In addition to the size of the site, the topography of the terrain plays a major role. On sites with a gentle slope, the building can be arranged so that it faces south, providing the best possible orientation for patient areas. With regard to the orientation of rooms, the respective function is the deciding factor. Treatment and functional rooms are best arranged to face north-west to north-east in order to benefit from good light conditions. Patient areas should be facing south-east to south-west so that they benefit from solar radiation without the excessive heat that tends to affect rooms facing east or west.

**Accessibility and Infrastructure**
Any such facility must have the benefit of good accessibility via private and public local transport. Ambulances and commercial delivery vehicles require separate access roads. Adequate parking facilities for staff and visitors, as well as bicycle parking areas, have to be provided in the proximity of the main and staff entrances respectively. →Table 4.8.1 and Figure 4.8.3

Figure 4.8.1
Refurbishment stages of a patient ward building during ongoing operation

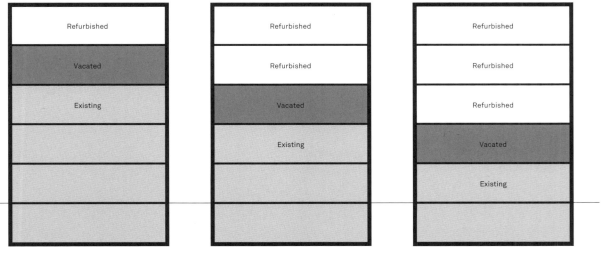

Stage of refurbishment 1    Stage of refurbishment 2    Stage of refurbishment 3

**Figure 4.8.2**
Examples of rural and
urban settings

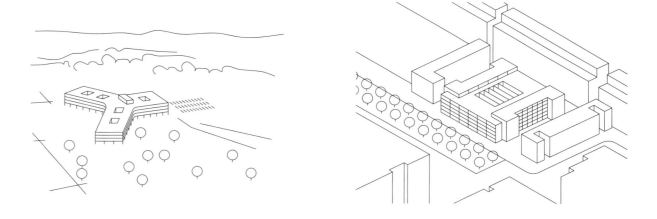

**Figure 4.8.3**
Site layout of a general hospital
with approximately 250 beds

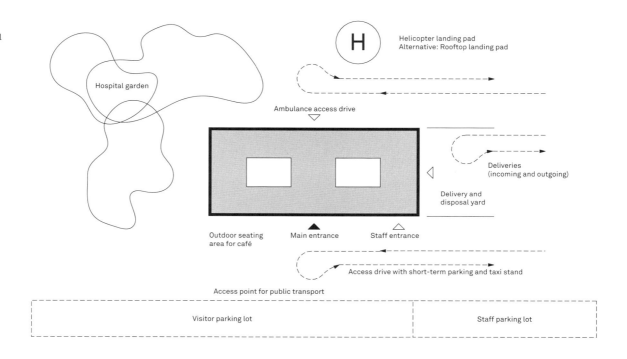

**Table 4.8.1**
Number of parking spaces
required

| Type of facility | Quantity of parking spaces | Percentage of visitors |
|---|---|---|
| University hospitals and other teaching hospitals | 1 parking space per 2–3 beds (additional parking spaces for frequently visited areas) | 50% |
| Hospitals, clinics, and sanitarium facilities | 1 parking space per 10–15 spaces | 60% |
| Nursing homes | 1 parking space per 10–15 spaces | 75% |

## 4.8.1.2 Building Forms

### Basic Structure

Large buildings such as hospitals usually have a large number of very similar rooms with the same orientation so that the most efficient layout can be obtained with an orthogonal system. With smaller buildings, special buildings, or individual areas such as oratories, a freer form can be adopted. → **Figures 4.8.4 and 4.8.5**

The functions of healthcare facilities broadly fall into two different categories with respect to construction, structure, and user requirements: the care areas where patients reside, and the examination and treatment areas where patients are diagnosed and treated, and where analyses are carried out. The varied story heights required for these different functions must be taken into account in the design. → **Table 4.8.2**

Table 4.8.2
Floor-to-floor heights in healthcare facilities

| Type of function | Floor-to-floor height in m |
|---|---|
| Care | 3.50 |
| Examination and treatment | 4.20 |
| Surgery | 4.20–4.50 |
| Technical installations | 4.50–6.00 |
| Supplies and disposal | 4.20–5.00 |

Figure 4.8.4
Examples of an orthogonal layout and a freer-form layout

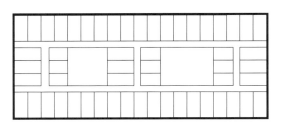
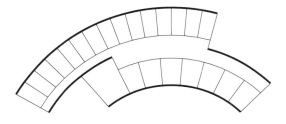

Figure 4.8.5
Typical building forms

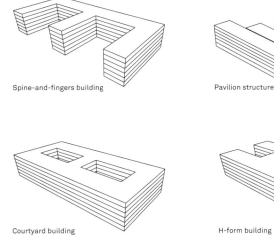
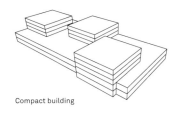
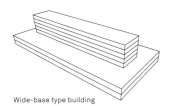

Spine-and-fingers building

Pavilion structure

Compact building

Courtyard building

H-form building

Wide-base type building

### Vertical Type

In vertical types, the care areas are arranged in one or several vertical building volumes above the examination and treatment area on the lower floors. As this type of layout requires a relatively small footprint area and different story heights are possible, this form of building is very economical. In addition, the internal organization is straightforward and circulation routes can be short. On the negative side, the care area cannot easily be extended and has a relatively poor connection to outside areas.

### Horizontal Type

In the horizontal type, the examination and treatment areas are on one level, with a distinction made between highly frequented and less busy areas. For example, a surgery department used only for inpatients may be placed on an upper floor, while areas for outpatients and visitors are located on the first floor. If both these areas are located on the same level of the building, the care function rooms have to have the same height as those of the examination and treatment areas. For this reason, this type of building is primarily suitable for smaller hospitals and care/health resort facilities, with few stories and only relatively few functional rooms with greater room heights.

### Hybrid Types

A great number of different combinations of forms are possible. One of the most common types has separate areas for outpatients and inpatients. The inpatient areas are sited next to the care facilities and have the same room height, while the outpatient areas are on other floors. In this way the respective different room heights are provided to the care areas and the examination and treatment facilities. Facilities with shared outpatient and inpatient functions and the resulting lack of flexibility can only be recommended in special cases. →**Figure 4.8.6**

Figure 4.8.6
Building types with different arrangements for the different functions

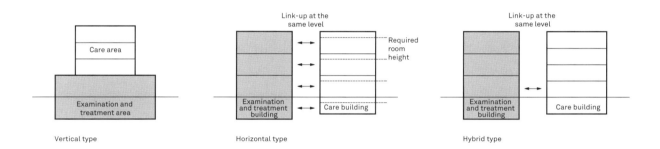

### 4.8.1.3 Circulation Systems

The access within a healthcare facility requires an internal circulation system; where a facility includes several buildings, additional circulation routes are required outside. Short routes without obstacles contribute significantly to the efficient operation of the facility. In addition, the circulation network must be barrier-free and straightforward in terms of orientation. If possible, concourses and corridors should have the benefit of natural light and ventilation, and be designed as comfortable spaces. It is also important to avoid the crossing of routes for visitors and patients in hospital trolley beds. Transporting patients in beds should be avoided near the main entrance. → **Figure 4.8.7**

The needs of sick and disabled persons must be taken into account in the design of signage and orientation systems. For example, people with visual impairment find it easier to distinguish signs with strong contrasting colors. ↗ **Chapter 2.1 Human Measure/Anthropometry and Barrier-Free Accessibility**

Figure 4.8.7
Separation of circulation flows in a hospital

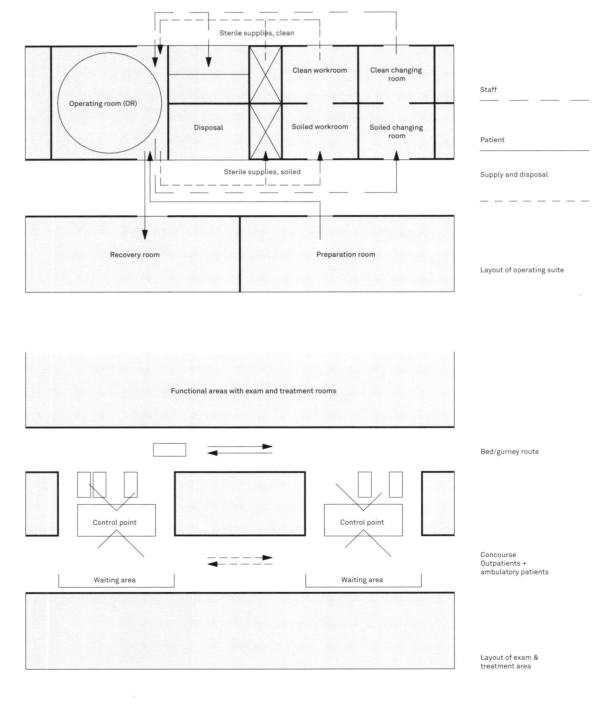

### Concourse

In larger facilities, the concourse functions as the main thoroughfare and connects the main entrance with all important functions and services, as well as with stairs and elevators. It also serves as a development axis of the building. In complex facilities, the functional areas are linked by main horizontal and vertical circulation routes with a concourse character. Except for control points with their associated waiting areas, no functional rooms should be located directly on the concourse. The design concept depends on the existing building and facility operating concept. In general, a distinction is made between an open and a closed structure. →Figure 4.8.8

### Corridors

Routes within the functional sections should provide a clear structure and should be designed to suit the expected traffic, including bed transport. The width of corridors must not be reduced by built-in structures, storage of items or similar. →Figure 4.8.9 and Table 4.8.3, ↗Chapter 3.2.2 Spaces/Internal Circulation/Corridors

### Elevators

In hospitals, clinics, etc., one general elevator per 100 beds must be provided for staff, patients, and visitors. In addition, special elevators for patient beds and gurneys have to be provided for the transport of patients on bed trolleys. In smaller establishments such as residential care homes, it is also possible to use these elevators for general purposes. A group arrangement with at least two elevators is a recommended solution. Optionally, it is possible to provide separate elevators for the transport of goods such as food or laundry. Sterile goods require separate elevators for clean and soiled materials. →Table 4.8.4

### Goods Transport Systems

In larger complexes, automatic goods transport systems and driverless transport systems may be used for the supply and disposal of goods such as food, laundry, waste, and consumables. These require the provision of dedicated elevators and storage areas on the supply levels, as well as a logistics center on the services level. In smaller establishments, goods are normally transported on manual transport carts, for which parking areas have to be provided in the respective functional areas. In larger facilities, smaller items such as medicines, samples, or letters are usually sent via pneumatic delivery systems. The receipt and delivery stations have to be integrated in the respective functional areas.

Figure 4.8.8
Concourse systems

Closed concourse

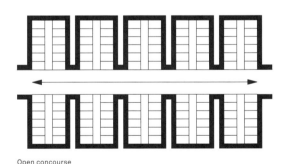

Open concourse

**Figure 4.8.9**
Requirements for corridors
in healthcare facilities

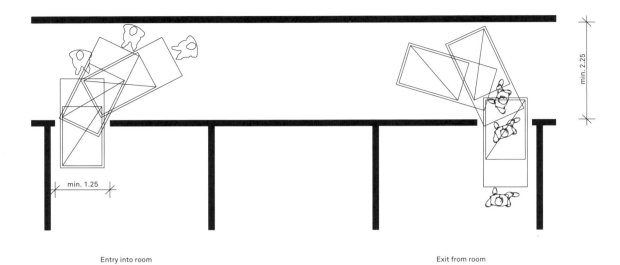

Entry into room    Exit from room

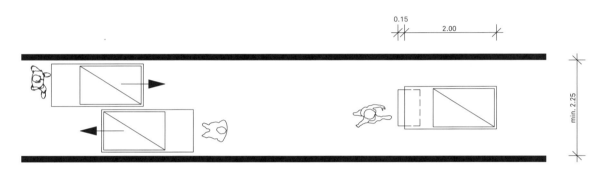

Meeting of two beds    Patient bed transport

**Table 4.8.3**
Corridor widths

| Function | Clear minimum width in m |
| --- | --- |
| General corridor/staff corridor without bed transport | 1.50 |
| Corridor with bed transport | 2.25 |
| ICU/IMC corridor | 2.30 |
| Concourse | 3.00 |
| Service corridor, supply/disposal | 3.50–4.00 |

**Table 4.8.4**
Dimensions of bed elevators

↗ Chapter 3.2.7 Spaces/Internal
Circulation/Elevators and
Conveying Systems

| Type of facility | Size of bed | Accompanying staff | Nominal load | Clear shaft width in m | Clear shaft depth, single door in m | Clear shaft depth, front and back doors in m |
| --- | --- | --- | --- | --- | --- | --- |
| Residential care homes | 90 × 200 cm | 1 person at the head end | 1,275 | 2.0 | 2.75 | 2.90 |
| Hospitals with average amount of traffic | 90 × 200 cm | 1–2 persons at the head end and/or side | 1,600 | 2.10 | 2.80 | 2.95 |
| Large hospitals with busy traffic | 90 × 200 cm | 1–2 persons at the head end and/or side | 2,000 | 2.40 | 3.10 | 3.25 |
| Vibration-free bed transport (OP area, ICU etc.) | 100 × 230 cm | max. 3 persons at the head end and/or side, incl. equipment for medical care and emergency treatment | 2,500 | 2.80 | 3.10 | 3.25 |

### 4.8.1.4 Construction and Technology

**Fit-out and Construction Grids**
Hospital design is likely to benefit from the use of modular grids. The construction grid has to be suitable for the accommodation of different functional areas (e.g. patient rooms and OP suites) and circulation layouts (e.g. foyers, staircases, corridors, possibly parking garages). A comparison of the different functional areas and the required space can lead to a suitable grid (for larger developments, usually between 7.20 m and 7.80 m). It is possible to use smaller construction grids when the proportion of larger rooms, such as operating rooms, is relatively small. For situations with identical fit-out and construction grids, a fit-out grid of 1.25 m with a construction grid of 7.50 m has proven to be useful. → **Figure 4.8.10** The 1.25 m system is suitable for both examination and treatment areas, and care zones. It is possible to use different fit-out grids for different functional areas, provided these areas are not arranged above each other or are based on the same base grid.

**Load-bearing Structure**
The structural system should have a high degree of flexibility. The structural system remains the determining structure of the building for fit-outs and conversions until it is demolished. In practice, neutral systems with individual columns and bracing cores have proved to be successful. Load-bearing walls should only be used for building components for which no change is expected in terms of position and function (staircases, elevators, and services cores). Floors are usually constructed as reinforced concrete slabs. Downstand beams are avoided in order to facilitate the installation of utility and medical services, and to limit the story height.

**M & E Installations and Medical Services Installations**
The service life of a hospital is, to a large extent, affected by its technical and medical services installations and their rapid development cycles. In most cases, the entire technical services installations are replaced within a period of approximately 15 years. Medical technical equipment is replaced within 5 to 10 years, depending on the function, and can have a significant effect on the design of the rooms (for example, magnetic resonance imaging, intracardiac catheter facilities, linear accelerator). The installation and removal of this type of equipment has to be taken into account in the design, and must be possible without altering the structural system.

**Hygiene**
Hospitals and other medical establishments have the highest hygiene requirements. For the design, this means that building components and surfaces have to be easy to clean and disinfect. Materials must be resistant to germs and pathogens, as well as to cleansing and disinfection agents and, if possible, should have antimicrobial properties. In order to reduce air-borne germs, areas such as OP suites, intensive care units, and laboratories are usually air-conditioned.

Figure 4.8.10
Application of fit-out and construction grids for a range of functional variations

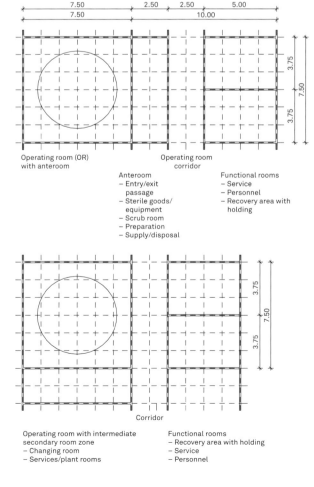

Operating room (OR) with anteroom

Operating room corridor

Anteroom
– Entry/exit passage
– Sterile goods/ equipment
– Scrub room
– Preparation
– Supply/disposal

Functional rooms
– Service
– Personnel
– Recovery area with holding

Operating room with intermediate secondary room zone
– Changing room
– Services/plant rooms

Functional rooms
– Recovery area with holding
– Service
– Personnel

Corridor

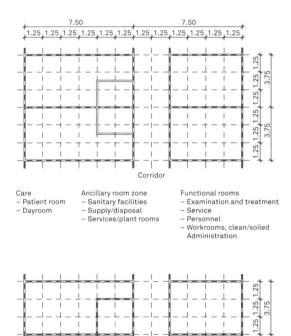

Corridor

Care
– Patient room
– Dayroom

Ancillary room zone
– Sanitary facilities
– Supply/disposal
– Services/plant rooms

Functional rooms
– Examination and treatment
– Service
– Personnel
– Workrooms, clean/soiled Administration

Examination and treatment
– Examination room with anteroom
– Preparation

Ancillary room zone
– Changing room
– Services/plant rooms

Functional rooms
– Examination and treatment
– Service
– Personnel
– Workrooms, clean/soiled Administration

Corridor

## 4.8.2  Program of Use

The design of healthcare facilities involves the provision of buildings with different requirements for patients, visitors, staff, students, and trainees. In spite of commercial and financial constraints, it must be the aim to create rooms and room ensembles that support the work, and the recovery of patients, beyond purely medical support. Research focused on subjects such as "healing architecture" or "evidence-based design" confirms that an agreeable working environment enhances the ability of staff to perform and that a patient-friendly environment supports the recovery process. The patient's health, mobility, and length of stay in hospital, and the required medical equipment, vary according to the respective type of clinic, but have a major influence on the design. Minimizing the effects of stress – such as from noise or a lack of privacy – contributes to patients' recovery. For visitors it is important to ensure easy access and straightforward orientation. In addition, ancillary areas such as those for cafeterias, dayrooms, extra beds, or parent accommodation are to be provided.

### 4.8.2.1  Hospitals and Clinics

As the requirement for diagnostic and therapeutic services increases, so does the complexity of healthcare facilities. For example, a university clinic will have numerous units such as diagnostics, therapy, care, administration, staff and services, supply and disposal, teaching, and research, which in turn are subdivided into numerous medical functional units. The design should not only reflect the relationships within a certain area, but should also integrate interdisciplinary cooperation between the different function groups and stations, and the overall operating concept. → **Tables 4.8.5 and 4.8.6,** ↗ **Chapter 4.9.3 Typologies/ Sports and Recreation/Areas and Rooms**

General medical hospitals are classified into levels of care in accordance with their size and number of medical specialties. → **Table 4.8.7** Clinics are subdivided by the specialist medical care they provide. Specialist hospitals such as psychiatric hospitals or trauma centers are specially equipped to treat certain types of conditions or groups of patients. Owing to the increase in specialization, the number of these specialist hospitals is increasing. The distinction between rehabilitation centers, health resort facilities, residential care homes, and geriatric facilities is often less than precise. ↗ **Chapter 4.1 Typologies/Housing**

### 4.8.2.2  Psychiatric Hospitals

Psychiatric facilities provide care for patients with psychiatric disorders. Treatment facilities range from outpatient or partial inpatient services to residential groups and specialist clinics. Psychiatric units are structured similar to a general care unit. They differ with respect to the additional safety measures for the protection of patients and staff. Forensic facilities for persons sectioned under the Mental Health Act require additional security measures. A simple difference exists between open and closed units; the latter refers to wards that patients cannot leave without permission.

The architecture/design of these units is determined in particular by the need to prevent suicide attempts, for example, by avoiding large drops; unused corners in corridors or rooms; providing security devices for stairs, doors, and windows; and the provision of crisis rooms with a monitoring facility. In addition, some clinics provide time-out rooms in which hard surfaces are padded and which are used to diffuse aggression. → **Table 4.8.8**

**Figure 4.8.11**
**User requirements**

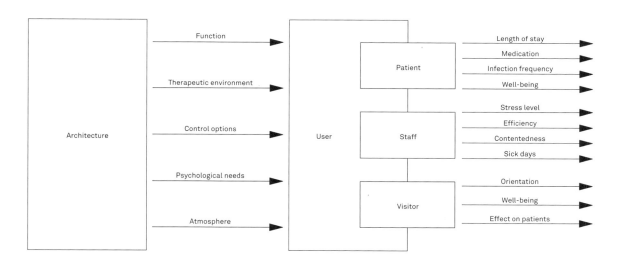

**Table 4.8.5**
Spatial relationships in hospitals

1 Strong relationship
2 Medium relationship
3 Slight relationship
4 No relationship
E Should be arranged on the same level if possible

| | Emergency | Reception | Main entrance | Examination & treatment | X-ray diagnostics | Endoscopy | OR suite | Obstetrics unit | Intensive care | Care | Physiotherapy | Laboratory | Sterilization | Pathology |
|---|---|---|---|---|---|---|---|---|---|---|---|---|---|---|
| Emergency | | 2 | 1 | 2 | 1E | 1 | 1 | 2 | 2 | 3 | 4 | 2 | 2 | 2 |
| Reception | 2 | | 1E | 2 | 3 | 3 | 3 | 3 | 3 | 3 | 3 | 4 | 4 | 4 |
| Main entrance | 1 | 1E | | 1 | 2 | 2 | 2 | 2 | 3 | 2 | 2 | 4 | 4 | 4 |
| Examination & treatment | 2 | 2 | 1 | | 1E | 1 | 2 | 2 | 2 | 2 | 4 | 1 | 2 | 2 |
| X-ray diagnostics | 1E | 3 | 2 | 1E | | 2 | 2 | 3 | 2 | 2 | 4 | 4 | 4 | 4 |
| Endoscopy | 1 | 3 | 2 | 1 | 2 | | 1E | 3 | 2 | 2 | 4 | 2 | 3 | 3 |
| OR suite | 1 | 3 | 2 | 2 | 2 | 1E | | 1E | 1E | 2 | 4 | 2 | 1 | 2 |
| Obstetrics unit | 2 | 3 | 2 | 2 | 3 | 3 | 1E | | 2 | 2 | 4 | 2 | 3 | 3 |
| Intensive care | 2 | 3 | 3 | 2 | 2 | 2 | 1E | 2 | | 2 | 4 | 2 | 2 | 3 |
| Care | 3 | 3 | 2 | 2 | 2 | 2 | 2 | 2 | 2 | | 2 | 2 | 3 | 3 |
| Physiotherapy | 4 | 3 | 2 | 4 | 4 | 4 | 4 | 4 | 4 | 2 | | 4 | 4 | 4 |
| Laboratory | 2 | 4 | 4 | 1 | 4 | 2 | 2 | 2 | 2 | 2 | 4 | | 2 | 4 |
| Sterilization | 2 | 4 | 4 | 2 | 4 | 3 | 1 | 3 | 2 | 3 | 4 | 2 | | 3 |
| Pathology | 2 | 4 | 4 | 2 | 4 | 3 | 2 | 3 | 3 | 3 | 4 | 4 | 3 | |

**Table 4.8.6**
Cooperation between medical specialist disciplines in hospitals

1 Intensive cooperation
2 Medium cooperation
3 Slight cooperation
4 Rare or no cooperation

| | Anesthesiology | Ophthalmology | Surgery | Gynecology | ENT | Internal medicine | Neonatal | Nuclear medicine | Orthopedics | Pediatrics | Psychiatry | Radiology | Radiotherapy | Urology |
|---|---|---|---|---|---|---|---|---|---|---|---|---|---|---|
| Anesthesiology | | 4 | 1 | 1 | 3 | 2 | 2 | 4 | 4 | 2 | 4 | 2 | 4 | 4 |
| Ophthalmology | 4 | | 3 | 4 | 2 | 4 | 4 | 4 | 4 | 2 | 4 | 3 | 4 | 4 |
| Surgery | 1 | 3 | | 1 | 3 | 2 | 1 | 3 | 1 | 1 | 4 | 1 | 2 | 2 |
| Gynecology | 1 | 4 | 1 | | 4 | 3 | 1 | 2 | 4 | 2 | 3 | 1 | 3 | 3 |
| ENT | 3 | 2 | 3 | 4 | | 3 | 3 | 3 | 4 | 1 | 4 | 2 | 3 | 4 |
| Internal medicine | 2 | 4 | 2 | 3 | 3 | | 3 | 3 | 4 | 3 | 3 | 1 | 3 | 3 |
| Neonatal | 2 | 4 | 1 | 1 | 3 | 3 | | 4 | 4 | 2 | 4 | 4 | 4 | 4 |
| Nuclear medicine | 4 | 4 | 3 | 2 | 3 | 3 | 4 | | 3 | 4 | 3 | 2 | 1 | 3 |
| Orthopedics | 4 | 4 | 1 | 4 | 4 | 4 | 4 | 3 | | 4 | 4 | 1 | 3 | 4 |
| Pediatrics | 2 | 2 | 1 | 2 | 1 | 3 | 2 | 4 | 4 | | 4 | 1 | 4 | 3 |
| Psychiatry | 4 | 4 | 4 | 3 | 4 | 3 | 4 | 3 | 4 | 4 | | 4 | 3 | 3 |
| Radiology | 2 | 3 | 1 | 1 | 2 | 1 | 4 | 2 | 1 | 1 | 4 | | 3 | 1 |
| Radiotherapy | 4 | 4 | 2 | 3 | 3 | 3 | 4 | 1 | 3 | 4 | 3 | 3 | | 3 |
| Urology | 4 | 4 | 2 | 3 | 4 | 3 | 4 | 3 | 4 | 3 | 3 | 1 | 3 | |

Table 4.8.7
Levels of care of different-sized hospitals in accordance with the Hospital Act of Rhineland-Palatinate

| Level | Number of regular beds | Services/Facilities |
|---|---|---|
| Maximum care | > 800 | • Main specialist departments for internal medicine and surgery<br>• At least ten other main specialist departments<br>• Special fields in advanced medical services, such as organ and bone marrow transplants<br><br>University clinics are considered to be maximum service clinics. In addition to the diagnostic and therapeutic facilities, these clinics also provide teaching and carry out research. |
| Extended care | 501–800 | • Main specialist departments for internal medicine and surgery<br>• At least six other main specialist departments |
| Regular care | 251–500 | • Main specialist departments (or units for affiliated consultants) for internal medicine and surgery<br>• At least one additional specialist department |
| Basic care | < 250 beds | • At least one main specialist department (or unit for affiliated consultants) for internal medicine<br>• One additional specialist field of care<br>• Usually, basic care hospitals provide the facilities of a surgery department. |

Table 4.8.8
Security and safety measures in psychiatric units

↗ Chapter 4.10 Typologies/Public Safety

| | |
|---|---|
| **Protection against escape** | • Design of closed wards<br>• Direct circulation routing<br>• Secure open areas/inner courtyards<br>• Eye contact from the control point to the ward/external doors<br>• Locks on windows/door furniture |
| **Protection against suicide** | • Avoidance of heights<br>• Securing stairwell openings<br>• Interior fit-out without hazardous furniture<br>• Avoidance of fixings that could be used for strangulation, etc.<br>• Locking of building elements such as inspection openings |
| **Monitoring facility** | • Provision of time-out rooms<br>• Interior fit-out without hazardous furniture, objects, etc.<br>• Monitoring via eye contact or monitor<br>• Sufficient space for monitoring person |
| **Restraint** | • Facility for restraining the patient to the bed, if necessary fixing the bed to the floor<br>• Option for arranging the bed into care position |

Figure 4.8.12
Vertical arrangement in a general hospital with approximately 250 beds

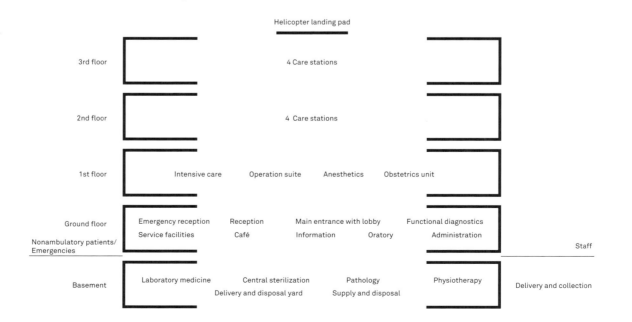

Helicopter landing pad

3rd floor — 4 Care stations

2nd floor — 4 Care stations

1st floor — Intensive care / Operation suite / Anesthetics / Obstetrics unit

Ground floor — Emergency reception / Reception / Main entrance with lobby / Functional diagnostics
Nonambulatory patients/ Emergencies — Service facilities / Café / Information / Oratory / Administration
Staff

Basement — Laboratory medicine / Central sterilization / Pathology / Physiotherapy / Delivery and collection
Delivery and disposal yard / Supply and disposal

### 4.8.2.3 Rehabilitation and Health Resort Facilities

Strengthening, preventative, and recovery/rehabilitation facilities are a necessity in order to keep the length of stay in hospitals as short as possible. There is a broad range of these facilities, which include rehabilitation clinics, therapy centers, sanitariums, and preventive care practices. The range of therapies covers treatment with medication through to healthcare and wellness treatments.

From the point of view of building typology, rehabilitation and health resort facilities can be described as hotel-like care facilities. The less prominent the degree of medical care, the more the design will be oriented toward a hotel establishment in terms of structure, rooms, and fit-out. A separation of therapy, patient, and guest rooms, as well as dayrooms, is recommended. In view of the fact that patients spend longer periods at these centers, there is a greater need for leisure facilities. This means that there is a need to create places for communication, cultural activities, and catering, as well as for retreat. ↗ **Chapter 4.1 Typologies/Housing**, ↗ **Chapter 4.7 Typologies/Lodging and Food Service**

### 4.8.2.4 Residential Care Homes

Residential care homes serve the care, nursing, and treatment of the elderly, the chronically ill, and all those requiring long-term care or assistance. These buildings are the home of their occupants, and the place around which their lives are centered. Therefore the top priority of the design must be the residents' need for security and well-being, independence, and self-determination. The range of facilities available includes traditional care homes through to supported residential groups and centers for dementia patients. Rooms with a clear layout, without obstacles, with good daylight and bright colors facilitate intuitive orientation, reduce anxiety, and support mobility. → **Figure 4.8.15**

**Figure 4.8.13**
Range of functions in residential care homes

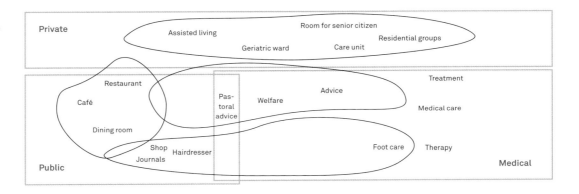

**Figure 4.8.14 (left)**
Schematic layout of care units in linear and square arrangements

**Figure 4.8.15 (right)**
View of corridor with communication zones in a residential care home

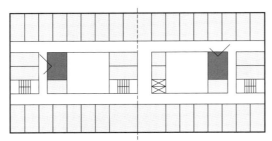

2 Wards in a linear arrangement

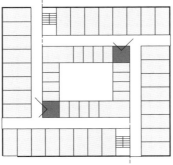

2 Wards in a square arrangement

### 4.8.2.5  Hospices and Palliative Care Wards

Hospices and palliative care wards occupy a special place in the healthcare system. In contrast to the other facilities, they do not provide treatment for the purpose of healing, but provide terminal care. The design of hospices is focused on the wishes and needs of the patients, with medical treatment usually restricted to pain management. While hospices work as independent units from the point of view of organization and management, palliative care wards are usually part of a hospital or a larger care home.

### 4.8.2.6  Group Practices and Doctor's Offices

Medical care provided by general practitioners (GPs) ranges from individual doctor's offices through to group practices, polyclinics, and community health centers (CHCs) which provide day-clinic and brief inpatient treatment. These CHCs and group practices require significantly less space while providing better service and more comfort to the patient because the use of diagnostic facilities such as x-ray, laboratory, and office facilities can be shared. →**Figures 4.8.16–4.8.18**

A good space concept will create a separation between patient and practice areas and the different fields of treatment while also achieving efficient use of the facilities. →**Table 4.8.9** While GP practices only need relatively straightforward rooms and equipment, larger specialist medical practices require special rooms for their respective specialism, as well as special medical equipment and instruments. Usually, specialist medical practices are significantly larger. →**Table 4.8.10**

The entrance area of the practice includes a reception zone with waiting area, coatrack, and toilet. This leads on to the examination and treatment room suite and additional diagnostic rooms such as X-ray, laboratory and additional examination facilities etc. Ancillary rooms such as staff and service rooms are located in areas less frequented by patients.

**Figure 4.8.16**
Functional layout of GP practice

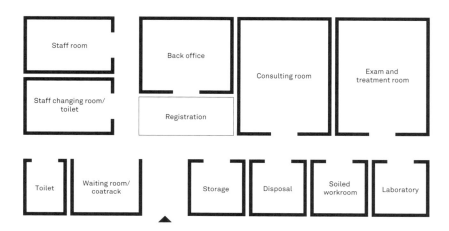

**Figure 4.8.17**
Functional layout of specialist practitioner practice

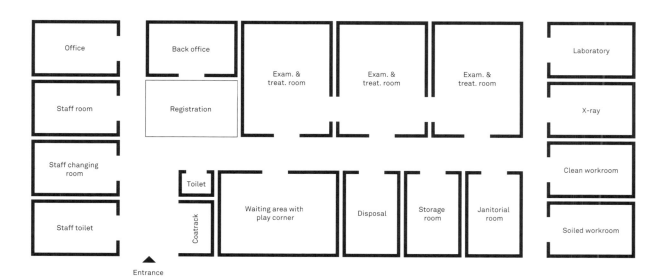

**Figure 4.8.18**
Functional layout of group practice

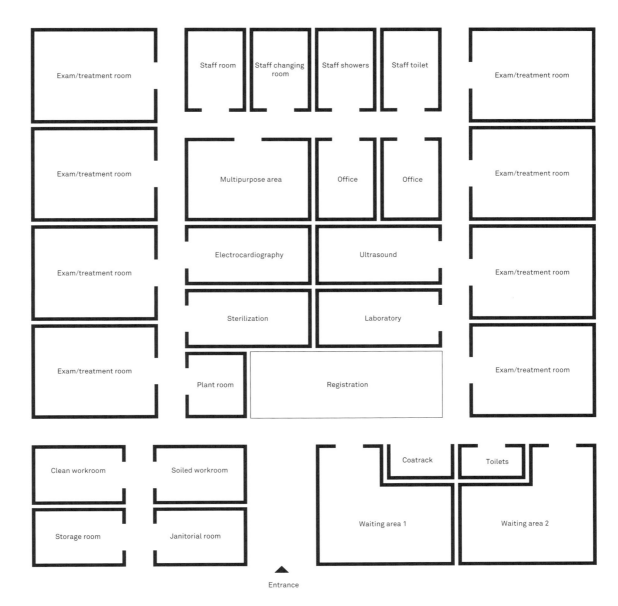

Table 4.8.9
Functional relationship between
rooms in medical practices

1 Strong functional relationship
2 Medium functional relationship
3 Low functional relationship
4 No functional relationship

| | Reception | Waiting area | Consulting room | Exam. & treat. rooms | Special-ists' rooms | Admin-istration rooms | Staff rooms | Supplies and disposal | Plant rooms |
|---|---|---|---|---|---|---|---|---|---|
| **Reception** | | 1 | 1 | 1 | 1 | 1 | 3 | 4 | 4 |
| **Waiting area** | 1 | | 1 | 1 | 1 | 2 | 4 | 4 | 4 |
| **Consulting room** | 1 | 1 | | 1 | 1 | 3 | 2 | 2 | 4 |
| **Exam. & treat. rooms** | 1 | 1 | 1 | | 1 | 3 | 2 | 2 | 3 |
| **Specialists' rooms** | 1 | 1 | 1 | 1 | | 3 | 2 | 2 | 1 |
| **Administra-tion rooms** | 1 | 2 | 3 | 3 | 3 | | 3 | 3 | 4 |
| **Staff rooms** | 3 | 4 | 2 | 2 | 2 | 3 | | 3 | 4 |
| **Supplies and disposal** | 4 | 4 | 2 | 2 | 2 | 3 | 3 | | 3 |
| **Plant rooms** | 4 | 4 | 4 | 3 | 1 | 4 | 4 | 3 | |

Table 4.8.10
Average room sizes in
medical practices

| Type of room | Small single-GP practice Size in m² | Large single-GP practice Size in m² | Small group practice Size in m² | Large group practice Size in m² |
|---|---|---|---|---|
| Patient rooms | 30 | 50 | 46 | 100 |
| Exam. & treat. rooms | 35 | 50 | 12 | 15 |
| Specialists' rooms | 10 | 10 | 75 | 200 |
| Service and staff rooms | 15 | 40 | 40 | 65 |
| Supplies and disposal | 10 | 20 | 15 | 55 |
| Administration | – | 10 | 12 | 30 |
| Training and teaching rooms | – | 18 | – | 30 |
| Plant rooms | – | 2 | – | 5 |
| Total | 100 | 200 | 200 | 500 |

## 4.8.3 Areas and Rooms

External circulation ↗Chapter 3.1

Parking lots ↗Chapter 3.1.2

Gates, ramps, loading bays ↗Chapter 3.1.2, ↗Chapter 3.1.3

Entrance areas ↗400 ↗Chapter 3.2.1, ↗Chapter 3.2.3

Staircases, elevators ↗Chapter 3.2.4, ↗Chapter 3.2.7

Escalators, moving walkways ↗Chapter 3.2.6

Corridors ↗Chapter 3.2.2, ↗Chapter 3.2.3

Workplaces ↗Chapter 3.3

Reception, emergency reception ↗400

Entrance for patients on beds or gurneys ↗400

Examination and treatment ↗402

Consulting room ↗402

Control station ↗402

Functional diagnostics ↗402

Endoscopy ↗404

Medical laboratory ↗404

Pathology ↗404

Radiological diagnostics ↗405

Operating rooms ↗406

Obstetrics ↗409

Physiotherapy/rehabilitation ↗410

Mechanical equipment rooms ↗Chapter 3.9

Patient room ↗411 ↗Chapter 4.1

Intensive care ↗413

Day care ↗413

Care control point ↗418

Workroom, clean/soiled ↗418

Patient bath ↗418 ↗Chapter 3.5

Waiting areas ↗420 ↗Chapter 3.4.2

Oratory ↗420

Bereavement room ↗420

Goods supply ↗422

Bed preparation ↗422

Food supply ↗422 ↗Chapter 4.7.3.3

Medication supply ↗422

Sterile goods supply ↗422

Storage – general ↗Chapter 3.7

Meeting rooms ↗Chapter 3.4.1

Kitchenettes ↗Chapter 3.6

Waste disposal ↗421 ↗Chapter 3.1.5

Staff room ↗Chapter 3.8.1

Lockers/changing rooms ↗Chapter 3.8.2

Toilets ↗Chapter 3.5

Janitorial rooms ↗Chapter 3.8.4

## 4.8.3.1 Diagnostics and Therapy

**Reception and Emergency Care**

In smaller practices and establishments, the reception is the central registration, information, and administration place. In larger practices, it is usual to provide a connection to separate offices. In clinics, a foyer with information, reception or emergency reception desks, and control points, form independent units. The reception area in medical establishments is necessary for recording general patient data, and is part of the clinic administration. The reception should be placed in the direct proximity of the main entrance on the entrance level. The reception area is usually designed as an open structure with several separate reception desks. → **Figure 4.8.19**

Emergency departments are staffed around the clock and deal with patients brought in by the ambulance service or arriving independently. Usually, an initial diagnosis and subsequent stabilization take place in the emergency room. Subsequent treatment of the patient may be carried out by a specialist on an outpatient or inpatient basis.

Irrespective of the size of a clinic, the emergency room should be located in one specific area. It must be easily accessible for accident patients or patients on stretchers or from the helicopter landing pad, as well as for ambulatory patients via the main entrance. Larger clinics consisting of several buildings should have an integrated emergency center with emergency facilities for the different specialist departments, which should also include radiological diagnostics.

The examination and treatment zone forms the core of the emergency care facility. As a rule, it comprises several examination rooms or separate cubicles and an associated service zone for documentation, material supply, and medical and care activities. → **Figure 4.8.20**

The nonambulatory patient entrance with drive must be easy to find and be close to the main entrance near the emergency care area. It is preferable to provide separate access for infectious patients and for multiple trauma patients, ideally with a direct connection to the trauma room and CT area. The drive for emergency access should be roofed over as a porte cochère. Either it or a separate ambulance bay should be large enough to accommodate three or more emergency vehicles parked next to each other.

Figure 4.8.19
Functional layout of reception

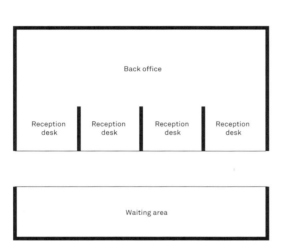

**Figure 4.8.20**
Functional layout of an emergency treatment center

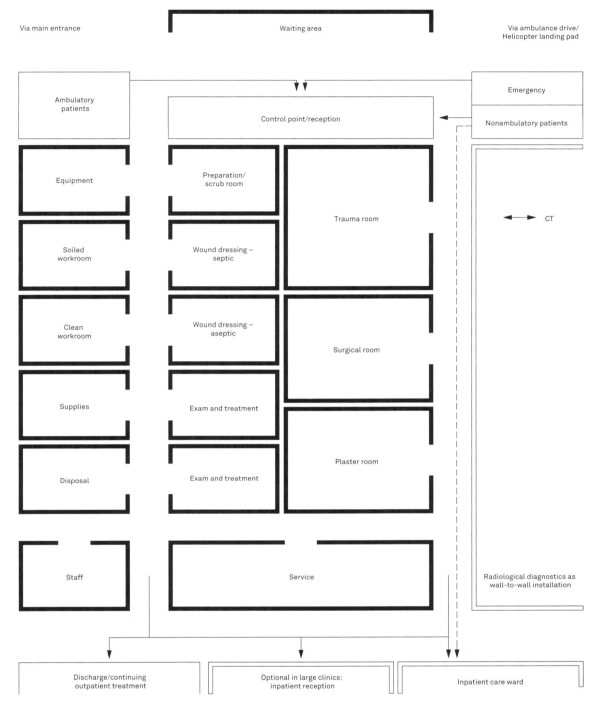

Via main entrance

Waiting area

Via ambulance drive/
Helicopter landing pad

Ambulatory patients

Control point/reception

Emergency

Nonambulatory patients

Equipment

Preparation/
scrub room

Trauma room

CT

Soiled workroom

Wound dressing – septic

Clean workroom

Wound dressing – aseptic

Surgical room

Supplies

Exam and treatment

Disposal

Exam and treatment

Plaster room

Staff

Service

Radiological diagnostics as wall-to-wall installation

Discharge/continuing outpatient treatment

Optional in large clinics: inpatient reception

Inpatient care ward

### Examination and Treatment

The examination and treatment section in clinics consists primarily of the consulting rooms and diagnostic and treatment rooms for medical specialist areas and subareas. The diagnostic rooms are the core of the examination and treatment zone, while the service rooms occupy a secondary position. Where examinations and treatment of inpatients cannot take place in the care area, the examination and treatment rooms must also be easily accessible for patients who are unable to walk or are bedridden.

The control point is where patients and staff register and obtain information, and is the organizational and administrative center for outpatients. → **Figure 4.8.21** The examination and treatment rooms of the different medical disciplines can be standardized in their basic structure, and therefore can be flexibly arranged in the building. Depend-ing on the requirement for examination, it is necessary to provide separate rooms or open cubicles with a form of screening. The area for doctors includes service and duty rooms. In addition, it is possible to provide a library, rest and staff rooms, and rooms for meetings and training events.

In GP or group practices the general examination and treatment room is the essential core. The adjoining spe-cialist rooms are needed for any further diagnostics and treatment. In larger practices or specialist practices, sep-arate consulting rooms are provided in addition to the ex-amination and treatment rooms. This means that the diag-nostic and therapeutic activities are separate from the patient/doctor consultation and can be performed by ap-propriate care personnel.

**Figure 4.8.21**
Functional layout of examination and treatment area with service rooms

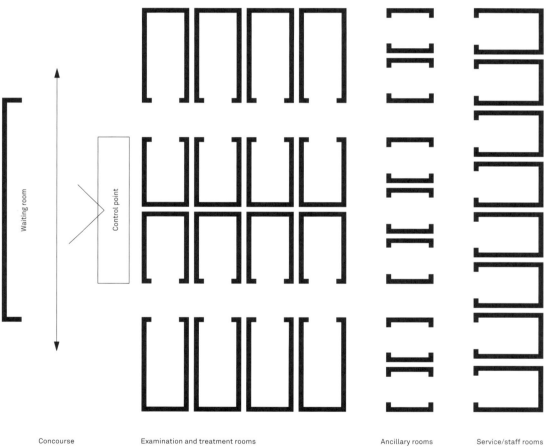

Waiting room

Control point

Concourse        Examination and treatment rooms        Ancillary rooms        Service/staff rooms

**Figure 4.8.22**
Minimum space requirement in an examination and treatment area

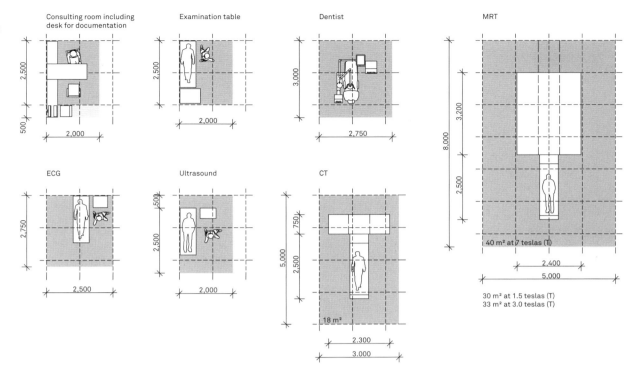

Consulting room including desk for documentation

Examination table

Dentist

MRT

ECG

Ultrasound

CT

2,500 / 500 / 2,000

2,500 / 2,000

3,000 / 2,750

8,000 / 3,200 / 2,500
40 m² at 7 teslas (T)
2,400 / 5,000
30 m² at 1.5 teslas (T)
33 m² at 3.0 teslas (T)

2,750 / 2,500

2,500 / 2,500 / 2,000

5,000 / 750 / 2,500
18 m²
2,300 / 3,000

**Figure 4.8.23**
Examination and treatment rooms in practices and clinics

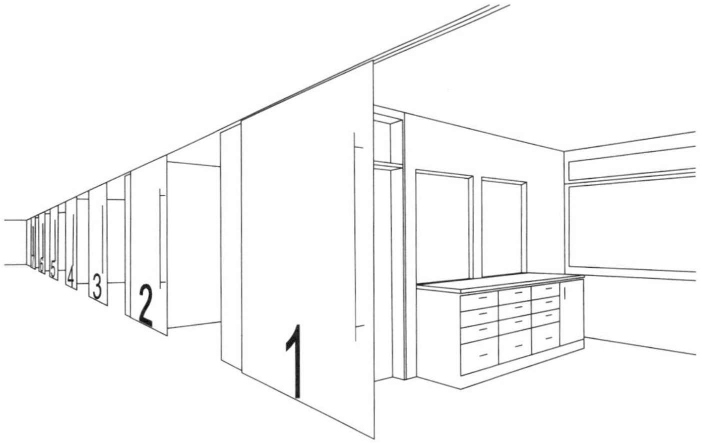

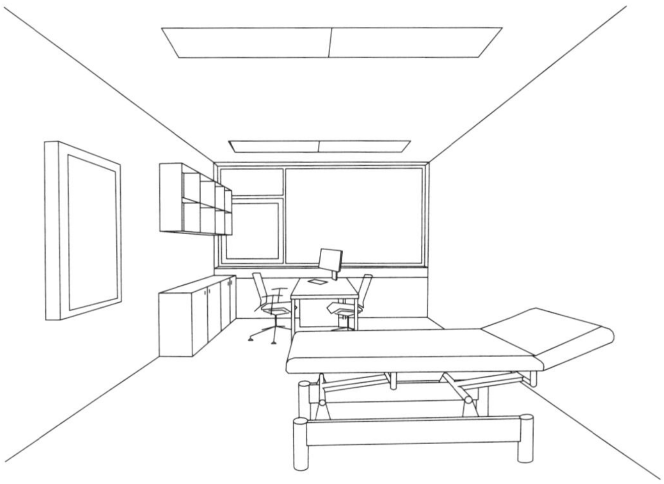

### Endoscopy

Endoscopy is one of the processes providing images and should therefore be located close to the operating area. In addition, it is important that there is good accessibility for ambulatory patients as well as for bedridden patients, and that there is appropriate space for waiting and for parking patient beds and gurneys. The units normally have a place for registration, examination and treatment rooms with nearby or integrated patient changing rooms, rooms for resting and for equipment preparation. → **Figure 4.8.24**

### Laboratory Medicine

Laboratory medicine is a discipline that works for all medical disciplines and is primarily concerned with analyzing blood, tissue, urine, and feces samples. Depending on the size of the medical establishment, the laboratory medicine may consist of just a single room through to central laboratories in separate buildings. In clinics it is usual to provide large laboratory rooms with standing and seated workplaces, which may be subdivided into clinical-chemical, hematological, and microbiological laboratories. Laboratories with special requirements, such as for gene technology work, are included separately. Depending on requirements it is also necessary to provide ancillary rooms with facilities such as wash-up, slops, disinfection and cooling, as well as the associated staff rooms. → **Figure 4.8.25**, ↗ **Chapter 4.5.3.5 Typologies/Education and Research/Areas and Rooms/Specialized Classrooms and Laboratories**

### Pathology

The pathology department deals with autopsies as well as histological and cytological analyses. The design for the unit should provide short transport routes and easy access for undertakers. For this reason, the department is often sited close to the delivery and disposal yard. If no separate bereavement room exists elsewhere, a dedicated room with separate access should be provided for laying out the corpse. → **Figure 4.8.26**

**Figure 4.8.24**
Functional layout of endoscopy unit

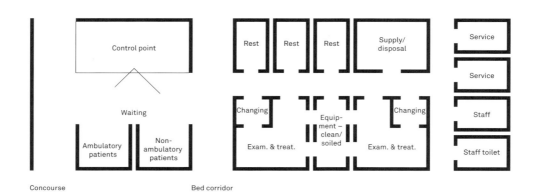

**Figure 4.8.25**
Functional layout of a laboratory medicine unit

For laboratories with safety levels S3 or S4, airlocks are required.

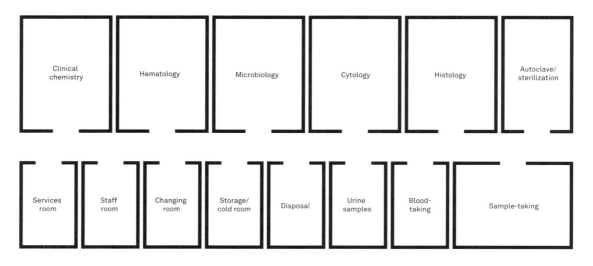

### Radiological Diagnostics

The discipline of radiological diagnostics includes all image-producing processes, with the exception of ultrasound diagnostics. This includes simple X-ray processes as well as computed tomography (CT), magnetic resonance tomography (MRT), electrocardiography (EKG) and diagnostic medical sonography (DMS) procedures among those of most importantance. In addition, therapeutic treatment such as radiation therapy is carried out.

In clinics, this department should be placed directly adjacent to the emergency care unit. From the reception area the patient will reach the diagnostic rooms via a patient zone with waiting area, changing rooms, and additional rooms for preparation, follow-up, and resting; if required by the procedure, there may also be installation and switch rooms. The CT and trauma rooms should be located close to each other. The latter is used for first aid care of patients with serious injuries or who have suffered multiple traumas, and is part of the emergency room area. Just outside the diagnostic core zone are facilities for evaluating the results, and service rooms. It is important to provide measures for radiation protection and electromagnetic screening. → **Figure 4.8.27**

**Figure 4.8.26**
Functional layout of
a pathology unit

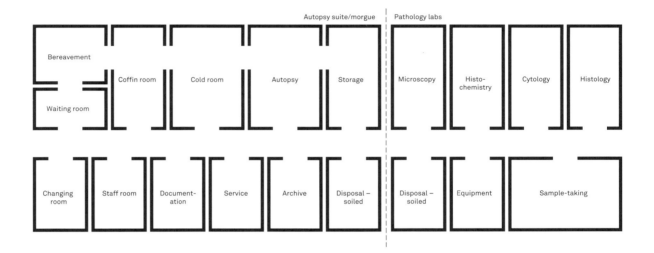

**Figure 4.8.27**
Functional layout of radiological
diagnostics unit

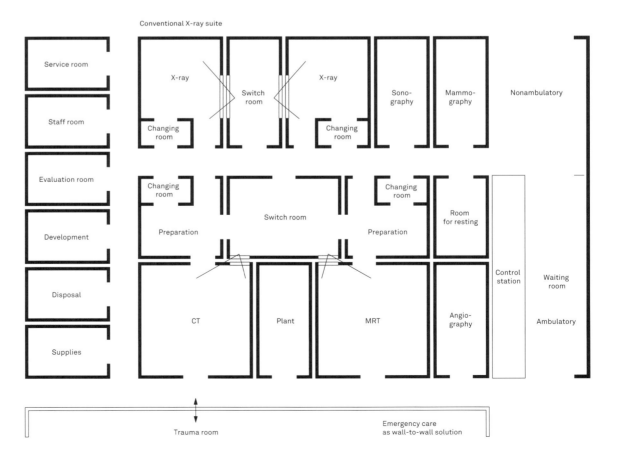

## Surgery

Usually, large surgery units are independent of inpatient facilities. Nowadays, the various medical disciplines are combined in a single department; furthermore, it is more and more common to carry out operations on an outpatient basis. This means that the number of operating rooms outside hospitals is increasing. Usually however, these are smaller intervention rooms and individual operating rooms.

The surgery department does not necessarily have to be linked to other departments, and is an independent unit that includes a hygiene lobby zone for persons and materials. This zone includes lobbies for patients, changing rooms and sanitary facilities for staff, and supply and disposal rooms. Before entering the operating rooms there are entrance and exit areas, as well as scrub room facilities. These days exit areas are often omitted, but entrance zones can range from an open central area with entrances through to dedicated rooms for each operating room. Sterile goods are supplied to the operating rooms from the rear. The sterile goods are prepared either in dedicated rooms or in a central preparation zone with places assigned for this task. →Figure 4.8.28

Operating rooms should ideally be square in layout and have a minimum floor area of 40 m²; usually they are equipped for interdisciplinary interventions. The color scheme for walls and floors should consist of shades from green to blue. Basic equipment includes a firmly anchored stand in the center of the room, upon which the variable and transportable operating table is mounted. Media and energy supplies are usually installed using systems suspended from the ceiling. Additional equipment consists of mobile units which are drawn upon as required by the respective medical discipline. →Figures 4.8.29–4.8.32

Following the operation the patient is moved to the recovery area, where postoperative monitoring takes place. As a rule, the recovery room is a large room with integrated monitoring space and a holding area for waiting, nonambulatory patients.

In order to reduce the transmission of germs, it makes sense to separate different work processes and circulation areas. Using a two-corridor system, it is possible to separate patients and staff/patients and clean goods from soiled goods. Operating rooms and departments are normally air-conditioned. In addition to providing a constant temperature and constant relative humidity, the air should be kept as free from germs as possible, and the concentration of anesthetic gases must be kept below the guide values. An air flow extremely low in germs (TAV) is conducted directly to the operating field from a ventilation field above the operating table. The operating room is pressurized so that no air can enter from the outside. In order to avoid uncontrolled air flow from adjoining rooms, the construction should be as airtight as possible. The air-conditioning of the surgery department requires appropriate plant installations for which space must be provided in the design. In addition, a backup power supply is required for emergencies. →Table 4.8.13

Table 4.8.11 (left)
Average space requirement of a surgery department

Table 4.8.12 (top right)
Requirements for special types of operations

Table 4.8.13 (bottom right)
Operating room requirements for air quality and sound

| Function | Size |
|---|---|
| Operating room | 40 m² |
| Entrance room | 15 m² |
| Exit room | 15 m² |
| Scrub room/area | 6 places |
| Preparation room/sterile goods | 10–15 m² |
| Control station | 10–15 m² |
| Dictation place/documentation | 6 m²/place |
| Operating equipment room | 20 m² |
| Recovery room | 1.5 × no. of operations = no. of beds |
| Disposal | 10–15 m² |
| Janitorial room | 5 m² |

| Type | Definition |
|---|---|
| Septic-operations | Special operating room in which operations on infected tissue are carried out. For this reason, it has separate ventilation ducts with exhaust air filters. |
| Hybrid operations | Modern operating rooms include large imaging devices, such as computers or magnetic resonance tomographs, and can also be used as a heart catheter laboratory using any existing angiography instruments. |

| Operating room requirements | |
|---|---|
| Temperature | 22°C–26°C |
| Relative humidity | 30%–65% rel. humidity |
| Air changes | 15–20 changes/h |
| Max. acoustic level | 40 dB(A) |

**Figure 4.8.28**
Functional layout of surgery
department with different version
of entrance and exit areas

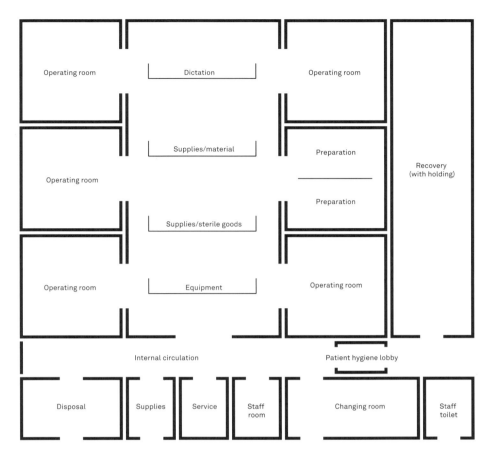

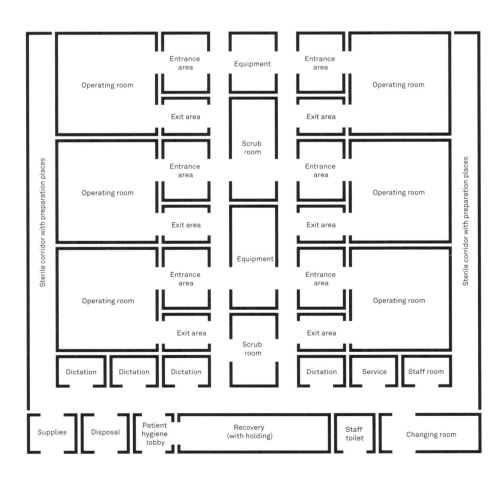

**Figure 4.8.29**
Space requirement and schematic
layout of operating room

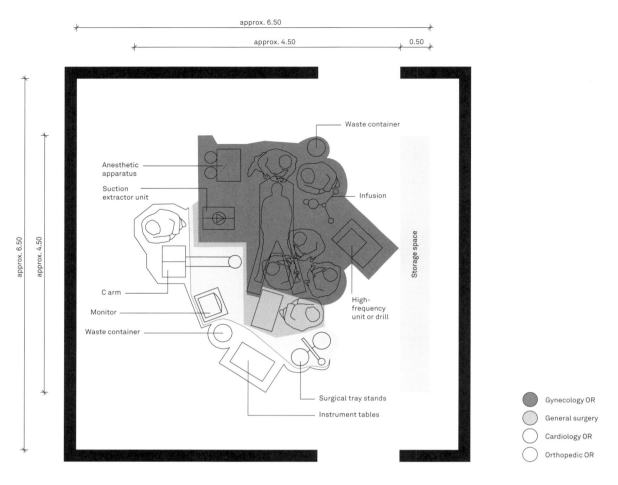

Waste container

Anesthetic
apparatus

Suction
extractor unit

Infusion

C arm

Monitor

Waste container

High-
frequency
unit or drill

Surgical tray stands

Instrument tables

Storage space

approx. 6.50

approx. 4.50

0.50

approx. 6.50

approx. 4.50

Gynecology OR

General surgery

Cardiology OR

Orthopedic OR

**Figure 4.8.30**
Schematic cross section through
operating room with ventilation
ceiling

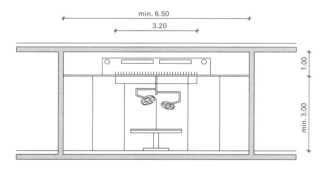

min. 6.50

3.20

1.00

min. 3.00

**Figure 4.8.31 (left)**
Operating room with supply unit
suspended from the ceiling

**Figure 4.8.32 (right)**
Sterile corridor with preparation
places

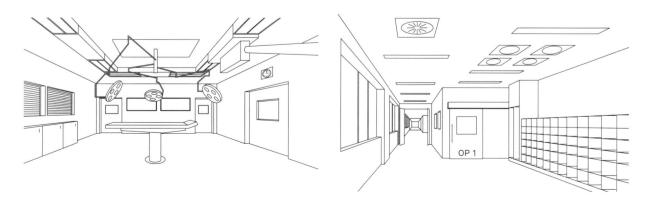

OP 1

### Obstetrics

Delivery rooms are found in hospitals, maternity units, and large midwifery or obstetrics practices. In most cases, the obstetrics department is spatially connected to the examination and treatment area. In larger hospitals with specialist departments for neonatal and intensive pediatric care, the units should be as close as possible. If the obstetrics department does not contain a dedicated operating room, it is essential that the distance to the surgery department be short.

A traditionally structured unit includes reception, a labor room, a delivery room and an initial care room, where-as multifunctional delivery units (also known as delivery apartments) nowadays integrate all steps from examination and monitoring (using a monitoring system) through to birth and initial care. The unit should have sufficient space for various birth aids, an accompanying person, and a separate sanitary unit. The option of an underwater birth should be provided in at least one delivery room. A separate, specially equipped initial care room can be omitted if a neonatal intensive care unit is available nearby. → **Figure 4.8.33**

**Figure 4.8.33**
Functional layout of obstetrics department

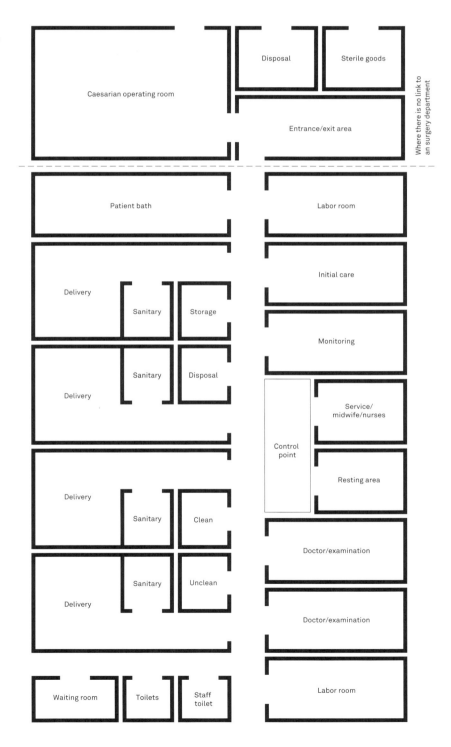

## Physical Therapy and Rehabilitation

In the context of clinical establishments, the forms of medical treatment required for prevention, therapy, and rehabilitation are combined in the physical therapy department. Patients who need further treatment following a medical intervention are increasingly treated on an outpatient basis or in special rehabilitation establishments and therapy centers. Depending on the medical orientation, a distinction is made between active measures in which the patient has to contribute (for example physiotherapy and remedial gymnastics) and passive measures (massage, electrotherapy, heat and cold treatment, inhalation, and climatotherapy, phototherapy, and hydrotherapy) and the type of treatment. An increased number of patients with movement restrictions must be taken into account in the design. →Figure 4.8.34

**Figure 4.8.34**
Functional layout of a physical therapy unit

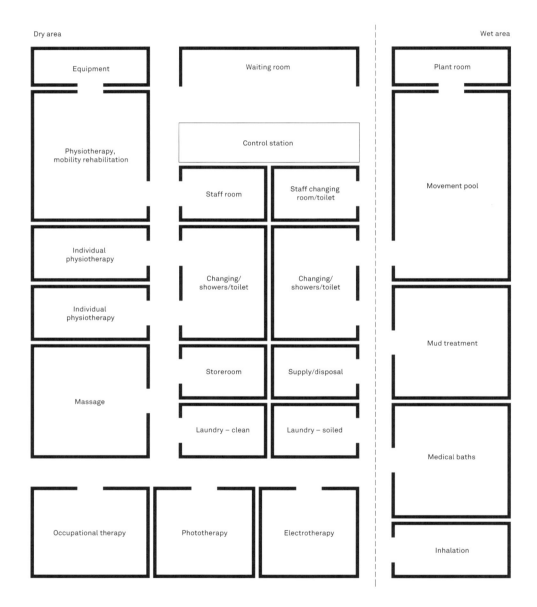

**Table 4.8.14**
Types of physical therapy treatment

| Type of treatment | Definition and space requirement |
|---|---|
| Dry | Movement therapy in gymnastic rooms, preferably with the option of subdivision; mobility rehabilitation with handrails and equipment, possibly also along corridors; rooms for massages and manual therapy as well as light treatment and short- and long-wave treatment |
| Wet | Gymnastics in pools of various sizes, bathtubs, hydrotherapy, poultices, inhalation |

### 4.8.3.2 Patient Rooms

There are different categories of care areas, which are classified by room size, degree of medical care and intensity, or the specific user groups. The boundaries between a room strictly used for care purposes and a residential room are somewhat fluid. The layout and fit-out of patient rooms depend largely on the degree of medical care required. The greater the requirement for medical equipment and the stricter the hygiene and security requirements (as in psychiatric units), the more the size/design of the room depends on technical/construction requirements. While rooms must be adequately sized for the number of beds, it is the atmosphere of the room that is most important for patients. Daylight, views to the outside, the use of light, color and materials play an important role in creating a room climate that supports healing.

**Room Layout and Size**
An important factor determining the size of a care room is the number and dimensions of patient beds (→ **Table 4.8.17**) and the necessary space for care, examination, and patient activities. The width of the room is determined by the space needed for moving beds without disturbing other patients. In addition, in a clinical environment, it must be possible to access each bed from three sides. Although three- and four-bed rooms are the most economical in terms of investment and operating costs, nowadays private and semiprivate rooms are the standard owing to the ubiquitous demand for privacy. These rooms are replicated many times in the building, and therefore represent an important design module. Since most new buildings are designed on the basis of a construction grid, it makes sense to provide private rooms of the same size as semiprivate rooms, which makes it possible to use these rooms flexibly to suit the demand/degree of utilization.

Each patient room should also have the benefit of an en-suite sanitary unit, which should be barrier-free if possible. These units are usually equipped with a toilet, washbasin, and a shower in most cases. ↗ **Chapter 3.5 Spaces/ Sanitary Facilities**

**Figure 4.8.35**
Patient room

- Service ducts for media and lighting with connections for oxygen, vacuum, and compressed air as well as sockets, reading lamp, nurse call aid (if required) and telephone
- Wall protection, height minimum 40–70 cm above floor level
- Corner protectors

Furniture:
- Table with chairs
- Wardrobe, closet, or clothes hooks
- Disinfection facility or small care work area

For each patient:
- Bedside table on castors
- Lockable patient cabinet with compartment for valuables
- Monitor at the patient bed for television, nurse call aid (if required) and telephone

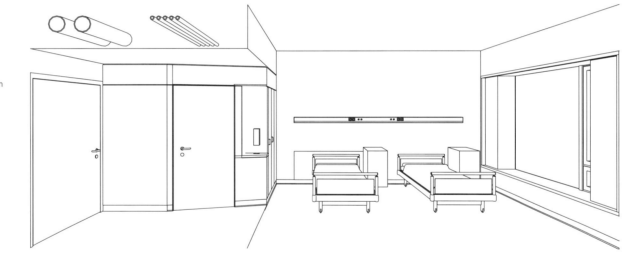

**Table 4.8.15 (left)**
Average dimensions of patient beds

**Table 4.8.16 (right)**
Average size of the different care units

| Type of use | ø Width in cm | ø Length in cm |
|---|---|---|
| Care bed | 100 | 200–210 |
| Clinic bed for normal care | 100–110 | 210–220 |
| Clinic bed – IMC/ICU | 110 | 215–230 |
| Clinic bed – children | 90–95 | 170 |
| Bed – newborns | 60 | 95 |
| Exam. & treat. couch/ doctor's couch | 80 | 200 |
| Occupational therapy couch | 80–100 | 200–220 |
| Operating table | 80 | 190 |

| Care area | No. of beds | Type of care |
|---|---|---|
| Intensive care unit (ICU) | 6–16 | Private/semiprivate room |
| Intermediate care (IMC) | 24–28 | Private/semiprivate room |
| Normal care (NC) | 32–36 | Private/semiprivate room |
| Normal care for children (NC) | 24–28 | Private/semiprivate room to max. 4-bed room/family room |
| Neonatal care | 6–12 | Private room/multiple-bed room |
| Postdelivery care | 24–28 | Private/semiprivate room/ family room |
| Psychiatry | 16–18 | Private/semiprivate room |
| Geriatrics | 24 | Private/semiprivate room |

**Table 4.8.17**
Average sizes of patient rooms

| Type | Size |
|---|---|
| Private room | 16 m² |
| Semiprivate room | 24 m² |
| Three-bed room | 32 m² |
| Four-bed room | 48 m² |

**Figure 4.8.36**
Layout examples of general care patient rooms

Private room, standard

Private room suite

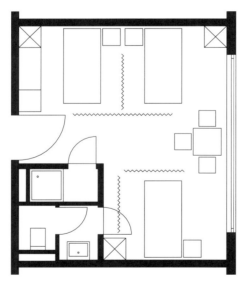

Two-bed deep three-bed room

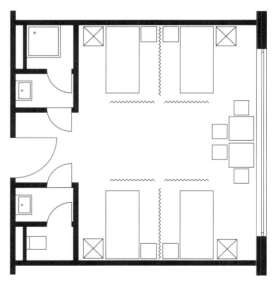

Four-bed room

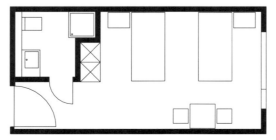

Semiprivate room (2 beds)

### Medical Degree of Care and Care Intensity

#### Day Care/Low Care

Both these degrees of care are for patients with a low requirement for care or for short-stay inpatients. Day care units function as intake stations, relief care areas or day clinics/emergency treatment areas (ETAs). While day care units are not attended during the night, low care (LC) units are normally attended around the clock.

#### General Care/Normal Care

General care or normal care (NC) refers to general inpatient care that is primarily for short-stay patients and does not require permanent monitoring of the patient. In order to achieve better utilization, the units should be designed so that they can be combined and their functions switched. For this reason, at least two units per level are recommended.

#### Intermediate Care

In intermediate care (IMC), patients are treated whose illness requires a high degree of monitoring and medical treatment but who do not require intensive care; they nevertheless require more input than patients in normal care.

Usually, intermediate care patients are accommodated in private or semiprivate rooms with en-suite sanitary facilities. Where the necessary connection is available for artificial respiration and an uninterruptible power supply, it is possible – using the ceiling-mounted service facilities – to provide intensive care also in rooms equipped for IMC.

#### Intensive Care

Intensive care units (ICUs) belong among those functional units for which the hygiene requirements are particularly exacting, requiring special attention in the functional and spatial design. The whole unit should be air-conditioned to a relative humidity of 50–70 percent in order to prevent dehydration in patients. Private and semiprivate rooms have low air pressure in order to prevent germs reaching the corridor. The center of each intensive care unit is an open service station with the associated control monitors. Patients in intensive care require constant monitoring and possibly also artificial respiration. For patients with infectious diseases it is necessary to provide private rooms with anteroom that functions as an airlock. → **Figures 4.8.37 and 4.8.38**

**Figure 4.8.37**
Example of an IMC/ICU room

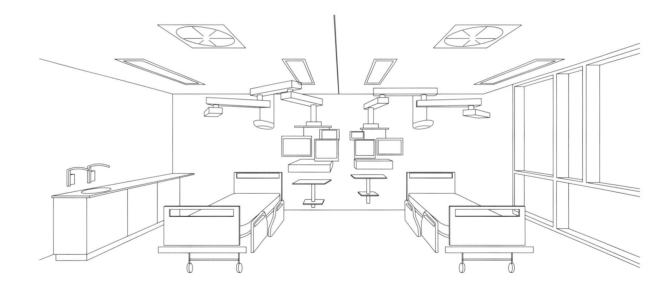

**Figure 4.8.38**
Functional layout of an intensive care unit (ICU)

Possible additional rooms
• a dedicated resuscitation room where there is no link to a surgery/emergency facility
• bed preparation room for IMC/ICU beds

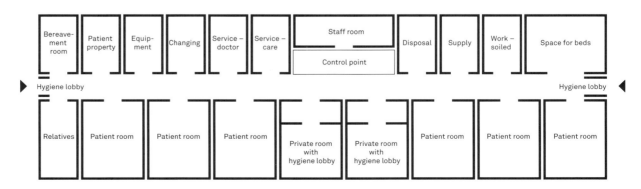

**Care According to User Group**

<u>Postdelivery Care</u>
Where the care of newborn infants is arranged in a centralized unit, the care unit for newborn babies is placed next to or within the postdelivery care unit. With rooming-in arrangements (where both infant and mother are accommodated in the same room), semiprivate rooms require more space for normal care than standard rooms. Private rooms are usually big enough to be modified into family rooms. → **Figure 4.8.39**

<u>Infant, Child, and Adolescent Care</u>
For the care of infants, children, and adolescents, the presence of an attachment figure is important for the patient's well-being and recovery. For this purpose, patient rooms and units have to provide appropriate space. Where several child care units are grouped together, it may be appropriate to provide playrooms, schooling, and backup rooms for teachers, speech therapists, psychologists, and social workers. The pediatrics department is a specialist area in which newborn infants are treated. In practice, these units comprise private rooms through to eight-bed rooms. The rooms should provide an anteroom with changing, bathing, and documentation areas. → **Figure 4.8.40**

<u>Dialysis</u>
Dialysis units are often operated as day clinics in which patients arrive by appointment and only stay for treatment for a few hours. For chronic dialysis patients, four- to six-bed rooms are suitable. For infectious patients, private or semiprivate rooms must be provided. Dialysis couches should be accessible from both sides and should be curtained to provide privacy. It is important that all places can be viewed from the control point.

<u>Care of Patients with Infectious Diseases</u>
Patients with infectious diseases require private rooms with a hygiene lobby. Depending on the size of the establishment and the type of illness, these rooms can form a separate unit or be part of a general care unit. → **Figure 4.8.41**

<u>Nuclear Medicine Care</u>
It is imperative that nuclear medicine care units be designed with a vestibule and be free of any through traffic. Patient rooms should contain a work station for the care staff, which must be screened from the patient bed. → **Figure 4.8.42**

**Figure 4.8.39**
Postdelivery rooms

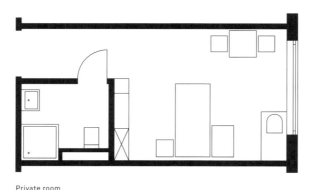

Private room

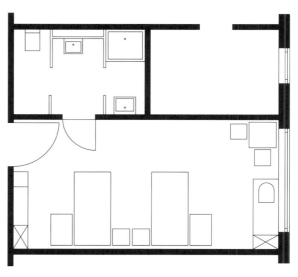

Semiprivate room

**Figure 4.8.40**
Rooms for child and
adolescent care

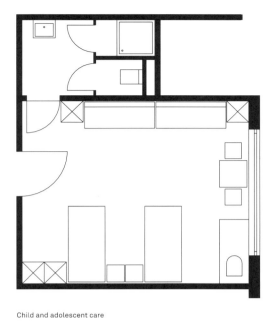

Child and adolescent care

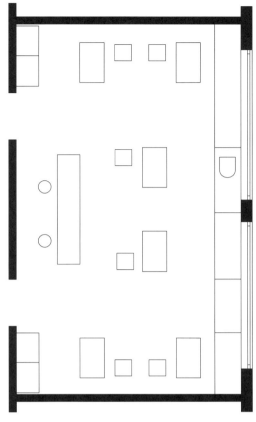

Pediatrics

**Figure 4.8.41 (left)**
Private room with hygiene lobby
for a patient with an infectious
disease

**Figure 4.8.42 (right)**
Semiprivate room for nuclear
medicine care

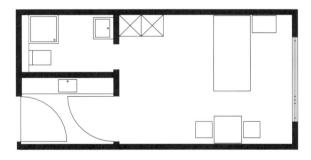

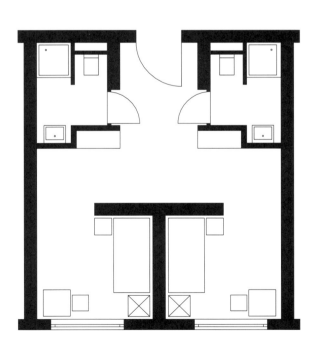

### Psychiatric Patients

The care areas for psychiatric patients should be as close as possible to normal residential accommodation. At the same time, provisions must be in place to avoid suicide and the violation of others. As a rule, private and semiprivate rooms are provided. Since psychiatric units do not require many care activities, it is not necessary for the beds in the patient rooms to be accessible from three sides. → **Figure 4.8.43**

### Health Resorts and Rehabilitation

The main focus of healthcare facilities in health resorts and rehabilitation centers is on improving the mobility of patients. This means that, in addition to the required care facilities, space must be provided for movement, communication, and therapy. Patient rooms are usually provided in the form of private and semiprivate rooms which, compared to the rooms in normal care units, are equipped more comfortably, approaching the standard of hotel rooms.

### Palliative Care

Palliative care is the process of assisting terminal patients; units normally comprise private rooms with optional additional beds or separate rooms for relatives. Rooms for medical functions are of secondary importance and should be placed accordingly. The main focus of the design is on providing a residential feel with plenty of light, air, and a view to nature.

### Geriatrics/Care of the Elderly

A variety of different establishments exist for the care and treatment of older patients and those in need of care; the design takes into account the medical conditions of the residents and the degree of medical care required. All rooms, apartments, and units should be completely barrier-free. → **Figure 4.8.45**, ↗ **Chapter 4.1 Typologies/Housing**

**Figure 4.8.43**
Territories in psychiatric patients' rooms

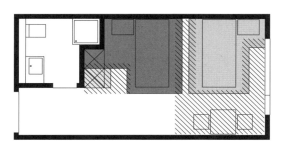

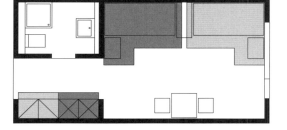

⊘ Territorial infringement

**Figure 4.8.44**
Monitoring patient rooms in a psychiatric unit

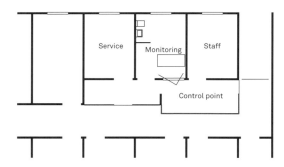

**Figure 4.8.45**
Geriatric and elderly care units

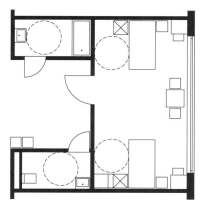

Semiprivate room in a geriatric care unit

Private room in a geriatric care unit

Shared accommodation

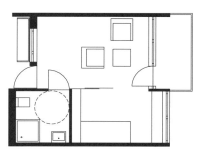

Room in a care home for the elderly

Assisted housing

**Additional Design Considerations for Care Units**

A number of different concepts exist for the basic structure of care units. Linear arrangements have the disadvantage of long distances, but may be appropriate for units with a small number of patient rooms. The proportion of circulation space required by double-loaded systems and systems with two parallel corridors is often relatively large and, in the latter, the internal rooms are without daylight unless inner courtyards or atria are provided. Inner courtyards are a favored solution as enclosed open areas for patients with psychiatric conditions or dementia requiring secure/safe environments. Patient rooms should be arranged along the outside elevations, providing a view to the outside, while staff and functional rooms can be placed around inner courtyards. The maximum walking distance for staff should be limited to 30 m.

### Care Control Point

The care control point should be located as centrally as possible within the unit and feature a glazed information counter with visual and speech contact toward the corridor. In addition, there must be sufficient space for work on documentation. A direct connection to the service and staff rooms is beneficial.

### Clean Workroom

The clean workroom is used for storing and dispensing medication. Medicine cabinets, special refrigerators and narcotics safes must be provided for the storage of medicines.

### Soiled workroom

One decentralized, soiled workroom should be provided for every eight beds. These rooms require cleaning and disinfection sinks, hand wash basins, a worktop, cabinets, and shelving.

### Patient Dayrooms

Dayrooms are used as general meeting areas for patients and visitors and, in some cases, as dining rooms. This room should be located centrally in the unit, and may be open to the corridor or separated by a glass wall. Furnishing should include several seating areas, possibly a drinks bar or drink dispensers. It may be possible to provide smaller dayrooms between two adjoining patient rooms.

### Patient Bathroom

The patient bathroom is used for the ablution of patients requiring help. The equipment includes a bathtub with hoist accessible from three sides, and a washbasin. It may be useful to provide, in addition, a shower suitable for the disabled. If the patient rooms do not have sanitary facilities with showers, an additional patient bathroom with shower cubicles should be provided. → **Figure 4.8.47**, ↗ **Chapter 3.5 Spaces/Sanitary Facilities**

**Figure 4.8.46**
Position of care control points

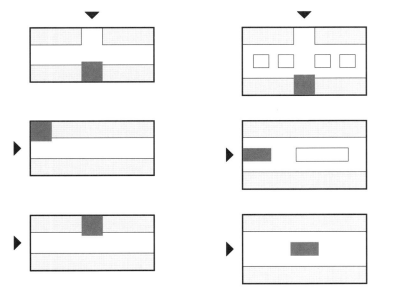
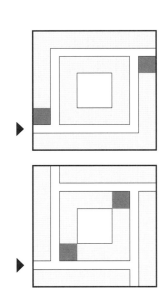

Table 4.8.18
Average number and size of rooms in a general care unit/station with 32 beds

| Use | Number | Size | Required |
|---|---|---|---|
| Private room (1 bed) | 4 | | |
| Semiprivate room (2 beds) | 14 | | |
| Control point | 1 | 25–30 m² | per station |
| Staff room | 1 | 20 m² | per station |
| Service room – doctor | 1 | 16 m² | for 2 stations |
| Service room – head nurse | 1 | 12–16 m² | per station |
| Exam & treatment room | 1 | 16–20 m² | for 2 stations |
| Workroom – clean | 1 | 12–20 m² | per station |
| Workroom – soiled | 2–4 | 8–10 m² | per station |
| Kitchenette | 1 | 8 m² | per station |
| Patient dayroom | 1 | 22–25 m² | per station |
| Patient bathroom | 1 | 18 m² | for 2 stations |
| Visitor toilet | 2 (m/f) | 2.50 m² | for 2 stations |
| Disabled (accessible) toilet | 1 | 5 m² | for 2–4 stations or integrated into patient toilet |
| Equipment room | 1 | 16 m² | for 2 stations |
| Supply room | 1 | 14 m² | per station |
| Disposal room | 1 | 10 m² | per station |
| Janitorial room | 1 | 4 m² | per station |
| Plant room | 1 | 8 m² | per station |
| Bed preparation | 1 | 36 m² | per station level; alternatively, central bed preparation |
| Room for deceased | 1 | 8 m² | per station level |

Figure 4.8.47 (left)
Patient sanitary units

Figure 4.8.48 (right)
Example of a care control point

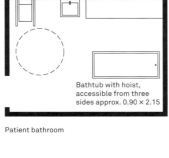

Bathtub with hoist, accessible from three sides approx. 0.90 × 2.15

Patient bathroom

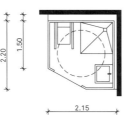

Prefabricated sanitary unit

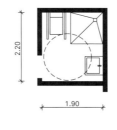

Sanitary unit

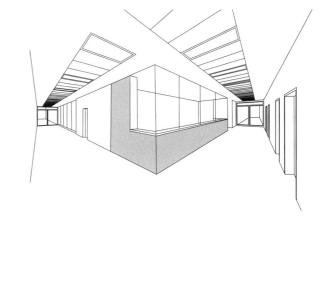

### 4.8.3.3 General Service and Special Areas

**Waiting Areas**
The size of waiting areas in doctors' practices and medical institutions depends on the number and frequency of visits to the doctors providing treatment, the average treatment time and opening hours, and the arrangements for appointments. The number of patients waiting for each doctor should not exceed five. In larger practices and care centers, it may be appropriate to provide several waiting areas. The additional waiting rooms can also be used for patients who are at risk of infection. It is recommended to provide a play corner for children within a waiting area.

Larger establishments require waiting areas near the reception, control points, and therapy facilities. They should be visible from the respective area and, if possible, should have natural light and ventilation. Where patient pagers are used, waiting areas can be smaller because patients can freely move around the building and can still be called up for their treatment.

**Foyer**
In larger medical establishments, the entrance lobby is also the central distribution point for the building/ensemble. These areas include information desks as well as central service facilities such as shops and a cafeteria. ↗Chapter 3.2.1 Spaces/Internal Circulation/Entrance Areas

**Oratory**
Larger establishments provide an oratory as a place for contemplation and retreat. It should be located centrally, but in a quiet environment. This facility may be denominational, depending on the ownership of the medical establishment.

**Bereavement Room**
A bereavement room is used to provide a suitable setting for relatives/friends to take leave of the deceased. In clinics, this room should be located close to the pathology department. In hospices and residential care homes, a quiet area should be chosen. Bereavement rooms may also be appropriate in palliative care units.

**Administration**
While in doctors' practices administrative tasks are carried out at the reception or in single office rooms, larger establishments will have their own departments. The size and location depend on the size of the establishment. ↗Chapter 4.2 Typologies/Office and Administration

Figure 4.8.49
Waiting areas at control points in hospitals and doctors' practices

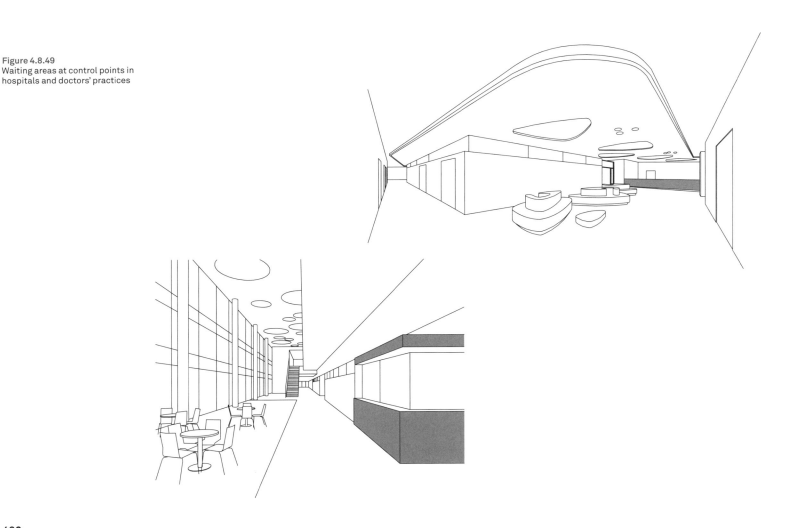

### 4.8.3.4 Supply and Disposal

The organization of the supply and disposal systems determines the position of these rooms in the building. Where external service providers are used (laundry, food), the in-house service areas are restricted to delivery and storage areas. In very large establishments with their own supply facilities, a supply center may be appropriate as an independent building which is connected via underground links. As a rule, supply units in buildings with about 250 beds are located in a general supply and disposal level beneath the main building. Deliveries and collections are made via the delivery and disposal yard. In addition to an incoming goods area with appropriate space for storage and the movement of vehicles, areas for different types of waste, utility installations such as emergency power aggregate, sprinkler, oxygen and compressed-air centers, as well as smaller workshops for metal workers, joiners, and electricians, should be provided. → **Figure 4.8.50**

Figure 4.8.50
Functional layout of supply and disposal area

**Supply of Materials/Bed Preparation**
A logistics room close to the delivery and disposal yard is recommended for the distribution and storage of materials; internal distribution within the building is coordinated from here. Any automatic goods transport systems or driverless transport systems in the building are controlled from the logistics room.

Bed preparation can be arranged centrally, or may be carried out part-centralized or decentralized at the respective unit, in which case two to four units usually share a disinfection room. In the case of decentralized preparation, a separate mattress disinfection facility must be provided in the service area. The bed preparation facility is divided into soiled and clean sides, which can be reached via separate hygiene lobbies for staff. The zones for disinfection and cleaning (if appropriate) lie between these. Adequate space for beds must be provided on both sides. → **Figure 4.8.51**

**Supply of Meals**
The place where meals are taken and how the meals are taken there are important considerations for the supply of meals. A distinction is made between traditional meal preparation (cook & serve) and precooked meal concepts. While for the latter the position of the kitchen is of secondary importance, in the traditional method of providing meals, proximity to the wards and staff restaurant is recommended. Allocating the kitchen to the service level, with short connections, guarantees an efficient workflow for the delivery, preparation, and serving of meals. ↗ **Chapter 4.7 Typologies/Lodging and Food Service**

**Dispensary**
Maximum service clinics usually have their own dispensary in which required medicines are prepared and stored for a short period. Dispensaries should be located close to elevators, pneumatic delivery system outlets, etc. In smaller hospitals, health resort, and rehabilitation establishments, medicines requiring prescriptions are dispensed by the dispensaries. → **Figure 4.8.52**

**Sterile Goods Supply**
The central sterile goods supply unit is used for preparing, disinfecting, and supplying all required instruments and medical products. In view of the fact that in clinics, about 40 percent of the instruments to be cleaned come from the surgery department, the central sterilization unit should be nearby. This unit is divided into soiled and clean areas, which are hygienically separated from each other. → **Figure 4.8.53**

Figure 4.8.51
Functional layout of a bed preparation facility

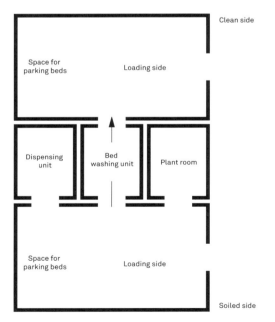

**Figure 4.8.52**
Functional layout of a dispensary

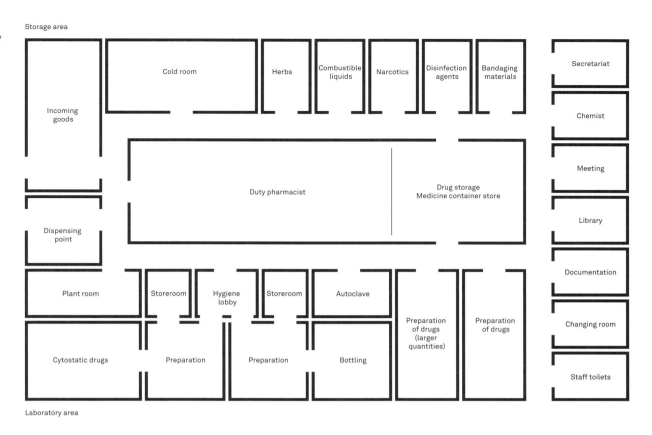

**Figure 4.8.53**
Functional layout of sterile
material supply unit

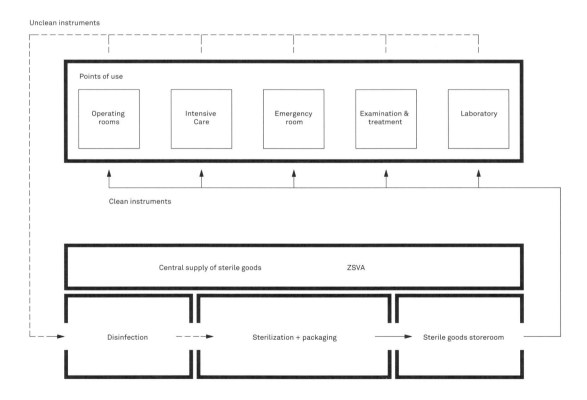

**Palazetto dello Sport,** Rome, Italy, Pier Luigi Nervi and Annibale Vitellozzi, 1957

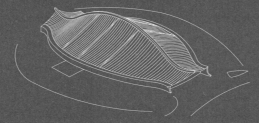

**Ingalls Rink ("The Whale"),** Yale University, New Haven, CT, USA, Eero Saarinen, 1958

**Yoyogi National Gymnasium,** Tokyo, Japan, Kenzo Tange, 1964

**Olympic Stadium,** Munich, Germany, Behnisch/ Frei Otto, 1972

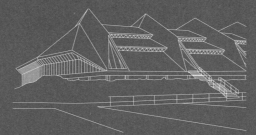

**Helmut-Körnig-Halle indoor athletics facility,** Dortmund, Germany, Klippel, Scheiding und Saitner, 1980

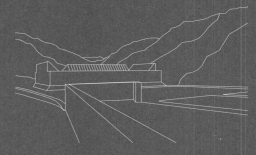

**Sporthalle Monte Carasso,** Monte Carasso, Switzerland, Luigi Snozzi, 1984

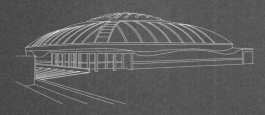

**Sporthalle Sant Jordi,** Barcelona, Spain, Arata Isozaki, 1992

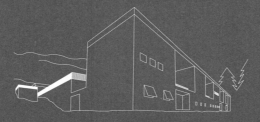

**Therme Vals,** Vals, Switzerland, Peter Zumthor, 1996

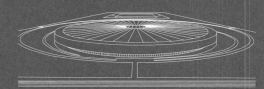

**Indoor Swimming Pool and Velodrome,** Berlin, Germany, Dominique Perrault, 1999

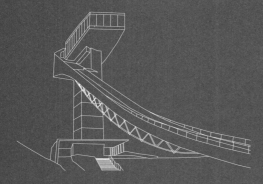

**Skischanze Innsbruck,** Innsbruck, Austria, Zaha Hadid, 2002

**Tschuggen Bergoase wellness center,** Arosa, Switzerland, Mario Botta, 2006

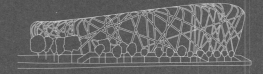

**National Stadium (Bird's Nest),** Beijing, China, Herzog & de Meuron, 2008

# 4 Typologies
## 4.9 Sports and Recreation

Bert Bielefeld

### 4.9.1 Building Concept ↗426

4.9.1.1 Planning Parameters ↗426
4.9.1.2 Building Forms ↗426
4.9.1.3 Circulation Systems ↗427
4.9.1.4 Construction and Technology ↗429

### 4.9.2 Program of Use ↗431

4.9.2.1 Ancillary Buildings for Outdoor Sports Facilities ↗431
4.9.2.2 Gymnasiums ↗431
4.9.2.3 Stadiums ↗434
4.9.2.4 Swimming Pools ↗438
4.9.2.5 Indoor Ice Rinks ↗440
4.9.2.6 Riding Halls ↗444
4.9.2.7 Climbing Gyms ↗445
4.9.2.8 Fitness and Wellness ↗446

### 4.9.3 Areas and Rooms ↗448

4.9.3.1 Entrance Areas ↗449
4.9.3.2 Sports Areas ↗450
4.9.3.3 Equipment for Sports and Games ↗460
4.9.3.4 Tiered Seating and Spectator Areas ↗467
4.9.3.5 Changing Areas and Sanitary Facilities ↗472
4.9.3.6 Ancillary Spaces ↗472

# 4.9 Sports and Recreation

## 4.9.1 Building Concept

### 4.9.1.1 Planning Parameters

The design and outward configuration of buildings for sports and recreation strongly reflect the activities they accommodate. They can be designed specifically for a particular sport or made to be multifunctional and flexible. The spectrum ranges from clubhouses, gymnasiums, and indoor swimming pools to major projects like multifunctional stadiums. Particularly for sport activities that draw large numbers of spectators, it is important not only to provide optimal conditions for sporting purposes, but also to focus on the interests of the spectators and the logistical aspects of places of assembly.

For sports and recreation buildings, urban and infrastructural integration (accessibility by car and public transit, environmental impact, etc.) are essential factors in selecting the site. Especially for activities that attract many spectators, large streams of visitors and users must be accommodated at peak times and sufficiently dimensioned parking areas must be provided accordingly. Beyond that, many outdoor sports facilities also require large, usable outdoor areas and sports fields close to the building.

Typical planning parameters are:
- Place, context, and site geometry
- Infrastructure and public transit connections
- Building code restrictions
- Unique requirements for use
- Additional spatial program/needs
- Ancillary uses
- Needs of the user groups
- Layout type and building form
- Presentational purposes
- Public–private relationship
- Barrier-free accessibility
- Budget and deadlines

The areas needed for the specific sports that will be played constitute the starting point for the design of sports buildings (↗4.9.3.2 Areas and Rooms/Sports Areas). Generally, the dimensions and ceiling heights needed for the actual sports areas (for instance, a playing field, court, or lane) are specified by the pertinent sport associations or the provisions of applicable standards, which are supplemented by perimeter areas to allow for safety clearances and free movement. The arrangement of the necessary auxiliary areas, such as changing rooms, equipment storage, and areas for building services, must be such that the shortest possible circulation paths result along with clearly definable zoning. If spectator areas are needed, not only are tiered seating areas along the playing field required, but also additional facilities such as sanitary facilities solely for public use, food service, separate entrances with access control, ticket booths, etc. → Figure 4.9.1

### 4.9.1.2 Building Forms

Because sports and recreation activities typically require large spaces and high ceilings, these activity areas play a decisive role in shaping the building form, such that, at least with monofunctional facilities, the building's purpose is often legible from outside. The clear space needed in cross section can be rationally enclosed with an outer covering that drapes over it, or the exterior can be freely sculpted. Further geometric opportunities present themselves when there is tiered seating surrounding the sports area, so one encounters sports and recreation buildings of many shapes and forms, including rectangular, rounded, oval, circular, and organic. → Figure 4.9.2

The layout of multiple playing fields, which usually dictates much of the total area, and the combination of various types of sports or recreational facilities, requires a

Figure 4.9.1
Systematization of the space requirements

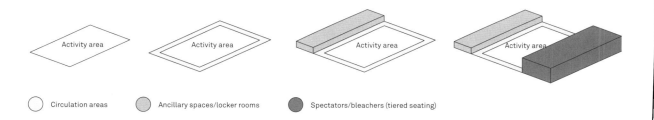

○ Circulation areas    ● Ancillary spaces/locker rooms    ● Spectators/bleachers (tiered seating)

carefully planned arrangement of the functional areas in order to minimize circulation paths and create space-efficient buildings. For instance, functional areas can be arranged in rows (typical for uniformly sized playing fields like tennis, bowling, etc.) or stacked vertically (locating locker rooms beneath tiered seating, for example). The various activities can be grouped around a central service facility or they can be served by decentralized facilities. → **Figure 4.9.3** The internal organization also has an impact on the building's outer appearance, which can either depict the individual activity areas as distinguishable elements or integrate them into an overall form.

### 4.9.1.3 Circulation Systems

It is important to distinguish between the building's internal circulation and its integration with the urban context and surrounding infrastructure, which is particularly key for areas that draw public attention.

The internal circulation of sports facilities is divided into separate functional areas for athletes, spectators, and support. Changing from street clothes to sports attire or leisurewear is part of the recreational experience, and the necessary facilities should be designed accordingly. For sports that require a change of clothes or shoes (indoor sports, swimming, ice sports, bowling, etc.) changing rooms, lockers, and sanitary facilities are usually posi-

tioned in such a way as to control the flow of people between a street-shoe zone and an athletic-shoe or barefoot zone. → **Figure 4.9.4** Otherwise, these can be added as secondary spaces. For changing areas that also serve an outdoor area, separate exits should be planned, along with direct access to the outdoor areas when possible. If additional functions such as equipment rental or food services are to be integrated in the recreation area, the circulation systems should be geared to typical user behavior and the sequence of use. → **Figure 4.9.5**, ↗ **Chapter 4.7 Typologies/Lodging and Food Service**

If the activity calls for spectator areas, the needs of the sport's typical visitor structure and any requirements attributable to league affiliations are decisive for the design. If, as for most amateur sports, the visitors consist mainly of groups of family and friends, separate entrances and circulation paths can be largely dispensed with. When the sports to be accommodated are more professional or of higher rank, the security and control requirements also increase correspondingly for spectators. The practical experience of athletes and fan representatives as well as the stipulations of the governing bodies generally provide information about the extent to which spectators and players/officials and supporters of different teams should be separated and protected from one another. For major events, such as those in stadiums, flows of spectators are usually split into multiple streams that pass through staggered access controls and security checkpoints. → **Figure 4.9.6**

**Figure 4.9.2**
Cross sections of various building forms with integrated bleacher seating

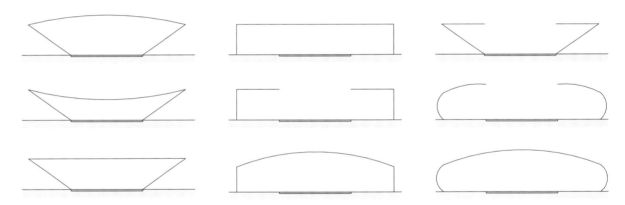

**Figure 4.9.3**
Configuration of multiple sports and leisure activities

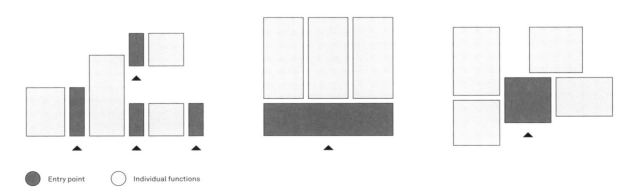

● Entry point     ○ Individual functions

Table 4.9.1
Number of parking spaces necessary for sports and recreation buildings

As per State Building Regulations for the State of North Rhine-Westphalia (BauO NRW)

| Type of facility | Number of parking spaces |
|---|---|
| Places of assembly in general | 1 parking space per 5–10 seats |
| Sports fields | 1 parking space per 250 m² sports area, plus 1 parking space per 10–15 visitors |
| Multipurpose gyms | 1 parking space per 50 m² indoor activity area, plus 1 parking space per 10–15 visitors |
| Outdoor and open-air swimming pools | 1 parking space per 200–300 m² site area |
| Indoor ice rinks | 1 parking space per 30–40 m² ice surface (public)<br>60 parking spaces per standard rink<br>150 parking spaces per speed skating rink<br>6 parking spaces per ice stock sport/curling sheet |
| Riding stables | 1 parking space per 4 horse stalls |
| Indoor swimming pools | 1 parking space per 5–10 lockers/clothes hooks, plus 1 parking space per 10–15 visitors |
| Fitness centers | 1 parking space per 15 m² activity area |
| Tennis facilities | 4 parking spaces per playing field, plus 1 parking space per 10–15 visitors |
| Bowling alleys | 4 parking spaces per lane |
| Boathouses and boat berths | 1 parking space per 2–5 boats |
| Dance halls, discotheques | 1 parking space per 4–8 m² guest area |

Figure 4.9.4 (left)
Changing areas as means for controlling access

Figure 4.9.5 (right)
Typical schematic layout for sports venues and recreational facilities

Simplified from DIN 18036

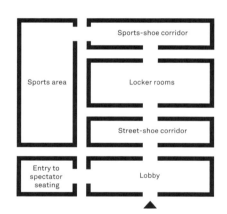

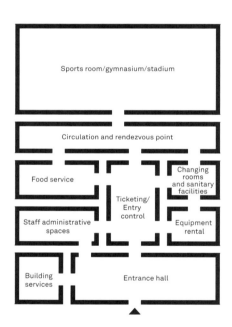

Figure 4.9.6
Access controls in a stadium

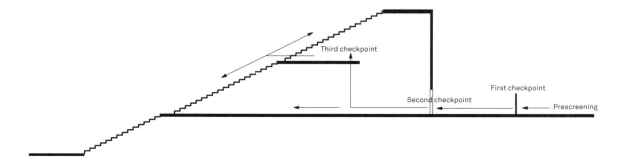

## 4.9.1.4  Construction and Technology

### Load-Bearing Structure

Since most sports activities require large, column-free spaces, the building's roof structure is an important parameter of design. When determining the span length, the depth of any spectator bleachers must be taken into consideration. → **Figure 4.9.7** Depending on the proportions of the area to be spanned, linear structures as well as shells and space frame structures are used. Due to the height needed and the presence of the roof structure, very com-

plex and costly construction methods are frequently used, either visibly exposing the roof structure on the interior, and thus increasing the volume of space within, or constructing it as an external structure, which has a consequent impact on the building's outward appearance. ↗ **Chapter 4.4.1.4 Typologies/Industry and Production/ Building Concept/Construction and Technology**

Figure 4.9.7
Determining the span length

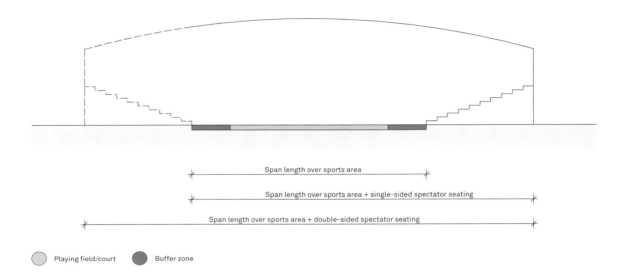

Span length over sports area

Span length over sports area + single-sided spectator seating

Span length over sports area + double-sided spectator seating

Playing field/court       Buffer zone

Figure 4.9.8
Structural design concepts
for gymnasiums (left) and
stadiums (right)

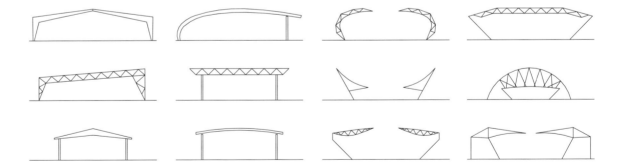

**Building Services**

Sports and recreation buildings generally need various technical installations. Due to large spatial volumes and the high rates of air change needed for sports areas and changing rooms, supplying fresh air and hot water as well as maintaining specific room temperatures often requires large areas for building services equipment and sufficient utility connections. ↗ **Chapter 3.9 Spaces/Technical Equipment Rooms**

In addition, there are use-specific technical installations such as public address systems, floodlights, media walls, broadcasting technology (radio/TV), water treatment for swimming pools, cooling plants for ice rinks, pinspotting equipment for bowling alleys, etc.

Especially at semipublic facilities such as stadiums, considerations such as weather protection and solar altitude/shadow casting need to be taken into account. → **Figure 4.9.9** If the immediate vicinity contains uses, such as residential areas, that require protection from the detrimental impact of aspects like noise and stray light, built measures for their abatement must be incorporated. → **Figure 4.9.10**

**Specific Building Construction**

For floors and walls, the demands of playing fields and recreational areas often dictate specific constructive requirements. These include grass or artificial turf surfaces, sand and clay surfaces compacted to varying degrees (for tennis, jumping events, or beach volleyball, for instance), cinder or synthetic running tracks, floors for riding halls and ice rinks. Depending on the type of activity, different types of sports floors and impact walls as well as movable partitions are used for the interiors of gymnasiums.

**Figure 4.9.9**
Casting of shadows
on the playing field

Source: FIFA

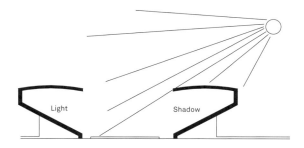 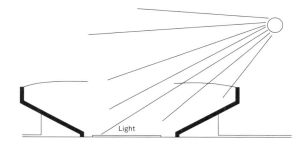

**Figure 4.9.10**
Noise and light emissions
from a stadium

Source: FIFA

Noise emissions

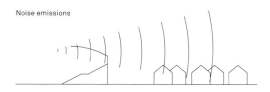 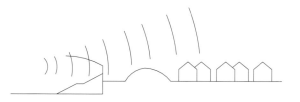

Light emissions

## 4.9.2 Program of Use

When planning sports and recreation facilities, the needs of the athletes/users and the spectators are of prime concern. When the number of anticipated spectators warrant such accessory functions, various lounge and entertainment areas, food services, shops, and the like can be added. The larger the building, the more functions it accommodates, and the greater its number of users, the more important it becomes to address issues of support and logistics, necessitating separate receiving areas, storage areas, distribution systems, etc. ↗Chapter 4.7 Typologies/ Lodging and Food Service, ↗Chapter 4.3 Typologies/ Logistics and Commerce

### 4.9.2.1 Ancillary Buildings for Outdoor Sports Facilities

Outdoor sports facilities ordinarily need ancillary buildings that accommodate changing rooms and sanitary facilities, storage areas, and club-related uses. Depending on the size of the club or the school, additional rooms may be provided for seminars, conferences, parties, or other recreational and sports activities. The spectrum ranges from basic sanitary facilities and sheds with locker rooms to multifunctional clubhouses with many amenities. → Figure 4.9.11

### 4.9.2.2 Gymnasiums

Gymnasiums and other indoor sports facilities are either for general-purpose use and school physical education, in which case they must allow for many types of sports, or they are geared specifically to one sport. When accommodating several types of sports, the dimensions of the largest sports fields (such as soccer, football, handball, hockey, etc.) and the specific requirements of the league classes using the facility are relevant for planning. In addition, due regard must be given to suitably accommodating the equipment necessary for all the sports. Such equipment includes, for example, climbing and gymnastic apparatus on walls and ceilings, fixed or portable goals and baskets that fold out or down from walls and ceilings, and various insert sleeves in the floor for poles and nets. In addition, equipment storage rooms for portable sports equipment must adjoin the sports areas. The layout of individual courts must ensure that the respective boundary markings on the sports floor can be clearly distinguished from one another.

Gymnasiums for general and school use are often designed as spaces that can be subdivided with movable partitions, so that the room can be used simultaneously by several groups or as one large space for major events. Attention must be given to ensure that all parts of the gymnasium are accessible from the sports-shoe corridor and that the escape routes function from all the different parts of the gym, even when the movable partitions are closed. → Figure 4.9.13

Depending on the sports to be practiced, not only are sports flooring and wall padding important, but also the impact resistance of other surfaces (especially where hockey is played). Load-carrying elements, in particular the roof structure, should be designed so that they cannot trap balls.

Figure 4.9.11
Schematic layout of an ancillary building

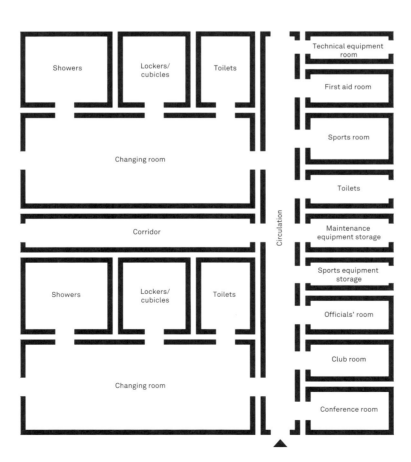

Table 4.9.2
Spatial program for ancillary buildings used by clubs and schools

a If more than two teams are to use a changing room at the same time, games must be scheduled to ensure that the matches do not run concurrently.
b A dedicated first aid room is only necessary when the trainers' and officials' room cannot be located at the playing-field level.
c For a maximum capacity of 1,000 spectators, also sufficient for spectator use. With more than 1,000 seats, additional toilets are required.
d Only when maintenance machinery remains on the sports grounds
e Divisible into 2 half spaces, each with 4 showers and 2 washing stations

**Spatial program for a sports building for club and school use**

| Number of teams | Number of classes for school use | Changing rooms[a] each with 12 m balcony length | Team locker rooms per changing room | Showers and washrooms, each with 8 showers and 4 washing positions | Toilets in the changing area | Room size m² (approx.) | Room for trainers, referees, and first aid[b] Showers/toilets | Clothing lockers | Toilets | Toilets for athletes in exterior areas[c] Men's toilet Urinals | Women's toilet Toilets | Room for groundskeeper (m² approx.) | Youth room/meeting room | Room for building services and handover station | Sports equipment storage | Maintenance equipment storage Machine storage[d] m² (approx.) | Manual tools m² (approx.) |
|---|---|---|---|---|---|---|---|---|---|---|---|---|---|---|---|---|---|
| 4 | 1 or 2 | 2 | 2 | 1 or 2 | 2 | 16 | 1/1 | 6 | 1 | 2 | 2 | 8 | As required, up to approx. 30 m² | Dependent on the technical facilities | m² sports area (net sports area) 0.15 m² | 20 | – |
| 6 | 2 | 2 | 3 | 2 | 2 | | | | | | | | | | | | |
| 8 | 2 | 3 | 3+2+2 | 1+1[e] | 3 | | 1/1 | 8 | 2 | 4 | 4 | | | | | | 10 |
| 8 | 3 | 4 | 2 | 2+1[e] | 4 | | | | | | | | | | | | |
| 12 | 5 | 4 | 3 | 4 | 4 | 24 | 2/1 | 12 | 3 | 6 | 6 | | | | | 50 | 15 |
| 12 | 6 | 6 | 2 | 6 | 6 | | | | | | | | | | | | |

**Figure 4.9.12**
Schematic layout of a single gym

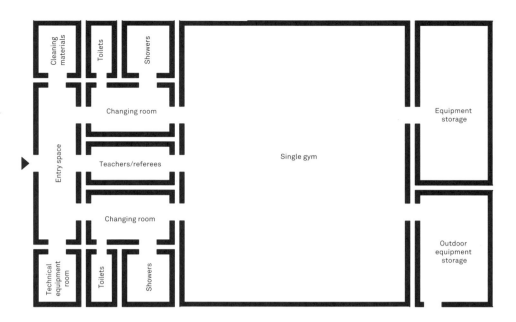

**Figure 4.9.13**
Schematic layout of a triple gymnasium

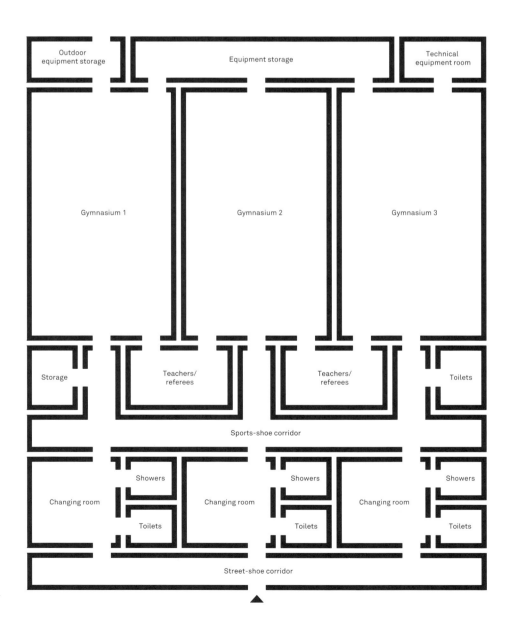

### 4.9.2.3 Stadiums

Stadiums accommodate large numbers of spectators at sports competitions. They can be monofunctional or allow for many types of sports (such as track and field plus soccer) along with other events, such as concerts. Their basic form is derived from the size of the playing field, which is typically bounded either partially or completely by grandstands. →Table 4.9.3 With stadiums that are used for track and field sports, a distinction is made between 3 different types. →Figure 4.9.14

Generally, specific requirements for the infrastructural design (→Table 4.9.4) and the technical equipment and facilities as well as the egress and evacuation routes (→Table 4.9.5) for stadiums are specified by the sports associations or defined in statutory regulations such as those governing places of assembly. Stadiums are constructed either without a roof, with a covered grandstand, or with a movable/retractable roof over the playing field (for concerts and other open-air events). They usually have floors covered with sports turf, elastic synthetic material, or compacted or loose granular material such as clay or sand (for tennis or beach volleyball, for example).

Table 4.9.3
Typical sports for various building forms

| Building form | Exemplary sports |
| --- | --- |
| Rectangular | Tennis, Soccer (Association Football), Equestrian sports, (Beach) Volleyball, Basketball |
| Oval | Track and field (possibly including soccer), Horse racing, Motorcycle racing, Ice sports, Track cycling |
| Circular | Cricket, Baseball, Soccer |
| Linear | Motor racing, Shooting sports |

Figure 4.9.14
Track and field – competition facility types A/B/C

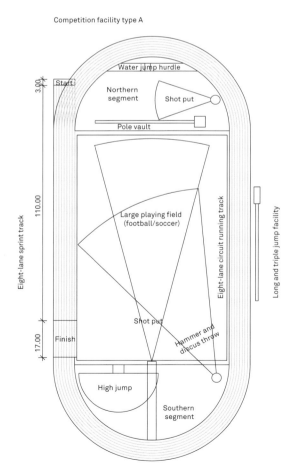

Competition facility type A

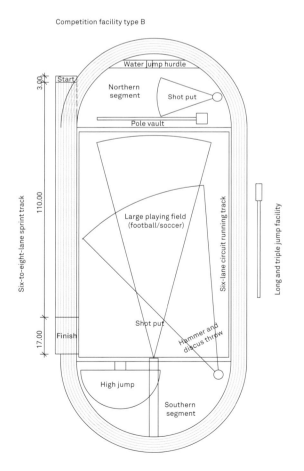

Competition facility type B

**Figure 4.9.14 (continuation)**
Track and field – competition
facility types A/B/C

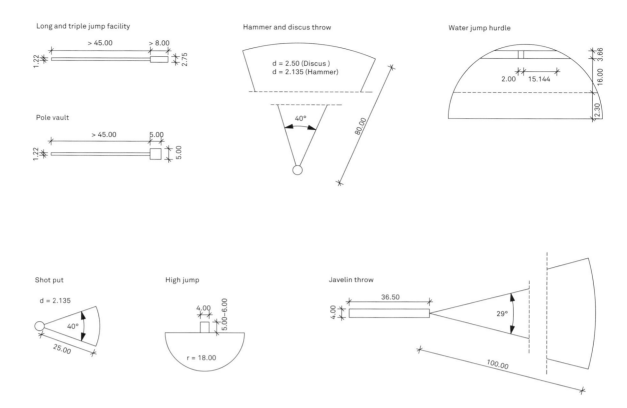

Long and triple jump facility

Pole vault

Hammer and discus throw

d = 2.50 (Discus )
d = 2.135 (Hammer)

40°

80.00

Water jump hurdle

2.00   15.144

3.66
16.00
2.30

Shot put

d = 2.135

40°

25.00

High jump

4.00

5.00–6.00

r = 18.00

Javelin throw

36.50

4.00

29°

100.00

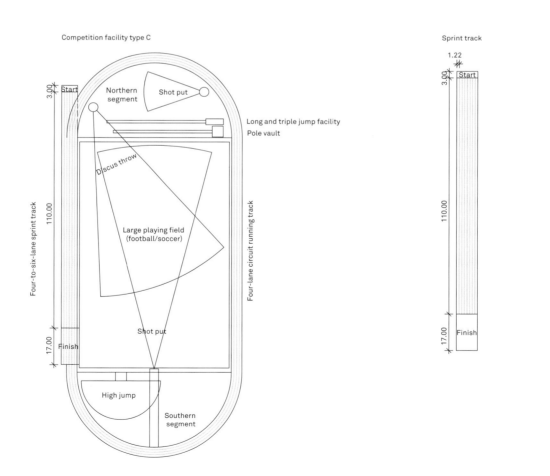

Competition facility type C

Start

3.00

Northern
segment

Shot put

Discus throw

Long and triple jump facility
Pole vault

Four-to-six-lane sprint track

110.00

Large playing field
(football/soccer)

Four-lane circuit running track

Shot put

17.00   Finish

High jump

Southern
segment

Sprint track

1.22

Start

3.00

110.00

17.00   Finish

Table 4.9.4 (this page)
Stadium criteria as per UEFA

Table 4.9.5 (facing page)
Requirements for soccer stadiums

| Requirements | Category I | Category II | Category III | Category IV (elite station) |
|---|---|---|---|---|
| **Stadium capacity** (At least 5% of the total capacity of the stadium must be reserved in a separate sector for fans of the visiting team.) | One grandstand with at least 200 seats | Minimum 3,000 seats | | Minimum 30,000 seats; of which at least 22,500 are roofed over |
| **Stands** (The use of provisional bleachers is prohibited.) | Standing room for spectators is permitted. | Only seating is permitted. Standing accommodations must remain closed. | | |
| **VIP seats** (The VIP seats must be located on the main grandstand between the two penalty areas, but preferably at the halfway line.) | Minimum of 50; 20 for the visiting team | Minimum of 400; 200 for the visiting team | Minimum of 750; 200 for the visiting team | Minimum of 1,500; 200 for the visiting team; Exclusive hospitality area 400 m² |
| **Floodlight system** (average illuminance in EV[lx]) | In the direction of permanently installed cameras: 800–1,400, In the direction of mobile cameras: 500–1,000 | | In the direction of permanently installed cameras: 1,200–1,400, In the direction of mobile cameras: 800–1,000 | In the direction of permanently installed cameras: min. 1,400, In the direction of mobile cameras: min. 1,000 |
| **Independent emergency generator** | | The generator must provide at least two-thirds of the required lighting capacity. | The generator must immediately and without interruption provide 100% of the required lighting capacity. | |
| **Video surveillance** | | | Continual video surveillance system, both inside and outside the stadium. The cameras must have a still-image function and be connected to color monitors that are located in the control room. | |
| **Playing field** (of natural or artificial turf) | Length: 100–110 m Width: 64–75 m | | Length: 105 m Width: 68 m | Length: 105 m Width: 68 m no fences whatsoever |
| **Parking spaces** (Parking spaces for at least 2 buses and 10 cars from the teams) | Minimum number of VIP seats in secure area: 20 | Minimum number of VIP seats in secure area: 100 | Minimum number of VIP seats in secure area: 100 + parking spaces for at least 400 buses in the vicinity of the stadium | |
| **Media-related areas** | Working area: min. 50 m² Platform for main camera: min. 4 m², space for 1 camera Press box: min. 20 seats TV/radio commentary positions: min. 2 Room capable of being used as a TV studio: 1 Outside broadcast van area: 100 m² | Working area: min. 100 m², for at least 50 media representatives Platform for main camera: min. 6 m², space for 2 cameras Press box: min. 20 seats, 10 with tables TV/radio commentary positions: min. 3 Room as TV studio (L × W × H): 5 × 5 × 2.30 m Outside broadcast van area: 200 m² Press room: Table, camera platform, podium, split box, sound system, chairs; min. 30 seats for media representatives Mixed zone: must be able to be set up between the dressing rooms and the parking areas for the team buses | Working area: min. 100 m², for at least 50 media representatives; Area for at least 15 photographers Platform for main camera: min. 6 m², space for 2 cameras Press box: min. 50 seats, 25 with tables TV/radio commentary positions: min. 5 Room as TV studio (L × W × H): 2, ea. 5 × 5 × 2.30 m Outside broadcast van area: 200 m² Press room: Table, camera platform, podium, split box, sound system, chairs; min. 50 seats for media representatives Mixed zone: must be able to be set up between the dressing rooms and the parking areas for the team buses | Working area: min. 200 m², for at least 75 media representatives; Area for at least 15 photographers Platform for main camera: min. 10 m², space for 4 cameras Press box: min. 100 seats (covered), 50 with tables TV/radio commentary positions: min. 25 Room as TV studio (L × W × H): 2, ea. 5 × 5 × 2.30 m, one of which is a presentation studio with a view of the playing field; 4 flash interview positions (2.50 m × 2.50 m) Outside broadcast van area: 1,000 m² Press room: Table, camera platform, podium, split box, sound system, chairs; min. 75 seats for media representatives Mixed zone: covered, for 50 media representatives |

| | | | |
|---|---|---|---|
| **Capacity** | 1st + 2nd national leagues min. 15,000 spectators, with a min. of 3,000 seats; 10% of the total capacity (seats and standees) shall be provided for fans of the visiting team. | 3rd league: min. 10,000 spectators, with a min. of 2,000 seats; 10% of the total capacity (seats and standees) shall be provided for fans of the visiting team. | Regional (minor) league: min. 5,000 spectators, with a min. of 2,000 seats; At least 10% of the total capacity must be reserved for fans of the visiting team, with a minimum of 500 persons. |
| **Sanitary facilities/ toilets** | Per 100 (for max. 1,000 people) Women's toilets: 1.2 Men's toilets: 0.8 Men's urinals: 1.2 | Per 100 (above 1,000 people) Women's toilets: 0.8 Men's toilets: 0.4 Men's urinals: 0.6 | Per additional 100 (above 20,000 people) Women's toilets: 0.4 Men's toilets: 0.3 Men's urinals: 0.6 |
| **Additional requirements** | One dressing room for each team, with a minimum of five showers, three individual seated toilets, seating for at least 25 people, one massage table, and one tactical board | Dressing room for referees, with one shower, one individual seated toilet, five seats, and a desk | Dedicated, direct, and secure access for both teams and the referees when going from their dressing rooms to the playing area and when arriving at or departing the stadium |
| **Facilities for spectators with disabilities** | The stadium must have dedicated access and seats for spectators with disabilities and their helpers. | In addition, persons with disabilities must have dedicated sanitary facilities as well as refreshment and catering facilities in the vicinity of the sector designated for their use. | One toilet for the disabled must be available for every 15 wheelchair users, but at least 1 in each stadium. |
| **External evacuation routes** | For emergency and rescue vehicles, special approach routes and deployment and maneuvering areas must be provided. The entrances to the stadium must be directly accessible from the approaches and deployment areas. | A two-lane evacuation route outside of the stadium shall be kept free with a no-parking zone; At least one vehicle access approach to the stadium interior shall be provided for emergency and rescue vehicles. | |
| **Internal evacuation routes** | Evacuation routes: Aisles and stepped aisles, exits from assembly rooms, necessary corridors and necessary stairways, exits to the outside, balconies serving as evacuation routes, roof terraces, exterior stairs, and outdoor evacuation routes on the premises shall all be kept free and accessible at all times. | Each story with occupiable rooms shall have at least two mutually independent physical evacuation routes; the same applies for blocks in the grandstands; routing on the same floor level within a shared necessary corridor is permissible; Evacuation routes may also lead to the outside on balconies, roof terraces, and exterior stairs. | Each story with more than 800 spectator positions needs its own evacuation route; Assembly spaces and other occupiable rooms with a minimum of 100 m² must each have at least two exits that are located as far apart as possible and which lead to the outside or to escape routes; The distance from any spectator position or from the grandstand to an exit from an assembly space may not exceed 30 m; if an assembly space has a clear height of more than 5 m, it is permissible to extend the distance to the nearest exit by 5 m for each 2.50 m of additional headroom, up to a maximum distance of 60 m. |
| **Width of rescue routes** | Width shall be calculated based on the maximum number of persons; clear width min. 1.20 m; Stadiums, whose roof cannot be closed: 1.20 m per 600 persons; in other closed areas: 1.20 m per 200 persons; widths only in 0.60 m increments | Clear width of necessary stairs shall not be more than 2.40 m; wider stairs are only permissible when the width is subdivided by handrails at a spacing of at least 2.40 m. | Evacuation gates shall be single-leaf and min. 1.80 m wide, with panic hardware, its outline highlighted with a contrasting color, identified with numerals or letters on both sides; can only be opened manually from the interior; doors in evacuation routes. |
| **Active fire protection** | In stadiums with more than 1,000 m² floor area, wall hydrants shall be installed; stadiums with more than 3,600 m² require an automatic fire-extinguishing system. | Assembly spaces, open kitchens, or similar facilities with a floor area of more than 30 m² must have a suitable automatic fire extinguishing system. | Assembly spaces and other occupiable spaces with more than 200 m² floor area and assembly spaces in basement levels must have a means of smoke extraction. |
| **Gates, approaches, grounds** | Walkways to the stadium shall be of sufficient dimensions for the volume of pedestrian traffic, shall preferably not cross vehicular traffic routes, and shall be adequately lit and signposted. | An outer fence shall amply surround and enclose the entire stadium complex site; minimum 2.20 m high; not easy to climb over, to pass through, to crawl under, or to remove. | At pedestrian and vehicular entrances, facilities with devices for entry control shall be installed; ticket booths and control devices shall be incorporated into the outer fence enclosure. |
| **Seating, aisles, stepped aisles** | At most 10 seats from the side of an aisle, in stadiums a max. 20 seats. Max. 20 seats between two side aisles; in stadiums max. 40 seats. In assembly spaces, there may be a maximum of 50 seats between two side aisles if, on each side of the assembly space, there is a door with a clear width of 1.20 m for each four rows of seats. | Stepped walkways Riser: 0.10–0.19 m Tread: min. 0.26 m; the floor of the space between rows of seating, and the floor of standee rows, must be at the same level as the adjacent tread of the stepped aisle; Stepped aisles must be made clearly distinguishable from the surrounding surfaces through the use of color markings. | |
| **Sectors, blocks, and barriers** | Subdivision of the spectator areas into at least 4 sectors, each with its own entrances, toilets, and kiosks; at boundaries of sectors and between seating and standing areas, partitions with a height of at least 2.20 m shall be installed and outfitted with 1.80 m wide, inward-opening evacuation gates. | Standing room must be arranged in blocks for a maximum of 2,500 spectators each, separated by barriers that are at least 2.20 m high and have separate entries. | Barriers, such as guards, railings, crush barriers, fences, barricades, or glass walls shall have a minimum height of 1.10 m; in front of rows of seats: guardrails 0.90 m high; with a parapet width of at least 0.20 m, the guardrail may be 0.80 m high; with a parapet width of at least 0.50 m, the guardrail may be 0.70 m high. |
| **Miscellaneous** | In standee areas, safety railings known as crush barriers are necessary; at a spacing of every 5 rows of steps: crush barriers with a height of 1.10 m and lengths of 3–5.50 m; at least 0.25 m longer at both ends, as lateral clearance between the crush barriers, max. 5 m. | Lateral clearance between the crush barriers behind the endlines and the sidelines (touchlines): safety clearances of 7.50 m and 6 m; outside the boundary lines of the field of play: min. 1.5 m wide natural or artificial turf surface, the overall playing area should measure 120 m × 80 m. | The field of play (pitch) is to be separated from the spectator areas by an enclosure (metal fence, laminated safety glass, etc.) with a height of min. 2.20 m, a trench that is difficult to pass, a combination of enclosure and trench, or by raising the first spectator row at least 2 m above the level of the playing field. |

## 4.9.2.4 Swimming Pools

Swimming pools serve the purposes of competitive and general sports, recreation, or relaxation and can be categorized according to the type of facility, their nature of use, or the individual types of pool basins. → **Figure 4.9.15** As a rough guide, the land required per square meter of water surface is 6–8 m² for indoor swimming pools, up to 12 m² for recreational pools, and up to 16 m² for outdoor swimming pools.

Pools for leisure and relaxation are usually designed without constraint, whereas recreational and competitive swimming pools are much more systematized and regulated. Typical swimming pools are constructed in lengths of 25 m or, for competition conditions, 50 m. → **Figures 4.9.17 and 4.9.18** In smaller facilities, different types of pools are often combined as a single surface of water with distinct areas, in which case transitions between different depths may only have a maximum slope of 30°. → **Table 4.9.6**

The swimming areas are flanked by the entrance area, changing rooms, and sanitary facilities, the internal management, including pool supervisor, and very extensive technical equipment, most of which is located below the swimming pool itself. → **Figure 4.9.16**

Figure 4.9.15
Categorization of swimming pools

Figure 4.9.16
Schematic layout of an indoor swimming pool

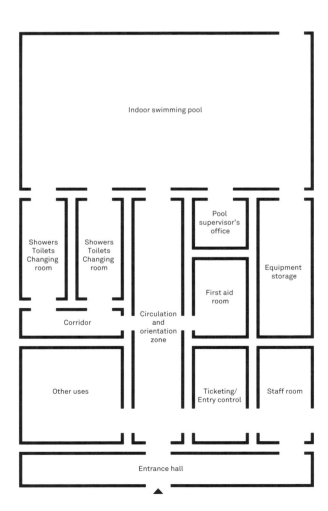

Table 4.9.6
Water depths of swimming pools

| Pool type | Water depth |
|---|---|
| Wading pool | max. 0.50/0.60 m |
| Nonswimmer pool | max. 1.35 m |
| Swimmer pool | min. 1.35 m, 1.80 m recommended |
| Water polo pool | min. 1.80 m, 2.00 m recommended |
| Olympic swimming pool | min. 2.00 m, 3.00 m recommended |
| Diving pool | min. 3.20 m, up to 4.50 m (depending on tower height) |
| Movable floor pools | Depth adjustable |

Figure 4.9.17
Swimming pool (50 m lanes)
for competitions

Source: FINA

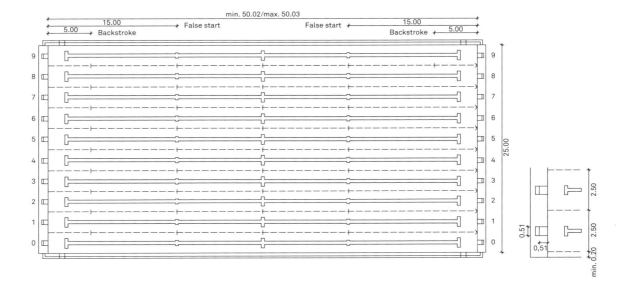

Figure 4.9.18
Diving pool for competitions

Source: FINA

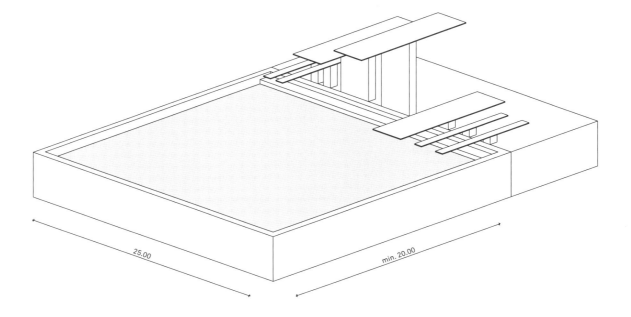

## 4.9.2.5 Indoor Ice Rinks

Ice rinks serve leisure activities as well as a variety of ice sports. German standards make a distinction between outdoor rinks (with no protection against weather), semienclosed rinks (horizontal weather protection), enclosed rinks (horizontal and vertical partial protection against the weather; min. 30 percent open), and indoor rinks (not directly influenced by weather). The ice rinks themselves constitute the heart of the building and their dimensions are determined by the sport activities they support. ↗ 4.9.3.2 Areas and Rooms/Sports Areas The ice rinks are surrounded by rink boards (dasher boards) approximately 1.20 m high, and for hockey rinks, this is augmented for a distance up to 4.00 m in front of the goal line by a dimensionally stable, transparent material to a height of 1.60–2.00 m (with nets above). Due to the use of ice skates, the floors and the walls must be designed to be particularly hard-wearing (up to a height of 0.60 m). Besides typical ancillary spaces such as changing rooms and administrative areas, ice rinks need special back-of-house facilities such as refrigeration chillers, a room for the ice resurfacer, a melting pit for ice rub, and various workshops. → Table 4.9.7 and Figure 4.9.19

**Typical ice sports are:**
- Figure skating
- Speed skating
- Short track speed skating
- Ice dancing
- Ice hockey
- Curling
- Ice stock sport

**Figure 4.9.19**
Schematic layout of an indoor ice rink

As per DIN 18036

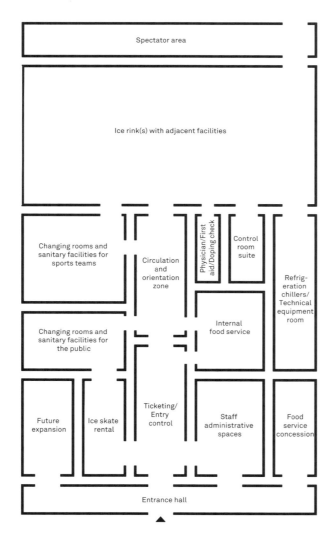

Table 4.9.7
Ancillary spaces for indoor
ice rinks

Source: DIN 18036

| Spatial group | Rooms/areas | Quantity Minimum size | | | Remarks |
|---|---|---|---|---|---|
| | | a | b | c | |
| Entrance area | Entry court | 1 | 1 | 1 | |
| | | 120 m² | 120 m² | 180 m² | |
| | Entrance area with vestibule, ticket counter, cash office, entry control, and toilets | 1 | 1 | 1 | Possibly just as covered outdoor entry area |
| | | 80 m² | 80 m² | 120 m² | |
| | Ice skate rental | 1 | 1 | 1 | With sharpening booth |
| | | 30 m² | 40 m² | 55 m² | |
| Area for public skating | Changing room for public skating | 1 | 1 | 1 | |
| | | 150 m² | 150 m² | 300 m² | |
| | Toilets for public skating | 2 | 2 | 2 | |
| | | 20 m² | 20 m² | 30 m² | |
| | First aid room | 1 | 1 | 1 | |
| | | 10 m² | 10 m² | 10 m² | |
| Athletes' zone | Changing room for team sports and figure skating | 4 | – | 4 | Calculation basis: 23 ice hockey players + 2 officials |
| | | 45 m² | – | 45 m² | For top-class sport events |
| | Sanitary facilities for team sports and figure skating | 4 | – | 4 | • Changing room 75 m² • Sanitary facilities 30 m² |
| | | 20 m² | – | 20 m² | • Drying room 20 m² |
| | Drying room for sports clothing | 4 | – | 4 | |
| | | 10 m² | – | 10 m² | |
| | Equipment and laundry room | 4 | – | 4 | |
| | | 5 m² | – | 5 m² | |
| | Skate sharpening room | 5 m² | 5 m² | 5 m² | |
| | Referees'/trainers' room with sanitary facilities | 2 | 2 | 3 | For all ice sports |
| | | 10 m² | 10 m² | 10 m² | |
| | Changing room for speed skating | – | 2 | 2 | Calculation basis: 20 to 30 speed skaters |
| | | – | 20 m² | 20 m² | |
| | Sanitary facilities for speed skating | – | 2 | 2 | |
| | | – | 10 m² | 10 m² | |
| Ice rink zone | Room for rink supervisor | 1 | 1 | 1 | For all ice sports, except speed skating |
| | | 10 m² | 10 m² | 10 m² | |
| | Room for director, finish line judge, and timekeeping | – | 1 | 1 | Only for speed skating |
| | | – | 20 m² | 20 m² | |
| | Scoring room (evaluation room) | – | 1 | 1 | For speed skating, if required also for figure skating, ice dancing, and ice stock sport (Bavarian curling) |
| | | – | 10 m² | 10 m² | |
| | Storage room for ice sports equipment | 1 | 1 | 1 | For ice hockey: Goals (for speed skating: curve guards) |
| | | 20 m² | 100 m² | 120 m² | |
| | Staff room with lounge area, 2 changing room zones, 2 sanitary facility zones | 1 | 1 | 1 | For operating personnel (supervisor, technicians, sales, rentals) |
| | | 30 m² | 30 m² | 45 m² | |

Table 4.9.7 (continuation)
Ancillary spaces for indoor
ice rinks

Source: DIN 18036

| Spatial group | Rooms/areas | Quantity | | | Remarks |
|---|---|---|---|---|---|
| | | Minimum size | | | |
| | | a | b | c | |
| Ice rink zone | Resting places for ice skaters and companions | 100 | 100 | 200 | As seating in the surrounding area, if there are no dedicated spectator seats |
| | | – | – | – | |
| | Concession stand (snacks), possibly with warming room | To suit local circumstances | | | For skaters and companions |
| Building services area | Room for chiller equipment | 1 | 1 | 1 | Guideline values for the spatial program of an ice sport facility with no spectator area |
| | | 80 m² | 130 m² | 170 m² | |
| | Room for low-voltage network main distribution | 1 | 1 | 1 | |
| | | 10 m² | 15 m² | 20 m² | |
| | Battery room | 1 | 1 | 1 | |
| | | 10 m² | 10 m² | 15 m² | |
| | Room for medium voltage switchgear | 1 | 1 | 1 | |
| | | 15 m² | 25 m² | 35 m² | |
| | Transformer room | 1 | 1 | 1 | |
| | | 5 m² | 15 m² | 20 m² | |
| | Room for ventilation equipment | 1 | – | 1 | Only for indoor ice rinks. An additional room for ventilation equipment must be provided for a standard speed skating track. |
| | | 80 m² | – | Dependent on number of spectators | |
| | Room for heating system for the premises | 1 | 1 | 1 | |
| | | 20 m² | 20 m² | 30 m² | |
| | Room for utility connections | 1 | 1 | 1 | |
| | | 10 m² | 10 m² | 10 m² | |
| | Room for ice resurfacing machine | 1 | 1 | 1 | Possibly with greasing pit |
| | | 25 m² | 40 m² | 40 m² | |
| | Melting pit for ice rub | 1 | 1 | 1 | Minimum 2 m depth |
| | | 15 m² | 30 m² | 40 m² | |
| | Workshop with rink supervisor's room | 1 | 1 | 1 | |
| | | 20 m² | 20 m² | 20 m² | |
| | Storage rooms | 1 | 1 | 1 | With connection to operational yard. The room sizes do not take into account multipurpose use. |
| | | 30 m² | 100 m² | 130 m² | |
| | Garage for motor vehicles (snow removal equipment, maintenance equipment) | 1 | 1 | 1 | Possibly combined with the room for ice resurfacing machine; gas station |
| | | 30 m² | 60 m² | 75 m² | |
| Supplementary rooms (as required) | Lobby for events | 1 | 1 | 1 | Toilets in sufficient quantity; 1 ticket booth (possibly mobile) per 1,000 spectator positions; for multipurpose use, possibly spectator coat check. |
| | | For capacities over 500 spectators, enlarge the entrance hall by 5 m² for each additional 100 spectators | | | |
| | Service businesses, such as a sports boutique or hairstylist | To suit local circumstances | | | |
| | Administrative spaces | To suit local circumstances | | | |

Table 4.9.7 (continuation)
Ancillary spaces for indoor
ice rinks

Source: DIN 18036

| Spatial group | Rooms/areas | Quantity Minimum size | | | Remarks |
|---|---|---|---|---|---|
| | | a | b | c | |
| Supplementary rooms (as required) | Cafeteria or restaurant | To suit local circumstances | | | |
| | Gymnastics room with apparatus storage | 1 + 1 | | | Square, minimum height 4 m |
| | | 150 + 15 m² | | | |
| | Conditioning room | 1 | | | Minimum 3.5 m ceiling height |
| | | 80 m² | | | |
| | Sauna | 1 | 1 | 1 | |
| | | To suit local circumstances | | | |
| | Club rooms | To suit local circumstances | | | |
| | Spectator positions | Depending on local conditions, predominantly as seats | | | Seating position: minimum 0.5 m wide, minimum 0.8 m deep (including circulation space of minimum 0.45 m directly in front of the seat) and 0.4 m high. Standing position (tiered): minimum 0.5 m wide, minimum 0.4 m/maximum 0.45 m deep, and minimum 0.2 m high. |
| | Control room | 1 | 1 | 1 | For all ice sports, except speed skating |
| | | 10 m² | 10 m² | 10 m² | |
| | Room for fire and police department use | 1 | 1 | 1 | |
| | | 20 m² | 20 m² | 20 m² | |
| | Room for security service | 1 | 1 | 1 | |
| | | 15 m² | 15 m² | 15 m² | |
| | Training room/conference room for judges/referees | 1 | 1 | 1 | |
| | | 40 m² | 40 m² | 40 m² | |
| | Positions for the press | To suit local circumstances | | | Seat with desk 0.75 m × min. 0.8 m |
| | Positions for radio | To suit local circumstances | | | Commentator's booth 1.8 m × 2 m |
| | Positions for television | To suit local circumstances | | | Television production and camera positions: In stadiums, it must be ensured that the cameras necessary for producing the television signal have fixed positions (on platforms where appropriate) in the grandstand area and optionally in the area surrounding the playing field. There must be an unobstructed view of the entire playing field from all the camera positions at all times. Commentator's booth 1.80 m × 2.00 m |
| | Guest dressing room | To suit local circumstances | | | |
| | Media workroom | | | | |
| | Interview room | | | | |
| | Room for medical care | 1 | 1 | 1 | Not essential for doping control area |
| | | 30 m² | 30 m² | 30 m² | |
| | Doping control area (waiting room, control room) | 1 | 1 | 1 | Toilet, washbasin |
| | | 40 m² | 40 m² | 40 m² | |
| | Caretaker's apartment | | | | |

### 4.9.2.6 Riding Halls

Riding arenas offer riders and horses free movement regardless of the weather conditions and should not be smaller than 15 × 30 m so that horses are able to gallop without any basic restrictions. As a rule, tournament dimensions of 20 × 40 m, 20 × 60 m, or 25 × 65 m are used. → **Figure 4.9.20** For longeing (lungeing) horses, there are also round and square longeing halls with diameters of 16–24 m. Riding halls are constructed as open, unheated buildings usually made with steel or laminated wood beams and roofed over with sandwich panels. To protect from the wind, open portions of the facade are typically covered with nets or

clad with perforated metal sheets. The halls are usually lined along the perimeter with wood kickboards measuring approximately 1.50–1.60 m high, with entrance doors that are approximately 4.00 m wide. → **Figure 4.9.21** This allows two horses with riders to safely enter the building at the same time. The riding hall floor is ordinarily made from a sand mixture (such as sand combined with sawdust or fleece shreds). For dust control and maintenance, an automatic sprinkler system is often installed within the roof structure or an irrigation system is built into the floor (so-called ebb and flow system).

**Figure 4.9.20**
Dimensions of riding halls

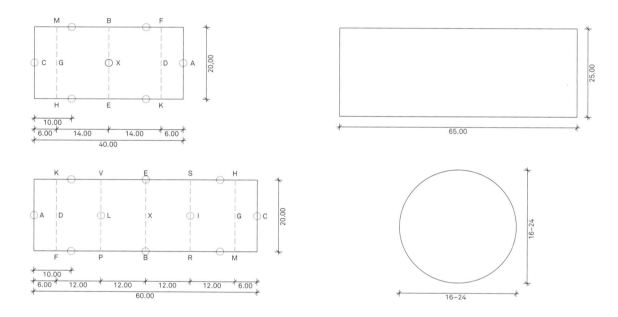

**Figure 4.9.21**
Cross section of a riding hall

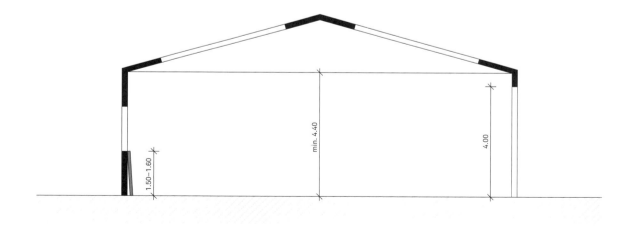

### 4.9.2.7 Climbing Gyms

Climbing gyms offer opportunities to climb at various levels of difficulty under controlled conditions, even during inclement weather. Besides various climbing walls, such facilities ordinarily have bouldering areas, ropes courses, outdoor areas, and auxiliary functions such as a ticket counter/information desk, retail store, restaurant, seminar room, and changing rooms. →**Figure 4.9.22** Climbing walls are installed in the space on steel or wood substructures and have variable options for mounting the hand holds and changing the overall configuration, thus making it possible to continually offer new climbing routes. The bouldering area is usually no more than 3–4 m high and is equipped with mats and impact-absorbing floor surfaces for unsecured climbing. A climbing gym should have a clear height of at least 10 m, ideally 15 m. A combination of indoor and outdoor facilities is advantageous to encourage year-round use.

**Figure 4.9.22**
Schematic layout of
a climbing gym

**Figure 4.9.23**
Examples of climbing walls

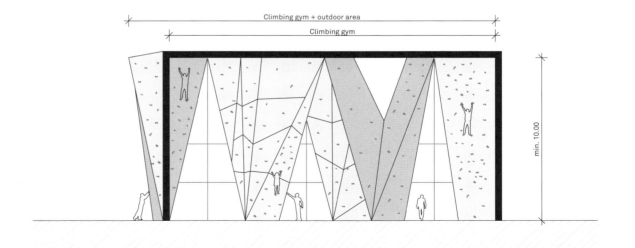

## 4.9.2.8 Fitness and Wellness

Fitness and wellness facilities appear as stand-alone typologies or they are integrated into other sports facilities and typologies, such as hotels. Fitness areas not only accommodate classic strength training on exercise equipment, but also often cater to diverse activities in the fields of preventative health, gymnastics, yoga, or various trend sports. →Figure 4.2.24 All areas should be capable of being furnished and used flexibly so they can be adapted to changing offers without any construction measures.

**Typical areas and rooms in fitness centers are:**
- Equipment for targeted strength training (such as cable machines, leg press, universal gym trainer)
- Cardiovascular exercise devices, such as ergometers, rowing machines, spin bikes, treadmills, and step machines
- Area for dumbbells and weights, including weight benches
- Rooms/areas for group sports (such as yoga, gymnastics, aerobics, Pilates)
- Where applicable, preventative health fields (such as consultation, physical therapy, back training)
- Trainer
- Changing areas, including sanitary facilities
- Bar

Wellness, spa, massage, and sauna facilities are, depending on the typology, often grouped together or integrated into other facilities, such as hotels, fitness studios, or sports areas. →Figure 4.9.25 Sauna facilities generally include indoor and outdoor areas with different types of saunas, along with steam baths, showers, plunge pools, and relaxation areas, which are combined according to the specific concepts of each operator. Massage facilities include individual rooms or larger rooms subdivided by curtains, with massage tables, washbasins, and cabinets. Wellness and spa facilities should offer diverse options to support techniques for relaxation and stress management within a suitably tranquil environment.

Figure 4.9.24
Schematic layout of a fitness area

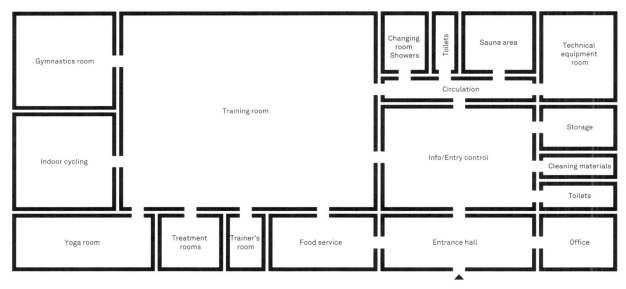

Figure 4.9.25
Schematic layout of a hotel
spa/wellness facility

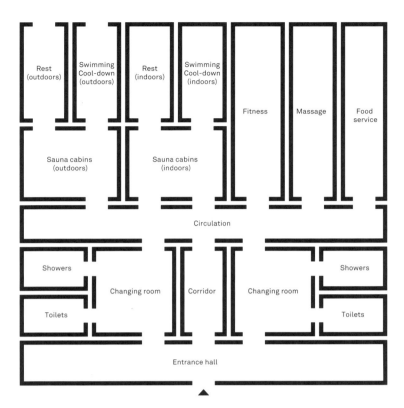

### 4.9.3  Areas and Rooms

**External circulation**  ↗Chapter 3.1

**Entrance area**  ↗449  ↗Chapter 3.2.1

**Custodian's office, ancillary rooms**  ↗449, ↗472

**Stairs, elevators**  ↗Chapter 3.2.4, ↗Chapter 3.2.7

**Corridors, internal circulation**  ↗Chapter 3.2.2

**Workplaces**  ↗Chapter 3.3.1

**Payment/ticketing areas**  ↗449

**Sports areas**  ↗450

**Sports equipment**  ↗460

**Equipment storage**  ↗460

**Stands/spectator areas**  ↗467  ↗Chapter 3.4

**Conference rooms**  ↗Chapter 3.4.1

**Staff kitchens**  ↗Chapter 3.6

**Cafeterias/canteens**  ↗Chapter 4.7, ↗Chapter 3.4.3

**Break rooms**  ↗Chapter 3.8.1

**Toilets, sanitary facilities**  ↗472  ↗Chapter 3.5.3

**Changing rooms/lockers**  ↗472  ↗Chapter 3.8.2

**Storage/archive rooms**  ↗472  ↗Chapter 3.7.2

**Server rooms**  ↗Chapter 3.9.8

**First aid rooms**  ↗Chapter 3.8.3

**Janitor's closets**  ↗Chapter 3.8.4

**Mechanical equipment rooms**  ↗Chapter 3.9

## 4.9.3.1 Entrance Areas

The entrance areas of sports and recreation buildings usually experience high traffic at peak times and must therefore be designed for the anticipated streams of visitors. The spectrum ranges from a sports team or school class waiting in front of a gymnasium to thousands of spectators entering a sports stadium. Entrance areas serve as meeting places and zones where people wait for entry or seek ride sharing opportunities to travel to away games, and need places where, among other things, people can sit or stand and momentarily put down their sport bags without obstructing the circulation areas. Where appropriate, large vestibule areas can function as buffer zones for this purpose. More importantly, requirements for security and access control must be taken into account. Such considerations range from custodians' offices that enable staff to maintain a general overview and payment/ticketing zones for controlling admittance to turnstiles and security screening of individuals at sports stadiums. → **Figures 4.9.26 and 4.9.27,** ↗ Chapter 3.2.1 Spaces/Internal Circulation/Entrance Areas

**Figure 4.9.26**
Payment/ticketing areas
for patrons

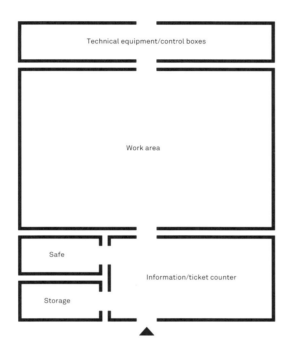

Technical equipment/control boxes

Work area

Safe

Information/ticket counter

Storage

**Figure 4.9.27**
Example of a combination
custodian's office and payment/
ticketing counter

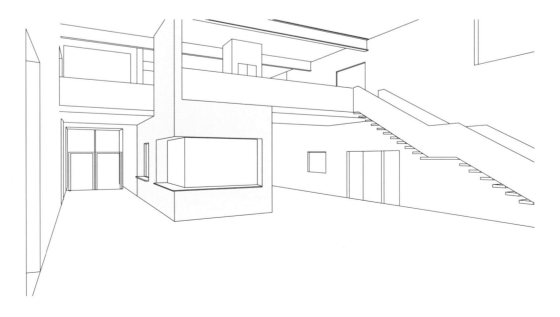

### 4.9.3.2 Sports Areas

The space requirements for individual sports areas are generally specified by the governing bodies, which establish differentiated requirements for many sports according to league or class affiliation in regard to the dimensions of the playing surface, movement and clearance areas, ceiling heights, surface qualities, physical conditions, and other parameters.

Table 4.9.8
Playing field sizes of various sports

Source: DIN 18032-1

| Sport | Area of playing field, court, or lane/track | | | Delineated space including clearances | | | Clear height | Remarks |
|---|---|---|---|---|---|---|---|---|
| | Length | Width | Area | Length | Width | Area | | |
| Acrobatic gymnastics | 12.00 m | 12.00 m | 144 m² | 14.00 m | 14.00 m | 196 m² | 5.50 m | |
| American football | 109.72 m | 48.76 m | 5,350 m² | 113.75 m | 50.80 m | 5,779 m² | | |
| Apparatus gymnastics | 29.00 m | 16.00 m | 464 m² | 36.00 m | 16.00 m | 576 m² | 7.00 m | For national and international events: 1 m clearance required on the long sides and 3 m at the ends |
| Archery | 30.00–90.00 m | 4.00–5.00 m | 120–450 m² | 280.00–340.00 m | 4.00–5.00 m | 1,120–1,700 m² | | |
| Artistic (trick) cycling | 14.00 m | 11.00 m | 154 m² | 16.00–18.00 m | 11.00–13.00 m | 176–234 m² | 4.00 m | |
| Badminton | 13.40 m | 6.10 m | 82 m² | 15.50 m | 6.70 m | 122 m² | 9.00 (7.00) m | 7 m is sufficient for national events |
| Baseball | 27.43 m | 27.43 m | 753 m² | 121.92 m | 121.92 m | 14,864 m² | | Diagonal playing direction |
| Basketball | 28.00 m | 15.00 m | 420 m² | 32.00 m | 19.00 m | 608 m² | 7.00 m | |
| Beach ball | 20.00–30.00 m | 10.00–20.00 m | 200–600 m² | 30.00 m | 20.00 m | 600 m² | | |
| Beachvolleyball | 16.00 m | 8.00 m | 128 m² | 22.00 m | 14.00 m | 308 m² | | |
| Boules | 27.50 m | 2.50–4.00 m | 69–110 m² | 27.50 m | 2.50–4.00 m | 69–110 m² | | |
| Bowling | 19.20 m | 1.06 m | 20 m² | 23.73 m | 1.04 m | 25 m² | | |
| Boxing | 4.90–6.10 m | 4.90–6.10 m | 24–38 m² | 5.90–7.10 m | 5.90–7.10 m | 35–51 m² | 4.00 m | |
| Casting | 100.00 m | 50.00 m | 5,000 m² | 100.00 m | 50.00 m | 5,000 m² | | |
| Cricket | 20.12 m | 2.05 m | 62 m² | 150.00 m | 90.00 m | 13,500 m² | | Field has elliptical shape |
| Curling | 45.72 m | 5.02 m | 230 m² | 46.00 m | 6.25 m | 269 m² | 4.00–7.00 m | min. 3 curling sheets per facility |
| Cycle ball/cycle polo | 14.00 m | 11.00 m | 154 m² | 16.00–18.00 m | 11.00–13.00 m | 176–234 m² | 4.00 m | |
| Darts | 2.37 m | 1.00 m | 2.37 m² | | | | | Side clearance from sheet to wall: min. 0.90 m; between two sheets: min. 1.80 m |
| Dressage | 20.00 m | 40.00–60.00 m | 800–1,200 m² | 20.00 m | 40.00–60.00 m | 800–1,200 m² | | Standardized dressage arena |
| Equestrianism (horseback riding) | 16.00–25.00 m | 20.00–65.00 m | 320–1,625 m² | 18.00–27.00 m | 22.00–67.00 m | 396–1,809 m² | 4.40 m | |

## 4.9.3 Areas and Rooms

Table 4.9.8 (continuation)
Playing field sizes of various sports

Source: DIN 18032-1

| Sport | Area of playing field, court, or lane/track | | | Delineated space including clearances | | | Clear height | Remarks |
|---|---|---|---|---|---|---|---|---|
| | Length | Width | Area | Length | Width | Area | | |
| Fencing | 14.00 m | 1.50–2.00 m | 21–48 m² | 19.00–30.00 m | 7.80–8.00 m | 148–240 m² | 4.00 m | |
| Field hockey | 91.40 m | 55.00 m | 5,027 m² | 101.40 m | 63.00 m | 6,389 m² | 5.50 m | |
| Fistball | 50.00 m | 20.00 m | 1,000 m² | 66.00 m | 32.00 m | 2,112 m² | | |
| Football tennis | 12.80–18.00 m | 8.20 m | 105–148 m² | 19.80–25.00 m | 14.20 m | 282–355 m² | | |
| Futsal (five-a-side indoor soccer) | 38.00–42.00 m | 20.00–25.00 m | 760–1,050 m² | 39.00–46.00 m | 21.00–26.00 m | 819–1,196 m² | | |
| Handball | 40.00 m | 20.00 m | 800 m² | 44.00 m | 22.00 m | 968 m² | 7.00 m | |
| Ice hockey | 60.00 m | 26.00–30.00 m | 1,560–1,800 m² | 59.00–64.00 m | 30.50–34.50 m | 1,800–2,208 m² | | 3 m safety clearance at access area |
| Indoor hockey | 36.00–44.00 m | 18.00–22.00 m | 648–968 m² | 40.00–48.00 m | 19.00–23.00 m | 760–1,104 m² | 5.50 m | |
| Judo | 8.00–10.00 m | 8.00–10.00 m | 64–100 m² | 14.00–16.00 m | 14.00–16.00 m | 196–256 m² | 4.00 m | |
| Lacrosse | 102.00 m | 55.00 m | 5,610 m² | 115.00 m | 60.00 m | 6,900 m² | | |
| Netball | 30.00 m | 15.00 m | 450 m² | 32.00 m | 17.00 m | 544 m² | 5.50 m | |
| Nine-pin bowling | 19.50 m | 1.50 m | 30 m² | 25.00 m | 1.50 m | 38 m² | | |
| Polo | 274.00 m | 146.00 m | 40,004 m² | 274.00 m | 146.00 m | 40,004 m² | | |
| Rhythmic gymnastics | 13.00 m | 13.00 m | 169 m² | 14.00 m | 14.00 m | 196 m² | 8.00 m | |
| Rugby | 120.00 m | 68.00 m | 8,160 m² | 125.00 m | 73.00 m | 9,125 m² | | |
| Schlagball (rounders) | 70.00 m | 25.00 m | 1,750 m² | 80.00 m | 45.00 m | 3,600 m² | | |
| Soccer (FIFA standard) | 105.00 m | 68.00 m | 7,140 m² | 120.00 m | 80.00 m | 9,600 m² | 5.50 m | |
| Soccer, general | 90.00–120.00 m | 45.00–90.00 m | 4,050–10,800 m² | 94.00–124.00 m | 47.00–92.00 m | 4,418–11,408 m² | 5.50 m | |
| Squash | 9.75 m | 6.40 m | 63 m² | 9.75 m | 6.40 m | 63 m² | 2.13–4.57 m | |
| Table tennis | 2.74 m | 1.525 m | 4.20 m² | 14.00 m | 7.00 m | 98 m² | 5.00 m | |
| Tennis | 23.77 m | 8.23–10.97 m | 196–261 m² | 36.57 m | 18.27 m | 669 m² | 7.00 m | |
| Trampoline | 7.57 m | 3.03 m | 23 m² | 15.57 m | 11.03 m | 172 m² | 8.00 m | |
| Ultimate Frisbee | 109.73 m | 36.58 m | 4,014 m² | 112.00 m | 39.00 m | 4,368 m² | | |
| Volleyball | 18.00 m | 9.00 m | 162 m² | 24.00 m | 15.00 m | 360 m² | 7.00 m | |
| Weightlifting | 4.00 m | 4.00 m | 16 m² | 10.00 m | 10.00 m | 100 m² | 4.00 m | |
| Wrestling | 9.00–12.00 m | 9.00–12.00 m | 81–144 m² | 13.00–16.00 m | 13.00–16.00 m | 169–256 m² | 4.00 m | |
| Wheel gymnastics | 23.00 m | 3.00 m | 69 m² | 27.00 m | 15.00 m | 405 m² | 4.00 m | |

**Figure 4.9.28**
Playing field dimensions for soccer (association football)

Soccer

Indoor soccer (Futsal)

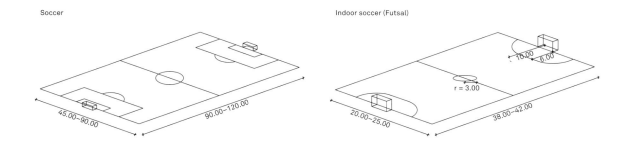

Soccer (as per FIFA standard)

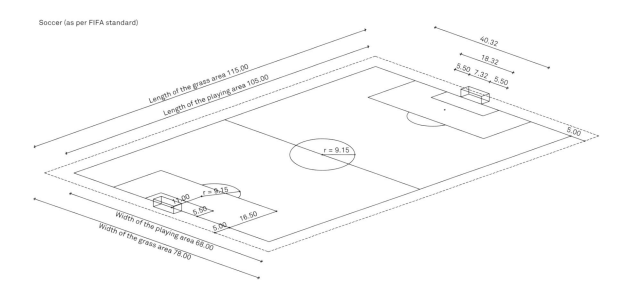

**Figure 4.9.29 (left)**
Court dimensions for handball

**Figure 4.9.30 (right)**
Court dimensions basketball

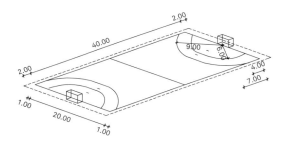

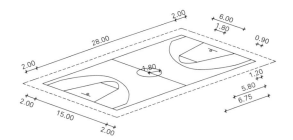

**Figure 4.9.31 (left)**
Court dimensions for volleyball

**Figure 4.9.32 (right)**
Court dimensions for beach volleyball

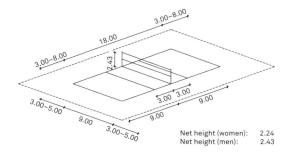

Net height (women):  2.24
Net height (men):  2.43

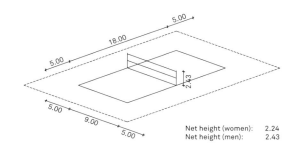

Net height (women):  2.24
Net height (men):  2.43

**Figure 4.9.33**
Playing field dimensions
for fistball

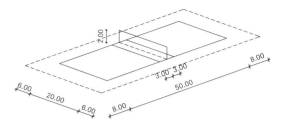

Net height (women): 1.90
Net height (men):    2.00

**Figure 4.9.34**
Playing field dimensions
for rugby

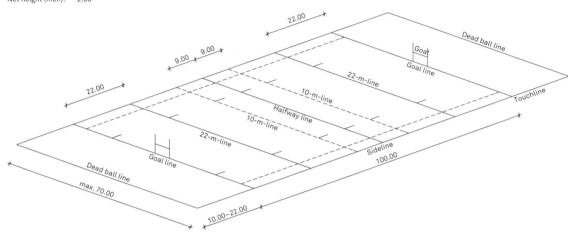

**Figure 4.9.35**
Playing field dimensions
for American football

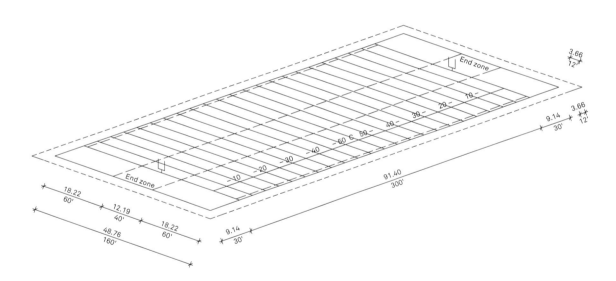

**Figure 4.9.36 (left)**
Baseball diamond

**Figure 4.9.37 (right)**
Dimensions for schlagball

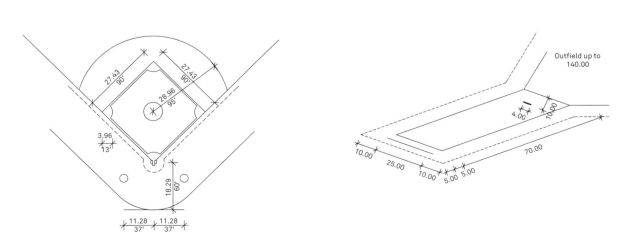

**Figure 4.9.38**
Playing field dimensions
for lacrosse

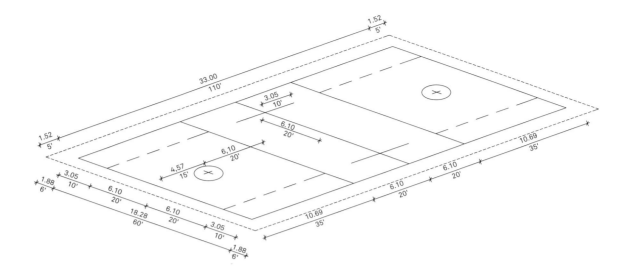

**Figure 4.9.39**
Playing field dimensions
for cricket

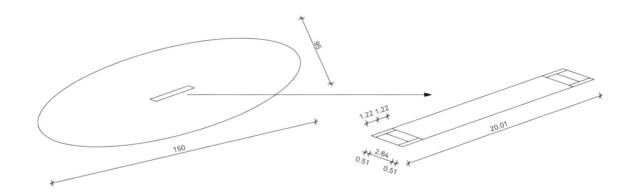

**Figure 4.9.40**
Playing field dimensions
for polo

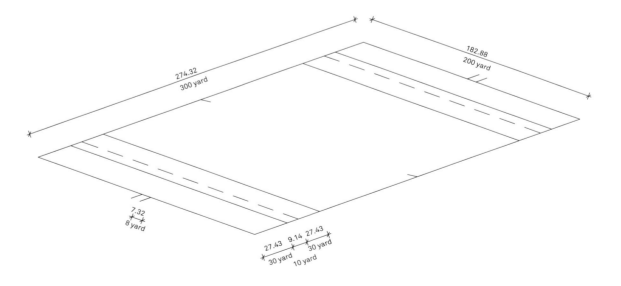

**Figure 4.9.41**
Playing field dimensions
for field hockey

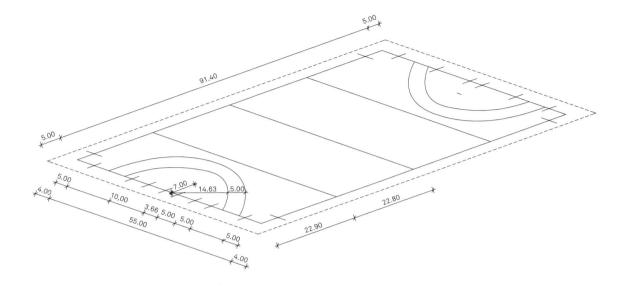

**Figure 4.9.42**
Court dimensions for tennis

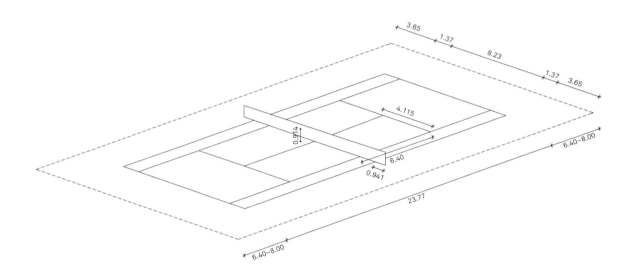

**Figure 4.9.43**
Court dimensions for badminton

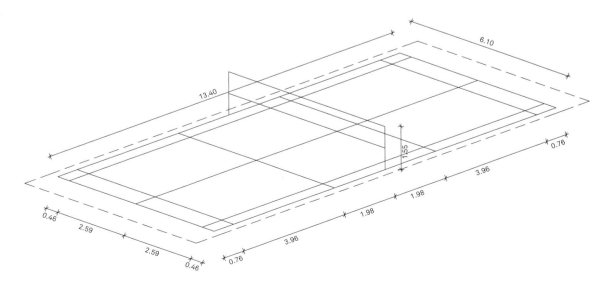

**Figure 4.9.44**
Court dimensions for squash

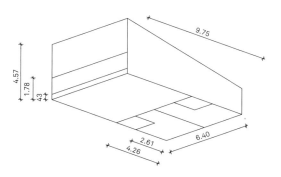

**Figure 4.9.45**
Lane dimensions for (ten-pin)
bowling/nine-pin bowling

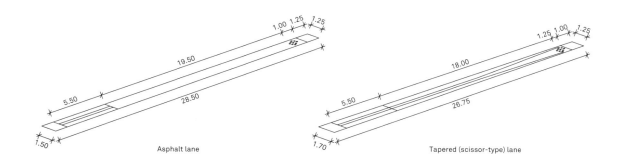

Asphalt lane                    Tapered (scissor-type) lane

**Figure 4.9.46 (left)**
Dimensions for judo

**Figure 4.9.47 (right)**
Dimensions for fencing

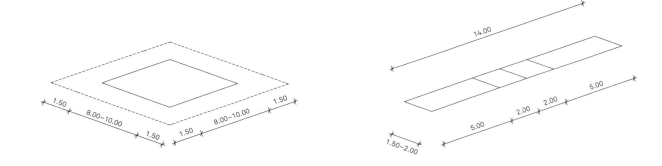

**Figure 4.9.48**
Ice hockey rink

Source: DIN 18036

1  Goal judge
2  Goal crease
3  Goal line, red, 0.05 m wide
4  Radius, 7.00 to 8.00 m
5  Blue line, 0.30 m wide
6  Players' bench, team A
7  Players' bench, team B
8  Penalty bench, team A
9  Penalty bench, team B
10  Scorekeeper's bench
11  End zone face-off spot and
    circle
12  Neutral zone face-off spot
13  Center line, red, 0.30 m wide
14  Center face-off spot and circle

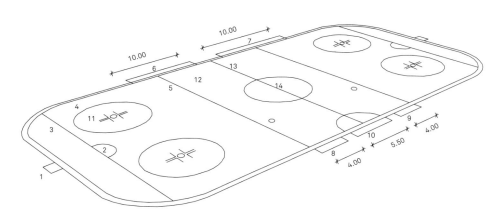

**Figure 4.9.49**
Various speed skating rinks

Source: DIN 18036

Left
1  Start for 300 m and 5,000 m
2  Start for 1,000 m
3  Start for 1,500 m
4  Start for 500 m
5  Start for 10,000 m
6  Finish for 1,000 m
7  Finish for 500 m, 1,500 m, 3,000 m, 5,000 m, 10,000 m

Right
1  Start for 1,000 m and 500 m
2  Start for 1,000 m, 3,000 m, 5,000 m
3  Finish line

Below
1  Start for semifinal
A  2 × A = 57.71 m
B  radius = 2 × 8.50 m × π
   = 53.71 m
   = 1 round = 111.12

Standard speed skating track with markings

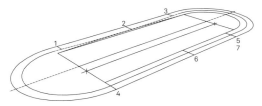

Starting positions for short track speed skating

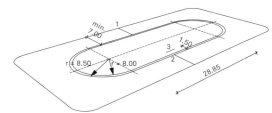

Oval for 111.12 m short track speed skating

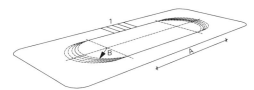

**Figure 4.9.50**
Dimensions for curling

1  Hack
2  Back line
3  Tee line
4  Free guard zone
5  Hog line
6  Center line

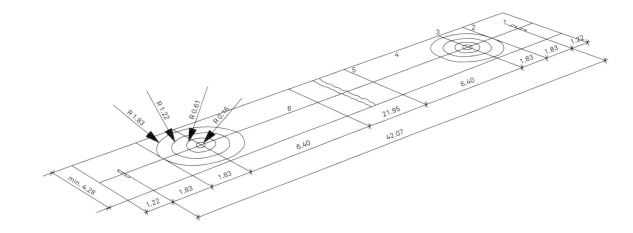

**Figure 4.9.51**
Bavarian curling

Source: DIN 18036

1  Houses 1–14
2  Scoreboard
3  Ice stock cushion
4  House length
5  Foot mark
6  Row of starting houses
7  Row of houses

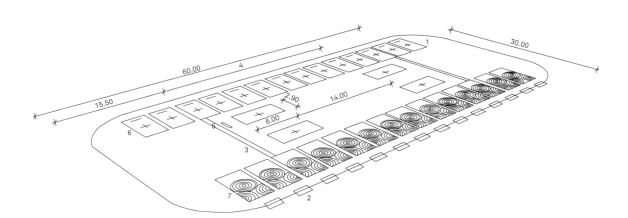

**Figure 4.9.52**
Dimensions of release areas
for discus and hammer

Hammer throw

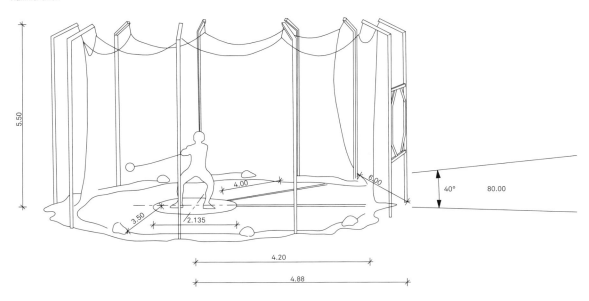

Discus throw

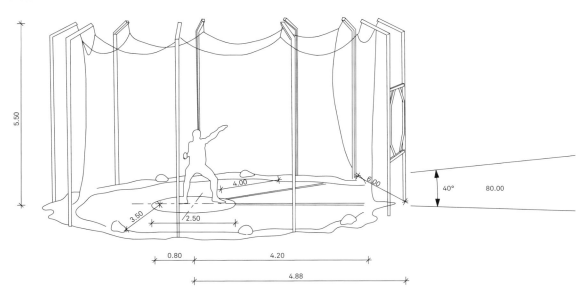

**Figure 4.9.53**
Dimensions for shot put
and javelin throw

Shot put

Javelin throw

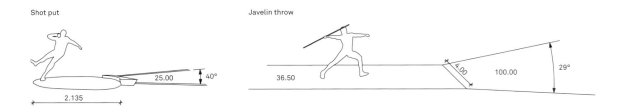

**Figure 4.9.54**
Dimensions for high jump
and pole vault

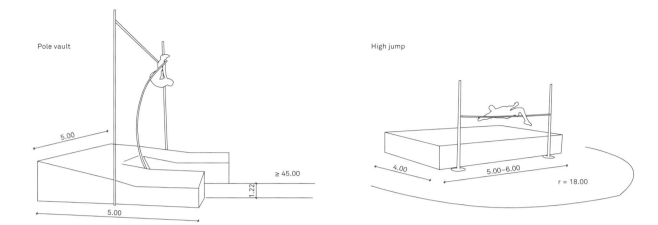

Pole vault

High jump

**Figure 4.9.55**
Dimensions for long jump
and triple jump

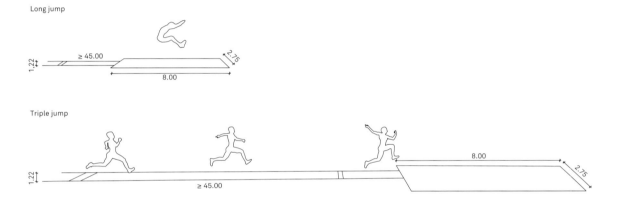

Long jump

Triple jump

**Figure 4.9.56**
Dimensions for running tracks
and hurdle tracks

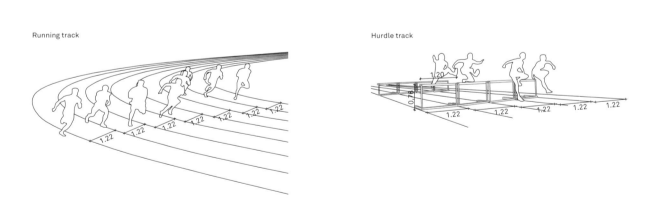

Running track

Hurdle track

### 4.9.3.3 Equipment for Sports and Games

Especially when sports groups simultaneously need to use several items of the same sports equipment, the quantity and dimensions of the movable sports and game equipment determine both the space needed for equipment in use and the space needed for storage. →**Table 4.9.9** Corresponding layout plans for equipment storage rooms, for instance, are to be prepared on this basis. →**Figure 4.9.66 and Table 4.9.10**

Table 4.9.9
Space requirements for gymnastics apparatus

| Apparatus | Obstacle-free zone | | | | Safety clearance | | | | Total area |
|---|---|---|---|---|---|---|---|---|---|
| | Length | Width | Height | Area | Lateral | Front | Rear | Side-by-side | |
| Floor performance area | 14.00 m | 14.00 m | 4.50 m | 196 m² | | | | | 196 m² |
| Pommel horse | 4.00 m | 4.00 m | 4.50 m | 16 m² | | | | | 16 m² |
| Vault | 36.00 m | 2.00 m | 5.50 m | 72 m² | | | | | 72 m² |
| Rings (steady rings) | 8.00 m | 6.00 m | 5.50 m | 64 m² | | | | | 64 m² |
| Bars | 6.00 m | 9.50 m | 4.50 m | 57 m² | 2.00 m | 4.00 m | 3.00 m | 4.50 m | 176 m² |
| Horizontal bar (high bar) | 12.00 m | 6.00 m | 7.00 m | 72 m² | 1.50 m | 6.00 m | 6.00 m | | 216 m² |
| Uneven bars | 12.00 m | 6.00 m | 5.50 m | 72 m² | 1.50 m | 6.00 m | 6.00 m | | 216 m² |
| Balance beam | 12.00 m | 6.00 m | 4.50 m | 72 m² | | | | | 72 m² |
| Flying rings | 18.00 m | 4.00 m | 5.50 m | 72 m² | 1.50 m | 10.50 m | 7.50 m | 1.50 m | 252 m² |
| Climbing ropes | | | | | 1.50 m | 4.50 m | 4.50 m | 1.00 m | 27 m² |
| Gymnastics wall bars | | | | | | 4.00 m | 4.00 m | 2.00 m | |

Table 4.9.10
Need for equipment storage rooms in gymnasiums

| Attribute of changing room | Equipment storage | |
|---|---|---|
| | Minimum dimensions | Minimum area |
| For 2 small units (≥ 28.00 m²) | 4.50 m × 15.00 m × 2.50 m | 67.50 m² |
| For 2 large units or 4 small units (≥ 56.00 m²) | 4.50 m × 21.00 m × 2.50 m | 94.50 m² |
| For 3 large units or 6 small units (≥ 84.00 m²) | 4.50 m × 27.00 m × 2.50 m | 121.50 m² |
| Outdoor equipment storage | 3.00 m × 5.00 m | 15.00 m² |

**Figure 4.9.57**
Space requirements for portable gymnastics apparatus

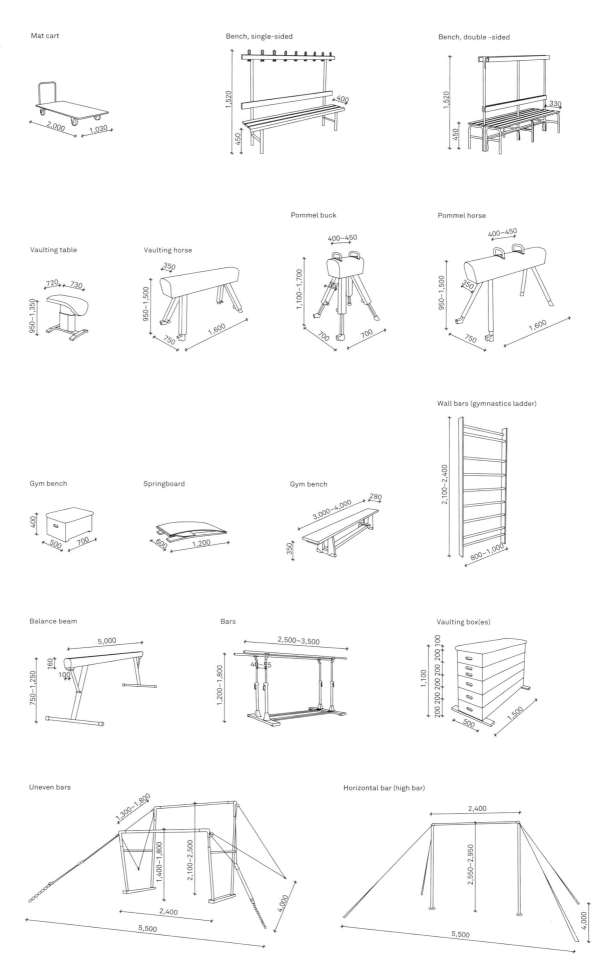

**Figure 4.9.58**
Space requirements for horizontal bars with removable and in-floor uprights

Horizontal bar apparatus

Floor sleeve for horizontal bar

Horizontal bar, sinkable in floor

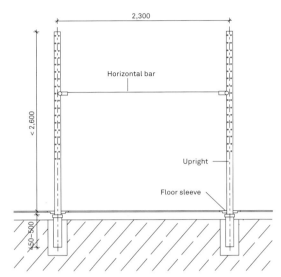

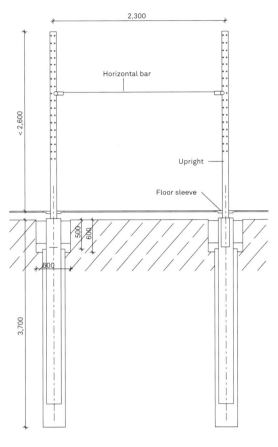

**Figure 4.9.59**
Space requirements for wall bars

Single and double section wall bars mounted within niches

Raisable wall bars

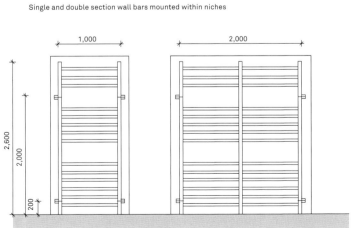

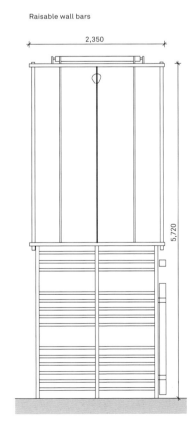

**Figure 4.9.60**
Construction principle for flying rings and climbing ropes

Flying rings

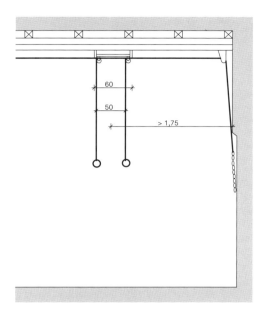

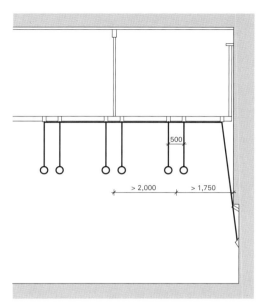

Climbing ropes

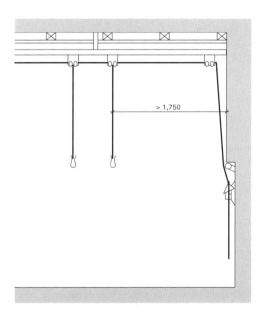

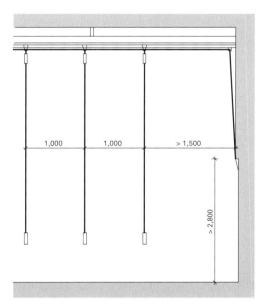

**Figure 4.9.61**
Space requirements for climbing poles

Climbing poles mounted in niches

| Quantity of poles | a | b | Width of niche |
|---|---|---|---|
| 3 poles | 1,600 mm | 1,100 mm | 1,800 mm |
| 4 poles | 1,750 mm | 1,400 mm | 1,950 mm |
| 5 poles | 2,300 mm | 1,650 mm | 2,500 mm |
| 6 poles | 2,850 mm | 2,200 mm | 3,050 m |

Climbing poles – raisable

| Quantity of poles | a | b |
|---|---|---|
| 3 poles | 1,640 mm | 1,100 mm |
| 4 poles | 1,890 mm | 1,650 mm |
| 5 poles | 2,440 mm | 2,200 mm |
| 6 poles | 2,990 mm | 2,750 mm |

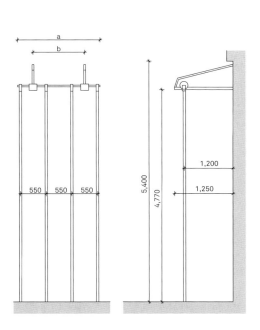

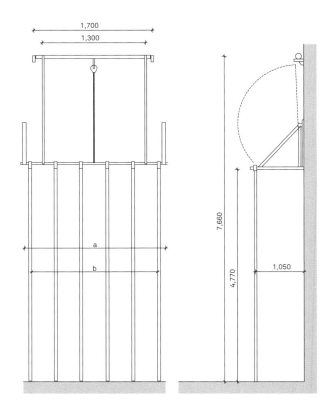

**Figure 4.9.62**
Space requirements for grid ladders

Grid ladder mounted in a niche

| Number of panels | a | b | Width of niche |
|---|---|---|---|
| 3-panel | 1,720 mm | 1,120 mm | 2,020 mm |
| 4-panel | 2,280 mm | 1,680 mm | 2,580 mm |

Grid ladder – raisable

| Number of panels | a |
|---|---|
| 3-panel | 2,240 mm |
| 4-panel | 2,740 mm |

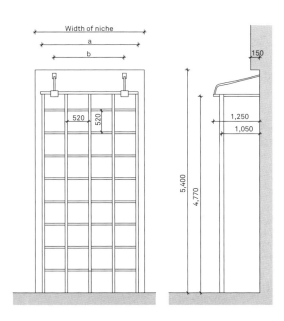

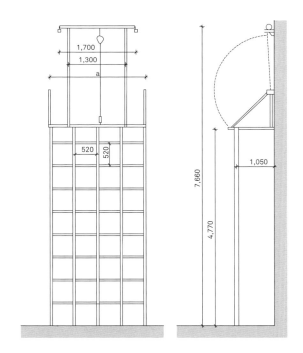

**Figure 4.9.63**
Ceiling- and wall-mounted
basketball backboards

Rear-folding retractable
ceiling-mounted backstop
frame for ceiling heights
up to 8,000 mm

Rear-folding retractable
ceiling-mounted backstop
frame for ceiling heights from
8,100 to 9,600 mm

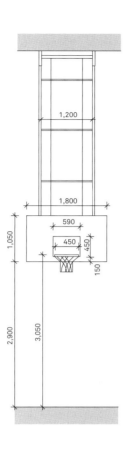

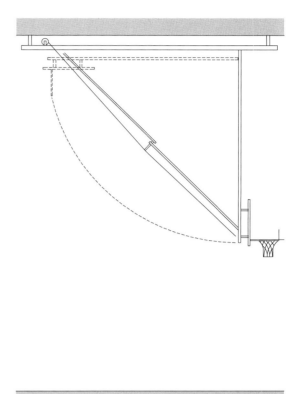

Side-folding backstop

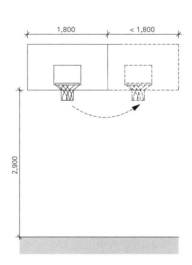

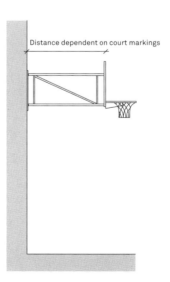

**Figure 4.9.64**
Goal for handball/indoor soccer, with anchorage

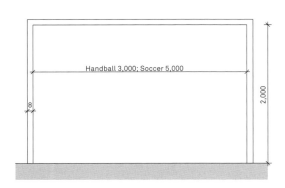

**Figure 4.9.65**
Various gaming tables

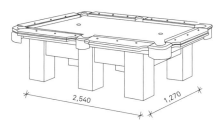

Billiards

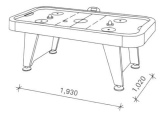

Air hockey

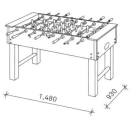

Foosball (table soccer)

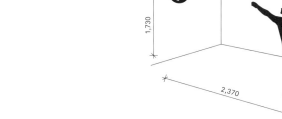

Darts

**Figure 4.9.66**
Example of apparatus storage in the equipment room

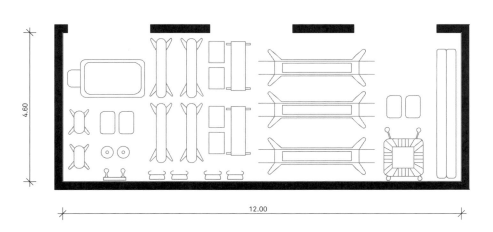

### 4.9.3.4  Tiered Seating and Spectator Areas

Basic tiered seating, especially if only needed temporarily for limited numbers of spectators, can be provided as portable bleachers with or without seats, or as permanently installed rows of seats, galleries, folding bleachers, or telescopic bleachers. → **Figure 4.9.67** With 200 or more spectators in buildings or with 5,000 or more spectators in stadiums, the regulations for places of assembly must be observed. These specify detailed requirements for escape routes and the characteristics of various building parts. The planning of tiered seating must therefore take account of the legal requirements as well as aspects of space efficiency and sight lines for good visibility of the playing area from all positions. → **Figure 4.9.68** In addition to determining the heights and angle of the tiered spectator seating → **Figure 4.9.70**, above all it is crucial to define the positions of the access points in such a way as to limit any lost seat positions and any restrictions on the spectators' lines of sight. → **Figures 4.9.69 and 4.9.71** Furthermore, rescue and panic situations must be simulated for large grandstands.

Seating positions can be along continuous benches or consist of individual seats. The minimum width of each seating position is 0.50 m, and the depth is about 0.35–0.40 m. The aisles must have a clear width of at least 0.40 m. For standing areas, crush barriers with a minimum height of 1.10 m must be provided.

Figure 4.9.67
Bleacher types for temporary use

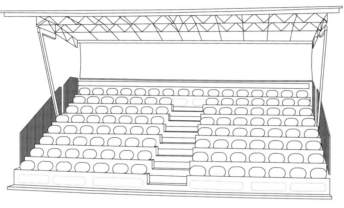

Portable bleacher

Telescopic bleacher

Gallery

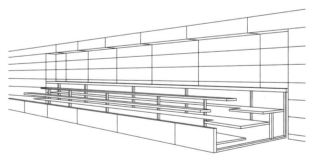

Folding bleacher

**Figure 4.9.68**
Dimensions of a stadium block

Source: VStättVO

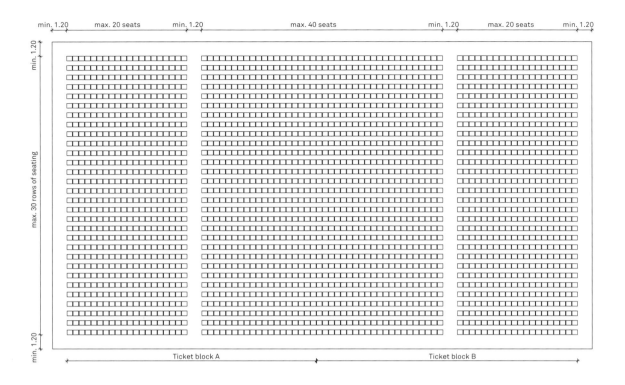

**Figure 4.9.69**
View of the playing field

Data source: FIFA: Football Stadiums – Technical Recommendations and Requirements

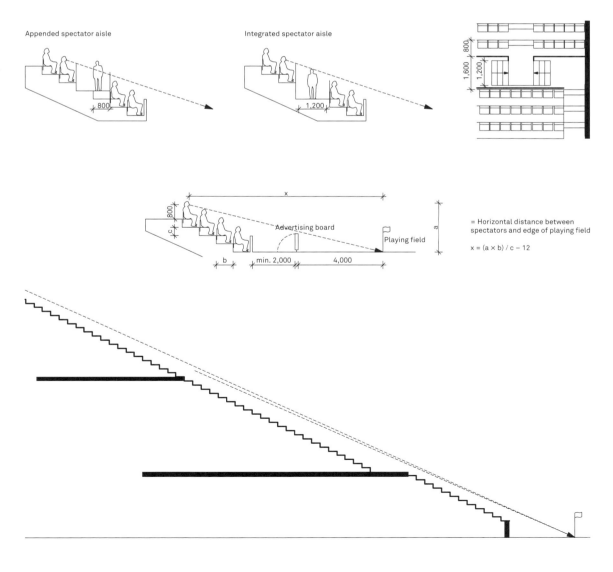

**Figure 4.9.70**
Distance between spectators
and playing field

As per FIFA

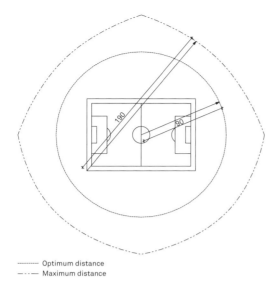

............... Optimum distance
—·—·— Maximum distance

**Figure 4.9.71**
Options for excluding
spectators from playing
area without restricting
sightlines

Source: FIFA

Minimum distances to avoid restricted sight lines

Fence or divider

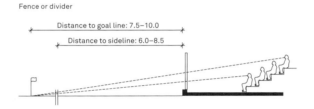

Trench

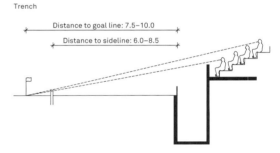

Raised tiered seating

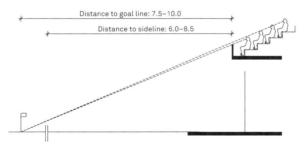

**Figure 4.9.72**
Options for grandstand access
in a stadium

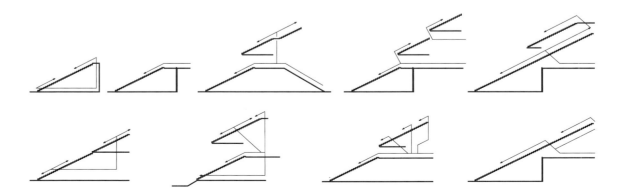

Figure 4.9.73
Access to stadium seating tiers

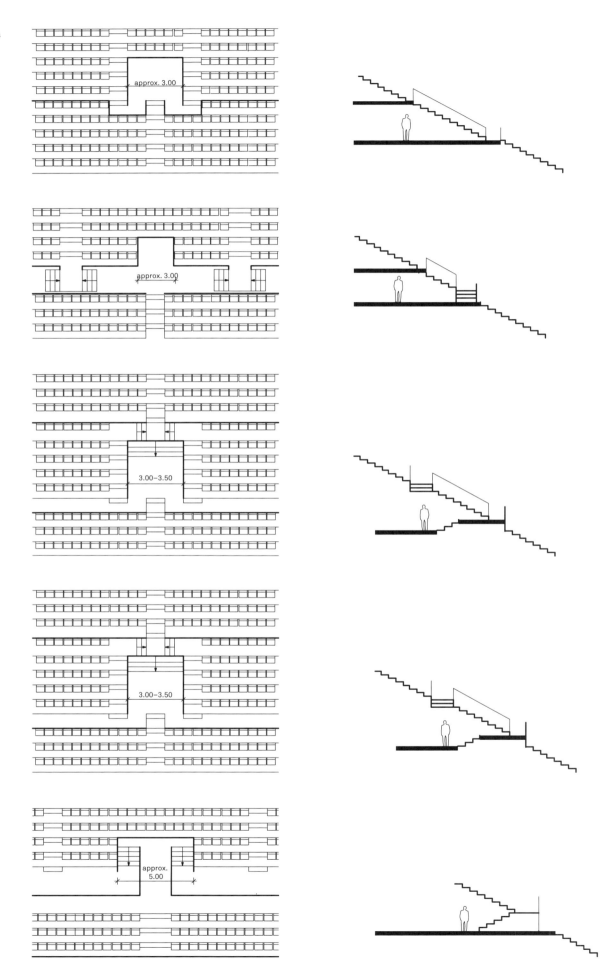

**Figure 4.9.74**
Necessary heights of barriers

Source: VStättVO

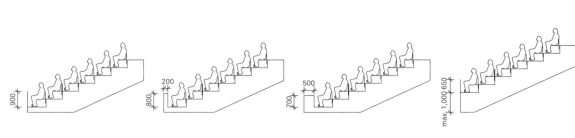

**Figure 4.9.75**
Arrangement of seats

Source: FIFA

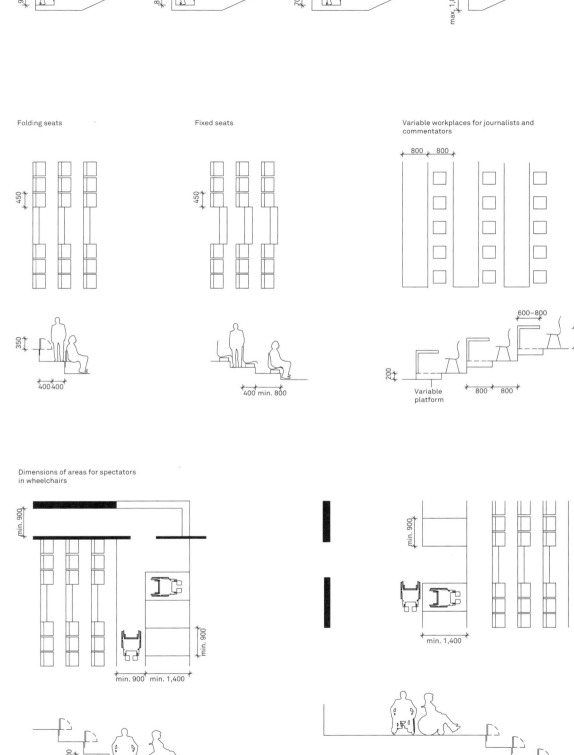

### 4.9.3.5 Changing Areas and Sanitary Facilities

Changing areas are to be dimensioned according to the number of athletes and the simultaneity of use by teams or groups. For team sports, each team should be provided with its own changing area, although these can be made available for use by several groups at different times. →**Tables 4.9.13 and 4.9.14** For individual sports, fitness areas, or swimming pools, communal changing rooms are typically separated by gender. →**Table 4.9.11** A separate changing room should be provided for wheelchair users. Depending on the sport, separate referees' or teachers' changing rooms with a minimum size of 10 m² are also required. These should be equipped with a lavatory, shower and changing stall, and lockers.

In general, all sports facilities should include spectator restrooms, and where many spectators are accommodated in stands, sanitary facilities should be located within a short distance to the seating. →**Table 4.9.12**, ↗**Chapter 3.5.3 Spaces/Sanitary Facilities/Public and Commercial Sanitary Facilities**, ↗**Chapter 3.8.2 Spaces/Ancillary and Staff Rooms/Locker and Changing Rooms**

### 4.9.3.6 Ancillary Spaces

For sports that are subject to doping control, a doping control station of at least 20 m² is to be incorporated in each case. →**Figure 4.9.76** In addition to sport-specific building services and storage areas, general-purpose building services and storage rooms are also required. For club use, separate storage accommodations should be made available for each of the individual teams. For multifunctional use, 0.05–0.06 m² storage space per seat should be planned for tables and chairs, and 0.12 m² storage space per m² stage area should be planned for stage platforms. Likewise, sufficient custodial rooms/janitor's closets are needed, each approximately 3 m² in size, including utility sink, cold and hot water connections, storage shelves, and a floor drain. ↗**Chapter 3.7 Spaces/Storage Spaces**, ↗**Chapter 3.8 Spaces/Ancillary and Staff Rooms**

Table 4.9.11
Number of plumbing fixtures according to sports activity

Source: VDI 3818

| Building type | Reference unit (RU) | Number of plumbing fixtures | | | | |
| --- | --- | --- | --- | --- | --- | --- |
| | Parameter | Women's toilets | Lavatories | Men's toilets | Urinals | Lavatories |
| Outdoor swimming pools | Water surface in m² | 1 toilet per 250 patrons | 1 lavatory per 3 toilets or 1 lavatory per max. 330 patrons | 1 per 500 patrons | 1 per 250 patrons | 1 lavatory per 3 toilets or 1 lavatory per max. 330 patrons |
| Saunas | Sauna capacity | 1 toilet per 10–15 patrons | 1 lavatory per toilet or 1 lavatory per max. 3–8 patrons | 1 per 20–25 patrons | 1 per 20–25 patrons | 1 lavatory per toilet or 1 lavatory per max. 3–8 patrons |
| Gymnasiums | Sports area in m² | 1 toilet per 50–100 patrons | 1–2 lavatories per toilet, or 1 lavatory per max. 10–20 patrons | 1 per 50–100 patrons | 1 per 150–200 patrons | 1–2 lavatories per toilet, or 1 lavatory per max. 10–20 patrons |
| Medical pools | Treatment capacity | 1 toilet per 10–15 patrons | 1 lavatory per toilet | 1 per 20–25 patrons | 1 per 20–25 patrons | 1 lavatory per toilet |

Table 4.9.12 (left)
Number of spectator toilets

Source: DIN 18035-1, special requirements specified in state and local regulations on places of assembly

Figure 4.9.76 (right)
Doping control station

| | For Women | For Men | |
| --- | --- | --- | --- |
| | Toilets | Toilets | Urinals |
| < 1,000 spectators | 1 | 1 | 2 |
| > 1,000 spectators, for each 1,000 spectators | 4 | 2 | 4 |
| For each 10 spectators in wheelchairs | 1 handicap-accessible toilet room | | |

Minimum size 20 m²

7.90

3.90

3.95

5.75

Clothing lockers

Working area

Refrigerator

**Table 4.9.13**
Changing areas and sanitary facilities for club use

Source: DIN 18035-1

a If more than two teams are to use a changing room at the same time, the games must be scheduled to ensure that the matches do not run concurrently.
b A dedicated first aid room of approximately 8 m² is only required when the room is not at ground level.
c In sports facilities for up to 1,000 simultaneous spectators, these sanitary facilities are also sufficient for the spectators. In larger facilities, separate toilets must be provided for the spectators.
d Only valid when maintenance machinery remains on the site. If maintenance is conducted by central or external crews that transport machinery to and from the site, this room can be omitted.
e Can be divided into 2 half-room units, each with 4 showers and 2 washing positions.

| Number of teams | Changing rooms ᵃ, each with 12 m bench length | Team locker rooms per changing room | Showers and washrooms, each with 8 showers and 4 washing positions | Toilets in the changing area | Number of classes for school use | Room for trainers, referees, and first aid ᵇ — Room size (m²) | Showers/toilets | Clothing lockers | Toilets for athletes in exterior areas ᶜ — Toilets (Men) | Urinals (Men) | Toilets (Women) | Room for groundskeeper (m²) | Youth room/club room | Room for building services and handover station | Sports equipment storage | Machine storage ᵈ | Manual tools |
|---|---|---|---|---|---|---|---|---|---|---|---|---|---|---|---|---|---|
| 4 | 2 | 2 | 1 or 2 | 2 | 1 or 2 | approx. 16 | 1/1 | 6 | 1 | 2 | 2 | approx. 8 | As needed | Size and any needed subdivisions are determined by the type of building services equipment contained within and the local utilities providers | 0.15 m² equipment storage per 100 m² sports area (net sports area) | approx. 20 | – |
| 6 | 2 | 3 | 2 | 2 | 2 | | | | | | | | | | | | |
| 8 | 3 | 3 + 2 + 3 | 1 + 1ᵉ | 3 | 2 | | 1/1 | 8 | 2 | 4 | 4 | | | | | | 10 |
| 8 | 4 | 2 | 2 + 1ᵉ | 4 | 3 | | | | | | | | | | | | |
| 12 | 4 | 3 | 4 | 4 | 5 | approx. 24 | 2/1 | 12 | 3 | 6 | 6 | | | | | approx. 50 | 15 |
| 12 | 6 | 2 | 6 | 6 | 6 | | | | | | | | | | | | |

**Table 4.9.14**
Changing areas and sanitary facilities for school use

Source: DIN 18035-1

a If more than two teams are to use a changing room at the same time, the games must be scheduled to ensure that the matches do not run concurrently.
b A dedicated first aid room of approximately 8 m² is only required when the room is not at ground level.
c In sports facilities for up to 1,000 simultaneous spectators, these sanitary facilities are also sufficient for the spectators. In larger facilities, separate toilets must be provided for the spectators.
d Only valid when maintenance machinery remains on the site. If maintenance is conducted by central or external crews that transport machinery to and from the site, this room can be omitted.
e Can be divided into 2 half-room units, each with 4 showers and 2 washing positions.

| Number of school classes | Changing rooms ᵃ, each with 12 m bench length | Showers and washrooms, each with 8 showers and 2 washing positions | Toilets in the changing area | Number of teams for club use | Team locker rooms | Room for trainers, referees, and first aid ᵇ — Room size (m²) | Showers/toilets | Clothing lockers | Toilets for athletes in exterior areas ᶜ — Toilets (Men) | Urinals (Men) | Toilets (Women) | Room for groundskeeper (m²) | Youth room/club room | Room for building services and handover station | Sports equipment storage | Machine storage ᵈ m² | Manual tools m² |
|---|---|---|---|---|---|---|---|---|---|---|---|---|---|---|---|---|---|
| Up to 2 | 2 | 1ᵉ | 2 | 2 | 0 | Approx. 16 m² | 1/1 | 6 | 1 | 2 | 2 | Approx. 8 m² | As needed | Size and any needed subdivisions are determined by the type of building services equipment contained within and the local utilities providers | 0.15 m² equipment storage per 100 m² sports area (net sports area) | Approx. 20 | – |
| | | 2 | 2 | Up to 6 | 3 + 3 | | | | | | | | | | | | |
| 4 | 4 | 4 | 4 | 4 | 0 | | 1/1 | 8 | 2 | 4 | 4 | | | | | | 10 m² |
| | | | | Up to 6 | 2 + 2 + 2 + 2 | | | | | | | | | | | | |
| 6 | 6 | 6 | 8 | 6 | 0 | Approx. 24 m² | 2/1 | 12 | 3 | 6 | 6 | | | | | Approx. 50 | 15 m² |
| | | | | Up to 12 | 2 + 2 + 2 + 2 | | | | | | | | | | | | |

**Tower of London,** London, Great Britain, 1078

**Peace Palace,** The Hague, The Netherlands, Louis M. Cordonnier, 1913

**Supreme Court,** Washington, DC, USA, Cass Gilbert, 1935

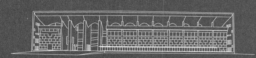

**High Court,** Chandigarh, India, Le Corbusier, 1956

**Supreme Court,** Brasilia, Brazil, Oscar Niemeyer, 1964

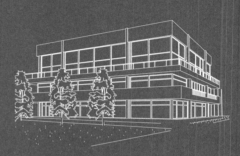

**Federal Constitutional Court,** Karlsruhe, Germany, Paul Baumgarten, 1965

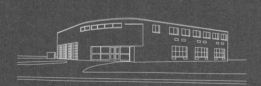

**Dixwell Fire Station,** New Haven, CT, USA, Robert Venturi and John Rauch, 1973

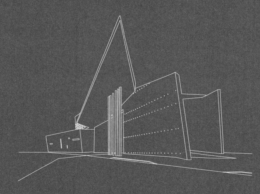

**Vitra Fire Station,** Weil am Rhein, Germany, Zaha Hadid, 1993

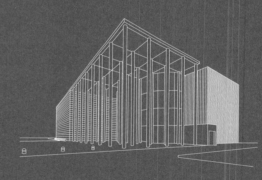

**Okayama West Police Station,** Okayama, Japan, Arata Isozaki, 2000

**Service Center (police station) on Theresienwiese,** Munich, Germany, Volker Staab, 2004

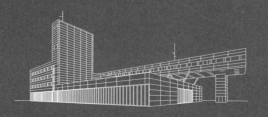

**Heidelberg Fire Station,** Heidelberg, Germany, Peter Kulka, 2007

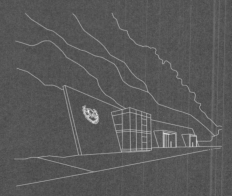

**Margreid Fire Station,** Margreid an der Weinstraße, Italy, Bergmeisterwolf, 2010

# 4 Typologies
## 4.10 Public Safety

Roland Schneider
Markus Stark

### 4.10.1 Building Concept ↗476

4.10.1.1 Planning Parameters ↗476
4.10.1.2 Building Forms ↗476
4.10.1.3 Circulation Systems ↗477
4.10.1.4 Construction and Technology ↗477

### 4.10.2 Program of Use ↗479

4.10.2.1 Fire Stations ↗479
4.10.2.2 Police Stations ↗481
4.10.2.3 Prisons ↗482
4.10.2.4 Courthouses ↗483

### 4.10.3 Areas and Rooms ↗484

4.10.3.1 Entrance Areas ↗485
4.10.3.2 Vehicles ↗485
4.10.3.3 Duty Rooms ↗487
4.10.3.4 Workshops ↗488
4.10.3.5 Practice Rooms ↗489
4.10.3.6 Courtrooms ↗491
4.10.3.7 Prison Cells ↗491
4.10.3.8 Office and Administrative Spaces ↗492
4.10.3.9 Ancillary Spaces ↗493

# 4.10 Public Safety

## 4.10.1 Building Concept

### 4.10.1.1 Planning Parameters

Public buildings have to fulfill a wide range of different functions. Internal processes and safety considerations determine the program and functional arrangement of spaces. For example, the built structure of fire stations is a vital factor in the reaction time to an emergency. In prisons, police stations, and some courthouses, security and clear zoning and access are of prime importance, so as to be able to separate groups of persons and minimize potential dangers in the buildings.

**Typical planning parameters are:**
- Place, context, and infrastructure
- Geometry of the site
- Building code restrictions
- Quantity of vehicles
- Program of use, spatial program, and space requirements
- Security issues
- Number of workplaces for regular work and standby duty
- Necessary secondary functions
- Requirements of user groups
- Type of function – public/internal
- Operating costs

At the beginning of the design phase, a needs analysis should fundamentally be carried out with the client and/or users in order to specify the particular functional requirements, the spatial program, and the space requirement in general. In the case of fire and police stations, for example, the catchment area and the classification level are essential for determining the functions to be accommodated. For prisons and courthouses, safety considerations are of utmost importance and have to be coordinated in detail. Buildings for uses with large space needs and high security requirements are significantly more complex to design for a central urban context, due to high building densities and tight lot configurations, than new builds in a rural context.

In general: for all building typologies the usually clearly defined patterns of use must be represented efficiently and clearly via the building layout – from internal circulation and security zoning to the traffic safety of the adjoining streets.

### 4.10.1.2 Building Forms

The forms of buildings vary greatly depending on their type of use. Prisons, for example, have clearly recognizable basic arrangement principles that result from the requirements for optimized circulation patterns and good surveillance. → **Figure 4.10.1**

Fire stations can be designed in very different forms. It is possible to combine all the functional areas, including the apparatus bay (vehicle garage), in one building or to arrange them in separate volumes that are joined to each other. The hose-drying tower will in any case be a conspicuous feature protruding from the rest of the building. → **Figure 4.10.2** Where offices and administrative facilities are included as separate elements, classic office building layouts may serve as a basis for design. ↗ **Chapter 4.2 Typologies/Office and Administration**

Figure 4.10.1
Building forms for prison facilities

○ Cell blocks

● Central and ancillary functions

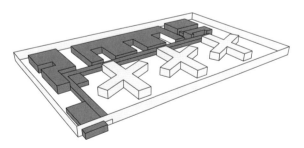

Cell blocks in cruciform layout

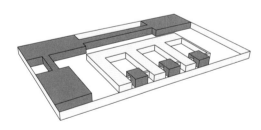

Cell blocks in a spine-and-fingers type layout

Figure 4.10.2
Typical building forms for fire stations

○ Apparatus bay and workshops

● Administrative and staff rooms

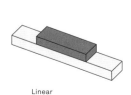

Linear

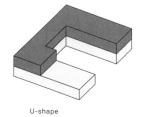

U-shape

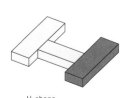

H-shape

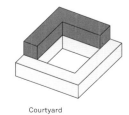

Courtyard

## 4.10.1.3 Circulation Systems

In addition to the required width of rescue and escape routes, all corridors and stair enclosures of duty departments and operational areas must be sufficiently dimensioned for all situations. To avoid collisions, it is especially important to ensure the strict separation of people arriving at the station from departing emergency services personnel. → **Figures 4.10.3 and 4.10.4** For conventional office and administrative spaces or wings, classic circulation systems with cellular, group, or open-plan offices can be used. ↗ **Chapter 4.2 Typologies/Office and Administration**

Depending on the building's function, internal circulation elements may need to be separated from publicly accessible areas. Where buildings are used by several different services, separate access must be provided to the different functions.

In addition to stairs and ramps, fire stations also have special poles and slides (→ **Figure 4.10.6**), whose use when responding to an emergency are prioritized as follows:

1. Fireman's shaft enclosure with fire pole
2. Fireman's slide
3. Staircase

In buildings for voluntary fire departments without professional firefighters, accident prevention dictates that no fire poles be installed.

## 4.10.1.4 Construction and Technology

Police stations and courthouses are preferentially built in the form of office/administration buildings using solid construction with drywall interior partitions. Fire and rescue stations must also have large clear spans for spaces housing vehicles and to accommodate exercises and other functions. Here, too, special technical installations must be taken into account, in particular in the control center and the workshop area. Control and monitoring centers, detention areas, and weapons rooms are normally subject to state-specific security requirements. Prisons and detention areas should generally be built of solid construction in order to minimize the risk of breakouts. Furthermore, the facade needs to be constructed with sufficient strength and durability; built-in components such as windows, windowsills, and doors may require special properties or forms (bullet and impact resistance, slanted installation, etc.). Unauthorized entry from the outside and the possibility of bringing in dangerous or hazardous substances must be precluded. For police stations in particular, projections, slots or other types of openings, ledges, and canopies should be avoided on the facade.

In terms of providing utility connections for building services, the design of public safety buildings requires giving special attention to security issues such as ensuring continuous availability and operations, supplying emergency power, maintaining the security systems in the case of a power failure, etc. Alarm and notification systems in prisons must be coordinated with the responsible authorities and integrated in the overall security concept. In principle, service lines entering the building must be installed underground and designed to be sabotage-proof.

**Figure 4.10.3 (left)**
Internal circulation – principle of short distances for emergency response (example: fire station)

The building layout must enable direct connections for emergency response situations in order to minimize the time needed for personnel to leave in the case of an alarm/service call.

**Figure 4.10.4 (right)**
Separation of incoming circulation routes from those of outgoing service personnel responding to an alarm

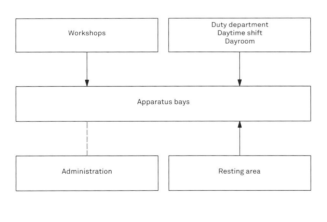

| Workshops | Duty department Daytime shift Dayroom |
|---|---|
| Apparatus bays | |
| Administration | Resting area |

⟶ Direct spatial connection for emergency response

**Figure 4.10.5**
Hazardous situations of incoming and outgoing vehicles (example: fire station)

Example of hazard reduction: the situation on the left has four points where there is a danger of collision between incoming and outgoing vehicles or normal traffic; in the situation on the right, a better design reduces the points of potential collision to two.

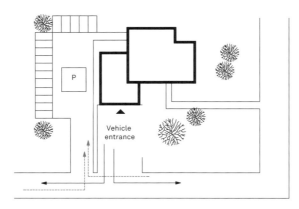

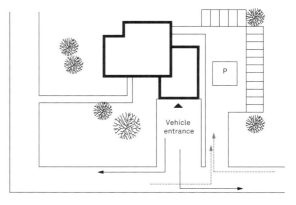

Four hazards

Two hazards

**Figure 4.10.6**
Quick-access facilities with fire pole and fireman's slide

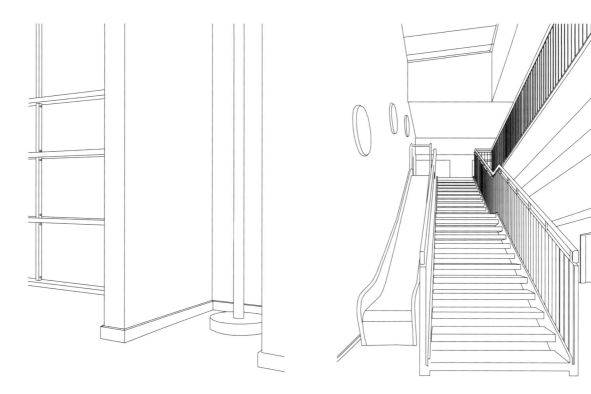

## 4.10.2 Program of Use

All buildings associated with public safety share high demands for safety and security. In the case of fire and rescue stations, this especially pertains to the safety of emergency services crews as they are leaving in response to an alarm. Police stations have a similar focus, but may also have to provide secure cells for detention on a small scale. Buildings with control centers, deployment control stations and the like must be protected using appropriate layouts and construction measures. Courthouses must fulfill the utmost security requirements in order to prevent transgressions during court hearings. For this reason, security checks at the entrances are of great importance. Prisons are a unique type of building, for which consideration must be given not only to the security of the inmates, but also to the safety of personnel and visitors.

### 4.10.2.1 Fire Stations

Fire stations are primarily functional buildings designed for efficiency and safety. Generally, all fire stations have to comply with the provisions of the applicable workplace regulations. This includes changing rooms (lockers), sanitary facilities, staff areas, and break rooms as important components for future use. There are also a number of safety-relevant issues intended to prevent injuries and accidents when responding to emergencies. Most countries have detailed design guidelines for newly constructed fire stations (for example, in Germany: DIN 14092, Parts 1, 3 and 7, along with DIN 14093 and 14097 for practice facilities).

Buildings of this type must differentiate among various types of fire departments:

- Professional fire department with 24-hour standby duty
- Full-time voluntary fire department with 24-hour standby duty
- Voluntary fire department, unpaid duty with on-call service
- Rescue service/ambulance corps with 24-hour standby duty

If several of these types of fire department services are to be accommodated in one building, the main zones of use should be separated from each other, and shared functional areas should be accessible to all. It follows that a fire station has to accommodate mixed functions.

Typical spaces in fire stations are:
- Apparatus bays
- Standard workshops
  - Motor vehicle repair shop
  - Metal workshop
  - Saddlery, etc.
- Workshops unique to fire departments
  - Hose maintenance
  - Fire extinguisher workshop
  - Care of chemical protection gear and breathing apparatus, etc.
- Duty department
  - Locker rooms
  - Quiet rooms
  - Dayroom, etc.
- Control center and crisis management
- Offices and administration
- Training, education, and practice facilities
- Sports and fitness
- Kitchen/canteen

**Figure 4.10.7 (left)**
General schematic layout of a fire station

CR = Changing room
SF = Sanitary facilities

**Figure 4.10.8 (right)**
Example of a fire station layout with basic facilities

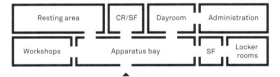

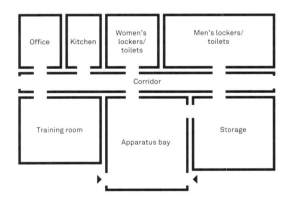

**Figure 4.10.9**
Example layout of a major fire station

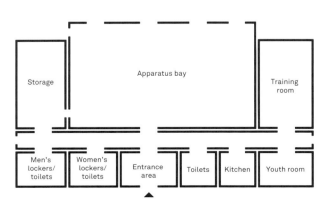

**Soiled/Clean Separation**

Service clothing (→ **Figure 4.10.10**), also referred to as personal protective equipment (PPE), can be accommodated in lockers or – for faster access – also in open wardrobes. Storage facilities for turnout gear (service clothing) are often provided in the form of stands next to the emergency vehicle. Following a service call it is important that a separation between clean and soiled turnout gear be maintained in order to uphold hygiene standards and protect against contamination. → **Figure 4.10.11** One way to achieve this is to arrange the changing rooms in such a way that the showers function as a transitional space between the soiled and clean areas. In all cases it is necessary to provide areas with containers for depositing contaminated service clothing and areas for storing clean private clothing. It is likewise necessary to provide a soiled/clean separation in the maintenance areas for breathing apparatus and hoses. Differentiated facilities result depending on the size and function of the fire department. → **Figure 4.10.12**

Figure 4.10.10
Open wardrobe for personal protective equipment, and changing locker

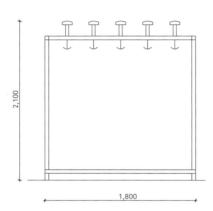
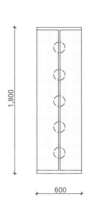

Figure 4.10.11 (left)
Diagram of the transition from soiled to clean areas

Figure 4.10.12 (right)
Example layout with soiled/clean separation

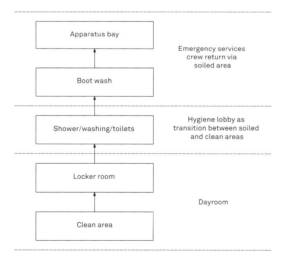
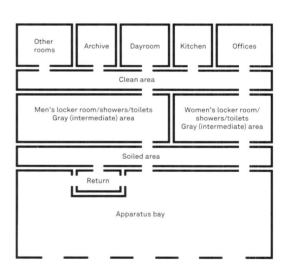

## 4.10.2.2 Police Stations

The design of police stations is strongly affected by regional differences in organizational and administrative structures as well as state-specific regulations. For this reason, the requirements for new buildings must be considered individually for each project. Building security is an important design objective for police organizations. Generally speaking, a distinction can be made between the local police station (precinct house) and a police administration building, which essentially consists of numerous office spaces. The same applies to higher-level service buildings such as criminal investigation offices, state and federal agencies, and intelligence services. For effective police operations and proximity to the public, the administration building should be sited in a central and easily accessible location. ↗ Chapter 4.2 Typologies/Office and Administration

Local police stations have a public entrance area that also serves as a transition zone for security purposes. This entrance area usually has a waiting area associated with it and is located in front of the duty room. The duty room ordinarily has a visitor desk or counter area with a back office. Members of the public are able to speak with the duty officers here at the counter. A quiet room and a kitchenette should be situated behind the duty room. A secure area should be established within a nearby storage area to accommodate an evidence room. On-duty police officers are provided with an internal corridor to reach other spaces such as changing areas, sanitary facilities, and – if applicable – detention rooms for temporary detainment of people in custody until they are released, granted a hearing, or transported to a prison. Police officers and civilian staff members may require a separate entrance. Additional departments are often accommodated on the upper floors of a police station. The offices are usually organized in an arrangement comprising cellular, shared, and group offices, and they typically have separate archive/storage rooms for each department. Each floor generally has its own entry controls at the point where the horizontal and vertical circulation systems meet.

**Police stations typically contain the following spaces:**
- Duty room
- Quiet room
- Waiting areas
- Changing areas
- Sanitary facilities
- Office and administration areas
- Storage room with evidence room
- Detention cells
- Interrogation room
- Lineup room
- Locker rooms
- Garages for service vehicles
- Tactical meeting rooms
- Rooms for press conferences

Police administration buildings have additional, higher-level divisions within the police department. These include various detectives' offices, workshops, training facilities (such as shooting ranges), the commissioner's office, and the deployment control station. Security issues have the highest priority in the detention areas and the deployment control station. Therefore these areas must have security checkpoints and separate entrances and exits. The other uses are similar to those found in a typical office structure. Changing rooms, workshops, and training facilities must be integrated into the functional scheme of the building.

**Figure 4.10.13**
Schematic layout of a police station

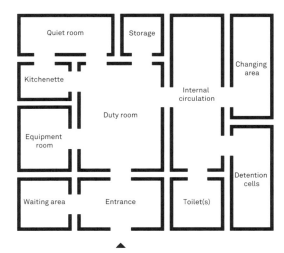

### 4.10.2.3 Prisons

When designing a prison, there are essentially three different groups of people that have to be taken into account: staff, inmates, and visitors. For security reasons, the building's design should ensure a strict physical separation of these three user groups. Furthermore, prisons or prison wings are always segregated by gender (separation principle); this pertains not only to the general accommodations during rest times, but also to the entire daily routine during imprisonment. In the case of sociotherapeutic correctional institutions and in prison hospitals as well as pretrial detention, the separation principle need not be applied.

Safety and security issues have top priority and are not to be understood only as preventing breakouts and escape, but also as providing for the safety of staff members, visitors, and inmates alike from attack by other detainees. This generally means that persons can only enter the building by passing individually through a security checkpoint and that vehicles must pass a controlled vehicle entrance. Both of these security facilities are located directly adjacent to a gatehouse. Beyond the security checkpoints, the administrative offices are assembled along with storage rooms, an evidence room, and ancillary rooms such as toilet facilities and kitchenettes. In addition to offices and administrative spaces, there may also be medical and psychological facilities integrated within the building.

Inmates are received and discharged at a central point in close proximity to the entrance area. They must hand over all their personal effects and civil clothing, and then receive a uniform at the clothing issue room. Similar to the visitor area, the reception and discharge area should have a separate waiting zone and sanitary facilities.

As a rule, the inmates' accommodations are arranged in multiple cell blocks. Each of these cell blocks may have rooms for guards, a dining hall, and a separately assigned outdoor exercise yard. Depending on the type of prison, it is also possible that yards and facilities such as gymnasiums or areas for leisure activities are provided in a central location for shared use. Good planning and an appealing design of the correctional environment can have a positive effect on the social behavior of the inmates and can also help achieve the penal objectives more quickly.

Alongside accommodations for the inmates, the facility also has places of work – either workshops where products intended for sale are produced, or facilities such as kitchens and laundries, which are needed for the running and maintenance of the correctional institution. →**Figure 4.10.14**

Visitor rooms should be placed such that they are accessible from outside quickly and easily via the security control points, and such that security screening is possible on both sides. The visitor area needs a waiting area with separate toilets. In addition to visitor rooms for individuals, group visitor rooms can be provided. Where such group visitor rooms have no protective separation between inmates and visitors, all furniture and equipment should be firmly anchored to the floor so that these items cannot be misused as weapons. A separating barrier between inmates and prisoners can, for instance, be provided by means of a glass partition. In that case, communication takes place via microphones and loudspeakers or with telephones. Some prisons may also make special accommodations for spousal visits by providing so-called conjugal visiting rooms, which are equipped with a bed or a couch.

**Figure 4.10.14**
Schematic layout of a prison

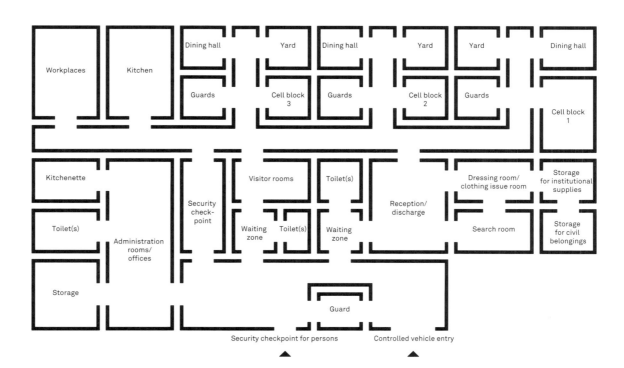

## 4.10.2.4 Courthouses

Owing to international differences in legal and judicial systems, courthouses may vary significantly in their design requirements. In Germany, various jurisdictions are represented by institutions at the federal and state level, such as the constitutional court, courts of law, labor courts, fiscal courts, social welfare courts, and administrative courts. Local district courts are the first level of ordinary jurisdiction and take on civil as well as criminal cases.

What unites all courthouses is that security measures play an important role in their design. Especially where cases involve confrontational litigation, physical attacks and attempts at vigilante justice are not uncommon and have to be prevented by appropriate means.

For this reason, the entrances to these buildings should always have a security screening area, including scanning equipment for both persons and hand-carried items; there should be sufficient space at the entrance to allow time-consuming searches to be carried out for larger numbers of people attending cases of public interest. The guard room and affiliated security office should be located directly adjacent to the screening area. On the internal side beyond the security checkpoint, the court registry office should be located in close proximity to the building entrance. The court registry is a facility for citizens to lodge an official action or make an application, even without representation by a lawyer. There should also be a general information point, which may be designed in the form of a desk or counter with a back office. The public entrance area should be supplemented by a waiting area with seating and restrooms. Facilities for secretaries and possibly court reporters should also be provided in the form of cellular offices. Depending on the type of court, additional rooms may also be needed for the land office, foreclosure auctions, compulsory execution proceedings, and an evidence room.
→ Figure 4.10.15

Central elements are the courtrooms, which should each have a separate consulting room to which the judges can withdraw and conduct consultations. Next to the courtrooms are a great many rooms for judges and attorneys. A legal library should be provided for routine use. Where a room for archiving files is provided, an adjoining room for viewing the documents must be included. Files are increasingly archived digitally, which can potentially reduce the space requirement for a physical archive. This part of the courthouse usually also accommodates offices and administrative departments, which, similar to office buildings, can be organized using different types of layouts.
↗ Chapter 4.2 Typologies/Office and Administration

Figure 4.10.15
Schematic layout of a courthouse

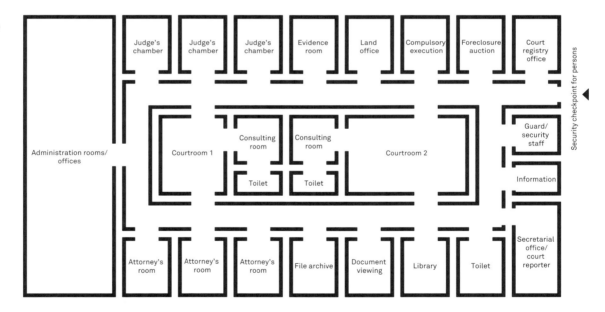

### 4.10.3  Areas and Rooms

**External circulation**  ↗Chapter 3.1

**Entrance hall**  ↗485  ↗Chapter 3.2.1

**Apparatus bay**  ↗485

**Security checkpoint for persons**  ↗485

**Guard room, ancillary rooms**  ↗485

**Stairs, elevators**  ↗Chapter 3.2.4,  ↗Chapter 3.2.7

**Corridors, internal circulation**  ↗Chapter 3.2.2

**Offices**  ↗492  ↗Chapter 3.3.1

**Control centers**  ↗487

**Duty rooms**  ↗487  ↗Chapter 3.4.1

**Workshops**  ↗488  ↗Chapter 3.3.2,  ↗Chapter 4.4

**Hose maintenance**  ↗488

**Care of PPE and hazmat suits**  ↗488

**Practice rooms**  ↗489

**Sports and fitness**  ↗490  ↗Chapter 4.9

**Courtrooms**  ↗491

**Prison cells**  ↗491

**Meeting rooms**  ↗492  ↗Chapter 3.4.1

**Kitchenettes**  ↗492  ↗Chapter 3.6

**Cafeteria**  ↗Chapter 4.7,  ↗Chapter 3.4.3

**Lunchrooms**  ↗492  ↗Chapter 3.8.1

**Toilets**  ↗493  ↗Chapter 3.5

**Storage/archive rooms**  ↗492  ↗Chapter 3.7.2

**Server rooms**  ↗Chapter 3.9.8

**First aid rooms**  ↗Chapter 3.8.3

**Janitor's closets**  ↗Chapter 3.8.4

**Mechanical equipment rooms**  ↗Chapter 3.9

### 4.10.3.1  Entrance Areas

#### Guard, Security Staff
The facilities for guards and security staff are often combined in the entrance areas. Entrance control buildings positioned outside the main building are secured by two-stage gate facilities providing an intermediate space in which security staff can carry out checks on persons and vehicles. The staff must be able to communicate with the outside and with the protected inside areas while also being protected against attack through security measures such as the installation of protective glass screens. The entire entrance area must be able to be monitored using cameras and panoramic mirrors.

#### Waiting Area
Waiting areas must be of a scale to suit the function and size of the building and should be located behind the entrance control area and security checkpoints. The space must be easily supervised from outside and the furniture must be fixed firmly in place. Where several security checkpoints establish successive zones, each zone must have its own separate waiting area.

#### Security Checkpoints for Persons
In addition to the prison entry security checkpoints for persons and vehicles described above, scanners for people and hand-carried items are also used in courthouses and other public buildings. → **Figure 4.10.16** These facilities require sufficient space for waiting lines in front of the scanning equipment and for sorting tables behind the scanners. ↗ **Chapter 3.1.3 Spaces/External Circulation/Private Exterior Circulation**

### 4.10.3.2  Vehicles

#### Vehicle Lot
In fire department and police buildings with emergency vehicles, the vehicle lot should take into account minimum turning curves and space for maneuvering the vehicles. For fire stations, adequate loading space must be provided in front of the gates (roughly the size of the vehicle bay). The number of parking spaces required for cars can be determined in accordance with the number of seats for personnel in all emergency vehicles, although a minimum of 12 spaces for cars should generally be provided. In addition, a training area of at least 250 m² should be included for fire stations with at least four emergency vehicles. ↗ **Chapter 3.1.1 Spaces/External Circulation/Public Access**, ↗ **Chapter 3.1.2 Spaces/External Circulation/Parked Vehicles**

#### Apparatus Bay
As a rule, apparatus bays are only provided for the emergency vehicles of the fire department and rescue services; outdoor parking is normally provided for police vehicles. For the design of an apparatus bay it is important to allow for the number of emergency vehicles as well as any anticipated future additions to the fleet. Any future expansions that may have to be accommodated in the design should be discussed with the client at an early stage. The clear height for vehicles must be at least 4.00 m and the clear width of garage doors and gates must be at least 3.60 m. A minimum clear space of 0.50 m should be provided between the parking areas (→ **Table 4.10.1**) and adjoining parts of buildings. → **Figures 4.10.17 and 4.10.18** The apparatus bay must also be equipped with mechanical exhaust extraction.

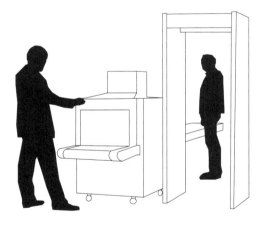

**Figure 4.10.16**
Security checkpoint with an X-ray scanner for hand-carried items

**Table 4.10.1 (left)**
Parking space sizes within apparatus bay

Based on DIN 14092-1

**Figure 4.10.17 (right)**
Minimum requirements for the apparatus bay of a fire station

| Size of parking space | Dimensions | Vehicle lengths |
| --- | --- | --- |
| 1 | 4.50 m × 8.00 m | maximum 6.00 m |
| 2 | 4.50 m × 10.00 m | 6.00–8.00 m |
| 3 | 4.50 m × 12.50 m | 8.00–10.00 m |
| 4 | 4.50 m × 12.50 m | maximum 10.00 m with a height of over 3.50 m |

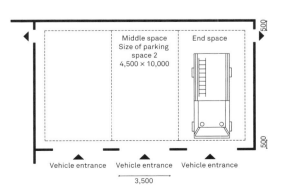

Figure 4.10.18
Required parking space size and minimum dimensions for clear passage as a function of vehicle type/size

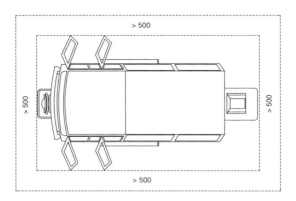
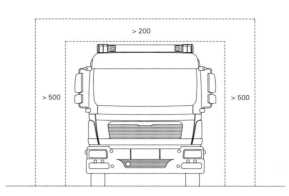

Figure 4.10.19
Vehicle pit beneath parking space

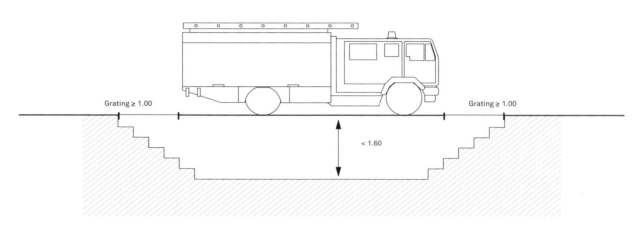

Figure 4.10.20
Variants of fire station doors

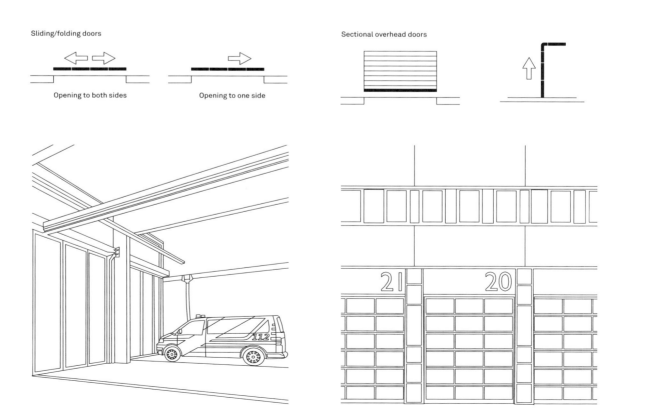

Sliding/folding doors

Opening to both sides

Opening to one side

Sectional overhead doors

### 4.10.3.3 Duty Rooms

**Control Center and Crisis Management Team**

Control centers of nonpolice organizations often vary significantly in different regions and may serve a variety of responsibilities, including firefighting, disaster management, or medical and technical rescue services. Generally there is a tendency to establish ever-larger control centers that cover greater areas of responsibility (fire and rescue dispatch centers, disaster management, etc.), sometimes referred to as cooperative control centers (or integrated control centers, ICCs); these centers integrate various hazard response teams. Control centers for the police (emergency operations centers, EOCs) should always be designed to be self-sufficient. In so doing, the various security zones (police vs. other emergency services) can be accommodated in the same building but must operate as independent entities. Exceptions are the control centers in English-speaking countries, where the centers may also have an internal division of responsibilities. Control centers are usually staffed around the clock. These centers receive all emergency calls and coordinate the deployments of emergency responders. During deployments, contact is maintained between the center and the responders on-site. Quiet rooms for resting, staff rooms for communal interaction, changing rooms, and dayrooms must also be provided. → **Figure 4.10.21**

Situation rooms and crisis management rooms are permanently equipped spaces used in cases of crisis and emergency, and are separately located within close proximity of the control center. The situation room is where information is gathered and also disseminated to the public. The size of control centers and crisis management rooms depends directly on the number of persons staffing the facility and the technology to be incorporated. This must be coordinated with the user and varies greatly depending on the size of the area of jurisdiction and the number of organizations involved.

**Duty Rooms**

Duty rooms can be combined with training rooms, thus reducing the overall space required. The size of these rooms is determined by the number of staff on duty. Generally, spaces functioning purely as duty rooms should not be smaller than 15 m². Where emergency responders have standby duty around the clock, it may be appropriate to provide additional television and/or reading rooms that are separate from the dayrooms. Depending on the need, kitchens may take the form of a kitchenette, a reheating room, or, in the case of larger buildings, a fully equipped industrial kitchen. ↗ **Chapter 3.6 Spaces/Kitchens**

Dining areas should always be provided in rooms with a welcoming atmosphere and good daylight. Where employees have 24-hour duty, a separate food locker for personal items should be provided in the dining or kitchen area for each staff member. The food lockers can be located either directly in the dining room or in a separate locker room nearby. The connection to the kitchen can be made with a pass-through opening; alternatively, a counter within an open-plan layout can serve as the link. ↗ **Chapter 3.4 Spaces/Communication Spaces and Dining Rooms**

Changing rooms for full-time/employed staff members should have double lockers (for private and service clothing). The firefighters' special turnout gear, such as personal protection equipment (PPE), should be kept in separate locker rooms for reasons of hygiene and odor. Where personnel have 24-hour standby duty, quiet rooms that provide opportunities to lie down for rest (but not conceived as bedrooms) must be provided. Quiet rooms can also be used as first aid rooms, for postcrisis care, and for duty meetings, and they should have a size of at least 15 m².

Figure 4.10.21 (left)
Schematic layout of a control center

Figure 4.10.22 (right)
Example of a control center layout for fire and rescue departments, operations management, and emergency management

Figure 4.10.23
Examples of a fire department control center and a situation room

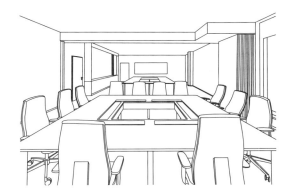

### 4.10.3.4  Workshops

**Hose Workshop**

In fire stations, hose maintenance can take place in the hose-drying tower by hanging the hoses to dry; alternatively, a separate hose maintenance facility may be provided independent of the tower. As a rule, hoses will be brought by various fire departments from the district, and delivery should take place via a direct connection from outside. It is imperative to ensure that a soiled/clean separation is maintained in order to prevent contamination within the building. Workrooms must have the benefit of natural daylight. The area for the hose maintenance workshop, including soiled/clean separation, storage, and logistics areas, should be at least roughly 80 m². The actual size depends on the cleaning method (hose maintenance along (1) full-length lines = approx. 24 m long, (2) half-length lines = approx. 12 m long, or (3) compact system = approx. 10 m²) and on the method used for drying (natural or mechanical). The hose-drying tower should follow in direct continuation from the cleaning line. → **Figure 4.10.25**

**Breathing Apparatus Workshop and Clothing Storage**

For organizational reasons, in particular soiled/clean separation and for better space efficiency, it is desirable to combine the acceptance of hoses, PPE (personal protective equipment) and hazmat suits (for protection from hazardous materials). The size of a breathing apparatus workshop, including soiled/clean separation, storage, and logistics areas, should total approximately 100 m². Due to the loudness of compressors, these units should be installed in a separate room measuring at least 9 m². → **Figure 4.10.26**

**Figure 4.10.24 (left)**
View into a hose-drying tower

**Figure 4.10.25 (right)**
Hose maintenance facility

Fire hoses come in lengths of up to approximately 35 m. Depending on the type of deployment (filling hose, turntable ladder, etc.), standardized lengths of hoses in Germany vary between 5 and 35 m.

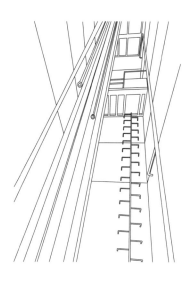

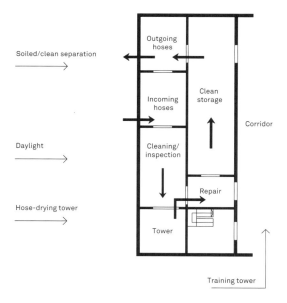

**Figure 4.10.26**
Layout example of a breathing apparatus workshop

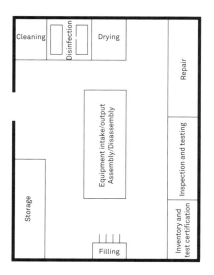

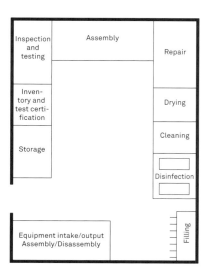

## 4.10.3.5 Practice Rooms

### Breathing Apparatus Practice Area

A breathing apparatus practice area is used by firefighters for operational training and should be close to the fitness room so that it is possible for staff training with full breathing protection equipment to share fitness equipment such as an endless ladder, a treadmill, or a bicycle ergometer. For training purposes, firefighters can be exposed to high temperatures in a controlled manner in a heat-acclimatizing room. At points of ingress and egress to/from the practice area it is necessary to provide vestibules in order to prevent the spread of smoke to clean areas. A visual connection must exist between the control station and the conditioning, training, and target rooms; when these rooms are filled with smoke, the connection must be maintained via infrared cameras. During training, paramedics must be present for checking blood pressure and monitoring general health. A first aid room must be provided so that emergency medical care can be administered when needed. → Figure 4.10.27

### Fire Room

Fire rooms are used to become accustomed to different types of fires and the appropriate extinguishing methods. Due to the flames and high temperatures generated by combustion, the building materials of the fire room must be particularly fire-resistant. Furniture made of stainless steel is used to simulate different types of rooms. Fire rooms can also be used to simulate flameover/flashover situations (sudden ignition of fire gas).

### Training Tower

It is usual to combine hose-drying towers and training towers in one structure. For training purposes there should be balconies and window openings for practicing the positioning of ladders of various types, such as scaling ladders, hook ladders, and aerial (turntable) ladders. Typical training towers are approximately 14 m high. If the structure is also used for hose-drying purposes, the tower may need to be up to 24 m high. In addition, hose-drying towers are often used for the installation of antenna masts. → Figure 4.10.29

Figure 4.10.27
Schematic layout of a breathing apparatus practice area

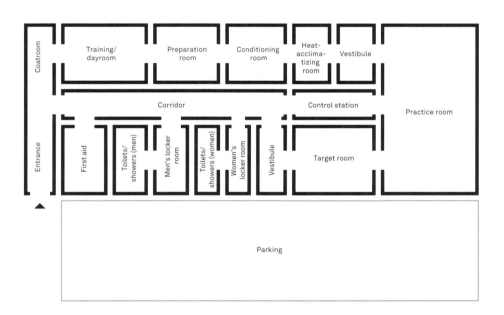

Figure 4.10.28 (left)
Example of a breathing apparatus practice area as an obstacle course built with mesh compartments

Figure 4.10.29 (right)
Examples of hose-drying and training towers with antenna masts

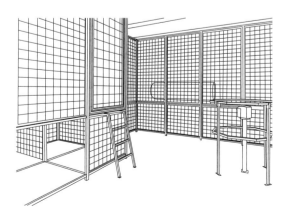

### Training Hall

Training halls can be used to simulate various different scenarios:

- Single-family house
- Multifamily dwelling
- High-rise building
- Retail store
- Workshop with loading ramp
- School
- etc.

Additional facilities may be provided, such as railroad tracks, practice areas for airport firefighting teams, industrial simulations, and other situations for specialized units. →Figure 4.10.30

### Shooting Ranges

Police stations may have shooting ranges or galleries which are not only used for training and practicing the use of firearms, but also for training appropriate responses in different situations and scenarios. In modern shooting ranges it is common to use computer-aided interactive video shooting simulation systems. Shooting ranges should always be designed for simultaneous use by several shooters, including variable shooting positions. An indoor shooting range is inherently enclosed on all sides, and all the enclosing building elements and components must be bulletproof. The location within a building should be carefully chosen to prevent disruption to or annoyance of other functions from noise or other emissions. It may be necessary to provide larger ventilation systems and ducts, because otherwise gunpowder residues might accumulate in the facility. Shooting ranges can also be combined with classrooms and other facilities in a training center housed in a separate building complex, thus making it possible for several police units to share the range and training facilities. →Figure 4.10.32

### Sports and Fitness

Facilities for sports and fitness are provided to enable the personnel to maintain physical fitness and can also be used by on-duty staff as a leisure activity. These facilities include gymnasiums for ball sports as well as strength and endurance training, or, where less space is available, may solely consist of small fitness rooms for strength and endurance training. ↗Chapter 4.9 Typologies/Sports and Recreation

**Figure 4.10.30 (left)**
Example of a fire department training hall

**Figure 4.10.31 (right)**
Example of an indoor shooting range

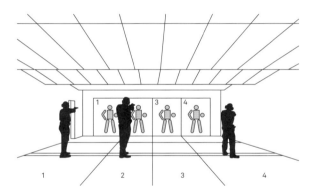

**Figure 4.10.32**
Schematic layout of an indoor shooting range

The bullet trap of shooting ranges should measure at least 7 × 8 m. Scenario rooms (blue box) should measure at least 5 × 8 m.

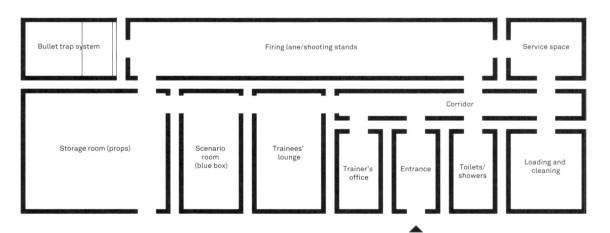

### 4.10.3.6 Courtrooms

The design of courtrooms depends on the type of court, the participants involved (such as lay judges, jurors), and the number of visitors to be accommodated. If multiple judges and/or a jury will be present, the room must have adequate seating and desks/tables in the judge's area. For large criminal procedures where several parties and joint plaintiffs may be involved, it is also necessary to provide sufficient seating for spectators and the media. In addition, courtrooms should have a separate consulting room to which the judges can withdraw and conduct consultations. → **Figure 4.10.33**

### 4.10.3.7 Prison Cells

Penal law contains minimum requirements for the design of detention cells as habitable rooms, which must provide accommodation fit for humans. A rule of thumb is that approximately 10 m² are required for a single detention room. The custody guidelines valid for the specific area of jurisdiction must be observed. → **Figure 4.10.34**

Figure 4.10.33
Schematic layout of a courtroom

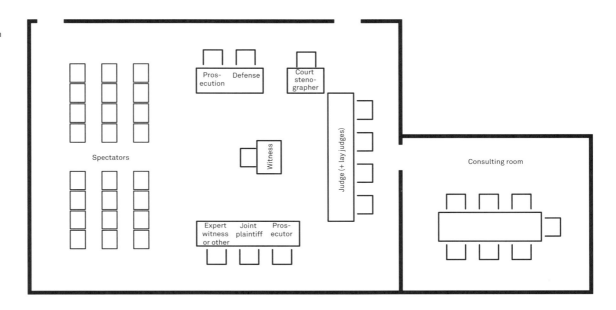

Figure 4.10.34
Example of layout and minimum dimensions for an individual cell and a cell for two inmates

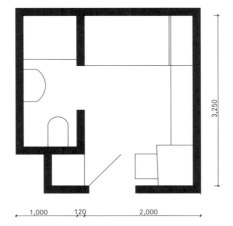
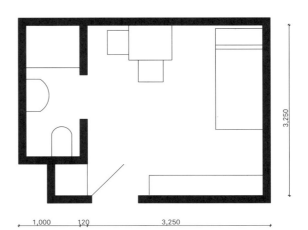

491

### 4.10.3.8  Office and Administrative Spaces

**Administration**

All public safety buildings also include offices and administrative spaces to varying degrees. These may be allocated to various departments and areas of responsibility at a supraregional level, as with criminal investigation departments, or may solely serve a specific local district. ↗ **Chapter 4.2 Typologies/Office and Administration**

**Typical fire department administration areas are:**
- Department head
- Duty manager
- Shift coordinator
- Preventive fire protection
- Preventive fire protection
- Municipal fire inspector
- Training
- Meeting rooms
- Ancillary spaces

**Typical administration areas of police departments are:**
- Department head
- Hazard prevention/response
- Traffic
- Crime
- Central tasks
- Prevention
- Training
- Meeting rooms
- Ancillary spaces

**Training, Education, Preparation for Practice Sessions**

Training rooms in public safety buildings are used for the basic and advanced theoretical and practical training of service personnel, and they are equipped with common items such as a projection screen and video projector along with loudspeakers/microphone. Fire stations may also require a fume hood (extraction system/laboratory) for demonstration and practice purposes.

Rooms for tactical deployment games (for fire and police departments) constitute a special type of training room. These are used to learn various deployment scenarios through theoretical but realistic simulations. A breathing apparatus practice area should simulate realistic situations as closely as possible. ↗ 4.10.3.5 **Practice Rooms**

**Table 4.10.2**
Space requirements for training, offices, and administration in fire stations

Based on DIN 14092-1

| Space | Size | Remarks |
|---|---|---|
| Training rooms | min. 30 m² | Necessity and size depend on the use concept. Recommendation: 1.5 m² per participant |
| Room for youth and junior fire department | min. 20 m² | Recommendation: 2 m² per user |
| Kitchenettes | min. 8 m² | – |
| Teaching supplies | min. 6 m² | – |
| First aid room and quiet room (also for duty meetings) | min. 15 m² | Can be designed as a multifunctional room with at least 15 m². Additional functions may include: Emergency pastoral (spiritual) guidance Recuperation for users of breathing apparatuses after longer deployments Crisis aftercare |
| Duty room/dayroom | min. 15 m² | Can be combined with training room |
| Administration/office unit | min. 12 m² | Quantity based on needs assessment. If there is only one office, a minimum size of 15 m² is recommended. |
| General storage | min. 12 m² | |

**Table 4.10.3**
Requirements for office and administration space in police stations

| Space | Size | Remarks |
|---|---|---|
| Administration/office unit | min. 12 m² | Quantity based on needs assessment. If there is only one office, a minimum size of 15 m² is recommended. |
| Kitchenettes | min. 4 m² | – |
| Dayroom | min. 15 m² | Size in accordance with use concept and number of persons |

## 4.10.3.9  Ancillary Spaces

All public safety buildings need locker rooms where personnel can change between private to service clothing. With the exception of courthouses, these buildings also need dayrooms and duty rooms as well as adequate sanitary facilities with showers. Table 4.10.4 lists exemplary space requirements for ancillary rooms in fire stations. The minimum space requirement per person for changing rooms is also applicable to police stations.

**Table 4.10.4**
Space requirement for ancillary rooms in the duty and practice facilities, with connection to the apparatus bay

Based on DIN 14092-1

↗ Chapter 3.5 Spaces/Sanitary Facilities
↗ Chapter 3.8 Spaces/Ancillary and Staff Rooms

| Space | Size | Remarks |
|---|---|---|
| PPE storage/changing room | min. 1.2 m² | Gender-specific |
| For female service personnel | | For each active member of the firefighting team |
| For male service personnel | | For each active member of the firefighting team |
| Sanitary facilities: toilets, washrooms/showers | – | At least one facility per gender, or additional as required |
| Female service personnel | – | Minimum sanitary facilities:<br>1 × toilet<br>1 × washbasin<br>1 × shower |
| Male service personnel | – | Minimum sanitary facilities:<br>1 × toilet<br>2 × urinals<br>1 × washbasin<br>1 × shower |
| Drying room | min. 6 m² | For drying wet service clothing |

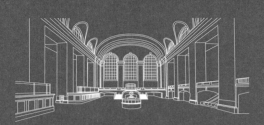

**Grand Central Station,** New York, NY, USA, Warren & Wetmore and Reed & Stern, 1913

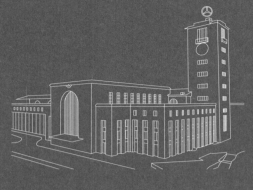

**Central Station,** Stuttgart, Germany, Paul Bonatz, 1922

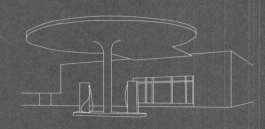

**Gas Station,** Skovshoved, Denmark, Arne Jacobsen, 1936

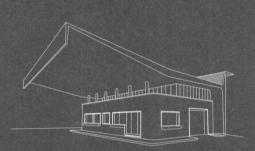

**Agip gas stations,** Italy, Mario Bacciocchi, 1950s

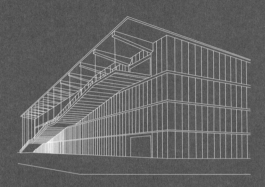

**Haniel Garage,** Düsseldorf, Germany, Paul Schneider-Esleben, 1951

**TWA Flight Center,** New York, NY, USA, Eero Saarinen, 1962

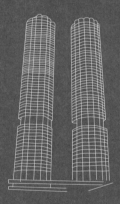

**Marina City,** Chicago, IL, USA, Bertrand Goldberg, 1964

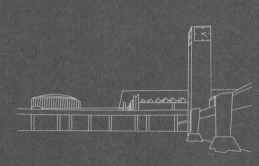

**Atocha Railway Station,** Madrid, Spain, Rafael Moneo, 1992

**Kansai Airport,** Japan, Renzo Piano, 1994

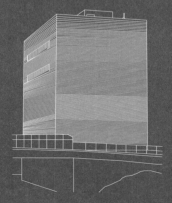

**Central Signal Box,** Basel, Switzerland, Herzog & de Meuron, 1998

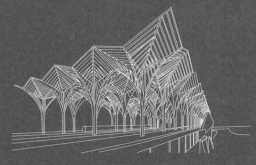

**Lisbon Orient Station,** Lisbon, Portugal, Santiago Calatrava, 1998

**Berlin Central Station,** Germany, gmp, 2006

Bert Bielefeld
Jasmin Sowa

# 4 Typologies
## 4.11 Transportation and Infrastructure

### 4.11.1 Building Concept ↗496

4.11.1.1 Planning Parameters ↗496
4.11.1.2 Building Forms ↗496
4.11.1.3 Circulation Systems ↗497
4.11.1.4 Construction and Technology ↗500

### 4.11.2 Program of Use ↗502

4.11.2.1 Railroad Stations ↗502
4.11.2.2 Bus Stations and Terminals ↗505
4.11.2.3 Airports ↗506
4.11.2.4 Ports ↗513
4.11.2.5 Parking Garages ↗515
4.11.2.6 Gas Stations/Car Washes/Auto Repair Shops ↗520

### 4.11.3 Areas and Rooms ↗523

4.11.3.1 Entrance Areas and Circulation Zones ↗524
4.11.3.2 Ticket Counters and Access Control Systems ↗526
4.11.3.3 Train Platforms ↗528
4.11.3.4 Bus platforms ↗528
4.11.3.5 Runways ↗530
4.11.3.6 Jetways ↗532
4.11.3.7 Baggage Claim ↗532
4.11.3.8 Equipment for Gas Stations and Car Repair Workshops ↗532

# 4.11 Transportation and Infrastructure

## 4.11.1 Building Concept

### 4.11.1.1 Planning Parameters

Means of transportation such as cars, buses, railroads, and airplanes are used by everyone in their daily lives. The buildings required for this purpose, in particular for changing between different means of travel and for the purposes of waiting, obtaining service, refueling, and parking, are determined to a large degree by the technical requirements of the respective means of transport and the number of users or volume of freight. Thus the various building typologies differ in significant ways.

A general distinction is made between transportation buildings that are used for mixed forms of transport and those used to exclusively serve passengers or freight. Transportation buildings are always part of regional or transregional infrastructure systems and transportation networks. Working from this context, the development of a project begins by defining the primary types of use and determining levels of user traffic and/or freight volumes.

Typical planning parameters are:
- Place, context
- Infrastructure, accessibility
- Type of use, primary function
- Passenger and/or freight transport
- Frequency of use, freight volumes
- Site geometry and topography
- Building code restrictions, noise abatement
- Spatial program and needs
- Ancillary uses
- User group needs
- Efficient logistics (passengers, freight, utilities)
- Presentational purposes
- Barrier-free accessibility
- Security (and access control where needed)
- Budget and deadlines

Due to their specific characteristics, every different means of transportation requires a specific approach that results from the space needs – including safety clearances (such as for jet airplanes), movement principles (such as the turning radius of a car or bus), and the type of access or method of loading (such as the height of train platforms or airplane doors) – or also from the necessity to limit emissions. Beyond that, essential planning parameters for the architect are the logistics processes for the flow of passengers or freight, which should be as unhindered as possible, and the necessary considerations. Furthermore, in order to ensure the attractiveness and popularity of many large transportation facilities, it is important to provide associated amenities such as hotels, conference areas, restaurants, stores, leisure facilities, and the like. Many transportation buildings also function as a landmark or an emblem for the city, and are therefore designed as prestigious edifices with a focus on accommodating high numbers of users.

Frequency of use is particularly important at intermodal interchanges (such as railroad stations or airports), where peak volumes have to be taken into consideration. Interchanges may involve a change between the same means of transport (from train to train, for example, or airplane to airplane) or an intermodal change, for example changing from public transit (such as a regional train or bus) or a private means of transport (such as a car or bicycle) to a transregional means of transport (such as an airplane, a long-distance train or bus, etc.). Appropriate parking areas must be provided for buses, cars, and bicycles.

In view of the constantly changing requirements, technical progress, and changing user expectations, another aspect in the design of transportation and infrastructure buildings is to achieve the greatest possible flexibility. Additionally, because security controls are becoming increasingly strict – particularly at airports and train stations – buildings need to offer space to accommodate future developments.

### 4.11.1.2 Building Forms

The forms taken on by transportation and infrastructure buildings are primarily determined at a technical level by the particular means of transport and logistical processes, and at a design level by the expectations of its users. Building forms range from basic utilitarian structures (such as roof canopies) to monumental and sculptural complex-

Figure 4.11.1
Basic building forms

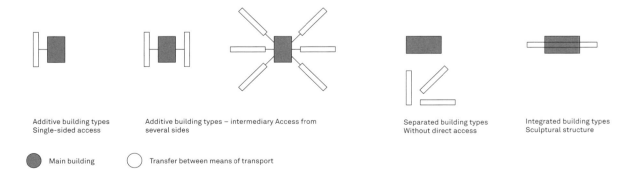

Additive building types
Single-sided access

Additive building types – intermediary Access from
several sides

Separated building types
Without direct access

Integrated building types
Sculptural structure

⬤ Main building          ◯ Transfer between means of transport

es for large airports and train stations. A common feature of all these typologies is that they require large spaces, which means that the structural system must offer large span widths.

In view of the linear nature of most transport routes (airport runways, railroad tracks, roads, etc.), the buildings have to be positioned accordingly. A distinction can be made between additive, separated, and integrated building types. → **Figure 4.11.1** In additive building types, different areas with varying requirements are coupled together. The components of large buildings such as airport or railroad terminals are joined with platforms or departure gates; the overall form of an additive building responds to functional needs by means of various decentralized facilities such as waiting areas, roofed areas, or access tunnels. Separated elements are independent buildings that accommodate ancillary functions needed beyond the actual use of the means of transport, for example a building for ticketing and information next to a bus terminal. These buildings are not directly connected with the actual transport routes, which means that in certain cases – for example in airports – a bus transfer may be required. Integrated types of building accommodate not only the connection to the means of transport but also all the ancillary functions and transfer links within one large volume or under one roof. Integrated building forms often have a sculptural character that also impacts the surrounding urban space (such as with a major train station or international airport), and thereby possess high representational value for a city or region.

### 4.11.1.3 Circulation Systems

Most transportation buildings serve as an interchange between different transportation systems (train, subway, bus, car, etc.). The routes to be taken by passengers when transferring between the different means of transport provide the basis for organizing the external circulation. → **Figure 4.11.2**, ↗ **Chapter 3.1.1 Spaces/External Circulation/Public Access**

Within the building, passenger circulation routes may be arranged on several levels (underground, at ground level, and via bridges). The organization of routes and weighting of the different passenger flows have a significant impact on the layout of functions and the volume of the building. → **Figure 4.11.3**

An important design task is the organization of the many individual movements within the building. Pedestrian flows can either be clearly directed or spread via large areas; they can be differentiated by separating the different flows according to their purposes, or they can be distributed by routing via different access points. In well-laid-out circulation systems, it is possible to accommodate larger numbers of persons or quantity of freight with the same amount of space/equipment. → **Figure 4.11.4**

Depending on the security and access concept (such as security check at airports or ticket check at railroad stations), it is also necessary to integrate the various passenger and luggage check zones into the circulation concept. In view of the fact that security checkpoints and access controls always represent points of congestion in the circulation, it may be appropriate to provide additional space (such as for turnstiles or identity checks) in order to compensate for slowdowns in the traffic flow. It is necessary to carry out risk analyses at an early stage in order to clearly define the different security areas and their interfaces, as these may also be relevant for ancillary functions and members of staff. The security concept may also be used to define further requirements for technical control measures such as door control systems, nonreturn gates, turnstiles, etc.

All major transportation buildings need a well-planned guide system to provide users with quick and reliable orientation. In a parking garage, a two-part guide system helps drivers to find empty parking spaces and also helps returning pedestrians to find their way back to the vehicle. In airports and railroad stations it is necessary to provide signage to identify the different areas, direction signs and display boards with the current arrival/departure times, as well as layout plans of the entire facility. There will also be information desks at strategic places, where personal advisors are available.

It is important to ensure that all routes are barrier-free. Where longer distances are involved, appropriate guide systems, lifts, moving walkways and escalators, as well as support vehicles for older persons and those with restricted mobility, need to be taken into consideration. ↗ **Chapter 3.2 Spaces/Internal Circulation**

Figure 4.11.2
Schematic diagram of a
transport interchange

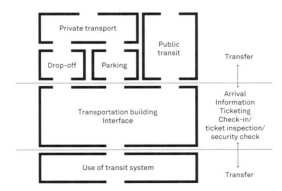

Figure 4.11.3
Examples of connections
to means of transport

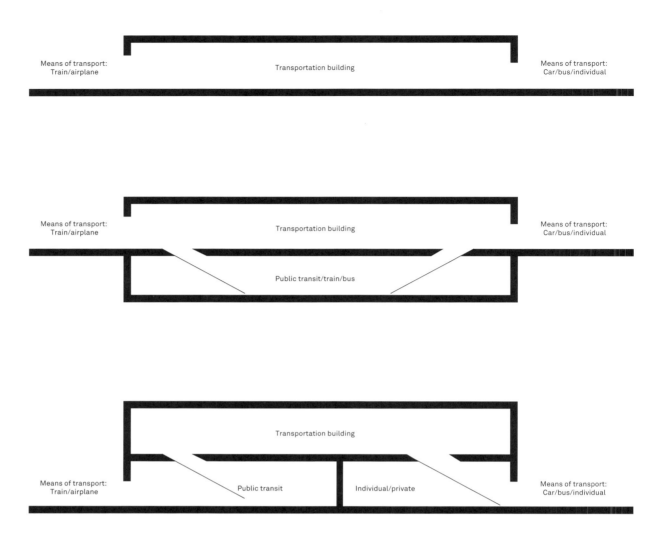

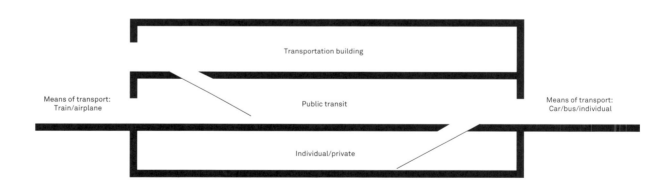

Figure 4.11.4
Typical sequence of security
checks in airports

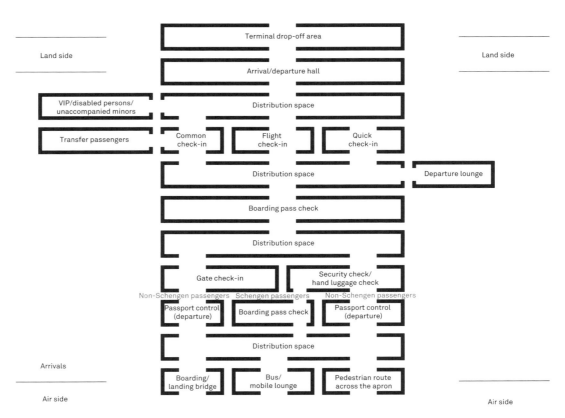

Figure 4.11.5
Schematic routing layout

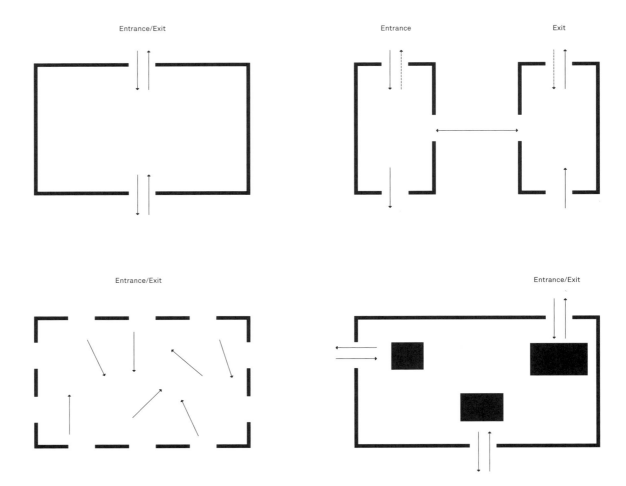

### 4.11.1.4 Construction and Technology

As a rule, the specific functions required of transport buildings mean that large spans without columns are required. For this reason, typical structures involve steel and/or concrete girders, barrel construction, space framing or tree column construction. → **Figure 4.11.6** In railroad stations and airport buildings, the load-bearing structures are usually very extensive and are often exposed to the view on the inside, providing a style element. → **Figure 4.11.7**

In parking garages, the load-bearing grid and hence the column grid have an important impact on the efficient use of space. Popular options involve optimized load-bearing systems as additive systems comprising steel columns and girders and trapeze sheet constructions with infill concrete, because the decks of this construction are less thick and the system is quick and relatively economical to build. → **Figure 4.11.8** In addition, it is necessary for the load-bearing elements and the facade to be able to withstand impact loads.

Figure 4.11.6
Common examples of
load-bearing structures

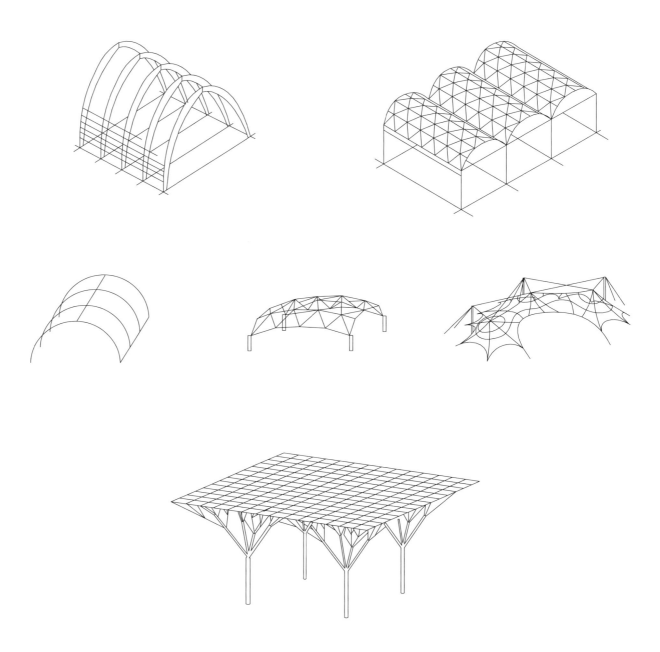

Figure 4.11.7
Construction examples for
railroad buildings

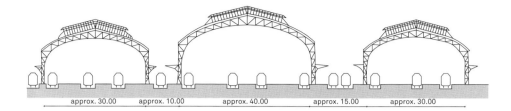

approx. 30.00     approx. 10.00     approx. 40.00     approx. 15.00     approx. 30.00

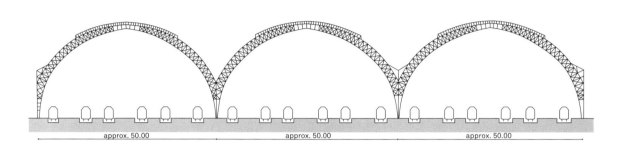

approx. 50.00          approx. 50.00          approx. 50.00

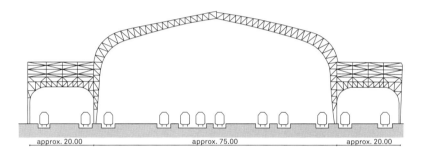

approx. 20.00          approx. 75.00          approx. 20.00

Figure 4.11.8
System sketches of parking
garage systems

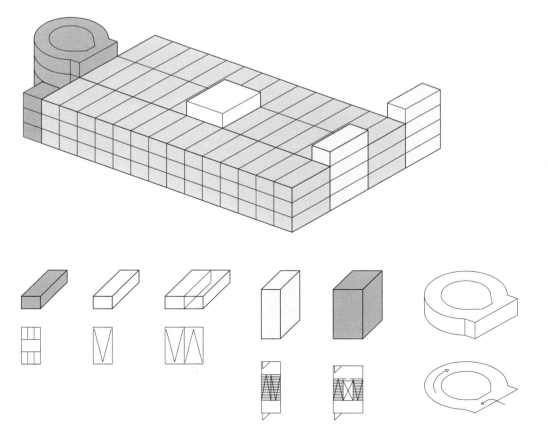

## 4.11.2 Program of Use

### 4.11.2.1 Railroad Stations

A distinction is generally made to distinguish between train stations that are used as passenger stations, freight stations, or depots. The design of railroad stations is primarily determined by the number and layout of the main and secondary tracks, the associated platforms – if any – and the functions to be accommodated in the buildings. →**Figure 4.11.10**

In addition, the design of railroad stations varies according to the direction of the train traffic (linear, changing direction, crossing over, terminal line) and the position of the station building (placed laterally, at the head, as an island, above or below the tracks). →**Figure 4.11.9**

**Railroad Stations for Passenger Traffic**
Passenger stations range from single-track platforms with a shelter in local passenger transport through to the main stations in large cities, which usually include numerous additional functions, such as:

- Drop-off area/deliveries
- Arrivals concourse
- Waiting areas
- Sales/retail shops
- Cafés/restaurants
- Toilets
- Information
- Ticketing (information/sales)
- Security check
- Lockers
- Travelers' aid (railway mission)
- Police/Customs
  ↗Chapter 4.10 Typologies/Public Safety
- Lost and found (lost property)

Usually, all functions of relevance to railroad passengers and passers-by are accommodated near the entrance or in the central station building. →**Figure 4.11.11** This includes the ticket sales, information booth, and various shops and cafés/restaurants. Where rather more incidental functions are provided, such as lounge areas, hotels, shopping centers, lost property offices, railway mission halls, these are usually placed somewhat apart from the main thoroughfare. ↗Chapter 3.4.2 Spaces/Communication Spaces and Dining Rooms/Waiting and Seating Areas, ↗Chapter 4.3 Typologies/Logistics and Commerce, ↗Chapter 4.7 Typologies/Lodging and Food Service

It is common practice to provide a circulation zone between the concourse or entrance and the platforms, which helps passengers with their orientation, makes it possible to change directly from platform to platform, and may also include checking functions for tickets and/or security. Where, in subway stations, these circulation zones are located directly beneath the street level, they may also be used as pedestrian underpasses. →**Figure 4.11.12**

The layout of and access to the platforms may be arranged directly from the station concourse or via transverse paths above or below the tracks. In the case of two-track railroad stations, such as in local passenger transport systems, it is possible to provide two platforms outside the two tracks, each of them serving the track from one side only; in this system, the tracks can carry on in a linear layout such as through tunnel tubes; alternatively, one platform can be placed centrally between the two tracks. In the case of multitrack stations, it is usual to combine both systems for more efficient use of the space, which means that a platform is placed between pairs of tracks. →**Figure 4.11.13**

Figure 4.11.9
Basic types of railroad stations

○ Train station building

● Main and secondary entrances

→ Access to tracks

Terminal station

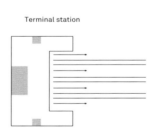

Through station

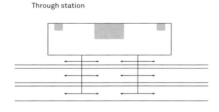

Elevated station

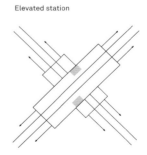

Island station

Cross-rail station

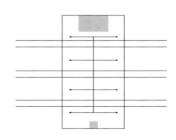

**Figure 4.11.10 (left)**
Track elements in a railroad station

**Figure 4.11.11 (right)**
Different types of platform layout

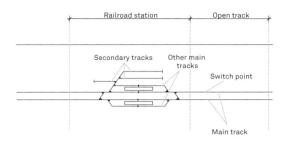

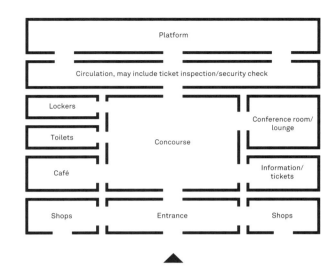

**Figure 4.11.12**
Layout of subway stations for local passenger transport

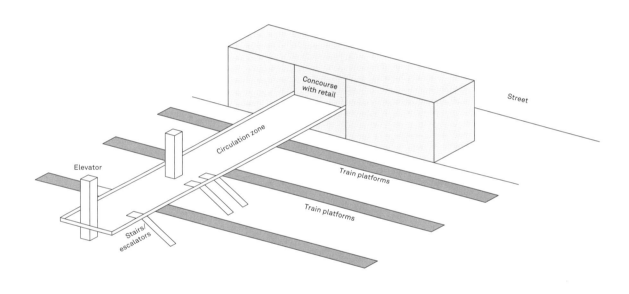

**Figure 4.11.13**
Different types of platform layout

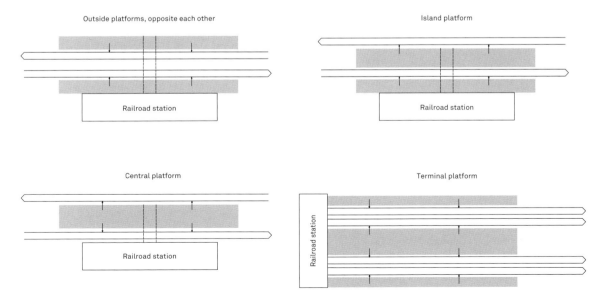

### Interlocking Towers

In view of the fact that interlocking towers (signal towers) are part of any larger track system, they are also considered as design tasks where they occur in an urban context. The following different technical versions exist:

- Mechanical signal towers (transmission via cable pulls or linkages)
- Electromechanical signal towers (mechanical operation assisted with electric motors)
- Track image or relay interlockings (control panels with image of track system)
- Electronic signaling centers (control via computer systems)

The interlocking tower comprises a main room with the control apparatus. In the case of mechanical interlocking towers, another room has to be provided beneath the main room. In addition, the buildings may include staff rooms and sanitary facilities, and even meeting rooms and other administration areas. → **Figure 4.11.14** In spite of their relatively small space requirement, interlocking towers are often arranged on several levels in the station area in order to ensure that operators have a good view of the entire track system.

### Freight Station

As a rule, the design of freight stations is largely determined by the track layout rather than the buildings. It is common to combine loading and unloading areas with other logistics functions and to provide appropriate service areas (registration, staff areas, etc.) in separate buildings. Extensive roof constructions covering the tracks and sheds are only rarely required owing to the reduction in individual goods rail transport, which is why these spaces are considered in the design as potential conversion areas.
→ **Figure 4.11.15**

Figure 4.11.14
Schematic layout of an
interlocking tower

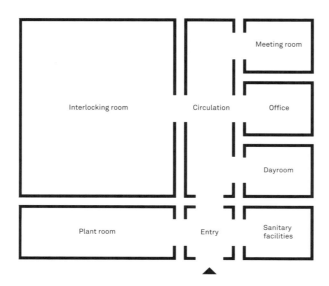

Figure 4.11.15
Switching yard or train
assembly yard

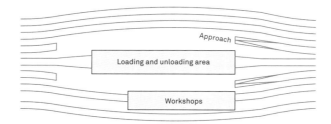

## 4.11.2.2 Bus Stations and Terminals

Bus stations and terminals serve as central points of arrival/departure or transfer in the vicinity of airports or train stations. Where a number of different buses have to be accommodated at the same time, various layouts can be adopted, such as parallel bus lanes, circular access and docking road, and layouts with parking berths (similar to a train terminal). → **Figure 4.11.16**

Bus terminals usually have raised platforms for the boarding/disembarking of passengers; they are also usually roofed over, with the design variations ranging from simple shelters through to platform roofs and roof systems covering the entire bus station/terminal area. In very busy bus stations it is common to integrate additional functions similar to railroad stations, that is, toilets, information and service points, catering facilities, shops, lounges, etc. The accommodation for these functions can be arranged in the fashion of a terminal layout or in parallel, over or under the bus platform. Accordingly it is necessary to provide appropriate circulation space, staircases, and lifts that allow for the number of passengers with their luggage. ↗ **Chapter 3.1.1 Spaces/External Circulation/Public Access**, ↗ **Chapter 3.1.2 Spaces/External Circulation/Parked Vehicles**, ↗ **Chapter 4.3 Typologies/Logistics and Commerce**, ↗ **Chapter 4.7 Typologies/Lodging and Food Service**

**Figure 4.11.16**
Layout options for bus terminals

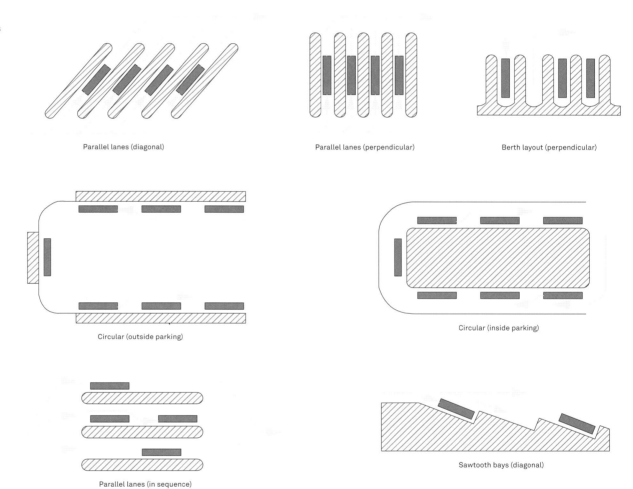

Parallel lanes (diagonal)

Parallel lanes (perpendicular)

Berth layout (perpendicular)

Circular (outside parking)

Circular (inside parking)

Parallel lanes (in sequence)

Sawtooth bays (diagonal)

**Figure 4.11.17**
Schematic layout of a bus station with high passenger volume

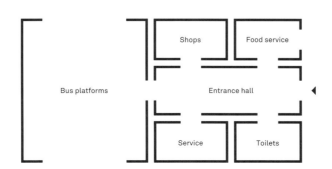

Bus platforms

Shops

Food service

Entrance hall

Service

Toilets

### 4.11.2.3 Airports

The design of airports is a very complex task, in which many standards of international and national organizations have to be taken into account; examples are the International Civil Aviation Organization (ICAO), the International Air Transport Association (IATA), the American Federal Aviation Administration (FAA), the European Joint Aviation Authorities (JAA) or the European Aviation Safety Agency (EASA).

Airports consist of a number of basic elements which are initially arranged to produce an overall concept and master plan. → Figure 4.11.18

A general distinction is made between the air side and the land side. The following elements should be provided on the air side:

- Air traffic control
- Tower
- Beacon systems
- Markings, signage
- Runways (takeoff and landing strips)
- Apron
- Taxiways/aircraft wait positions
- Hangars
- Catering
- Cleaning of aircraft
- Fueling of aircraft
- Storage of operating materials

- Freight handling
- Workshops
- Electricity supply
- Meteorological systems
- Fire Department (↗ Chapter 4.10 Typologies/Public Safety)

The general layout of runways and their length and number, as well as their extendability, are crucial factors when deciding on a location for a new airport. → Figure 4.11.19 Primary considerations for selecting the location for an airport are the topographical and meteorological conditions and the environmental impact of the flight operations.

On the land side, the design should provide for parking and traffic circulation, a link to local public transit, and various supporting functions. These may include:

- Security systems and services
- Delivery and logistics areas
- Supply facilities (such as catering, fuel)
- Administrative areas
- Commercial and hotel premises

↗ Chapter 4.3 Typologies/Logistics and Commerce
↗ Chapter 4.7 Typologies/Lodging and Food Service
↗ Chapter 4.10 Typologies/Public Safety

Figure 4.11.18
Basic elements of an airport

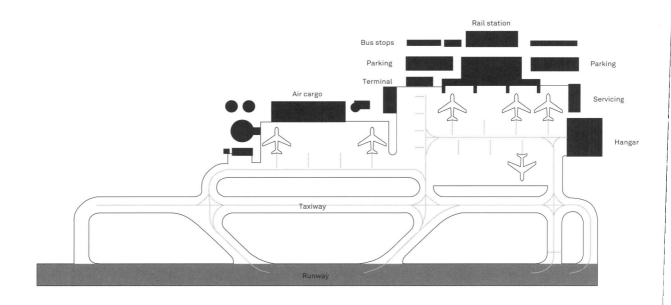

Figure 4.11.19
Runway configurations

Runway

Terminal

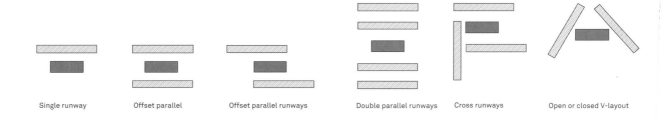

Single runway    Offset parallel    Offset parallel runways    Double parallel runways    Cross runways    Open or closed V-layout

**Passenger Transport within the Terminal**

The main buildings of an airport are the terminals, which act as interfaces between the airside and the landside and which need to accommodate the following three functions. →**Figure 4.11.20**

Terminals consist of many passenger-handling, security, and waiting areas:

- Boarding gates
- Gate check-in
- Flight check-in
- Sufficient circulation space and waiting areas throughout
- Lounge/VIP areas
- Information systems
- Security checks
- Boarding pass/passport control
- Food services and retail shops
- Duty-free shops
- Baggage claim
- Customs
- Various ancillary functions

For large community airports in particular, multiples of the above facilities are provided in order to be able to cope with large numbers of passengers. →**Table 4.11.1**

Various terminal concepts have evolved to achieve efficient passenger handling. →**Table 4.11.2** Of key importance are the spatial options for layout of the runways and the number of gates and total passengers. With large hub airports in particular, it is important to keep the distances and times for transfer between gates as short as possible.

The passenger flows within terminals are governed by international handling and safety/security standards. →**Figure 4.11.21** Ticket and check-in counters are arranged in the main concourse. As a rule, this area also accommodates many commercial functions such as food service outlets, shops, rental car companies, etc. Likewise, the areas beyond the security check zone will often include food service facilities, duty-free shops, and extensive waiting areas. ↗**Chapter 3.4.2 Spaces/Communication Spaces and Dining Rooms/Waiting and Seating Areas**

In designing a new airport, a key decision is how to arrange passenger access to the aircraft. Available options are transport by bus, moving walkway, and gangways for direct connections, or footpaths on the apron; the chosen option determines the organization of the building levels. →**Figure 4.11.23** As a rule, one gangway is used per aircraft; for larger machines (such as an Airbus 380) possibly also two or three in order to reduce time spent on the apron.

As a rule, arriving passengers are routed directly through the departure area; alternatively they are routed via a separate story/layout organization to the baggage collection area, passing passport control if necessary. From there, the route leads through customs control to the land side. The handling of baggage follows its own logistics path separate from the passengers, involving connections with the check-in and bulk baggage counters, the baggage conveyors, the security installations and finally the apron. →**Figure 4.11.22**

Figure 4.11.20
Mobility relationships of an airport

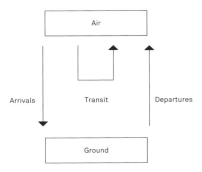

Table 4.11.1
Classification of airports

As per European Commission

| | |
|---|---|
| Large community airports | > 10 million passengers/year |
| National airports | 5–10 million passengers/year |
| Large regional airports | 1–5 million passengers/year |
| Small regional airports | < 1 million passengers/year |

Table 4.11.2
Typical terminal concepts

| Terminal concept | Description | Access to terminal – aircraft | Transit/transfer | Basic layout examples |
|---|---|---|---|---|
| Open apron | Passengers are driven by bus to the aircraft on the apron. | Not direct – only via buses | Not direct – only via the terminal | |
| Linear concept | Gates next to each other on one side of the building | Direct | Direct via the terminal | |
| Spine-and-fingers concept | Individual gates are located on both sides of the "fingers" (main gates), which are connected via the main building | Direct | Direct; any transfer to another terminal via the main building | |
| Satellite concept | Standalone buildings with individual gates all round, access via means of transport at ground level or below ground | Direct | Direct; may require change to another satellite | |
| Unit/cluster concept | Gate clusters serving different parts of a building | Direct | Direct; may require change to another unit | |

Figure 4.11.21
Schematic layout of an airport

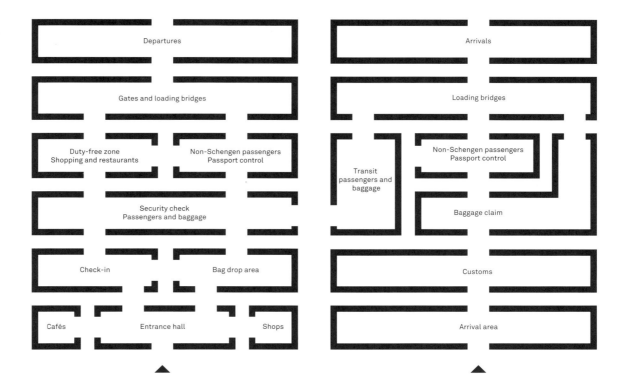

Figure 4.11.22
Schematic layout of baggage
logistics at airports

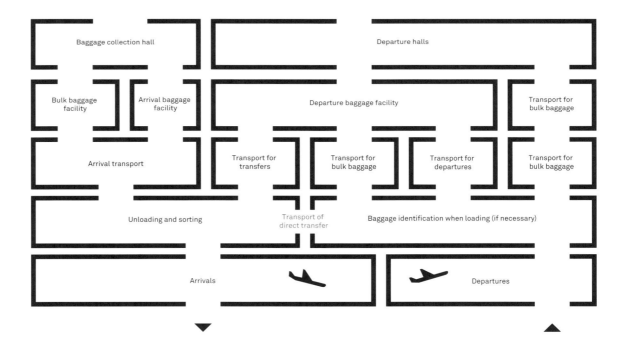

Figure 4.11.23
Terminal connections

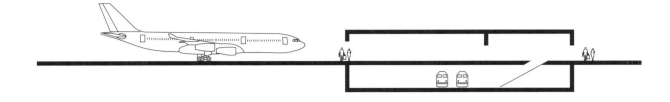

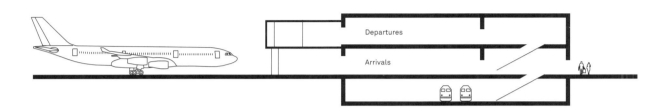

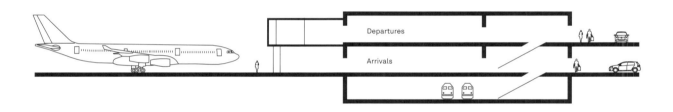

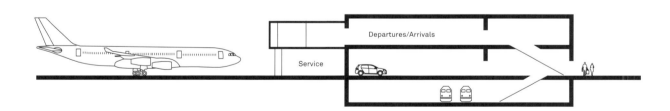

### Freight Facilities

In addition to the areas reserved for transporting passenger luggage, there are also facilities within the airport complex specifically for the handling of freight, which are categorized by the turnover quantity. →**Table 4.11.3**

Freight terminals and handling facilities involve heavy goods vehicle (HGV) logistics on the land side, inbound and outbound goods areas, and extensive storage and sorting areas, which may be subdivided by the type of freight (such as refrigerated goods, valuable goods, animals, hazardous goods, etc.). In addition to the logistics areas, there will be administration facilities for customs, the airlines, and service providers. →**Figure 4.11.24**

### Helicopter Landing Pads

Helicopter landing pads require much less area than the runways needed by aircraft; however, owing to the strong air turbulence involved, landing lanes (takeoff and landing are into the wind) and safety distances must be accounted for. Landing pads can be provided either at ground level adjacent to airports or on buildings or ships. The landing pad is marked with an "H" and, if also used for night flights, must have navigation lights and a wind sock. Helicopters are transported to nearby hangars using transport platforms. Key dimensions are the external dimensions of the helicopter and its rotor blades.

Figure 4.11.24
Schematic layout of
a freight terminal

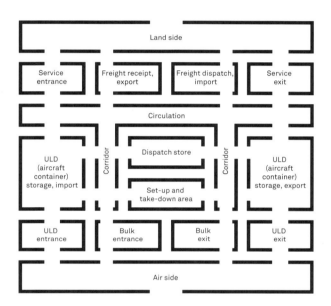

Table 4.11.3
Freight terminal categories

| Name | Turnover quantity | Degree of automation |
|---|---|---|
| Shed terminal | < 75,000 t | Low degree of automation, no separate inward and outward deliveries |
| Station terminal | 75,000–250,000 t | May have fixed transport media, direct access to the apron |
| Center terminal | 250,000–1,000,000 t | Conveyor systems, mostly separate for inward and outward deliveries, high proportion of transfer items |
| Hub terminal | > 1,000,000 t | High degree of automation, very high proportion of transfer items |

Table 4.11.4
Typical dimensions of helicopters

| Helicopter type | Length | Height | Main rotor diameter |
|---|---|---|---|
| Light multipurpose helicopter | 10.00–18.00 m | 3.00–4.00 m | 10.00–13.00 m |
| Multipurpose helicopter | 10.00–13.00 m | 3.00–4.00 m | 10.00–12.00 m |
| Medium-lift transport helicopter | 16.00–30.00 m | 4.00–7.00 m | 15.00–19.00 m |
| Transport helicopter | 12.00–14.00 m | 3.00–5.00 m | 10.00–12.00 m |
| Light helicopter | 6.00–9.00 m | 2.00–3.00 m | 7.00–10.00 m |
| Rescue helicopter | 14.00–15.00 m | 4.50–5.50 m | 9.00–11.00 m |

## Control Tower

The control tower is a landmark at any airport that can be seen from afar; it contains part of the air traffic control, giving instructions and clearance to aircraft for taking off and landing. For this purpose, air traffic controllers need an unobstructed view of the runway, the apron, and the adjoining taxiways next to the main runway. Thus the system for determining obstacle-free areas makes it possible to calculate the necessary height of the control tower.

## Hangar

Hangars are built to accommodate airplanes (and helicopters), making it necessary for these buildings to have large roof spans (mostly space-frame structures, tunnels, or dome structures) that reflect the geometric dimensions of the aircraft and hangar doors of adequate width. For smaller aircraft, T-hangars or aircraft carousels are often used.
→ Figures 4.11.25 and 4.11.26

Figure 4.11.25
Layout principle of T-hangars and aircraft carousels

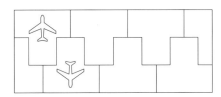 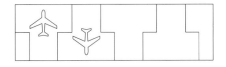 

Figure 4.11.26
Example of a hangar for large aircraft

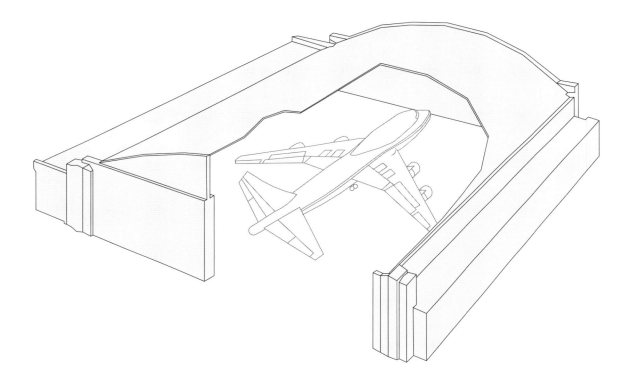

### 4.11.2.4 Ports

Ports are subdivided into inland ports along rivers and waterways/canals, and into seaports at the coast or river estuaries. The water level in a port may fluctuate (as in ports protected by breakwaters) or remain constant (such as impounded docks, dry docks, and wet docks), which affects the embankment walls, the design of the shipping channels, and the heights and construction of the wharves. → **Figure 4.11.27**

The dimensions of the actual waterways and anchoring berths largely depend on the types and size of ships. → **Table 4.11.5** Ports generally need buildings for the purpose of storage, for production requiring port access, and for the transshipment of freight. Marinas (→ **Figure 4.11.28**) are an exception that represent a different typology, with clubhouses and boathouses as well as terminals for passenger ships.

#### Boathouses

Boathouses are needed to store sailboats, rowboats, and motorboats. They can be designed purely as storage premises with or without direct access to the water, include auxiliary functions such as changing rooms and workshops, or even incorporate various restaurant and club facilities to form comprehensive clubhouses. → **Figure 4.11.29**

#### Passenger Ship Terminals

Since the provision of services is an important component in passenger shipping – particularly in the case of cruise ships – the design of terminals increasingly involves provisions for additional and associated functions. Along with the actual passenger-handling facilities, various additional spaces (waiting areas, viewing platforms, etc.) and ancillary functions, such as shops, restaurants, and leisure facilities, must also be provided. → **Figure 4.11.30** Depending on the security concept, access controls can range from simply checking tickets upon boarding to airport-type security checks, and in consequence, it may be necessary to provide ancillary functions for multiple security zones.

**Figure 4.11.27**
Typical elements of a port

Port connection to the mainland

Facilities for unloading vessels

Storage and transshipment areas

Elements of a port

Infrastructural facilities and services

Facilities for loading vessels

**Table 4.11.5**
Typical dimensions of various types of cargo vessels

| Type of ship/boat | Length | Width | Draft |
|---|---|---|---|
| Built on/after 1960 | 137–192 m | 29 m | 10 m |
| Built on/after 1969 | 200–220 m | 29 m | 11–12 m |
| Built on/after 1971 | 260–290 m | 32–33 m | 12–13 m |
| Built on/after 1988 | 290–300 m | 32–33 m | 13–14 m |
| Built on/after 1997 | 320–370 m | 42–46 m | 13–15 m |
| Panamax | max. 425 m | max. 32.3 m | max. 12.5 m |
| Suezmax | | max. 64 m | max. 20 m |
| Malaccamax | max. 470 m | max. 60 m | max. 20 m |
| Inland cargo ship | 38–135 m | 5–11.5 m | 2–3.5 m |

**Figure 4.11.28**
Options for the design of
yacht harbors

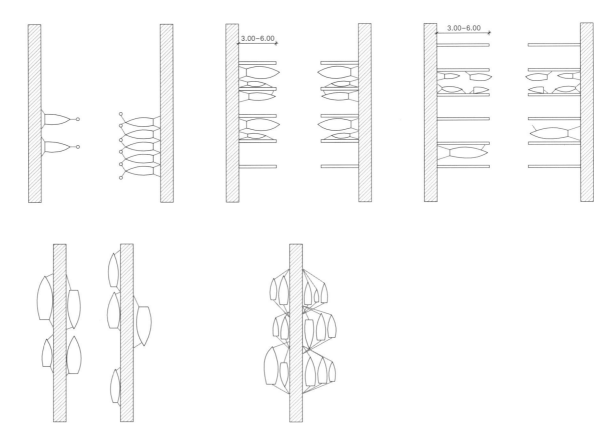

**Figure 4.11.29 (left)**
Schematic layout of a clubhouse

**Figure 4.11.30 (right)**
Schematic layout of a passenger
ship terminal

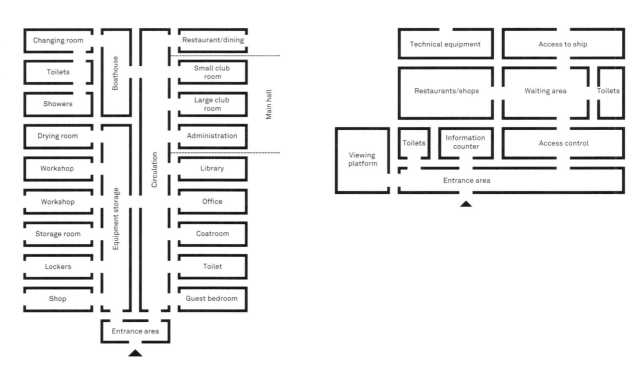

### 4.11.2.5 Parking Garages

Parking garages are built wherever there is insufficient ground-level space for the number of cars that need to be accommodated, which typically includes inner cities, shopping centers, office buildings, airports, hotels, and large housing complexes. Parking garage dimensions are based on the legally required number of parking spaces, the expected number of users, or the maximum number of parking spaces that can be accommodated on the site. ↗ Chapter 3.1.2 Spaces/External Circulation/Parked Vehicles

Garages with a usable area of up to 100 m² are classified as small garages, those between 100 m² and 1,000 m² as medium-sized garages, and garages with over 1,000 m² of usable area as large garages. Parking garages can be built above- or belowground. → Figure 4.11.32 As a general guideline for preliminary design, space needs of about 25–30 m² per parking space can be assumed.

Multistory parking garages can be designed with various access concepts. → Figure 4.11.33 For very large parking garages with a high turnover of vehicles, it makes sense to opt for a full-story system accessed by straight or circular ramps because there are few crossover points for vehicles entering and leaving. Generally more economical is the split-level system with offset half-story levels and more variable access, because this demands less space and can accommodate a higher density of vehicles. The type of ramps and the selection of a column grid suited to the use are the determining elements of a parking garage.

In the design of ramp systems it is important to take into account the gradients and transition areas between ramp and horizontal, as well as the accessibility, and the turning radii of vehicles. ↗ Chapter 3.1.1 Spaces/External Circulation/Public Access

The footprint of a parking garage is often determined by the size and shape of the site or by building geometries, making it necessary to define appropriate grid dimensions that also take into account multilane traffic aisles. → Figure 4.11.34 In order to provide column-free traffic aisles, multistory parking garages are often built of steel structures with grids of up to 18 m. Underground parking garages built of reinforced concrete usually only permit much smaller column grids due to the superimposed loads involved, making it necessary to position columns along the traffic aisle, thus reducing the efficiency of the parking layout. → Figure 4.11.35 Where underground parking garages are located beneath buildings, it is also necessary to take into account the load-bearing grid of the building, which may make it necessary to combine different layout variations.

Figure 4.11.31
Schematic layout of a parking garage

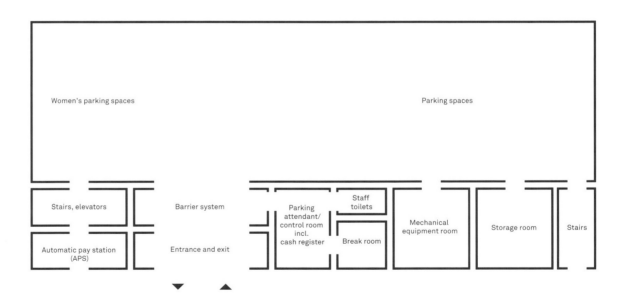

Figure 4.11.32
Aboveground and underground parking garages

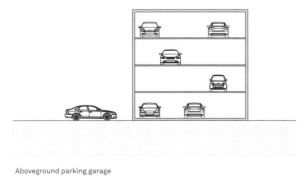

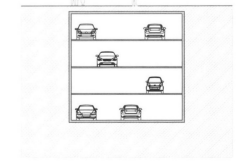

Aboveground parking garage

Underground parking garage

Table 4.11.6 (left)
Required lengths of ramps in
parking garages

Table 4.11.7 (right)
Minimum width of traffic aisles

| Floor-to-floor height | 2.50 m | 3.00 m | 3.50 m | 4.00 m |
|---|---|---|---|---|
| Ramp length | 20.83 m | 25.00 m | 29.17 m | 33.33 m |
| Transition zone | 3.00 m | 3.00 m | 3.00 m | 3.00 m |
| Total length | 24.00 m | 28.00 m | 32.17 m | 36.33 m |

| Layout of parking spaces relative to the traffic aisle | Minimum width of aisle for a parking space width of | | |
|---|---|---|---|
| | 2.30 m | 2.40 m | 2.50 m |
| 90° | 6.50 m | 6.00 m | 5.50 m |
| 45° | 3.50 m | 3.25 m | 3.00 m |

Figure 4.11.33
Vehicular access options
for parking garages

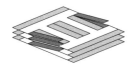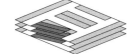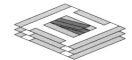

Straight full-story ramp

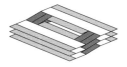

Straight half-story ramp

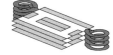

Full-story circular ramp

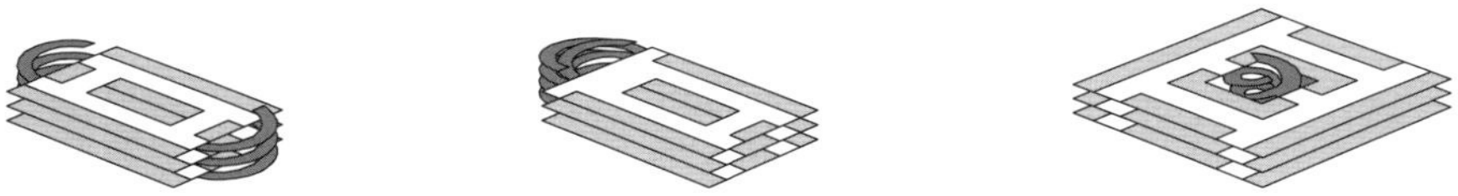

Half-story circular ramp

**Figure 4.11.34**
Load-bearing grid alternatives
for parking garages

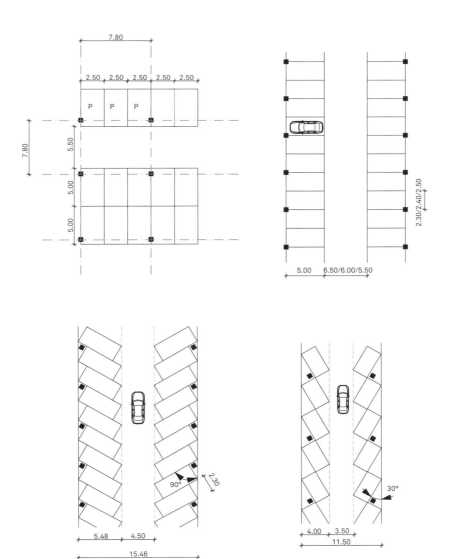

**Figure 4.11.35**
Possible positioning of columns
in parking garages

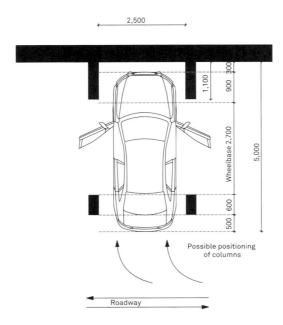

**Automatic Parking Systems**
Partially or fully automated systems are also available, which can save space but are also more expensive to build. Partially automated systems that are used in order to increase the space efficiency include lift systems, double parkers, lift/slide systems or rotating plate systems. → **Figures 4.11.36 and 4.11.37**

Fully automated parking systems require significantly less story height and a much reduced circulation area since only the transmission space is entered by the driver and the cars are parked using lift or paternoster systems. → **Figure 4.11.38**

Figure 4.11.36
Lift systems for garages

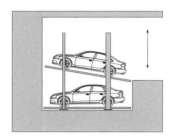

Double parker

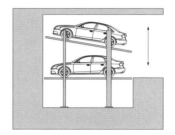

Lift systems

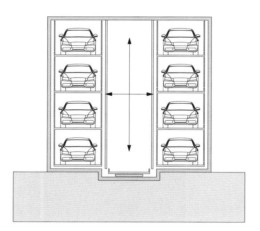

Lift/slide systems

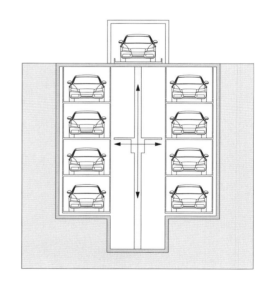

Figure 4.11.37
Examples of parking pallets and
rotating plate systems

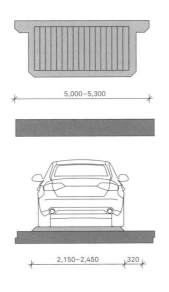

5,000–5,300

2,150–2,450   320

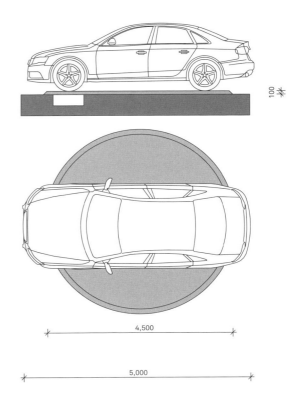

100

4,500

5,000

Figure 4.11.38
Example of a fully automated
parking system

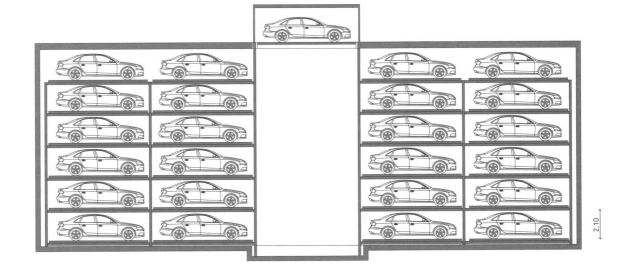

2.10

### 4.11.2.6 Gas Stations/Car Washes/ Auto Repair Shops

**Gas Stations**

The design of gas stations is determined by the connection to the road network, the drive layout on the site itself, and any additional secondary functions to be accommodated. It is important to prevent vehicles causing an obstruction to each other in the roofed-over area. → **Figure 4.11.39** Efficient organization is particularly important where there is a high turnover of vehicles, such as at freeways; typical designs involve the separation of HGV and car areas, and predetermined, one-way driving directions. ↗ **Chapter 3.1.1 Spaces/External Circulation/Public Access**

Often, gas stations are located near parking lots and rest stops and therefore need to accommodate additional functions such as shops, restaurants, car washes, car service points (air pressure, vacuum cleaner, water, etc.), workshops, and toilets. → **Figure 4.11.41**

**Typical elements/rooms at a gas station:**
- Pumps
- Roof/rain cover
- Price mast
- Parking spaces
- Self-service point (water, pressurized air)
- Cash register/POS, incl. night counter
- Kiosk/sales room
- Food services
- Workshop, incl. repair and service bays and tool storage
- Toilets (customers and staff)
- Fuel storage
- Car wash
- Office
- Staff room
- Stockroom

In view of the fact that many gas stations are operated by national operators, the corporate design – including signage and lighting – and the standardization of construction elements play an important role.

As a rule, the fuel tanks are installed underground but sometimes also aboveground in an area that cannot be seen by the public. For the filling of the tanks, adequately sized areas are required for the tankers; in an ideal situation fueling operations are not interrupted while the tanks are being filled. In the pump and tank-filling areas the ground has to be sealed to prevent any fuel entering the subsoil.

**Car Washes**

Car-wash facilities are often found with gas stations, but can also be provided on their own. A distinction is made between individual self-service wash bays and automated car-wash systems in the form of in-bay systems or conveyor systems. → **Figure 4.11.42** In-bay systems work on the basis of the equipment moving along a rail system straddling the stationary vehicle; they take up significantly less space than conveyor systems, in which the vehicle passes through the various service stations on a conveyor belt. In this case, the design parameters and building geometries are directly dependent on the car-wash system used. Most car-wash facilities also have areas for precleaning using high-pressure jets, and vacuum cleaner berths.

**Figure 4.11.39**
Drive-in systems with different arrangements of pump islands

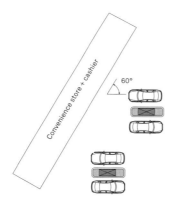
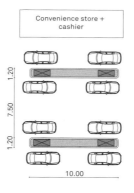
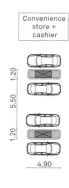

**Figure 4.11.40**
Typical roofing options for gas stations (examples)

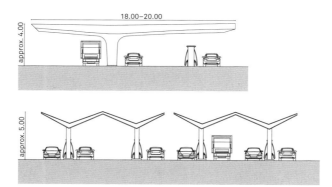
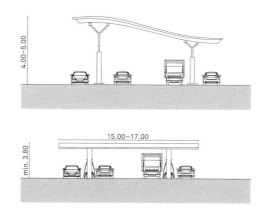

**Figure 4.11.41**
Schematic layout of a gas station

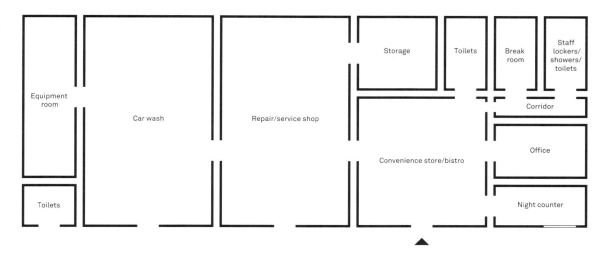

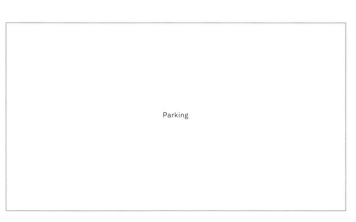

**Figure 4.11.42**
Automated car-wash systems
and self-service facilities

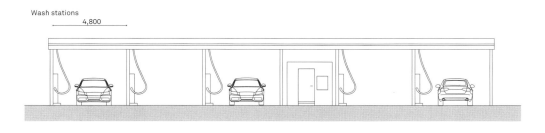

**Auto Repair Shops/Service Stations**

Auto Repair shops and service stations need to provide work spaces for mechanics, including hoists, equipment, and work areas, as well as adjoining storage and administration rooms. Lift platforms are the most ubiquitous work equipment and come in a variety of designs (hydraulically and electrically operated, drive-on ramps with workshop pit, etc.), depending on the particular service function. All necessary equipment is provided either behind or on the side of the lifting platform. This may include:

- Brake test stand
- Axle measurement stand
- Diagnostic instruments/devices
- Headlight adjustment unit
- Diagnostic instruments/devices
- Floor standing press
- Brake venting unit
- Air-conditioning service unit
- Tire-mounting machine
- Balancing machine
- Various tool carts

Access to the lift platforms may either be directly from the outside via an industrial door or in a large service area with the appropriate driving and shunting space. Close to the service area may be special workshops and storage areas as well as staff and office spaces. → **Figure 4.11.43**

Figure 4.11.43
Car workshops

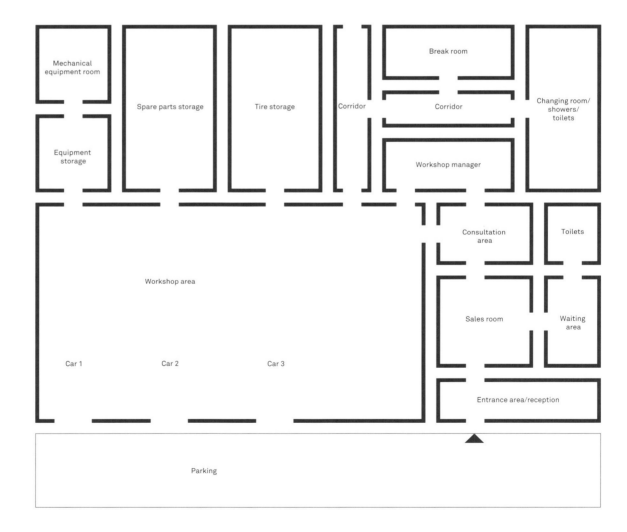

## 4.11.3 Areas and Rooms

**External circulation**  ↗Chapter 3.1

**Entrance area**  ↗524  ↗Chapter 3.2.1

**Access/security control**  ↗526  ↗Chapter 3.1.3

**Stairs, elevators**  ↗Chapter 3.2.4, ↗Chapter 3.2.7

**Corridors, internal circulation**  ↗Chapter 3.2.2

**Workplaces**  ↗Chapter 3.3.1

**Waiting areas**  ↗Chapter 3.4.2

**Cash registers/ticket counters**  ↗526

**Check-in counters**  ↗526

**Train platforms**  ↗528

**Bus platforms**  ↗528  ↗Chapter 3.1.2

**Runways**  ↗530

**Jetways**  ↗532

**Baggage claim**  ↗532

**Pumps**  ↗532

**Lift platforms**  ↗532

**Meeting rooms**  ↗Chapter 3.4.1

**Staff kitchens**  ↗Chapter 3.6

**Canteens, catering outlets**  ↗Chapter 4.7, ↗Chapter 3.4.3

**Break rooms**  ↗Chapter 3.8.1

**Toilets, sanitary facilities**  ↗Chapter 3.5.3

**Changing rooms, cloakrooms**  ↗Chapter 3.8.2

**Storage/archive rooms**  ↗Chapter 3.7.2

**Server rooms**  ↗Chapter 3.9.8

**First aid rooms**  ↗Chapter 3.8.3

**Janitor's closets**  ↗Chapter 3.8.4

**Mechanical equipment rooms**  ↗Chapter 3.9

### 4.11.3.1 Entrance Areas and Circulation Zones

Especially in larger transport buildings, the entrance areas have to fulfill highly representational functions. For example, the concourses in railroad stations and airport terminals are rarely designed purely to satisfy functional aspects. At the same time, these areas are used by large numbers of people and function as circulation areas connecting many different functions and means of transport. → **Figure 4.11.44** For this reason it is important to take into account the aspects of connection, and of direction of traffic flows dealt with in ↗ **4.11.1.3 Building Concept/Circulation Systems.** For example, the concourse in a railroad station or airport terminal can be accessed at different levels or from different entrances or sides.

Within the entrance area there should be sufficient space for placing all the information and wayfinding systems as well as ticket sales counters and vending machines. As a rule, various ancillary functions such as public lockers, toilets, lounge/VIP areas, food service outlets, and shops are accessed from the main entrance.

At main railroad stations and airports the lockers are located separately from the main circulation routes. Lockers are available in a range of sizes. Given that this facility requires a large amount of space, systems have been devised in which only the deposit and retrieval counter is located in the main concourse, with the actual storage area being elsewhere, such as in the basement. → **Figure 4.11.46**

The circulation areas at the transition between different means of transport should be generously dimensioned to allow adequate space for the number of people expected. Within these zones many different kinds of information and guide systems, aids, and additional services are provided. ↗ **Chapter 3.4.2 Spaces/Communication Spaces and Dining Rooms/Waiting and Seating Areas**

**Figure 4.11.44**
Example of public access on the land side of an airport

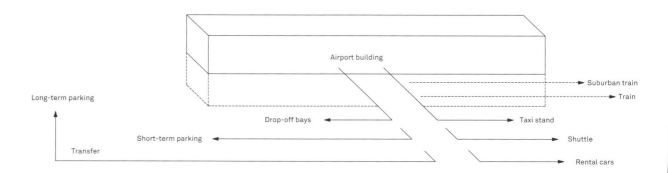

**Figure 4.11.45**
Luggage carts (baggage trolleys)

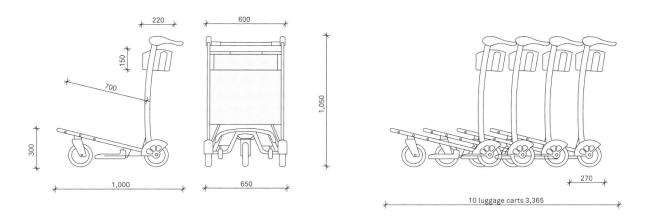

**Figure 4.11.46**
Manual and automated
luggage lockers

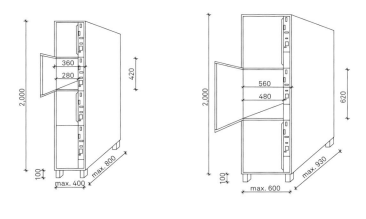

Manual luggage lockers

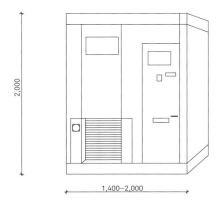

Automated luggage lockers

## 4.11.3.2 Ticket Counters and Access Control Systems

### Ticket Counters and Ticket Machines

All transport buildings except those serving individual motorized traffic require ticket counters or ticket machines which, depending on the layout concept, are located in the entrance area, the circulation zones, or within the actual means of transport. All main modes of transport nowadays have an adequate number of ticket-vending machines as well as centralized ticket counters offering personal assistance. → **Figures 4.11.47 and 4.11.48**

### Check-in counters

Air travelers hand in their baggage at check-in counters, where they also receive their boarding passes unless these have already been obtained online or from a check-in kiosk. Check-in counters consist of the counter itself with the work place behind and a baggage conveyor with integrated scale. Above the check-in counter is a monitor displaying check-in information. → **Figure 4.11.49**

### Access and Security Control Systems

Depending on the means of transport and the operator requirements, a number of different access control systems can be used to control access or to check ID documents or tickets. These include turnstiles, interlocking doors, or personal checkpoints with appropriate reading devices. ↗ **Chapter 3.1.3 Spaces/External Circulation/Private Exterior Circulation**

The security requirements at airports are very extensive, which is why both travelers and baggage are checked very thoroughly. All travelers and members of staff have to pass through security control before entering the security area. Equipment includes metal detectors for persons and X-ray equipment for checking hand luggage. The design should include adequate surfaces for depositing hand luggage, metal objects, and clothes before passing through the detection frame, and for picking these items up after passing the control, allowing for separate manual searches, in order to ensure a smooth process without hold-ups. Nowadays some facilities may include full-body scanners. Similarly, the main luggage and bulky items are checked with large X-ray equipment; however, this normally takes place outside the areas used by passengers. → **Figure 4.11.50**

Figure 4.11.47
Ticket-vending and parking payment machines

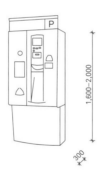

Figure 4.11.48
Ticket counter

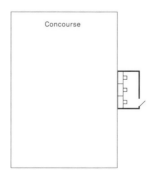
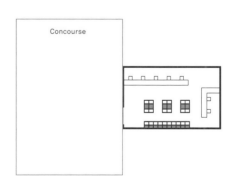

Figure 4.11.49
Various check-in counters
at an airport

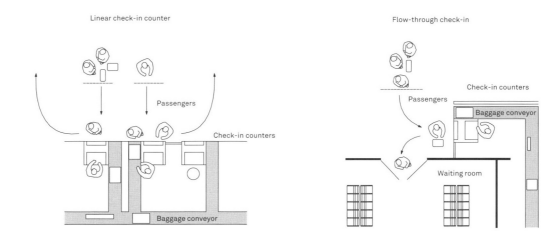

Linear check-in counter

Flow-through check-in

Passengers

Check-in counters

Check-in counters

Baggage conveyor

Baggage conveyor

Passengers

Waiting room

Island check-in counter

Passengers

Baggage conveyor

Check-in counters

Check-in counters

Figure 4.11.50
Passenger screening at an airport

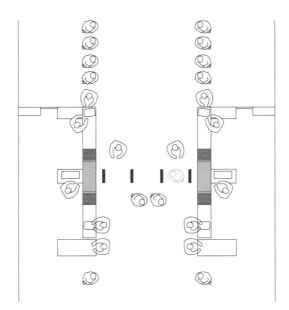

### 4.11.3.3 Train Platforms

The design of platforms is based on the geometry of the track structures (definition of elements → **Figure 4.11.51**) and the national regulations governing clear spaces between trains; these mandatory clearances – as well as those between the tracks – vary between different states and application areas (city, regional and long-distance railways). → **Figures 4.11.52 and 4.11.53**

Taking the applicable minimum clearance outline into account, platforms should be roofed over whenever possible so as to ensure that passengers can board trains without inconvenience from the weather or hindrance by columns. The width of platforms between tracks should be sufficient to accommodate not only walking and waiting passengers, but also space in the middle for stairs, escalators, elevators, seats, vending machines, waste receptacles, information boards, and possibly also kiosks. → **Figures 4.11.54 and 4.11.55** Depending on local regulations, the typical heights platforms are 55, 76, 92–96, and 130 cm. Markings in the flooring can define the safety clearance and also serve as guidance for barrier-free routes. ↗ **Chapter 3.4.2 Spaces/Communication Spaces and Dining Rooms/Waiting and Seating Areas**

### 4.11.3.4 Bus platforms

Bus platforms are usually built similar to sidewalks, with a height of 16 to 24 cm above the roadway. To enable the use of platforms by wheelchair users and to provide enough space for travelers with luggage, a clear width of at least 1.50 m should be maintained, resulting in total widths of at least 2.50 to 3.00 m. For additional dimensions for buses and bus platforms, see ↗ **Chapter 3.1.1 Spaces/External Circulation/Public Access.**

**Figure 4.11.51 (left)**
Railway components

**Figure 4.11.52 (right)**
Standard track clearances
for railway lines

As per German Ordinance on
the Construction and Operation
of Railways (EBO)

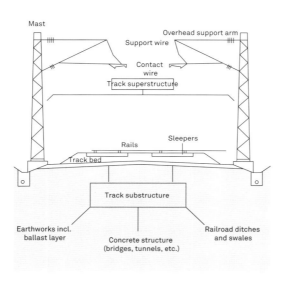

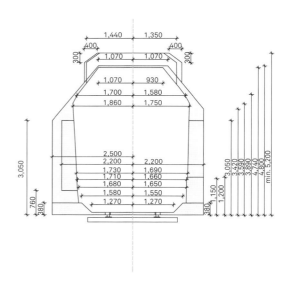

**Figure 4.11.53**
Common railroad track
gauges in mm

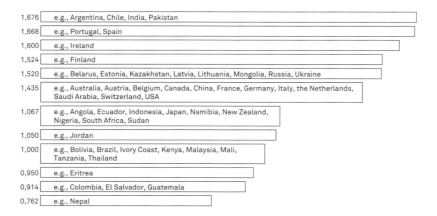

**Figure 4.11.54**
Schematic cross section (above) and plan (below) of a train platform, with minimum dimensions for local public transport

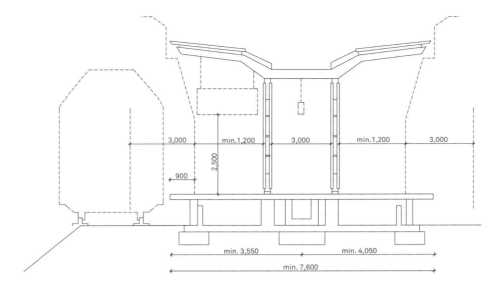

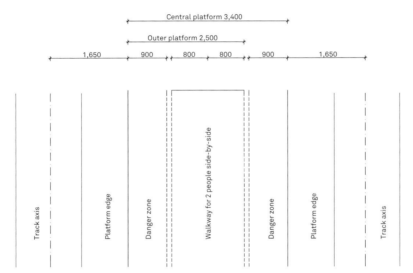

**Figure 4.11.55**
Platform furniture

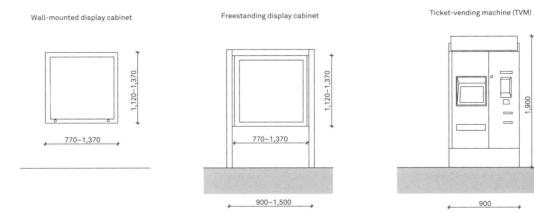

Wall-mounted display cabinet

Freestanding display cabinet

Ticket-vending machine (TVM)

### 4.11.3.5 Runways

The design of runways for takeoff and landing is subject to extensive and complex regulations issued by international organizations. Aspects of importance are the provision of obstacle-free areas adjacent to the runways, and the abatement of noise emissions during takeoff and landing. →Figure 4.11.57

The following key parameters have to be taken into account when designing takeoff and landing runways:

- Takeoff Run Available (TORA)
- Takeoff Distance Available (TODA)
- Accelerate Stop Distance Available (ASDA)
- Landing Distance Available (LDA) →Table 4.11.8 and Figure 4.11.56

Similarly, the taxiways between the apron and takeoff and landing runways are subject to complex rules and must be designed in accordance with the traffic expected and the overall airport organization. Additional areas to be provided are those for the cleaning and deicing of aircraft. All runways and taxiways must be equipped with lighting systems; the lighting required for landing runways may have to extend beyond the actual airport area.

Table 4.11.8
Structure of airport
reference codes

Source: ICAO

| Code Element 1 | | Code Element 2 | | |
|---|---|---|---|---|
| Code number | Length of takeoff runway | Code letter | Wingspan | Track width of undercarriage |
| 1 | < 800 m | A | < 15 m | < 4.50 m |
| 2 | 800–1,200 m | B | 15–24 m | 4.50–6 m |
| 3 | 1,200–1,800 m | C | 24–36 m | 6–9 m |
| 4 | > 1,800 m | D | 36–52 m | 9–14 m |
| | | E | 52–65 m | 9–14 m |
| | | F | 65–80 m | 14–16 m |

Figure 4.11.56
Designations used for the
dimensions used in the design
of takeoff and landing runways

Use orientation from left to right

Source: ICAO

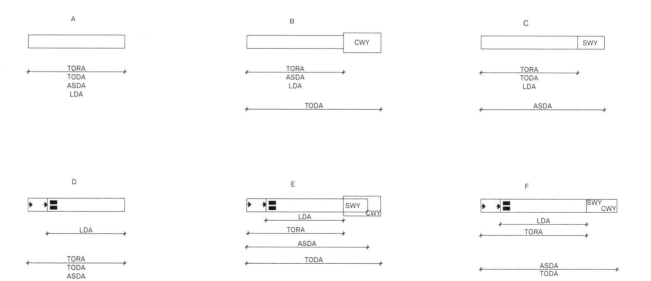

**Figure 4.11.57**
Areas with obstacle restrictions
for takeoff and landing

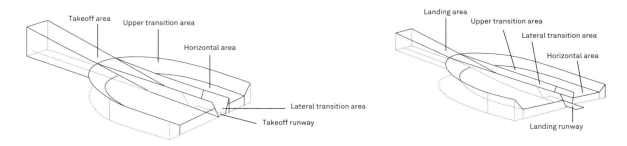

**Figure 4.11.58**
Determination of the length of
takeoff and landing runways

Source: ICAO

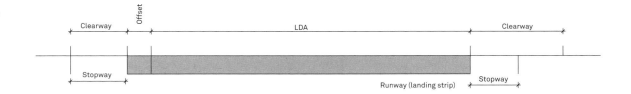

### 4.11.3.6 Jetways

Gangways and jetways provide a direct connection between the gate and the aircraft. They are designed to be flexible so that they can be adapted in length, radius and height to suit all types of aircraft. →**Figure 4.11.59** For large aircraft, double jetways are built, and for the A380, there are even triple jetways.

### 4.11.3.7 Baggage Claim

The Baggage claim area at airports operates with baggage conveyors or carousels that are usually grouped together. There are flat and slanted baggage belts; usually, they have an extended run in order to allow more people direct access to the belt. →**Figure 4.11.60** As a rule, close to the baggage reclaim area are a lost property office, toilets, bulky items collection, information for onward travel, and, at the transition to the land side, customs control.

### 4.11.3.8 Equipment for Gas Stations and Car Repair Workshops

Normally, gas stations are fitted with the standard equipment by the respective mineral oil company. The dimensions and layout systems of gas pumps are proprietary. Different designs are used depending on the number of fuels; also, operating may be from one or both sides, and there may be additional operating and information elements. →**Figure 4.11.61**

Pumps and surface fuel tanks must be protected against impact and other mechanical damage by providing appropriate protection elements in concrete or steel. →**Figure 4.11.62**

The equipment of auto repair shops largely depends on the respective specialization. The type of hydraulic lift should be determined at an early stage so that any foundations, workshop pits, and service lines required can be included in the design. →**Figure 4.11.64**

Figure 4.11.59
Various types of gangways/jetways

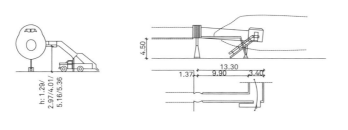
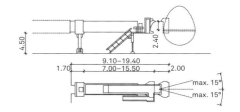
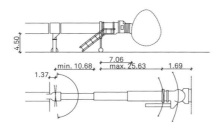
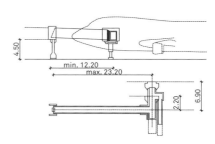

Figure 4.11.60
Flat and slanted circulating baggage belts

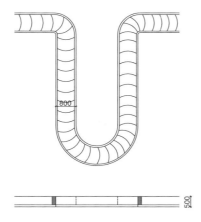
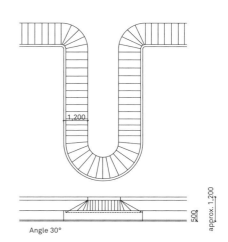

**Figure 4.11.61**
Dimensions of pumps
at gas stations

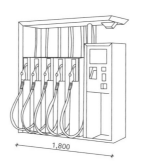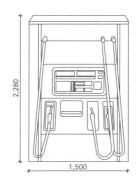

**Figure 4.11.62**
Protection elements for pumps
at a gas station

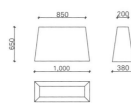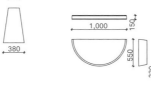

**Figure 4.11.63**
Tanks installed below ground
and at ground level

Pump at gas station – Tank installed below ground

Pump

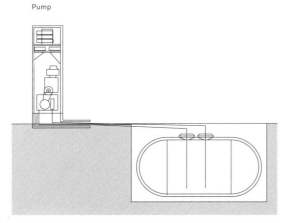

Pump at gas station – Tank installed at ground level

Pump

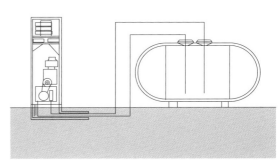

**Figure 4.11.64**
Different types of car lifts

Two-post lift

Four-post lift

Scissor lift

In-ground lift

# 5 Reference Guide

## 5.1 Standards and Regulations ↗537

## 5.2 References ↗553

## 5.3 Index ↗559

## 5.4 Picture Credits ↗565

## 5.5 The Authors ↗567

# 5.1 Standards and Regulations

## Dimensions and Units

Table 5.1.1
Common US/Imperial units of measurement and their equivalents in the metric system

| Unit | Abbreviation | Size | Metric equivalent |
|---|---|---|---|
| inch | in., " | – | 0.0254 meter |
| foot | ft., ' | 12 inches | 0.3048 meter |
| yard | yd. | 3 feet | 0.9144 meter |
| mile (statute mile) | mi., m. | 8 furlongs 1,760 yards 5280 feet | 1,609.344 meters |
| square foot | sq. ft., ft2 | 144 in² | 0.092903 square meter |

Table 5.1.2
Common metric units and their equivalents in the US/Imperial measurement system

| Unit | Abbreviation | Size | US/Imperial equivalent |
|---|---|---|---|
| millimeter | mm | – | 0.0393701 inch |
| centimeter | cm | 10 mm | 0.0328084 foot |
| meter | m | 100 cm 1,000 mm | 1.09361 yards |
| kilometer | km | 1,000 m | 0.621371 mile |
| square meter | m² | 100,000 mm² | 10.7639 square feet |

## General

Readers should be advised that although DIN standards are generally also given English titles, which are used here, that provides no indication of whether a particular standard has actually been published in English – and hence it may be solely available in German. Many but not all of the standards listed below are officially available in English. Documents for which an English title is given below in square brackets are available only in German and typically known only by their German title or abbreviation.

| Document | Title | Edition |
|---|---|---|
| BauNVO | Federal Land Utilization Ordinance (Baunutzungsverordnung) | 1990-01-23 |
| MBO | Model Building Code (Musterbauordnung) | 2002-11 |
| MVStättV | Model Ordinance on Places of Assembly (Musterversammlungsstättenverordnung) | 2014-07 |
| ArbStättV | Ordinance on Workplaces (Arbeitsstättenverordnung) | 2004-08-12 |
| BImschG | Federal Immission Control Act (Bundes-Immissionsschutzgesetz) | 2002-09-26 |
| DIN 277-1 | Areas and Volumes of Buildings – Part 1: Building Construction | 2016-01 |
| DIN 18000 | Modular Coordination in Building | 1984-05 (withdrawn) |
| DIN 18205 | Brief for Building Design | 2015-11 (draft) |
| BGV | Regulations of the Institutions for Statutory Accident Insurance and Prevention (Berufsgenossenschaftliche Vorschriften) | |
| BGR | Rules of the Institutions for Statutory Accident Insurance and Prevention (Berufsgenossenschaftliche Regeln) | |
| BGI | Information booklets of the Institutions for Statutory Accident Insurance and Prevention (Berufsgenossenschaftliche Informationen) | |
| VDS | Guidelines of the Association of Property Insurers (Richtlinien des Verbandes der Sachversicherer) | |
| VDE | Regulations of the Association for Electrical, Electronic & Information Technologies | |

## Chapter 2.1  Anthropometry and Barrier-Free Accessibility

| Document | Title | Edition |
|---|---|---|
| DIN 18024-1 | Barrier-free Built Environment – Part 1: Streets, Squares, Paths, Public Transport, Recreation Areas And Playgrounds – Design Principles | 1998-01 (withdrawn) |
| DIN 18025-1 | Accessible Dwellings; Dwellings for Wheelchair Users – Design Principles | 1992-12 (withdrawn) |
| DIN 18040-2 | Construction of Accessible Buildings – Design Principles – Part 2: Dwellings | 2011-09 |
| DIN 33402-1 | Ergonomics – Body Dimensions of People – Part 1: Terms and Definitions, Measuring Procedures | 2008-03 |
| DIN 33402-2 | Ergonomics – Human Body Dimensions – Part 2: Values | 2005-12 |
| DIN 33408-1 | Body Templates – Part 1: For Seats of All Kinds | 2008-03 |
| DIN 33411-1 | Physical Strengths of Man; Concepts, Interrelations, Defining Parameters | 1982-09 |
| DIN EN ISO 7250-1 | Basic Human Body Measurements for Technological Design – Part 1: Body Measurement Definitions and Landmarks | 2010-06 |
| BS EN ISO 7250:1998 | Basic Human Body Measurements for Technological Design. Body Measurement Definitions and Landmarks | 1998-02-15 |
| ISO 7250-1:2008 | Basic Human Body Measurements for Technological Design – Part 1: Body Measurement Definitions and Landmarks | 2013-10-21 |
| BIP 2228:2013 | Inclusive Urban Design: A Guide to Creating Accessible Public Spaces | 2013-10-02 |
| BS 8300:2009+A1:2010 | Design of Buildings and Their Approaches to Meet the Needs of Disabled People. Code of Practice | 2009-02 |

## Chapter 2.2  Comfort and Physical Spatial Qualities

| Document | Title | Edition |
|---|---|---|
| ASR A3.5 | Raumtemperatur [Room temperature] | 2010-06 |
| ASR A3.6 | Lüftung [Ventilation] | 2012-01 |
| DIN 1946-6 | Ventilation and Air Conditioning – Part 6: Ventilation for Residential Buildings – General Requirements, Requirements for Measuring, Performance and Labeling, Delivery/Acceptance (Certification) and Maintenance | 2009-05 |
| DIN 4102-1 | Fire Behaviour of Building Materials and Building Components – Part 1: Building Materials; Concepts, Requirements and Tests | 1998-05 |
| DIN 4108-2 | Thermal Protection and Energy Economy in Buildings – Part 2: Minimum Requirements to Thermal Insulation | 2013-02 |
| DIN 4109 | Sound Insulation in Buildings; Requirements and Testing | 1989-11 |
| DIN 5034-1 | Daylight in Interiors – Part 1: General Requirements | 2011-07 |
| DIN 5035-3 | Artificial Lighting – Part 3: Lighting of Health Care Premises | 2006-07 |
| DIN 5035-7 | Artificial Lighting – Part 7: Lighting of Interiors with Visual Displays Work Stations | 2004-08 |
| DIN 18041 | Acoustic Quality in Rooms – Specifications and Instructions for the Room Acoustic Design | 2015-02 (draft) |
| DIN EN 12464-1 | Light and Lighting – Lighting of Work Places – Part 1: Indoor Work Places | 2011-08 |
| DIN EN 12831 | Heating Systems in Buildings – Method for Calculation of the Design Heat Load | 2003-08 |
| TA Lärm | Technische Anleitung zum Schutz gegen Lärm [Technical Instructions on Noise Abatement] | 1998-08-26 |
| VDI 4100 | Sound Protection in Buildings – Housing – Assessment and Proposals for Enhanced Sound Protection | 2012-10 |
| BS EN 12831:2003 | Heating Systems in Buildings. Method for Calculation of the Design Heat Load | 2003-08-22 |
| BS EN 12464-1:2011 | Light and Lighting. Lighting of Work Places. Indoor Work Places | 2011-06-30 |

| Document | Title | Edition |
|---|---|---|
| BS EN 12665:2002 | Light and Lighting. Basic Terms and Criteria for Specifying Lighting Requirements | 2002-09-20 |
| BS 8206-2:2008 | Lighting for Buildings. Code of Practice for Daylighting | 2008-09-30 |
| BS EN ISO 17624:2004 | Acoustics. Guidelines for Noise Control in Offices and Workrooms by Means of Acoustical Screens | 2005-01-24 |
| ISO 11855-1:2012 | Building Environment Design – Design, Dimensioning, Installation and Control of Embedded Radiant Heating and Cooling Systems – Part 1: Definition, Symbols, and Comfort Criteria | 2012-07-25 |
| ISO 8995-1:2002 | Lighting of Work Places – Part 1: Indoor | 2002-05 |
| ANSI/IESNA RP-1-12 | Office Lighting | 1994-04-12 |
| IES RP-5-13 | Recommended Practice for Daylighting Buildings | 2013-12-15 |
| ISO 17624:2004 | Acoustics – Guidelines for Noise Control in Offices and Workrooms by Means of Acoustical Screens | 2004-12 |

## Chapter 2.3  Spatial Perception

| Document | Title | Edition |
|---|---|---|
| ASR A1.2 | Technische Regel für Arbeitsstätten – Raumabmessungen und Bewegungsflächen [Technical rules for workplaces – Room dimensions and circulation areas] | 2013-09 |

## Chapter 3.1  External Circulation

| Document | Title | Edition |
|---|---|---|
| ISO 612 | Road Vehicles – Dimensions of Motor Vehicles and Towed Vehicles – Terms and Definitions | 1978-03 |
| DIN 14090 | Areas for the Fire Brigade on Premises | 2002-05 |
| DIN 32984 | Ground Surface Indicators in Public Areas | 2011-10 |
| DIN EN 13724 | Postal Services – Apertures of Private Letter Boxes and Letter Plates – Requirements and Test Methods, German version of EN 13724:2013 | 2013-07 |
| DIN EN 840-1 | Mobile Waste and Recycling Containers – Part 1: Containers with 2 Wheels with a Capacity up to 400 L for Comb Lifting Devices – Dimensions and Design | 2013-03 |
| SN 640238 | Fußgänger- und leichter Zweiradverkehr – Rampen, Treppen und Treppenwege | 2007-10 |
| FGSV 287 | Bemessungsfahrzeuge und Schleppkurven zur Überprüfung der Befahrbarkeit von Verkehrsflächen | 2001 |
| RASt 06 FGSV 200 | Directives for the Design of Urban Roads (Richtlinien für die Anlage von Stadtstraßen) | 2006, rectified 2008-12-15 |
| ERA 10 | Guidelines for Cycling Facilities (Empfehlungen für Radverkehrsanlagen) | 2010 |
| EAR 05 | Guidelines for Parking Facilities (Empfehlungen für Anlagen des ruhenden Verkehrs) | 2005-02 |
| RAS-EW | Directive for Road Construction – Part: Drainage (Richtlinie für die Anlage von Straßen, Teil: Entwässerung) | 2005-11 |
| BS EN 13724:2013 | Postal Services. Apertures of Private Letter Boxes and Letter Plates. Requirements and Test Methods | 2013-04-30 |
| BS EN 840-1:2012 | Mobile Waste and Recycling Containers. Containers with 2 Wheels with a Capacity up to 400 L for Comb Lifting Devices. Dimensions and Design | 2012-12-31 |
| BS EN 840-1:2012 | Mobile Waste and Recycling Containers. Containers with 2 Wheels with a Capacity up to 400 L for Comb Lifting Devices. Dimensions and Design | 2012-12-31 |

## Chapter 3.2  Internal Circulation

| Document | Title | Edition |
|---|---|---|
| ASR A1.8 | Technische Regel für Arbeitsstätten – Verkehrswege [Technical rules for workplaces – Circulation paths] | 2012-11 |
| ASR A2.3 | Technische Regel für Arbeitsstätten – Fluchtwege und Notausgänge, Flucht- und Rettungsplan [Technical rules for workplaces – Escape routes, emergency exits, escape and rescue plan] | 2007-08 |
| DIN 15306 | Lifts – Passenger Lifts in Residential Buildings – Functional Dimensions | 2002-06 |
| DIN 15309 | Lifts – Passenger Lifts in Non-Residential Buildings and Bed Lifts – Functional Dimensions | 2002-12 |
| DIN 18065 | Stairs in Buildings – Terminology, Measuring Rules, Main Dimensions | 2015-03 |
| DIN 18650-1 | Powered Pedestrian Doors – Part 1: Product Requirements and Test Methods | 2010-06 |
| DIN 51130 | Testing of Floor Coverings – Determination of the Anti-slip Property – Workrooms and Fields of Activities with Slip Danger – Walking Method – Ramp Test | 2013-05-21 (withdrawn) |
| DIN EN 115-1 | Safety of Escalators and Moving Walks – Part 1: Construction and Installation | 2015-08 (draft) |
| DIN EN 13724 | Postal Services – Apertures of Private Letter Boxes and Letter Plates – Requirements and Test Methods | 2011-04 (withdrawn) |
| ÖNORM S 2025 | Locations for Waste Containers – Dimensions | 2010-02-01 |
| ÖNORM B 5371 | Stairs, Guard-rails and Parapets in Buildings and Landscapes – Dimensions | 2010-09-01 |
| VDI 2160 | Waste Management in Buildings and on Ground – Requirement[s] for Bins, Locations and Transportation Routes | 2007-12 |
| DGUV Regel 108-003 (formerly BGR 181) | BG-Regel – Fußböden in Arbeitsräumen und Arbeitsbereichen mit Rutschgefahr | 2003-10 |
| BGI/GUV-I 561, DGUV Information 208-005 | Information – Treppen | 2010-07 |
| GUV-I 8527 | GUV-Informationen – Bodenbeläge für nassbelastete Barfußbereiche | 2004-08 |
| GUV-V C 27 DGUV Vorschrift 44 | Unfallverhütungsvorschrift "Müllbeseitigung" mit Durchführungsanweisungen | 1999 |
| bfu-Fachdokumentation 2.032 (CH) | Anforderungsliste Bodenbeläge | 2012 |
| bfu-Fachdokumentation 2.027 | Bodenbeläge | 2011 |
| bfu (CH) | Swiss Council for Accident Prevention: Stairs | 2009 |
| ISO 4190-1:1999 | Lift (US: Elevator) installation. Class I, II, III and VI lifts | 2002-10-08 |

## Chapter 3.3  Workrooms and Production Spaces

| Document | Title | Edition |
|---|---|---|
| ASR A1.2 | Technische Regel für Arbeitsstätten – Raumabmessungen und Bewegungsflächen [Technical rules for workplaces – Room dimensions and circulation areas] | 2013-09 |
| DIN EN 527-1 | Office Furniture – Work Tables and Desks – Part 1: Dimensions | 2011-08 |
| DGUV Information 209-069 | Ergonomische Maschinengestaltung von Werkzeugmaschinen der Metallbearbeitung, Deutsche Gesetzliche Unfallversicherung | 2010-12 |

## Chapter 3.4 Communication Spaces and Dining Rooms

| Document | Title | Edition |
|---|---|---|
| DIN EN 13200-1 | Spectator Facilities – Part 1: General Characteristics for Spectator Viewing Area | 2011-04 (withdrawn) |

## Chapter 3.5 Sanitary Facilities

| Document | Title | Edition |
|---|---|---|
| ASR A4.1 | Technische Regel für Arbeitsstätten – Sanitärräume [Technical rules for workplaces – Sanitary facilities] | 2013-09 |
| VDI 3818 | Public Sanitary Facilities | 2008-02 |
| VDI 6000 Part 1 | Provision and Installation of Sanitary Facilities – Private Housing | 2008-02 |
| VDI 6000 Part 2 | Provision and Installation of Sanitary Facilities – Workplaces and Work Stations | 2007-11 |
| VDI 6000 Part 3 | Provision and Installation of Sanitary Facilities – Public Buildings and Areas | 2011-06 |

## Chapter 3.6 Kitchens

| Document | Title | Edition |
|---|---|---|
| DIN 66354 | Kitchen Equipment; Forms, Planning Principles | 1986-12 |
| DIN EN 1116 | Kitchen Furniture – Co-ordinating Sizes for Kitchen Furniture and Kitchen Appliances | 2004-09 |
| BS 3705:1972 | Recommendations for Provision of Space for Domestic Kitchen Equipment | 1972-04 |
| BS EN 1116:2004 | Kitchen Furniture. Co-ordinating Sizes for Kitchen Furniture and Kitchen Appliances | 2004-07-21 |
| ISO 3055:1985 | Kitchen Equipment – Coordinating Sizes | 2014-05-23 |

## Chapter 3.7 Storage Spaces

| Document | Title | Edition |
|---|---|---|
| ASR A1.8 | Technische Regel für Arbeitsstätten – Verkehrswege [Technical rules for workplaces – Circulation paths] | 2012-11 |
| DIN 15141-1 | Transportation Chain; Pallets; Types and Principal Dimensions of Flat Pallets | 1986-01 (withdrawn) |
| DIN 15142-1 | Load Boards; Box Pallets, Post Pallets, Principal Dimensions and Stacking Devices | 1973-02 |
| DIN EN 1398 | Dock Levellers – Safety Requirements | 2009-07 |
| DIN ISO 668 | Series 1 Freight Containers – Classification, Dimensions and Ratings (ISO 668:1995) | 1999-10 |
| BS ISO 668:2013 | Series 1 Freight Containers. Classification, Dimensions and Ratings | 2013-08-31 |

## Chapter 3.8 Ancillary and Staff Rooms

| Document | Title | Edition |
|---|---|---|
| ASR A4.2 | Technische Regel für Arbeitsstätten – Pausen- und Bereitschaftsräume [Technical rules for workplaces – Break and on-call rooms] | 2012-08 |
| ASR A4.3 | Technische Regel für Arbeitsstätten – Erste-Hilfe-Räume, Mittel und Einrichtungen zur Ersten Hilfe [Technical rules for workplaces – First aid rooms, means and facilities for first aid] | 2010-12 |
| DIN EN 840-1 | Mobile Waste and Recycling Containers – Part 1: Containers with 2 Wheels with a Capacity up to 400 L for Comb Lifting Devices – Dimensions and Design | 2013-03 |

## Chapter 3.9  Technical Equipment Rooms

| Document | Title | Edition |
|----------|-------|---------|
| ASR A3.6 | Lüftung [Ventilation] | 2012-01 |
| DIN 18012 | House Service Connections Facilities – Principles for Planning | 2007-06 |
| DIN 18015-3 | Electrical Installations in Residential Buildings – Part 3: Wiring and disposition of electrical equipment | 2016-02 (draft) |

## Chapter 4.1  Housing

| Document | Title | Edition |
|----------|-------|---------|
| BauNVO | Baunutzungsverordnung [Federal land utilization ordinance] | 1990-01-23 |
| BauO NRW | North Rhine-Westphalia Building Code | 2005-09-01 |
| WoFlV | Wohnflächenverordnung [Living space ordinance] | 2003-11-25 |
| DIN 277-1 | Areas and Volumes of Buildings – Part 1: Building Construction | 2016-01 |
| DIN 1946-6 | Ventilation and air conditioning – Part 6: Ventilation for Residential Buildings – General Requirements, Requirements for Measuring, Performance and Labeling, Delivery/Acceptance (Certification) and Maintenance | 2009-05 |
| DIN 4109 | Sound Insulation in Buildings; Requirements and Testing | 1989-11 |
| DIN 5034-1 | Daylight in Interiors – Part 1: General Requirements | 2011-07 |
| DIN 18011 | Areas Required for the Furniture etc., Spacings and Activity Spaces in Housing | 1967-03 (withdrawn) |
| DIN 18015-1 | Electrical Installations in Residential Buildings – Part 1: Planning Principles | 2013-09 |
| DIN 18017-1 | Ventilation of Bathrooms and WCs without Outside Windows; single Shaft Systems without Ventilators | 1987-02 (withdrawn) |
| DIN 18022 | Domestic Kitchens, Bathrooms and WCs; Design Principles | 1989-11 (withdrawn) |
| DIN 18024-1 | Barrier-free Built Environment – Part 1: Streets, Squares, Paths, Public Transport, Recreation Areas and Playgrounds – Elements for Design | 1998-01 (withdrawn) |
| DIN 18025-1 | Accessible Dwellings; Dwellings for Wheelchair Users; Elements for Design | 1992-12 (withdrawn) |
| DIN 18040-2 | Construction of Accessible Buildings – Design Principles – Part 2: Dwellings | 2011-09 |
| DIN 18065 | Stairs in Buildings – Terminology, Measuring Rules, Main Dimensions | 2015-03 |
| DIN 66354 | Kitchen Equipment; Forms, Planning Principles | 1986-12 |
| DIN 68881-1 | Concepts for Kitchen Furniture; Kitchen Cupboards | 1979-02 |
| DIN 68878 | Chairs for Domestic Use – Performance Characteristics – Requirements and Test Methods | 2011-11 |
| DIN 68880-1 | Furniture; Concepts | 1973-10 |
| DIN 68890 | Wardrobes for Domestic Use – Fitness for Purpose Requirements – Testing | 2009-05 |
| DIN 68935 | Coordinating Dimensions for Bathroom Furniture, Appliances and Sanitary Equipment | 2009-10 |
| DIN 77800 | Quality Requirements for Providers of "Assisted Living for the Elderly" | 2006-09 |
| DIN EN 716-1 | Furniture – Children's Cots and Folding Cots for Domestic Use – Part 1: Safety Requirements | 2015-10 (draft) |
| DIN EN 747-1 | Furniture – Bunk Beds and High Beds – Part 1: Safety, Strength and Durability Requirements | 2015-08 |
| DIN EN 1116 | Kitchen Furniture – Co-ordinating Sizes for Kitchen Furniture and Kitchen Appliances | 2004-09 |
| VDI 6000 Part 1 | Provision and Installation of Sanitary Facilities – Private Housing | 2008-02 |
| DD 266:2007 | Design of accessible housing. Lifetime home. Code of Practice | 2007-12-31 |
| DI-MISC-81049 | Family Housing Inventory Designation and Assignment Report | |

## Chapter 4.2 Office and Administration

| Document | Title | Edition |
|---|---|---|
| ASR A1.2 | Technische Regel für Arbeitsstätten – Raumabmessungen und Bewegungsflächen [Technical rules for workplaces – Room dimensions and circulation areas] | 2013-09 |
| ASR A1.8 | Technische Regel für Arbeitsstätten – Verkehrswege [Technical rules for workplaces – Circulation paths] | 2012-11 |
| ASR A2.3 | Technische Regel für Arbeitsstätten – Fluchtwege und Notausgänge, Flucht- und Rettungsplan [Technical rules for workplaces – Escape routes, emergency exits, escape and rescue plan] | 2007-08 |
| ASR A4.2 | Technische Regel für Arbeitsstätten – Pausen- und Bereitschaftsräumen [Technical rules for workplaces – Break and on-call rooms] | 2012-08 |
| ASR V3a.2 | Technische Regel für Arbeitsstätten – Barrierefreie Gestaltung von Arbeitsstätten [Technical rules for workplaces – Barrier-free design of workplaces] | 2012-08 |
| DIN 4543-1 | Office Work Place – Part 1: Space for the Arrangement and Use of Office Furniture; Safety Requirements, Testing Safety Requirements | 1994-09 |
| DIN 5035-8 | Artificial Lighting – Part 8: Workplace Luminaries – Requirements, Recommendations and Proofing | 2007-07 |
| DIN 16555 | Office Work Place – Space for Communication Work Places in Office Buildings – Requirements, Testing | 2002-12 |
| DIN 18040-1 | Construction of Accessible Buildings – Design Principles – Part 1: Publicly Accessible Buildings | 2010-10 |
| DIN EN 16139 | Furniture – Strength, Durability And Safety – Requirements For Non-domestic Seating | 2014-03 |
| ÖNORM B 2471 | Lifts for Office and Administration Buildings, Hotels and Schools; Recommended Functional Dimensions of Lifts with Friction-Disk-Drive | 1982-07-01 |
| VDI 2569 | Sound Protection and Acoustical Design in Offices | 2016-02 (draft) |
| VDI 3804 | Air-conditioning – Office Buildings (VDI ventilation code of practice) | 2009-03 |
| VDI 6000 Part 2 | Provision and Installation of Sanitary Facilities – Workplaces and Work Stations | 2007-11 |
| DGUV Information 215-443 | Akustik im Büro – Hilfen für die akustische Gestaltung von Büros | 2012-09 |
| BüroFlRL BR | Richtlinie zum Flächenstandard bei Büroräumen | 2010-02-23 |
| licht.wissen 04 | Office Lighting: Motivating and Efficient | 2012-04 |
| Licht Heft 13 | Good Lighting for Local Authority Buildings and Amenities | 1989-01 |
| AWV Büro, Akustik | Der Mensch im Büro; Gestaltung der Arbeitsumgebung; Lärm und Akustik | 1988-01 |

## Chapter 4.3 Logistics and Commerce

| Document | Title | Edition |
|---|---|---|
| ArbStättV | Ordinance on Workplaces (Arbeitsstättenverordnung) | 2004-08-12 |
| ASR | Technische Regel für Arbeitsstätten [Technical rules for workplaces] | |
| VkVO | Verkaufsstättenverordnung [Ordinance governing sales premises] | |
| IndBauRL | Industriebaurichtlinie [Industrial buildings directive] | |
| DIN 1045-3 | Concrete, Reinforced and Prestressed Concrete Structures – Part 3: Execution of Structures | 2012-03 |
| DIN 4102-1 | Fire Behaviour of Building Materials and Building Components – Part 1: Building Materials; Concepts, Requirements and Tests | 1998-05 |
| DIN 5034-1 | Daylight in Interiors – Part 1: General Requirements | 2011-07 |
| DIN 5035-3 | Artificial Lighting – Part 3: Lighting of Health Care Premises | 2006-07 |

| Document | Title | Edition |
|---|---|---|
| DIN 10505 | Food Hygiene – Ventilation Equipment for Sales Arrangements of Foodstuffs – Requirements, Testing | 2009-04 |
| DIN 15141-4 | Transportation Chain; Pallets; Four Way Timber Perimeter-Base Pallets; 1,000 mm × 1,200 mm Brewery Pallets | 1985-11 |
| DIN 15185-1 | Warehouse Systems with Guided Industrial Trucks; Requirements on the Ground, the Warehouse and Other Requirements | 1991-08 |
| DIN 15185-2 | Industrial Trucks – Safety Requirement – Part 2: Use in Narrow Aisles | 2013-10 |
| DIN 18005-1 | Noise Abatement in Town Planning – Part 1: Fundamentals and Directions for Planning | 2002-07 |
| DIN 18040-1 | Construction of Accessible Buildings – Design Principles – Part 1: Publicly Accessible Buildings | 2010-10 |
| DIN 18065 | Stairs in Buildings – Terminology, Measuring Rules, Main Dimensions | 2015-03 |
| DIN 18202 | Tolerances in Building Construction – Buildings | 2013-04 |
| DIN 18225 | Industrial Construction; Traffic Ways in Industrial Buildings | 1988-06 |
| DIN 18230-1 | Structural Fire Protection in Industrial Buildings – Part 1: Analytically Required Fire Resistance Time | 2010-09 |
| DIN 18560-7 | Floor Screeds – Part 7: Heavy-duty Screeds (Industrial Screeds) | 2004-04 |
| DIN EN 528 | Rail Dependent Storage and Retrieval Equipment – Safety Requirements | 2009-02 |
| DIN EN 12464-1 | Light and Lighting – Lighting of Work Places – Part 1: Indoor Work Places; German version | 2011-08 |
| DIN EN 13698-1 | Pallet Production Specification – Part 2: Construction Specification for 1,000 mm × 1,200 mm Flat Wooden Pallets | 2004-01 |
| DIN EN ISO 3691-1 | Industrial Trucks – Safety Requirements and Verification – Part 1: Self-Propelled Industrial Trucks, Other than Driverless Trucks, Variable-Reach Trucks and Burden-Carrier Trucks | 2015-12 |
| BGV | Regulations of the Institutions for Statutory Accident Insurance and Prevention (Berufsgenossenschaftliche Vorschriften) | 2014-10-15 |
| BGR | Rules of the Institutions for Statutory Accident Insurance and Prevention (Berufsgenossenschaftliche Regeln) | |
| BGI | Information booklets of the Institutions for Statutory Accident Insurance and Prevention (Berufsgenossenschaftliche Informationen) | |
| VDS | Guidelines of the Association of Property Insurers (Richtlinien des Verbandes der Sachversicherer) | |
| EAR 05 | Guidelines for Parking Facilities (Empfehlungen für Anlagen des ruhenden Verkehrs) | 2005-02 |
| VO (EG) Nr. 852/2004 | Lebensmittelhygiene [Food hygiene] | |
| HACCP | Hazard Analysis and Critical Control Point | |
| VDI 2082 | Air-conditioning – Sales Outlets (VDI Ventilation Code of Practice) | 2009-03 |
| VDI 3564 | Recommendations for Fire Protection in High-Bay Warehouses | 2011-01 |
| VDI 3590, Part 1 | Order Picking Systems | 1994-04 |
| VDI 3818 | Public Sanitary Facilities | 2008-02 |
| BGN | Guidelines of the Berufsgenossenschaft für Nahrungsmittel und Gastgewerbe | |
| BGHW | Guidelines of the Berufsgenossenschaft für Handel und Warenlogistik | |
| EC Machinery Directive | EC Machinery Directive "Directive 98/37/EC of the European Parliament and of the Council of 22 June 1998 on the Approximation of the Laws of the Member States Relating to Machinery" | 1998-06-22 |
| EMC Directive | EMC Directive "Directive 2004/108/EC of the European Parliament and of the Council of 15 December 2004 on the Approximation of the Laws of the Member States relating to Electromagnetic Compatibility and Repealing Directive 89/336/EEC" | 2004-12-15 |
| FEM Rules | FEM Rules of the European Federation of Materials Handling | 2015-12 |
| VDE | VDE Regulations of the Association for Electrical, Electronic & Information Technologies | |

| Document | Title | Edition |
| --- | --- | --- |
| BGR 234 | Berufsgenossenschaftliche Regeln für Sicherheit und Gesundheit bei der Arbeit Lagereinrichtungen und -geräte [Industrial rules for safety and health at work: storage facilities and equipment] | 2003 |
| TRGS | Technical Rules for Hazardous Substances (Technische Regeln für Gefahrstoffe) | 2015-06-15 |
| TRbF | Technische Regeln für brennbare Flüssigkeiten [Technical rules for flammable liquids] | 2015-07-27 |
| LöRüRL | Richtlinie zur Bemessung von Löschwasser- Rückhalteanlagen beim Lagern wasser-gefährdender Stoffe [Directive for the calculation of fire-water retention facilities with the storage of materials hazardous to water] | 2003-01 |
| KLR | Kunststofflager-Richtlinie [Plastics storage directive] | 2003-01 |
| BS EN 61812-1:2011 | Time Relays for Industrial and Residential Use. Requirements and Tests | 2011-08-31 |
| PD 6512-3:1987 | Use of Elements of Structural Fire Protection with Particular Reference to the Recommendations given in BS 5588 | 1987-03-31 |
| NFPA 557-2012 | Standard for Determination of Fire Loads for Use in Structural Fire Protection Design, 2012 Edition | 2012 |
| ASCE/SEI/SFPE 29-05 | Standard Calculation Methods for Structural Fire Protection | 2007 |
| EN 61812-1 | Time Relays for Industrial and Residential Use – Part 1: Requirements and Tests (IEC 61812-1:2011) | 2011-08 |

## Chapter 4.4  Industry and Production

| Document | Title | Edition |
| --- | --- | --- |
| IndBauRL | Richtlinie über den baulichen Brandschutz im Industriebau [Directive on structural fire protection in industrial buildings] | 2015-02-04 NRW |
| M-IndBauRL | Muster-Richtlinie über den baulichen Brandschutz im Industriebau [Model Industrial Buildings Directive] | |
| DIN 18225 | Industrial Construction; Traffic Ways in Industrial Buildings | 1988-06 |
| DIN 18230-1 | Structural Fire Protection in Industrial Buildings – Part 1: Analytically Required Fire Resistance Time | 2010-09 |
| AWE 64 | Lichttechnische Gestaltung von Halleneinfahrten; Verbesserung der innerbetrieblichen Verkehrssicherheit [Lighting design of industrial hall entries; Improvement of internal traffic safety] | 1988 |
| VdS 2038 | Allgemeine Sicherheitsvorschriften der Feuerversicherer für Fabriken und gewerbliche Anlagen [General safety regulations of the fire insurers for factories and commercial plants] (ASF) | 2008-01 |
| VDI 3644 | Analysis and Planning of Factory Areas Fundamentals, Application and Examples | 2010-08 |
| BS EN 61812-1:2011 | Time Relays for Industrial and Residential Use. Requirements and Tests | 2011-08-31 |
| PD 6512-3:1987 | Use of Elements of Structural Fire Protection with Particular Reference to the Recommendations given in BS 5588 | 1987-03-31 |
| NFPA 557-2012 | Standard for Determination of Fire Loads for Use in Structural Fire Protection Design, 2012 Edition | 2012 |
| ASCE/SEI/SFPE 29-05 | Standard Calculation Methods for Structural Fire Protection | 2007 |
| EN 61812-1 | Time Relays for Industrial and Residential Use – Part 1: Requirements and Tests (IEC 61812-1:2011) | 2011-08 |

## Chapter 4.5  Education and Research

| Document | Title | Edition |
| --- | --- | --- |
| BImSchG | Federal Immission Control Act (Bundes-Immissionsschutzgesetz) | 1974-03 |
| ASiG | Occupational Safety Act (Arbeitssicherheitsgesetz) | 2013-04-20 |

| Document | Title | Edition |
|---|---|---|
| | Day care Facility Laws of the German States | |
| ArbSchG | Safety and Health at Work Act (Arbeitsschutzgesetz) | 1996-08-07 |
| ArbStättV | Ordinance on Workplaces (Arbeitsstättenverordnung) | 2004-08-12 |
| ASR | Technische Regel für Arbeitsstätten [Technical rules for workplaces] | |
| | Regulations on Minimum Requirements in Day Care Facilities for Children | |
| VStättVO | Ordinance on the Construction and Operation of Places of Public Assembly (Versammlungsstättenverordnung) | |
| BioStoffV | Ordinance on Safety and Health Protection for Work with Biological Agents (Verordnung über Sicherheit und Gesundheitsschutz bei Tätigkeiten mit Biologischen Arbeitsstoffen) | 2013-07-15 |
| GenTG | Act on the Regulation of Genetic Engineering (Gesetz zur Regelung der Gentechnik) | 1993-12-16 |
| GenTSV | Genetic Engineering Safety Ordinance (Gentechnik-Sicherheitsverordnung) | 1990-10-24 |
| GefStoffV | Hazardous Substances Ordinance (Gefahrstoffverordnung) and Regulations on Explosives Law | 2010-11-26, rectified |
| DIN 1946-7 | Ventilation and Air Conditioning – Part 7: Ventilation Systems in Laboratories | 2009-07 |
| DIN 4108-2 | Thermal Protection and Energy Economy in Buildings – Part 2: Minimum Requirements to Thermal Insulation | 2013-02 |
| DIN 4109-1 | Sound Insulation in Buildings – Part 1: Requirements for Sound Insulation | 2013-06 |
| DIN 5034-1 | Daylight in Interiors – Part 1: General Requirements | 2011-07 |
| DIN 5035-7 | Artificial Lighting – Part 7: Lighting of Interiors with Visual Displays Work Stations | 2004-08 |
| DIN 7914 | Gymnastic Equipment – Mats – Dimensions | 2005-01 (withdrawn) |
| DIN 7926-1 | Playground Equipment for Children; Concepts, Safety Requirements, Testing | 1985-08 |
| DIN 18024-1 | Barrier-free Built Environment – Part 1: Streets, Squares, Paths, Public Transport, Recreation Areas and Playgrounds | 1998-01 (withdrawn) |
| DIN 18032-1 | Sports Halls – Halls and Rooms for Sports and Multi-Purpose Use – Part 1: Planning Principles | 2014-11 |
| DIN 18034 | Playgrounds and Outdoor Play Areas – Requirements on Planning, Building and Operation | 2012-09 |
| DIN 18040-1 | Construction of Accessible Buildings – Design Principles – Part 1: Publicly Accessible Buildings | 2010-10 |
| DIN 18041 | Acoustic Quality in Rooms – Specifications and Instructions for the Room Acoustic Design | 2015-02 |
| DIN 33942 | Barrier-free Accessible Playground Equipment – Safety Requirements and Test Methods | 2015-04 (draft) |
| DIN EN 1729-1 | Furniture – Chairs and Tables for Educational Institutions – Part 1: Functional Dimensions | 2016-02 |
| DIN EN 1176-1 | Playground Equipment and Surfacing, Part 1: General Safety Requirements and Test Methods | 2014-11 |
| DIN EN 1177 | Impact Attenuating Playground Surfacing – Determination of Critical Fall Height | 2008-08 |
| DIN EN 14056 | Laboratory Furniture – Recommendations for Design and Installation | 2003-07 |
| GUV-SR 2002 | Richtlinien für Kindergärten – Bau und Ausrüstung | 2006-01 |
| GUV-SI 8017 | Außenspielflächen und Spielplatzgeräte | 2008-09 |
| GUV-SI 8464 | Erste Hilfe in Kindertageseinrichtungen | 2004-09 |
| VDI 6000 Part 3 | Provision and Installation of Sanitary Facilities – Public Buildings and -Areas | 2011-06 |
| VDI 6000 Part 6 | Provision and Installation of Sanitary Facilities – Kindergartens, Day-care Centres, Schools | 2006-11 |
| GUV-SI 2001 | Richtlinien für Schulen; Bau und Ausrüstung | 1987-01 |
| GUV-SI 8070 | Richtlinien zur Sicherheit im Unterricht | 2003-03 |
| DIN EN 12464-1 | Light and Lighting – Lighting of Work Places – Part 1: Indoor Work Places | 2011-08 |

| Document | Title | Edition |
|---|---|---|
| VDI 6040 Part 1 | Air-conditioning – Schools – Requirements (VDI Ventilation Code of Practice, VDI Code of Practice for School Buildings) | 2011-06 |
| GUV-SI 8011 | Richtig sitzen in der Schule – Mindestanforderungen an Tische und Stühle in allgemeinbildenden Schulen | 1999-04 |
| GUV-SI 8018 | GUV-Informationen – Giftpflanzen – Beschauen, nicht kauen | 2005 |
| GUV-V S 1 | Unfallverhütungsvorschrift "Schule" mit Durchführungsanweisungen | 2002-06 |
| GUV-V S 2 | Unfallverhütungsvorschrift: Kindertageseinrichtungen | 2007-05 |
| DGUV Regel 102–002 | Unfallverhütungsvorschrift: Kindertageseinrichtungen | 2009-04 |
| BGI/GUV-I 561 | Information – Treppen | 2008-07 |
| UKH Series, Vol. 8 | Kindertageseinrichtungen sicher gestalten | 2015-07 |
| Prävention in NRW 51 | Die sichere Kindertageseinrichtung Eine Arbeitshilfe zur Planung und Gestaltung | 2012-06 |
| Prävention in NRW 40 | Sicher bilden und betreuen – Gestaltung von Bewegungs- und Bildungsraumen für Kinder unter drei Jahren | 2010-12 |
| UKBW publication | Unfallkasse BW Kinder unter drei Jahren sicher betreuen – Sichere und kindgerechte Gestaltung von Kinderkrippen | |

# Chapter 4.6  Culture and Performing Arts

| Document | Title | Edition |
|---|---|---|
| VStättV | German State Regulations on Places of Assembly | |
| DIN 15905-1 | Entertainment Technology – Audio-, Video- and Communication Audio Engineering for Purposes in Theatres and Multi-purpose Halls – Part 1: Requirements for Own Productions, Co-Productions and Foreign Productions | 2010-07 |
| DIN 56930-1 | Stage Lighting Systems – Part 1: Definitions, Requirements | 2000-03 |
| DIN 56950-4 | Entertainment Technology – Machinery Installations – Part 4: Safety Requirements for Serially Manufactured Projection Screens | 2015-12 |
| VdS 2847 | Notfallprävention und -planung für Museen, Galerien und Archive [Emergency prevention and planning for museums, galleries, and archives] | 2007-12 |
| VdS 3434 | Leitfaden für die Erstellung von Evakuierungs- und Rettungsplänen für Kunst und Kulturgut [Guidelines for the development of evacuation and rescue plans for art and cultural heritage] | 2005-09 |
| VdS 3511en | Security Guidelines for Museums and Showrooms | 2008-09 |
| Info on museum lighting | Museumsbeleuchtung – Strahlung und ihr Schädigungspotenzial – Konservatorische Maßnahmen – Grundlagen zur Berechnung (special supplement to German edition of licht. wissen 18) | 2006-12 |
| DGUV Information 215-313 | Sicherheit bei Veranstaltungen und Produktionen – Leitfaden für Theater, Film, Hörfunk, Fernsehen, Konzerte, Shows, Events, Messen und Ausstellungen | 2015-03 |
| BGI 5036 | BG-Information – Sicherer Betrieb von Lichtspieltheatern | 2006-10 |
| licht.wissen 18 | Good Lighting for Museums, Galleries and Exhibitions | 2006-12 |
| NF S27-100 | Cinematography – Electronic Projection Rooms of Digital Cinema Type | 2006-07-01 |

# Chapter 4.7  Lodging and Food Service

| Document | Title | Edition |
|---|---|---|
| MBeVO | Muster-Verordnung über den Bau und Betrieb von Beherbergungsstätten [Model ordinance on the construction and operation of accommodation establishments] | 2014-05 |
| BStättV BY | Verordnung über den Bau und Betrieb von Beherbergungsstätten [Ordinance on the construction and operation of accommodation establishments] for Bavaria | 2007-07-02 |

| Document | Title | Edition |
|---|---|---|
| BeBauV BB | Verordnung über den Bau und Betrieb von Beherbergungsstätten [Ordinance on the construction and operation of accommodation establishments] for Brandenburg | 2001-06-15 |
| BeStättV MV | Beherbergungsstättenverordnung [Accommodation establishments ordinance] for Mecklenburg-Western Pomerania | 2002-02-12 |
| GastBauVO NW | Verordnung über den Bau und Betrieb von Gaststätten [Ordinance on the construction and operation of restaurants establishments] for North Rhine-Westphalia | 1983-12-09 |
| GastbarrierefreiV ND | Verordnung über die Mindestanforderungen an die barrierefreie Gestaltung von Gaststätten [Ordinance on the minimum requirements for barrier-free design of restaurants] for Lower Saxony | 2014-10-07 |
| DIN 1116 | Kitchen Furniture – Co-ordinating Sizes for Kitchen Furniture and Kitchen Appliances | 2004-09 |
| DIN 10506 | Food Hygiene – Mass Catering | 2012-03 |
| DIN 10510 | Food Hygiene – Commercial Dishwashing with Multitank-Transport Dishwashers – Hygiene Requirements, Procedure Testing | 2013-10 |
| DIN 10512 | Food Hygiene – Commercial Dishwashing with One-Tank Dishwashers – Hygiene Requirements, Type Testing | 2008-06 |
| DIN 10535 | Food Hygiene – Retail Bake-off Stations – Hygienic Requirements | 2014-09 |
| DIN 15906 | Convention Centers | 2009-06 |
| DIN 18854 | Equipment for Commercial Kitchens – Multiple Deck Ovens – Requirements and Testing | 2015-03 |
| DIN 18860-2 | Equipment for Commercial Kitchens – Working Tables – Part 2: Working Tables with Substructures; Requirements and Testing | 2000-06 |
| DIN 18865-1 | Equipment for Commercial Kitchens – Food Distribution Equipment – Part 1: Dimensions, Requirements, Testing | 2003-05 |
| DIN 18872-1 | Equipment for Commercial Kitchens – Refrigeration Technology Equipment – Part 1: Refrigerators and Refrigerated Counters; Requirements and Testing | 2011-05 |
| DIN EN 454 | Food Processing Machinery – Planetary Mixers – Safety and Hygiene Requirements | 2015-02 |
| DIN EN 16282-6 | Equipment for Commercial Kitchens – Components for Ventilation of Commercial Kitchens – Part 6: Aerosol Separators – Design and Safety Requirements | 2014-11 (draft) |
| DIN EN ISO 18513 | Tourism Services – Hotels and Other Types of Tourism Accommodation – Terminology | 2003-12 |
| ÖNORM B 1603 | Accessible Facilities for Tourism and Leisure – Design Principles | 2013-10-01 |
| ÖNORM EN ISO 18513 | Tourism Services – Hotels and Other Types of Tourism Accommodation – Terminology | 2013-12-01 |
| VDI 2160 | Waste Management in Buildings and on Ground – Requirement[s] for Bins, Locations and Transportation Routes | 2008-10 |
| VDI 3726 | Noise Reduction in Restaurants and Skittle-Alleys | 1991-01 |
| licht.wissen 11 | Good Lighting for Hotels and Restaurants | 1990-11 |
| ASTM E1661 – 95a(2012) | Standard Classification for Serviceability of an Office Facility for Meetings and Group Effectiveness | 1995 |
| ISO 18513:2003 | Tourism Services. Hotels and Other Types of Tourism Accommodation. Terminology | 2003-10-28 |

## Chapter 4.8  Healthcare

| Document | Title | Edition |
|---|---|---|
| KHG | Gesetz zur wirtschaftlichen Sicherung der Krankenhäuser und zur Regelung der Krankenhauspflegesätze [Hospital Financing Act] | 1972-06 |
| | Hospital Building Codes of the Respective German States | |
| | German State Regulations on Hospital Funding | |
| ArbStättV | Ordinance on Workplaces (Arbeitsstättenverordnung) | 2004-08-12 |
| HeimMindBauV | Ordinance on Structural Minimum Requirements for Homes and Hostels for the Elderly and Nursing Homes for Adults (Heimmindestbauverordnung) | 1978-01 |

| Document | Title | Edition |
|---|---|---|
| DIN 277-1 | Areas and volumes of buildings – Part 1: Building Construction | 2016-01 |
| DIN 1946-4 | Ventilation and air conditioning – Part 4: Ventilation in Buildings and Rooms of Health Care | 2008-12 |
| DIN 5035-3 | Artificial Lighting – Part 3: Lighting of Health Care Premises | 2006-07 |
| DIN 12924-4 | Laboratory Furniture – Fume Cupboards – Part 4: Fume Cupboards for Pharmacies | 2012-02 |
| DIN 13080 | Division of Hospitals into Functional Areas and Functional Sections | 2015-04 (draft) |
| DIN 13411 | Protection of Walls and Apparatus in Medical Facilities – Terms, Specific Data | 1999-02 (withdrawn) |
| DIN 18000 | Modular Coordination in Building | 1984-05 (withdrawn) |
| DIN 18030 | Barrierfree Building – Design Principles | 2006-01 (withdrawn) |
| DIN 18205 | Brief for Building Design | 2015-11 (draft) |
| DGUV | Unfallverhütungsvorschriften [Accident prevention regulations] | |
| BGI/GUV-I 8681 | Information – Neu- und Umbauplanung im Krankenhaus unter Gesichtspunkten des Arbeitsschutzes | 2008-09 |
| RKI | Richtlinie für Krankenhaushygiene und Infektionsprävention [Guidelines for hospital hygiene and infection prevention] | 2004-04 |
| KRINKO | Guidelines of the Commission for Hospital Hygiene and Infection Prevention | |
| StrlSchV | Directive on the Ordinance on the Protection against Damage and Injuries Caused by Ionizing Radiation (Strahlenschutzverordnung) | 2001-07-20 |
| | Richtlinie über das Verfahren über die Gewährung von Fördermitteln nach § 9 Abs. 1 KHG | 2004-11-01 |

# Chapter 4.9  Sports and Recreation

| Document | Title | Edition |
|---|---|---|
| DIN 18032-1 | Sports Halls – Halls and Rooms for Sports and Multi-purpose Use – Part 1: Planning Principles | 2014-11 |
| DIN 18035-1 | Sports Grounds – Part 1: Outdoor Play and Athletics Areas, Planning and Dimensions | 2003-02 |
| DIN 18035-4 | Sports Grounds – Part 4: Sports Turf Areas | 2012-01 |
| DIN 18036 | Ice-sport Facilities – Ice-sport Facilities with Artificial Ice – Rules for Planning and Construction | 2010-03 |
| DIN EN 1069-1 | Water Slides – Part 1: Safety Requirements and Test Methods | 2015-09 (draft) |
| DIN EN 12193 | Light and Lighting- Sports Lighting | 2008-04 |
| DIN EN 13200-1 | Spectator Facilities – Part 1: General Characteristics for Spectator Viewing Area | 2012-11 |
| DIN EN 13451-1 | Swimming Pool Equipment – Part 1: General Safety Requirements and Test Methods | 2011-11 |
| DIN EN 15288-1 | Swimming Pools – Part 1: Safety Requirements for Design | 2010-12 |
| VDI 3770 | Characteristic Noise Emission Values of Sound Sources – Facilities for Recreational and Sporting Activities | 2012-09 |
| GUV-R 1/111 | Sicherheitsregeln für Bäder [Safety rules for pools] | 2005-06 |
| GUV-I 8527 | Bodenbeläge für nassbelastete Barfußbereiche | 1999-07 |
| PD ISO/TR 20183:2015 | Sports and Other Recreational Facilities and Equipment | 2015-06-30 |
| BS EN 12231:2003 | Surfaces for Sports Areas. Method of Test. Determination of Ground Cover of Natural Turf | 2003-08-15 |
| ASTM F2442 – 07 | Standard Guide for Layout of Ice Arena | 2007 |
| ASTM F2270 – 12 | Standard Guide for Construction and Maintenance of Warning Track Areas on Athletic Fields | 2012 |

## Chapter 4.10  Public Safety

| Document | Title | Edition |
| --- | --- | --- |
| DIN 14090 | Areas for the Fire Brigade on Premises | 2002-05 |
| DIN 14092-1 | Fire Stations – Part 1: Elements for Design | 2012-04 |
| DIN 14093 | Equipment for Practicing Respiratory Protective Devices – Elements of Design | 2014-04 |
| DIN 14097 | Fire Brigade Training Houses | 1989-07 |
| GUV-V C 53 | Unfallverhütungsvorschrift "Feuerwehren" mit Durchführungsanweisungen | 2005 |
| GUV-I 8554 | GUV-Information – Sicherheit im Feuerwehrhaus – Sicherheitsgerechtes Planen, Gestalten und Betreiben | 2008-07 |
| MRFlFw | Muster-Richtlinien über Flächen für die Feuerwehr | 2009-10 |
| ÖBFV-RL FH01 | Errichtung von Feuerwehrhäusern | 2012-06-05 |
| 2012-06-05 | Specification for ropes and lines for fire service use other than for rope rescue purposes | 1999-10 |
| BS 3367:1980 | Specification for Fire Brigade and Industrial Ropes and Rescue Lines | 1980-10 |
| BS 3367:1961 | Fire Brigade Rescue Lines | 1961-04 (withdrawn) |
| NFPA 1500-2002 | NFPA 1500: Standard on Fire Department Occupational Safety and Health Program, 2002 Edition | 2002 |
| NFPA 1914-1997 | NFPA 1914: Standard for Testing Fire Department Aerial Devices, 1997 Edition | 1997 |

## Chapter 4.11  Transportation and Infrastructure

| Document | Title | Edition |
| --- | --- | --- |
| ArbStättV | Ordinance on Workplaces (Arbeitsstättenverordnung) | 2004-08-12 |
| ASR A | Technische Regel für Arbeitsstätten [Technical rules for workplaces] | |
| BetrSichV | Betriebssicherheitsverordnung [Industrial safety ordinance] | 2015-02-03 |
| LuftVO | Luftverkehrsordnung [Air traffic ordinance] | 2015-10-29 |
| LuftVZO | Luftverkehrs-Zulassungs-Ordnung [Air traffic licensing ordinance] | 2008-07-10 |
| SBauVO | Sonderbauverordnung [Special construction regulation] | |
| GarVO | Garagenverordnung [Garage ordinance] | 2000-02-20 |
| GaVAAErl BW | Erlaß über die Anwendung der Garagenverordnung; Ausführungsanweisung zur Garagenverordnung | 1976-09-08 |
| MGaV | Muster einer Verordnung über den Bau und Betrieb von Garagen [Model ordinance on the construction and operation of garages] | 2008-05 |
| VStättVO | Ordinance on the Construction and Operation of Places of Public Assembly (Versammlungsstättenverordnung) | 2004-04-28 |
| EBO | EBO – Eisenbahn-Bau- und Betriebsordnung [Ordinance on the construction and operation of railways] | |
| DIN 4054 | Correction of waterways; Terms | 1977-09 |
| DIN 12464-2 | Light and Lighting – Lighting of Work Places – Part 2: Outdoor Work Places | 2014-05 |
| DIN 24446 | Safety of Machinery – Vehicle Washing Machines – Safety Requirements, Test Methods | 1998-08 |
| DIN EN 1360 | Rubber and Plastic Hoses and Hose Assemblies for Measured Fuel Dispensing Systems – Specification | 2011-10 (draft) |
| DIN EN 12285-1 | Workshop Fabricated Steel Tanks – Part 1: Horizontal Cylindrical Single Skin and Double Skin Tanks for the Underground Storage of Flammable and Non-Flammable Water Polluting Liquids | 2014-05 (draft) |

| Document | Title | Edition |
|---|---|---|
| DIN EN 13012 | Petrol Filling Stations – Construction and Performance of Automatic Nozzles for Use on Fuel Dispensers | 2010-07 (draft) |
| DIN EN 13160-1 | Leak Detection Systems – Part 1: General Principles | 2014-10 (draft) |
| DIN EN 13617-1 | Petrol Filling Stations – Part 1: Safety Requirements for Construction and Performance of Metering Pumps, Dispensers and Remote Pumping Units | 2012-08 |
| DIN EN 14503 | Inland Navigation Vessels – Harbours for Inland Navigation | 2004-03 |
| DIN EN 15268 | Petrol Filling Stations – Safety Requirements for the Construction of Submersible Pump Assemblies | 2008-11 |
| DIN EN 15273-1 | Railway Applications – Gauges – Part 1: General – Common Rules for Infrastructure and Rolling Stock | 2014-06 |
| DIN EN 16082 | Airport and Aviation Security Services | 2011-11 |
| DIN EN 16495 | Air Traffic Management – Information Security for Organisations Supporting Civil Aviation Operations | 2014-05 |
| DIN EN 16584-1 | Railway Applications – Design for PRM Use – General Requirements – Part 1: Contrast; German version | 2013-07 |
| GrSchRaumBahnBek | Notification of the Structural Principles for Large Shelters of Basic Protection in Connection with Underground Railways | |
| GUV-V D 30.1 | Unfallverhütungsvorschrift "Eisenbahnen" mit Durchführungsanweisunge | 1998-09 |
| DGUV Information 214-009 (BGI 770) | Gestaltung von Sicherheitsräumen, Sicherheitsabständen und Verkehrswegen bei Eisenbahnen | 2011-07 |
| UIC 140 | Accessibility to Stations in Europe | |
| XP X43-105 | Air Quality – Auditing of Air Quality in Non-industrial Premises – Public Transport Means and Stations | |
| ÖAL Directive 24, Part 1 | Lärmschutzzonen in der Umgebung von Flughäfen – Planungs- und Berechnungsgrundlagen | 2008-03-01 |
| HTG EAU 2012:2012-11 | Empfehlungen des Arbeitsausschusses "Ufereinfassungen" – Häfen und Wasserstraßen | 2012-11 |
| ANSI/NFPA 88A | Standard for Parking Structures | 2011 |
| DBV Bulletin | Merkblatt – Parkhäuser und Tiefgaragen | 2010-09 |
| NF P91-100 | Public Car-Parks: Criteria for Functional Capability – Design and Dimensions | 1994-05-01 |
| VDI 4466 Part 1 | Automatic Parking Systems – Basic Principles | 2001-01 |
| EAR 05 | Empfehlungen für Anlagen des ruhenden Verkehrs | 2005-02 |
| AWE 86 | Kfz-Werkstätten – Gestaltung von Arbeitsplätzen und Arbeitsumgebung in Kfz-Werkstätten | 1993 |
| FGSV 219 RAT | Richtlinien für die Anlage von Tankstellen an Straßen; RAT | 1985 |
| RAA | Richtlinien für die Anlage von Autobahnen | 2008-06 |
| VDA | Kriterien für VDA-konforme Waschanlagen | 2007-01 |
| VwV | Anforderungen an Abfüllanlagen für Tankstellen [Requirements for filling systems for fueling stations] | 1998-02-04 |
| TRbF | Technische Regeln für brennbare Flüssigkeiten [Technical rules for flammable liquids] | 2015-07-27 |
| TRGS | Technical Rules for Hazardous Substances (Technische Regeln für Gefahrstoffe) | 2015-06-15 |
| ZH 1/543 | Richtlinien für Fahrzeugwaschanlagen | 1986-10 |

# 5.2 References

## General References

American Institute of Architects. *Architectural Graphic Standards*, 12th ed. Hoboken: Wiley, 2006.

American Planning Association (APA). *Planning and Urban Design Standards*. Hoboken: Wiley, 2006.

Bielefeld, Bert, and Isabella Skiba. *Basics Technical Drawing*, 2nd rev. ed. Basel: Birkhäuser, 2013.

Ching, Francis D. K., and Steven R. Winkel. *Building Codes Illustrated: A Guide to Understanding the International Building Code*, 4th ed. Hoboken: Wiley, 2012.

De Chiara, Joseph, and Mike Crosbie. *Time-Saver Standards for Building Types*, 4th ed. New York: McGraw-Hill, 2001.

De Chiara, Joseph, Julius Panero, and Martin Zelnik. *Time-Saver Standards for Interior Design and Space Planning*, 2nd ed. New York: McGraw-Hill, 2001.

Deplazes, Andrea, ed. *Constructing Architecture: Materials, Processes, Structures*, 3rd ed. Basel: Birkhäuser, 2013.

Harmon, Sharon K., and Katherine E. Kennon. *The Codes Guidebook for Interiors*, 6th ed., Hoboken: Wiley, 2014.

Harris, Charles, and Nicholas Dines. *Time-Saver Standards for Landscape Architecture: Design and Construction Data*, 2nd ed. New York: McGraw-Hill, 1998.

Heiss, Oliver, Christine Degenhart, and Johann Ebe. *Barrier-Free Design: Principles, Planning, Examples*, translated by Gerd H. Söffker and Philip Thrift. Edition Detail. Basel: Birkhäuser, 2010.

International Code Council: *International Building Code*, 2015 edition, ICC/Cengage Learning, Clifton Park, NY 2014. The 2012 edition is availa online at http://publicecodes.cyberregs.com/icod/, last accessed June 11, 2016.

Littlefield, David, ed. *Metric Handbook: Planning and Design Data*. 4th ed. New York: Routledge, 2012.

Neufert, Ernst, and Peter Neufert. *Architect's Data*, 4th ed., updated by Johannes Kister et al., translated by David Sturge. Chichester: Wiley-Blackwell, 2012.

Watson, Donald, and Michael J. Crosbie, eds. *Time-Saver Standards for Architectural Design: Technical Data for Professional Practice*, 8th ed. New York: McGraw-Hill, 2004.

Zimmermann, Astrid, ed. *Constructing Landscape: Materials, Techniques, Structural Components*, 3rd ed. Basel: Birkhäuser, 2015.

Zimmermann, Astrid. *Planning Landscape: Dimensions, Elements, Typologies*. Basel: Birkhäuser, 2015.

## Chapter 2.1 Anthropometry and Barrier-Free Accessibility

Flügel, Bernd, Holle Greil, and Karl Sommer. *Anthropologischer Atlas*. Frankfurt am Main: Wötzel, 1986.

Jürgens, Hans, Ivar Aune, and Ursula Pieper. *International Data on Anthropometry*. Geneva: International Labour Office, 1990.

Panero, Julius, and Martin Zelnik. *Human Dimension & Interior Space: A Source Book of Design Reference Standards*. New York: Whitney Library of Design, 1979.

Pheasant, Stephen. *Bodyspace: Anthropometry, Ergonomics and the Design of Work*. London: Taylor & Francis Ltd, 2005.

Skiba, Isabella, and Rahel Züger. *Basics Barrier-Free Planning*. Basel: Birkhäuser, 2009.

## Chapter 2.2 Comfort and Physical Spatial Qualities

DiLaura, David L., Kevin W. Houser, Richard G. Mistrick, and Gary Steffy, eds. *The Lighting Handbook: Reference and Application*, 10th ed. New York: Illuminating Engineering Society of North America, 2011.

Frank, Walther. *Raumklima und Thermische Behaglichkeit*. Berlin: Wilhelm Ernst & Sohn, 1975.

Glück, Bernd. *Wärmtechnisches Raummodell*. Heidelberg: Müller, 1997.

Klein, Oliver, and Jörg Schlenger. *Basics Room Conditioning*. Basel: Birkhäuser, 2008.

Leusden, F., and H. Freymark. "Darstellungen der Raumbehaglichkeit für den einfachen praktischen Gebrauch," *Gesundheitsingenieur* 72, no. 16 (1951): 271–73.

Maas, Anton, ed. *Umweltbewusstes Bauen*. Stuttgart: Fraunhofer IRB, 2008.

Mayer, Erhard, ed. *Menschengerechte Raumklimatisierung durch Quelllüftung und Flächenkühlung*. Stuttgart: Fraunhofer IRB, 1995.

Nocke, Christian. *Raumakustik im Alltag: Hören – Planen – Verstehen*. Stuttgart: Fraunhofer IRB, 2014.

Pistohl, Wolfram, Christian Rechenauer, and Birgit Scheuerer. *Handbuch der Gebäudetechnik*, vol. 2, *Heizung, Lüftung, Beleuchtung, Energiesparen*, 8th ed. Cologne: Werner , 2013.

Watson, Donald, and Kenneth Labs. *Climatic Building Design: Energy-Efficient Building Principles and Practices*. New York: McGraw-Hill, 1993.

Willems, Wolfgang. *Wärme- und Feuchteschutz, Behaglichkeit, Lüftung*. Wiesbaden: Vieweg, 2006.

## Chapter 2.3 Spatial Perception

Bogardus, Emory S. "Measuring Social Distances," *Journal of Applied Sociology* 9 (1925): 299–308.

Bundesministerium für Gesundheit. *Handbuch für Planer und Praktiker*. Bad Homburg, 1996.

Gehl, Jan. *Life Between Buildings: Using Public Space*, rev. ed., translated by Jo Koch. New York: Van Nostrand Reinhold, 1987. Originally published as *Livet mellem husene* (1971).

Hall, Edward T. *The Hidden Dimension*. Garden City, NY: Doubleday, 1966.

Le Corbusier. *The Modulor* and *Modulor 2*. Basel: Birkhäuser, 2000.

Roedler, F. "Wärmephysiologische und hygienische Grundlagen," in H. Rietschels, *Lehrbuch der Heiz- und Lüftungstechnik*, 284–316. Berlin: Springer, 1960.

Stolzenberg, H., H. Kahl, and K. E. Bergmann. "Körpermaße bei Kindern und Jugendlichen in Deutschland," *Bundesgesundheitsblatt – Gesundheitsforschung – Gesundheitsschutz* 50, no. 5–6 (2007): 659–69.

## Chapter 3.1 External Circulation

Auhagen, Axel, Klaus Ermer, Klaus, and Rita Mohrmann. *Landschaftsplanung in der Praxis*. Stuttgart: Ulmer, 2002.

Booth, Norman K. *Basic Elements of Landscape Architectural Design*. Long Grove, IL: Waveland Press, 1990.

Kirchhoff, Peter. *Städtische Verkehrsplanung: Konzepte, Verfahren, Maßnahmen*. Wiesbaden: Vieweg+Teubner, 2002.

Köhler, Uwe. *Einführung in die Verkehrsplanung*. Stuttgart: Fraunhofer IRB, 2014.

Lohse, Dieter. *Verkehrsplanung*, 3rd ed. Berlin: Beuth, 2011.

Weidinger, Jürgen, ed. *Atmosphären Entwerfen*. Berlin: TU Berlin, 2014.

Weiland, Ulrike. *Einführung in die Raum- und Umweltplanung*. Stuttgart: UTB, 2007.

## Chapter 3.2 Internal Circulation

Schittich, Christian, ed. *Designing Circulation Areas, Staged Paths and Innovative Floorplan Concepts*. Berlin: Edition Detail, 2013.

## Chapter 3.3 Workrooms and Production Spaces

Grundig, Claus-Gerold. *Fabrikplanung – Planungssystematik – Methoden – Anwendungen*, 5th ed. Munich: Carl Hanser, 2014.

Wiendahl, Hans-Peter, Jürgen Reichardt, and Peter Nyhuis. *Handbook Factory Planning and Design.* Heidelberg: Springer, 2015.

## Chapter 3.4 Communication Spaces and Dining Rooms

Ausschuss für staatlichen Hochbau, Bauministerkonferenz. *Planung und Bau von Küchen und Kantinen für 50 bis 1000 Verpflegungsteilnehmer.* Hanover: HIS Hochschul-Informations-System, 2002. Available online: https://www.is-argebau.de/Dokumente/4231417.pdf

## Chapter 3.5 Sanitary Facilities

Feurich, Hugo. *Grundlagen der Sanitärtechnik, Sanitärräume, Sanitäreinrichtung, Krankenhauseinrichtungen, physikalische Therapie-Einrichtungen, Wasserversorgung*, 10th exp. ed. Düsseldorf: Krammer, 2011.

Pistohl, Wolfram, Christian Rechenauer, and Birgit Scheuerer. *Handbuch der Gebäudetechnik*, vol. 1, *Planungsgrundlagen und Beispiele*, 8th ed. Cologne: Werner, 2013.

Wellpott, Edwin, and Dirk Bohne. *Technischer Ausbau von Gebäuden*, 9th rev. and upd. ed., Stuttgart: Kohlhammer, 2006.

## Chapter 3.6 Kitchens

Aicher, Otl. *Die Küche zum Kochen: Werkstatt einer neuen Lebenskultur*, 3rd ed. Staufen bei Freiburg: Ökobuch, 2005.

Loeschke, Gerhard, and Jutta Höfs. *Großküchen*. Wiesbaden: Bauverlag, 1985.

## Chapter 3.7 Storage Spaces

Heinrich, Martin. *Transport- und Lagerlogistik: Planung, Struktur, Steuerung und Kosten von Systemen der Intralogistik*, 9th ed. Wiesbaden: Springer Vieweg, 2014.

Ten Hompel, Michael, Thorsten Schmidt, and Lars Nagel. *Materialflusssysteme: Förder- und Lagertechnik*, 3rd rev. ed. Berlin: Springer, 2001.

## Chapter 3.8 Ancillary and Staff Rooms

Streit, Wilhelm, and Ernst-Friedrich Pernack, eds. *Arbeitsstätten*, 8th ed. Heidelberg: ecomed Sicherheit, 2011.

## Chapter 3.9 Technical Equipment Rooms

Grondzik, Walter T., and Alison G. Kwok. *Mechanical and Electrical Equipment for Buildings*, 12th ed. Hoboken: Wiley, 2014.

Klein, Oliver, and Jörg Schlenger. *Basics Room Conditioning*. Basel: Birkhäuser, 2008.

Pistohl, Wolfram, Christian Rechenauer, and Birgit Scheuerer. *Handbuch der Gebäudetechnik*, vol. 2, *Heizung, Lüftung, Beleuchtung, Energiesparen*, 8th ed. Cologne: Werner, 2013.

RWE. *Bau-Handbuch*. Frankfurt: EW Medien und Kongresse Buchverlag, 2014.

Trost, Frederick Jerome, and Ifte Choudhury. *Design of Mechanical and Electrical Systems in Buildings*, Upper Saddle River, NJ: Pearson, 2003.

TÜV Rheinland. *Kriterienkatalog zum Audit von Serverräumen und Rechenzentren.* n.p., n.d.

Wellpott, Edwin, and Dirk Bohne. *Technischer Ausbau von Gebäuden*, 9th rev. and up. ed. Stuttgart: Kohlhammer, 2006.

## Chapter 4.1 Housing

Arc-en-rêve, ed. *New Forms of Collective Housing in Europe*. Basel: Birkhäuser, 2009.

Bott, Helmut, and Volker von Haas. *Verdichteter Wohnungsbau*. Wiesbaden: Vieweg+Teubner, 1996.

Ebner, Peter, et al. *typology+, Innovative Residential Architecture*. Basel: Birkhäuser, 2009.

Gast, Klaus-Peter. *Living Plans: New Concepts for Advanced Housing*. Basel: Birkhäuser, 2005.

Heckmann, Oliver, and Friederike Schneider. *Floor Plan Manual: Housing*, 4th ed. Basel: Birkhäuser, 2011.

Heisel, Joachim. *Planungsatlas: Das kompakte Planungsbuch für den Bauentwurf mit Projektbeispielen*, 4th ed. Berlin: Beuth, 2004.

Huber, Andreas, ed. *New Approaches to Housing for the Second Half of Life*. Basel: Birkhäuser, 2008.

Klaffke, Julius, and Peter Ebner. *Living Streets*. Vienna: Springer, 2009.

Kliment, Stephen A., ed. *Building Type Basics for Housing*, 2nd ed. Hoboken: Wiley, 2010.

König, Roland. *Leitfaden barrierefreier Wohnungsbau*, 3rd ed. Stuttgart: Fraunhofer IRB, 2005.

Kramer, Klaus. *Das private Hausbad 1850–1950*. Schiltach: Hansgrohe, 1997.

Krebs, Jan. *Basics Design and Living*. Basel: Birkhäuser, 2007.

Leupen, Bernard, and Harald Mooij. *Housing Design: A Manual*, 2nd ed. Rotterdam: nai010, 2012.

Manser, Joe A., Eric Bertels, Andreas Stamm, and Thomas Brenner. *Wohnungsbau hindernisfrei – anpassbar,* 3rd ed. Zurich: Schweizerische Fachstelle für Behindertengerechtes Bauen, 2009.

Noever, Peter, ed. *Die Frankfurter Küche von Margarete Schütte-Lihotzky: die Frankfurter Küche aus der Sammlung des MAK – Österreichisches Museum für Angewandte Kunst, Wien*. Berlin: Ernst & Sohn, 1992.

Perkins, Bradford, and J. David Hoglund. *Building Type Basics for Senior Living*, 2nd ed. Hoboken: Wiley, 2010.

Peters, Paulhans. *Häuser in Reihen*. Munich: Callwey, 1973.

Pfeifer, Günter, and Per Brauneck. *Courtyard Houses: A Housing Typology,* Basel: Birkhäuser, 2008.

———. *Freestanding Houses: A Housing Typology*, Basel: Birkhäuser, 2010.

———. *Row Houses: A Housing Typology*. Basel: Birkhäuser, 2007.

———. *Town Houses: A Housing Typology*, Basel: Birkhäuser, 2008.

Posener, Julius. *Anfänge des Funktionalismus: Von Arts and Crafts zum Deutschen Werkbund*. Bauwelt Fundamente 11. Basel: Birkhäuser, 2014.

Preiser, Wolfgang F. E., Jacqueline Vischer, and Edward T. White. *Design Intervention*. New York: Better World Books, 1991.

Sauter, Hanns M., et al. *Einführung in das Entwerfen*, vol. 1: *Entwurfspragmatik*. Wiesbaden: Springer Vieweg, 2011.

Schittich, Christian, ed. *In Detail: High-Density Housing: Concepts, Planning, Construction*. Basel: Birkhäuser, 2012.

———. *In Detail: Housing for People of All Ages*. Basel: Birkhäuser, 2013.

———. *In Detail: Semi-Detached and Terraced Houses*. Basel: Birkhäuser, 2012.

———. *In Detail: Single Family Houses*, 2nd ed. Basel: Birkhäuser, 2005.

Schneider, Friederike, and Oliver Heckmann. *Floor Plan Manual: Housing*, 4th ed. Basel: Birkhäuser, 2011.

Skiba, Isabella, and Rahel Züger. *Basics Barrier-Free Planning*. Basel: Birkhäuser, 2009.

Stamm-Teske, Walter, et al. *Raumpilot Wohnen*. Stuttgart: Krämer, 2010.

Weitz, Ewald, and Jürgen Friedenberg, eds. *Interbau Berlin 1957*. Berlin, 1957.

Wietzorrek, Ulrike. *Housing+*. Basel: Birkhäuser, 2014.

Yuen, Belinda, and Anthony Yeh, eds. *High-Rise Living in Asian Cities*. Dordrecht: Springer, 2011.

## Chapter 4.2  Office and Administration

Clements-Croome, Derek. *Creating the Productive Workplace.* New York: Taylor & Francis, 2006.

Eisele, Johann, and Bettina Staniek, eds. *BürobauAtlas: Grundlagen, Planung, Technologie, Arbeitsplatzqualitäten.* Munich: Callwey, 2005.

Gause, Jo Allen, et al. *Office Development Handbook*, 2nd ed. Washington, DC: Urban Land Institute, 1998.

Hascher, Rainer, Simone Jeska, Thomas Arnold, and Birgit Klauck. *Office Buildings, A Design Manual.* Basel: Birkhäuser, 2002.

Institut für Internationale Architektur-Dokumentation, ed. *Büro/ Office.* Munich: Detail, 2013.

Kohn, A. Eugene, and Paul Katz. *Building Type Basics for Office Buildings.* Hoboken: Wiley, 2002.

Marmot, Alexi, and Joanna Eley. *Office Space Planning: Designs for Tomorrow's Workspace.* New York: McGraw Hill, 2000.

Ostertag, Roland. *Rathäuser und kommunale Zentren: Entwurf und Planung.* Munich: Callwey, 1983.

Oswald, Ansgar. *Offices.* Berlin: DOM Publishers, 2012.


## Chapter 4.3  Logistics and Commerce

Beck, Eva-Maria. *Bauliche Sicherheit im Einzelhandel.* Berlin: Beuth, 2015.

Beyard, Michael D. *Developing Retail Entertainment Destinations*, 2nd ed. Washington, DC: Urban Land Institute, 2001.

Beyard, Michael D., and Paul W. O'Mara. *Shopping Center Development Handbook*, 3rd ed. Washington, DC: Urban Land Institute, 1999.

Coleman, Peter. *Shopping Environments: Evolution, Planning and Design.* Amsterdam: Elsevier, 2006.

Ebster, Claus, and Marion Garaus. *Store Design and Visual Merchandising*, Vienna: Facultas, 2015.

Gibbs, Robert J. *Principles of Urban Retail Planning and Development.* Hoboken: Wiley, 2012.

Gretz, Friedrich. *Läden richtig planen: Fehler vermeiden.* Stuttgart: Krämer, 2000.

Groenmeyer, Thomas. *Logistikimmobilien vom Band – Standardisierung im gewerblichen Hochbau am Beispiel von Warehouse-Logistikimmobilien.* Schriftenreihe Bauwirtschaft, Forschung 23. Kassel: Kassel University Press, 2012.

Gudehus, Timm. *Logistik: Grundlagen, Strategien, Anwendungen.* Berlin: Springer, 2010.

Gudehus, Timm, and Herbert Kotzab. *Comprehensive Logistics.* Berlin: Springer, 2012.

Heathcote, Edwin. *Bank Builders.* New York: Wiley, 2000.

Holfeld, Monika. *Licht und Farbe: Planung und Ausführung bei der Gebäudegestaltung.* Berlin: Beuth, 2013.

Hompel, Michael ten, and Thorsten Schmidt. *Warehouse Management: Automation and Organisation of Warehouse and Order Picking Systems.* Berlin: Springer, 2006.

Jerde Partnership, and Wilma Barr. *Building Type Basics for Retail and Mixed-Use Facilities.* Hoboken, Wiley, 2004.

Juhr, Michael. "Konstruktionsmerkmale Logistikgebäude," *industrieBau* 56, no. 3 (2010): 24ff.

Kielkopf, Jens. *Marktanalyse Logistikimmobilien.* Munich: GRIN, 2013.

Kramer, Anita. *Retail Development Handbook*, 4th ed. Washington, DC: Urban Land Institute, 2008.

Krämer, Karl, ed. *Commercial and Industrial Buildings.* Stuttgart: Krämer, 2006.

Kreft, Wilhelm. *Ladenplanung Merchandising-Architektur. Strategien für Verkaufsräume: Gestaltungs-Grundlagen, Erlebnis-Inszenierungen, Kundenleitweg-Planungen*, 2nd rev. ed. Leinfelden-Echterdingen: Koch, 2002.

Kusch, Clemens F. *Construction and Design Manual Exhibition Halls.* Berlin: DOM Publishers, 2013.

Lehder, Günter, and Dieter Uhlig. *Betriebsstättenplanung – Grundlagen, Methoden und Inhalte unter besonderer Berücksichtigung des Arbeitsschutzes.* Filderstadt: Weinmann, 1998.

Lopez, Michael J. *Retail Store Planning and Design Manual*, 2nd ed. New York: Wiley, 1995.

Lorenz, Peter. *Gewerbebau, Industriebau – Architektur, Planen, Gestalten.* Leinfelden-Echterdingen: Koch, 1991.

Lorenz, Peter, and Stephan Isphording. *Banken und Geldinstitute: Aktuelle Architektur und neue Entwicklungstendenzen.* Leinfelden-Echterdingen: Koch, 2003.

Mesher, Lynne. *Basics Interior Design 01: Retail Design.* London: Bloomsbury, 2010.

Messedat, Jons. *Retail Architecture S-XXL: Development, Design, Projects.* Stuttgart: Avedition, 2015.

Münchow, Malte-Maria, ed. *Kompendium der Logistikimmobile: Entwicklung, Nutzung und Investment.* Wiesbaden: IZ Immobilien Zeitung Verlagsgesellschaft, 2012.

Pracht, Klaus. *Läden: Planung und Gestaltung.* Basel: Birkhäuser, 2001.

Stark, Ulrike. *Lagerhallen I.* Stuttgart: Fraunhofer IRB, 1998.

Umdasch Shop Academy, ed. *Handbuch Ladenbau: Konzept – Planung – Realisierung.* Munich: Callwey, 2015.

———. *Ladenbau Lexikon: Ladenmarketing.* Munich: Callwey, 2011.


## Chapter 4.4  Industry and Production

Adam, Jürgen, and Katharina Hausmann. *Industrial Buildings, A Design Manual.* Basel: Birkhäuser, 2004.

Führer, Hansjakob, and Dorothea Stürmer, eds. *Grundlagen 1: Industriebau.* Darmstadt: Das Beispiel, 1999.

Grundig, Claus-Gerold. *Fabrikplanung: Planungssystematik – Methoden – Anwendungen*, 5th ed. Munich: Carl Hanser, 2014.

Heathcote, Edwin. *Factory Builders: The Influence of Industrial Architecture.* New York: Wiley-Academy, 2001.

Koengeter, Bernd. *Industrie- und Gewerbeparks.* Stuttgart: Fraunhofer IRB, 1998.

Schittich, Christian, ed. *In Detail: Work Environments.* Basel: Birkhäuser, 2011.

Sommer, Degenhard, ed. *Industriebauten gestalten.* Vienna: Picus, 1989.

van Uffelen, Chris. *Factory Design.* Salenstein: Braun, 2008.

Wiendahl, Hans-Peter, Jürgen Reichardt, and Peter Nyhuis. *Handbook Factory Planning and Design.* Heidelberg: Springer, 2015.


## Chapter 4.5  Education and Research

Braun, Hardo, and Dieter Grömling. *Research and Technology Buildings.* Basel: Birkhäuser, 2005.

Curtis, Eleanor. *School Builders.* Hoboken: Wiley, 2003.

Dubber, Geoff, and Kathy Lemaire. *Visionary Spaces: Designing and Planning a Secondary School Library.* Swindon: School Library Association, 2008.

Dudek, Mark. *Schools and Kindergartens, A Design Manual*, 2nd ed. Basel: Birkhäuser, 2011.

Gralle, Horst, and Christian Port. *Bauten für Kinder – Ein Leitfaden zur Kindergartenplanung.* Stuttgart: Kohlhammer, 2002.

Haas, Dirk E., ed. *Leitlinien für leistungsfähige Schulbauten in Deutschland.* Bonn: Montag Stiftung Urbane Räume, 2013.

Hille, R. Thomas. *Modern Schools: A Century of Design for Education.* Hoboken: Wiley, 2011.

Hubeli, Ernst, and Thomas Becker, eds. *Schulen Planen und Bauen – Grundlagen und Prozesse*, 2nd rev. ed. Berlin: Jovis, 2012.

ILA – Institut fur Landschaftsarchitektur, and University of Natural Resources and Life Sciences, Vienna, eds. *Schul:FREI – Empfehlungen für Schulfreiräume.* Vienna, 2004.

Khan, Ayub. *Better by Design: An Introduction to Planning and Designing a New Library Building.* London: Facet, 2009.

Kramer, Sibylle. *Colleges & Universities: Educational Spaces.* Salenstein: Braun, 2010.

Langmead, Stephen, and Margaret Beckman. *Guidelines to Planning Academic Library Buildings.* Hoboken: Wiley, 1971.

Lederer, Arno, Barbara Pampe, and Wüstenrot Stiftung, eds. *Raumpilot Lernen.* Stuttgart: Krämer, 2012.

Leighton, Philip D., and David C. Weber. *Planning Academic and Research Library Buildings.* Chicago: American Library Association, 1999.

Lippman, Peter C. *Evidence-Based Design of Elementary and Secondary Schools.* Hoboken: Wiley, 2010.

Lushington, Nolan. *Libraries Designed for Users*. New York: Neal-Schuman, 2002.

Macaluso, Joseph, Rosane Drummey, and David Lewek. *Building & Renovating Schools*. Kingston, MA: Reed Construction Data, 2004.

Martin, Ron G., and Pat Hawthorne. *Planning Additions to Academic Library Buildings*. Chicago: American Library Association, 1995.

Nair, Prakash, Randall Fielding, and Jeffery A. Lackney. *The Language of School Design: Design Patterns for 21st Century Schools*, rev. ed. Minneapolis: DesignShare, 2013.

Neuman, David J. *Building Type Basics for College and University Facilities*, 2nd ed. Hoboken: Wiley, 2013.

Niegaard, Hellen, ed. *Library Space: Inspiration for Building and Design*. Copenhagen: Danish Library Association, 2009.

Perkins, Bradford, and Raymond Bordwell. *Building Type Basics for Elementary and Secondary Schools*, 2nd ed. Hoboken: Wiley, 2010.

Roth, Manuela. *Library Architecture + Design*. Salenstein: Braun, 2011.

Rühm, Bettina. *Kindergärten, Krippen, Horte – Neue Architektur, Aktuelle Konzepte*. Munich: Deutsche Verlags-Anstalt, 2011.

Sannwald, William W. *Checklist of Library Building Design Considerations*, 4th ed. Chicago: American Library Association, 2001.

Schloz, Thomas. *Innenraumgestaltung in Bibliotheken und Büchereien*. Stuttgart: Fraunhofer IRB, 1998.

Schröteler-von Brandt, Hildegard, Thomas Coelen, Andreas Zeising, and Angela Ziesche, Angela, eds. *Raum für Bildung: Ästhetik und Architektur von Lern- und Lebensorten*. Bielefeld: transcript, 2012.

Sekretariat der Kultusministerkonferenz, and Zentralstelle für Normungsfragen und Wirtschaftlichkeit im Bildungswesen, eds. *Arbeitshilfen zum Schulbau*. Berlin: ZNWB, 2008.

Veatch, Julian Lamar. "Library Architecture and Environmental Design." PhD diss., Florida State University, 1979.

Watch, Daniel D.: *Building Type Basics for Research Laboratories,* 2nd ed. Hoboken: Wiley, 2008.

## Chapter 4.6  Culture and Performing Arts

Appleton, Ian. *Buildings for the Performing Arts: A Design and Development Guide*, 2nd ed. Oxford: Elsevier, 2008.

Armstrong, Leslie, and Roger Morgan. *Space for Dance: An Architectural Design Guide*. New York: Publishing Center for Cultural Resources, 1984.

Barron, Michael. *Auditorium Acoustics and Architectural Design*. London: Spon Press, 2009.

Cavanaugh, William J., Gregory C. Tocci, and Joseph A. Wilkes. *Architectural Acoustics: Principles and Practice*. Hoboken: Wiley, 2010.

Hardy, Hugh, and Stephen A. Kliment. *Building Type Basics for Performing Arts Facilities*. Hoboken: Wiley, 2006.

Heathcote, Edwin, and Iona Spens. *Church Builders of the Twentieth Century*. Chichester: Academy Press, 1997.

Lawson, Fred. *Congress, Convention and Exhibition Facilities: Planning, Design and Management*. Architectural Press Planning and Design Series. Oxford: Architectural, 2000.

Long, Marshall. *Architectural Acoustics*. Boston: Elsevier, 2014.

Mackintosh, Iain. *Architecture, Actor and Audience*. Theatre Concepts. London: Routledge, 2003.

Rosenblatt, Arthur. *Building Type Basics for Museums*. Hoboken: Wiley, 2001.

Schittich, Christian, ed. *In Detail: Exhibitions and Displays*. Basel: Birkhäuser, 2009.

Steele, James. *Museum Builders*. London: Academy Editions, 1994.

———. *Theatre Builders: A Collaborative Art*. London: Academy Editions, 1996.

Strong, Judith. *Theatre Buildings: A Design Guide*. Abingdon: Routledge, 2010.

van Uffelen, Chris. *Convention Centers*. Salenstein: Braun, 2012.

von Naredi-Rainer, Paul. *Museum Buildings: A Design Manual*. Basel: Birkhäuser, 2004.

## Chapter 4.7  Lodging and Food Service

Baraban, Regina S., and Joseph F. Durocher. *Successful Restaurant Design*, 3rd ed. Hoboken: Wiley, 2010.

Birchfield, John C. *Design and Layout of Foodservice Facilities*, 3rd ed. Hoboken: Wiley, 2007.

Hamer, Jan, and Christiane Pfau. *Holiday Architecture – Selection 2016*. Hannover: Urlaubsarchitektur, 2015.

Knirsch, Jürgen. *Hotels: Planen und Gestalten*, 4th ed. Leinfelden-Echterdingen: Knoch, 2001.

Lawson, Fred. *Hotels and Resorts: Planning, Design and Refurbishment*. Oxford: Butterworth Architecture, 1995.

McDonough, Brian, and John Hill. *Building Type Basics for Hospitality Facilities*. Hoboken: Wiley, 2001.

Miller, Richard. *Casino & Hotel Design Guidelines*. Charleston, SC: CreateSpace, 2012.

Payne-Palacio, June, and Monica Theis. *Introduction to Foodservice*, 11th ed. Upper Saddle River, NJ: Pearson/Prentice Hall, 2008.

Penner, Richard H., Lawrence Adams, and Stephani K. A. Robson. *Hotel Design: Planning and Development*, 2nd ed. New York: W. W. Norton, 2012.

Ronstedt, Manfred, and Tobias Frey. *Hotel Buildings: Construction and Design Manual*. Berlin: DOM Publishers, 2014.

Rutes, Walter, and Richard Penner. *Hotel Planning and Design*. New York: Architectural Press, 1985.

Thomas, Chris, Edwin J. Norman, and Costas Katsigris. *Design and Equipment for Restaurants and Foodservice: A Management View*, 4th ed. Hoboken: Wiley, 2013.

## Chapter 4.8  Healthcare Facilities

Feddersen, Eckhard, and Insa Lüdtke. *Living for the Elderly*. Basel: Birkhäuser, 2010.

Galindo, Michelle. *Doctor's Practices*. Salenstein: Braun, 2011.

Kobus, Richard L., et al. *Building Type Basics for Healthcare Facilities*, 2nd ed. Hoboken: Wiley, 2008.

Meuser, Philipp. *Medical Facilities and Health Care*. Berlin: DOM Publishers, 2011.

Miller, Richard L., Earl S. Swensson, and J. Todd Robinson. *Hospital and Healthcare Facility Design*, 3rd ed. New York: W. W. Norton, 2012.

Nickl-Weller, Christine, and Hans Nickl, eds. *Healing Architecture*. Salenstein: Braun, 2013.

universalRAUM ed. *Evidenzbasiertes Planungshandbuch Psychiatrie*. Dresden: UniversalRaum, 2012.

Whaley Gallup, Joan. *Wellness Centers: A Guide for the Design Professional*. Hoboken: Wiley, 1999.

Wischer, Robert, and Hans-Ulrich Riethmüller. *Zukunftsoffenes Krankenhaus – Ein Dialog zwischen Medizin und Architektur: Fakten, Leitlinien, Bausteine*. Vienna: Springer, 2007.

## Chapter 4.9  Sports and Recreation

Deutscher Schwimm-Verband e.V. *Bau- und Ausstattungsanforderungen für wettkampfgerechte Schwimmsportstätten*. 2012.

Diedrich, Richard J. *Building Type Basics for Recreational Facilities*. Hoboken: Wiley, 2005.

Forschungsgesellschaft Landschaftsentwicklung Landschaftsbau (FLL), in cooperation with the Deutsche Reiterliche Vereinigung (FN). *Empfehlungen für Planung, Bau und Instandhaltung von Reitplätzen*. 2014.

John, Geraint, Rod Sheard, and Ben Vickerey. *Stadia: The Populous Design and Development Guide*. London: Routledge, 2013.

Koordinierungskreis Bader. *Richtlinien für den Bäderbau*. KOK-Richtlinien. 2013.

Krämer, Thomas. *Outdoor Sportstätten: Ratgeber Planung & Bau*. Brühl: Stadionwelt, 2013.

Nixdorf, Stefan. *StadiumATLAS: Technical Recommendations for Grandstands in Modern Stadia*. Berlin Ernst & Sohn, 2008.

Sawyer, Thomas H. *Facility Planning Design for Health Physical Activity, Recreation, and Sport*, 12th ed. Urbana, IL: Sagamore, 2009.

Sheard, Rod, and Christopher Lee. *Sports Buildings: A Design Manual.* Basel: Birkhäuser, 2016.

Stürzebecher, Peter, and Sigrid Ulrich. *Architecture for Sport, New Concepts and International Projects for Sport and Leisure*, translated by Cybertechnics and Lucy Isenberg. Chichester: Wiley-Academy, 2001.

Vandenberg, M. *Stadium Builders*, Wiley-Academy.

van Uffelen, Chris. *Stadiums and Arenas: The Architecture of Games.* Architecture for Fun, Sports and Leisure. Salenstein: Braun, 2009.

Wimmer, Martin. *Stadium Buildings: Construction and Design Manual.* Berlin: DOM Publishers, 2016.

## Chapter 4.10  Public Safety

Bartezko, Dieter, ed. *Polizeipräsidium Frankfurt am Main/Police Headquarters Frankfurt.* Hamburg: Junius, 2005.

Der Hessische Minister der Justiz. *Empfehlungen für den Bau und die Einrichtung von Vollzugsanstalten.* Wiesbaden, 1967.

Fennel, Katja. *Gefängnisarchitektur und Strafvollzugsgesetz: Anspruch und Wirklichkeit.* Saarbrücken, VDM Verlag Dr. Müller, 2008.

Guyer, J. Paul. *An Introduction to Architectural Design: Fire Stations.* Charleston, SC: CreateSpace, 2013.

Klemmer, Klemens, Rudolf Wassermann, Rudolf, and Thomas Wessel. *Deutsche Gerichtsgebäude: Von der Dorflinde über den Justizpalast zum Haus des Rechts.* Munich: C. H. Beck, 1993.

Krämer, Karl-Heinz, ed. *Bauten für Polizei und Rettungsdienste/Buildings for Police and Rescue Services*, translated by Jo Desch. Stuttgart: Krämer, 2006.

Kunger, Dietrich. *Feuerwehrhäuser, Feuerwachen und Gerätehäuser.* Schöneiche bei Berlin: Bock & Kübler, 2000.

Meyer-Bohe, Walter. *Grundrisse öffentlicher Gebäude.* Berlin: Ernst & Sohn, 1997.

Mulcahy, Linda. *Legal Architecture: Justice, Due Process and the Place of Law.* Abingdon: Routledge, 2011.

Phillips, Todd S., and Michael A. Griebel. *Building Type Basics for Justice Facilities.* Hoboken: Wiley, 2003.

Richter, Klaudia. *Polizeidirektion Dresden und Polizeirevier Dresden-Altstadt – Umbau und Sanierung.* Dresden: Sächsischen Staatsregierung Immobilien- und Baumanagement, 2005.

Schreck-Offermann, Ursula. *Feuerwachen*, 4th exp. ed. Stuttgart: Fraunhofer IRB, 1994.

Simon, Jonathan, Nicholas Temple, and Renée Tobe. *Architecture and Justice.* Burlington, VT: Ashgate, 2013.

van Uffelen, Chris. *Fire, Crime & Accident: Fire Departments, Police Stations, Rescue Services*, Salenstein: Braun, 2012.

## Chapter 4.11  Transportation and Infrastructure

Ashford, Norman, Saleh Mumayiz, and Paul Wright. *Airport Engineering: Planning, Design and Development of 21st Century Airports.* Hoboken: Wiley, 2011.

Bayer, Edwin. *Parkhäuser – aber richtig: Ein Leitfaden für Bauherren, Architekten und Ingenieure*, 3rd ed. Düsseldorf: Bau + Technik, 2006.

Binney, Marcus. *Airport Builders.* Chichester: Academy Press, 1999.

De Neufville, Richard, Amedeo Odoni, Peter Belobaba, and Tom Reynolds. *Airport Systems: Planning, Design and Management*, 2nd ed. New York: McGraw-Hill, 2013.

Edwards, Bryan. *The Modern Airport Terminal: New Approaches to Airport Architecture*, 2nd. ed. London: Spon Press, 2005.

Fendrich, Lothar, and Wolfgang Fengler, ed. *Handbuch Eisenbahninfrastruktur*, 2nd rev. ed. Berlin: Springer Vieweg, 2013.

Frankel, Ernst G. *Port Planning and Development.* New York: Wiley, 1987.

Griffin, Kenneth W. *Building Type Basics for Transit Facilities.* Hoboken: Wiley, 2004.

*Häfen und Kaianlagen.* Berlin: Ernst, 2012.

Irmscher, Ilja; Kosarev, Ivan: Schiefenhövel, Angela: Parking structures – construction and design manual. Berlin: DOM Publishers, 2013.

Kähler, Gert, and Bund Deutscher Architekten. *Renaissance der Bahnhöfe.* Wiesbaden: Vieweg+Teubner, 1996.

Kleinmanns, Joachim. *Parkhäuser.* Marburg: Jonas, 2011.

Mensen, Heinrich. *Planung, Anlage und Betrieb von Flugplätzen.* Berlin: Springer Vieweg, 2007.

National Association of City Transportation Officials. *Transit Street Design Guide.* Washington, DC: Island Press, 2016.

National Association of City Transportation Officials. *Urban Bikeway Design Guide*, 2nd ed. Washington, DC: Island Press, 2014.

Richter, Andrè. *Gepäcklogistik auf Flughäfen.* Heidelberg: Springer, 2013.

Ross, Julian. *Railway Stations: Planning, Design and Management.* Oxford: Architectural Press, 2000.

Tsinker, Gregory. *Port Engineering: Planning, Construction, Maintenance and Security.* Hoboken: Wiley, 2004.

Wright, Paul, and Karen Dixon. *Highway Engineering*, intl. ed. Hoboken: Wiley, 2004.

Young, Seth B., and Alexander T. Wells. *Airport Planning and Management*, 6th ed. New York: McGraw-Hill, 2011.

Zilch, Konrad, Claus Jürgen Diederichs, Rolf Katzenbach, and Klaus J. Beckmann eds. *Raumordnung und Städtebau, Öffentliches und Verkehrsanlagen*, 2nd ed. Berlin: Springer Vieweg, 2013.

# 5.3 Index

## A

absence of PWIS — 285
access control — 428, 497
access control systems — 54–55, 526–27
accessible ramps — 54, 74
access via an outdoor gallery — 167
acoustics — 29, 92
additive model — 294, 295
administration building — 204, 205, 481
after-school care — 304, 305
air — 21, 22, 83, 143, 144, 146–47, 151, 152
air-conditioning equipment — 146, 203, 300, 356, 361, 406
air curtain system — 252, 254
air exchange — 22, 23, 279, 333
airlocks — 247, 285, 317, 320, 413
air quality — 23, 300, 384, 406
aisle principle — 244, 245
alternative energy sources — 143
American football — 431, 434–35, 450, 453
anchoring berths — 513
angled parking — 40, 43
anthropometry — 11–19
apartment entrance areas — 183
arcades — 231
arched structures — 278
arena principle — 244, 245
armchairs — 95
art museums — 328, 330
assembly line production — 283
athletic-shoe or barefoot zone — 83, 133, 427, 428
atrium — 194, 200, 231, 232, 331
atrium houses — 175
autoclave rooms — 310, 404, 423
automated storage and retrieval (S/R) equipment — 255
automatic door openers — 62, 67
auto repair shops — 522, 532

## B

baby changing areas — 105, 106
backflow level — 139, 148
backflow preventers — 148
badminton — 450, 455
baggage claim — 532
baggage trolleys — 525
balcony — 171, 194
ballet rehearsal — 351
banking hall — 207
banks — 207
barrier-free — 188
barrier-free accessibility — 11, 19, 40, 66, 77, 78, 105, 108, 180, 183, 188, 192
barrier gates — 54, 233, 266, 287
baseball — 450, 453
basketball — 450, 452
basketball backboards — 465
batch production — 283
bathroom — 104, 190–92
bathtubs — 103

bavarian curling — 457
beach volleyball — 452
beams — 273
bedrooms — 188–89
bereavement room — 420
bicycle — 41
bicycle parking spaces — 49, 50
big bags — 119, 122
bike boxes — 50
bike channels — 74
binder storage — 126
biosafety laboratories — 317
block development — 162, 163, 175, 195, 330
block storage — 123, 124, 242, 243
boathouses — 513
body heights — 11–13
boiler rooms — 143
bouldering areas — 445
bowling — 450, 451, 456
boxes — 347
Braille — 18
branch lines — 139
break area — 321
break line — 70
building depth — 164, 200, 201, 202, 203, 233
building drainage — 139, 148, 276
bus — 42
business club — 220
bus platforms — 528
bus stop — 53

## C

cafeterias — 323
care — 188
care areas — 411–19
care control point — 418
care of patients with infectious diseases — 414–15
care of the elderly — 416–17
carport — 46
car washes — 520, 521
cash-and-carry wholesalers — 246
ceiling heights — 65, 83, 146, 273, 274, 275, 426, 450–51
cellular layout — 169, 170, 184, 186
cellular offices — 202, 212, 213, 215, 217
centers for dementia patients — 180, 181, 395, 418
central kitchens — 375
CEP transshipment hubs — 239, 240
chain food outlets — 366
chairs — 97
changing areas — 132–35, 472–73
changing compartments — 133
check-in counter — 497, 507, 509, 526, 527
checkout — 246, 247, 259, 265
child day care center — 297, 303, 304, 305
children — 13, 188, 189
cinemas — 341, 350
circulation paths — 65, 75, 275, 308, 426–27
circulation pipes — 148

circulation routes — 127, 202, 234, 235, 236, 238
circulation without corridors — 201
classrooms — 21, 23, 25, 29, 90, 92, 292, 293, 315–20
clean room — 280, 285, 320
climbing gyms — 445
climbing poles — 464
climbing ropes — 460, 463
clinics — 392–94, 396–98, 400–23
closet — 159, 183, 190, 411
clubhouses — 431, 513, 514
cluster (sales premises) — 231, 232
cognition — 19
cold storage — 123, 247, 249, 267
colleges — 297, 309, 322, 324, 325
column — 228, 238, 272, 273, 276, 278, 332, 359, 391, 429, 500–501, 515, 517, 528
combi-offices — 200, 212–13, 217–18
comfort — 21–29
communal food service — 366–67
communication areas — 11, 63, 87–93, 169, 179, 204, 215, 217
compact storage — 123
comprehensive schools — 308
computer workstations — 83, 311
concert halls — 338, 340, 343, 345–49, 351
concourse — 388, 389, 390, 502–3, 507, 524
condominium — 159
conference rooms — 21, 29, 87, 90, 222–23, 361
construction grids — 391
construction site fabrication — 283
construction vehicles — 42
consulting rooms — 396, 398, 402, 403, 483, 491
container — 52, 119, 121, 136
control point — 388, 389, 394, 400, 401, 402, 404, 409, 413, 414, 416, 418, 419, 420
control tower — 512
conveyor systems — 123, 129, 233, 239, 242, 255, 257, 511, 520, 526, 527, 532
conveyor vehicles — 127
cooktops — 112, 113, 114
corner buildings — 173, 176
corridor access — 166–68
corridors — 25, 63–65, 83, 105, 163, 167, 168, 170, 171, 178, 200, 201, 202, 233, 234, 235, 236, 275, 297, 299, 331, 344, 350, 358, 389, 390, 418
council chambers — 29, 204, 205
counter system — 378
courier, express, and parcel services (CEP) — 233, 239, 240, 252
courtyard buildings — 199, 386
courtyard houses — 175
craftsmen's workshops — 48, 282, 284, 287
crèche (day nursery) — 304, 305, 325
cricket — 450, 454
cross-docking — 228, 233, 252

crush barriers — 437, 467
cultural buildings — 328
curling — 450, 457
custodian's office — 209, 211, 338, 449
customer route planning — 229
customer toilets — 244, 248, 263, 266, 267
cycling — 40, 446, 450

## D

dance rehearsal — 338, 351
data systems technology — 29, 304, 305, 413
day care — 29, 304, 305, 413
daylight — 25, 26, 28, 31, 131, 161, 173, 175, 176, 200, 201, 224, 272, 273, 292, 296, 298, 301–2, 332, 395, 411, 487, 488
delivery yard — 235, 237, 250, 421
department stores — 21, 23, 146, 231, 237, 245, 262, 267
design of sales premises — 229
desks — 209, 212, 214, 216, 220, 259, 263, 306, 311, 323, 335, 339, 341, 352, 360, 371, 400, 420, 443, 445, 481, 483, 491, 497
desk sharing — 220
diagnostics — 400, 402–5
dialysis — 414
dining area — 23, 97–99, 159, 169, 184, 185, 186, 323, 365, 378, 381, 487
dirty laundry chute — 190
disabilities — 19, 47, 48, 133
discus — 434, 435, 458
dispatchers' rooms — 266
display area — 244
display fixtures — 259
disposal yard — 385, 394, 404, 421, 422
distribution kitchens — 375
dock levelers — 51
doctor's offices — 396–97
domed skylights — 279
doorbell — 56
doors — 66–68
door types — 66
double corridors — 199, 200, 202
double-loaded corridor — 164, 166, 167, 199, 200, 202, 297, 299, 358, 418
double wall construction — 109
drainage — 139, 148–49, 193, 272, 276
dressing rooms — 25, 161, 329, 338, 352
drying rooms — 132, 193, 284, 441, 488, 514
duplex apartments — 167, 172, 178
duplex houses — 162, 173
dwelling unit size — 158–59

## E

e-fulfillment centers — 239
electrical wiring — 150
elevator groups — 178
elevators — 77–81, 210, 235, 266
elevators for patient beds and gurneys — 77, 79, 389, 390

emergency departments — 400, 401
endoscopy — 393, 404
entrance areas — 61–62, 83, 183, 209–11, 252–54, 287, 303, 306, 309, 311, 313, 330, 334, 338, 343, 358, 369, 396, 420, 441, 449, 481, 483, 485, 524
entrance mat — 183, 252, 254
equipment rental — 427, 428, 440, 441
equipment room — 466
ergonomics — 11
escalators — 25, 75–76, 235
escape route length — 65, 166, 233, 237, 275, 297
escape routes — 63, 64, 65, 66, 68, 73, 84, 85, 164, 178, 201, 229, 236, 275, 331, 358, 431, 437
events area — 361
examination and treatment room — 402
examination and treatment zone — 400
exhibition spaces — 344
exhibits — 329, 332
experiment bench — 318
explosion protection — 285
express elevator — 77, 178
external factors of production — 271

## F

factory outlet — 246
factory production — 282
fencing — 451, 456
field hockey — 451, 455
filing shelves — 126
fire brigade elevators — 178
fire compartments — 64, 85, 199, 201, 233, 235, 236, 271, 274, 285
fire dampers — 142, 146
fireplaces — 142, 143, 145
first aid room — 83, 136, 431, 432, 438, 441, 473, 487, 489, 492
fistball — 451, 453
fitness — 446
fit-out grid — 177, 193, 203, 215, 216, 228, 238, 285, 356, 364, 369, 370, 391, 395, 411
fitting rooms — 259, 264
flex office — 220
floodlight system — 436
floor-to-floor height — 72, 75, 146, 203, 273, 386, 516
flow of materials — 280
flow rack storage — 123, 124
flues — 142, 143, 145
flying rings — 460, 463
fly loft — 330, 338
food logistics — 247, 249
food-processing plants — 285
foreman's office — 284, 288
forensic facilities — 392
forklifts — 127, 128, 246, 255
frame structure — 276, 278, 429, 512
freight centers — 231
freight elevators — 77, 257, 267, 358, 389
freight transport network — 233

"front-to-back" layout — 161, 177, 178
frozen storage warehouses — 247
full climate-control systems — 22
fume hood — 22, 317, 318, 319, 492
functional units — 61, 150, 209, 225, 308, 392, 413

## G

game equipment — 460, 466
gaming tables — 466
gangways — 507, 532
garage — 46, 47, 162, 168, 173, 177, 195, 203, 211, 235, 358, 359, 391, 476, 485, 500, 501, 515–19
garbage chutes — 195
garbage collection points — 195
garbage disposal — 195
gas pumps — 532, 533
gas stations — 48, 520, 521, 532, 533
gas supply — 140, 318
gate — 54, 94, 127, 228, 239, 240, 252, 287, 437, 485, 497, 508, 532
general care — 392, 412, 413, 419
geriatrics — 392, 395, 411, 416, 417
glare protection — 23, 27, 28, 254
goods to man — 242, 243
goods transport systems — 229, 233, 389, 422
grid ladders — 464
groceries — 247
group offices — 200, 201, 202, 212, 213, 215, 216, 481
group production (cell production) — 283
group room — 29, 301, 303, 313, 314
groups of people — 11, 14, 15
guide system — 211, 244, 299, 309, 313, 497, 524
gymnasiums — 23, 132, 429, 431–33, 460, 472
gymnastics — 443, 446, 450, 451, 460, 461

## H

habitable rooms — 25, 28, 159, 161, 168, 184, 194, 491
hammer — 434, 435, 458
hammerhead turnaround — 43
handball — 451, 452, 466
handling space — 235
hand pallet trucks — 128
hangar — 506, 511, 512
heat gain — 21
heating production halls — 85
heating system — 141, 143, 144, 148
heat transfer stations — 143, 145
helicopter — 384, 385, 394, 400, 401, 511
high-bay warehouses — 230, 239, 256
high jump — 434, 435, 459
high-rack storage — 125, 128
high-rise apartment buildings — 177–78
high-rise buildings — 200, 201
horizontal bars — 460, 461, 462
horizontal carousel storage — 123, 124

hose-drying tower — 476, 488, 489
hospices — 396, 420
hot water demand — 148
housing form — 158
hurdle tracks — 459
hydraulic lift — 532
hygiene — 285, 391

**I**

ice hockey — 451, 456
ice rinks — 440–43
illuminance — 24, 25, 28, 332
impact walls — 430
individual food service — 366
indoor air — 22–23, 83, 285
indoor air humidity — 21
indoor shopping streets — 231
indoor swimming pools — 438–39
industrial architecture — 270
industrial sheds — 272, 278
industrial trucks — 127, 255, 257
infrastructure — 39, 84, 94, 152, 160, 231, 239, 328, 384, 496–522
inland ports — 513
installation height — 55, 113, 325
integrated model — 294, 295
intensive care — 391, 393, 411, 413
intercity bus (coach) — 42
intermediate bulk containers (IPC) — 119, 121
intermediate care — 411, 413
intermediate landing — 69
internal circulation — 61
ISO containers — 119, 121

**J**

janitor's closets — 137, 200, 225, 381, 472
javelin throw — 435, 458
jetways — 532
judo — 451, 456

**K**

kitchen appliances — 111, 112, 115
kitchen fixtures — 111, 374
kitchens — 111–17, 179, 185–87, 224, 365, 375, 376, 377, 378

**L**

laboratories — 310, 317
laboratory benches — 93, 317, 318
laboratory medicine — 404
lacrosse — 451, 454
laundry rooms — 190, 193, 441
layout concepts — 245
lecterns — 93
lecture hall — 23, 25, 29, 87, 88, 89, 91, 315, 316
levels of care — 392, 394
lifting platform — 77
lighting — 150, 213
lighting, artificial — 24, 25, 28, 213
lighting, natural — 24, 25, 28, 213, 279
lighting conditions — 24
light source — 24
line — 124

linear apartment buildings — 175
linear buildings — 166, 176, 199, 232, 296
linear development — 163, 357
linear storage — 123, 242
linked townhouses — 175
living room — 184
loading platforms — 252, 287
loan associations — 207
lockers — 133, 525
loggia — 177, 178, 194
logistics — 119
logistics centers — 231, 389, 421
logistics zones — 231
longeing halls — 444
long jump — 459
lounge areas — 96, 289, 363
low care — 413
lunchrooms — 83, 131, 200, 224

**M**

machine deployment — 84
mailbox units — 56
mail slots — 56
main lecture hall — 309
makeup rooms — 352, 353
malls — 231
manager's offices — 266, 287, 309
maneuvering zones — 45, 63, 64, 84, 101, 102, 103, 133
man to goods — 242, 243
media equipment — 88, 222
medical services installations — 391
meeting rooms — 204, 207, 215, 222, 223, 306, 310, 324
merchandise zones — 229
mezzanine level — 266, 313
middle zone — 200
minimization of living space — 159
minimum ceiling heights — 83
mobile pallet storage — 124
mobile shelving — 123, 126, 243
motorcycle — 41
motor functions — 16
movable partitions — 321, 344, 430, 431
movement sequences — 16, 84
movie theaters — 31, 341, 350
moving walkways — 75, 76, 235
multifamily dwellings — 172, 173, 193
multigenerational home — 179
multipurpose arenas — 341
multipurpose rooms — 321, 322, 363
multistory buildings — 230, 231, 245, 273, 274, 276, 277, 279, 281, 306
multistory residential buildings — 162, 163, 172, 176, 183, 193, 195
museums — 21, 23, 328, 329, 330, 331, 332, 333, 334, 335, 336, 352

**N**

natural history museums — 328
necessary corridors — 63, 168, 178, 297, 437
necessary stairs — 168, 437
needs analysis — 158, 476

net and nest — 220
nine-pin bowling — 451, 456
noise abatement parameters — 29
nonambulatory patient entrance — 394, 400, 401, 404, 405, 406
nonterritorial work environments — 220, 221
normal care — 411, 413, 414, 416
nuclear medicine — 393, 414, 415
nursery school — 48, 303, 304, 305

**O**

obstetrics — 393, 394, 409
occupied spaces — 31, 32
office spaces — 25, 212–21
omnichannel retail — 239
open area — 162, 194, 266, 271, 302, 314, 321, 418
open layout — 169
open-plan offices — 21, 200, 201, 203, 212, 213, 216, 219
opera houses — 329, 338, 339, 343, 345–49, 351, 352, 353
operator zone — 241
oratory — 420
orchestra pit — 347, 349
order picking — 241, 242, 255
orientation of rooms — 161
outdoor sports — 431
owner-occupant — 158
owner's association — 172

**P**

pallets — 119, 120, 128, 228
pallet trucks — 127, 128
palliative care — 416
palliative care wards — 396
parking garages — 195, 515–19
parking spaces — 236, 428, 436, 485, 486, 515–19
parliament halls — 205
passenger cars — 41, 45
passenger conveyors — 75
passenger elevators — 77, 78, 162, 178, 210, 211, 266, 358, 389, 503, 515
pathology department — 393 404, 405, 420
patient rooms — 391, 398, 411–19
patio — 161, 171, 194
pedestrian zones — 231, 232
pediatrics — 393, 414–15
physical therapy — 410, 446
piping routes — 109
places of assembly — 47, 65, 70, 108, 205, 315, 331, 352, 358, 426, 428, 434, 467, 472
planning of goods flows — 228
plant rooms — 195, 248, 338, 391, 398, 410, 419, 421, 423, 504
plenary rooms — 205
plumbing fixtures — 101, 102, 103, 104, 105, 107, 108, 109, 353, 472
pneumatic delivery system — 389, 422
point-block buildings — 199, 357
pole vault — 434, 435, 459
polo — 451, 454

porch — 194
portal frames — 278
portal line — 345
ports — 513
postdelivery care — 411, 414
precast reinforced concrete (PRC)
    elements — 278
pressurized ventilation
    system — 168
preventative health — 446
primary schools — 308, 323
private exterior circulation — 54
production conditions — 270
production layout — 271, 272, 273,
    279, 288
production spaces — 84
production workflow — 270, 272,
    273
projection room — 350
projection surfaces — 88, 93
psychiatric hospitals — 392
public access — 39
public transit bus — 42
public utilities — 139
pump stations — 148

R

rack-serving equipment — 127
rack storage — 123, 124, 128
rack systems — 255
radiators — 143, 144, 168, 279
radiological diagnostics — 400, 401,
    405
railroad stations — 500, 501, 502–4
raised seating rows — 89
ramps — 42, 54, 74, 75, 83, 252
reach ranges — 16
reading areas — 311, 323
receiving — 270, 280, 281, 284, 287,
    375, 431
reception — 210, 211, 222, 281, 287,
    334, 335, 341, 364, 369, 393, 394,
    396, 400, 482, 522
recovery room — 388, 406
rehabilitation — 384, 392, 395, 410,
    416
rehearsal rooms — 339, 340, 351
rehearsal stage rooms — 339, 351
release area — 458
rental apartments — 115, 159
rescue routes — 63, 66, 69, 85, 168,
    236, 315, 331, 437
reserve room or stockroom — 267
residential care homes — 390, 392,
    395, 420
residential environment — 160
residential group housing — 180
retail shop — 175, 178, 230, 238,
    245, 502, 507
retirement homes — 180
reverberation time — 29, 301, 345
revolving door — 55, 66, 68, 253
riding arenas — 444
riding hall floor — 444
risers — 142
roof structures — 272, 276
room acoustics — 29, 301
room lighting — 24, 371
rooms for children and
    teenagers — 188, 189

room temperature — 21, 430
room ventilation — 22
ropes courses — 445
routing for installations — 168
routing of utility lines — 279
row houses — 162, 173, 174, 175
rugby — 451, 453
running tracks — 434, 435, 459
runways — 506, 511, 530, 531

S

safe deposit boxes — 207
sales approach — 229
sales premises — 229, 231, 235,
    236, 237, 239, 244–49, 252, 266,
    267
sales system — 229
sanitariums — 358, 385, 395
sanitary facilities — 101, 105–6
Sankey diagram — 280
sauna — 179, 190, 361, 364, 443,
    446, 447, 472
savings associations — 207
sawtooth roof — 279
seaports — 513
seating areas — 94–96
seating circle — 313
seating furniture — 91, 218
seating groups — 96
seating rows — 88, 89, 315
secondary schools — 25, 297, 308,
    322, 323, 324, 325
security concept — 209, 477, 497,
    513
seminar — 87, 88, 89, 90, 91, 93,
    204, 220, 292, 309
semiprivate rooms — 411, 412, 413,
    414, 415, 416, 417, 419
sensory perception — 17
server cabinets — 151
server rooms — 151–53
service connection room — 140–41
service elevator — 77, 381, 389
service feed — 141
serving area — 323, 375, 378
serving food — 378
shafts — 142
shaft ventilation — 142, 147
shared units — 179
shelf storage — 242, 243
shelving systems — 123, 124, 242,
    243, 259, 323, 352
shop-in-shop principle — 244, 245
shopping cart — 235, 259, 262
shot put — 434, 435, 458
shower — 101, 103, 104
shower areas — 23, 83, 101, 105, 106
side tables — 96
silo-type construction — 230
single-family dwellings — 173, 176
single-loaded corridor — 166, 167,
    200, 202, 297, 299
single-sided delivery — 233
single-story buildings — 230, 302
sinks — 105, 111, 112, 113, 114
slab building — 163, 176, 199
slip resistance — 83, 101, 285
soccer — 434, 435, 436–37, 451, 452,
    466
sofas — 95

solitary buildings — 176, 330
sound-absorbing surfaces — 92,
    216, 351
sound attenuators — 146
spa — 446
space frame — 272, 278, 429, 512
span lengths — 76, 272, 273, 277, 429
spatial feeling — 186
specialist hospitals — 392
specialized classrooms — 308, 309,
    317–21, 324
specialty food store — 247–49
spectator areas — 29, 333, 339,
    340, 347, 426, 427, 428, 429, 440,
    467–71
speed skating rinks — 441–43, 457
spine-and-fingers buildings — 199,
    201, 296, 386, 476, 508
split-level — 169, 170, 515
sports floors — 430, 431
squash — 451, 456
stadium block — 468
stadiums — 341, 426, 427, 429, 430,
    434–37
staff kitchens — 200, 204, 215, 217,
    218, 224
stage theaters — 338, 339, 345–49,
    352, 353
stair — 69–73, 165, 166, 168, 174,
    178, 201, 237, 297, 331
stair railings — 69, 70, 72
stair risers and treads — 70
stair types — 70
stairway widths — 73
stand-up tables — 99
stepped buildings — 175
sterile goods supply — 389, 406,
    407, 422, 423
storage containers — 121
storage management system — 242
storage rooms — 119, 137, 159, 169,
    194, 224, 352, 377, 431, 441, 442,
    460, 471, 481, 482, 490
storage systems — 123
storage units — 255
storage volume — 228
storage zone — 241, 242
storerooms — 137
street-shoe zone — 427, 428
street spaces — 39, 40
strength training — 446
student housing — 179
student laboratory — 319
studio apartments — 169, 171, 172
sun shading — 27
supermarkets — 230, 244, 247, 259,
    262
supply center — 421
supply of meals — 422
surface temperature — 21
swimming pools — 438–39

T

tables — 91, 96, 97, 99, 131, 222, 259,
    260, 261, 316, 323, 366, 408, 446,
    466
teachers' room — 303, 306, 307, 308,
    324
technical equipment rooms — 139–
    53, 200, 224, 279, 429

telecommunications — 139, 140, 141, 150, 239, 371
teller stations — 207
tennis — 451, 455
therapy centers — 395, 410
three-hinged frame — 278
ticket counters — 526, 527
ticket-vending machines — 526. 529
tiered seating — 89, 426, 427, 467, 469
total runs (stairs) — 72
tower building — 163
track structures — 528
trade fair buildings — 250
trade schools — 308
train platforms — 528, 529
transportation buildings — 496–522
transport pallets — 120
trash compactor — 59
triple jump — 434, 435, 459
truck — 41, 43, 44, 52, 54, 233, 236, 239, 240, 242, 249, 250, 252, 267, 284, 287
truss — 272, 277
turning curves — 44, 485
two-sense principle — 17

**U**

universities — 295, 297, 309, 315, 317, 318, 322, 324
utility connections — 139, 141, 172, 430, 442, 477
utility lines — 139, 273, 279
utility rooms — 159, 172, 173, 193

**V**

vault rooms — 207
ventilation stations — 279
ventilation systems — 22, 139, 146, 147, 168, 285, 300, 320, 333, 490
vertical carousel storage — 124
vertical gardens — 178
vestibules — 62, 132, 136, 153, 183, 252, 369, 414, 489
video projectors — 88, 93, 492
visual screening — 106, 194, 242
vocational schools — 308, 325
volleyball — 451, 452

**W**

waiting areas — 40, 53, 94–96, 204, 205, 207, 209, 210–11, 307, 343, 388, 389, 396, 397, 398, 400, 401, 420, 481, 482, 483, 485, 497, 522
walking aid — 19, 54, 66
warehouse aisles — 255
warehouse operations — 127
warm-up kitchens — 375
washrooms — 105, 132, 267, 289, 310, 325, 432, 473, 493
waste disposal rooms — 237, 239, 244, 247, 249, 265, 267, 270, 287, 377, 386, 388, 389, 390, 391, 392, 394, 396, 398, 401, 404, 405, 406, 407, 410, 413, 419, 421
waste receptacles — 57–59, 195, 263, 408
water heaters — 148, 149

water supply — 148, 318
weighing rooms — 310
wellness hotel — 361
wheelchair — 16, 19
wheelchair-accessible toilets — 103, 104
wheelchair-accessible toilets and shower rooms (publicly accessible) — 101, 103, 105
wheelchair-accessible water closets — 101, 103, 104, 105
wholesale market — 239, 246
window seating — 314
winter garden — 194
workbench production — 282
workplaces — 83, 107, 198, 212
workshop production — 282

**Y**

yoga — 446

**Z**

zones of impact and reach — 244

# 5.4 Picture Credits

## Chapter 4.3 Logistics and Commerce

Page 226, Southdale Center: after a photo from Minnesota Historical Society, ID number MH5 9 ED3 1 p4
Page 226, High-bay warehouse, Sedus Stoll AG: after a photo from Sedus Stoll AG
Page 226, BMW Welt: after a photo from BMW AG
Page 226, Westside Shopping and Leisure Center: after a photo by Migros Aare/Westside
Page 226, Logistics Center, Ernsting's family: after a photo from Ernsting's real estate
Page 226, G. Park Blue Planet: after a photo by IDI Gazeley

## Chapter 4.4 Industry and Production

Page 272, Cromford Mill textile factory: after a photo by Hans Peter Schaefer GNU
Page 272, Hackesche Höfe: after a photo by Manfred Brückels GNU
Page 272, AEG Turbine Factory: after a photo by Doris Antony GNU
Page 272, Fagus Factory: after a photo by Carsten Janssen
Page 272, Friedrich Steinberg Hat Factory: after a photo by lumu
Page 272, Fiat Factory, Lingotto: after a photo by Dgtmedia
Page 272, Van Nelle Factory: after a photo by Avalphen
Fig. 4.4.18: fastplan GmbH, Velbert

## Chapter 4.6 Culture and Performing Arts

Page 326, Solomon R. Guggenheim Museum: after a photo by Jean-Christophe Benoist
Page 326, Philharmonie Berlin: after a photo by Manfred Brückels

Page 326, Neue Nationalgalerie: after a photo by Manfred Brückels
Page 326, Sydney Opera House: after a photo by Steve Collis
Page 326, Louvre (entrance pavilion): after a photo by ros k @ getfunky_paris
Page 326, Museu de Arte Contemporânea: after a photo by Marcusrg
Page 326, Guggenheim Museum, Bilbao: after a photo by Ardfern
Page 326, Jewish Museum, Berlin: after a photo by Studio Daniel Libeskind
Page 326, Royal Opera House, Copenhagen: after a photo by Adam Mork
Page 326, Palau de les Arts Reina Sofia: after a photo by Zibi
Page 326, Kolumba: after a photo by Elke Wetzig
Page 326, Opera House, Oslo: after a photo by dalbera
Fig. 4.6.21: after photos by Nic Lehoux (top left), Piotrus (top right), MrEnglish (bottom left), Adam Mork (bottom right)
Fig. 4.6.25: MrEnglish
Fig. 4.6.26: Peter Csaba Rákoczy
Fig. 4.6.32 (right): based on photo by Adam Mork
Figs. 4.6.38–4.6.40 (photos): Adam Mork

## Chapter 4.8 Healthcare

Page 382, General Hospital, Vienna: after an illustration from Josef & Peter Schafer, *600 Jahre Almer Mater Rudolphina*, Eigenverlag Universität Wien, 1965, p. 96
Page 382, Terrace Hospital, Waiblingen: after a photo by Bildarchiv Marburg
Page 382, Aachen University Clinic: after a photo by Michael Jeiter, Bildarchiv Marburg
Page 382, AZ Groeninge Hospital: after a photo by Werner Huthmacher, Baumschlager Eberle

Editor: Bert Bielefeld

Authors: Bert Bielefeld (Chapter 1–3, 4.2, 4.9, 4.11); Alexander Görg (Chapter 4.1); Roland Schneider (Chapter 4.1, 4.2, 4.10); Bettina Sigmund (Chapter 4.3); Nils Kummer (Chapter 4.4); Mareike Borkeloh (Chapter 4.5); Mathias Hölzinger (Chapter 4.5, 4.6); Ann-Christin Siegemund (Chapter 4.7); Barbara Weyand (Chapter 4.8); Markus Stark (Chapter 4.10); Jasmin Sowa (Chapter 4.11)

Drawings: David Hollnack and Viktouria Kezir, with assistance from Katharina Holterhof and Alexander Pilar

Book concept and editing: Annette Gref

Project management: Petra Schmid

Translation from German into English: David Koralek/ArchiTrans, with assistance from Hartwin Busch

Copy editing: Keonaona Peterson

Production: Katja Jaeger

Layout (basic concept): Hug & Eberlein
Layout (revision and realization): Res Eichenberger, Sven Schrape

Typesetting and cover design: Sven Schrape

Paper: 130 g/m² Amber Graphic
Printing: Kösel GmbH & Co. KG, Altusried-Krugzell

The technical recommendations contained in this book reflect the current state of technology but expressly require explicit coordination by the responsible specialist planners to ensure compliance with the applicable and current laws, regulations, and standards of the country concerned. Neither the author nor the publisher can be held in any way accountable for the design, planning or execution of faulty work.

Library of Congress Cataloging-in-Publication data
A CIP catalog record for this book has been applied for at the Library of Congress.

Bibliographic information published by the German National Library
The German National Library lists this publication in the Deutsche Nationalbibliografie; detailed bibliographic data are available on the Internet at http://dnb.dnb.de.

This publication is also available in a German language edition (ISBN 978-3-0356-0318-7, Hardcover; ISBN 978-3-0356-0320-0, Softcover).

© 2016 Birkhäuser Verlag GmbH, Basel
P.O. Box 44, 4009 Basel, Switzerland
Part of Walter de Gruyter GmbH, Berlin/Boston

Printed on acid-free paper produced from chlorine-free pulp. TCF ∞

Printed in Germany

ISBN 978-3-0356-0323-1 (Hardcover)
ISBN 978-3-0356-0324-8 (Softcover)

9 8 7 6 5 4 3 2 1                    www.birkhauser.com

# 5.5 The Authors

## Acknowledgments

Such a comprehensive undertaking would not have been possible without the dedicated efforts of many people. In my capacity as editor I would therefore like to thank all the authors who have contributed their time and their expertise to this endeavor and, together with everyone else, have produced a very sound and conceptually successful book. In this regard, I would especially like to thank Annette Gref, who assisted me in the process of developing positions through many discussions in which we repeatedly scrutinized and improved concepts and organizational structures. I would also like to thank David Hollnack and Viktouria Kezir, who selflessly took care of preparing the extensive illustrations.

## Authors

Bert Bielefeld, Prof. Dr.-Ing., is an architect, professor of building economics and construction management at the University of Siegen, and founding partner of the planning firm bertbielefeld&partner architekten ingenieure, based in Dortmund.

Mareike Borkeloh, B. A. in architecture, M. Eng. in urban planning, is a lecturer for urban design at Frankfurt University of Applied Sciences, and a planner at BS+ städtebau und architektur, based in Frankfurt am Main.

Alexander Görg, Dipl.-Ing. (FH), M. A., is an architect, a partner in the architecture firm Modulbüro in Siegen, and a lecturer at the University of Siegen.

Mathias Hölzinger, Dr.-Ing., M. Sc., is an architect, a lecturer on housing, urban development, and neighborhood planning at RheinMain University of Applied Sciences and at Frankfurt University, and a project manager at PROPROJEKT Planungsmanagement und Projektberatung GmbH in Frankfurt am Main.

Nils Kummer, Dipl.-Ing., is an architect who has worked for the public and the private sector, including the central factory planning division of a German automotive supplier.

Roland Schneider, Dipl.-Ing. (FH), M. Sc., is an architect and the managing director of art schneider architekten in Schwäbisch Hall.

Ann-Christin Siegemund, B. Sc., studied architecture, construction management, and real estate management at the University of Siegen and TU Dortmund, and is an employee with the firm bertbielefeld&partner.

Bettina Sigmund, Dipl.-Ing. in architecture, M. A. in architecture media management, is an author and specialized trade journalist as well as proprietor of the architectural communication agency aboutarchitecture.

Jasmin Sowa, Dipl. Ing. (FH), is an architect, a project supervisor at the German Federal Office for Building and Regional Planning in Bonn, and a research associate with the Chair of Construction Economics and Construction Management at the University of Siegen.

Markus Stark, Dipl. Ing. BDA, is an architect and the proprietor of the planning firm starkarchitekten in Siegen.

Barbara Weyand, Dipl.-Ing., M. A. in architecture media management, is an architect, a freelance writer based in Munich, and a public relations specialist for various renowned architecture firms working in the fields of research, education, and health.